Alexander Gühler

(privat)

PONS
Fachwörterbuch
Marketing

PONS

Fachwörterbuch Marketing

Englisch - Deutsch
Deutsch - Englisch

von

P. H. Collin
A. Ivanovic
Dorothee Lantemann
Rupert Livesey

Ernst Klett Verlag für Wissen und Bildung
Stuttgart · Dresden

PONS Fachwörterbuch Marketing
Englisch - Deutsch/Deutsch - Englisch

Von/by P. H. Collin, A. Ivanovic, Dorothee Lantemann, Rupert Livesey

auf der Basis von/based on

Dictionary of Marketing
first published by
Peter Collin Publishing Ltd

Warenzeichen
Wörter, die unseres Wissens eingetragene Warenzeichen darstellen, sind als solche gekennzeichnet. Es ist jedoch zu beachten, daß weder das Vorhandensein noch das Fehlen derartiger Kennzeichnungen die Rechtslage hinsichtlich eingetragener Warenzeichen berührt.

CIP-Titelaufnahme der Deutschen Bibliothek
PONS Fachwörterbuch Marketing: englisch-deutsch,
deutsch-englisch/von P. H. Collin ...-
1. Aufl. - Stuttgart; Dresden: Klett, Verlag für Wissen und Bildung, 1991
ISBN 3-12-517980-7
NE: Collin, Peter H.; Fachwörterbuch Marketing

1. Auflage 1991

Einbandentwurf: Erwin Poell, Heidelberg
Computer processing by Compulexis, Oxford
Computer typesetting by Systemset, Stotfold, Hertfordshire
Druck: Clausen & Bosse, Leck
Printed in Germany
ISBN 3-12-517980-7

Vorwort

Das PONS Fachwörterbuch Marketing enthält einen etwa 3500 Stichwörter und Wendungen umfassenden Basiswortschatz aus allen relevanten Teilbereichen des Marketing von Gütern und Dienstleistungen, darunter unter anderem Termini aus Marktforschung, Produktpräsentation, Verkaufsförderung und Werbung.

Die Stichwörter und Wendungen werden in leicht verständlichem Englisch erklärt, um den Bedürfnissen des Fremdsprachenlerners Rechnung zu tragen. Der Bedeutungserklärung folgt jeweils die deutsche Entsprechung. Zahlreiche englische Beispiele zeigen die Verwendung der Fachterminologie in typischen Kontexten auf.

Das Wörterbuch enthält eine Vielzahl von Zitaten aus einem breiten Spektrum englischsprachiger Fachzeitungen und -zeitschriften, die dem Wörterbuchbenutzer einen Einblick in authentische Verwendungszusammenhänge vermitteln.

Im zweiten Teil des Wörterbuchs sind die übersetzten deutschen Fachtermini mit ihren englischen Entsprechungen in einem alphabetischen Register aufgelistet. Das bietet den Vorteil, daß das Nachschlagen sowohl ausgehend vom Englischen als auch vom Deutschen erfolgen kann. Damit vereinigt das PONS Fachwörterbuch Marketing die Vorzüge eines einsprachigen Erklärungswörterbuchs mit denen eines zweisprachigen Nachschlagewerks.

Wir möchten Herrn Dr. Rudolf Richard Gerharz für seine Hilfe bei der Übersetzung dieses Wörterbuchs ins Deutsche danken.

Preface

This ENGLISH-GERMAN DICTIONARY OF MARKETING contains some 3,500 words and phrases with their German equivalents. The subject matter covers such aspects as market research, advertising and publicity, promotional aids, presentation and packaging, as well as various selling techniques.

The words and phrases are clearly defined in simple English and many examples are given to show how the words are used in context. In cases where English and German terminology or institutions do not correspond, the expression is explained by a definition in German. In addition, there are numerous quotations from various magazines and journals which give an idea of how the terms are used in real life.

In the second part of the dictionary, a Glossary lists the translated German terms in alphabetical order, together with their English equivalents, thus enabling the user to refer to words both in English and in German. The supplement at the back of the book gives some further information which may be helpful to the user.

We would like to thank Dr. Rudolf Richard Gerharz for his assistance in the the translation of this dictionary.

Englisch-Deutsches Wörterbuch

Aa

ABC method = ATTENTION, BENEFIT, CLOSE sales method, where the customer's Attention is attracted, the salesman then shows the Benefits of the product to the customer, and finally Closes the deal **ABC-Methode (Aufmerksamkeit, Nutzen, Abschluß)**

above-the-line advertising *noun* advertising for which a payment is made (such as an ad in a magazine or a stand at a trade fair) and for which a commission is paid to the advertising agency **Werbung ‚über dem Strich', vergütungsfähige Werbung;** *Compare* BELOW-THE-LINE

absolute *adjective* complete *or* total **absolut, unbeschränkt; absolute advantage** = advantage enjoyed by an area of the world which can produce a product more cheaply than other areas **absoluter Vorteil;** *for climatic reasons, tropical countries have an absolute advantage in that type of production;* **absolute monopoly** = situation where only one producer or supplier produces or supplies something **unumschränktes Monopol;** *the company has an absolute monopoly of imports of French wine; the company can fix high prices since it has an absolute monopoly; the supplier's absolute monopoly of the product meant that customers had to accept his terms*

absorb *verb*
(a) to take in a small item so as to form part of a larger one **absorbieren, aufnehmen; to absorb a surplus** = to take back surplus stock so that it does not affect a business **Warenbestände zurücknehmen; overheads have absorbed all our profits** = all our profits have gone into paying overhead expenses **die laufenden Kosten haben unsere ganzen Gewinne geschluckt; to absorb a loss by a subsidiary** = to write a subsidiary company's loss into the main accounts **den Verlust einer Tochtergesellschaft auffangen**
(b) a business which has been absorbed by a competitor = a small business which has been made part of a larger one **Unternehmen, das von der Konkurrenz übernommen wurde**

◇ **absorption** *noun* making a smaller item *or* business part of a larger one **Übernahme absorption costing** = allocation of fixed or indirect costs as well as variable or direct costs to the actual products or services produced **Vollkostenrechnung**

accelerator *noun* theory that a change in demand for consumer goods will result in a greater change in demand for the capital goods used in their production **Akzelerationsprinzip**

accept *verb*
(a) to agree formally to receive something *or* to be responsible for something **annehmen; to accept a bill** = to sign a bill of exchange to indicate that it will be paid **einen Wechsel akzeptieren; accepted bill** = bill of exchange which has been signed, and therefore accepted by the buyer **akzeptierter Wechsel; to accept delivery of a shipment** = to take goods into the warehouse officially when they are delivered **eine Warensendung annehmen**
(b) to take something which is being offered *or* to say "yes" *or* to agree to something **akzeptieren, annehmen;** *she accepted the offer of a job in Australia; he accepted £200 for the car*

◇ **acceptable** *adjective* which can be accepted **akzeptabel, annehmbar;** *both parties found the offer acceptable*

◇ **acceptance** *noun*
(a) signing a bill of exchange to show that you agree to pay it **Akzept, Annahme; to present a bill for acceptance** = to send a bill for payment by the person who has accepted it **einen Wechsel zum Akzept vorlegen; acceptance house** *or* *(US)* **acceptance bank** = ACCEPTING HOUSE
(b) acceptance of an offer = agreeing to an offer **Annahme eines Angebotes; to give an offer a conditional acceptance** = to accept provided that certain things happen *or* that certain terms apply **ein Angebot unter Vorbehalt annehmen; we have his letter of acceptance** = we have received a letter from him accepting the offer **wir haben seine Annahmeerklärung erhalten; clean acceptance** = unconditional acceptance of a bill of lading **vorbehaltloses Akzept; irrevocable acceptance** = acceptance which cannot be withdrawn **unwiderrufliches Akzept; acceptance against documents** = transaction where the seller takes charge of the shipping documents for a consignment of goods when a buyer accepts a bill of exchange **Akzeptleistung gegen Dokumente;** *sellers sometimes insist on acceptance against documents; acceptance against documents protects the seller when sending*

goods which are not yet paid for; **acceptance sampling** = testing a small part of a batch to see if the whole batch is good enough **Qualitätskontrolle mittels Stichprobe**

◇ **accepting house** *noun* firm which accepts bills of exchange (i.e. promises to pay them) and is paid a commission for this **Akzeptbank**

◇ **acceptor** *noun* person who accepts a bill of exchange by signing it, thus making a commitment to pay it by a certain specified date **Akzeptant**

access

1 *noun* **to have access to something** = to be able to obtain *or* reach something **zu etwas Zugang haben;** *he has access to large amounts of venture capital;* **access to the market** = (i) legal right to sell in a particular market; (ii) ability to reach a market by promotion and distribution **(i) Verkaufsrecht; (ii) Marktzugang; access time** = time taken by a computer to find data stored in it **Zugriffszeit**

2 *verb* to call up (data) which is stored in a computer **aufrufen, zugreifen auf;** *she accessed the address file on the computer*

◇ **accessibility** *noun* ability of a market to be reached by promotion and distribution **(Markt)zugänglichkeit;** *there is much demand in the market, but, because of the great distances involved, accessibility is a problem; we must analyse the geographical aspects in assessing the market's accessibility*

accommodation

accommodation *noun* **accommodation bill** = bill of exchange which the person signs in order to help someone raise a loan **Gefälligkeitswechsel**

account

1 *noun*

(a) record of money paid *or* owed **Abrechnung; Konto;** *please send me your account or a detailed or an itemized account;* **expense account** = money which a businessman is allowed by his company to spend on travelling and entertaining clients in connection with his business **Spesenkonto;** *he charged his hotel bill to his expense account*

(b) *(in a shop)* arrangement whereby a customer pays for the goods he or she buys at a later date (usually the end of the month) **Kunden(kredit)konto;** *to have an account or a charge account or a credit account with Harrods; put it on my account or charge it to my account; (of a customer)* **to open an account** = to ask a shop to supply goods which will be paid for at a later date **ein Kundenkonto eröffnen, einrichten;** *(of a shop)* **to open an account** *or* **to close an account** = to start *or* to stop supplying a customer on credit **ein Kundenkonto eröffnen/einrichten; ein Kundenkonto sperren; to settle an account** = to pay all the money owed on an account **ein Konto be-, ausgleichen; to stop an account** = to stop supplying a customer until he or she has paid what is owing **ein Kundenkonto sperren; on account** = as part of a total bill **als Teilzahlung; to pay money on account** = to pay money in settlement of part of a bill **eine Anzahlung leisten, Geld anzahlen; advance on account** = money paid as a part payment **eine Teilzahlung leisten**

(c) arrangement which a company has with an advertising agency, where the agency deals with all promotion for the company **Werbeetat (des Kunden einer Werbeagentur);** *the company has moved its $3m account to another agency; the small agency lost the account when the company decided it needed a different marketing approach; three agencies were asked to make presentations, as the company had decided to switch its account*

(d) customer who does a large amount of business with a firm and has an account with it **Kreditkunde;** *he is one of our largest accounts; our salesmen call on their best accounts twice a month;* **fringe accounts** = accounts that are not very profitable for the supplier **Sekundärkunden; national account** = customer with branches or offices all over the country **Kunde auf nationaler Ebene**

(d) the accounts of a business *or* **a company's accounts** = detailed record of a company's financial affairs **Geschäftsbücher, Bücher; to keep the accounts** = to write each sum of money in the account book **die Bücher führen;** *the accountant's job is to enter all the money received in the accounts;* **annual accounts** = accounts prepared at the end of a financial year **Jahresabschluß, Jahresbilanz; management accounts** = financial information (sales, expenditure, credit, and profitability) prepared for a manager so that he or she can take decisions **Rechnungsbericht für die besonderen Zwecke der Unternehmensleitung; Geschäftsbilanz; profit and loss account** = accounts for a company with expenditure and income balanced to show a final profit or loss **Gewinn- und Verlustrechnung; accounts department** = department in a company which deals with money paid, received, borrowed or owed **Buchhaltung; accounts manager** = manager of an accounts department **Leiter/-in der Buchhaltung; accounts payable** = money owed by a company **Verbindlichkeiten; accounts receivable** = money owed to a company **Außenstände**

(e) bank account *or* *(US)* **banking account** = arrangement to keep money in a bank

Bankkonto; budget account = bank account where you plan income and expenditure to allow for periods when expenditure is high **Budget-Konto; current account** *or* **cheque account** *or (US)* **checking account** = account which pays no interest but from which the customer can withdraw money at any time by writing cheques **laufendes Konto, Girokonto; deposit account** = account which pays interest but from which money can usually be withdrawn only after notice has been given **Sparkonto (ohne gesetzliche Kündigungsfrist); external account** = account with a British bank held by someone who is living in another country **Auslandskonto; frozen account** = account where the money cannot be used or moved because of a court order **gesperrtes Konto; joint account** = account for two people **gemeinsames Konto, Gemeinschaftskonto;** *most married people have joint accounts so that they can each take money out when they want;* **overdrawn account** = account where you have taken out more money than you have put in (i.e. where the bank is lending you money) **überzogenes Konto; savings account** = account where you put money in regularly and which pays interest, often at a higher rate than a deposit account **Sparkonto; to open an account** = to start a bank account by putting money in **ein Konto eröffnen/einrichten; to close an account** = to take all money out of a bank account and stop the account **ein Konto auflösen**

(f) *(Stock Exchange)* period of credit (usually fourteen days) at the end of which you must pay for shares you have bought **(14-tägige) Abrechnung; account day** = day on which shares which have been bought must be paid for **Abrechnungstag;** *share prices rose at the account end or the end of the account*

(g) notice **Berücksichtigung; to take account of inflation** *or* **to take inflation into account** = to assume that there will be a certain percentage inflation when making calculations **die Inflation in Betracht ziehen**

2 *verb* **to account for** = to explain and record a money deal **Rechenschaft ablegen, sich verantworten;** *to account for a loss or a discrepancy; the reps have to account for all their expenses to the sales manager*

◇ **account executive** *noun*

(a) employee who looks after certain customers *or* who is the link between certain customers and the company **Kundenbetreuer**

(b) *(also* **account handler)** person who works in an advertising agency, and who is responsible for a particular client **Kontakter, Kundenbetreuer**

> QUOTE we have moved the account because we thought it would be better suited in a smaller agency
>
> *Marketing Week*

accountancy *noun* work of an accountant **Buchhaltung, Rechnungswesen;** *he is studying accountancy or he is an accountancy student*

◇ **accountant** *noun* person who keeps a company's accounts *or* person who advises a company on its finances *or* person who examines accounts **Buchhalter/-in; Steuerberater/-in; Rechnungs-, Wirtschaftsprüfer/-in; certified accountant** = accountant who has passed the professional examinations and is a member of the Association of Certified Accountants; *(entspricht)* **amtlich zugelassener Wirtschaftsprüfer;** *(US)* **certified public accountant** = accountant who has passed professional examinations; *(entspricht)* **Wirtschaftsprüfer; chartered accountant** = accountant who has passed the professional examinations and is a member of the Institute of Chartered Accountants; *(entspricht)* **beeidigter Wirtschaftsprüfer; cost accountant** = accountant who gives managers information about their business costs **Kostenrechner/-in; management accountant** = accountant who prepares financial information for managers so that they can take decisions **Finanzbuchhalter**

◇ **accounting** *noun* work of recording money paid, received, borrowed or owed **Buchhaltung, Rechnungswesen;** *accounting machine; accounting methods or accounting procedures; accounting system;* **accounting period** = period usually covered by a firm's accounts **Abrechnungszeitraum; cost accounting** = preparing special accounts of manufacturing and sales costs **Kostenrechnung; current cost accounting** = method of accounting which values assets at what it would cost to replace them now, rather than at their original cost **Rechnungslegung zum Wiederbeschaffungswert**

> QUOTE applicants will be professionally qualified and have a degree in Commerce or Accounting
>
> *Australian Financial Review*

accredited agent *noun* agent who is appointed by a company to act on its behalf **Bevollmächtigte(r), Kommissionär**

acct = ACCOUNT

accurate *adjective* correct **genau, exakt, fehlerfrei; accurate description** = honest and true description of a product *or* service in an advertisement or catalogue **korrekte Beschreibung;** *as the advertisement was clearly not an accurate description of the product, the company had to pay a fine; it is not an accurate description of the product to state that it gives out more light than the sun*

◇ **accurately** *adverb* correctly **genau, exakt, fehlerfrei;** *the computer accurately forecast that sales would drop in the second quarter*

acknowledge *verb* to inform a sender that a letter *or* package *or* shipment has arrived **bestätigen;** *he has still not acknowledged my letter of the 24th; we acknowledge receipt of your letter of June 14th*

◇ **acknowledgement** *noun* act of acknowledging **Bestätigung;** *she sent an acknowledgement of receipt; they sent a letter of acknowledgement*

ACORN = A CLASSIFICATION OF RESIDENTIAL NEIGHBOURHOODS classification of residential areas by the type of people who live in them, much used in consumer research **ACORN (eine Wohngegendklassifikation);** *ACORN will help us plan where to concentrate our sales visits*

acquire *verb* to buy **erwerben;** *to acquire a company*

◇ **acquirer** *noun* person *or* company which buys something **Erwerber, Ankäufer**

◇ **acquisition** *noun* thing bought; act of getting *or* buying something **Anschaffung, Erwerb;** *the chocolate factory is his latest acquisition;* **data acquisition** *or* **acquisition of data** = obtaining and classifying data **Datenerfassung**

acronym *noun* word which is made up from the initials of other words **Akronym, Initialwort;** *the name of the company was especially designed to provide a catchy acronym; BASIC is an acronym for Beginner's All-purpose Symbolic Instruction Code*

across-the-board *adjective* running an ad or radio or TV commercial for five consecutive days (from Monday to Friday) **werktäglich zur selben Zeit**

action *see* AIDA

◇ **action shot** *noun* scene with movement (either in a film or on TV) **Aufnahme von Aktion, Bewegungsaufnahme**

ad = ADVERTISEMENT

adapt *verb* to change something a little to fit in with changing circumstances **anpassen;** *this product must be adapted in line with recent technological developments; the device has been adapted for use on board aircraft*

◇ **adaptation** *noun* small change; thing which has been adapted **Anpassung; überarbeitetes/angepaßtes Stück;** *this machine is an adaptation of our original model; with a few minor adaptations, the machine will cut square holes as well as round ones*

◇ **adaptive control model** *noun (US)* model for planning advertising expenditure in line with changes in consumer responses to advertising **anpassungsfähiges Kontrollmodell**

ad hoc *adjective* irregular *or* done only occasionally **ad hoc, besondere(r,s);** *they run ad hoc surveys to test customer reaction when new products are launched; shipping by airfreight was an ad hoc arrangement because of the strike in the docks*

adjust *verb* to change to fit new circumstances **anpassen, angleichen; seasonally adjusted figures** = statistics which are adjusted to take account of seasonal variations **saisonbereinigte Beträge**

adman *noun (informal)* man who works in advertising **Werbefachmann;** *the admen are using balloons as promotional material*

administer *verb* to organize *or* to manage **verwalten;** *he administers a large pension fund;* **administered channel** = distribution channel in which there is cooperation between businesses **verwalteter Vertriebsweg;** *(US)* **administered price** = price fixed by a manufacturer which cannot be varied by a retailer **Preisbindung zweiter Hand; vertikale Preisbindung;** *compare* RESALE PRICE MAINTENANCE

◇ **administration** *noun* organization *or* control *or* management of a company **Verwaltung, Führung; the expenses of the administration** *or* **administration expenses** = costs of management, not including production, marketing or distribution costs **Verwaltungskosten; letters of administration** = letter given by a court to allow someone to deal with the estate of a person who has died **Bestallungsurkunde zum Nachlaßverwalter**

◇ **administrative** *adjective* referring to administration **administrativ, verwaltungstechnisch;** *administrative details; administrative expenses*

◊ **administrator** *noun*
(a) person who directs the work of other employees in a business **Verwalter; Bürovorsteher**
(b) person appointed by a court to manage the affairs of someone who has died without leaving a will **Nachlaßverwalter**

adopt *verb*
(a) to agree to (something) *or* to accept (something) **annehmen;** *to adopt a new marketing strategy*
(b) to decide to buy and continue to use a particular product **akzeptieren**

◊ **adopter** *noun* customer who adopts a particular product **Akzeptierende(r); early adopters** = category of adopters of a product who use it or buy it later than innovators, but earlier than the late majority **früh Akzeptierende, Frühadopter**

◊ **adoption** *noun* decision to buy *or* use a particular product **Adoption, Akzeptanz;** *more promotion was needed to speed up adoption of the product; widespread adoption of its new shampoo range has made the company the market leader;* **adoption curve** = line on a graph showing how many consumers adopt or buy a new product at various time periods after the launch date **Adoptionskurve(nlinie);** *the adoption curve shows that most people who buy the product do so at a fairly late stage*

adshel *noun* trade mark for a poster site for advertisements in a bus shelter **Anschlagwerbewarenzeichen (an Bus-Unterständen)**

ad valorem duty *noun* duty calculated on the sales value of the goods **Wertsteuer**

advance
1 *noun*
(a) money paid as a loan or as a part of a payment to be made later **Vorschuß; Anzahlung; Darlehen**
(b) in advance = early *or* before something happens **im voraus, vorab;** *to pay in advance; freight payable in advance; price fixed in advance;* **advance freight** = freight which is payable in advance **im voraus zu leistende Frachtkosten;** *(US)* **advance man** = person who publicizes a performance and sells tickets for it before the performers arrive **Werber, Vorverkäufer**
(c) increase **Fortschritt, Verbesserung; Erhöhung;** *advance in trade; advance in prices*
2 *adjective* early **im voraus, vorab;** *advance booking; advance payment; you must give seven days' advance notice of withdrawals from the account*
3 *verb*
(a) to lend **leihen; vorschießen;** *the bank advanced him £10,000 against the security of his house*
(b) to increase **steigen, anziehen;** *prices generally advanced on the stock market*
(c) to make something happen earlier **vorverlegen;** *the date of the AGM has been advanced to May 10th; the meeting with the German distributors has been advanced from 11.00 to 09.30*

advertise *verb* to announce that something is for sale *or* that a job is vacant *or* that a service is offered **eine Anzeige schalten, annoncieren; per Anzeige suchen; Reklame machen für;** *to advertise a vacancy; to advertise for a secretary; to advertise a new product*

◊ **ad** *noun (informal)* = ADVERTISEMENT *we put an ad in the paper; she answered an ad in the paper; he found his job through an ad in the paper;* **backup ad** = advertisement designed to accompany editorial material in a publication **textanschließende Anzeige; classified ads** *or* **small ads** *or* **want ads** = advertisements listed in a newspaper under special headings (like "property for sale","jobs wanted") **Kleinanzeigen;** *look in the small ads to see if anyone has a computer for sale;* **coupon ad** = advertisement with a form attached, which is to be cut out and returned to the advertiser with your name and address for further information **Kuponanzeige; display ad** = advertisement which is set apart from other advertisements by having its own typeface, borders, illustrations, etc. **Großanzeige; house ad** = advertisement in a publication which is placed by the publication itself (such as one offering a readers' advice service, or selling back numbers of the publication) **Eigenanzeige**

◊ **advert** *noun (GB) informal* = ADVERTISEMENT *to put an advert in the paper; to answer an advert in the paper; classified adverts; display advert*

◊ **advertisement** *noun* notice which shows that something is for sale *or* that a service is offered *or* that someone wants something *or* that a job is vacant, etc.; short film on television, short announcement on the radio, which tries to persuade people to use a certain product or service **Anzeige, Annonce; Reklame, Werbung;** *to put an advertisement in the paper; to answer an advertisement in the paper;* **classified advertisements** = advertisements listed in a newspaper under special headings (such as "property for sale" or "jobs wanted") **Kleinanzeigen; display advertisement** = advertisement which is set apart from other advertisements by having its own typeface, borders, illustrations, etc.

Großanzeige; advertisement manager = manager in charge of the advertisement section of a newspaper **Anzeigenleiter**

◇ **advertiser** *noun* person *or* company which advertises **Inserent, Anzeigenkunde;** *the catalogue gives a list of advertisers*

◇ **advertising** *noun* business of announcing that something is for sale *or* of trying to persuade customers to buy a product or service **Werbewesen, Werbung(sbranche);** *she works in advertising; he has a job in advertising; the company has asked an advertising agent to prepare a presentation; our advertising budget has been cut again; the advertising campaign was a flop;* **advertising agency** = office which plans, designs and manages advertising for other companies **Werbeagentur; advertising appropriation** *or* **advertising budget** = money set aside by an organization for its advertising **(bewilligtes) Werbebudget;** *the marketing director and the chief accountant have yet to fix the advertising appropriation; we cannot afford as large an advertising appropriation as last year; if the market turns out to be bigger than expected, we will increase our advertising appropriation;* **advertising control** = legislative and other measures to prevent abuses in advertising **Überprüfung der Werbung;** *if voluntary advertising control doesn't work, then the government will step in with legislation;* **advertising hoarding** = billboard *or* wooden surface onto which advertising posters are stuck **Werbeanschlagfläche;** *advertising hoardings have been taken down in that town since the council banned posters; giant advertising hoardings were placed in fields on either side of the road;* **advertising manager** = manager in charge of advertising a company's products **Werbeleiter; advertising media** = types of communication used in advertising such as television or the press **Werbemedien;** *which advertising media would get our message across best? television is not considered the most effective advertising medium for industrial products;* **advertising message** = whatever a company is trying to communicate in an advertisement **Werbeaussage, Werbebotschaft;** *bad copywriting made the advertising message unclear; the advertising message was aimed at the wrong target audience and therefore got little response; the poster does not use words to get its advertising message across;* **advertising rates** = amount of money charged for advertising space in a newspaper *or* advertising time on TV **Anzeigenkosten; Werbetarif; advertising space** = space in a newspaper set aside for advertisements **Anzeigenraum; to take advertising space in a paper** = to put an advertisement in a newspaper **in einer Zeitung inserieren; Anzeigenraum in einer Zeitung belegen; advertising time** = time on television or radio set aside for advertising **Werbe(sende)zeit;** *advertising time is cheapest in the afternoon; he spent a month selling advertising time over the telephone; how much advertising time does this programme allow for?; see also* ADVOCACY, AERIAL, COMPARATIVE, DIRECT-ACTION, EDUCATIONAL, ENDORSEMENT, INVESTMENT, NATIONAL, REMINDER, SATURATION, TESTIMONIAL etc.

◇ **Advertising Standards Authority (ASA)** *noun* independent body which oversees the system of self-regulation in the British advertising industry **(Britischer) Werberat**

> QUOTE The objective of advertising for new products differs from that of advertising for improved products
>
> ***International Journal of Advertising***
>
> QUOTE in 1987, the advertising expenditure total was £6,264m
>
> ***Precision Marketing***
>
> QUOTE as media costs have spiralled, more financial directors are getting involved in the advertising process
>
> ***Marketing Week***

advice *noun* notification *or* telling someone what has happened **Benachrichtigung, Mitteilung; advice of dispatch** = communication from seller to buyer stating that goods have been sent, specifying time and place of arrival **Versandanzeige, Avis;** *we have paid for the goods but as yet have received no advice of dispatch; the advice of dispatch informed the buyer that the goods would arrive at Southampton on the morning of the 10th;* **advice note** *or* **letter of advice** = written notice to a customer giving details of goods ordered and shipped but not yet delivered **Versandanzeige, Avis; as per advice** = according to what is written on the advice note **laut Benachrichtigung/Avis**

advise *verb* to tell someone what has happened **in Kenntnis setzen, informieren, unterrichten;** *we are advised that the shipment will arrive next week*

advocacy advertising *noun* advertising by a business that expresses a particular point of view on a certain issue **engagierte Werbung;** *because of its prestige as a producer, the company's advocacy advertising had great influence; the food company's advocacy advertising condemned unhealthy additives in canned produce; advocacy advertising has changed the public's attitude to smoking*

aerial advertising *noun* advertising displayed in the air from balloons or planes or in smoke designs **Luftwerbung;** *aerial advertising proved to be an effective gimmick; aerial advertising was used to attract the attention of people on the beach*

affordable method *noun* method of budgeting how much can be spent on marketing and promotion, which is based on what you can afford, rather than what you want to achieve **finanzmittelbezogene Werbebudgetierung;** *affordable method appeals to accountants, but won't help us achieve a high enough market share for the product*

after-date *noun* reference on a bill of exchange to the length of time allowed for payment after a certain date **Verfallsdatum;** *the after-date allowed the buyer three months in which to pay*

◊ **after-sales service** *noun* service of a machine carried out by the seller some time after the machine has been purchased **Kundendienst**

◊ **after-sight** *noun* type of bill of exchange which is due to be paid on a certain day after acceptance **nach Sicht**

agate *noun (US)* measurement of advertising space in a newspaper, equal to one-fourteenth of an inch **Agate(-Zeile)**

age group *noun* category including all people whose ages fall between two established points **Altersgruppe;** *what age groups is this product meant to appeal to? research shows an increase in smoking among the 18-20 age group*

agency *noun*
(a) office *or* job of representing another company in an area **Agentur, Vertretung;** *they signed an agency agreement or an agency contract;* **sole agency** = agreement to be the only person to represent a company *or* to sell a product in a certain area **Alleinvertretung; Alleinvertrieb;** *he has the sole agency for Ford cars;* **agency bill** = bill of exchange which is accepted by the London branch of an overseas bank **Wechsel, der von einer Londoner Niederlassung einer ausländischen Bank akzeptiert wird**
(b) office *or* business which arranges things for other companies **Agentur; employment agency** = office which finds jobs for people **Stellenvermittlung; estate agency** = office which arranges for the sale of properties **Grundstücks- und Immobilienmakler(büro); news agency** = office which distributes news to newspapers and television stations **Nachrichtenagentur, Nachrichtendienst; travel agency** = office which arranges travel for customers **Reisebüro**
(c) advertising agency = office which plans *or* designs and manages advertising for companies **Werbeagentur; house agency** = advertising agency owned and used by a large company, but which can be used by other companies also **hauseigene Werbeagentur, Hausagentur**

agent *noun*
(a) person who represents a company *or* another person in an area **Vertreter/-in;** *to be the agent for IBM;* **sole agent** = person who has the sole agency for a company in an area **Alleinvertreter;** *he is the sole agent for Ford cars;* **agent's commission** = money (often a percentage of sales) paid to an agent **Vertreterprovision**
(b) person in charge of an agency **Makler/-in, Agent/-in;** *advertising agent; estate agent; travel agent;* **commission agent** = agent who is paid by commission, not by fee **Provisionsvertreter, Kommissionsagent; Kommissionär; forwarding agent** = person *or* company which arranges shipping and customs documents **Spediteur; insurance agent** = person who arranges insurance for clients **Versicherungsvertreter; land agent** = person who runs a farm *or* a large area of land for the owner **Gutsverwalter**
(c) *US* **(business) agent** = chief local official of a trade union **Gewerkschaftsfunktionär**

aggregate *adjective* total *or* with everything added together **Gesamt-, gesamt, angesammelt; aggregate demand** = total demand for goods and services in a country **gesamte/aggregierte Nachfrage;** *economists are studying the recent fall in aggregate demand; as incomes have risen, so has aggregate demand;* **aggregate supply** = all goods and services on the market **gesamtes/aggregiertes Angebot;** *is aggregate supply meeting aggregate demand?*

agree *verb*
(a) to approve **genehmigen, sich einverstanden erklären;** *the auditors have agreed the accounts; the figures were agreed between the two parties; we have agreed the budgets for next year; terms of the contract are still to be agreed; he has agreed your prices*
(b) to say yes *or* to accept **vereinbaren; zustimmen;** *it has been agreed that the lease will run for 25 years; after some discussion he agreed to our plan; the bank will never agree to the terms of the loan*
(c) to agree to do something = to say that you will do something **sich einverstanden od**

bereit erklären, etwas zu tun; *she agreed to be chairman; will the finance director agree to resign? the bank agreed to lend the company $250,000*
(d) *(of a group of people)* **to agree on something** = to come to a joint decision about something **sich einigen über etwas;** *they have finally agreed on a new marketing strategy; can we agree on a date for the new product launch?*
(e) to think the same *or* to be the same **einverstanden sein; übereinstimmen;** *I think it's an excellent plan, but the marketing director doesn't agree; the two sets of calculations do not agree*

◇ **agree with** *verb*
(a) to say that your opinions are the same as someone else's **übereinstimmen mit;** *I agree with the chairman that the figures are lower than normal*
(b) to be the same as **übereinstimmen mit;** *the auditors' figures do not agree with those of the accounts department*

◇ **agreed** *adjective* which has been accepted by everyone **vereinbart, abgemacht;** *an agreed amount; on agreed terms*

◇ **agreement** *noun* contract between two parties which explains how they will act **Vereinbarung, Abkommen, Abmachung;** *written agreement; unwritten or verbal agreement; to draw up or to draft an agreement; to break an agreement; to sign an agreement; to witness an agreement; agreement has been reached or concluded or come to; to reach or to come to an agreement on prices or salaries; an international agreement on trade; collective wage agreement; an agency agreement; a marketing agreement;* **blanket agreement** = agreement which covers many different items **Gesamtvereinbarung; exclusive agreement** = agreement whereby a company is appointed sole agent for a product in a market **Alleinvertretungsvereinbarung; gentleman's agreement** = verbal agreement between two parties who trust each other **Vereinbarung auf Treu und Glauben, Gentleman's Agreement**

AIDA

AIDA = ATTENTION, INTEREST, DESIRE, ACTION model showing stages in the effects of advertising on consumers **AIDA-Modell (Aufmerksamkeit, Interesse, (Kauf)wunsch, Handlung)**

aid

1 *noun* something which helps **Hilfsmittel; dealer aids** = types of advertising material which can be used in shops as a way of attracting customers **Werbematerial, Händlerhilfen; sales aids** = advertising materials used to help sales, such as sample packs, sales literature, display cases, etc. **Verkaufshilfen**
2 *verb* to help **helfen; aided recall** = test to see how well someone remembers an advertisement by giving the respondent some help (such as a picture which he or she might associate with it) **gestützte Erinnerung;** *even aided recall brought no reaction from the respondent; aided recall has shown that we must make our advertising more striking*

◇ **aids-to-trade** *noun* services which support trade, such as banking and advertising **Hilfsbetriebe des Handels;** *the recession has affected aids-to-trade and the industries they support and supply; at that time, advertising was the fastest expanding aid-to-trade*

aim

1 *noun* something which you try to do **Ziel, Bestrebung;** *one of our aims is to increase the quality of our products;* **the company has achieved all its aims** = the company has done all the things it had hoped to do **das Unternehmen hat seine Ziele erreicht**
2 *verb* to try to do something **streben nach;** *we aim to be No. 1 in the market in two years' time; each salesman must aim to double his previous year's sales*

air

air *noun*
(a) method of travelling *or* sending goods using aircraft **auf dem Luftwege, per Luftpost;** *to send a letter or a shipment by air;* **air carrier** = company which sends cargo *or* passengers by air **Flug-, Luftfahrtgesellschaft; air forwarding** = arranging for goods to be shipped by air **Luftfrachtspedition; air letter** = special sheet of thin blue paper which when folded can be sent by air mail without an envelope **Luftpostbrief(papier)**
(b) medium for broadcasting (i.e., radio or television) **(auf) Sendung; im Rundfunk;** *two of our advertisements will be on the air this morning*

◇ **air cargo** *noun* goods sent by air **Luftfracht**

◇ **air freight** *noun* method of shipping goods in an aircraft **Luftfracht;** *to send a shipment by air freight; air freight charges or rates*

◇ **airfreight** *verb* to send goods by air **per Luftfracht senden;** *to airfreight a consignment to Mexico; if you run out of stock, we will airfreight the goods to you*

◇ **airline** *noun* company which carries passengers or cargo by air **Fluggesellschaft, Airline**

◇ **airmail**
1 *noun* way of sending letters *or* parcels by air **Luftpost;** *to send a package by airmail;*

airmail charges have risen by 15%; **airmail envelope** = very light envelope for sending airmail letters **Luftpostumschlag; airmail sticker** = blue sticker with the words "by air mail" which can be stuck to an envelope or packet to show it is being sent by air **Luftpostaufkleber**
2 *verb* to send letters *or* parcels by air **per Luftpost schicken;** *to airmail a document to New York*

◊ **airtight** *adjective* which does not allow air to get in **luftdicht;** *the goods are packed in airtight containers*

◊ **air time** *noun* time set aside for advertising on television or radio **Werbezeit;** *how much air time do we need for this commercial? we should look for air time on the new radio station; all the air time in the world won't sell this product*

aisle *noun* space or passageway between the shelves of products on display in a supermarket **Gang**

à la carte *adjective* system whereby advertisers use the services of a whole range of businesses rather than relying on one agency over a long period **nach der (Speise)karte**

all-in price *noun* price which covers all items in a purchase (shipping, insurance, packing, as well as the item bought) **Inklusivpreis**

ambush marketing *noun* linking a promotion campaign to an event (such as a sporting contest which is sponsored by another manufacturer) without paying a fee **Windschattenmarketing**

analyse *or* **analyze** *verb* to examine in detail **analysieren, auswerten;** *to analyse a statement of account; to analyse the market potential*

◊ **analysis** *noun* detailed examination and report **Analyse, Auswertung;** *job analysis; market analysis; sales analysis; to carry out an analysis of the market potential; to write an analysis of the sales position;* **contribution analysis** = analysis of how much each product contributes to profit **Beitragsanalyse; cost analysis** = examination in advance of the costs of a new product **Kostenanalyse; systems analysis** = using a computer to suggest how a company can improve efficiency by analysing the way in which it works at present **Systemanalyse** *see also* CRITICAL PATH ANALYSIS

◊ **analyst** *noun* person who analyses **Analytiker/-in;** *market analyst; systems analyst*

ancillaries-to-trade *noun* services which support trade, such as banking and advertising **Hilfsbetriebe des Handels;** *the recession has affected ancillaries-to-trade and the industries they support and supply; advertising was the fastest expanding ancillary-to-trade at that time*

animatic *noun* rough outline version of a television commercial shown to the advertiser for approval **Probewerbesendung;** *the animatic was sent back to the agency with several criticisms; the animatic impressed the advertiser because it put the message over stylishly; if the animatic is approved, the creative team will begin work on the final product*

◊ **animation** *noun* film made from drawings *or* a cartoon film **Zeichentrickfilm**

anonymous product *noun* product with no apparent brand name, used in advertisements to highlight the product being promoted **anonyme Ware;** *Brand X is the anonymous product which never gets your washing completely white; we must choose an anonymous product which performs badly enough; no one watching the commercial would believe the anonymous product was as bad is it seemed; what happens if the respondent chooses the anonymous product instead of ours?*

anti- *prefix* against **Anti-**

◊ **anti-trust** *adjective* which attacks monopolies and encourages competition **Antitrust-;** *anti-trust laws or legislation*

appeal *noun* being attractive **Reiz, Anziehungskraft; customer appeal** = being attractive to customers **Kundenattraktivität; sales appeal** = quality which makes customers want to buy **Kaufanreiz**

apperception *see* THEMATIC

appraiser *noun (US)* person who estimates how much money something is worth **Schätzer;** *although he is our chief buyer, he is a poor appraiser*

appro *noun* = APPROVAL; **to buy something on appro** = to buy something which you will only pay for if it is found to be satisfactory after a trial period **etwas zur Probe/zur Ansicht kaufen**

approach
1 *noun*
(a) getting in touch with someone with a proposal **Herantreten, Herangehen(sweise);** *the company made an approach to the supermarket chain; the board turned down all approaches on the subject of mergers; we have had an approach from a Japanese company to buy our car division*
(b) method of dealing with a problem *or* subject **Betrachtungsweise, Art und Weise ein Problem in Angriff zu nehmen;** *if you are selling to the teenage market, you will need a different approach; I like the agency's approach to the problem of marketing our products*
2 *verb*
(a) to get in touch with someone with a proposal **herantreten an, sich wenden an;** *he approached the bank with a request for a loan; the company was approached by an American publisher with the suggestion of a merger; we have been approached several times but have turned down all offers*
(b) to try to deal with a problem **herangehen;** *perhaps we should approach the problem of selling to the children's market from a different angle?*

appropriation *noun* act of putting money aside for a special purpose **Zuweisung, Bereitstellung;** *appropriation of funds to the reserve;* **appropriation account =** part of a profit and loss account which shows how the profit has been dealt with (i.e. how much has been given to the shareholders as dividends, how much is being put into the reserves, etc.) **Gewinnverteilungsrechnung; advertising appropriation =** money set aside by an organization for its advertising **Werbebudget, Werbeetat;** *the marketing director and the chief accountant have yet to fix the advertising appropriation; we cannot afford as large an advertising appropriation as last year; if the market turns out to be bigger than expected, we will increase our advertising appropriation*

approve *verb*
(a) to approve of = to think something is good **billigen, gutheißen;** *the chairman approves of the new company letter heading; the sales staff do not approve of interference from the accounts division*
(b) to agree to something officially **genehmigen; ratifizieren;** *to approve the terms of a contract; the proposal was approved by the board*
◇ **approval** *noun*
(a) agreement **Genehmigung;** *to submit a budget for approval;* **certificate of approval =** document showing that an item has been officially approved **Genehmigungszertifikat**
(b) on approval = sale where the buyer only pays for goods if they are found to be satisfactory after a trial period **zur Probe; versuchsweise;** *the office has bought a photocopier on approval*

area *noun* part of a country, a division for commercial purposes **Gebiet;** *his sales area is the North-West; he finds it difficult to cover all his area in a week*
◇ **area code** *noun* special telephone number which is given to a particular area **Vorwahl, Ortsnetzkennzahl;** *the area code for central London is 071*
◇ **area manager** *noun* manager who is responsible for a particular part of the country **Bezirks-, Gebietsleiter**

arithmetic mean = AVERAGE

armchair research *noun* looking for information that has already been compiled and published in reference books such as directories **Sekundärforschung;** *most of our armchair research can be done in libraries; if we cannot find all the data through armchair research, we shall have to do a market survey of our own*

art director *noun* coordinator of creative work in advertising **Leiter/-in der Grafikabteilung, Art-Direktor/-in;** *the art director briefed the copywriter and illustrator on the main points of the campaign; after three years as an agency photographer, he was made art director*

article *noun*
(a) product *or* thing for sale **Artikel;** *to launch a new article on the market; a black market in luxury articles*
(b) section of a legal agreement **Artikel, Paragraph, Absatz, Klausel;** *see article 8 of the contract*

artificial obsolescence *noun* deliberately making old models seem out-of-date by bringing out new ones with changes and additional features which will attract the customer **künstliche Obsoleszenz, geplante Veralterung;** *artificial obsolescence is making our products seem cheap and disposable; artificial obsolescence means that no product can be fashionable for very long*

artwork *noun* original work (such as drawings, layouts, photographs) to be used for an advertisement **Werbegrafik, Illustrationen**

ASA = ADVERTISING STANDARDS AUTHORITY

asking price *noun* price which the seller is hoping will be paid for the item being sold **geforderter Preis; Verhandlungsbasis;** *the asking price is £24,000*

assembly *noun*
(a) putting an item together from various parts **Montage, Zusammenbau;** *we can't put the machine together because the instructions for assembly are in Japanese;* **car assembly plant** = factory where cars are put together from parts made in other factories **Auto-Montagewerk**
(b) meeting **Versammlung**

◊ **assembly line** *noun* production system in which the product (such as a car) moves slowly through the factory with new sections being added to it as it goes along **Montageband, Fließband, Fertigungsstraße;** *he works on an assembly line or he is an assembly line worker*

asset *noun* thing which belongs to company or person, and which has a value **Aktiva, Vermögenswert;** *he has an excess of assets over liabilities; her assets are only £640 as against liabilities of £24,000;* **capital assets** *or* **fixed assets** = property *or* machinery which a company owns and uses **Anlagevermögen; current assets** = assets used by a company in its ordinary work (such as materials, finished goods, cash) **Umlaufvermögen; frozen assets** = assets of a company which cannot be sold because someone has a claim against them **eingefrorene/blockierte Vermögenswerte; intangible assets** = assets which have a value, but which are not solid objects (such as goodwill. or a patent, or a trademark) **immaterielle Vermögenswerte; liquid assets** = cash, or bills which can be quickly converted into cash **flüssige Mittel; personal assets** = movable assets which belong to a person **bewegliches Privatvermögen; tangible assets** = assets which are solid objects (such as furniture or jewels or cash) **materielle Vermögenswerte; bilanzirbare Sachwerte; asset stripper** = person who buys a company to sell its assets **Aufkäufer (un)rentabler Unternehmen, der anschließend deren Vermögenswerte verkauft; asset stripping** = buying a company to sell its assets **Aufkauf (un)rentabler Unternehmen, deren Vermögenswerte anschließend verkauft werden; asset value** = value of a company calculated by adding together all its assets **Vermögenswert**

> QUOTE many companies are discovering that a well-recognised brand name can be a priceless asset that lessens the risk of introducing a new product
>
> *Duns Business Month*

assortment *noun* combination of goods sold together **Sortiment, Zusammenstellung;** *the box contains an assortment of chocolates with different centres*

asterisk law *noun (US)* law which forces telemarketing agencies not to try to sell to people who have indicated that they do not want to be approached by telephone salesmen (by putting an asterisk against their names in the phone book) **Sternzeichen-Gesetz** *(entspricht etwa)* **Robinsonliste**

atmosphere *noun* effect that the medium itself through which the advertisement is presented has on the audience **Atmosphäre**

◊ **atmospherics** *noun* creating an overall image of a company through the design of its premises and products **Gestaltung des Fimenimages**

ATR = AWARENESS, TRIAL, REPEAT model showing stages in the effects of advertising on the consumer, where the customer becomes aware of the product, buys it once to try it and the buys it again when he finds it is satisfactory **ATR-Modell (Bewußtheit, Probe, Wiederkauf)**

atrium *noun* very large open space in a building, usually with a glass roof, fountains and plants, which acts as a central meeting point, linking with shopping and office areas and restaurants **Atrium**

attention *noun*
(a) careful consideration and treatment **Aufmerksamkeit, Beachtung;** *for the attention of the Managing Director; your orders will have our best attention*
(b) receiving the message conveyed by an advertisement and retaining it in the mind **Aufmerksamkeit;** *see also* AIDA

attitude *noun* way in which a person views someone *or* something **Einstellung, Haltung; attitude measurement** *or* **attitude testing** = ascertaining the way in which a person views something by assigning scores to various factors **Einstellungsmessung; Einstellungstesten;** *attitude measurement has given us a good idea of how consumers view our product; will attitude testing lead to* *the redesigning of these heaters?;* **attitude research** = carrying out surveys to discover people's attitudes to products, advertisements or the companies producing them **Einstellungsforschung; attitude scale** = device which measures or tests attitudes by analysing a subject's responses **Einstellungsskala**

attrition *noun* decrease in the loyalty of consumers to a product, due to boredom, desire for a change, etc. **Kundenverlust(rate);** *we must adapt our products if we are to avoid attrition; attrition showed the company that brand loyalty could not be taken for granted; a survey was done to find reasons for the unexpected attrition*

auction
1 *noun* method of selling goods where people make bids, and the item is sold to the person who makes the highest offer **Auktion, Versteigerung;** *sale by auction; auction rooms; to sell goods by auction or ; (US) at auction;* **to put something up for auction** = to offer an item for sale at an auction **etwas zur Versteigerung anbieten; Dutch auction** = auction where the auctioneer offers an item for sale at a high price and gradually reduces the price until someone makes a bid **holländische Versteigerung**
2 *verb* to sell at an auction **versteigern;** *the factory was closed and the machinery was auctioned off*
◇ **auctioneer** *noun* person who conducts an auction **Auktionator/-in**

audience *noun* (i) number of people who watch a TV programme or listen to a radio programme; (ii) number of people who are exposed to an advertisement **(i) Zuschauer-, Zuhörerschaft; (ii) Publikum, Reichweite; captive audience** = people who cannot avoid being exposed to an advertisement **unfreiwilliges Publikum; target audience** = consumers at whom an advertisement is aimed **Zielgruppe;** *TV advertising will fail unless we have a clear idea of who the target audience is for our product*

audio-visual *adjective* media that can be seen and heard (such as a TV commercial) **audiovisuell;** *the exhibition was devoted to the latest in audio-visual equipment*

audit *noun* checking on figures **Rechnungsprüfung; home audit** = survey method whereby a panel of householders keep records of purchases so that these can be regularly checked for quantity and brands **Haushaltsbuchforschung; social audit** = analysis of the social consequences of a particular marketing strategy **Überprüfung der Sozialfolgen;** *see also* RETAIL, SALES, SHOP

automation *noun* use of machines to do work with very little supervision by people **Automatisierung**

automatic *adjective* which works *or* takes place without any person making it happen **(voll)automatisch; automatic selling** *or* **automatic vending** = selling through a machine **automatischer Verkauf, Automatenvertrieb;** *automatic selling is popular because of the low labour costs involved;* **automatic vending machine** = machine which provides drinks, cigarettes, etc. when a coin is put in **Automat**

average
1 *noun* number calculated by adding several figures together and dividing by the number of figures added **Durchschnitt, Mittelwert;** *the average for the last three months or the last three months' average; sales average or average of sales;* **moving average** = method for working out averages while taking into account seasonal variations **gleitender Durchschnitt; weighted average** = average which is calculated taking several factors into account, giving some more value than others **gewogener Durchschnitt; on (an) average** = in general **im Durchschnitt, durchschnittlich;** *on an average, £15 worth of goods are stolen every day*
2 *adjective*
(a) middle (figure) **durchschnittlich;** *average cost per unit; average price; average sales per representative; the average figures for the last three months; the average increase in prices;* **average cost pricing** = pricing based on the average cost of producing one unit of a product **durchschnittliche Kostenpreisberechnung; average frequency** = average number of times a consumer will see a particular advertisement **durchschnittliche Kontakthäufigkeit;** *we will have to buy a lot of advertising time to attain a high average frequency; what average frequency do we need to get this advertisement across to the target audience?*
(b) not very good **durchschnittlich, Durchschnitts-;** *the company's performance has been only average; he's only an average worker*
3 *verb* to be on average **sich durchschnittlich belaufen auf, durchschnittlich betragen;** *price increases have averaged 10% per annum; days lost through sickness have averaged twenty-two over the last four years*
◇ **average due date** *noun* date when several payments (due at different dates)

are settled in one payment **mittlerer Zahlungstermin**

◊ **average out** *verb* to come to a figure as an average **durchschnittlich betragen;** *it averages out at 10% per annum; sales increases have averaged out at 15%*

awareness *noun* being conscious of an advertisement's message *or* of a brand's existence and qualities **Bewußtheit, Bekanntheit;** *the survey after the campaign showed advertising awareness had remained low; brand awareness began to develop satisfactorily six months after the launch; see also* ATR, MAXIMAL AWARENESS

Bb

baby boomers *noun* market composed of people born during the period from 1945 to 1965, when the population of the UK and the USA increased rapidly **Babyboomer**

back
1 *noun* opposite side to the front **Rückseite;** *write your address on the back of the envelope; the conditions of sale are printed on the back of the invoice; please endorse the cheque on the back* ; **back cover** = back of a magazine cover, which can be used for advertising **letzte/vierte Umschlagseite, U4; inside back cover** = advertising page on the inside of the back cover **dritte Umschlagseite, U3;** *we have advertised on the back cover of every issue this year; the survey is trying to establish how much notice readers take of the back cover*
2 *adjective* referring to the past **zurück, Rück-; back interest** = interest not yet paid **Zinsrückstand; back orders** = orders received in the past and not fulfilled (usually because the item is out of stock) **unerledigte Aufträge;** *after the strike it took the factory six weeks to clear all the accumulated back orders*
3 *verb*
(a) to back someone = to help someone financially **jdn (finanziell) unterstützen;** *the bank is backing him to the tune of £10,000; he is looking for someone to back his project*
(b) to back a bill = to sign a bill promising to pay it if the person it is addressed to is not able to do so **(als Dritter) einen Wechsel unterzeichnen**

◊ **backdoor selling** *noun* bypassing an organization's bureaucracy and selling direct to the chief decision-maker in it **Realisierung des Verkaufs durch die Hintertür, Verkauf unter Umgehung der festgelegten Absatzwege;** *if we did not resort to backdoor selling the right department might never hear of us; the chairman was asked out for a meal by the sales director of the other company to try a little backdoor selling*

◊ **backer** *noun*
(a) person who backs someone **Geldgeber; Sponsor; Hintermann;** *he has an Australian backer; one of the company's backers has withdrawn*
(b) backer of a bill = person who backs a bill **Wechselgarant**

◊ **backing** *noun*
(a) financial support **finanzielle Unterstützung;** *he has the backing of an Australian bank; the company will only succeed if it gets sufficient backing; who is providing the backing for the project or where does the backing for the project come from?*
(b) currency backing = gold or government securities which maintain the strength of a currency **Währungsgarantie**

◊ **backload** *verb* to make sure that most of the costs of a promotional campaign come in the later stages, so that they can be regulated according to the response received (the campaign can then be cut back if the response rate is inadequate - this is opposed to frontloading, where most of the costs are incurred in the early stages) **Werbebudget für die letzte Hälfte einer Planperiode aufbewahren**

◊ **backlog** *noun* work (such as orders *or* letters) which has piled up waiting to be done **Rückstand;** *the warehouse is trying to cope with a backlog of orders; my secretary can't cope with the backlog of paperwork*

◊ **backup** *adjective* supporting *or* helping **zusätzlich, Unterstützungs-;** *we offer customers a free backup service; after a series of sales tours by representatives, the sales director sends backup letters to all the contacts;* **backup ad** = advertisement designed to accompany editorial material in a publication **textanschließende Anzeige; backup copy** = copy of a computer disk to be kept in case the original disk is damaged **Sicherungskopie**

◊ **backward integration** *noun* process of expansion in which a business becomes its own supplier (as opposed to forward integration, where the company becomes its own distributor) **Rückwärtsintegration;** *buying up rubber plantations is part of the tyre company's backward integration policy; backward integration will ensure cheap supplies but forward integration would bring us nearer to the market*

◇ **backwardation** *noun* penalty paid by the seller when postponing delivery of shares to the buyer **Deport**

> QUOTE the company has received the backing of a number of oil companies who are willing to pay for the results of the survey
> *Lloyd's List*

bait *noun* article which is sold at a loss to attract customers **Lock(vogel)angebot;** *this is an attractive enough product to use as bait; the shop's best bargains were displayed in the window as bait*

band *noun* strip of paper or rubber ring put round articles to attach them together **Papierstreifen; Gummiband**

◇ **banded** *adjective* attached with a band **mit einem Band/Streifen versehen; banded offer** = type of sales promotion involving the offer of an additional item along with the main one **Combipack-Angebot;** *the banded offer consisted of a full-sized bottle of shampoo along with a small bottle of hair conditioner;* **banded pack** = pack which includes an additional item along with the main one **Verbundpackung;** *these banded packs have been specially designed for our sales promotion drive*

bank bill *noun*
(a) *GB* order by one bank telling another bank (usually in another country) to pay money to someone **Bankwechsel**
(b) *US* piece of printed paper money **Banknote, Schein**

◇ **bank draft** *noun* order by one bank telling another bank (usually in another country) to pay money to someone **Banktratte; Bankwechsel**

◇ **banker** *noun* person who is in an important position in a bank **Bankier, Banker; banker's bill** *or* **bank bill** = order by one bank telling another bank (usually in another country) to pay money to someone **Bankwechsel; banker's order** = order written by a customer asking a bank to make a regular payment **Dauerauftrag;** *he pays his subscription by banker's order*

◇ **bank giro** *noun (GB)* method used by clearing banks to transfer money rapidly from one account to another **Bankgiro**

banner *noun* material stretched between two walls or buildings, carrying an advertising message **Spann-, Spruchband, Banner, Transparent;** *there were banners across the street advertising the charity run*

bar chart *noun* chart where values *or* quantities are shown as thick columns of different heights **Balken-, Stab-, Säulendiagramm**

◇ **bar code** *noun* system of lines printed on a product which when read by a computer give a reference number or price **Strichkodierung, Bar-Code**

bargain
1 *noun*
(a) agreement on the price of something **Handel, Geschäft;** *to make a bargain;* **to drive a hard bargain** = to sell only at terms which are favourable to yourself **hart verhandeln, harte Bedingungen stellen; to strike a hard bargain** = to agree a deal which is favourable to you **ein Geschäft zufriedenstellend abschließen; it's a bad bargain** = it's not worth the price **das ist ein schlechtes Geschäft**
(b) thing which is cheaper than usual **Schnäppchen, Gelegenheitskauf;** *that car is a (real) bargain at £500;* **bargain hunter** = person who looks for cheap deals **jd, der auf Sonderangebote aus ist**
(c) sale of one lot of shares on the Stock Exchange **Börsengeschäft, Abschluß; bargains done** = number of deals made on the Stock Exchange during a day **Anzahl der Abschlüsse/Börsengeschäfte**
2 *verb* to discuss a price for something **(aus)handeln;** *you will have to bargain with the dealer if you want a discount; they spent two hours bargaining about or over the price*

◇ **bargain basement** *noun* basement floor in a shop where goods are sold cheaply **Abteilung für Sonderangebote im Untergeschoß eines Kaufhauses; I'm selling this at a bargain basement price** = I'm selling this very cheaply **ich verkaufe dies zu einem Sonderpreis**

◇ **bargain counter** *noun* counter in a shop where goods are sold cheaply **Sonderangebotsstand, Sondertisch**

◇ **bargain offer** *noun* sale of a particular type of goods at a cheap price **Sonderangebot, günstiges Angebot;** *this week's bargain offer - 30% off all carpet prices*

◇ **bargain price** *noun* cheap price **Sonderpreis, Spottpreis;** *these carpets are for sale at a bargain price*

◇ **bargain sale** *noun* sale of all goods in a store at cheap prices **Ausverkauf**

◇ **bargaining** *noun* act of discussing a price, usually wage increases for workers **Handeln, Aushandeln; (free) collective bargaining** = negotiations between employers and workers' representatives over wage increases and conditions **(autonome) Tarifverhandlungen; bargaining power** = strength of one person or group when discussing prices *or* wage settlements **Verhandlungsstärke; bargaining position** =

statement of position by one group during negotiations **Verhandlungsposition**

barrier *noun* thing which stops someone doing something, especially sending goods from one place to another **Schranke; customs barriers** *or* **tariff barriers** = customs duty intended to make trade more difficult **Zollschranken; to impose trade barriers on certain goods** = to restrict the import of certain goods by charging high duty **bestimmte Güter mit Handelsschranken belegen;** *the unions have asked the government to impose trade barriers on the import of foreign cars;* **to lift trade barriers from imports** = to remove restrictions on imports **Handelsschranken für Importe aufheben; barriers to entry into a market** = things which make it difficult for a company to enter a new market (such as start-up costs) **Einführungsprobleme**

barter
1 *noun* system where goods are exchanged for other goods, not sold for money **Tauschhandel; barter agreement** *or* **barter arrangement** *or* **barter deal** = agreement to exchange goods by barter **Tauschabkommen;** *the company has agreed a barter deal with Bulgaria*
2 *verb* to exchange goods for other goods, not for money **Tauschhandel treiben;** *they agreed a deal to barter tractors for barrels of wine*
◊ **bartering** *noun* act of exchanging goods for other goods and not for money **Tauschhandel**

> QUOTE under the barter agreements, Nigeria will export 175,000 barrels a day of crude oil in exchange for trucks, food, planes and chemicals
> *Wall Street Journal*

base
1 *noun*
(a) lowest or first position **Basis, Ausgangspunkt, Grundlage;** *turnover increased by 200%, but started from a low base;* **base line** = part of promotional material that contains basic information about the organization such as its name and address **Schlußzeile; base year** = first year of an index, against which changes in later years are measured **Basis-, Vergleichsjahr; bank base rate** = basic rate of interest which a bank charges on loans to its customers **Eckzins;** *see* DATABASE
(b) place where a company has its main office or factory *or* place where a businessman has his office **Sitz, Standort;** *the company has its base in London and branches in all European countries; he has an office in Madrid which he uses as a base while travelling in Southern Europe*
2 *verb* to set up a company *or* a person in a place **stationieren;** *the European manager is based in our London office; our overseas branch is based in the Bahamas; a London-based sales executive*
◊ **basement** *noun* section of a shop which is underground **Untergeschoß; bargain basement** = basement floor in a shop where goods are sold cheaply **Abteilung für Sonderangebote im Untergeschoß eines Kaufhauses;** *I'm selling this at a bargain basement price*

> QUOTE the base lending rate, or prime rate, is the rate at which banks lend to their top corporate borrowers
> *Wall Street Journal*
> QUOTE other investments include a large stake in the Chicago-based insurance company
> *Lloyd's List*

basic
1 *adjective*
(a) normal **Grund-, Basis-; eigentlich; basic discount** = normal discount without extra percentages **Grundrabatt;** *our basic discount is 20%, but we offer 5% extra for rapid settlement;* **basic price** *or* **basic rate** = price of a product *or* service that does not include any extras **Grundpreis;** *this is a rather high basic price; please make clear whether £1000 is the basic rate or inclusive of spare parts*
(b) most important **wesentlich, hauptsächlich, Haupt-; basic commodities** = ordinary farm produce, produced in large quantities (such as corn, rice, sugar, etc.) **Grundstoffe**
(c) simple *or* from which everything starts **Grund-, elementar;** *he has a basic knowledge of the market; to work at the cash desk, you need a basic qualification in maths*
◊ **basics** *plural noun* simple and important facts **Grundlagen, Grundsachverhalt;** *he has studied the basics of foreign exchange dealing;* **to get back to basics** = to consider the basic facts again **zum Kern der Sache/zu den Grundlagen zurückkommen**

basis *noun*
(a) point *or* number from which calculations are made **Grundlage, Basis;** *we forecast the turnover on the basis of a 6% price increase*
(b) general terms of agreement **Basis, Grundlage; on a short-term** *or* **long-term basis** = for a short *or* long period **kurzfristig** *or* **langfristig;** *he has been appointed on a short-term basis; we have three people working on a freelance basis*

batch
1 *noun* group of items which are made at one time **Serie; Auflage;** *this batch of shoes*

has the serial number 25-02; **batch production** = production of goods in batches or small groups **Serienfertigung**
2 *verb* to put items together in groups **stapeln;** *to batch invoices or cheques*

◇ **batch number** *noun* number attached to a batch **Seriennummer; Auflagennummer;** *when making a complaint always quote the batch number on the packet*

battle *noun* fight **Kampf;** *(US)* **battle of the brands** = competition in the market between existing product brands **Markenkampf;** *this battle of the brands will lead to dramatic price-cutting;* **circulation battle** = fight between newspapers to sell more copies in the same section of the market **Kampf um die Auflagenhöhe (verschiedener Zeitungen)**

Bayesian decision theory *noun* method for helping decision-making, often applied to new product development **Bayes(sches)-Theorem**

behavioural segmentation *noun* segmentation or division of the market according to customers' buying habits and usage of a product **Marktsegmentierung aufgrund von Verhaltensmerkmalen;** *behavioural segmentation will mean there are several distinct target audiences for our product*

below-the-line *adjective* **below-the-line advertising** = advertising which is not paid for (such as work by staff members at an exhibition) and for which no commission is paid to the advertising agency **Werbung ‚unter dem Strich', vergütungsunfähige Werbung; below-the-line expenditure** = exceptional payments which are separated from a company's normal accounts **außerordentliche Aufwendungen;** *Compare* ABOVE-THE-LINE

benefit *noun* **benefit segmentation** = division of a market into segments according to the types of benefit obtained by the customer from a product (such as ease of availability, light weights, etc.) **Marktsegmentierung aufgrund von Nutzen; fringe benefits** = extra items given by a company to workers in addition to their salaries (such as company cars, private health insurance) **Leistungsanreize für Arbeitnehmer**

berth
1 *noun* place in a harbour where a ship can tie up **Liegeplatz; berth cargo** = cargo carried at especially low rates **Auffülladung;** *if we do not send the goods as berth cargo we will have to charge the buyer more*
2 *verb* to tie up at a berth **anlegen;** *the ship will berth at Rotterdam on Wednesday*

BES = BUSINESS EXPANSION SCHEME

bias *noun* prejudice *or* subjective feeling on the part of a researcher that distorts the results of a survey or test **Voreingenommenheit, Vorurteil; systematische Fehler;** *a postal survey will do away with bias; the trainee interviewers were taught how to control bias and its effects*

bid
1 *noun*
(a) offer to buy something at a certain price **Gebot, Angebot; to make a bid for something** = to offer to buy something **ein Angebot/Gebot für etwas machen;** *he made a bid for the house; the company made a bid for its rival;* **to make a cash bid** = to offer to pay cash for something **ein Bargebot machen; to put in a bid for something** *or* **to enter a bid for something** = to offer (usually in writing) to buy something **ein Angebot abgeben;** *(at an auction)* **opening bid** = first bid **Eröffnungsgebot; closing bid** = last bid at an auction *or* the bid which is successful **Höchstgebot**
(b) offer to do stated work at a certain price **Kosten(vor)anschlag, Angebot;** *he made the lowest bid for the job; (US)* offer to sell something at a stated price **Angebot;** *they asked for bids for the supply of spare parts*
(c) takeover bid = offer to buy all or a majority of the shares in a company so as to control it **Übernahmeangebot;** *to make a takeover bid for a company; to withdraw a takeover bid;* **the company rejected the takeover bid** = the directors recommended that the shareholders should not accept it **das Unternehmen hat das Übernahmeangebot zurückgewiesen**
2 *verb (at an auction)* **to bid for something** = to offer to buy something **für/auf etwas bieten; he bid £1,000 for the jewels** = he offered to pay £1,000 for the jewels **er bot £1.000 für den Schmuck**

◇ **bidder** *noun* person who makes a bid (usually at an auction) **Bieter/-in;** *several bidders made offers for the house;* **the property was sold to the highest bidder** = to the person who had made the highest bid *or* who offered the most money **der Besitz wurde an den Meistbietenden verkauft; the tender will go to the lowest bidder** = to the person who offers the best terms *or* the lowest price for services **der Auftrag wird an den Mindestbietenden vergeben**

◇ **bidding** *noun* action of making offers to buy (usually at an auction) **Bieten, Gebot; Abgabe von Angeboten; the bidding started at £1,000** = the first and lowest bid was £1,000 **£1.000 war das Mindestgebot; the bidding stopped at £250,000** = the final (successful) bid was for £250,000 **£250.000 war das Höchstgebot; the auctioneer started the bidding at £100** = he suggested a first bid of £100 **der Auktionator setzte das Erstgebot mit £100 an**

bilateral *adjective* between two parties *or* countries **bilateral, zweiseitig;** *the minister signed a bilateral trade agreement*

◇ **bilateralism** *noun* system whereby a country balances its trade with another **Zweiseitigkeit, zweiseitiges Handelsabkommen;** *with luck, bilateralism will put an end to the trade war*

bill
1 *noun*
(a) written list of charges to be paid **Rechnung, Faktura;** *the salesman wrote out the bill; does the bill include VAT? the bill is made out to Smith Ltd; the builder sent in his bill; he left the country without paying his bills;* **to foot the bill** = to pay the costs **die Rechnung begleichen/bezahlen**
(b) list of charges in a restaurant **Rechnung;** *can I have the bill please? the bill comes to £20 including service; does the bill include service? the waiter has added 10% to the bill for service*
(c) small poster **Plakat, Anschlagzettel**
(d) written paper promising to pay money **Wechsel; Tratte; bill of exchange** = document which tells a bank to pay a person (usually used in payments in foreign currency) **Wechsel; Tratte; accommodation bill** = bill of exchange which the person signs in order to help someone raise a loan **Gefälligkeitswechsel; bank bill** = bill of exchange endorsed by a bank **Bankwechsel, Bankakzept; demand bill** = bill of exchange which must be paid when payment is asked for **Sichtwechsel; to accept a bill** = to sign a bill of exchange to show that you promise to pay it **einen Wechsel akzeptieren; to discount a bill** = to buy a bill of exchange at a lower price than that written on it in order to cash it later **einen Wechsel diskontieren; bills payable** = bills which a debtor will have to pay **Wechselverbindlichkeiten; bills receivable** = bills held by a creditor awaiting payment **Wechselforderungen**
(e) bill of entry = written details of goods to go through customs **Zolleinfuhrerklärung, Zolldeklaration**
(f) *US* piece of paper money **Banknote, Schein;** *a $5 bill*
(g) bill of sale = document which the seller gives to the buyer to show that the sale has taken place **Kaufvertrag**
(h) draft of a new law which will be discussed in Parliament **Gesetzesvorlage, Gesetzentwurf**
2 *verb* to present a bill to someone so that it can be paid **berechnen, in Rechnung stellen;** *the plumbers billed him for the repairs*

◇ **billboard** *noun*
(a) poster site of double crown size (30 x 20 inches) **Anschlagbrett**
(b) *US* large outdoor poster site (measuring 12 feet by 25) **großformatige Außenplakatwand;** *the railway track was lined with billboards specially set up for election propaganda; a shortage of billboards has led to an increase in press advertising*

◇ **billing** *noun*
(a) total annual turnover of an advertising agency **Umsatz;** *with such an impressive billing, the agency decided to expand; our billings have gone down this year because many producers have left the area*
(b) *US* writing of invoices or bills **Ausstellen von Rechnungen, Fakturieren**

◇ **bill of lading** *noun* list of goods being shipped,which the transporter gives to the person sending the goods to show that the goods have been loaded **Konnossement clean bill of lading** = bill of lading stating that the goods arrived on board in good condition **reines Konnossement; dirty bill of lading** *or* **foul bill of lading** = bill of lading stating that the goods did not arrive on board in good condition **unreines Konnossement**

bin *noun* large container; separate section of shelves in a warehouse **Behälter, Kiste; dump bin** = display container like a large box, filled with goods for sale **Wühltisch**

Bingo card *noun* printed card bound into a magazine, with a matrix of numbers and letters which a reader can mark; the numbers refer to products advertised in the magazine, and the card is returned post free to the publisher, who sends out further information on the product to the reader **Bingo-Karte, Kennzifferkarte**

bipolar scale *noun* scale used in questionnaires which contains two extreme points within which an interviewee can choose an answer **bipolare Skala**

black
1 *adjective*

(a) black market = buying and selling goods when this is not allowed by law **Schwarzmarkt;** *there is a flourishing black market in spare parts for cars; you can buy gold coins on the black market;* **to pay black market prices** = to pay high prices to get items which are not easily available **Schwarzmarktpreise bezahlen**
(b) black economy = business activity which is paid for in cash, and therefore not declared for tax **Schattenwirtschaft**
(c) in the black = in credit **in den schwarzen Zahlen;** *the company has moved into the black; my bank account is still in the black*
2 *verb* to forbid trading in certain goods or with certain suppliers **boykottieren;** *three firms were blacked by the government; the union has blacked a trucking firm*

◇ **black list** *noun* list of goods *or* people *or* companies which have been blacked **schwarze Liste**

◇ **blacklist** *verb* to put goods *or* people *or* a company on a black list **auf die schwarze Liste setzen;** *his firm was blacklisted by the government*

blanket *noun* **blanket agreement** = agreement which covers many items **Gesamtvereinbarung; blanket branding** = giving a whole group *or* line of products the same brand name **die Schöpfung einer Markenfamilie; Markenfamilienbranding;** *blanket branding will make the brand a household name;* **blanket coverage** = advertising to the general public with no particular target audience in mind **Zufallsstreuung;** *we will go for blanket coverage first and then see what kind of people buy the product;* **blanket insurance** = insurance which covers various items (such as a house and its contents) **Kollektivversicherung; blanket refusal** = refusal to accept anything, although many different items have been suggested **allgemeine Ablehnung**

bleed *verb* to allow advertising space to run to the edge of a printed page **anschneiden**

blind testing *noun* testing a product on consumers without their knowing what brand it is **Blindtesten, anonymer Warentest;** *plain wrappers are put round the products in the blind testing sessions*

blister pack *noun* type of packing where the item for sale is covered with a stiff plastic sheet sealed to a card backing **Schrumpffolienverpackung**

blitz *noun* marketing campaign which starts at full pressure (as opposed to a gradual build-up) **intensive/explosionsartige Werbekampagne**

blurb *noun* brief description of a book, printed in a publisher's catalogue or on the cover of the book itself **Klappentext;** *the author was asked to write his own brief blurb; the blurb instantly aroused his interest in the book;* **mandatory blurb** = certain words which are required by law to be included in an advertisement (such as a health warning on cigarette advertisements) **rechtsverbindlicher Text/Warnhinweis**

body copy *noun* main part of the text of an advertisement **Body Copy, Haupttextteil;** *the body copy will do, though the company's address needn't be included; the body copy on the poster is too long for passers-by to read it all*

body language *noun* communication by people using gestures or movements of the body **Körpersprache;** *trainee salesmen learn how to interpret a customer's body language; the interviewer of prospective marketing managers observed the body language of the candidates very carefully; the candidate claimed to be very confident about taking the job, but his body language was saying the opposite*

bonded warehouse *noun* warehouse where goods are stored until excise duty has been paid **Zollager**

bonus *noun* extra payment **Prämie, Zulage, Bonus; bonus size** = extra large size of pack sold at the usual price as a form of sales promotion **Riesenpackung;** *we are offering bonus packs in order to attract new customers to the product; bonus size packs are 20% larger, but are sold at the normal price;* **bonus spot** = free television or radio spot offered to an advertiser as part of an advertising package **Gratiswerbesendung; productivity bonus** = extra payment made because of increased productivity **Produktivitätsprämie;**

book
1 *noun* **a company's books** = the financial records of a company **Geschäftsbücher; account book** = book which records sales and purchases **Rechnungsbuch; cash book** = record of cash transactions **Kassenbuch; order book** = record of orders **Auftragsbuch, Bestellbuch; the company has a full order book** = it has sufficient orders to keep the

workforce occupied **das Unternehmen hat volle Auftragsbücher; purchase book** = record of purchases **Wareneingangsbuch; sales book** = record of sales **Warenverkaufsbuch; book sales** = sales as recorded in the sales book **Absatz laut Verkaufsbuch; book value** = value as recorded in the company's books **Buch-, Bilanzwert**

boom

1 *noun* time when sales *or* production *or* business activity are increasing **Aufschwung, Boom, Hochkonjunktur, Hausse;** *a period of economic boom; the boom of the 1970s;* **boom industry** = industry which is expanding rapidly **Konjunkturindustrie; a boom share** = share in a company which is expanding **eine steigende Aktie; the boom years** = years when there is an economic boom **die Jahre des Aufschwungs**
2 *verb* to expand *or* to become prosperous **einen Aufschwung haben;** *business is booming; sales are booming*

◇ **booming** *adjective* which is expanding *or* becoming prosperous **florierend, blühend;** *a booming industry or company; technology is a booming sector of the economy*

> QUOTE starting in 1981, a full-blown real estate boom took off in Texas
> *Business*

Boston matrix *noun* type of product portfolio analysis, in which products are identified as stars, question marks, cash cows or dogs **Vierfelder-Portfolio-Matrix**

bottle hanger *noun* advertisement in the form of a card which hangs round the neck of a bottle **Flaschenanhänger**

bottleneck *noun* inability of one section of the operation to cope with the amount of work it has to do, which slows down the later stages of the operation and business activity in general **Engpaß;** *a bottleneck in the supply system; there are serious bottlenecks in the production line*

bottom

1 *noun* lowest part *or* point **Tiefpunkt; Tiefststand; sales have reached rock bottom** = the very lowest point of all **die Verkaufszahlen haben einen Tiefpunkt erreicht; the bottom has fallen out of the market** = sales have fallen below what previously seemed to be the lowest point **die Marktpreise haben einen Tiefststand erreicht; bottom price** = lowest price **niedrigster Preis; rock-bottom price** = lowest price of all **Tiefst-, Schleuderpreis;**
2 *verb* **to bottom (out)** = to reach the lowest point **den tiefsten Stand erreichen; the market has bottomed out** = has reached the lowest point and does not seem likely to fall further **der Markt hat seinen tiefsten Stand erreicht**

◇ **bottom line** *noun*
(a) the last line on a balance sheet indicating profit or loss **Saldo; the boss is only interested in the bottom line** = he is only interested in the final profit **der Chef ist nur am Saldo interessiert**
(b) the most significant point **das Wichtigste/Wesentlichste;** *we have to position the product on the market before 1995, and that is the bottom line*

boutique *noun* small specialized shop, especially for up-to-date clothes; section of a department store selling up-to-date clothes **Boutique;** *a jeans boutique; a ski boutique*

box *noun* cardboard *or* wood *or* plastic container **Schachtel, Kasten;** *the goods were sent in thin cardboard boxes; the watches are prepacked in plastic display boxes;* **paperclips come in boxes of two hundred** = packed two hundred to a box **Büroklammern sind in Schachteln zu zweihundert erhältlich;** *(US)* **box store** = supermarket like a warehouse, with not much service or promotion, where goods are sold from their original packing cases; *(entspricht)* **(Verbraucher-)Abholmarkt;** *the school bought stationery in large quantities from the box store; with low overheads, box stores can offer cut-rate prices*

◇ **boxed** *adjective* put in a box *or* sold in a box **in Kisten od Schachteln verpackt/verkauft; boxed set** = set of items sold together in a box **in einer Schachtel verpacktes Set; Bände in einem Schuber**

boycott

1 *noun* refusal to buy *or* to deal in certain products **Boykott;** *the union organized a boycott against or of imported cars*
2 *verb* to refuse to buy *or* to deal in a certain product **boykottieren;** *we are boycotting all imports from that country;* **the management has boycotted the meeting** = has refused to attend the meeting **die Leitung hat das Treffen boykottiert**

BRAD = BRITISH RATE AND DATA

brainstorming *noun* intensive discussions in small groups as a way of producing new ideas or solutions to problems, from the spontaneous exchanges between people taking part

Diskussionssitzung, Brainstorming; *brainstorming generated a method of revolutionizing our distribution; the new sales manager showed his brilliance in the brainstorming sessions on new approaches to customers*

branch

1 *noun* local office of a bank or large business; local shop which is part of a large chain **Filiale, Geschäfts-, Zweigstelle, Niederlassung;** *the bank or the store has branches in most towns in the south of the country; the insurance company has closed its branches in South America; he is the manager of our local branch of Lloyds bank; we have decided to open a branch office in Chicago; the manager of our branch in Lagos or of our Lagos branch;* **branch manager** = manager of a branch **Filialleiter**
2 *verb* **to branch out** = to start a new (but usually related) type of business **in fremde/andere Branchen einsteigen;** *from car retailing, the company branched out into car leasing*

> QUOTE a leading manufacturer of business, industrial and commercial products requires a branch manager to head up its mid-western Canada operations based in Winnipeg
> *Globe and Mail (Toronto)*

brand

brand *noun* make of product, which can be recognized by a name or by a design **Marke;** *the top-selling brands of toothpaste; the company is launching a new brand of soap;* **brand awareness** = consciousness by the public of a brand's existence and qualities **Markenbekanntheit, Markenbewußtsein;** *how can you talk about brand awareness when most people don't even know what the product is supposed to do? our salesmen must work harder to increase brand awareness in this area;* **brand image** = ideas which the public associate with a particular brand **Markenimage, Markenprofil;** *the brand image is too cheap and old-fashioned to attract young customers; our brand image is sophisticated and appeals to the sophisticated buyer;* **brand leader** = brand with the largest market share **Markenführer;** *despite one of its products being a brand leader, the company's profits were bad for the year;* **brand loyalty** = inclination of the customer to keep on buying the same brand **Markentreue; brand manager** = manager or executive responsible for the marketing of a particular brand **Marketingleiter eines Markenproduktes;** *the brand manager and the production manager met to discuss changes to be made to the company's leading brand of soap;* **brand name** = name of a brand **Markenname; brand positioning** = acquiring a position for a brand in a market, so that it is recognizable to the public **Markenproduktpositionierung;** *intensive television advertising is a key part of our brand positioning strategy;* **brand recognition** = being able to recognize or identify a brand on sight **Markenwiedererkennung;** *the packaging needs to be more original to improve brand recognition; brand recognition depends on having a catchy attractive brand name;* **brand switching** = changing from buying one brand to another, showing little brand loyalty **Markenwechsel;** *we can't rely on steady sales with such a lot of brand switching going on; brand switching makes shopping more fun for consumers;* **brand X** = the anonymous brand which is used on TV commercials as a comparison to the named brand being advertised **Marke X; own brand** = products which are specially packed for a store and carry its name on the label **Eigenmarke;** *see also* DEALER'S BRAND, DISTRIBUTOR'S BRAND, HOUSE BRAND, PRIMARY BRAND, PRIVATE BAND

◇ **branded** *adjective* **branded goods** = goods sold under brand names **Markenartikel**

◇ **branding** *noun* the action of giving brand names to products **Markengebung; family branding** = selling a variety of goods under the same brand name **Markenfamilienverkauf**

> QUOTE you have to look much further down the sales league to find a brand which has not been around for what seems like ages
> *Marketing*
>
> QUOTE major companies are supporting their best existing brands with increased investment
> *Marketing Week*

breach

breach *noun* failure to carry out the terms of an agreement **Verletzung, Verstoß; breach of contract** = failing to do something which is in a contract **Vertragsbruch; the company is in breach of contract** = it has failed to carry out its duties under the contract **das Unternehmen ist vertragsbrüchig geworden; breach of warranty** = supplying goods which do not meet the standards of the warranty applied to them **Garantieverletzung; Verletzung der Gewährleistungspflicht**

break even

break even *verb* to balance costs and receipts, but not make a profit **kostendeckend arbeiten;** *last year the company only just broke even; we broke even in our first two months of trading*

◇ **breakeven analysis** *noun* analysis of fixed and variable costs and sales to determine at what level of production the breakeven point will be reached **Break-**

Even-Analyse, Gewinnschwellen-, Rentabilitätsanalyse; *the breakeven analysis showed that the company will only break even if it sells at least 1000 bicycles a month;* **breakeven point** = point at which sales cover costs, but do not show a profit **Break-Even-Punkt, Gewinn-, Rentabilitätsschwelle**

◇ **breaking bulk** *noun* buying in bulk and then selling in small quantities to many customers **Aufteilen der Menge**

◇ **break up** *verb* to split something large into small sections **aufteilen;** *the company was broken up and separate divisions sold off;* **break-up value** = (i) value of the material of a fixed asset; (ii) value of various parts of a company taken separately **(i) & (ii) Auflösungswert;** *what would the break-up value of our old machinery be? scrap merchants were asked to estimate the tractors' break-up value*

bridge *verb* to print an advertisement across the centre of a double page spread in a magazine **im Bundsteg angeschnittene Anzeige**

brief
1 *noun* basic objectives and instructions concerning an advertising campaign, given by an advertiser to an advertising agency **Einweisung;** *the brief stressed the importance of the market segment to be targeted; the brief was not detailed enough and did not show what sort of product image the advertiser wanted to create*
2 *verb* to explain to someone in detail **briefen, informieren, instruieren;** *the salesmen were briefed on the new product; the managing director briefed the board on the progress of the negotiations*

◇ **briefing** *noun* telling someone details **Briefing, Einweisungs- und Einsatzbesprechung;** *all salesmen have to attend a sales briefing on the new product*

British Rate and Data (BRAD) a regular publication which lists British newspapers and magazines, giving all relevant information about their circulation, rates, frequency and other advertising services offered **britische Zeitungs- und Zeitschriftenpublikation (BRAD);** *you should consult BRAD first to find the most suitable newspaper to carry our advertising*
NOTE: the comparable American publication is **Standard Rate and Data Service (SRDS)**

broadsheet *noun* large size of newspaper page (as opposed to tabloid) **großformatige(s) Zeitung(sblatt), Planobogen**

broadside *noun (US)* publicity leaflet **Prospekt, Werbezettel**

brochure *noun* publicity booklet **Prospekt, Broschüre;** *we sent off for a brochure about holidays in Greece or about postal services*

broken lot *noun* incomplete set of goods for sale **unvollständiger Satz;** *we'll give you a discount since it is a broken lot, with two items missing*

broker *noun*
(a) dealer **Makler, Händler; foreign exchange broker** = person who buys and sells foreign currency on behalf of other people **Devisenhändler, Devisenmakler; insurance broker** = person who sells insurance to clients **Versicherungsvertreter; media broker** = business which offers companies a media buying service **Media-Agentur; ship broker** = person who sells shipping *or* transport of goods to clients **Schiffsmakler**
(b) (stock)broker = person who buys or sells shares for clients **Börsenmakler**

◇ **brokerage** *or* **broker's commission** *noun* payment to a broker for a deal carried out **Maklergebühr; Courtage**

bubble card *or* **bubble pack** *noun* type of packaging, where the item for sale is covered by a stiff plastic sheet sealed to a card backing **Schrumpffolienverpackung**

budget
1 *noun*
(a) plan of expected spending and income (usually for one year) **Budget; Haushalt; Etat;** *to draw up a budget; we have agreed the budgets for next year;* **advertising budget** = money planned for spending on advertising **Werbeetat; cash budget** = plan of cash income and expenditure **Einnahmen- und Ausgabenplanung; overhead budget** = plan of probable overhead costs **Festkostenvoranschlag; publicity budget** = money allowed for expected expenditure on publicity **Werbeetat; sales budget** = plan of probable sales **Absatzplanung**
(b) the Budget = the annual plan of taxes and government spending proposed by a finance minister **der Staatshaushalt;** *the minister put forward a budget aimed at boosting the economy;* **to balance the budget** = to plan income and expenditure so that they balance **den Etat ausgleichen;** *the president is planning for a balanced budget*
(c) *(in a bank)* **budget account** = bank account where you plan income and expenditure to allow for periods when

expenditure is high, by paying a set amount each month **Budget-Konto**

(d) *(in shops)* cheap **Billig-; budget department** = cheaper department **Sonderangebotsabteilung; budget prices** = low prices **Sparpreise**

2 *verb* to plan probable income and expenditure **das Budget planen, budgetieren;** *we are budgeting for £10,000 of sales next year*

◇ **budgetary** *adjective* referring to a budget **Finanz-, Budget-, Etat-, Haushalts-; budgetary policy** = policy of planning income and expenditure **Budgetpolitik; budgetary control** = keeping a check on spending **Budgetkontrolle; budgetary requirements** = spending or income required to meet the budget forecasts **Budgetbedarf**

◇ **budgeting** *noun* preparing budgets to help plan expenditure and income **Budgetierung, Finanzplanung; Kalkulation**

> QUOTE he budgeted for further growth of 150,000 jobs (or 2.5 per cent) in the current financial year
>
> *Sydney Morning Herald*
>
> QUOTE the minister is persuading the oil, gas, electricity and coal industries to target their advertising budgets towards energy efficiency
>
> *Times*
>
> QUOTE the Federal government's budget targets for employment and growth are within reach according to the latest figures
>
> *Australian Financial Review*

built-in *adjective* forming part of the system *or* of a machine **eingebaut;** *the micro has a built-in clock; the accounting system has a series of built-in checks;* **built-in obsolescence** = method of ensuring continuing sales of a product by making it in such a way that it will soon become obsolete **eingebaute/geplante, qualitative Obsoleszenz**

bulk *noun*

(a) large quantity of goods **Masse, Menge; in bulk** = in large quantities **en gros, in Massen, in Mengen;** *to buy rice in bulk;* **bulk buying** *or* **bulk purchase** = buying large quantities of goods at a lower price **Mengen-, Posteneinkauf; bulk carrier** = ship which carries large quantities of loose goods (such as coal) **Massengutfrachter; bulk discount** = discount on the basis of quantity bought **Mengenrabatt;** *if we buy all our supplies together we can get a bulk discount; it was worth buying two more refrigerators to get the bulk discount;* **bulk shipments** = shipments of large quantities of goods **Massengütertransport**

(b) bulk rate = cheap rate offered to advertisers who take large amounts of advertising space **Mengenrabatt**

◇ **bulk-breaking** *or* **breaking bulk** *noun* buying in bulk and then selling small quantities on to retail customers **Aufteilen der Menge**

◇ **bulky** *adjective* large and awkward **sperrig;** *the Post Office does not accept bulky packages*

bulldog *noun* first edition of a daily newspaper **Bulldoggenausgabe**

bulletin *noun* short note *or* newsletter *or* report, issued regularly **Bulletin, Nachrichtenblatt;** *bulletins were regularly sent to the sales force; the bulletin contained sales figures for the month*

buppies *noun (US)* Black Upwardly-Mobile Professionals **Bups**

burst *noun* many advertisements for a product placed over a short period **stoßweise Werbung;** *shall we go for a burst or for a more prolonged campaign?*

business *noun*

(a) work in buying or selling **Geschäft; Gewerbe;** *we do a lot of business with Japan; business is expanding; business is slow; repairing cars is 90% of our business; we did more business in the week before Christmas than we usually do in a month; strikes are very bad for business; what's your line of business?;* **business call** = visit to talk to someone on business **Geschäftsbesuch; business centre** = part of a town where the main banks, shops and offices are located **Geschäftsviertel; business class** = type of airline travel which is less expensive than first class and more comfortable than tourist class **Business Class; business college** *or* **business school** = place where commercial studies are taught **Wirtschaftsinstitut; business correspondent** = journalist who writes articles on business news for newspapers **Wirtschaftskorrespondent; business cycle** = movement of trade from a point of high activity down to a point of low activity and upwards again in the form of a regular cycle **Konjunkturzyklus;** *the recession is a low point in the business cycle;* **business efficiency exhibition** = exhibition which shows products (computers, word-processors, etc.) intended to help a business to be more efficient **Ausstellung von arbeitssparenden Büroeinrichtungen; business environment** = elements *or* factors outside a business organization which directly affect it, such as supply of raw materials and product demand **Aufgabenumwelt, Mikro-Umwelt;** *the unreliability of supplies is one of the worst* *features of our business environment;* **business games** = games, often run on computers, in which individuals or teams compete to do business in a hypothetical market **handelsthematische Computerspiele;** *students on management courses are often asked to take part in business games to improve their decision-making skills;* **business letter** = letter about commercial matters **Geschäftsbrief; business lunch** = lunch to discuss business matters **Geschäftsessen; business portfolio analysis** = method of categorizing a firm's products according to their relative competitive position and business growth rate in order to lay the foundations for sound strategic planning **Produktportfolio-Analyse; business publications** = magazines or newspapers which are only concerned with business matters (such as trade journals) **Wirtschafts-, Handelszeitschriften/-zeitungen; business trip** = trip to discuss business matters with clients **Geschäftsreise, Dienstreise; to be in business** = to be engaged in commercial activities **im Geschäft sein; to go into business** = to start a commercial firm **ein Geschäft gründen;** *he went into business as a car dealer;* **to go out of business** = to stop trading **das Geschäft aufgeben;** *the firm went out of business during the recession;* **on business** = for commercial purposes *or* as part of a one's job **geschäftlich, dienstlich;** *he had to go abroad on business; the chairman is in Holland on business*

(b) commercial company **Unternehmen, Geschäft, Betrieb;** *he owns a small car repair business; she runs her business from home; he set up in business as an insurance broker;* **business address** = details of number, street and town where a company is located **Geschäftsadresse; business card** = card showing a businessman's name and the name and address of the company he works for **Visitenkarte; business correspondence** = letters concerned with a business **Geschäftskorrespondenz; business equipment** = machines used in an office **Büroeinrichtung, Büroausstattung; business expansion scheme** = system in Britain where money invested for some years in a new company is free from tax **Steuerbefreiung bei Investitionen in Betriebsneugründung; business expenses** = money spent on running a business, not on stock or assets **Betriebskosten; business hours** = time (usually 9 a.m. to 5 p.m.) when a business is open **Geschäftsstunden, Geschäftszeit; big business** = very large commercial firms **Großunternehmertum, Großindustrie**

(c) affairs discussed **Angelegenheit, Sache;** *the main business of the meeting was finished by 3 p.m.;* **any other business** = item at the end of an agenda, where any matter can be raised **Verschiedenes**

◇ **business agent** *noun (US)* chief local official of a trade union **Gewerkschaftsfunktionär**

◇ **businessman** *or* **businesswoman** *noun* man *or* woman engaged in business **Geschäftsmann; Geschäftsfrau; she's a good businesswoman** = she's good at commercial deals **sie ist eine gute Geschäftsfrau; a small businessman** = man who owns a small business **Kleinunternehmer**

buy

1 *verb* to get something by paying money **(ein)kaufen;** *he bought 10,000 shares; the company has been bought by its leading supplier; to buy wholesale and sell retail; to buy for cash;* **to buy a pup** = to buy something which is worthless **Schund/die Katze im Sack kaufen; to buy forward** = to buy foreign currency before you need it, in order to be sure of the exchange rate **auf Termin kaufen; buy classes** = categories of buying based on how much the purchasing decisions of an organization have changed from the time of the previous purchase **Kaufkategorien; buy grid** = method used for objective assessment of competing products, especially when purchasing industrial supplies **Gitterkarte(methode); buy phases** = phases in the buying of industrial products (the main phases are the recognition of a want, the identification of a product, comparison with other competing products on the the market, evaluation of possible courses of action and final decision-making) **Kaufphasen;**

2 *noun* **good buy** *or* **bad buy** = thing bought which is *or* is not worth the money paid for it **guter Kauf; schlechter Kauf;** *that watch was a good buy; this car was a bad buy;* **new buy** = type of organizational buying, where a completely new product is bought **Neuproduktaufnahme**

◇ **buy back** *verb* to buy something which one has sold **zurückkaufen;** *he sold the shop last year and is now trying to buy it back;* **buy-back agreement** = agreement that a producer will buy back goods from a distributor on a certain date if the distributor has not been able to sell them **Rückkaufsvertrag, Rücknahmevereinbarung; Remission (Buchhandel)**

◇ **buyer** *noun*

(a) person who buys **Käufer/-in; there were no buyers** = no one wanted to buy **es gab keine Käufer; buyers' market** = market where products are sold cheaply because there are few buyers **Käufermarkt; buyer's risk** = risk taken by a buyer when accepting goods or services with no guarantee **Käuferrisiko; buyer's surplus** = difference between what a buyer would be willing to pay for something and what he or she does pay for it in the end **Käuferrente;** *when the brand manager realized how great the buyer's surplus was, he decided to raise the price of the product; because prices had not changed in line with an increase in demand, there was a considerable buyer's surplus;* **impulse buyer** = person who buys something when he sees it, not because he was planning to buy it **Impuls-, Spontankäufer; media buyer** = person in an advertising agency who places advertisements in the media on behalf of clients **Streuplaner, Kontakter zu den Werbemedien; space buyer** = person who buys advertising space in magazines and newspapers **Anzeigen(ver)mittler, Werbungtreibende(r); time buyer** = person who buys advertising time on radio or TV **Funkmedienkontakter**

(b) person who buys a certain type of goods wholesale for a large store to stock and sell **Einkäufer; head buyer** = most important buyer in a store **Einkaufsleiter;** *she's the shoe buyer for a London department store*

◇ **buy in** *verb*

(a) *(of a large store or of a company)* to buy a large stock of something which is likely to be needed later on

(b) *(of a seller at an auction)* to buy the thing which you are trying to sell because no one will pay the price you want **rückkaufen**

◇ **buying** *noun* getting something for money **Kaufen, Einkaufen; bulk buying** = getting large quantities of goods at low prices **Mengen-, Posteneinkauf; forward buying** *or* **buying forward** = buying shares *or* commodities *or* currency for delivery at a later date **Terminkauf; habit buying** = buying a particular product again and again by force of habit, without making a conscious decision to buy **Gewohnheitskauf; impulse buying** = buying items which you have just seen, and did not originally plan to buy **Impuls-, Spontankäufe; panic buying** = rush to buy something at any price because stocks may run out **Panikkäufe; buying agent** = person who buys for a business *or* another person, and earns a commission **Provisionseinkäufer, Kommissionär;** *our buying agent is presently looking for materials in Portugal; the buying agent knows a whole network of suppliers round the country;* **buying department** = department in a company which buys raw materials or goods for use in the company **Einkaufsabteilung; buying power** = ability to buy **Kaufkraft;** *the buying power of the pound has fallen over the last years*

by-product *noun* product made as a result of manufacturing a main product **Neben-, Abfallprodukt;** *soap is a useful by-product of oil*

Cc

CA = CONSUMERS ASSOCIATION **Verbraucherverband**

cable television *noun* television service which a viewer receives via a cable from a particular station and pays for on subscription **Kabelfernsehen**

call

1 *noun*

(a) visit **Besuch;** *the salesmen make six calls a day;* **business call** = visit to talk to someone on business **Geschäftsbesuch; cold call** = sales visit where the salesman has no appointment and the client is not an established customer **unangemeldeter Besuch; call bird** = low-priced product advertised to attract customers to the point-of-sale where they can then be sold more profitable goods **Lockvogel;** *we need a call bird to bring round more customers;* **call cycle** = time between a salesman's visits to the same customer **Besuchszyklus;** *because we now have more customers to deal with, call cycles are getting longer;* **call frequency** = the number of times a salesman visits a particular customer during a certain period **Besuchshäufigkeit; call rate** = number of calls made by a salesman on customers in a specific period **Besuchsrate; call report** = report made by a salesman after a visit to a customer **Besuchsbericht;** *in his call report, the salesman explained why he was experiencing sales resistance; the call reports have to be handed in each week to the sales manager*

(b) *US* **call letters** = series of letters used to identify a radio station **Sender-, Stationsabkürzung**

2 *verb* **to call on someone** = to visit **jdn besuchen;** *our salesmen call on their best accounts twice a month*

◇ **call in** *verb*

(a) to visit **vorbeikommen;** *the sales representative called in twice last week*

(b) to telephone to make contact **anrufen;** *we ask the reps to call in every Friday to report the weeks' sales*

(c) to ask someone to help **hinzuziehen;** *we called in an outside agency to handle all our promotion*

campaign *noun* series of co-ordinated activities to reach an objective **Kampagne, Aktion; sales campaign** = co-ordinated activities to achieve higher sales **Verkaufsaktion; publicity campaign** *or* **advertising campaign** = co-ordinated publicity or advertising drive to sell a product **Werbekampagne, Werbeaktion;** *they built the whole campaign round a well-known TV personality; the campaign was launched with a series of ads on prime-time television; they are working on a campaign to launch a new brand of soap*

canned presentation *noun* standard sales presentation which some salesmen use all the time **routinemäßige/stereotype Vorführung;** *when trainee salesmen are not sure how to approach customers they fall back on canned presentations; the sales manager feels that the artificiality of canned presentations makes them ineffective*

cannibalism *noun* situation where one of a company's products is selling well at the expense of another **Kannibalisierungseffekt;** *though the new product sold well, the resultant cannibalism damaged the company's overall profits for the year; cannibalism became a real problem because the new product made the existing line seem obsolete*

canvass *verb* to visit people to ask them to buy goods *or* to vote *or* to say what they think **werben; Wahlwerbung betreiben; befragen;** *he's canvassing for customers for his hairdresser's shop; we've canvassed the staff about raising the prices in the staff restaurant*

◇ **canvasser** *noun* person who canvasses **Vertreter; Wahlhelfer; Meinungsforscher**

◇ **canvassing** *noun* asking people to buy *or* to vote *or* to say what they think **Vertreterbesuche; Wahlwerbung; Meinungsumfrage;** *canvassing techniques; door-to-door canvassing*

capital *noun*
(a) money, property and assets used in a business **Kapital;** *a company with £10,000 capital or with a capital of £10,000 ;* **authorized capital** = maximum capital which is permitted by a company's articles of association **genehmigtes Grundkapital; capital account** = account of dealings (money invested in the company, or taken out of the company) by the owners of a company **Kapitalkonto; capital assets** = property *or* machines, etc. which a company owns and uses **Anlagevermögen; capital bonus** = bonus payment by an insurance company which is produced by capital gain **Bonus aus Kapitalerträgen; capital equipment** = equipment which a factory or office uses to work **Produktionsmittel; capital expenditure** *or* **investment** *or* **outlay** = money spent on fixed assets (property, machines, furniture) **Investitionen; capital gains** = money made by selling a fixed asset *or* by selling shares **Veräußerungsgewinn; capital gains tax** = tax paid on capital gains **Veräußerungsgewinnsteuer; capital goods** = goods used to manufacture other goods (i.e. machinery) **Anlagegüter; capital levy** = tax on the value of a person's property and possessions **Vermögenssteuer; capital loss** = loss made by selling assets **Kapitalverlust; capital reserves** = part of share capital which can be used only when a company is wound up **Kapitalreserven; capital structure of a company** = way in which a company's capital is set up **Kapitalstruktur eines Unternehmens; capital transfer tax** = tax on gifts or bequests of money or property **Kapitaltransfersteuer; circulating capital** = capital in the form of raw materials, finished products and work in progress required for a company to carry on its business **Umlaufvermögen; equity capital** = amount of a company's capital which is owned by the shareholders **Eigenkapital; fixed capital** = capital in the form of buildings and machinery **Anlagevermögen; issued capital** = amount of capital issued as shares to the shareholders **ausgegebenes Kapital; paid-up capital** = amount of money paid for the issued capital shares **einbezahltes Kapital; risk capital** *or* **venture capital** = capital for investment which may easily be lost in risky projects **Risiko-, Wagniskapital; share capital** = value of the assets of a company held as shares, less its debts **Aktienkapital; working capital** = capital in cash and stocks needed for a company to be able to work **Working Capital**
(b) money for investment **Kapital; movements of capital** = changes of investments from one country to another **Kapitalverkehr; flight of capital** = rapid movement of capital out of one country because of lack of confidence in that country's economic future **Kapitalflucht; capital market** = places where companies can look for investment capital **Kapitalmarkt**

◇ **capitalism** *noun* economic system where each person has the right to invest money, to work in business, to buy and sell, with no state restrictions **Kapitalismus**

◇ **capitalist**
1 *adjective* which practises or believes in capitalism **kapitalistisch;** *we work in a capitalist system*

2 *noun* person who possesses capital and invests it in business **Kapitalist/-in**

◊ **capitalize on** *verb* to make a profit from **Kapital schlagen aus;** *to capitalize on one's market position*

captain *see* CHANNEL CAPTAIN

caption *noun* short description above, below *or* next to an illustration *or* photograph **Bildüberschrift, Bildunterschrift, Legende;** *having no caption at the bottom of the illustration created more reader interest in the product; it took the copywriter days to think of a suitable caption for the photograph*

captive audience *noun* people who cannot avoid being exposed to an advertisement **unfreiwilliges Publikum;** *advertisers like to have their posters in underground stations where there is a large captive audience*

◊ **captive market** *noun* market where one supplier has a monopoly and the buyer has no choice over which product to purchase **monopolistischer Absatzmarkt**

capture *verb* to take *or* to get control of something **erobern, einnehmen; to capture 10% of the market** = to sell hard, and so take a 10% market share **10% des Marktes erobern; to capture 20% of a company's shares** = to buy shares in a company rapidly and so own 20% of it **Firmenanteile von 10% erwerben**

card *noun*
(a) printed piece of cardboard with information on it **Karte; car card** = advertisement display card which is placed in a vehicle (as in a bus or taxi or train) **Verkehrsmittelanschlag; rate card** = list of charges for advertising issued by a newspaper, magazine or other media owner **Anzeigenpreisliste; card rate** = advertising charge which is based on the charges listed in a rate card (i.e. without any discounts) **Listenpreis;** *see also* ESCALATOR CARD, SHOWCARD
(b) piece of plastic, usually with information printed on it magnetically **Karte; cash card** = card used to take money from one's account through a cash dispenser **Geldautomatenkarte; credit card** = card which allows the owner to borrow money or to buy goods and pay for them at a later date **Kreditkarte; store card** = credit card issued by a particular store, and which can only be used for purchases in that store **Kundenkarte, Membercard**

cargo *noun* load of goods which are sent in a ship *or* plane, etc. **Fracht, Ladung, Kargo; the ship was taking on cargo** = was being loaded with goods **das Schiff nahm Fracht auf; to load cargo** = to put cargo on a ship **Fracht verladen; air cargo** = goods sent by air **Luftfracht; berth cargo** = cargo carried at specially low rate **Auffülladung; deck cargo** = cargo carried on the open deck of a ship, rather than in the hold **Deckladung; cargo liner** = cargo ship with a regular schedule **(Linien)frachtschiff;** *if the cargo liner's schedule doesn't suit us, we'll have to charter a ship; the cargo liner makes regular trips between Southampton and Lisbon;* **cargo ship** *or* **cargo plane** = ship *or* plane which carries only cargo and not passengers **Frachter, Fracht-, Transportschiff; Transportflugzeug**

carnet *noun* international document which allows dutiable goods to cross several European countries by road without paying duty until the goods reach their final destination **Carnet**

carriage *noun* transporting goods from one place to another; cost of transport of goods **Transport; Transportkosten;** *to pay for carriage; to allow 10% for carriage; carriage is 15% of the total cost;* **carriage free** = deal where the customer does not pay for the shipping **frachtfrei; carriage paid** = deal where the seller has already paid for the shipping **frachtfrei; carriage forward** = deal where the customer will pay for the shipping when the goods arrive **Frachtnachnahme**

carrier *noun*
(a) company which transports goods **Spedition, Transportunternehmen;** *we only use reputable carriers;* **air carrier** = company which sends cargo *or* passengers by air **Flug-, Luftfahrtgesellschaft; common carrier** = firm which carries goods or passengers, and which can be used by anyone **öffentliches Fuhr- und Transportunternehmen; carrier's risk** = responsibility of the carrier to pay for any damage to goods **Spediteursrisiko**
(b) vehicle *or* ship which transports goods **Transporter; bulk carrier** = ship which carries large quantities of loose goods (such as corn) **Massengutfrachter**

carry *verb*
(a) to take from one place to another **befördern;** *to carry goods; a tanker carrying oil from the Gulf; the train was carrying a consignment of cars for export*
(b) to keep in stock **führen, auf Lager haben;** *to carry a line of goods; we do not carry pens*

◇ **carrying** *noun* transporting from one place to another **Beförderung, Transport;** *carrying charges; carrying cost*

◇ **carry over** *verb*

(a) to carry over a balance = to take a balance from the end of one page or period to the beginning of the next **einen Saldo vortragen**

(b) to carry over stock = to hold stock from the end of one stocktaking period to the beginning of the next **Waren übertragen (in das neue Finanzjahr)**

◇ **carry-over effect** *noun* effect of something after it has happened **Carryover-Effekt, Übertragungswirkung;** *the carry-over effect of the currency devaluation was a good few years of lucrative exporting; the political unrest in our key export markets had disastrous carry-over effects on our international marketing*

cartage *noun* carrying goods by road **Transport**

cartel *noun* group of companies which try to fix the price *or* to regulate the supply of a product so that they can make more profit **Kartell**

carter *noun* person who transports goods by road **Fuhrunternehmer**

carton *noun* box made of cardboard **Pappkarton, Karton;** *(Zigaretten)* **Stange;** *(Milch)* **Tüte;** *a carton of cigarettes*

case *noun*

(a) cardboard or wooden box for packing and carrying goods **Kiste; six cases of wine =** six boxes, each containing twelve bottles **sechs Kisten Wein; packing case =** large wooden box for carrying items which can be easily broken **Kiste**

(b) display case = table or counter with a glass top, used for displaying items for sale **Schau-, Glaskasten, Vitrine**

◇ **case study** *noun* true or invented business situation used in business training to practise decision-making **Fall-, Projektstudie;** *the marketing case study consisted of a long history of the company, the present situation and a choice of strategic plans; the case study was about territory-planning in a city in which there were a number of accounts of varying importance*

cash

1 *noun*

(a) money in coins or notes **Bargeld; cash in hand =** money and notes in the till, kept to pay small debts **Barbestand, Bargeld; hard cash =** money in notes and coins, as opposed to cheques or credit cards **Bargeld; petty cash =** small amounts of money (for example, money kept in an office for making small payments) **Porto-, Barkasse; ready cash =** money which is immediately available for payment **Bargeld; cash account =** account which records the money which is received and spent **Kassen-, Kassakonto; cash advance =** loan in cash against a future payment **Barvorschuß; cash balance =** balance in cash, as opposed to amounts owed **Bar-, Kassenbestand; cash book =** book in which cash transactions are entered **Kassenbuch; cash box =** metal box for keeping cash **Geldkassette; cash budget =** plan of cash income and expenditure **Einnahmen- und Ausgabenplanung; cash card =** card used to obtain money from a cash dispenser **Geldautomatenkarte; cash cow =** in the Boston matrix, a product that consistently generates good profits and maintains its market share, but will not provide growth **Milchkuh;** *with reliable sales and a low production cost, the cash cow produced steady if unspectacular profits;* **cash desk =** place in a store where you pay for the goods you have bought **Kasse; cash dispenser =** machine which gives out money when a special card is inserted and instructions given **Geldautomat; cash float =** cash put into the cash box at the beginning of the day or week to allow business to start **Wechselgeld; cash offer =** offer to pay in cash **Barzahlungsangebot; cash payment =** payment in cash **Barzahlung; cash purchases =** purchases made in cash **Barkäufe; cash register** *or* **cash till =** machine which shows and adds the prices of items bought, and which has a drawer for keeping the cash received **Registrierkasse; cash reserves =** a company's reserves in cash, deposits or bills, kept in case of urgent need **Bar-, Liquiditätsreserven**

(b) using money in coins or notes **Barzahlung; to pay cash down =** to pay in cash immediately **(in) bar zahlen; cash against documents =** system whereby a buyer receives documents for the goods on payment of a bill of exchange **Zahlung gegen Dokumente; cash discount** *or* **discount for cash =** discount given for payment in cash **Barzahlungsrabatt, Diskont;** *the seller offered a 15% cash discount for payment within 2 weeks; a generous cash discount is found to be a good incentive for early payment;* **cash price** *or* **cash terms =** (i) price of goods when cash is used for payment; (ii) lower price *or* terms which apply if the customer pays cash **Bar(zahlungs)preis; Barzahlungsbedingungen;** *the cash price of the article is low because the seller needs the money urgently;* **cash sale** *or* **cash transaction =** transaction paid for in cash

Bar-, Kassegeschäft; cash settlement *or* **settlement in cash** = paying a bill in cash **Barzahlung; terms: cash with order** = terms of sale showing that payment has to be made in cash when the order is placed **Bedingungen: Barzahlung bei Bestellung; cash on delivery** = payment in cash when goods are delivered **per Nachnahme;** (NOTE: US English is **collect on delivery)**
2 *verb* **to cash a cheque** = to exchange a cheque for cash **einen Scheck einlösen**

◇ **cashable** *adjective* which can be cashed **einlösbar;** *a crossed cheque is not cashable at any bank*

◇ **cash and carry** *noun* large store, selling goods at low prices, where the customer pays cash and has to take the goods away himself **(Verbraucher-)Abholmarkt;** *cash and carry warehouse*

◇ **cash flow** *noun* cash which comes into a company from sales less the money which goes out in purchases or overhead expenditure **Cashflow; cash flow forecast** = forecast of when cash will be received or paid out **Cashflow-Prognose; cash flow statement** = report which shows cash sales and purchases **Cashflow-Bericht; discounted cash flow** = calculating the forecast return on capital investment in current terms, with reductions for current interest rates **diskontierter Cashflow; net cash flow** = difference between the money coming in and the money going out **Netto-Cashflow; negative cash flow** = situation where more money is going out of a company than is coming in **negativer Cashflow; positive cash flow** = situation where more money is coming into a company than is going out **positiver Cashflow; the company is suffering from cash flow problems** = cash income is not coming in fast enough to cover expenditure **das Unternehmen hat Cashflow-Probleme**

◇ **cashier** *noun* person who takes money from customers in a shop; person who deals with customers' money in a bank **Kassierer/-in**

catalogue *or* *(US)* catalog

1 *noun* publication which lists items for sale, usually showing their prices **Katalog, Prospekt, Liste;** *an office equipment catalogue; they sent us a catalogue of their new range of desks;* **classified catalogue** = catalogue where the items are listed in categories **nach Fachgebieten gegliederter Katalog; mail-order catalogue** = catalogue from which a customer orders items to be sent by mail **Versandhauskatalog; catalogue price** = price as marked in a catalogue **Katalog-, Listenpreis**
2 *verb* to put an item into a catalogue **katalogisieren**

> QUOTE a 112-page international stock photo catalogue can provide images for every conceivable use
> ***Sales & Marketing Management***
> QUOTE the catalogue, containing card and gift offers, will have been sent to 500,000 people by the end of September
> ***Precision Marketing***

catchpenny

noun article which has only superficial appeal, but which attracts buyers **Schundware;** *a closer look at the doll showed it to be just a shoddily made catchpenny*

cater for

verb to deal with *or* to provide for **ausgerichtet sein auf;** *the store caters mainly for overseas customers*

◇ **caterer** *noun* person who supplies food and drink, especially for parties **Lebensmittellieferant**

◇ **catering** *noun*
(a) supplying food and drink for a party, etc. **gastronomische Betreuung; the catering trade** = food trade, especially the sector which supplies food ready to eat **Gaststättengewerbe**
(b) catering for = which provides for **ausgerichtet auf;** *store catering for overseas visitors*

caveat emptor

= LET THE BUYER BEWARE phrase meaning that the buyer himself is responsible for checking that what he buys is in good order **Ausschluß der Gewährleistung**

Ceefax

teletext services broadcast by the BBC **Bildschirmzeitung (von der BBC)**

ceiling

noun highest point **Höchstgrenze;** *output has reached a ceiling; to fix a ceiling for a budget;* **ceiling price** *or* **price ceiling** = highest price that can be reached **oberste Preisgrenze**

census

noun official count of a country's population, including such data as the age, sex, and occupation of individuals **Volkszählung;** *the market research department made a careful study of the census in different areas of the country to see where demand would be highest; see also* DISTRIBUTION CENSUS

Central Office of Information (COI)

British government organization which provides a publicity service and advice on international trade for British companies wishing to export **Informationsamt der (britischen) Regierung**

centre *or (US)* **center** *noun* group of items in an account **Kosten; cost centre** = person or group whose costs can be itemized **Kostenstelle; profit centre** = person or department which is considered separately for the purposes of calculating a profit **Profit Center**

◇ **centre spread** *noun* two facing pages in the centre of a newspaper *or* magazine used by an advertiser for one advertisement **Mittelseiten; doppelseitige Anzeige in der Heftmitte;** *the whole centre spread for three days cost the advertiser £150,000; the centre spread was taken up with a large advertisement for a new model of car*

chain *noun* series of stores belonging to the same company **Kette;** *a chain of hotels or a hotel chain; the chairman of a large do-it-yourself chain; he runs a chain of shoe shops; she bought several shoe shops and gradually built up a chain*

◇ **chain store** *noun* one store in a chain **Filiale, Kettenladen**

challenger *noun* company which challenges other companies which are already established in the marketplace **Herausforderer; market challenger strategy** = strategy adopted by a company which is challenging the market leaders by pricing, aggressive advertising or product design **Marktherausfordererstrategie**

Chamber of Commerce *noun* group of local businessmen who meet regularly to discuss problems which they have in common and to promote business in their town; similar group of businesses whose aim is promote business links with a certain foreign country **Handelskammer;** *the British Chamber of Commerce in Spain*

channel *noun*
(a) means by which information or goods pass from one place to another **Kanal, Weg; to go through the official channels** = to deal with government officials (especially when making a request) **den Amtsweg/Dienstweg beschreiten; to open up new channels of communication** = to find new ways of communicating with someone **neue Kommunikationswege erschließen; distribution channels** *or* **channels of distribution** = means by which goods pass from the manufacturer to the consumer, via wholesalers and retailers **Vertriebswege; channel members** = the various companies which form a distribution channel **Vertriebswegmitglieder; channels of influence** = ways in which a company can influence consumers to buy their products, i.e. personal influence channels such as salesmen, or non-personal channels such as press advertising **Einflußwege, Beeinflussungsmöglichkeiten; Werbekanäle;** *owing to lack of capital there were not many channels of influence open to the company; it was decided that personal selling was the most effective channel of influence for such a specialized product*
(b) trading channel = series of purchases and sales from company to company which are made until the finished product is purchased by the customer **Absatzweg; channel power** = the influence which one company in a trading channel has over the other companies in the channel **Absatzwegkapitänseinfluß**

◇ **channel captain** *noun (US)* business which controls or has the most influence in a distribution channel **Absatzwegkapitän;** *the production company became a channel captain by acquiring a number of important retail outlets; only businesses with enough financial resources to acquire other companies can become channel captains*

◇ **channel strip** *noun* front edge of a shelf on which details of the products displayed can be put (such as price, weight, code numbers, etc.) **Regal-, Werbeleiste**

charge
1 *noun*
(a) money which must be paid *or* price of a service **Gebühr, Kosten;** *to make no charge for delivery; to make a small charge for rental; there is no charge for service or no charge is made for service;* **admission charge** *or* **entry charge** = price to be paid before going into an exhibition, etc. **Eintritt(sgebühr); bank charges** = charges made by a bank for carrying out work for a customer **Bankgebühren; handling charge** = money to be paid for packing *or* invoicing *or* dealing with goods which are being shipped **Bearbeitungsgebühr; inclusive charge** = charge which includes all items **Gesamtgebühr, Pauschale; interest charges** = money paid as interest on a loan **Zinsbelastung, Sollzinsen; scale of charges** = list showing various prices **Gebührenordnung; service charge** = charge added to a bill in a restaurant to pay for service **Bedienung;** *a 10% service charge is added; does the bill include a service charge?;* **charges forward** = charges which will be paid by the customer **Nachnahme; token charge for heating** = a small charge which does not cover the real costs at all **nominelle Heizkostenpauschale; free of charge** = free *or* with no payment to be made **kostenlos, gebührenfrei;** *see also* DATE-IN-CHARGE

(b) debit on an account **Belastung;** *it appears as a charge on the accounts*
2 *verb*
(a) to ask someone to pay for services later **in Rechnung stellen, berechnen; to charge the packing to the customer** = the customer has to pay for packing **dem Kunden Verpackungskosten in Rechnung stellen**
(b) to ask for money to be paid **erheben, berechnen, in Rechnung stellen;** *to charge £5 for delivery; how much does he charge?;* **she charges £6 an hour** = she asks to be paid £6 for an hour's work **sie nimmt £6 pro Stunde**

◇ **chargeable** *adjective* which can be charged **anrechenbar, zu berechnen;** *repairs chargeable to the occupier;* **sums chargeable to the reserve** = sums which can be debited to a company's reserves **Beträge, die von den Rücklagen getragen werden**

◇ **charge account** *noun*
(a) arrangement which a customer has with a store to buy goods and pay for them at a later date, usually when the invoice is sent at the end of the month **Kunden(kredit)konto**
(b) *US* system whereby a customer can pay a supplier at the end of an agreed period for all goods or services bought **Kunden(kredit)konto;** *the seller would not agree to a charge account as he needed money from sales immediately*

◇ **charge card** *noun* plastic card which allows the user to purchase items and charge them to a charge account **Kunden(kredit)karte**

charity *noun* organization which offers free help or services to those in need **karitative Organisation, wohltätige Stiftung;** *because the organization is a charity it does not have to pay taxes; the charity owes its success to clever marketing strategies in its fund-raising*

chart *noun* diagram showing information as a series of lines *or* blocks, etc. **Diagramm; bar chart** = diagram where quantities and values are shown as thick columns of different heights *or* lengths **Balken-, Stabdiagramm; flow chart** = diagram showing the arrangement of various work processes in a series **Arbeitsablauf-, Flußdiagramm; line chart** = chart which indicates values using lines of different lengths **Linien-, Strichdiagramm; organization chart** = diagram showing how a company *or* an office is organized **Stellenbesetzungsplan; Diagramm der Unternehmensstruktur, Organigramm; pie chart** = diagram where information is shown as a circle cut up into sections of different sizes **Kreisdiagramm; sales chart** = diagram showing how sales vary from month to month **Umsatz-, Absatzdiagramm**

charter
1 *noun*
(a) hiring transport for a special purpose **Chartern; Charterung; charter flight** = flight in an aircraft which has been hired for that purpose **Charterflug; charter plane** = plane which has been chartered **Charterflugzeug; boat on charter to Mr Smith** = boat which Mr Smith has hired for a voyage **Boot, das von Mr Smith gechartert wurde**
(b) statement of rights **Rechtsbewilligung; shoppers' charter** = law which protects the rights of shoppers against dishonest shopkeepers **Verbraucherschutzgesetz**
2 *verb* to hire for a special purpose **chartern; mieten;** *to charter a plane or a boat or a bus*

◇ **chartered** *adjective* **chartered ship** *or* **bus** *or* **plane** = ship *or* bus *or* plane which has been hired for a special purpose **gechartertes Schiff od Flugzeug; gemieteter Bus**

◇ **charterer** *noun* person who hires a ship, etc., for a special purpose **Charterer; Mieter/-in**

◇ **chartering** *noun* act of hiring for a special purpose **Chartern; Mieten**

◇ **charter party** *noun* contract between owner and charterer of a ship **Chartepartie, Frachtvertrag**

checklist *noun* list of items which have to be checked, especially as a way of evaluating a promotional campaign or a single advertisement **Kontrolliste, Checkliste**

checkout *noun (Supermarkt)* place where goods are paid for in a shop or supermarket **Kasse;** *the new supermarket has sixteen checkouts, each equipped with EPOS systems*

cherry-picking *noun (US)* going from shop to shop or from supplier to supplier, looking for special bargains **Sonderangebotsankaufen;** *(metaphorisch)* **das Herauspicken von Rosinen;** *cherry-picking has become so widespread that prices may be forced down*

cheque *or (US)* **check** *noun* note to a bank asking them to pay money from an account to the account of the person whose name is written on the note **Scheck; cheque account** = bank account which allows the customer to write cheques **laufendes Konto, Girokonto; cheque to bearer** = cheque with no name written on it, so that the person who holds it can cash it **Überbringer-, Inhaberscheck; crossed cheque** = cheque with two lines across it showing that it can only be deposited at a bank and not exchanged for cash **Verrechnungsscheck;**

open *or* **uncrossed cheque** = cheque which can be cashed anywhere **Barscheck; blank cheque** = cheque with the amount of money and the payee left blank, but signed by the drawer **Blankoscheck; pay cheque** *or* **salary cheque** = monthly cheque by which an employee is paid **Lohn-, Gehaltsscheck; traveller's cheques** = cheques taken by a traveller, which can be cashed in a foreign country **Reiseschecks; dud cheque** *or* **bouncing cheque** *or* **cheque which bounces** *or* *(US)* **rubber check** = cheque which cannot be cashed because the person writing it does not have enough money in the account to pay it **ungedeckter Scheck**
(b) to cash a cheque = to exchange a cheque for cash **einen Scheck einlösen; to endorse a cheque** = to sign a cheque on the back to show that you accept it **einen Scheck girieren; to make out a cheque to someone** = to write someone's name on a cheque **jdm einen Scheck ausstellen;** *who shall I make the cheque out to?;* **to pay by cheque** = to pay by writing a cheque, rather than using cash or a credit card **mit (einem) Scheck bezahlen; to pay a cheque into your account** = to deposit a cheque **einen Scheck auf das Konto einzahlen; the bank referred the cheque to drawer** = returned the cheque to the person who wrote it because there was not enough money in the account to pay it **die Bank gab den Scheck zurück an den Aussteller; to sign a cheque** = to sign on the front of a cheque to show that you authorize the bank to pay the money from your account **einen Scheck unterschreiben; to stop a cheque** = to ask a bank not to pay a cheque which you have written **einen Scheck sperren lassen**

◇ **cheque book** *noun* booklet with new cheques **Scheckheft**

◇ **cheque guarantee card** *noun* plastic card from a bank which guarantees payment of a cheque up to a certain amount, even if there is no money in the account **Scheckkarte**

c.i.f. = COST, INSURANCE AND FREIGHT **Kosten, Versicherung und Fracht; cif**

circular
1 *adjective* sent to many people **Rund-; circular letter of credit** = letter of credit sent to all branches of the bank which issues it **Akkreditiv**
2 *noun* leaflet *or* letter sent to many people **Rundschreiben, Umlauf;** *they sent out a circular offering a 10% discount*

◇ **circularize** *verb* to send a circular to **Rundschreiben verschicken;** *the committee has agreed to circularize the members; they circularized all their customers with a new list of prices*

◇ **circulate** *verb*
(a) *(Geld)* **to circulate freely** = to move about without restriction by the government **in freiem Umlauf sein**
(b) to send information to **in Umlauf bringen;** *they circulated a new list of prices to all their customers*

◇ **circulation** *noun (von Zeitungen)* number of copies sold **Auflage, Auflagenhöhe;** *the audited circulation of a newspaper; the new editor hopes to improve the circulation;* **circulation battle** = competition between newspapers to try to sell more copies in the same market **Kampf um die Auflagenhöhe (verschiedener Zeitungen); paid circulation** = the number of copies of a newspaper or magazine which have been bought **Verkaufsauflage;** *see also* CONTROLLED CIRCULATION, SUBSCRIBED CIRCULATION

CKD = COMPLETELY KNOCKED DOWN

classify *verb* to put into classes *or* categories **klassifizieren, einstufen; classified advertisements** = advertisements listed in a newspaper under special headings (such as "property for sale" or "jobs wanted") **Kleinanzeigen; classified directory** = book which lists businesses grouped under various headings (such as computer shops *or* newsagents) **Branchenverzeichnis; classified display advertising** = advertising that, although it is classified, may also have individual features such as its own box border or the company logo **rubrizierte Großanzeigenwerbung**

◇ **classified catalogue** *noun* catalogue which groups articles into certain categories **nach Fachgebieten gegliederter Katalog;** *the classified catalogue is divided into two sections, electrical and non-electrical products; the department store publishes a classified catalogue with a section for each department; there is no entry for garden furniture in the classified catalogue*

clause *noun* section of a contract **Klausel, Paragraph, Absatz;** *there are ten clauses in the contract; according to clause six, payments will not be due until next year;* **exclusion clause** = clause in a contract *or* insurance policy *or* warranty which says which items are not covered by it **Ausschlußklausel, Freizeichnungsklausel; penalty clause** = clause which lists the penalties which will be imposed if the contract is not fulfilled **Strafklausel; termination clause** = clause which explains how and when a contract can be terminated **Kündigungsklausel**

◇ **claused** *adjective* **claused bill of lading** = bill of lading stating that goods did not arrive on board in good condition **unreines Konnossement**

clean *adjective* straightforward *or* with no complications **rein, sauber; einwandfrei, vorbehaltlos; clean acceptance** = unconditional acceptance of a bill of lading **vorbehaltloses Akzept;** *a clean acceptance ensures a quick and uncomplicated transaction;* **clean bill of lading** = bill of lading stating that goods arrived on board in good condition **reines Konnossement**

clear *verb* to sell cheaply in order to get rid of stock **räumen; ab-, ausverkaufen;** *"demonstration models to clear"*

◇ **clearance** *noun*
(a) customs clearance = passing goods through customs so that they can enter or leave the country **Zollabfertigung; to effect customs clearance** = to clear goods through customs **die Zollabfertigung vornehmen; clearance certificate** = certificate showing that goods have been passed by the customs **Zollabfertigungs-, Ausklarierungsschein**
(b) clearance sale = sale of items at low prices to get rid of stock **Räumungsverkauf**
(c) clearance of a cheque = passing of a cheque through the banking system, transferring money from one account to another **Einlösen eines Schecks;** *you should allow six days for cheque clearance*

client *noun* person with whom business is done *or* person who pays for a service **Kunde/Kundin, Auftraggeber/-in**

◇ **clientele** *noun* all the clients of a business; all the customers of a shop **Kundschaft, Kundenkreis, Klientel**

clip *noun* short extract from a film **kurzer Filmausschnitt**

◇ **clipping** *noun* cutting out pieces from publications which refer to an item of particular interest **Ausschneiden; clipping service** = service which cuts out references to a customer from newspapers and magazines and sends them to him **Presseausschnittdienst**

close
1 *noun* end (of a sales negotiation) **Abschluß; concession close** = act of ending a sale by offering a concession to the purchaser **Abschlußrabatt**
2 *verb*
(a) to bring to an end **(ab)schließen, beenden; to close a sale** = to end a sales negotiation and persuade a buyer to make a purchase **ein Geschäft abschließen**
(b) to shut *or* to stop commercial work **schließen, zumachen;** *the shop closes at 5.30; the office is closed on Saturdays*
(c) to stop something being open **sperren, löschen, auflösen; to close an account** = (i) to stop supplying a customer on credit; (ii) to withdraw all money from a bank account and stop using it **(i) ein Kundenkreditkonto sperren; (ii) ein Konto auflösen; to close a market** = to restrict a market to one agent or distributor, and refuse to allow others to deal in the area **einen Markt schließen; closed market** = market where the supplier supplies only one agent or distributor **geschlossener Markt;**

◇ **close down** *verb* to stop business permanently **schließen; stillegen; closing-down sale** = sale of goods when a shop is closing for ever **Totalaus-, Räumungsverkauf**

closing
1 *adjective*
(a) final *or* coming at the end **Abschluß-, Schluß-, abschließend; closing bid** = last bid at an auction *or* the bid which is successful **Höchstgebot; closing date** = last date **Schließungstag;** *(für Inserate)* **Anzeigenschluß;** *(für Ausschreibungsangebot)* **Ausschreibungsschluß;** *the closing date for tenders to be received is May 1st;* **closing price** = price of a share at the end of a day's trading **Schlußkurs, Schlußnotierung**
(b) at the end of an accounting period **Abschluß-;** *closing balance; closing stock*
2 *noun*
(a) closing a sale = point where a salesman persuades a buyer to actually place an order **Abschluß eines Verkaufs;** *the trainee salesmen discovered that closing a sale needs patience and persistence; special discounts for first-time buyers were sometimes used as incentives in closing a sale;* **closing techniques** = special techniques of persuasion used by salesmen to close sales **Abschlußtechnik;** *the training manager demonstrated some presentation and closing techniques; most of our salesmen develop their own selling methods, including closing techniques*
(b) shutting of a shop *or* being shut **Schließung; Sunday closing** = not opening a shop on Sundays **geschäftsfreier Sonntag; closing time** = time when a shop or office stops work **Geschäftsschluß; Ladenschluß; early closing day** = weekday (usually Wednesday or Thursday) when many shops close in the afternoon **Tag mit frühem Ladenschluß**

(c) closing of an account = act of stopping supply to a customer on credit **Sperrung eines Kundenkreditkontos**
◇ **closure** *noun*
(a) act of closing **Schließung; Stillegung**
(b) psychological process whereby a person supplies an ending (such as a brand name) which is implied, but not stated by a stimulus, such as an advertisement **Wahrnehmung einer Verstandswerbung;** *the advertisement only showed part of the brand name, relying on closure to get the whole message across; by means of closure the target audience received the advertiser's intended message*

cluster *noun* group of things together **Gruppe, Klumpen; cluster analysis** = method whereby samples are classified into groups according to certain characteristics **Clusteranalyse; cluster sampling** = sampling on the basis of well-defined groups **Klumpenauswahl;** *cluster sampling was used in the survey since there were several very distinct groups in the population under study*

COD *or* **c.o.d.** = CASH ON DELIVERY

code *noun* system of signs or numbers or letters which has a meaning **Code, Chiffre; bar code** = system of lines printed on a product which, when read by a computer, indicate a reference number and price **Strichkodierung, Bar-Code;**
◇ **code of practice** *noun* formally established ways in which members of a profession agree to work **Richtlinien;** *advertisers have agreed to abide by the code of practice set out by the advertising council*

coefficient of correlation *noun* measurement of correlation *or* relationship between two sets of data on a continuum from -1 to +1 **Korrelationskoeffizient**

cognitive dissonance *noun* conflict experienced by a person who cannot resolve apparently contradictory information, as when making buying decisions or evaluating purchases which have been made **kognitive Dissonanz**

COI = CENTRAL OFFICE OF INFORMATION

cold *adjective* without previous preparation **unvorbereitet; cold call** = sales call where the salesman has no appointment and the client is not an established customer **unangemeldeter Vertreterbesuch; cold start** = starting a new business *or* opening a new shop where there was none before **ein völliger Neubeginn**

collect
1 *verb*
(a) to make someone pay money owing **einziehen, eintreiben; to collect a debt** = to go and make someone pay a debt **Schulden einziehen/eintreiben** *(US)* **collect on delivery** = payment in cash when goods are delivered **per Nachnahme;** NOTE: GB English is **cash on delivery**
(b) to fetch things from a place **abholen;** *we have to collect the stock from the warehouse; can you collect my letters from the typing pool?;* **letters are collected twice a day** = the post office workers take them from the letter box to the post office for dispatch **die Briefkästen werden zweimal täglich geleert**
2 *adverb & adjective (US)* (phone call) which the person receiving the call agrees to pay for **R-Gespräch;** *to make a collect call; he called his office collect*
◇ **collecting agency** *noun* agency which collects money owed to other companies for a commission **Inkassobüro**

colour supplement *noun* magazine which accompanies a newspaper and contains a lot of advertising **Supplement, illustrierte/bunte Beilage, Farbbeilage;** *the spring colour supplements were mostly devoted to holiday advertising; the tobacco company bought advertising space on three pages of the colour supplement*

column *noun* section of printed words in a newspaper *or* magazine **Kolumne, Spalte; column-centimetre** *or* **column inch** = unit of measurement of space in a newspaper column (one column one centimetre or one inch in depth) used for calculating charges for advertising **Maß der Spaltenbreite in Zentimeter (od Zoll); Zentimeterpreis**

comeback *noun* means of getting compensation for complaints or claims **Rückforderung(sanspruch);** *if you throw away the till receipt you will have no comeback if the goods turn out to be faulty*

commando selling *noun* hard intensive selling **aggressive Verkaufsstrategie;** *commando selling campaigns were started in all the new markets where the company's products were virtually unknown; commando selling is needed to obtain a reasonable market share in a market dominated by a powerful competitor*

commerce *noun* business *or* buying and selling of goods and services **Handel, Handelsverkehr; Chamber of Commerce** = group of local businessmen and women who meet to discuss common problems and to promote business in their town **Handelskammer**

◇ **commercial**
1 *adjective*
(a) referring to business **Handels-, Geschäfts-, kommerziell; commercial agent** = person *or* business selling a company's products or services for a commission **Handelsvertreter, Provisionsagent;** *the marketing director decided to set up a network of commercial agents in Europe; the commercial agent earned a 30% commission on sales he made; as a commercial agent, she represents several companies;* **commercial aircraft** = aircraft used to carry cargo *or* passengers for payment **Verkehrsflugzeug; commercial artist** = artist who designs advertisements *or* posters, etc. for payment **Werbegrafiker; commercial attaché** = diplomat who represents and tries to promote his country's business interests **Handelsattaché; commercial break** = time set aside for commercials on television **Programmunterbrechung/Sendepause für Werbung;** *the advertiser wished to specify exactly when in the commercial break the advertisements were to appear; the advertising manager placed one advertisement in each commercial break of the day on the radio channel;* **commercial college** = college which teaches business studies **Handelsinstitut; commercial counsellor** = person who advises on commercial matters in an embassy **Handelsberater, Handelsattaché;** *the commercial counsellor gave us sound advice on marketing in the country he represented;* **commercial course** = course in which students study business skills **kaufmännischer Lehrgang, Handelskurs;** *he took a commercial course by correspondence;* **commercial directory** = book which lists all the businesses and business people in a town **Branchenadreßbuch; commercial district** = part of a town where most offices and shops are **Gewerbegebiet; commercial law** = laws which relate to business **Handelsrecht (Teil des Wirtschaftsrechts); commercial load** = amount of goods *or* number of passengers which a bus *or* train *or* plane has to carry to make a profit **wirtschaftliche Auslastung; commercial port** = port which has only goods traffic **Handelshafen; commercial services** = services which support trade, such as banking and advertising **Hilfsbetriebe des Handels;** *the recession has affected commercial services and the industries they support and supply;* **commercial traveller** = salesman who travels round an area visiting customers on behalf of his company *or* several companies; *(old-fashioned)* **Handelsreisende(r); Handelsvertreter(in); commercial vehicle** = van *or* truck, etc. used for business purposes **Nutzfahrzeug; sample only - of no commercial value** = not worth anything if sold **unverkäufliche Warenprobe**
(b) profitable **wirtschaftlich, gewinnbringend; not a commercial proposition** = not likely to make a profit **kein gewinnbringendes Geschäft;**
2 *noun* advertisement on television **Werbespot, Werbung; combination commercial** = television advertisement which combines still pictures with action shots **Werbesendung, in der verschiedene Werbetechniken kombiniert werden; commercial protection** = guarantee that rival products will not be advertised directly before or after a particular advertisement **Sendezeitabstand für Konkurrenten; commercial time** = time that a television or radio station devotes to advertising **Gesamtwerbezeit;** *the TV station is extending its commercial time in order to increase revenue*

◇ **commercialization** *noun*
(a) the launch of a product onto the market **Kommerzialisierung;** *the pilot tests have proved successful, and full-scale commercialization will begin in the spring*
(b) making something into a business proposition **Kommerzialisierung;** *the commercialization of museums*

◇ **commercialize** *verb* to make something into a business **kommerzialisieren;** *the holiday town has become unpleasantly commercialized*

◇ **commercially** *adverb* as regards business **geschäftlich, gewerblich, kommerziell; not commercially viable** = not likely to make a profit **unrentabel**

commission *noun* money paid to a salesman *or* an agent, usually a percentage of the sales made **Provision, Kommission(sgebühr), Maklergebühr;** *she gets 10% commission on everything she sells;* **he charges 10% commission** = he asks for 10% of sales as his payment **er erhebt 10% Provision; commission agent** = agent who is paid a percentage of sales **Provisionsvertreter, Kommissionsagent; Kommissionär; commission rebating** = advertising agency's discounting of invoices for media costs sent to clients, in effect taking them out of its own commission or profit margin **Kommissionsrabatt; commission rep** =

representative who is not paid a salary, but receives a commission on sales **Provisionsvertreter; commission sale** *or* **sale on commission** = sale where the salesman is paid a commission **Verkauf auf Kommissionsbasis**

commodity *noun* thing sold in very large quantities, especially a raw material such as a metal and food such as corn **Ware; primary** *or* **basic commodities** = farm produce grown in large quantities, such as corn, rice, cotton, etc. **Grundstoffe; staple commodity** = basic food or raw material which is vital to a country's economy **Haupterzeugnis; commodity market** *or* **commodity exchange** = place where people buy and sell commodities **Warenbörse; commodity futures** = trading in commodities for delivery at a later date **Warentermingeschäft;** *silver rose 5% on the commodity futures market yesterday;* **commodity trader** = person whose business is buying and selling commodities **Warenterminhändler**

common *adjective*
(a) which happens frequently **häufig, weitverbreitet, allgemein, normal;** *putting the carbon paper in the wrong way round is a common mistake; getting caught by customs is becoming more common*
(b) belonging to several different people or to everyone **gemeinsam, Gemeinschafts-, Gemein-; common carrier** = firm which carries goods or passengers, and which anyone can use **öffentliches Fuhr- und Transportunternehmen; common ownership** = ownership of a company *or* a property by a group of people **Miteigentum; common pricing** = illegal fixing of prices by several businesses so that they all charge the same price **Preisabsprache;** *(US)* **common stock** = ordinary shares in a company, giving shareholders a right to vote at meetings and to receive dividends **Stammaktien; Common Agricultural Policy** = agreement between members of the EC to protect farmers by paying subsidies to fix prices of farm produce **Agrarpolitik der Europäischen Gemeinschaft**

◇ **Common Market** *noun* **the European Common Market** = the European Economic Community *or* organization which links several European countries for the purposes of trade **der Gemeinsame Markt; the Common Market finance ministers** = the finance ministers of all the Common Market countries meeting as a group **die Finanzminister der Europäischen Gemeinschaft**

communisuasion *noun* *(US)* communication that is intended to persuade **überzeugende Kommunikation;** *the salesmen are being trained in the subtleties of communisuasion*

comparative *adjective* which can be compared with something else **vergleichend; comparative advertising** = advertising which compares a company's product with competing brands to its own advantage **Vergleichswerbung;** *disparaging remarks in comparative advertising were strongly discouraged in the industry; the company uses comparative advertising to highlight the advantages of its products;* **comparative analysis** = analysis of different media and vehicle options by an advertiser **vergleichende Analyse;** *a tight advertising budget made a thorough comparative analysis essential; comparative analysis is difficult when the various media offer such different advantages*
◇ **comparison** *noun* action of comparing one thing with another **Vergleich; intermedia comparison** = comparison of different media as vehicles for advertising **Intermediavergleich; intercompany comparison** = comparing different companies to see how much they spend on promotion, what their return-on-investment is, what their profits are, etc. **zwischenbetrieblicher Vergleich; paired comparison** = tests in which respondents compare two brands on the basis of certain attributes which are common to both **Paarvergleich**

compete *verb* **to compete with someone** *or* **with a company** = to try to do better than another person *or* another company **mit jdm od mit einem Unternehmen konkurrieren;** *we have to compete with cheap imports from the Far East; they were competing unsuccessfully with local companies on their home territory;* **the two companies are competing for a market share** *or* **for a contract** = each company is trying to win a larger part of the market *or* to win the contract **die beiden Unternehmen stehen in Konkurrenz um einen Marktanteil od einen Vertrag**
◇ **competing** *adjective* which competes **konkurrierend; competing firms** = firms which compete with each other **konkurrierende Unternehmen; competing products** = products from different companies which have the same use and are sold in the same markets at similar prices **Konkurrenzprodukte**
◇ **competition** *noun*
(a) trying to do better than another supplier or to win over some of its customers

Wettbewerb, Konkurrenz; free competition = being free to compete without government interference **freier Wettbewerb; keen competition** = strong competition **scharfer Wettbewerb;** *we are facing keen competition from European manufacturers; see also* IMPERFECT COMPETITION, PERFECT COMPETITION

(b) the competition = companies which are trying to compete with your product **die Konkurrenz;** *we have lowered our prices in order to beat the competition; the competition have brought out a new range of products*

(c) competitions = type of sales promotions which enables consumers who can show that they have bought a certain minimum number of purchases to compete in games **Preisausschreiben;** *the company uses competitions to sell off an excess supply of tinned food; competitions involve prizes ranging from washing-machines to holidays abroad; competitions and free gifts make up a large part of the company's sales promotions*

◇ **competitive** *adjective* which competes fairly **wettbewerbs-, konkurrenzfähig; competitive demand** = demand for products that are competing for sales **Konkurrenzproduktnachfrage; competitive edge** *or* **competitive advantage** = advantage that one company *or* product has over its rivals in the market **Wettbewerbsvorteil;** *any competitive edge we have in this market is due to our good after-sales service; why does this product have the competitive edge over its rivals?;* **competitive parity** = method of budgeting marketing or promotional expenses according to the amounts being spent by competitors **Wettbewerbsparität; competitive price** = price which is kept low to compete with a rival product **wettbewerbs-, konkurrenzfähiger Preis; competitive pricing** = putting low prices on goods so as to compete with other products **wettbewerbs-, konkurrenzfähige Auspreisung; competitive products** = products made to compete with existing products **Konkurrenzartikel, Konkurrenzprodukte; konkurrenzfähige Produkte; competitive separation** = guarantee that rival products will not be advertised directly before or after a particular advertisement **Sendezeitabstand für Konkurrenten;** *if our advertising campaign is to be really effective, we must insist on competitive separation*

◇ **competitively** *adverb* **competitively priced** = sold at a low price to compete with the price of similar products from other companies **mit wettbewerbsfähigen Preisen**

◇ **competitiveness** *noun* being competitive **Wettbewerbs-, Konkurrenzfähigkeit**

◇ **competitor** *noun* person *or* company which competes **Konkurrent/-in;** *those two German firms are our main competitors*

QUOTE whereas Japanese companies might be able to emulate competitors originally, this has now moved on to researching a product/market from fundamentals
Quarterly Review of Marketing

QUOTE profit margins in the industries most exposed to foreign competition are worse than usual
Sunday Times

QUOTE competition is steadily increasing and could affect profit margins as the company tries to retain its market share
Citizen (Ottawa)

QUOTE the company blamed fiercely competitive market conditions in Europe for a £14m operating loss last year
Financial Times

QUOTE the one thing for certain is that in a more competitive market, new creative ideas will be very necessary
Marketing

QUOTE the growth of increasingly competitive global markets and the pace of technological innovation are forcing manufacturers to take new approaches
Management Today

QUOTE farmers are increasingly worried by the growing lack of competitiveness for their products on world markets
Australian Financial Review

QUOTE sterling labour costs continue to rise between 3% and 5% a year faster than in most of our competitor countries
Sunday Times

complaints department *noun* department in a company *or* store to which customers can send or bring complaints about its products or service **Beschwerde-, Reklamationsabteilung;** *the customer brought his faulty CD player to the complaints department*

complementary *adjective* which adds to or completes something else **ergänzend, komplementär; complementary demand** = demand for two or more products that are needed together **Komplementärgüternachfrage;** *the demand for cars and petrol was an example of complementary demand; complementary demand means that manufacturers of cigarette lighters are heavily dependent on the tobacco industry;* **complementary supply** = supply of two or more products from the same production process **Komplementärgüterangebot; complementary product** = product for which demand is dependent on the demand for another product **Komplementärprodukt;** *when demand for our product fell, producers of* *complementary products also suffered; Compare* COMPLIMENTARY

Completely Knocked Down products (CKD products) *noun* products which are sold unassembled, and therefore at reasonably low prices **in Einzelteile zerlegte, preiswerte Produkte; Selbstbauprodukte;** *many low-income buyers buy CKD products; CKD products are popular with DIY enthusiasts*

complimentary *adjective* **complimentary ticket** = free ticket, given as a present **Freikarte;** *Compare* COMPLEMENTARY

◊ **compliments slip** *noun* piece of paper with the name of the company printed on it, sent with documents *or* gifts, etc. instead of a letter **Kurzmitteilung**

component *noun* piece of machinery *or* section which will be put into a final product **Bestandteil;** *the assembly line stopped because the supply of a vital component was delayed;* **components factory** = factory which makes parts which are used in other factories to make finished products **Zulieferant**

composite demand *noun* total demand for a product that has many uses **Gesamtnachfrage;** *composite demand for the construction equipment came from construction companies and DIY enthusiasts*

computer *noun* electronic machine which calculates *or* stores information and processes it automatically **Computer, Rechner; computer bureau** = office which offers to do work on its computers for companies which do not have their own computers **Rechenzentrum; EDV-Servicebüro; computer department** = department in a company which manages the company's computers **EDV-Abteilung; computer error** = mistake made by a computer **Computerfehler; computer file** = section of information on a computer (such as the payroll, list of addresses, customer accounts) **Computerdatei; computer language** = system of signs, letters and words used to instruct a computer **Computersprache; computer listing** = printout of a list of items taken from data stored in a computer **Computerausdruck; computer manager** = person in charge of a computer department **Leiter der EDV-Abteilung; computer program** = instructions to a computer, telling it to do a particular piece of work **Computerprogramm; computer programmer** = person who writes computer programs **Computerprogrammierer, Programmierer; computer services** = work using a computer, done by a computer bureau **EDV-Service; computer time** = time when a computer is being used (paid for at an hourly rate) **Betriebszeit;** *running all those sales reports costs a lot in computer time;* **business computer** = powerful small computer which is programmed for special business uses **kommerzieller Rechner; personal computer** *or* **home computer** = small computer which can be used in the home **Personalcomputer, PC**

◊ **computerize** *verb* to change from a manual system to one using computers **computerisieren, auf Computer/Datenverarbeitung/EDV umstellen;** *our stock control has been completely computerized*

◊ **computerized** *adjective* worked by computers **computerisiert, EDV-;** *a computerized invoicing system*

◊ **computer-readable** *adjective* which can be read and understood by a computer **computerlesbar;** *computer-readable codes*

◊ **computing** *adjective & noun* referring to computers *or* work done on computers **Computer-, Rechen-, Datenverarbeitungs-, EDV-; Computing; computing speed** = speed at which a computer calculates **Rechengeschwindigkeit**

concentrated marketing *noun* promotion of a product aimed at one particular area of the market **gezieltes Marketing;** *when it became obvious that the general public were interested in our product, we switched from concentrated marketing to a much broader approach*

◊ **concentration** *noun* degree to which a small number of businesses control a large section of the market **Konzentration;** *too much concentration created resentment among small businesses trying to enter the market; concentration has meant too little competition and therefore higher prices to the consumer*

concept *noun* idea **Konzept; marketing concept** = business idea based on the importance of profit and consumer satisfaction **Marketingkonzept; concept testing** = evaluating a new product idea, usually by consulting representatives from all the main departments in a company, and/or by interviewing a sample of consumers **Durchführung eines Konzepttests;** *the new product idea did not survive concept testing because it didn't answer an existing demand; after thorough concept testing the idea of a disposable pen was rejected as the* *company's production capacity was too limited*

concession *noun*
(a) right to use someone else's property for business purposes **Konzession; mining concession** = right to dig a mine on a piece of land **Abbaurecht, Bergbaukonzession**
(b) right to be the only seller of a product in a place **Alleinvertrieb;** *she runs a jewellery concession in a department store*
(c) allowing something to be done, which is not normally done **Zugeständnis; concession close** = offering a concession to a potential buyer in order to close a sale **Abschlußrabatt;** *the trainee salesmen were told to resort to concession closes only when meeting with strong sales resistance; a full morning's bargaining finally ended with a concession close*
◇ **concessionnaire** *noun* person or business that has the right to be the only seller of a product in a particular place **Konzessionär**

condition *noun* term of a contract *or* duties which have to be carried out as part of a contract *or* something which has to be agreed before a contract becomes valid **Bedingung, Kondition, Auflage; conditions of employment** *or* **conditions of service** = terms of a contract of employment **Arbeitsvertragsbedingungen; conditions of sale** = agreed ways in which a sale takes place (such as discounts *or* credit terms) **Verkaufsbedingungen; on condition that** = provided that **unter der Bedingung, daß ...;** *they were granted the lease on condition that they paid the legal costs*
◇ **conditional** *adjective* provided that certain things take place **mit Auflagen, unter Vorbehalt, bedingt; to give a conditional acceptance** = to accept, provided that certain things happen *or* certain terms apply **unter Vorbehalt annehmen; the offer is conditional on the board's acceptance** = provided the board accepts **das Angebot ist abhängig von der Zustimmung des Vorstands; he made a conditional offer** = he offered to buy, provided that certain terms applied **er machte ein bedingtes Angebot**

conference *noun* meeting of people to discuss problems **Konferenz, Besprechung, Tagung; to be in conference** = to be in a meeting **sich in einer Konferenz/Besprechung befinden; conference room** = room where small meetings can take place **Besprechungszimmer; kerbside conference** = discussion of sales techniques between a trainee salesman and the person training him, after making a sales call **Besprechung am Straßenrand; press conference** = meeting where newspaper and TV reporters are invited to hear news of a new product *or* a takeover bid, etc. **Pressekonferenz; sales conference** = meeting of sales managers, representatives, publicity staff, etc. to discuss future sales plans **Konferenz zur Absatzförderung**

confidence *noun* feeling sure *or* being certain **Vertrauen;** *the sales teams do not have much confidence in their manager; the board has total confidence in the managing director;* **confidence level** = measurement, shown as a percentage, of how reliable *or* accurate the results of a survey can be expected to be **Signifikanzniveau (im Vertrauensbereich)**

confirm *verb* to say that something is certain **bestätigen, bekräftigen;** *to confirm a hotel reservation or a ticket or an agreement or a booking;* **to confirm someone in a job** = to say that someone is now permanently in the job **jdn nach einer Probezeit fest anstellen; confirmed credit** = credit that is official and binding **unwiderruflicher Kredit; confirming house** = organization that confirms a buyer's order with a supplier and makes transport arrangements **Auftragsbestätigungsunternehmen, institutioneller Zahlungsgarant;** *a reputable confirming house acted for the buyers of the machinery; we will need a confirming house to arrange for a new supply of office furniture to be delivered to our shop by December*
◇ **confirmation** *noun*
(a) making certain **Bestätigung, Bekräftigung; confirmation of a booking** = checking that a booking is certain **Buchungsbestätigung**
(b) document which confirms something **Bestätigungsschreiben;** *he received confirmation from the bank that the deeds had been deposited*

conflict *noun* **conflict of interest** = situation where a person may profit personally from decisions which he takes in his official capacity **Interessenkonflikt**

conglomerate *noun* group of subsidiary companies under a holding company, each making very different types of products **Mischkonzern**

consign *verb* **to consign goods to someone** = to send goods to someone for him to use or to sell on your behalf **Waren in Kommission geben**
◇ **consignation** *noun* act of consigning **Versand, Versenden**

◇ **consignee** *noun* person who receives goods from someone for his own use or to sell for the sender **Empfänger**

◇ **consignment** *noun*
(a) sending of goods to someone who will sell them for you **Versand, Versenden; consignment note** = note saying that goods have been sent **Versandanzeige, Frachtbrief; goods on consignment** = goods kept for another company to be sold on their behalf for a commission **Konsignationsgüter**
(b) group of goods sent for sale **Warensendung, Lieferung;** *a consignment of goods has arrived; we are expecting a consignment of cars from Japan; the electrical fitting which you ordered are being sent as a separate consignment*

◇ **consignor** *noun* person who consigns goods to someone **Ab-, Versender**

consolidate *verb* to group goods together for shipping **zusammenlegen consolidated shipment** = goods from different suppliers which are grouped together in one shipment **Sammelgut, Sammelladung**

◇ **consolidation** *noun* grouping of goods together for shipping **Zusammenlegung**

◇ **consolidator** *noun* company which groups together various goods from different suppliers to form one large shipment **Sammelgutunternehmen**

consortium *noun* group of companies which work together **Konsortium;** *a consortium of Canadian companies or a Canadian consortium; a consortium of French and British companies is planning to build the new aircraft*

consult *verb* to ask an expert for advice **konsultieren, zu Rate ziehen;** *he consulted his accountant about his tax*

◇ **consultancy** *noun* act of giving specialist advice **Beratung;** *a consultancy firm; he offers a consultancy service*

◇ **consultant** *noun* specialist who gives advice **Berater/-in, Gutachter/-in;** *engineering consultant; management consultant; tax consultant*

◇ **consulting** *adjective* (person) who gives specialist advice **beratend**

consumable *adjective* **consumable goods** = goods which are bought by members of the public and not by companies **Verbrauchs-, Konsumgüter**

◇ **consumables** *plural noun* = CONSUMABLE GOODS

consumer *noun* person *or* company which buys and uses goods and services **Verbraucher/-in, Konsument/-in;** *gas consumers are protesting at the increase in prices; the factory is a heavy consumer of water;* **end consumer** = person who actually uses a product (not necessarily the person who has bought it) **Endverbraucher; consumer cooperative** = retailing business owned by consumers who share in its profits **Konsumgenossenschaft; consumer council** = group representing the interests of consumers **Verbraucherberatung; consumer credit** = credit given by shops, banks and other financial institutions to consumers so that they can buy goods **Kundenkredit; Abzahlungskredit; consumer durables** = relatively expensive items bought by the public, which can be used for several years (such as washing machines *or* refrigerators *or* cookers) **langlebige Gebrauchs-, Konsumgüter; consumer goods** = goods bought by consumers *or* by members of the public **Verbrauchs-, Konsumgüter; consumer magazine** = magazine published for consumers, giving details of product tests, special legal problems regarding services offered, etc.; **consumer market** = customers who buy consumer goods **Konsumenten-, Verbrauchermarkt;** *there is a growing consumer market for construction materials owing to the increased popularity of DIY; both consumer markets and industrial markets have been affected by the recession;* **consumer panel** = group of consumers who report over a period of time on products they have used so that the manufacturers can improve them or use what the panel says about them in advertising **Verbraucherpanel;** *(US)* **consumer price index** = index showing how prices of consumer goods have risen over a period of time, used as a way of measuring inflation and the cost of living **Verbraucherpreisindex; consumer protection** = legislation to protect the rights of consumers against unfair *or* illegal traders **Verbraucherschutz; consumer research** = research into why consumers buy goods and what goods they really want to buy **Konsumforschung; consumer resistance** = lack of interest by consumers in buying a product **Kaufunlust;** *the latest price increases have met with considerable consumer resistance;* **consumer society** = type of society where consumers are encouraged to buy goods **Konsumgesellschaft; consumer sovereignty** = the power of consumers to influence trends in production and marketing **Konsumentensouveranität; consumer spending** = spending by consumers **Ausgaben der Privathaushalte; consumer's surplus** = difference between what a consumer is willing to pay for something and what he or she actually does pay for it **Konsumentenrente;** *when the brand manager realised how big the consumer's surplus was he decided to raise the price of the product ;* **consumer survey** = survey of existing and potential demand for a product **Konsumenten-, Verbraucherbefragung**

◇ **Consumers Association (CA)** an independent organization which protects consumers and represents their interests, and reports on the quality of products and services in its regular magazine **Verbraucherverband**

◇ **consumerism** *noun* activities concerned with protecting the rights and interests of consumers **Konsumerismus, Verbraucherschutzpolitik**

> QUOTE forecasting consumer response is one problem which will never be finally solved
> *Marketing Week*
>
> QUOTE companies selling in the UK market are worried about reduced consumer spending as a consequence of higher interest rates and inflation
> *Business*
>
> QUOTE consumer tastes in the UK are becoming much more varied
> *Marketing*

consumption *noun* buying or using goods or services **Konsum, Verbrauch;** *a car with low petrol consumption; the factory has a heavy consumption of coal;* **conspicuous consumption** = consumption of goods for show *or* to get approval, rather than because they are useful **Prestigekonsum, auffälliger/demonstrativer Konsum;** *conspicuous consumption is responsible for much resentment among poorer sections of society; the recession has led to a fall in conspicuous consumption;* **home consumption** *or* **domestic consumption** = use of something in the home *or* in one's own country **Heimverbrauch; Inlandsverbrauch**

contain *verb* to hold something inside **enthalten;** *each crate contains two computers and their peripherals; a barrel contains 250 litres; we have lost a file containing important documents*

◇ **container** *noun*

(a) box *or* bottle *or* can, etc. which can hold goods **Behälter;** *the gas is shipped in strong metal containers; the container burst during shipping*

(b) very large metal case of a standard size for loading and transporting goods on trucks, trains and ships **Container;** *container ship; container berth; container port; container terminal; to ship goods in containers;* **a container-load of spare parts** = a shipment of spare parts sent in a container **eine Containerladung mit Ersatzteilen**

◇ **containerization** *noun* putting into containers; shipping in containers **Umstellung auf Containertransport**

◇ **containerize** *verb* to put goods into containers; to ship goods in containers **auf Container umstellen**

contest *noun* type of promotion where prizes are given to people who give the right answers to a series of questions **Preisausschreiben; sales contest** = incentive scheme that rewards the salesman who has the best results **Verkaufswettbewerb**

continuity *noun* maintaining a continuous, stable, level of advertising activity **(Werbe)kontinuität;** *continuity must be the watchword of this promotional campaign to keep the product firmly in the minds of the target audience; shall we aim for a sudden short blast of advertising or should continuity be the essence of our strategy?*

◇ **continuous** *adjective* with no end *or* with no breaks **kontinuierlich, stetig, gleichmäßig; continuous process production** = automated production of many identical products **kontinuierlicher Produktionsprozeß, Fließbandherstellung; continuous research** = regular ongoing market research **kontinuierliche/fortlaufende Marktforschung;** *continuous research will tell us if sales are dropping off;* **continuous stationery** = paper made as one long sheet, used in computer printers **Endlospapier**

contra

1 *noun* **contra account** = account which offsets another account **Gegenkonto; Gegenrechnung; contra deal** = deal between two businesses to exchange goods and services; **contra entry** = entry made on the opposite side of an account to make an earlier entry worthless (i.e. a debit against a credit) **Gegenbuchung; per contra** *or* **as per contra** = words showing that a contra entry has been made **als Gegenbuchung**

2 *verb* **to contra an entry** = to enter a similar amount on the opposite side of an account **einen Eintrag zurückbuchen**

contraband *noun* **contraband (goods)** = goods brought into a country illegally, without paying customs duty **Schmuggelware**

contract

1 *noun*

(a) legal agreement between two parties **Vertrag, Vereinbarung;** *to draw up a contract; to draft a contract; to sign a contract;* **the contract is binding on both parties** = both parties signing the contract must do what is agreed **beide Vertragspartner sind an den Vertrag gebunden; to be under contract** = bound by the terms of a contract **unter Vertrag stehen;** *the firm is under contract to deliver the goods by November;* **to void a contract** = to make a contract invalid **einen Vertrag aufheben/für nichtig erklären; exchange of contracts** = point in the sale of a property when the buyer and seller both sign the contract of sale which then becomes binding **Unterzeichnung des Kaufvertrages (bei Grundbesitz)**

(b) contract law *or* **law of contract** = laws relating to agreements **Vertragsrecht; Schuldrecht; by private contract** = by private legal agreement **durch Privatvertrag; contract note** = note showing that shares have been bought or sold but not yet paid for **Ausführungsanzeige**

(c) agreement for supply of a service or goods **Dienstleistungsvertrag; Liefervertrag;** *contract for the supply of spare parts; to enter into a contract to supply spare parts; to sign a contract for £10,000 worth of spare parts;* **to put work out to contract** = to decide that work should be done by another company on a contract, rather than employing members of staff to do it **Auftragsarbeit vergeben; to award a contract to a company** *or* **to place a contract with a company** = to decide that a particular company will get the contract to do work **einen Auftrag an eine Firma vergeben; to tender for a contract** = to put forward an estimate of costs for work under contract **ein Angebot/eine Offerte unterbreiten; breach of contract** = breaking the terms of a contract **Vertragsbruch; the company is in breach of contract** = the company has failed to do what was agreed in the contract **die Firma ist vertragsbrüchig geworden; contract carrier** = carrier *or* transportation company which has special contracts with businesses **Vertragslieferant;** *a contract carrier which ships coffee beans from Brazil to coffee wholesalers in Britain;* **contract manufacturing** = agreement which allows an overseas manufacturer to manufacture or assemble one's products in that country for sale there **Herstellung unter Vertrag;** *under a contract manufacturing agreement a local company is making our cars in France;* **contract work** = work done according to a written agreement **Auftragsarbeit**

2 *verb* to agree to do some work by contract **sich vertraglich verpflichten;** *to contract to supply spare parts or to contract for the supply of spare parts;* **the supply of spare parts was contracted out to Smith Ltd** = Smith Ltd was given the contract for supplying spare parts **der Vertrag für den Ersatzteilevertrieb wurde an Smith Ltd vergeben; to contract out of an agreement** = to withdraw from an agreement with the written permission of the other party **sich von einer vertraglichen Verpflichtung befreien**

◊ **contracting** *adjective* **contracting company** = independent broadcasting company that sells advertising time **Rundfunkwerbungtreibender;** *with two new contracting companies being set up this year, advertisers will have more choice;* **contracting party** = person or company signing a contract **Vertragspartner**

◊ **contractor** *noun* person or company which does work according to a written agreement **Auftragnehmer; Unternehmer; haulage contractor** = company which transports goods by contract **Transport-, Fuhrunternehmer; Spediteur; government contractor** = company which supplies the government with goods by contract **Unternehmen mit Staatsaufträgen**

◊ **contractual** *adjective* **vertraglich, vertragsmäßig; contractual liability** = legal responsibility for something as stated in a contract **Vertragshaftung; to fulfill your contractual obligations** = to do what you have agreed to do in a contract **seine vertraglichen Verpflichtungen erfüllen; he is under no contractual obligation to buy** = he has signed no agreement to buy **er ist vertraglich nicht verpflichtet zu kaufen**

◊ **contractually** *adverb* according to a contract **vertraglich, durch Vertrag;** *the company is contractually bound to pay his expenses*

contribute

contribute *verb* to give money *or* to add to money **beisteuern, einen Beitrag leisten;** *to contribute 10% of the profits; he contributed to the pension fund for 10 years*

◊ **contribution** *noun* something that is contributed **Beitrag; contribution analysis** = analysis of how much each of a company's products contributes to fixed costs, based on its profit margin and sales **Beitragsanalyse;** *contribution analysis helps to streamline production and marketing; thorough contribution analysis led to six products being dropped from the product range;* **contribution of capital** = money paid to a company as additional capital **Investition; contribution pricing** = pricing method based on maximizing the contribution of each product to fixed costs **Deckungsbeitragsrechnung**

◊ **contributor** *noun* **contributor of capital** = person who contributes capital **Investor**

control

1 *noun*

(a) power *or* being able to direct something **Leitung, Kontrolle, Macht, Aufsicht;** *the company is under the control of three* *shareholders; the family lost control of its business;* **to gain control of a business** = to buy more than 50% of the shares so that you can direct the business **die Aktienmehrheit an einem Unternehmen erwerben; to lose control of a business** = to find that you have less than 50% of the shares in a company, and so are not longer able to direct it **die Aktienmehrheit an einem Unternehmen verlieren**

(b) restricting *or* checking something *or* making sure that something is kept in check **Kontrolle, Überwachung; under control** = kept in check **unter Kontrolle;** *expenses are kept under tight control; the company is trying to bring its overheads back under control;* **out of control** = not kept in check **außer Kontrolle;** *costs have got out of control;* **budgetary control** = keeping check on spending **Budgetkontrolle; credit control** = checking that customers pay on time and do not exceed their credit limits **Kreditkontrolle; quality control** = ensuring that the quality of a product is satisfactory **Qualitätskontrolle;** *too many defective watches are getting through to the shops so we will have to tighten up our quality control;* **stock control** = recording movements of stock **Lagersteuerung**

(c) exchange controls = government restrictions on changing the local currency into foreign currency **Devisenkontrollen;** *the government has imposed exchange controls; they say the government is going to lift exchange controls;* **price controls** = legal measures to prevent prices rising too fast **Preiskontrollen; Preisüberwachung; Preisbindung**

(d) control group = group which is identical to another group being used for research purposes and which serves as a comparison **Kontrollgruppe; control question** = question in a questionnaire designed to check that answers are consistent **Kontrollfrage;** *a control question was included to check that respondents were not lying about their age; if control questions show that answers are not honest, the interview is ended ;* **control systems** = systems used to check that a computer system is working correctly **Steuerungssysteme**

2 *verb*

(a) to control a business = to direct a business **die Mehrheit an einem Unternehmen haben;** *the business is controlled by a company based in Luxembourg; the company is controlled by the majority shareholder*

(b) to make sure that something is kept in check *or* is not allowed to develop **kontrollieren, steuern;** *the government is fighting to control inflation or to control the rise in the cost of living*

◇ **controllable** *adjective* which can be controlled **kontrollierbar; controllable variables** = variables *or* factors that can be controlled such as a company's marketing mix **kontrollierbare Variablen;** *because there were so few controllable variables the outcome of the marketing plan was very uncertain; although our advertising expenditure is a controllable variable, our main competitor's is not*

◇ **controlled** *adjective* ruled *or* kept in check **kontrolliert, gesteuert; government-controlled** = ruled by a government **unter staatlicher Aufsicht; controlled circulation** = distribution of a publication to a specialist readership who are members of a particular organization or profession (often a free controlled circulation, where the magazine is distributed free to key executives, and is paid for by the advertisers) **Gratisverteilung, Freiversand, Gratis-, Freivertrieb;** *the professional institute publishes a quarterly magazine with a controlled circulation; the newspaper has a controlled circulation and is suitable for advertisements for highly specialized products;* **controlled economy** = economy where the most business activity is directed by orders from the government **staatlich gelenkte Wirtschaft**

convenience *noun* **at your earliest convenience** = as soon as you find it possible **baldmöglichst; convenience foods** = food which is prepared by the shop before it is sold, so that it only needs to be heated before eating **Fertiggerichte; convenience goods** = ordinary everyday products that people have to buy but which command little or no brand loyalty **Convenience Goods, Verbrauchsgüter des täglichen Bedarfs;** *price competition is very fierce in the convenience goods market ;* **ship sailing under a flag of convenience** = flying the flag of a country which may have no ships of its own but allows ships of other countries to be registered in its ports **ein Schiff, das unter Billigflagge fährt**

◇ **convenient** *adjective* suitable *or* handy **passend; praktisch;** *a bank draft is a convenient way of sending money abroad; is 9.30 a convenient time for the meeting?*

cooling-off period *noun* (i) during an industrial dispute, a period when negotiations have to be carried on and no action can be taken by either side; (ii) period during which a person who has agreed to buy something on hire-purchase is given time to reconsider and possibly change his mind; *(Arbeitskampf)* **Friedenspflicht;** *(vor Vertragsabschluß)* **Überlegungs-, Rücktrittsfrist;** *New York has a* *three day cooling-off period for telephone sales; (US)* **cooling-off laws** = state laws allowing cancellation of an order within a specific period after signing an agreement **Rücktrittsfristgesetze;** *cooling-off laws are making buyers less hesitant about placing large orders*

co-op *noun* = CO-OPERATIVE 2

◊ **co-operate** *verb* to work together **kooperieren, zusammenarbeiten;** *the governments are co-operating in the fight against piracy; the two firms have co-operated on the computer project*

◊ **co-operation** *noun* working together **Kooperation, Zusammenarbeit, Mitarbeit;** *the project was completed ahead of schedule with the co-operation of the workforce*

◊ **co-operative**

1 *adjective* willing to work together **kooperativ;** *the workforce has not been co-operative over the management's productivity plan;* **co-operative advertising** = sharing by two companies (often a producer and a distributor) of advertising costs **gemeinsame/kooperative Werbung;** *a co-operative advertising agreement means that two companies can enjoy quantity discounts offered by the media;* **co-operative marketing** = arrangement whereby various producers co-operate in the marketing of their products or services **kooperatives Marketing;** *co-operative marketing proved an economic method of selling for companies with few financial resources;* **co-operative society** = society where the customers and workers are partners and share the profits **Genossenschaft**

2 *noun* business run by a group of workers who are also the owners and who share the profits **Kooperative;** *they set up a workers' co-operative to take over the factory which was about to be closed down*

copy

1 *noun* **publicity copy** = text of a proposed advertisement before it is printed **Copy, Werbetextentwurf;** *she writes copy for a travel firm;* **disparaging copy** *or* **knocking copy** = advertising material which criticizes competing products **herabsetzende Werbung; copy approach** = COPY PLATFORM; **copy brief** = instructions from an advertiser to a copywriter explaining the objectives of an advertising campaign **Copy-Einweisung;** *the copy brief made it clear that the advertisements were to be aimed at young people; the copy brief gave the copywriter little idea as to what image to create; the advertisers blamed the agency for not paying enough attention to the copy brief;* **copy clearance** = passing of an advertiser's copy as neither misleading nor offensive **Drehbuch-, Manuskriptannahme;** *it is doubtful the advertisement will get copy clearance since it directly disparages the competition; the advertisement has received copy clearance because all its claims can be substantiated; you will not get copy clearance for this ad because the caption is sure to offend a lot of women readers;* **copy date** = date by which an advertisement must be delivered to the media concerned **Anzeigenschluß;** *the creative teams are working flat out because the copy date is only one week away; let's work on the advertisements with the earliest copy dates;* **copy fitting** = arrangement of advertising text so it fits the space allowed for it **Satzumfangsberechnung; copy platform** = main theme of an advertisement's copy **Copy-Plattform, Werbe(grund)konzept;** *there is no point in discussing details until we decide on a copy platform;* **copy testing** = testing the effectiveness of an advertisement's copy **Copytesten;** *copy testing led to the copywriter having to rethink the wording of the message; copy testing will tell us whether or not the advertisements are offensive to the public in general*

2 *verb* to make a second document which is like the first **kopieren; einen Durchschlag/eine Abschrift machen;** *he copied the company report and took it home*

◊ **copier** *or* **copying machine** *noun* machine which makes copies of documents **Kopierer**

copywriter *noun* person who writes copy for advertisements **Werbetexter/-in**

corner *verb* **to corner the market** = to gain control of a market in such a way that one can dictate prices and terms **den Markt beherrschen;** *they succeeded in cornering the market when their main rival was forced to raise its prices*

corporate *adjective* referring to a whole company **Firmen-, Unternehmens-; corporate advertising** = advertising an organization rather than a product **Firmen-, Unternehmenswerbung;** *our corporate advertising is designed to present us as a caring organization; no amount of corporate advertising will ever persuade the consumer that the company stands for quality;* **corporate image** = idea which a company would like the public to have of it **Firmenimage; corporate plan** = plan for the future work of a whole company **langfristiger Unternehmensplan; corporate planning** = planning the future work of a whole company **langfristige Unternehmensplanung; corporate profits** =

profits of a corporation **Unternehmensgewinne**

◇ **corporation** *noun*
(a) large company **Unternehmen; Kapitalgesellschaft; finance corporation** = company which provides money for hire purchase **Finanzierungsgesellschaft; corporation tax** = tax on profits made by companies **Körperschaftssteuer**
(b) *US* company which is incorporated in the United States **Kapital-, Aktiengesellschaft; corporation income tax** = tax on profits made by incorporated companies **Körperschaftssteuer**

> QUOTE the prime rate is the rate at which banks lend to their top corporate borrowers
> *Wall Street Journal*
>
> QUOTE corporate profits for the first quarter showed a 4 per cent drop from last year
> *Financial Times*
>
> QUOTE if corporate forecasts are met, sales will exceed $50 million in 1985
> *Citizen (Ottawa)*

correlation *noun* degree to which there is a relationship between two sets of data **Korrelation;** *is there any correlation between people's incomes and the amount they spend on clothing?; see also* COEFFICIENT, MULTIPLE

cosmetic *adjective* referring to the appearance of people or things **kosmetisch;** *we've made some cosmetic changes to our product line; packaging has both practical as well as cosmetic importance*

cost
1 *noun*
(a) amount of money which has to be paid for something **Kosten; Preis;** *what's the cost of a first class ticket to New York? computer costs are falling each year; we can't afford the cost of two telephones;* **to cover costs** = to produce enough money in sales to pay for the costs of production **die Kosten decken;** *the sales revenue barely covers the costs of advertising or the manufacturing costs;* **to sell at cost** = to sell at a price which is the same as the cost of manufacture or the wholesale cost **zum Selbstkostenpreis verkaufen; fixed costs** = business costs which do not rise with the quantity of the product made **Fixkosten; Gemeinkosten; labour costs** = cost of paying workers employed to make a product **Lohnkosten; manufacturing costs** *or* **production costs** = cost of making a product **Herstellungs-, Produktionskosten; marginal cost** = cost of making a single extra unit above the number already planned **Grenzkosten; operating costs** *or* **running costs** = cost of the day-to-day organization of a company **Betriebskosten; variable costs** = production costs which increase with the quantity of the product made (such as wages, raw materials) **variable Kosten; cost accountant** = accountant who gives managers information about their business costs **Kostenrechner/-in; cost accounting** = specially prepared accounts of manufacturing and sales costs **Kostenrechnung; cost analysis** = calculating in advance what a new product will cost **Kostenanalyse; cost and freight** = estimate of a price, which includes the cost of the goods and the transport charges **Kosten und Fracht;** *the quoted price is $500, cost and freight;* **cost centre** = aspect of a business which can account for part of the costs, such as a machine, worker or department **Kostenstelle; cost, insurance and freight** = estimate of a price, which includes the cost of the goods, the insurance and the transport charges **Kosten, Versicherung und Fracht, cif; cost per inquiry** = the average cost for each inquiry in response to an advertisement **Kosten pro Anfrage; cost per thousand (CPT)** = cost of an advertisement, calculated as the cost for every thousand people reached **Tausenderpreis;** (NOTE: in US English shortened to **CPM)** *this newspaper has the highest cost per thousand but a very high proportion of its readers fall within our target audience;* **cost price** = selling price which is the same as the price which the seller paid for the item (i.e. either the manufacturing cost or the wholesale price) **Selbstkostenpreis; cost of sales** = all the costs of a product sold, including manufacturing costs and the staff costs of the production department **Absatz-, Vertriebskosten**
(b) costs = expenses involved in a court case **Gerichtskosten; to pay costs** = to pay the expenses of a court case **Gerichtskosten tragen;** *the judge awarded costs to the defendant; costs of the case will be borne by the prosecution*
2 *verb*
(a) to have a price **kosten;** *how much does the machine cost? this cloth costs £10 a metre*
(b) to cost a product = to calculate how much money will be needed to make a product, and so work out its selling price **den Preis eines Produktes kalkulieren**

◇ **cost-effective** *adjective* which gives value, especially when compared with something else **kostenwirksam;** *we find advertising in the Sunday newspapers very cost-effective*

◇ **cost-effectiveness** *noun* being cost-effective **Kostenrentabilität;** *can we calculate the cost-effectiveness of air freight against shipping by sea?*

◇ **costing** *noun* calculation of the manufacturing costs, and so the selling price of a product **Kostenberechnung;** *the costings give us a retail price of $2.95; we cannot do the costing until we have details of all the production expenditure*

◇ **costly** *adjective* expensive *or* costing a lot of money **teuer, kostspielig**

◇ **cost of living** *noun* money which has to be paid for food, heating, rent, etc. **Lebenshaltungskosten;** *to allow for the cost of living in the salaries;* **cost-of-living allowance** = addition to normal salary to cover increases in the cost of living **Lebenshaltungskostenzuschuß; cost-of-living bonus** = extra money paid to meet the increase in the cost of living **Teuerungszulage; cost-of-living increase** = increase in salary to allow it to keep up with the increased cost of living **Gehaltszulage zur Anpassung an gestiegene Lebenshaltungskosten; cost-of-living index** = way of measuring the cost of living which is shown as a percentage increase on the figure for the previous year **Lebenshaltungskostenindex**

◇ **cost plus** *noun* system of calculating a price, involving taking the cost of production or of a service and adding a percentage to them to cover overheads and profit margin (also used in charging for advertising by an agency, the actual cost of the ad being increased by an agreed percentage to cover the agency's overheads) **Kosten-Plus-System; cost-plus charging** *or* **charging on a cost-plus basis** = system of charging, where the buyer pays the costs plus a percentage commission to the seller **Kostenberechnung plus prozentualer Aufschlag;** *we are charging for the work on a cost-plus basis;* **cost-plus pricing** = pricing method that involves basing the price on the production costs and adding a certain percentage for margin **Kostenpreiskalkulation plus prozentualer Aufschlag**

cottage industry *noun* industry based in the producer's own home **Heimarbeit;** *cottage industries are disappearing now that mass production has taken over; as the demand for hand-made goods rises, so do the profits of cottage industries*

counter *noun* long flat surface in a shop for displaying and selling goods **Ladentisch, Tresen; over the counter** = legally **legal (verkaufen); goods sold over the counter** = retail sales of goods in shops **im Einzelhandel gegen bar verkaufte Waren;** *some drugs are sold over the counter, but others are only sold on prescription;* **over-the-counter sales** = legal selling of shares which are not listed in the official Stock Exchange list **Verkauf im Freiverkehr; under the counter** = illegally **(illegal) unter dem Ladentisch; under-the-counter sales** = black market sales **ungesetzliche Verkäufe; bargain counter** = counter where things are sold cheaply **Sonderangebotsstand, Sondertisch; ticket counter** = place where tickets are sold **Kartenschalter; trade counter** = shop in a factory *or* warehouse where goods are sold to retailers **Warenausgabe für den Einzelhandel, Großhandelsverkauf; glove counter** = section of a shop where gloves are sold **Handschuhabteilung; counter staff** = sales staff who serve behind counters **Verkaufspersonal hinter dem Ladentisch**

◇ **counter-jumper** *noun (informal)* person who sells goods over the counter **Ladenschwengel;** *he was a counter-jumper for many years before he became a manager; five years as a counter-jumper gave her plenty of experience of customer relations*

◇ **counterpack** *noun* box for the display of goods for sale, placed on the counter or on another flat surface in a shop **Thekenaufstellpackung**

counter- *prefix* against **Gegen-**

◇ **counteradvertising** *noun* advertising aimed as a reply to a competitor's advertisements **Gegenwerbung**

◇ **counterbid** *noun* higher bid in reply to a previous bid **Gegengebot;** *when I bid £20 he put in a counterbid of £25*

◇ **countermand** *verb* to cancel (an order) **(einen Auftrag) stornieren**

◇ **counter-offer** *noun* higher offer made in reply to another offer **Gegengebot;** *Smith Ltd made an offer of £1m for the property, and Blacks replied with a counter-offer of £1.4m*

◇ **countersign** *verb* to sign a document which has already been signed by someone else **gegenzeichnen;** *all cheques have to be countersigned by the finance director; the sales director countersigns all my orders*

coupon *noun*

(a) piece of paper used in place of money **Gutschein; gift coupon** = coupon from a store which is given as a gift and which must be exchanged in that store **Geschenkgutschein**

(b) piece of paper which replaces an order form **Coupon; coupon ad** = advertisement with a form attached, which is to be cut out and returned to the advertiser with one's name and address if one wants further information about the product advertised **Couponanzeige; reply coupon** = form attached to a coupon ad, which must be

filled in and returned to the advertiser **Antwortcoupon**
(c) interest coupon = slip of paper attached to a government bond certificate which can be cashed to provide the annual interest **Zinsschein; cum coupon** = with a coupon attached **cum/mit Kupon; ex coupon** = without the interest coupon **ex/ohne Kupon**
◊ **couponed** *adjective* with a coupon attached **mit Coupon versehen;** *the agency is using couponed direct response advertising*

> QUOTE it employs selective mailings and package inserts such as the couponed offers sent out with credit card statements
> *PR Week*

course *noun* series of lessons **Kurs(us), Lehrgang;** *she's finished her marketing course; the company has paid for him to attend a course for trainee sales managers*

courtesy *noun* supplied free of charge **gratis;** *a courtesy sample is sent with the sales literature;* **courtesy car** = use of a car offered free to a customer **Ersatzfahrzeug, kostenloser Leihwagen, Kundentransportwagen, Serviceauto**

cover *noun*
(a) one of the outside pages of a publication (the four cover pages are: front cover, inside front cover, inside back cover and back cover); *(Buch)* **Einband;** *(Zeitschrift)* **Umschlag; cover page** = the front or back cover of a publication **vorderer/hinterer Einbanddeckel; Umschlagseite eins/vier;** *we could never afford to advertise on the cover of this magazine*
(b) coverage *or* proportion of a target audience reached by advertising **Reichweite; four-plus cover** = situation where the target audience will have seen the advertisement at least four times **mehr als vier Kontakte; net cover** = proportion of a target audience exposed to an advertisement at least once **Nettoreichweite**
◊ **coverage** *noun*
(a) press coverage *or* **media coverage** = reports about something in the newspapers *or* on TV, etc. **Berichterstattung durch die Presse od die Medien;** *the company had good media coverage for the launch of its new model*
(b) proportion of a target market that is reached by an advertisement **Reichweite;** *the advertisement itself was effective but it had very poor coverage; we must consider both the cost of the advertisement and its coverage before committing ourselves any further*
◊ **cover charge** *noun (in a restaurant)* charge for a seat and a table, in addition to the charge for food and drink **Gedeck, Couvert;** *it's not worth having just a cup of coffee since the cover charge is so high; the cover charge ensures that the restaurant makes a profit on every customer*

> QUOTE from a PR point of view it is easier to get press coverage when you are selling an industry and not a brand
> *PR Week*

CPM *(US)* = COST PER THOUSAND

CPT = COST PER THOUSAND

creaming *noun* fixing a high price for a product in order to achieve high short-term profits **Abschöpfungsstrategie, Absahnungspolitik**

create *verb* to make something new **schaffen;** *by acquiring small unprofitable companies he soon created a large manufacturing group; the government scheme aims to create new jobs for young people*
◊ **creative** *adjective* relating to the conceptual or artistic side of advertising **kreativ, schöpferisch, künstlerisch;** *there are three copywriters and four illustrators in the agency's creative department; he has had good experience working on both the creative and the administrative sides of advertising;* **creative shop** = highly specialized business offering creative customer advertising services **künstlerische Werbeagentur;** *a group of copywriters and designers have left the agency to set their own creative shop; the creative shop made short advertising films and designed some press ads for us*

credere *see* DEL CREDERE AGENT

credibility gap *noun* discrepancy between claims for a product made by the manufacturer and acceptance of these claims by the target audience **Glaubwürdigkeitslücke;** *the credibility gap that we face is partly due to our product's bad performance record*

credit
1 *noun*
(a) time given to a customer before he has to pay **Kredit, Darlehen;** *to give someone six months' credit; to sell on good credit terms;* **extended credit** = credit on very long repayment terms **verlängerter/prolongierter Kredit; interest-free credit** = arrangement to borrow money without paying interest on the loan **zinsloses Darlehen; long credit** = terms allowing the borrower a long time to

pay **Kredit mit langer Laufzeit; open credit** = bank credit given to good customers without security **offener (ungedeckter) Kredit, Blankokredit; short credit** = terms allowing the customer only a short time to pay **kurzfristiger Kredit; credit account** = account which a customer has with a shop which allows him or her to buy goods and pay for them later **Kundenkreditkonto;** *to open a credit account;* **credit agency** *or (US)* **credit bureau** = company which reports on the creditworthiness of customers to show whether they should be allowed credit **Kreditauskunftei; credit bank** = bank which lends money **Kreditbank; credit control** = ensuring that customers pay on time and do not owe more than their credit limit **Kreditkontrolle; credit facilities** = arrangement with a bank or supplier to have credit so as to buy goods **Kreditmodalitäten; credit freeze** *or* **credit squeeze** = period when lending by banks is restricted by the government **Einfrieren von Krediten; letter of credit** = letter from a bank, allowing someone credit and promising to repay at a later date **Akkreditiv; irrevocable letter of credit** = letter of credit which cannot be cancelled **unwiderrufliches Akkreditiv; credit limit** = fixed amount which is the most a customer can owe on credit **Kreditlinie, Kreditlimit; he has exceeded his credit limit** = he has borrowed more money than he is allowed **er hat seinen Kredit überzogen; to open a line of credit** *or* **a credit line** = to make credit available to someone **eine Kreditlinie einräumen; credit rating** = amount which a credit agency feels a customer should be allowed to borrow **Bonitätsbeurteilung; on credit** = without paying immediately **auf Kredit;** *to live on credit; we buy everything on sixty days credit; the company exists on credit from its suppliers*

(b) money received by a person *or* company and recorded in the accounts **Haben, Kredit;** *to enter £100 to someone's credit; to pay in £100 to the credit of Mr Smith;* **debit and credit** = money which a company owes and which it receives **Soll und Haben; credit balance** = balance in an account showing that more money has been received than is owed by the company **Kredit-, Aktivsaldo;** *the account has a credit balance of £1,000;* **credit column** = right-hand column in accounts showing money received **Kredit-, Habenspalte; credit entry** = entry on the credit side of an account **Habenbuchung, Gutschrift;** *(US)* **credit memorandum** *or* **credit memo** = note showing that money is owed to a customer **Gutschriftszettel;** *when the buyer paid too much money for the goods he was immediately sent a credit memorandum; I hope we receive a credit memo from the suppliers for the money they owe us;* **credit note** = note showing that money is owed to a customer **Gutschriftsanzeige;** *the company sent the wrong order and so had to issue a credit note;* **credit side** = right-hand side of accounts showing money received **Habenseite; account in credit** = account where the credits are higher than the debits **Konto, das nicht überzogen ist, Konto mit Habensaldo; bank credit** = loans or overdrafts from a bank to a customer **Bankkredit; tax credit** = part of a dividend on which the company has already paid tax, so that the shareholder is not taxed on it **Steuergutschrift**

2 *verb* to put money into someone's account; to note money received in an account **gutschreiben;** *to credit an account with £100 or to credit £100 to an account*

◇ **credit card** *noun* plastic card which allows you to borrow money and to buy goods without paying for them immediately **Kreditkarte**

◇ **creditor** *noun* person who is owed money **Gläubiger; creditors' meeting** = meeting of all persons to whom a bankrupt company owes money, to decide how to obtain the money owed **Gläubigerversammlung**

◇ **credit-worthy** *adjective* able to buy goods on credit **kreditwürdig**

◇ **creditworthiness** *noun* ability of a customer to pay for goods bought on credit **Kreditwürdigkeit, Bonität**

critical path analysis *noun* analysis of a project in terms of the minimum time it will take to complete and calculating which parts can be delayed without holding up the rest of the project **Critical-Path-Analyse/Methode;** *critical path analysis can be used to save time in carrying out a marketing plan*

cross *verb*

(a) to go across **überqueren;** *Concorde only takes three hours to cross the Atlantic; to get to the bank, you turn left and cross the street at the post office*

(b) to cross a cheque = to write two lines across a cheque to show that it has to be paid into a bank **einen Scheck zur Verrechnung ausstellen; crossed cheque** = cheque which has to be paid into a bank **Verrechnungsscheck**

◇ **cross elasticity of demand** *noun* changes in demand for an item depending on the selling price of a competing product **Kreuzpreiselastizität der Nachfrage**

◇ **cross tracks** *noun* poster site next to a railway track **Plakatposition gegenüber den Bahngleisen**

cumulative *adjective* added to regularly over a period of time **kumulativ, anhäufend; cumulative audience** *or* **cumulative reach** = number of people reached by an advertisement at least once over a period of time **kumuliertes Publikum; cumulative interest** = interest which is added to the capital each year **Zins und Zinseszins; cumulative quantity discount** = discount based on quantity bought *or* value of purchases over a period of time **kumulativer Mengenrabatt;** *we have purchased only from these suppliers over the last few months in order to enjoy a cumulative quantity discount*

currency *noun* money in coins and notes which is used in a particular country **Währung; convertible currency** = currency which can easily be exchanged for another **frei konvertierbare Währung; foreign currency** = currency of another country **Devisen, Fremdwährung; foreign currency account** = bank account in the currency of another country (e.g. a dollar account) **Devisen-, Fremdwährungskonto; foreign currency reserves** = a country's reserves in currencies of other countries **Devisenreserven; hard currency** = currency of a country which has a strong economy and which can easily be changed into other currencies **harte Währung;** *to pay for imports in hard currency; to sell raw materials to earn hard currency;* **legal currency** = money which is legally used in a country **gesetzliches Zahlungsmittel; soft currency** = currency of a country with a weak economy, which is cheap to buy and difficult to exchange for other currencies **weiche Währung; currency backing** = gold *or* securities which maintain the international strength of a currency **Währungsgarantie; currency note** = bank note **Banknote, Schein**

> QUOTE the strong dollar's inflationary impact on European economies, as national governments struggle to support their sinking currencies and push up interest rates
>
> *Duns Business Month*
>
> QUOTE today's wide daily variations in exchange rates show the instability of a system based on a single currency, namely the dollar
>
> *Economist*
>
> QUOTE the level of currency in circulation increased to N4.9 billion in the month of August
>
> *Business Times (Lagos)*

current *adjective* referring to the present time **derzeitig, gegenwärtig; current account** = bank account from which the customer can withdraw money at any time **laufendes Konto, Girokonto; current assets** = assets used by a company in its ordinary work (such as materials, finished products, cash) **Umlaufvermögen; current cost accounting** = method of accounting which values assets at what it would cost to replace them at current prices rather than at what they originally cost **Rechnungslegung zum Wiederbeschaffungswert; current liabilities** = debts which a company has to pay within the next accounting period **kurzfristige Verbindlichkeiten; current price** = today's price **Tagespreis; current rate of exchange** = today's rate of exchange **Tageskurs; current yield** = dividend calculated as a percentage of the price paid per share **laufende Ertrag**

> QUOTE crude oil output plunged during the past month and is likely to remain at its current level for the near future
>
> *Wall Street Journal*
>
> QUOTE customers' current deposit and current accounts also rose to $655.31 million at the end of December
>
> *Hongkong Standard*

curve *noun* line which is not straight (such as a line on a graph) **Kurve; experience curve** = graph showing the relationship between the cumulative amount of products produced and the production cost per unit **Erfahrungskurve; learning curve** = line on a graph which shows the relationship between experience in doing something and competence at carrying it out **Lernkurve**

custom *noun*

(a) use of a shop by regular shoppers **Kundschaft, Klientel; to lose someone's custom** = to do something which makes a regular customer go to another shop **jdn als Kunden verlieren; custom-built** *or* **custom-made** = made specially for one customer **spezialangefertigt;** *he drives a custom-built Rolls Royce*

(b) the customs of the trade = general way of working in a trade **Handelsbrauch, Usance**

◇ **customer** *noun* person *or* company which buys goods (note that the customer may not be the consumer or end user of the product) **Kunde/Kundin;** *the shop was full of customers; can you serve this customer first please? he's a regular customer of ours;* **customer appeal** = what attracts customers to a product **Kundenattraktivität; customer loyalty** = inclination of a customer to keep shopping at the same shop **Kundentreue; customer profile** = description of an average customer for a product or service **Kundenprofil; customer service** = service given to a customer once he has made his decision to buy (including delivery, after-sales service, installation, training, etc.) **Kundendienst; customer service department** = department which deals with customers and their complaints and orders **Kundendienst(abteilung)**

◇ **customize** *verb* to change something to fit the special needs of a customer **individuell anpassen, auf Bestellung anfertigen;** *we used customized computer terminals*

> QUOTE a difficult market to get into, China nevertheless offers a high degree of customer loyalty once successfully entered
> ***Economist***
>
> QUOTE the only leverage the manufacturer can now apply to the retailer is his relationship with the consumer - his customer
> ***Precision Marketing***
>
> QUOTE unless advertising and promotion is done in the context of an overall customer orientation, it cannot seriously be thought of as marketing
> ***Quarterly Review of Marketing***

◇ **customs** *plural noun* the government department which organizes the collection of taxes on imports; office of this department at a port *or* airport **Behörde für Zölle und Verbrauchssteuern; Zoll(behörden); to go through customs** = to pass through the area of a port or airport where customs officials examine goods **den Zoll passieren; to take something through customs** = to carry something illegal through the customs area without declaring it **etwas durch den Zoll schmuggeln;** *he was stopped by customs officials; her car was searched by customs;* **customs barrier** = customs duty intended to prevent imports **Zollschranke; customs broker** = person *or* company which takes goods through customs for a shipping company **Zollagent; customs clearance** = document given by customs to a shipper to show that customs duty has been paid and the goods can be shipped **Zollabfertigung;** *to wait for customs clearance;* **customs declaration** = statement showing goods being imported on which duty will have to be paid **Zollerklärung;** *to fill in a customs (declaration) form;* **customs duty** = tax paid on goods brought into or taken out of a country **Zoll(abgabe); the crates had to go through a customs examination** = the crates had to be examined by customs officials **die Kisten wurden vom Zoll untersucht; customs formalities** = declaration of goods by the shipper and examination of them by customs **Zollformalitäten; customs invoice** = customs form containing a list of goods with their values in both the exporter's and importer's countries **Zollfaktura; customs officers** *or* **customs officials** = people working for customs **Zollbeamten; customs tariff** = list of duties to be paid on imported goods **Zollgebühren; customs union** = agreement between several countries that goods can travel between them, without paying duty, while goods from other countries have to pay special duties **Zollunion customs warehouse** = government-run warehouse where goods are stored until duty is paid **Zollniederlage;** *the goods will remain in the customs warehouse until the buyer claims them*

cut-price *adjective* sold at a cheaper price than usual **zu herabgesetzten Preisen;** *cut-price goods; cut-price petrol;* **cut-price store** = store selling cut-price goods **Niedrigpreisgeschäft, Billigladen**

◇ **cut-throat competition** *noun* intense competition between rival companies where prices are considerably reduced and only the most efficient organizations can remain profitable and survive **mörderischer Wettbewerb** *cut-throat competition has forced several companies out of the market*

◇ **cutting** *noun*
(a) cost cutting = reducing costs **Kostensenkung;** *we have made three secretaries redundant as part of our cost-cutting programme;* **price cutting** = sudden lowering of prices **Preissenkung; price-cutting war** = competition between companies to get a larger market share by cutting prices **Preiskrieg**
(b) piece cut out of a publication which refers to an item of particular interest **Ausschnitt; press cutting agency** = company which cuts out references to a client from newspapers and magazines and sends them on to him **(Presse)ausschnittdienst; press cuttings** = references to a client *or* person *or* product cut out of newspapers or magazines **Zeitungs-, Zeitschriftenausschnitte;** *we have a file of press cuttings on our rivals' products*

> QUOTE state-owned banks cut their prime rates a percentage point to 11%
> ***Wall Street Journal***
>
> QUOTE the US bank announced a cut in its prime from 10.5 per cent to 10 per cent
> ***Financial Times***
>
> QUOTE Opec has on average cut production by one third since 1979
> ***Economist***

cycle *noun* events which happen in a regularly repeated sequence **Zyklus, Kreislauf; call cycle** = the time between a salesman's visits to the same customer **Besuchszyklus; economic cycle** *or* **trade cycle** *or* **business cycle** = period during which trade expands, then slows down and then expands again **Konjunkturzyklus; cycle models** = models which are used to explain cyclical change **zyklische Modelle;** *cycle models were used in the case study to show recent developments in retailing*

◇ **cyclical** *adjective* which happens in cycles **zyklisch; cyclical factors** = way in which a trade cycle affects businesses **zyklische Faktoren**

Dd

DAGMAR = DEFINING ADVERTISING GOALS FOR MEASURING ADVERTISING RESPONSE model showing stages in effect of advertising on a consumer, e.g. awareness, comprehension, conviction and action **DAGMAR(-Modell)**

data *noun* information (letters or figures) available on computer **Daten; primary data** = data from research carried out with the aim of providing specific information about a certain market segment **Primärdaten; secondary data** = data from research which has collected general information with no specific market in mind **Sekundärdaten; data acquisition** = getting information **Datenerfassung; data bank** *or* **bank of data** = store of information in a computer **Datenbank; data processing** = selecting and examining data in a computer to produce special information **Datenverarbeitung; data sheet** = leaflet with data *or* information about a product **Datenblatt**

NOTE: **data** is usually singular: **the data is easily available**

◇ **database** *noun* store of information in a large computer **Datenbank;** *we can extract the lists of potential customers from our database*

date *noun* number of day, month and year **Datum;** *I have received your letter of yesterday's date;* **closing date** = last date (for receipt of tenders, etc.) **Ausschreibungsschluß; launching date** = date when the sales of a new product officially begin **Einführungstermin; sell-by date** = date on a food packet which is the last date when the food is still guaranteed to be good **Mindesthaltbarkeitsdatum; date code** = showing the date by which a product should be consumed **Haltbarkeitskodierung; date stamp** = rubber stamp for marking the date on letters received **Datumsstempel; date of receipt** = date when something is received **Eingangs-, Empfangsdatum; date-in-charge** = date from which a poster site is charged **Anschlagbeginn;** *we will have three weeks of exposure from the date-in-charge*

day *noun* period of 24 hours **Tag;** *there are thirty days in June; the first day of the month is a public holiday;* **day after recall test** = advertising research test to see how much someone can remember of an advertisement, the day after it appeared or was broadcast **Werbeerinnerungstest einen Tag nach dem Werbemittelkontakt; days of grace** = days allowed for payment after it becomes due **Sichttage, Zahlungsfrist;** *let's send the cheque at once since we have only five days of grace left; because the shopowner has so little cash available, we will have to allow him additional days of grace;* **three clear days** = three whole working days **drei (volle) Werk-/Arbeitstage;** *to give ten clear days' notice; allow four clear days for the cheque to be paid into the bank*

◇ **daypart** *noun* section of a day, used for measuring audience ratings on TV **Tageszeitsegment**

dead *adjective* not working **unproduktiv, ertraglos; dead account** = account which is no longer used **umsatzloses Konto; the line went dead** = the telephone line suddenly stopped working **die Verbindung wurde unterbrochen; dead freight** = payment by a charterer for unfilled space in a ship *or* plane **Faut-, Fehlfracht;** *too much dead freight is making it impossible for the company to continue to charter ships;* **dead loss** = total loss **Totalverlust;** *the car was written off as a dead loss;* **dead season** = time of year when there is a slump in the tourist industry **Nebensaison;** *what do all the hotel staff do in the dead season? the waiters do odd jobs to get through the dead season*

◇ **deadline** *noun* date by which something has to be done **(letzter) Termin, Stichtag; to meet a deadline** = to finish something in time **eine Frist einhalten;** *we've missed our October 1st deadline*

◇ **deadweight** *noun* heavy goods like coal, iron or sand **schwere Güter; deadweight cargo** = heavy cargo which is charged by weight, not by volume **Schwergut; deadweight capacity** *or* **deadweight tonnage** = largest amount of cargo which a ship can carry safely **Gesamtzuladung, Tragfähigkeit**

deal

1 *noun* business agreement *or* affair *or* contract **Abkommen, Abschluß, Geschäft, Handel;** *to arrange a deal or to set up a deal or to do a deal; to sign a deal; the sales director set up a deal with a Russian bank; the deal* *will be signed tomorrow; they did a deal with an American airline;* **to call off a deal** = to stop an agreement **ein Abkommen rückgängig machen;** *when the chairman heard about the deal he called it off;* **cash deal** = sale done for cash **Barverkauf; package deal** = agreement where several different items are agreed at the same time **Pauschalarrangement, Verhandlungspaket;** *they agreed a package deal, which involves the construction of the factory, training of staff and purchase of the product;* **deal in** = sales promotion to the trade **Händlerabsatzförderung; deal out** = sales promotion to consumers **Verbraucherabsatzförderung**

2 *verb*

(a) to deal with = to organize **sich befassen mit;** *leave it to the filing clerk - he'll deal with it;* **to deal with an order** = to supply an order **eine Bestellung ausführen**

(b) to trade *or* to buy and sell **handeln, Handel treiben; to deal with someone** = to do business with someone **mit jdm Geschäfte machen, mit jdm in Geschäftsverbindung stehen; to deal in leather** *or* **to deal in options** = to buy and sell leather *or* options **in der Lederbranche tätig sein; Optionsgeschäfte machen; he deals on the Stock Exchange** = his work involves buying and selling shares for clients on the Stock Exchange **er ist als Börsenhändler tätig**

◇ **dealer** *noun* person who buys and sells **Händler/-in, Kaufmann/Kauffrau;** *dealer in tobacco or tobacco dealer;* **dealer aids** = types of advertising material used by shops to stimulate sales **Händlerhilfen; dealer's brand** = brand owned by a distributor rather than by a producer **Handelsmarke, Hausmarke;** *I bought the dealer's brand of soap since the store is well known for its high quality goods;* **dealer tie-in** = advertising which includes the names of local dealers that stock the product being advertised **Bezugsquellen-, Einzelhändlernachweis (in einer Anzeige); retail dealer** = person who sells to the general public **Einzelhändler; wholesale dealer** = person who sells in bulk to retailers **Großhändler**

◇ **dealership** *noun* the authority to sell certain products or services; business run by an authorized dealer

debit

1 *noun* money which a company owes **Schuldposten, Soll, Debet; debits and credits** = money which a company owes and money it receives **Soll und Haben; debit balance** = balance in an account, showing that the company owes more money than it has received **Sollsaldo; debit card** = plastic card used to transfer money directly from a customer's account to a retailer's account, without the use of cheques **Scheckkarte; debit column** = left-hand column in accounts showing the money paid or owed to others **Debetspalte; debit entry** = entry on the debit side of an account **Sollbuchung, Lastschrift; debit side** = left-hand side of an account showing the money paid or owed to others **Debetseite; debit note** = note showing that a customer owes money **Lastschriftanzeige;** *we undercharged Mr Smith and had to send him a debit note for the extra amount;* **direct debit** = system where a customer allows a company to charge costs to his bank account automatically and where the amount charged can be increased or decreased with the agreement of the customer **Direktabbuchung;** *I pay my electricity bill by direct debit*

2 *verb* **to debit an account** = to charge an account with a cost **ein Konto belasten;** *his account was debited with the sum of £25*

◇ **debitable** *adjective* which can be debited **belastbar**

debt *noun*

(a) money owed for goods or services **Schulden;** *the company stopped trading with debts of over £1 million;* **to be in debt** = to owe money **Schulden haben; he is in debt to the tune of £250** = he owes £250 **er hat Schulden in Höhe von £250; to get into debt** = to start to borrow more money than one can pay back **sich verschulden, Schulden machen; the company is out of debt** = the company does not owe money any more **das Unternehmen ist aus den Schulden heraus; to pay back a debt** = to pay all the money owed **Schulden zurückzahlen; to pay off a debt** = to finish paying money owed **Schulden begleichen/tilgen; to service a debt** = to pay interest on a debt **für Schulden Zinsen bezahlen;** *the company is having problems in servicing its debts;* **bad debt** = money owed which will never be paid back **uneinbringliche Forderung, nicht einziehbare Außenstände;** *the company has written off £30,000 in bad debts;* **secured debts** *or* **unsecured debts** = debts which are guaranteed or not guaranteed by assets **gesicherte Verbindlichkeiten; ungesicherte Verbindlichkeiten; debt collection** = collecting money which is owed **Forderungseinziehung, Schuldeneintreibung; debt collection agency** = company which collects debts for a commission **Inkassofirma; debt collector** = person who collects debts **Inkassobeauftragter;** *(umg)* **Schuldeneintreiber; debts due** = money owed which is due for repayment **fällige Schulden**

(b) funded debt = part of the British National Debt which pays interest, but where there is no date for repayment of the principal **fundierte Schuld; the National Debt** = money borrowed by a government **Staatsverschuldung**

◇ **debtor** *noun* person who owes money **Schuldner/-in; Kreditnehmer; debtor side** = debit side of an account **Soll-, Debetspalte; debtor nation** = country whose foreign debts are larger than money owed to it by other countries **Schuldnerland**

> QUOTE the United States is now a debtor nation for the first time since 1914, owing more to foreigners than it is owed itself
> *Economist*

decide *verb* to make up one's mind to do something **entscheiden, beschließen, sich entschließen;** *to decide on a course of action; to decide to appoint a new managing director*

◇ **deciding** *adjective* **deciding factor** = most important factor which influences a decision **entscheidender Faktor** *a deciding factor in marketing our range of sports goods in the country was the rising standard of living there*

decision *noun* the process of making up one's mind to do something **Entscheidung, Beschluß, Entschluß;** *to come to a decision or to reach a decision;* **decision-making** = act of coming to a decision **Entscheidungsfindung, Beschlußfassung; the decision-making process** = way in which decisions are reached **Entscheidungsprozeß; decision-making unit (DMU)** = group of people who decide on the purchase of a product (such as for the purchase of a new piece of equipment, the manager, the financial controller and the operator who will use the equipment) **Entscheidungseinheit; decision-maker** = person who has to decide **Entscheidungsträger; decision theory** = mathematical methods for weighing the various factors in making decisions **Entscheidungstheorie;** *in practice it is difficult to apply decision theory to our planning; students study decision theory to help them suggest strategies in case-studies;* **decision tree** = model for decision-making, showing the possible outcomes of different decisions **Entscheidungsbaum;** *this computer programme incorporates a decision tree*

deck *noun* flat floor in a ship **Deck; deck cargo** = cargo carried on the open top deck of a ship, rather than in the hold below **Deckladung;** *fragile goods should not be carried as deck cargo;* **deck hand** = ordinary sailor on a cargo ship **gemeiner Matrose**

decline

1 *noun* gradual fall; final stage in the life cycle of a product when the sales and profitability are falling off and the product is no longer worth investing in **Rückgang, Abnahme, Sinken; Degeneration(sphase)**
2 *verb* to fall slowly *or* to decrease **zurückgehen, abnehmen, sinken, geringer/weniger werden;** *shares declined in a weak market; imports have declined over the last year; the economy declined during the last government*

> QUOTE in 1984 the profits again declined to L185bn from the 1983 figure of L229.7bn
> *Financial Times*
>
> QUOTE Saudi oil production has declined by three quarters to around 2.5m barrels a day
> *Economist*
>
> QUOTE this gives an average monthly decline of 2.15 per cent during the period
> *Business Times (Lagos)*

deep-rooted demand *noun* brand loyalty which survives even if the product no longer offers value for money **tief verwurzelte Markentreue/Nachfrage;** *there is deep-rooted demand for this product which is a household name*

defer *verb* to put back to a later date *or* to postpone **ver-, aufschieben, zurückstellen, vertagen;** *to defer payment; the decision has been deferred until the next meeting*

◇ **deferment** *noun* postponement *or* putting back to a later date **Aufschub, Zurückstellung, Vertagung;** *deferment of payment; deferment of a decision*

◇ **deferred** *adjective* put back to a later date **aufgeschoben, vertagt; deferred creditor** = person who is owed money by a bankrupt but who is paid only after all the other creditors **nachrangiger (Konkurs)gläubiger; deferred payment** = payment for goods by instalments over a long period **Ratenzahlung; deferred rebate** = discount given to a customer who buys up to a specified quantity over a specified period **Abzahlungsrabatt; deferred stock** = shares which receive a dividend after all other dividends have been paid **Nachzugsaktien**

deficit *noun* amount by which spending is higher than income **Defizit, Minusbetrag, Verlust; the accounts show a deficit** = the accounts show a loss **die Bilanz weist einen Verlust auf; to make good a deficit** = to put money into an account to balance it **ein Defizit ausgleichen; balance of payments deficit** *or* **trade deficit** = situation when a country imports more than it exports **Zahlungsbilanzdefizit; deficit financing** = planning by a government to borrow money to cover the shortfall between tax income and expenditure **Defizitwirtschaft**

deflate *verb* **to deflate the economy** = to reduce activity in the economy by cutting the supply of money **eine restriktive Wirtschaftspolitik betreiben**

◇ **deflation** *noun* reduction in economic activity **Deflation**

◇ **deflationary** *adjective* which can cause deflation **deflationär;** *the government has introduced some deflationary measures in the budget*

> QUOTE the strong dollar's deflationary impact on European economies as national governments push up interest rates
> *Duns Business Month*

delay

1 *noun* time when someone *or* something is later than planned **Verspätung, Verzögerung, Verzug;** *there was a delay of thirty minutes before the AGM started or the AGM started after a thirty-minute delay; we are sorry for the delay in supplying your order or in replying to your letter*

2 *verb* to be late; to make someone late **sich verspäten/verzögern; aufhalten;** *he was delayed because his taxi had an accident; the company has delayed payment of all invoices;* **delayed response** = slower than expected response by consumers to a company's promotion **verzögerte Reaktion;** *if there is a delayed response we will only reap the benefits next year; a delayed response is hardly common in such a new product*

del credere agent *noun* agent who receives a high commission because he guarantees payment by customers **Delkredereagent**

delete *verb* to remove a product from a company's product range **eliminieren, streichen;** *we have decided to delete three old products as the new ones are coming on stream*

◇ **deletion** *noun* removing an old product from the market **Elimination, Streichung;** *the product has lost market share and is a candidate for deletion*

deliver *verb* to transport goods to a customer **liefern, zustellen; goods delivered free** *or* **free delivered goods** = goods transported to the customer's address at a price which includes transport costs **frei Haus gelieferte Waren; goods delivered on board** = goods transported free to the ship *or* plane but not to the customer's warehouse **frei Bord; delivered price** = price which includes packing and transport **Lieferpreis**

◇ **delivery** *noun*

(a) delivery of goods = transport of goods to a customer's address **Warenlieferung, Warenzustellung;** *parcels awaiting delivery; free delivery or delivery free; delivery date; delivery within 28 days; allow 28 days for delivery; delivery is not allowed for or is not included;* **delivery note** = list of goods being delivered, given to the customer with the goods **Lieferschein; delivery order** = instructions given by the customer to the person holding his goods, to tell him to deliver them **Lieferauftrag; delivery receipt** = delivery note when it has been signed by the person receiving the goods **Empfangsschein; the store has a delivery service to all parts of the town** = the store will deliver goods to all parts of the town **das Geschäft liefert in alle Stadtteile; delivery time** = number of days before something will be delivered **Lieferzeit; delivery van** = goods van for delivering goods to retail customers **Lieferwagen; express delivery** = very fast delivery **Eilzustellung;** *(US)* **general delivery** = post office service which receives parcels and letters for people and holds them until they are claimed **Ausgabe postlagernder Sendungen; recorded delivery** = mail service where the letters are signed for by the person receiving them **Einschreiben;** *we sent the documents (by) recorded delivery;* **cash on delivery** *or (US)* collect on delivery = payment in cash when the goods are delivered **gegen Nachnahme; to take delivery of goods** = to accept goods when they are delivered **eine Lieferung abnehmen/übernehmen;** *we took delivery of the stock into our warehouse on the 25th*

(b) goods being delivered **Lieferung;** *we take in three deliveries a day; there were four items missing in the last delivery*

(c) transfer of a bill of exchange **Übertragung**

delphi method *noun* method of forming strategies by soliciting individual estimates on the time-scale of projected developments and then inviting further estimates on the basis of all those already made until a consensus is reached **Delphi-Methode**

demand

1 *noun*

(a) asking for payment **Forderung, Aufforderung; payable on demand** = which must be paid when payment is asked for **zahlbar bei Sicht/auf Verlangen; demand bill** = bill of exchange which must be paid when payment is asked for **Sichtwechsel;** *(US)* **demand deposit** = money in a bank account which can be taken out when you want it by

writing a cheque **Kontokorrentkonto, laufendes Konto, Sichteinlage; final demand** = last reminder from a supplier, after which he will sue for payment **letzte Mahnung**
(b) need for goods at a certain price **Nachfrage, Bedarf;** *there was an active demand for oil shares on the stock market;* **to meet a demand** *or* **to fill a demand** = to supply what is needed **den Bedarf decken;** *the factory had to increase production to meet the extra demand; the factory had to cut production when demand slackened; the office cleaning company cannot keep up with the demand for its services;* **there is not much demand for this item** = not many people want to buy it **dieser Artikel ist nicht sehr gefragt; this book is in great demand** *or* **there is a great demand for this book** = many people want to buy it **dieses Buch ist sehr gefragt; effective demand** = actual demand for a product backed up by the ability to pay for it **effektive Nachfrage; elastic demand** = demand which experiences a comparatively large percentage change in response to a percentage change in price **elastische Nachfrage; demand forecasting** = estimating what demand would exist at various prices, used as a method of calculating prices **Nachfrageprognose; demand price** = price at which a certain quantity of goods will be bought **Nachfragepreis; demand schedule** = table showing demand for a product *or* service at different prices **Nachfragetabelle; demand theory** = branch of economics concerned with consumer buying habits and factors which determine demand **Nachfrageanalyse; supply and demand** = amount of a product which is available and the amount which is wanted by customers **Angebot und Nachfrage; law of supply and demand** = general rule that the amount of a product which is available is related to the needs of potential customers **Gesetz von Angebot und Nachfrage**
2 *verb* to ask for something and expect to get it **fordern, verlangen;** *she demanded a refund; the suppliers are demanding immediate payment of their outstanding invoices*

◇ **demand-led inflation** *noun* inflation caused by rising demand which cannot be met **Nachfrageinflation**

> QUOTE spot prices are now relatively stable in the run-up to the winter's peak demand
> *Economist*
>
> QUOTE the demand for the company's products remained strong throughout the first six months of the year with production and sales showing significant increases
> *Business Times (Lagos)*
>
> QUOTE growth in demand is still coming from the private rather than the public sector
> *Lloyd's List*

demarketing *noun* attempting to reduce the demand for a product **Demarketing, Reduktionsmarketing;** *demarketing was the keynote in the industry when rationing was introduced*

demography *noun* study of populations and relevant statistics (such as age, sex, income, education, etc.) **Demographie**

◇ **demographic** *adjective* referring to demography **demographisch;** *a full demographic study of the country must be done before we decide how to export there;* **demographic segmentation** = dividing a market up into segments according to the age, sex, income levels, etc., of the potential customers **demographische Marktsegmentierung**

demonstrate *verb* to show how something works **vorführen;** *he was demonstrating a new tractor when he was killed; the managers saw the new stock control system being demonstrated*

◇ **demonstration** *noun* showing how something works; explanation of how something works **Vorführung;** *we went to a demonstration of new telex equipment;* **demonstration effect** = theory stating that people buy products to impress or keep up with their neighbours **Mitläufereffekt;** *the promotion of luxury goods is intended to exploit the demonstration effect;* **demonstration model** = piece of equipment used in demonstrations and later sold off cheaply **Vorführmodell**

◇ **demonstrator** *noun* person who demonstrates pieces of equipment **Vorführer/-in**

demurrage *noun* money paid to a customer when a shipment is delayed at a port *or* by the customs **Liegegeld**

department *noun*
(a) specialized section of a large company **Abteilung;** *complaints department; design department; dispatch department; export department; legal department;* **accounts department** = section which deals with money paid or received **Buchhaltung; new issues department** = section of a bank which deals with issues of new shares **Emissionsabteilung; marketing department** = section of a company dealing with marketing and sales **Marketingabteilung; head of department** *or* **department head** *or* **department manager** = person in charge of a department **Abteilungsleiter**
(b) section of a large store selling one type of product **Abteilung;** *you will find beds in the furniture department;* **budget**

department = department in a large store which sells cheaper goods **Sonderangebotsabteilung**
(c) section of the British government containing several ministries **Ministerium;** *the Department of Trade and Industry; the Department of Education and Science*

◊ **department store** *noun* large store with sections for different types of goods **Kaufhaus**

depend *verb*
(a) to depend on = to need someone *or* something to exist **angewiesen sein auf;** *the company depends on efficient service from its suppliers; we depend on government grants to pay the salary bill*
(b) to happen because of something **abhängig sein von;** *the success of the launch will depend on the publicity;* **depending on** = which varies according to something **abhängig von, je nach;** *depending on the advertising budget, the new product will either be launched on radio or on TV*

◊ **dependent** *adjective* which depends on someone *or* something **abhängig, angewiesen; dependent variable** = variable or factor which changes as a result of a change in another **abhängige Variable;** *we are trying to understand the effects of several independent variables on one dependent variable, in this case, sales*

deposit *noun* money given in advance so that the thing which one wants to buy will not be sold to someone else **Anzahlung;** *to pay a deposit on a watch; to leave £10 as a deposit*

depot *noun* central warehouse for goods; centre for transport **Depot, Lagerhaus; Depot;** *bus depot; freight depot; goods depot; oil storage depot*

depress *verb* to reduce **herabsetzen, drücken, senken, vermindern, verringern;** *reducing the money supply has the effect of depressing demand for consumer goods*

◊ **depressed** *adjective* **depressed area** = part of a country suffering from depression **von einer Wirtschaftskrise betroffenes Gebiet; depressed market** = market where there are more goods than customers **flauer Markt**

◊ **depression** *noun* period of economic crisis with high unemployment and loss of trade **Depression, Flaute, Tiefstand;** *an economic depression;* **the Great Depression** = the world economic crisis of 1929-1933 **die Weltwirtschaftskrise (von 1929)**

dept = DEPARTMENT

depth *noun* variety in a product line **Umfang, Auswahl; depth interview** = interview with no preset questions and following no fixed pattern, but which can last a long time and allows the respondent time to express personal views and tastes **Intensiv-, Tiefeninterview;** *depth interviews elicited some very original points of view*

deregulation *noun* reducing government control over an industry **Deregulation, Abbau einschränkender Bestimmungen;** *the deregulation of the airlines*

derived demand *noun* demand for a product because it is needed to produce another product which is in demand **abgeleitete Nachfrage**

describe *verb* to say what someone *or* something is like **beschreiben, ausführen, schildern;** *the leaflet describes the services the company can offer; the managing director described the difficulties the company was having with cash-flow*

◊ **description** *noun* words which show what something is like **Beschreibung, Schilderung; false description of contents** = false statement about the contents of a packet to trick customers into buying it **unkorrekte Inhaltsbeschreibung; job description** = official document from the management which says what a particular job involves **Tätigkeitsbeschreibung; trade description** = description of a product used in advertising or promotional material **Warenkennzeichnung**

design
1 *noun* (i) planning *or* drawing of a product before it is built or manufactured; (ii) the planning of the visual aspect of an advertisement **(i) Design, Entwurf; (ii) künstlerische Gestaltung; industrial design** = design of products made by machines (such as cars and refrigerators) **Industriedesign; product design** = design of consumer products **Produktgestaltung; design department** = department in a large company which designs the company's products or its advertising **Design-Abteilung; Werbeabteilung; design factor** = ratio of sampling error of a complex sample *or* sample design to that of a completely random sample **Design-Faktor; design studio** = independent firm which specializes in creating designs **Design-Studio**
2 *verb* to plan *or* to draw something before it is built or manufactured **entwerfen;** *he designed a new car factory; she designs garden furniture*

◇ **designer** *noun* person who designs **Designer/-in;** *she is the designer of the new computer;* **designer products** = elegant products created by a well-known designer **Designerprodukte;** *recent wealth in the cities has increased the demand for designer products; designer jeans and sportswear are only some of our designer products*

desire *noun* wish to do something **Wunsch; desire to purchase** = feeling of a customer that he needs to purchase a product **Kaufwunsch;** *see also* AIDA

desk *noun* writing table in an office, usually with drawers for stationery **Schreibtisch;** *desk diary; desk drawer; desk light;* **desk pad** = pad of paper kept on a desk for writing notes **Schreibblock desk research** = looking for information that has already been compiled and published (as in directories) **Sekundärforschung;** *most of our desk research is done in libraries; will desk research be enough, or do we have to commission a survey?;* **desk researcher** = person who carries out desk research **Sekundärforscher, Desk Researcher; external desk research** = research based on material outside the company's own records, such as in libraries, government departments, etc. **außerbetriebliche Sekundärforschung; internal desk research** = research based on information in a company's own records, such as customer accounts, salesmen's reports, etc. **innerbetriebliche Sekundärforschung**

despatch *see* DISPATCH

devalue *verb* to reduce the value of a currency against other currencies **abwerten;** *the pound has been devalued by 7%; the government devalued the dollar by 7%*

◇ **devaluation** *noun* reduction in value of a currency against other currencies **Abwertung;**

develop *verb*

(a) to plan and produce **entwickeln;** *to develop a new product*

(b) to plan and build an area **erschließen;** *to develop an industrial estate*

◇ **developer** *noun* **a property developer** = person who plans and builds a group of new houses *or* new factories **Bauunternehmer**

◇ **developing country** *or* **developing nation** *noun* country which is not fully industrialized **Entwicklungsland**

◇ **development** *noun*

(a) planning the production of a new product and constructing the first prototypes **Entwicklung;** *research and development*

(b) industrial development = planning and building of new industries in special areas **industrielle Erschließung; development area** *or* **development zone** = area which has been given special help from a government to encourage the setting up of businesses and factories there **Förderungsgebiet**

deviation *noun* change of route *or* strategy **Abweichung;** *advertising in the tabloids will mean a deviation from our normal marketing strategy*

diadic test *noun* product test in which respondents compare two products **Paarvergleich**

diagram *noun* drawing which shows something as a plan or a map **Diagramm, graphische Darstellung, Schaubild;** *diagram showing sales locations; he drew a diagram to show how the decision-making processes work; there is a diagram on page 36 of the company's organizational structure;* **flow diagram** = diagram showing the arrangement of work processes in a series **Arbeitsablauf-, Flußdiagramm**

◇ **diagrammatic** *adjective* **in diagrammatic form** = in the form of a diagram **graphisch dargestellt, in einem Diagramm dargestellt;** *the chart showed the sales pattern in diagrammatic form*

◇ **diagrammatically** *adverb* using a diagram **in einem Diagramm/Schaubild;** *the chart shows the sales pattern diagrammatically*

diary *noun* book in which one can write notes or appointments for each day of the week **Terminkalender, Tagebuch;** *desk diary;* **diary method** = market research method whereby respondents keep a regular written account of advertising noticed *or* purchases made *or* products used **Tagebuchmethode**

dichotomous question *noun* question in a questionnaire that can only be answered by "yes" or "no" **Ja-Nein-Frage**

differential

1 *adjective* which shows a difference **unterschiedlich, verschieden; differential advantage** = advantage that one product has over rival products in the market **Unterscheidungsvorteil;** *we are confident that our toothpaste has a differential advantage;* **differential tariffs** = different tariffs for different classes of goods **Differential-, Staffeltarife**

2 *noun* **price differential** = difference in price between products in a range **Preisunterschied, Preisgefälle; semantic differential** = scaling technique which gives a range of possible answers between two opposite descriptive words **semantisches Differential; wage differentials** = differences in pay for workers doing different jobs in the same industry or profession **Lohngefälle; to erode wage differentials** = to reduce differences in pay gradually **Lohngefälle abbauen**

◇ **differentiation** *noun* ensuring that a product has some unique features that distinguish it from competing products **Differenzierung;** *we are adding some extra features to our watches in the interest of product differentiation; the aim of differentiation should be to catch the customer's eye*

diffusion *noun* process by which a product is adopted by consumers **Diffusion; diffusion curve** = geographical representation of how many consumers adopt a product at different times **Diffusionskurve;** *see also* EXPONENTIAL

diminishing returns *noun* **law of diminishing returns** = the general rule that beyond a certain point, an increase in one factor of production (land, capital or labour) while the other factors remain constant, will not produce an equal increase in output or profit **Gesetzmäßigkeit vom abnehmenden Ertragszuwachs**

Dinkies *noun* couple who are both wage-earners and have no children **kinderlose Doppelverdiener, DINKs;** (Short for **Double Income No Kids)**

direct
1 *verb* to manage *or* to organize **leiten, führen;** *he directs our South-East Asian operations; she was directing the development unit until last year*
2 *adjective* straight *or* with no interference **direkt, unmittelbar; direct action** = strike *or* go-slow, etc. **Arbeitskampfmaßnahmen; direct-action advertising** = advertising which aims to get a quick response **auf direkte (Kauf)reaktionen zielende Werbung, Aktions-, Kaufwerbung;** *we'll need some direct-action advertising if we're not to fall behind our competitors this spring; direct-action advertising will only help us in the short term;* **direct cost** = production cost of a product **Selbstkosten; direct debit** = system where a customer allows a company to charge costs to his bank account automatically and where the amount charged can be increased or decreased with the agreement of the customer **Direktabbuchung;** *I pay my electricity bill by direct debit;* **direct demand** = demand for a product *or* service for its own sake, and not for what can be derived from it **direkte Nachfrage; direct export** = selling a product direct to the overseas customer without going through a middleman **Direktexport;** *direct export is the only way to keep down the retail price; our overseas marketing consists mainly of direct export to German department stores;* **direct labour** = labour *or* workers employed to do a specific job for an organization and to do it under the direct control of that organization **direkte Arbeitskräfte; direct mail** = selling a product by sending publicity material to possible buyers through the post **Direktversand; Direktwerbung;** *these calculators are only sold by direct mail; the company runs a successful direct-mail operation;* **direct-mail advertising** = advertising by sending leaflets to people through the post **Briefwerbung; direct marketing (DM)** *or* **direct selling** = selling a product direct to the customer without going through a shop **Direktmarketing; Direktabsatz, Direktverkauf; direct response advertising** = advertising in such a way as to get customers to send in inquiries or orders directly by mail **Direct-Response-Werbung; direct services** = personal services to the public, such as catering or dentistry, hairdressers etc. **Dienstleistungen;** *there is little manufacturing industry in the area, and direct services account for most of the wealth*
3 *adverb* straight *or* with no third party involved **direkt, unmittelbar;** *we pay income tax direct to the government;* **to dial direct** = to contact a phone number yourself without asking the operator to do it for you **durchwählen;** *you can dial New York direct from London*

◇ **directly** *adverb* straight *or* with no third party involved **sofort, gleich;** *we deal directly with the manufacturer, without using a wholesaler*

> QUOTE after five years of explosive growth, fuelled by the boom in financial services, the direct marketing world is becoming a lot more competitive
>
> *Marketing Workshop*
>
> QUOTE all of those who had used direct marketing techniques had used direct mail, 79% had used some kind of telephone technique and 63% had tried off-the-page selling
>
> *Precision marketing*
>
> QUOTE direct marketing is all about targeting the audience, individualising the message and getting a response
>
> *PR Week*

direction *noun*
(a) organizing *or* managing **Leitung, Führung;** *he took over the direction of a multinational group*
(b) directions for use = instructions showing how to use something **Gebrauchsanweisung**

◇ **directive interview** *noun* interview using pre-set questions and following a fixed pattern **direktive Befragung**

◇ **director** *noun*
(a) person appointed by the shareholders to help run a company **Direktor/-in, Aufsichtsratsmitglied; managing director** = director who is in charge of the whole company **Generaldirektor, geschäftsführender Direktor, Geschäftsführer; chairman and managing director** = managing director who is also chairman of the board of directors **Vorsitzender und Geschäftsführer; board of directors** = all the directors of a company **Board of Directors;** *(entspricht)* **(Firmen)vorstand; Aufsichtsrat (nach britischem Recht); directors' report** = annual report from the board of directors to the shareholders **Jahresbericht; associate director** = director who attends board meetings but has not been elected by the shareholders; *(entspricht)* **außerordentliches Verwaltungsratsmitglied; executive director** = director who actually works full-time in the company **geschäftsführender Direktor; non-executive director** = director who attends board meetings only to give advice; *(entspricht)* **Aufsichtsratsmitglied; outside director** = director who is not employed by the company **unternehmensfremder Direktor; marketing director** = director who is responsible for an organization's marketing activities **Marketingdirektor; sales director** = director who is responsible for an organization's sales **Verkaufsdirektor**
(b) person who is in charge of a project, an official institute, etc. **Leiter/-in, Direktor/-in;** *the director of the government research institute; she was appointed director of the organization*

◇ **directorate** *noun* group of directors **Direktion, Direktorium, Geschäftsleitung; Aufsichtsrat**

◇ **directorship** *noun* post of director **Direktorenstelle;** *he was offered a directorship with Smith Ltd*

◇ **directory** *noun* reference book containing information on companies and their products **Adreßbuch; Telefonbuch;** *we use directories a lot in our desk research;* **classified directory** = book which lists businesses grouped under various headings **Branchenverzeichnis;**

> QUOTE what benefits does the executive derive from his directorship? In the first place compensation has increased sharply in recent years
> *Duns Business Month*

dirty *adjective* not clean **schmutzig; dirty bill of lading** = bill of lading stating that the goods did not arrive on board in good condition **unreines Konnossement**

discount
1 *noun*
(a) percentage by which the seller reduces the full price for the buyer **Rabatt, Preisnachlaß;** *to give a discount on bulk purchases;* **to sell goods at a discount** *or* **at a discount price** = to sell goods below the normal price **Waren mit Rabatt verkaufen; basic discount** = normal discount without extra percentages **Normal-, Grundrabatt;** *we give 25% as a basic discount, but can add 5% for cash payment;* **cash discount** = discount obtained by paying for goods in cash **Barzahlungsrabatt; quantity discount** = discount given to people who buy large quantities **Mengenrabatt; 10% discount for quantity purchases** = you pay 10% less if you buy a large quantity **10% Mengenrabatt; 10% discount for cash** *or* **10% cash discount** = you pay 10% less if you pay in cash **10% Skonto bei Barzahlung; trade discount** = discount given to a customer in the same trade **Händler-, Wiederverkäuferrabatt**
(b) discount house = (i) financial company which specializes in discounting bills; (ii) shop which specializes in selling cheap goods bought at a high discount **(i) Diskontbank; (ii) Diskonter, Diskonthaus, Diskontladen; discount rate** = percentage taken when a bank buys bills **Diskontsatz; discount store** = shop which specializes in cheap goods bought at a high discount **Diskontladen, Billigladen; table of discounts** *or* **discount table** = table showing discounts for various prices and quantities **Diskonttabelle;** *the price list was accompanied by a discount table; according to the table of discounts, there was no discount for purchases involving less than 100 items of each product*
2 *verb* to reduce prices (in order to increase sales) **Rabatt gewähren; to discount bills of exchange** = to buy bills of exchange for less than the value written on them in order to cash them later **Wechsel diskontieren; shares are discounting a rise in the dollar** = shares have risen in advance of a rise in the dollar price **die Aktien nehmen eine Aufwertung des Dollar vorweg; discounted cash flow** = calculating the forecast return on capital investment in current terms, with reductions for current interest rates **diskontierter Cashflow; discounted value** =

difference between the face value of a share and its lower market price **Diskontwert**

◇ **discountable** *adjective* which can be discounted **diskontfähig;** *these bills are not discountable*

◇ **discounter** *noun* (i) company which discounts bills; (ii) company which sells goods at a discount **(i) Diskonthaus; (ii) Diskontladen, Diskonter**

discretion *noun* being able to decide correctly what should be done **Ermessen, Entscheidungsfreiheit; I leave it to your discretion** = I leave it for you to decide what to do **ich stelle es in Ihr Ermessen, ich lasse Ihnen freie Hand; at the discretion of someone** = according to someone's decision **nach jds Ermessen;** *membership is at the discretion of the committee*

◇ **discretionary** *adjective* which can be done if someone wants **beliebig; the minister's discretionary powers** = powers which the minister could use if he or she wished **die Ermessensbefugnis des Ministers; discretionary income** = income left after fixed payments have been made and whose spending is therefore subject to advertising influence **verfügbares Einkommen;** *discretionary incomes generally increase in the recession*

discrimination *noun* treating people in different ways because of class, religion, race, language, colour or sex **Diskriminierung; sexual discrimination** *or* **sex discrimination** *or* **discrimination on grounds of sex** = treating men and women in different ways **Diskriminierung aufgrund des Geschlechts; discrimination test** = product test designed to show how one product differs from another **Unterscheidungstest;** *the discrimination test showed our product to be superior to that of our closest competitor*

diseconomies of scale *noun* situation where there are no longer economies of scale and increased production leads to a higher production cost per unit *or* average production cost **Größennachteile; Kostenprogression**

disequilibrium *noun* imbalance in the economy when supply does not equal demand **Gleichgewichtsmangel**

dishoarding *noun* putting goods back onto the market when they have been hoarded or stored for some time **Vermarktung des Lagerbestandes**

dishonour *verb* **to dishonour a bill** = not to pay a bill **einen Wechsel nicht bezahlen; dishonoured cheque** = cheque which the bank will not pay because there is not enough money in the account to pay it **nichteingelöster Scheck**

disintegration *noun* decision to stop producing certain goods or supplies and to buy them instead **Produktionseinstellung zugunsten Fremdbezugs;** *disintegration has meant we now have to buy all of our raw materials; part of the company's disintegration policy involved selling off the factories*

disparage *verb* to criticize **herabsetzen; disparaging copy** = advertising copy which is critical of another company's products **herabsetzende Werbung;** *their disparaging copy has given them a bad name in the industry*

dispatch
1 *noun*
(a) sending of goods to a customer **Versand;** *the strike held up dispatch for several weeks;* **dispatch department** = department which deals with the packing and sending of goods to customers **Versandabteilung; dispatch note** = note saying that goods have been sent **Versandschein; dispatch rider** = motorcyclist who delivers messages or parcels in a town **Motorrad-Bote**
(b) goods which have been sent **Sendung;** *the weekly dispatch went off yesterday*
2 *verb* to send goods to customers **(ver)senden, schicken**

◇ **dispatcher** *noun* person who sends goods to customers **Expedient; Absender**

dispenser *noun* machine which automatically provides something (an object *or* a drink *or* some food), often when money is put in **Automat;** *automatic dispenser; towel dispenser;* **cash dispenser** = machine which gives out money when a special card is inserted and instructions given **Geldautomat**

dispersion *noun* attempts by a middleman *or* distributor to distribute a product to a market **Streuung, Dispersion**

display
1 *noun* showing of goods for sale **Auslage;** *the shop has several car models on display; an attractive display of kitchen equipment;* **display advertisement** = advertisement in a publication which is set apart from other advertisements by having its own typeface, border, illustration, etc. **Großanzeige;** *the*

display advertisement for the perfume took up a quarter of the page; **display cabinet** *or* **display case** = piece of furniture with a glass top or glass doors for showing goods for sale **Vitrine, Schaukasten; display material** = posters, photographs, etc. to be used to attract attention to goods which are for sale **Dekorationsmaterial; display outer** = container for protecting goods in transit which can also be used as an attractive display container for the goods in a shop **Auslage-, Ausstellungskarton; display pack** *or* **display box** = special box for showing goods for sale **Schaupackung, Präsentationspackung;** *the watches are prepacked in plastic display boxes;* **display stand** *or* **display unit** = special stand for showing goods for sale **Auslagenstand, Vollsichtregal; visual display unit** *or* **visual display terminal** = screen attached to a computer which shows the information stored in the computer **Monitor, Bildschirm**
2 *verb* to show **ausstellen, zeigen;** *the company was displaying three new car models at the show*

dispose *verb* **to dispose of** = to get rid of *or* to sell cheaply **veräußern, losschlagen;** *(umg)* **verramschen;** *to dispose of excess stock; to dispose of one's business*

◇ **disposable** *adjective*
(a) which can be used and then thrown away **Wegwerf-, Einweg-;** *disposable cups*
(b) disposable personal income = income left after tax and national insurance have been deducted **(frei) verfügbares Einkommen nach Steuerabzug**

◇ **disposal** *noun* sale **Verkauf, Veräußerung, Absatz;** *disposal of securities or of property;* **lease** *or* **business for disposal** = lease *or* business for sale **langfristiger Pachtvertrag od Unternehmen zu verkaufen**

dissonance *noun* **cognitive dissonance** = conflict experienced by a person who cannot resolve apparently contradictory information, as when making buying decisions or evaluating purchases which have been made **kognitive Dissonanz; dissonance reduction** = reducing worries experienced by the purchaser after a product has been purchased, by increasing his awareness of the positive features of the product and reducing his fears about its negative features **Dissonanzreduktion**

distance freight *noun* freight charge based on the distance over which the goods are transported **Fernlast**

distinctive competence *noun* advantage that one company *or* producer has over competitors in the market **Unterscheidungskompetenz;** *our distinctive competence is a highly professional sales force; the company could not survive with high costs and no distinctive competence*

distress merchandise *noun (US)* goods sold cheaply to pay a company's debts **im Notverkauf abgesetzte Waren; distress sale** = sale of goods cheaply to pay off debts **Notverkauf; distress selling** = selling goods cheaply in order to pay off debts **Notverkauf;** *difficult circumstances forced the producers to resort to distress selling*

distribute *verb*
(a) to share out dividends **ausschütten;** *profits were distributed among the shareholders*
(b) to send out goods from a manufacturer's warehouse to retail shops **vertreiben;** *Smith Ltd distributes for several smaller companies*

◇ **distribution** *noun*
(a) act of sending goods from the manufacturer to the wholesaler and then to retailers **Vertrieb;** *distribution costs; distribution manager;* **channels of distribution** *or* **distribution channels** = means by which goods pass from the manufacturer to the consumer, via the wholesaler and retailer **Absatzkanäle, Vertriebswege; distribution census** = official statistics regarding the number of distributors and their businesses **Vertriebszählung;** *using the distribution census, we drew up a list of wholesalers who were worth approaching;* **distribution network** = series of points *or* small warehouses from which goods are sent all over a country **Verteiler-, Vertriebsnetz; intensive distribution** = the use by a producer of as wide a range of distributors as possible to sell his products **Intensivvertrieb**
(b) distribution slip = paper attached to a document *or* a magazine showing all the people in an office who should read it **Verteilerzettel**

◇ **distributive** *adjective* referring to distribution **Verteilungs-; distributive trades** = all businesses involved in the distribution of goods **Verteilerorganisationen**

◇ **distributor** *noun* company which sells goods for another company which makes them **Verteiler, Wiederverkäufer, Händler; sole distributor** = retailer who is the only one in an area allowed by the manufacturer to sell a certain product **Alleinvertrieb; network of distributors** = series of distributors spread all over a country **Verteilernetz; distributor's brand** = goods specially packed for a store with the store's name printed on them **Handelsmarke, Hausmarke;** *I bought the distributor's brand of soap because it was the cheapest*

◇ **distributorship** *noun* position of being a distributor for a company **Vertrieb**

> QUOTE there is evidence that distribution channels are supply driven
> *Quarterly Review of Marketing*
>
> QUOTE British distribution companies are poised to capture a major share of the European market
> *Management News*

divergent marketing *noun* separate marketing treatment for each of a company's products **getrenntes Marketing;** *divergent marketing is giving way to a more co-ordinated and integrated marketing effort*

diversification *noun* adding another quite different type of business to a firm's existing trade **Diversifikation; product diversification** *or* **diversification into new products** = adding new types of products to the range already made **Erweiterung des Produktangebots, Sortimentserweiterung; lateral diversification** = diversifying into quite a different type of business **seitliche Diversifikation**

◇ **diversify** *verb*
(a) to add new types of business to existing ones **diversifizieren, erweitern;** *to diversify into new products*
(b) to invest in different types of shares or savings so as to spread the risk of loss **verteilt/gestreut anlegen**

divestment *noun* the dropping or sale of a whole product line, to allow the company to concentrate on other products **Streichung**

division *noun*
(a) main section of a large company **Abteilung;** *marketing division; production division; retail division; the paints division of ICI; the hotel division of THF; he is in charge of one of the major divisions of the company*
(b) company which is part of a large group **Unternehmensbereich;** *Smith's is now a division of the Brown group of companies*

◇ **divisional** *adjective* referring to a division **Abteilungs-;** *a divisional director; the divisional headquarters*

DIY = DO-IT-YOURSELF

DM = DIRECT MARKETING

DMU = DECISION-MAKING UNIT

document *noun* paper, especially an official paper, with written information on it **Dokument, Urkunde, Akte; document of title** = document allowing the holder to handle certain goods as if he or she owns them **urkundlicher Rechtstitel; documents against acceptance** = arrangement whereby a buyer receives documents for the goods on his or her acceptance of a bill of exchange **Dokumente gegen Akzept; documents against cash** *or* **documents against presentation** = arrangement whereby a buyer receives documents for the goods on payment of a bill of exchange **Dokumente gegen Bezahlung** *or* **Wechsel**

◇ **documentary**
1 *adjective* in the form of documents **dokumentarisch, urkundlich;** *documentary evidence; documentary proof*
2 *noun* film concerning actual facts or real events **Dokumentarfilm**

◇ **documentation** *noun* all documents referring to something **Dokumentation;** *please send me the complete documentation concerning the sale*

dog *noun* product that has a low market share and a low growth rate, and so is likely to be dropped from the company's product line **Armer Hund**

do-it-yourself (DIY) *adjective* done by an ordinary person, not by a skilled worker **Do-it-yourself; do-it-yourself conveyancing** = the drawing up of a legal conveyance by the person selling a property, without the help of a lawyer **Übertragungsurkunde ohne notarielle Hilfe; do-it-yourself magazine** = magazine with articles on work which the average person can do to repair or improve his house **Do-it-yourself Magazin, Heimwerkermagazin; do-it-yourself store** = large store specializing in selling materials for the repair and improvement of houses **Heimwerkerladen, D-I-Y-Geschäft**

dollar *noun*
(a) money used in the USA and other countries **Dollar;** *the US dollar rose 2%; fifty Canadian dollars; it costs six Australian dollars;* **five dollar bill** = banknote for five dollars **Fünfdollarschein**
(b) the currency used in the USA **(US) Dollar; dollar area** = area of the world where the dollar is the main trading currency **Dollarzone; dollar balances** = a country's trade balances expressed in US dollars **Handelsbilanz in Dollar; dollar crisis** = fall in the exchange rate for the US dollar **Dollarkrise; dollar gap** *or* **dollar shortage** = situation where the supply of dollars is not enough to satisfy the demand for them

from overseas buyers **Dollarlücke; dollar stocks** = shares in US companies **US Aktien**
NOTE: usually written $ before a figure: **$250.** The currencies used in different countries can be shown by the initial letter of the country: **C$** (Canadian dollar) **A$** (Australian dollar), etc.

domestic *adjective*
(a) referring to the home market *or* the market of the country where the business is situated **Innen-, Binnen-, einheimisch, im Inland;** *domestic sales; domestic turnover;* **domestic consumption** = consumption on the home market **Inlandsverbrauch;** *domestic consumption of oil has fallen sharply;* **domestic market** = market in the country where a company is based **Binnen-, Inlandsmarkt;** *they produce goods for the domestic market;* **domestic production** = production of goods for domestic consumption **Inlandsproduktion**
(b) for use in the home **Haushalts-;** *glue which is intended for both domestic and industrial use;* **domestic appliances** = electrical machines (such as washing machines) which are used in the home **Haushaltsgeräte**

door *noun* **the store opened its doors on June 1st** = the store started in business on June 1st **das Geschäft öffnete am 1. Juni (erstmals) seine Türen; door drop** = delivering promotional literature by hand to each house in an area **Wurfsendung**
◇ **door-to-door** *adjective* going from one house to the next **(von) Haus zu Haus; door-to-door canvassing** = going from one house to the next, asking the occupiers to buy something or to vote for someone **Direkt-, Haustürverkauf; door-to-door salesman** = man who calls on people in their homes **Hausierer; Vertreter; door-to-door selling** = selling things from house to house **Haustürverkauf; Hausiergewerbe; door-to-door service** = transportation service that takes goods directly to the buyer's address **Hauslieferung**

dormant *adjective* no longer active *or* no longer operating **ruhend, still, untätig; dormant accounts** = past customers who are no longer buying **stille Kunden;** *let's re-establish contact with some of our dormant accounts; all the old reports on dormant accounts have been filed away*

> QUOTE the agency has been responsible for the dormant account since its last campaign was run three years ago
> *Marketing Week*

double
1 *adjective*
(a) twice as large *or* two times the size **doppelt;** *their turnover is double ours;* **to be on double time** = to earn twice the usual wages, for working on Sundays or other holidays **das Doppelte verdienen; double column** = two columns spanned by an advertisement **Doppelspalte; double crown** = basic poster size, 30 inches deep by 20 inches wide **Doppelkrone, Double Crown; double-decker** = two advertising panels, one on top of the other **Doppeldeckerplakat; double page spread** = two facing pages in a magazine *or* newspaper, used by an advertiser **doppelseitige Anzeige**
(b) in double figures = with two figures *or* 10 to 99 **zweistellig;** *inflation is in double figures; we've had double-figure inflation for some years*
2 *verb* to become twice as big; to make something twice as big **verdoppeln;** *we have doubled our profits this year or our profits have doubled this year; the company's borrowings have doubled*

◇ **double-pricing** *noun* showing two prices on a product, to make buyers think there has been a price reduction **(irreführende) Doppelpreisauszeichnung**

down
1 *adverb & preposition* in a lower position *or* to a lower position **unten, herunter, hinunter, niedrig, gefallen;** *the inflation rate is gradually coming down; shares are slightly down on the day; the price of petrol has gone down;* **to pay money down** = to make a deposit **Geld anzahlen;** *he paid £50 down and the rest in monthly instalments*
2 *verb* **to down tools** = to stop working **die Arbeit niederlegen**

◇ **down-market** *adverb & adjective* cheaper *or* appealing to a less wealthy section of the population **Billig-, Massen-; billig;** *the company has adopted a down-market image;* **the company has decided to go down-market** = the company has decided to make products which appeal to a wider section of the public **die Firma hat beschlossen, sich dem Massenmarkt zuzuwenden**

◇ **downside** *noun* **downside factor** = possibility of making a loss (in an investment) **Verlustfaktor; the sales force have been asked to give downside forecasts** = they have been asked for pessimistic forecasts **das Verkaufspersonal wurde aufgefordert, in der Prognose eine Abwärtsbewegung aufzuzeigen**

◇ **downturn** *noun* movement towards lower prices *or* sales *or* profits **Rückgang, Abflauen, Flaute;** *a downturn in the market price; the last quarter saw a downturn in the economy*

draft *noun* order for money to be paid by a bank **Bankwechsel; Banktratte;** *banker's draft;* **to make a draft on a bank** = to ask a bank to pay money for you **einen Wechsel auf eine Bank ziehen; sight draft** = bill of exchange which is payable when it is presented **Sichtwechsel, Sichttratte**

draw *verb*
(a) to take money away **abheben;** *to draw money out of an account;* **to draw a salary** = to have a salary paid by the company **ein Gehalt beziehen;** *the chairman does not draw a salary*
(b) to write a cheque **ausstellen;** *he paid the invoice with a cheque drawn on an Egyptian bank*

◇ **drawback** *noun*
(a) thing which is not convenient *or* which is likely to cause problems **Nachteil;** *one of the main drawbacks of the scheme is that it will take six years to complete*
(b) rebate on customs duty for imported goods when these are then used in producing exports **Zollrückvergütung, Rückzoll;** *the producer managed to get a drawback on rubber he had imported from Malaysia when making tyres for export to France and Italy*

◇ **drawee** *noun* person or bank asked to make a payment by a drawer **Bezogener, Trassat**

◇ **drawer** *noun* person who writes a cheque *or* a bill asking a drawee to pay money to a payee **Aussteller, Trassant; the bank returned the cheque to drawer** = the bank would not pay the cheque because the person who wrote it did not have enough money in the account to pay it **die Bank schickte den Scheck an den Aussteller zurück**

◇ **drawing account** *noun*
(a) current account *or* account from which the customer may take money when he or she wants **Kontokorrentkonto, laufendes Konto, Girokonto**
(b) advance payment to a salesman on commission in view of his or her expected future earnings **Kommissions-, Provisionsvorschuß;** *a drawing account made it possible for the new salesmen to get through the two months of training with no proper income*

drip *noun* placing of advertisements for a product at fairly long intervals, making a long-drawn-out advertising campaign **Tröpfelkampagne**

drive *noun* energy *or* energetic way of working **Elan, Schwung; economy drive** = vigorous effort to save money or materials **Sparkampagne; sales drive** = vigorous effort to increase sales **Verkaufskampagne; he has a lot of drive** = he is very energetic in business **er hat viel Elan**

drop
1 *noun*
(a) fall **Rückgang, Sturz;** *drop in sales; sales show a drop of 10%; a drop in prices*
(b) door drop = delivering promotional literature by hand to all the houses in an area **Wurfsendung**
(c) drop shipment = delivery of a large order from the manufacturer direct to a customer's shop or warehouse without going through an agent or wholesaler **Direktlieferung**
2 *verb*
(a) to fall **zurückgehen, stürzen, fallen;** *sales have dropped by 10% or have dropped 10%; the pound dropped three points against the dollar*
(b) not to keep in a product range **einstellen;** *we have dropped these items from the catalogue because they've been losing sales steadily for some time*

◇ **drop ship** *verb* to deliver a large order direct to a customer **direkt an den Kunden liefern**

QUOTE while unemployment dropped by 1.6 per cent in the rural areas, it rose by 1.9 per cent in urban areas during the period under review
Business Times (Lagos)

QUOTE corporate profits for the first quarter showed a 4 per cent drop from last year's final three months
Financial Times

QUOTE since last summer American interest rates have dropped by between three and four percentage points
Sunday Times

dud *adjective & noun (informal)* false *or* not good (coin or banknote) **gefälscht; Blüte;** *the £50 note was a dud;* **dud cheque** = cheque which the bank refuses to pay because the person writing it does not have enough money in his account to pay it **ungedeckter Scheck**

due *adjective*
(a) owed **fällig;** *sum due from a debtor; bond due for repayment;* **to fall due** *or* **to become due** = to be ready for payment **fällig sein/werden; bill due on May 1st** = bill which has to be paid on May 1st **eine am 1. Mai fällige Rechnung; balance due to us** = amount owed to us which should be paid **fälliger Rechnungsbetrag**
(b) expected to arrive **erwartet (werden); the plane is due to arrive at 10.30** *or* **is due at 10.30** = the plane is expected to arrive at 10.30 **das Flugzeug soll um 10.30 Uhr ankommen**

(c) in due form = written in the correct legal form **vorschriftsmäßig, rechtsgültig;** *receipt in due form; contract drawn up in due form;* **after due consideration** = after thinking seriously (about the problem) **nach reiflicher Überlegung**
(d) caused by **aufgrund, wegen;** *supplies have been delayed due to a strike at the manufacturers; the company pays the wages of staff who are absent due to illness*

◇ **dues** *plural noun*
(a) dock dues *or* **port dues** *or* **harbour dues** = payment which a ship makes to the harbour authorities for the right to use the harbour **Hafengebühren**
(b) orders taken but not supplied until new stock arrives **Vorbestellungen**

dummy *noun*
(a) imitation product to test the reaction of potential customers to its design **Aufmachungsmuster, Dummy;** *(von Buch)* **Blindband; dummy pack** = empty pack for display **Attrappe, Schau-, Leerpackung;**
(b) rough layout of an advertisement or publicity leaflet **Entwurf**
(c) person *or* company whose name is used in a sales transaction in order to hide the name of the actual principals **Scheinkommittent; Scheinfirma**

dump
verb **to dump goods on a market** = to get rid of large quantities of excess goods cheaply in an overseas market **Waren billig auf einen ausländischen Markt bringen/werfen; dump display** = goods on special display in a container for self-selection in a shop **Sonderwarenauslage;** *we will use dump displays with price reductions clearly marked; there are several dump displays near the counters in the supermarket*

◇ **dump bin** *noun* display container like a large box which is filled with goods for sale **Auslagekasten, Ausstellungsbehälter, Wühlkorb**

◇ **dumping** *noun* act of getting rid of excess goods cheaply in an overseas market **Dumping, Schleuderausfuhr;** *the government has passed anti-dumping legislation; dumping of goods on the European market;* **panic dumping of sterling** = rush to sell sterling at any price because of possible devaluation **Panik-Dumping von Sterling**

> QUOTE a serious threat lies in the 400,000 tonnes of subsidized beef in EEC cold stores. If dumped, this meat will have disastrous effects in Pacific Basin markets
> *Australian Financial Review*

duopoly
noun existence of only two producers *or* suppliers in a market **Dyopol;** *the duopoly meant that the two businesses collaborated to keep prices at very high levels; when they took over their only competitor in the market, the duopoly became a monopoly; compare* MONOPOLY

durable
1 *adjective* **durable goods** = goods which will be used for a long time (such as washing machines or refrigerators) **langlebige Güter; durable effects** = effects which will be felt for a long time **Dauereffekte;** *the strike will have durable effects on the economy*
2 *noun* **consumer durables** = goods bought by the public which will be used for a long time (such as washing machines or refrigerators) **langlebige Gebrauchsgüter**

dustbin check
noun consumer audit for which a panel of householders keep the empty containers of products bought so that these can be regularly checked for product type, size, and brand **Mülleimerkontrolle**

Dutch
adjective **Dutch auction** = auction where the auctioneer offers an item for sale at a high price and then gradually reduces the price until someone makes a bid **holländische Versteigerung**

dutiable
adjective **dutiable goods** *or* **dutiable items** = goods on which a customs duty has to be paid **zollpflichtige Güter**

◇ **duty** *noun* tax which has to be paid **Steuer;** *to take the duty off alcohol; to put a duty on cigarettes;* **ad valorem duty** = duty calculated on the sales value of the goods **Wertsteuer; customs duty** *or* **import duty** = tax on goods imported into a country **Zoll, Einfuhrzoll; excise duty** = tax on goods (such as alcohol and petrol) which are produced in the country **Verbrauchssteuer; goods which are liable to duty** = goods on which customs or excise tax has to be paid **zu verzollende Güter; duty-paid goods** = goods where the duty has been paid **verzollte Waren; stamp duty** = tax on legal documents (such as the conveyance of a property to a new owner) **Stempelgebühr; estate duty** *or (US)* **death duty** = tax paid on the property left by a dead person **Erbschaftssteuer**

◇ **duty-free** *adjective & adverb* sold with no duty to be paid **zollfrei;** *he bought a duty-free watch at the airport or he bought the watch duty-free;* **duty-free shop** = shop at an airport *or* on a ship where goods can be bought without paying duty **Duty-Free-Shop**

> QUOTE Canadian and European negotiators agreed to a deal under which Canada could lower its import duties on $150 million worth of European goods
> *Globe and Mail (Toronto)*

dynamic obsolescence *noun* redesign of a company's product in order to make previous models and other products on the market obsolete **geplante, funktionelle Obsoleszenz**

Ee

e. & o.e. = ERRORS AND OMISSIONS EXCEPTED

ear *noun* space at the top left or right corner of the front page of a newspaper, set aside for advertising **Titelbox**

early *adjective & adverb* before the usual time **frühzeitig, früher, vorzeitig; early closing day** = weekday when most shops in a town close in the afternoon **Tag, an dem die Geschäfte nachmittags geschlossen sind; at your earliest convenience** = as soon as possible **so bald wie möglich; at an early date** = very soon **bald early adopters** = category of adopters of a product who use it or buy it later than innovators, but earlier than the late majority **Frühadopter, früh Akzeptierende; early majority** = category of buyers of a product who use it or buy it later than the early adopters but before the late majority **frühe Mehrheit**

earnest *noun* money paid as a down payment by a buyer to a seller, to show commitment to the contract of sale **Hand-, Draufgeld**

ECGD = EXPORT CREDIT GUARANTEE DEPARTMENT

econometrics *noun* study of the statistics of economics, using computers **Ökonometrie**

economic *adjective*
(a) which provides enough money **rentabel;** *the flat is let at an economic rent; it is hardly economic for the company to run its own warehouse;* **economic order quantity** = concept or formula which indicates the most economic *or* profitable amount of supplies to order, taking into account stock holding costs and quantity discounts offered for large orders **optimale Bestellmenge, Andlersche Losgrößenformel**
(b) referring to the financial state of a country **Wirtschafts-;** *economic planner; economic planning; the government's economic policy; the economic situation; the country's economic system; economic trends;* **economic crisis** *or* **economic depression** = state of financial collapse in a country **Wirtschaftskrise;** *the government has introduced import controls to solve the current economic crisis;* **economic cycle** = period during which trade expands, then slows down, then expands again **Konjunkturzyklus; economic development** = expansion of the commercial and financial situation **wirtschaftliche Entwicklung;** *the government has offered tax incentives to speed up the economic development of the region; economic development has been relatively slow in the north, compared with the rest of the country;* **economic growth** = increase in the national income **Wirtschaftswachstum;** *the country enjoyed a period of economic growth in the 1960s;* **economic indicators** = statistics which show how the economy is going to perform in the short or long term **Schlüsselwerte für die Wirtschaft, Konjunkturindikatoren; economic sanctions** = restrictions on trade with a country in order to make its government change policy **Wirtschaftssanktionen;** *the western nations imposed economic sanctions on the country;* **the European Economic Community** = the Common Market **die Europäische Gemeinschaft**

◇ **economical** *adjective* which saves money or materials *or* which is cheap **sparsam, rationell; economical car** = car which does not use much petrol **im Benzinverbrauch sparsames Auto; economical use of resources** = using resources as carefully as possible **sparsamer Umgang mit Ressourcen**

◇ **economics** *noun*
(a) study of the production, distribution, selling and use of goods and services **Volkswirtschaft, Wirtschaftswissenschaft**
(b) study of financial structures to show how a product or service is costed and what returns it produces **ökonomischer Aspekt, Ökonomie;** *the economics of town planning; I don't understand the economics of the coal industry*

◇ **economist** *noun* person who specializes in the study of economics **Volkswirt, Wirtschaftswissenschaftler;** *government economists are forecasting a growth rate of 3% next year; an agricultural economist studies the economics of the agriculture industry*

> QUOTE each of the major issues on the agenda at this week's meeting is important to the government's success in overall economic management
>
> *Australian Financial Review*
>
> QUOTE believers in free-market economics often find it hard to sort out their views on the issue
>
> *Economist*

economy *noun*
(a) being careful not to waste money or materials **Sparsamkeit, Wirtschaftlichkeit; an economy measure** = an action to save money or materials **eine Sparmaßnahme; to introduce economies** *or* **economy measures** = to start using methods to save money or materials **Sparmaßnahmen einführen; economies of scale** = making a product more profitable by manufacturing it in larger quantities and lowering the unit cost **Größendegression; economy car** = car which does not use much petrol **im Benzinverbrauch sparsames Auto; economy class** = cheapest class on a plane **Touristenklasse;** *to travel economy class;* **economy drive** = campaign to save money or materials **Sparkampagne; economy size** = large size *or* large packet which is better value for money than a smaller size **Sparpackung;** *housewives are tempted by economy size packs of new brands; those on tight budgets only buy economy size packs*
(b) financial state of a country *or* way in which a country makes and uses its money **Wirtschaft;** *the country's economy is in ruins;* **black economy** = work which is paid for in cash or goods, but not declared to the tax authorities **Schattenwirtschaft; capitalist economy** = system where each person has the right to invest money, to work in business, and to buy and sell with no restrictions by the state **kapitalistisches Wirtschaftssystem; controlled economy** = system where business activity is controlled by orders from the government **staatlich gelenkte Wirtschaft; free market economy** = system where the government does not interfere in business activity in any way **freie Marktwirtschaft; mixed economy** = system which contains both nationalized industries and private enterprise **Mischwirtschaft; planned economy** = system where the government plans all business activity **Planwirtschaft**

> QUOTE the European economies are being held back by rigid labor markets and wage structures, huge expenditures on social welfare programs and restrictions on the free movement of goods within the Common Market
>
> *Duns Business Month*

editing *noun*
(a) checking the results of a survey to confirm that data has been collected correctly **Plausibilitätskontrolle**
(b) modifying or correcting a text or film **Bearbeiten, Redigieren; Schneiden;** *this sales literature needs editing to make it less long-winded*
◇ **edition** *noun* issue of a publication, such as a newspaper, trade magazine, book, etc. **Ausgabe;** *we are too late to advertise in this month's edition; there will be too many competing advertisements in that edition*
◇ **editorial**
1 *adjective* referring to an editor **redaktionell, Redaktions-; editorial advertisement** = advertisement in the form of text material in a magazine **redaktionell aufgezogene/gestaltete Anzeige; editorial board** = group of editors (on a newspaper, etc.) **Redaktion, Redaktionskomitee; editorial publicity** = free publicity which is given to a product by a newspaper or magazine in an editorial or article, rather than in an advertisement which must be paid for **redaktionelle Werbung**
2 *noun* main article in a newspaper, written by the editor **Leitartikel**

EDMA = EUROPEAN DIRECT MARKETING ASSOCIATION

educational advertising *noun* advertising that informs consumers about a product, particularly important when the product has only recently been introduced **informative Werbung;** *educational advertising has made the public aware that our product is as safe as more traditional devices on the market*

effect
1 *noun*
(a) result **Auswirkung, Effekt;** *the effect of the pay increase was to raise productivity levels;* **demonstration effect** = theory that people buy products to impress or keep up with their neighbours **Mitläufereffekt;** *see also* PARETO EFFECT
(b) terms of a contract which take effect *or* **come into effect from January 1st** = terms which start to operate on January 1st **Vertragsbedingungen, die am 1. Januar in Kraft treten; prices are increased 10% with effect from January 1st** = new prices will apply from January 1st **mit Wirkung vom 1. Januar werden die Preise um 10% erhöht; to remain in effect** = to continue to be applied **wirksam/gültig bleiben**
(c) meaning **Sinn; clause to the effect that** = clause which means that **Klausel, die zum Inhalt hat/Klausel, die ... beinhaltet; we have made provision to this effect** = we have put into the contract terms which will make

this work **wir haben für diesen Fall Klauseln eingebaut**
(d) personal effects = personal belongings **Gegenstände des persönlichen Gebrauchs**
2 *verb* to carry out **aus-, durchführen; to effect a payment** = to make a payment **eine Zahlung leisten; to effect customs clearance** = to clear something through customs **zollamtlich abfertigen lassen; to effect a settlement between two parties** = to bring two parties together and make them agree to a settlement **einen Vergleich zustande bringen**
◇ **effective** *adjective*
(a) actual (as opposed to theoretical) **tatsächlich; effective cover** = situation where consumers in the target audience will have seen the advertisement at least four times on average **tatsächliche/wirksame Reichweite; effective demand** = actual demand for a product backed up by the ability to pay for it **effektive Nachfrage;** *there is not enough effective demand in a depressed economy; is there effective demand yet for our computers, or only potential demand?*
(b) effective date = date on which a rule *or* a contract starts to be applied **Stichtag, Tag des Inkrafttretens; clause effective as from January 1st** = clause which starts to be applied on January 1st **Klausel mit Wirkung vom 1. Januar**
(c) which works *or* which produces results **effektiv, wirksam;** *advertising in the Sunday papers is the most effective way of selling ;* *see* COST-EFFECTIVE
◇ **effectiveness** *noun* working *or* producing results **Wirksamkeit;** *I doubt the effectiveness of television advertising;* *see* COST-EFFECTIVENESS
◇ **effectual** *adjective* which produces a correct result **wirksam**

eftpos *or* **EFTPOS** = ELECTRONIC FUNDS TRANSFER AT POINT OF SALE

ego *noun* psychological term for a person's consciousness of himself or herself **Ego;** *we are designing clothes to boost men's egos; glamorous advertising appeals to the customer's ego*

eighty/twenty rule *noun* rule that a small percentage of customers may account for a large percentage of sales **Achtzig/Zwanzig-Regel;** *see also* PARETO EFFECT

elastic *adjective* which can expand or contract easily because of small changes in price **elastisch elastic demand** = demand which experiences a comparatively large percentage change in response to a change in price **elastische Nachfrage; elastic supply** = supply which experiences a comparatively large percentage change in response to a change in price **elastisches Angebot**
◇ **elasticity** *noun* ability to change easily **Elastizität; elasticity of supply and demand** = changes in supply and demand of an item depending on its market price **Elastizität von Angebot und Nachfrage;** *see also* CROSS ELASTICITY

electronic *adjective* **electronic data processing** = selecting and examining data stored in a computer to produce information **elektronische Datenverarbeitung; electronic funds transfer at point of sale (eftpos)** = system where money is immediately debited from the customer's bank account to the store's account as the purchase is registered at the cash desk **elektronische Kasse; electronic mail** = system of sending messages from one computer terminal to another, via telephone lines **elektronische Post, E-Mail; electronic media** = electronic-based media, such as television and radio **elektronische Medien;** *advertising in the electronic media would certainly increase sales, but we can only afford to advertise in the press;* **electronic point of sale (epos)** = system where sales are charged automatically to a customer's credit card and stock is controlled by the shop's computer **(elektronischer) Kassenterminal, Datenkasse**
◇ **electronics** *noun* applying the scientific study of electrons to produce manufactured products, such as computers, calculators or telephones **Elektronik;** *the electronics industry; an electronics specialist or expert; electronics engineer*

eliminate *verb* to remove **eliminieren, streichen;** *we have decided to eliminate this series of old products from our range*
◇ **elimination** *noun* act of removing **Eliminierung, Streichung; product elimination** = removal of old products from the market as new ones are added to the company's range **Produktelimination**

embargo
1 *noun*
(a) government order which stops a type of trade **Embargo, Handelsverbot; to lay** *or* **put an embargo on trade with a country** = to say that trade with a country must not take place **ein Handelsembargo über ein Land verhängen;** *the government has put an embargo on the export of computer equipment;* **to lift an embargo** = to allow trade to start again **ein Embargo aufheben;**

the government has lifted the embargo on the export of computers; **to be under an embargo** = to be forbidden **einem Embargo unterliegen**
(b) period of time during which certain information in a press release must not be published **Informationsstop**
2 *verb*
(a) to stop trade *or* not to allow trade **ein Embargo verhängen;** *the government has embargoed trade with the Eastern countries*
(b) not to allow publication of information for a period of time **Informationsstop verhängen;** *the news of the merger has been embargoed until next Wednesday*

> QUOTE the Commerce Department is planning to loosen export controls for products that have been embargoed but are readily available elsewhere in the West
> *Duns Business Month*

emotional appeal *noun* attempt by advertising to persuade through an emotional rather than a rational message **emotionaler Appell;** *the charity used the emotional appeal of starving children to raise funds; emotional appeal was an obvious feature in all the political parties' campaign films*

empirical data *noun* data *or* information which comes from actual observation or which can be proved **empirische Daten;** *we have no empirical data concerning our competitors' sales last year*

emporium *noun* large shop **Warenhaus**
NOTE: plural is **emporia**

emptor *see* CAVEAT EMPTOR

EMS = EUROPEAN MONETARY SYSTEM

enclose *verb* to put something inside an envelope with a letter **beilegen, beifügen;** *to enclose an invoice with a letter; I am enclosing a copy of the contract; letter enclosing a cheque; please find the cheque enclosed herewith*

◊ **enclosure** *noun* document enclosed with a letter or package **An-, Beilage;** *the enclosure turned out to be a free sample of perfume; sales material on other products was sent out as an enclosure*

end *noun* final point *or* last part **Ende, Beendigung; end consumer** = person who uses a product **Endverbraucher;** *the survey was designed to assess the attitudes of end consumers to the product;* **end product** = manufactured product, made at the end of a production process **Endprodukt;** *after six months' trial production, the end product is still not acceptable;* **end user** = person who actually uses a product **Endverbraucher;** *the operating instructions must be simplified so that they can be easily understood by the end user; end users face fairly high prices because of the middlemen's profits*

endorse *verb*
(a) *(of someone who is not the producer)* to say that a product is good **werben für;** *the company has persuaded a famous scientist to endorse their product*
(b) to endorse a bill *or* **a cheque** = to sign a bill *or* a cheque on the back to show that you accept it **einen Wechsel indossieren; einen Scheck girieren**

◊ **endorsee** *noun* person whose name is written on a bill *or* a cheque as having the right to cash it **Indossat**

◊ **endorsement** *noun*
(a) act of endorsing; signature on a document which endorses it **Indossament**
(b) endorsement advertising = advertising which makes use of famous *or* qualified people to endorse a product **Leitbildwerbung, Testimonialwerbung;** *which celebrities have agreed to contribute to our endorsement advertising? endorsement advertising will, we hope, help our fund-raising campaign*

◊ **endorser** *noun* person who endorses a bill which is then paid to him **Indossant**

enterprise *noun*
(a) system of carrying on a business **Unternehmertum; free enterprise** = system of business free from government interference **freies Unternehmertum; private enterprise** = businesses which are owned privately not nationalized **Privatwirtschaft;** *the project is completely funded by private enterprise;* **enterprise zone** = geographical area which is given a special grant by the government towards its industrial and economic development **Förderungsgebiet;** *it has been declared an enterprise zone as a means of combating the unemployment there; it might be a good idea to move the company to an enterprise zone*
(b) business **Unternehmen; a small-scale enterprise** = a small business **ein Kleinbetrieb; a state enterprise** = a state-controlled company **ein staatliches Unternehmen, Staatsbetrieb;** *bosses of state enterprises are appointed by the government*

entrepot *noun* **entrepot port** = town with a large international commercial port dealing in re-exports **Wiederausfuhrhafen; entrepot trade** = exporting of imported goods **Wiederausfuhr**

entrepreneur *noun* person who directs a company and takes commercial risks **Unternehmer**
◇ **entrepreneurial** *adjective* taking commercial risks **unternehmerisch;** *an entrepreneurial decision*

envelope stuffer *noun* advertising material which is mailed in an envelope **Drucksachenbeilage**

environment *noun* area in which an organization works **Umgebung, Umwelt; immediate environment** = the elements outside an organization which directly affect its work, such as the supply of raw materials and the demand for its products **Aufgabenumwelt, Mikro-Umwelt;** *compare* MACRO-ENVIRONMENT
◇ **environmental analysis** *noun* analysis of factors outside an organization such as demography or politics, in order to make strategic planning more effective **Umweltsanalyse;** *our environmental analysis must cover all the countries we sell in; environmental analysis made clear that some markets were too unstable to enter*

epos *or* **EPOS** = ELECTRONIC POINT OF SALE

equilibrium *noun* state of balance in the economy where supply equals demand **Gleichgewicht**

error *noun*
(a) mistake **Fehler;** *he made an error in calculating the total; the secretary must have made a typing error;* **clerical error** = mistake made in an office **Schreibfehler; computer error** = mistake made by a computer **Computerfehler; margin of error** = number of mistakes which are accepted in a document *or* in a calculation **Fehlerspielraum; errors and omissions excepted (e. & o.e.)** = words written on an invoice to show that the company has no responsibility for mistakes in the invoice **Irrtümer und Auslassungen vorbehalten; error rate** = number of mistakes per thousand entries *or* per page **Fehlerquote;**
(b) (i) difference between the results achieved in a survey using a sample and what the results would be using the entire population; (ii) distortion of the results of a survey owing to bias and mistakes made **(i) Zufallsfehler; (ii) systematischer Fehler**

escalate *verb* to increase steadily **eskalieren, ansteigen**
◇ **escalation** *noun* **escalation of prices** = steady increase in prices **Preiseskalation, Preisanstieg; escalation clause** = ESCALATOR CLAUSE
◇ **escalator** *noun* moving staircase **Rolltreppe; escalator cards** = advertisements on either side of an escalator in underground stations **neben Rolltreppen hängende Plakatanschläge;** *the media buyer compared the cost of posters and escalator cards;* **escalator clause** *or* **escalation clause** = clause in a contract allowing for regular price increases because of increased costs **Preisgleitklausel**

escrow *noun* **in escrow** = held in safe keeping by a third party **treuhänderisch hinterlegt; document held in escrow** = document given to a third party to keep and to pass on to someone when money has been paid **bei einem Treuhänder verwahrtes Dokument;** *(US)* **escrow account** = account where money is held in escrow until a contract is signed *or* until goods are delivered, etc. **Treuhandkonto**

espionage *noun* **industrial espionage** = spying on a competitor, trying to find out the secrets of a competitor's work or products, usually by illegal means **Werks-, Wirtschaftsspionage**

essential *adjective* very important **wesentlich, unerläßlich, unbedingt notwendig;** *it is essential that an agreement be reached before the end of the month; the factory is lacking essential spare parts;* **essential goods** *or* **essential products** = basic goods or products necessary for everyday life **Güter des täglichen Bedarfs**

estimate
1 *noun*
(a) calculation of probable cost *or* size *or* time of something **Schätzung; rough estimate** = very approximate calculation **grobe Schätzung/Berechnung; at a conservative estimate** = calculation which probably underestimates the final figure **bei vorsichtiger Schätzung;** *their turnover has risen by at least 20% in the last year, and that is a conservative estimate;* **these figures are only an estimate** = these are not the final accurate figures **diese Beträge sind nur Schätzwerte;** *can you give me an estimate of how much time was spent on the job?*
(b) calculation by a contractor or seller of a service of how much something is likely to cost, given to a client so as to get him to make an order **Kostenvoranschlag;** *you should ask for an estimate before committing yourselves; before we can give the grant we must have an estimate of the total costs involved; unfortunately the bill was quite different from the estimate;* **to put**

in an estimate = to give someone a written calculation of the probable costs of carrying out a job **einen Kostenvoranschlag machen;** *three firms put in estimates for the job*

2 *verb*

(a) to calculate the probable cost *or* size *or* time of something **schätzen;** *to estimate that it will cost £1m or to estimate costs at £1m; we estimate current sales at only 60% of last year*

(b) to estimate for a job = to state in writing the future costs of carrying out a piece of work so that a client can make an order **einen Kostenvoranschlag für einen Auftrag einreichen;** *three firms estimated for the fitting of the offices*

◇ **estimated** *adjective* calculated approximately **geschätzt, veranschlagt;** *estimated sales; estimated figure*

◇ **estimation** *noun* approximate calculation **Schätzung**

◇ **estimator** *noun* person whose job is to calculate estimates for carrying out work **Schätzer/-in**

ethics *noun* moral aspects of decision-making **Ethik;** *whether or not we use such aggressive sales tactics is a matter of ethics*

ethnocentric stage *noun (US)* early stage in a company's marketing when goods are sent overseas with no concessions to local needs or tastes **ethnozentrische Phase**

European Direct Marketing Association (EDMA) organization based in Switzerland, which monitors new techniques in direct marketing and represents the interests of its members **europäischer Direkmarketing-Verband (EDMA)**

even numbers *noun* numbers (like 24 or 80) which can be divided by two **gerade Zahlen; odd-even pricing** = using either odd or even numbers in pricing, according to what seems to be most effective in persuading customers to buy **Odd-Even Pricing**

ex *preposition*

(a) out of *or* from **ab; price ex dock** *or* **price ex quay** = price that includes all costs up to delivery of goods on land at a port, including customs duty and unloading costs **Preis ab Hafen; Preis ab Kai; price ex ship** = price that includes all costs up to the arrival of the ship at port **Preis ab Schiff; price ex warehouse** = price for a product which is to be collected from the manufacturer's or agent's warehouse and so does not include delivery **Preis ab Lager; price ex works** *or* **ex factory** = price not including transport from the maker's factory **Preis ab Werk**

(b) without **ohne; ex coupon** = bond without the interest coupon **ohne/ex Kupon; share quoted ex dividend** = share price not including the right to receive the next dividend **ex Dividende notierte Aktie;** *the shares went ex dividend yesterday*

◇ **ex-** *prefix* former **ehemalig, Ex-;** *an ex-director of the company*

excess *noun* amount which is more than that allowed **Überschuß, Mehrbetrag;** *an excess of expenditure over revenue;* **excess baggage** = extra payment at an airport for taking baggage which is heavier than the normal passenger's allowance **Übergewicht; excess capacity** = more production capacity than is needed for present levels of demand **Überkapazität;** *we will be selling off machinery owing to our excess capacity; excess capacity is a waste of resources;* **excess demand** = more demand at the present price than sellers can satisfy **Nachfrageüberschuß;** *much more machinery and labour must be acquired to meet excess demand; excess demand has arisen owing to a sudden rise in incomes;* **excess profits** = profit which is more than that thought to be normal **Mehrgewinn; excess profits tax** = tax on excess profits **Steuer zur Abschöpfung von Höchstgewinnen; excess supply** = more supply at the present price than buyers want to buy **Angebotsüberschuß**

> QUOTE control of materials provides manufacturers with an opportunity to reduce the amount of money tied up in excess materials
> *Duns Business Month*

exchange

1 *noun*

(a) giving of one thing for another **Tausch, Austausch; to offer** *or* **take something in part exchange** giving *or* taking an old product as part of the payment for a new one **etwas in Zahlung geben od nehmen;** *to take a car in part exchange;* **exchange of contracts** = point in the sale of property when the buyer and the seller both sign the contract of sale which then becomes binding **Unterzeichnung des Kaufvertrags von Grundbesitz; exchange economy** = economy based on the exchange of goods and services **Tauschwirtschaft**

(b) foreign exchange = (i) exchanging the money of one country for that of another; (ii) money of another country **(i) Devisenhandel, Devisenverkehr; (ii) Devisen;** *the company has more than £1m in foreign exchange;* **foreign exchange broker** = person who buys and sells foreign currency on behalf of other people **Devisenhändler, Devisenmakler; foreign exchange market** = dealings in foreign currencies **Devisenmarkt;** *he trades on the foreign exchange market; foreign exchange markets were very active after the dollar devalued;* **rate of exchange** *or* **exchange rate** = rate at which one currency is exchanged for another **Wechselkurs;** *the current rate of exchange is 10.95 francs to the pound;* **exchange control** = control by a government of the way in which its currency may be exchanged for foreign currencies **Devisenkontrolle;** *the government had to impose exchange controls to stop the rush to buy dollars;* **exchange dealer** = person who buys and sells foreign currency **Devisenhändler; exchange dealings** = buying and selling foreign currency **Devisenhandel;** *(GB)* **Exchange Equalization Account** = account with the Bank of England used by the government when buying or selling foreign currency to influence the sterling exchange rate **Währungsausgleichsfonds; exchange premium** = extra cost above the normal rate for buying a foreign currency **Agio, Aufgeld**

(c) bill of exchange = document which tells a bank to pay a person (usually used in foreign currency payments) **Wechsel, Tratte**

(d) Stock Exchange = place where stocks and shares are bought and sold **Börse;** *the company's shares are traded on the New York Stock Exchange; he works on the Stock Exchange;* **commodity exchange** = place where commodities are bought and sold **Warenbörse**

2 *verb*

(a) to exchange one article for another = to give one thing in place of something else **einen Artikel gegen einen anderen umtauschen;** *he exchanged his motorcycle for a car; if the trousers are too small you can take them back and exchange them for a larger pair; goods can be exchanged only on production of the sales slip*

(b) to exchange contracts = to sign a contract when buying a property (done by both buyer and seller at the same time) **beim Kauf von Grundbesitz den Vertrag unterschreiben**

(c) to change money of one country for money of another **wechseln, tauschen;** *to exchange francs for pounds*

◇ **exchangeable** *adjective* which can be exchanged **austauschbar, umtauschbar**

◇ **exchanger** *noun* person who buys and sells foreign currency **Devisenhändler**

> QUOTE under the barter agreements, Nigeria will export crude oil in exchange for trucks, food, planes and chemicals
> ***Wall Street Journal***
>
> QUOTE can free trade be reconciled with a strong dollar resulting from floating exchange rates?
> ***Duns Business Month***
>
> QUOTE a draft report on changes in the international monetary system casts doubt on any return to fixed exchange-rate parities
> ***Wall Street Journal***

exclusion clause *noun* clause in a contract *or* insurance policy *or* warranty stating that some item is not covered by it **Ausschlußklausel, Freizeichnungsklausel**

◇ **exclusive** *adjective*

(a) exclusive agreement = agreement where a person is made sole agent for a product in a market **Alleinvertretungsvereinbarung; exclusive right to market a product** = right to be the only person to market the product **Recht zum Alleinvertrieb eines Produktes**

(b) exclusive of = not including **exklusive, ausschließlich;** *all payments are exclusive of tax; the invoice is exclusive of VAT*

◇ **exclusivity** *noun* exclusive right to market a product **Alleinvertrieb, Exklusivrecht**

exempt

1 *adjective* not covered by a law *or* not forced to obey a law **ausgenommen, befreit; exempt from tax** *or* **tax exempt** = not required to pay tax **von der Steuer befreit, steuerfrei;** *as a non-profit-making organization, we are exempt from tax;* **exempt rating** = legal right of a business not to add VAT to the prices of certain products *or* services **Mehrwertsteuerbefreiung; exempt supplies** = products *or* services on which the supplier does not have to charge VAT **von Mehrwertsteuer befreite Produkte**

2 *verb* to free something from having tax paid on it; to free someone from having to pay tax **befreien;** *non-profit-making organizations are exempted from tax; food is exempted from sales tax*

ex-gratia *adjective* done as a favour **aus Gefälligkeit, freiwillig; an ex-gratia payment** = payment made as a gift, with no other obligations **Kulanzzahlung, Zahlung ohne Anerkennung einer Rechtspflicht;** *the ex-gratia payment was a token of the buyer's appreciation of the supplier's reliable service over many years*

exhibit

1 *noun*

(a) thing which is shown **Ausstellungsstück;**

the buyers admired the exhibits on our stand
(b) single section of an exhibition **Ausstellungsstand;** *the British Trade Exhibit at the International Computer Fair*
2 *verb* **to exhibit at the Motor Show** = to display new models of cars **auf der Fahrzeugausstellung ausstellen**

◊ **exhibition** *noun* show of goods so that buyers can look at them and decide what to buy **Ausstellung;** *the government has sponsored an exhibition of British design; we have a stand at the Ideal Home Exhibition;* **exhibition room** *or* **hall** = place where goods are shown so that buyers can look at them and decide what to buy **Ausstellungsraum, Messehalle; exhibition stand** = separate section of an exhibition where a company exhibits its products or services **Messestand**

◊ **exhibitor** *noun* person *or* company which shows products at an exhibition **Aussteller**

exorbitant *adjective* unreasonably high **übertrieben, übermäßig, unverschämt;** *$10,000 a minute, that's exorbitant and quite unjustified; their fees may seem exorbitant, but their costs are very high*

expand *verb* to increase *or* to get bigger *or* to make something bigger **erweitern, (sich) ausweiten/vergrößern, expandieren, ausbauen;** *an expanding economy; the company is expanding fast; we have had to expand our sales force*

◊ **expansion** *noun* increase in size **Erweiterung, Ausweitung, Vergrößerung, Expansion, Ausbau;** *the expansion of the domestic market; the company had difficulty in financing its current expansion programme; (GB)* **business expansion scheme (BES)** = system where money invested in a new company for some years is free from tax **Steuerbefreiung bei Investition in Betriebsneugründung**

> QUOTE inflation-adjusted GNP moved up at a 1.3% annual rate, its worst performance since the economic expansion began
> *Fortune*
>
> QUOTE the businesses we back range from start-up ventures to established businesses in need of further capital for expansion
> *Times*
>
> QUOTE the group is undergoing a period of rapid expansion and this has created an exciting opportunity for a qualified accountant
> *Financial Times*

expect *verb* to hope that something is going to happen **erwarten;** *we are expecting him to arrive at 10.45; they are expecting a cheque from their agent next week; the house was sold for more than the expected price;* **expected price** = price of a product which consumers consider corresponds to its true value **erwarteter Preis**

◊ **expectancy** *noun* **life expectancy** = number of years a person is likely to live **Lebenserwartung**

> QUOTE he observed that he expected exports to grow faster than imports in 1985-86
> *Sydney Morning Herald*
>
> QUOTE American business as a whole has seen profits well above the levels normally expected at this stage of the cycle
> *Sunday Times*

expense *noun* money spent **Ausgabe, Kosten;** *the likely profits do not justify the expense of setting up the project; it was well worth the expense to get really high-quality equipment;* **expense account** = money which a businessman is allowed by his company to spend on travelling and entertaining clients in connection with his business **Spesenkonto;** *I'll put this lunch on my expense account; expense account lunches form a large part of our current expenditure*

◊ **expenses** *plural noun* money paid for doing something **Unkosten, Spesen;** *the salary offered is £10,000 plus expenses;* **all expenses paid** = with all costs paid by the company **mit Vergütung aller Unkosten;** *the company sent him to San Francisco all expenses paid;* **to cut down on expenses** = to try to reduce spending **die Unkosten einschränken; allowable expenses** = business expenses which are allowed against tax **abzugsfähige Ausgaben; business expenses** = money spent on running a business, not on stock or assets **Betriebskosten; entertainment expenses** = money spent on giving meals to business visitors **Bewirtungsspesen; fixed expenses** = money which is spent regularly (such as rent, electricity, telephone, etc.) **Fixkosten; incidental expenses** = small amounts of money spent at various times, in addition to larger amounts **Nebenkosten; legal expenses** = money spent on fees paid to lawyers **Anwaltskosten; overhead expenses** *or* **general expenses** *or* **running expenses** = money spent on the day-to-day cost of running a business **Betriebskosten, allgemeine Unkosten, Festkosten; travelling expenses** = money spent on travelling and hotels for business purposes **Reisespesen**

◊ **expensive** *adjective* which costs a lot of money **teuer, kostspielig;** *first-class air travel is becoming more and more expensive*

experience
1 *noun* knowledge or skill that comes from having lived through various situations **Erfahrung;** *he is a man of considerable*

experience; she has a lot of experience of dealing with German companies; he gained most of his experience in the Far East; some experience is required for this job; **experience curve** = graph showing the relationship between the cumulative amount of products produced and the production cost per unit **Erfahrungskurve;** *the experience curve shows how increasing efficiency has brought down our costs;* **experience effect** = the role of experience in improving business efficiency **Erfahrungseffekt;** *the experience effect is evident in the rise in our profits as our workforce becomes more skilled*

2 *verb* to live through a situation **durchmachen, erleben, erfahren;** *the company experienced a period of falling sales*

◇ **experienced** *adjective* person who has lived through many situations and has learnt from them **erfahren, sachkundig;** *he is the most experienced negotiator I know; we have appointed a very experienced sales director*

experimental method *noun* use of controlled experiments to discover the influence of various variables in marketing, such as types of promotion and sales training **Experiment-Methode**

expert *noun* person who knows a lot about something **Experte/Expertin, Fachmann, Sachverständiger;** *an expert in the field of electronics or an electronics expert; the company asked a financial expert for advice or asked for expert financial advice;* **expert's report** = report written by an expert **Sachverständigengutachten, Expertise**

◇ **expertise** *noun* specialist knowledge **Fachwissen, Sachkenntnis, Expertise;** *we hired Mr Smith because of his financial expertise or because of his expertise in the African market*

exploit *verb* to use something to make a profit **(aus)nutzen; ausbeuten;** *the company is exploiting its contacts in the Ministry of Trade; we hope to exploit the oil resources in the China Sea*

exponential *adjective* **exponential diffusion** *or* **exponential growth** = typical growth pattern of new products that involves a slow start, followed by acceleration and finally a slowing down **exponentieller Trend; exponential smoothing** = technique for working out averages while allowing for recent changes in values by moving forward the period under consideration at regular intervals **exponentielle Glättung**

export

1 *noun*

(a) exports = goods sent to a foreign country to be sold **Exporte;** *exports to Africa have increased by 25%*

(b) action of sending goods to a foreign country to be sold **Export, Ausfuhr;** *the export trade or the export market;* **direct export** = sending goods for sale direct to the overseas customer, without going through a middleman **Direktexport; export agent** = person who sells overseas on behalf of a company and earns a commission **Kommissionär;** *an export agent is developing our business in West Africa; he is working in London as an export agent for a French company;* **export bounty** = government payment to businesses to encourage certain types of export **Ausfuhrprämie; export department** = section of a company which deals in sales to foreign countries **Exportabteilung; export duty** = tax paid on goods sent out of a country for sale **Export-, Ausfuhrzoll; export house** = company which specializes in the export of goods made by other manufacturers **Exportfirma; export licence** = government permit allowing something to be exported **Exportlizenz;** *the government has refused an export licence for computer parts;* **export manager** = person in charge of an export department in a company **Exportleiter;** *the export manager planned to set up a sales force in Southern Europe; sales managers from all export markets report to our export manager;* **Export Credit Guarantee Department (ECGD)** = British government department which insures British businesses against losses incurred in exporting goods; *(entspricht)* **Hermes Kreditversicherung; staatliche Exportkreditversicherung**

2 *verb* to send goods to foreign countries for sale **exportieren, ausführen;** *50% of our production is exported; the company imports raw materials and exports the finished products*

◇ **exportation** *noun* act of sending goods to foreign countries for sale **Ausfuhr, Export**

◇ **exporter** *noun* person *or* company *or* country which sells goods in foreign countries **Exporteur, Exportfirma;** *a major furniture exporter; Canada is an important exporter of oil or an important oil exporter*

◇ **exporting** *adjective* which exports **Ausfuhr-, Export-; oil-exporting countries** = countries which produce oil and sell it to other countries **erdölexportierende Länder**

> QUOTE in the past, export documentation was a major stumbling block for some companies
> *Marketing & Sales Management*
> QUOTE in 1985, Europe's gross exports of white goods climbed to 2.4 billion, about a quarter of total production
> *Economist*
> QUOTE the New Zealand producers are now aiming to export more fresh meat as opposed to frozen which has formed the majority of its UK imports in the past
> *Marketing*

exposition *noun (US)* = EXHIBITION

exposure *noun*
(a) publicity given to an organization or product **Publicity, Publizität;** *our company has achieved more exposure since we decided to go public*
(b) total number of people who can be reached by a particular advertising medium **Gesamtkontakte**

express
1 *adjective* rapid *or* very fast **Expreß-, Eil-, per Expreß;** *express letter; express delivery*
2 *verb* to send very fast **per Expreß/ als Eilsendung schicken;** *we expressed the order to the customer's warehouse*

◇ **expressage** *noun (US)* very fast transport service **Sendung durch Paketförderungsgesellschaft**

extend *verb*
(a) to make available *or* to give **gewähren;** *to extend credit to a customer*
(b) to make longer **verlängern, prolongieren;** *to extend a contract for two years;* **extended credit** = credit allowing the borrower a very long time to pay **langfristiger Kredit;** *we sell to Australia on extended credit;* **extended guarantee** = guarantee offered by a dealer on consumer durables, such as dishwashers, which goes beyond the time specified in the manufacturer's guarantee **verlängerte Garantie**

◇ **extension** *noun* allowing more time **Verlängerung, Prolongation; to get an extension of credit** = to get more time to pay back **eine Kreditverlängerung gewährt bekommen; extension of a contract** = continuing the contract for a further period **Vertragsverlängerung extension strategy** = marketing strategy aimed at extending the life of a product either by making small changes in it, finding new uses for it or finding new markets **Revitalisierungs-Strategie;** *an extension strategy is needed to ensure demand for another few years; the extension strategy consisted in providing a greater choice of colours and upholstery for the range of cars*

◇ **extensive** *adjective* very large *or* covering a wide area **umfangreich, ausgedehnt, weit, breit, umfassend;** *an extensive network of sales outlets;* **extensive marketing** = using a wide network of distributors and a great variety of promotional activities to gain as large a section of the market as possible **flächendeckendes Marketing;** *only a company with vast resources could embark on this type of extensive marketing;* **extensive problem-solving** = detailed research and decision-making by a buyer who needs to examine carefully all options open to him or her **extensives Problemlösung**

external *adjective*
(a) outside a country **ausländisch; external account** = account in a British bank held by someone who is living in another country **Auslandskonto; external trade** = trade with foreign countries **Außenhandel**
(b) outside a company **außerbetrieblich, extern; external audit** = audit carried out by an independent auditor **außerbetriebliche/unabhängige Rechnungsprüfung/Revision**

extra
1 *adjective* which is added *or* which is more than usual **extra, zusätzlich;** *there is no extra charge for heating; to charge 10% extra for postage; we get £25 extra pay for working on Sunday; service is extra*
2 *noun* **extras** = items which are not included in a price **Nebenkosten, Neben-, Sonderausgaben;** *packing and postage are extras*

extrapolation *noun* forecasting technique which involves projecting past trends into the future **Extrapolation;** *we are using extrapolation to forecast demand for a new product based on the demand for a similar product over the last five years*

eye *noun* **eye-movement test** = advertising research test which involves recording the movement of a subject's eyes as he or she looks at an advertisement to see which parts are of special interest **Augenbewegungs-, Blickverlaufstest; Blickregistrierungsverfahren;** *the eye-movement test will tell us what to highlight in future advertisements;* **eye-wash** = inflated or exaggerated claims made for a product **leeres Geschwätz, Gewäsch, Quatsch;** *few were impressed by the advertisement which was dismissed as so much eye-wash*

Ff

face-lift *noun* improvement to the design of products and packaging *or* of an organization's image **Innovation, Aufmöbelung;** *these products need a face-lift if they are going to retain their appeal*

◇ **face out** *adverb* way of displaying books on bookshop shelves, showing the front cover **Titelpräsentation**

◇ **face-to-face selling** *noun* person-to-person *or* direct selling, involving a meeting between seller and buyer **persönlicher Verkauf, Direktverkauf;** *six months of face-to-face selling will give trainees direct experience of the market; we need confident outgoing people to do our face-to-face selling*

facia *see* FASCIA

facility *noun*
(a) total amount of credit which a lender will allow a borrower **Kredit; credit facilities** = arrangement with a bank *or* supplier to have credit so as to buy goods **Kreditmodalitäten; overdraft facility** = arrangement with a bank to have an overdraft **Überziehungskredit**
(b) facilities = equipment *or* buildings which make it easy to do something **Einrichtungen;** *storage facilities; harbour facilities; transport facilities; there are no facilities for passengers; there are no facilities for unloading or there are no unloading facilities*
(c) *US* single large building **Anlage, Betriebsanlage;** *we have opened our new warehouse facility*

facing *adjective* opposite **gegenüberliegend; facing page** = the page opposite **gegenüberliegende Seite; facing matter** *or* **facing text matter** = placing an advertisement on the page opposite to one containing editorial matter **gegenüber (redaktionellem) Text**

facsimile *noun* an exact copy of a text *or* illustration **Faksimile**

fact *noun* piece of information **Tatsache, Faktum; fact book** = data put together about a product on the market that can be used for reference by the producers or by an advertising agency **Informationsbuch; fact sheet** = sheet of paper giving information about a product *or* service which can be used for publicity purposes **Informationsblatt**

factor
1 *noun*
(a) thing which is important *or* which influences **Faktor;** *the drop in sales is an important factor in the company's lower profits;* **cost factor** = problem of cost **Kostenfaktor; cyclical factors** = way in which a trade cycle affects businesses **zyklische Faktoren; deciding factor** = most important factor which influences a decision **entscheidender/ausschlaggebender Faktor; design factor** = ratio of sampling error of a complex sample *or* sample design to that of a completely random sample **Design-Faktor; factor analysis** = process of identifying key factors that influence the results in an attitude research programme **Faktorenanalyse**
(b) (i) person who sells for a business or another person and earns a commission; (ii) person or company which is responsible for collecting debts for companies, by buying debts at a discount on their face value **(i) Kommissionär; (ii) Factor**
2 *verb* to buy debts from a company at a discount **Forderungen ankaufen**

◇ **factorage** *noun* commission earned by a factor **Provision, Kommissionsgebühr;** *what percentage is the factorage?*

◇ **factoring** *noun*
(a) selling for another person on commission **Kommissionshandel; factoring agent** = person who sells for a business or another person and earns a commission **Kommissionär**
(b) business of buying debts at a discount **Factoring; factoring charges** = cost of selling debts to a factor for a commission **Factoring-Gebühren**

fad *noun* short-lived fashion or craze **Mode(torheit), Marotte**

fair
1 *noun* **trade fair** = large exhibition and meeting for advertising and selling a certain type of product **Handels-, Fachmesse;** *to organize or to run a trade fair; the fair is open from 9 a.m. to 5 p.m.; the computer fair runs from April 1st to 6th; there are two trade fairs running in London at the same time - the carpet manufacturers' and the computer dealers'*
2 *adjective* honest *or* correct **gerecht, fair; fair deal** = arrangement where both parties are treated equally **faire Abmachung;** *the workers feel they did not get a fair deal from the management;* **fair dealing** = legal buying and selling of shares **geordneter Effektenhandel; fair price** = good price for both buyer and seller **angemessener Preis; fair trade** = (i) international business system whereby countries agree not to

charge import duties on certain items imported from their trading partners; (ii); *US* = RESALE PRICE MAINTENANCE **(i) Nichtdiskriminierung im Außenhandel; fair trading** *or* **fair dealing** = way of doing business which is reasonable and does not harm the consumer **lauterer Wettbewerb;** *(GB)* **Office of Fair Trading (OFT)** = government department which protects consumers against unfair or illegal business **Amt für Verbraucherschutz; fair wear and tear** = acceptable damage caused by normal use **normale Abnutzungs- und Verschleißerscheinungen;** *the insurance policy covers most damage, but not fair wear and tear to the machine*

fall

1 *noun* sudden drop *or* suddenly becoming smaller *or* loss of value **Sinken, Fallen;** *a fall in the exchange rate; fall in the price of gold; a fall on the Stock Exchange; profits showed a 10% fall*

2 *verb*

(a) to drop suddenly to a lower price **sinken, fallen;** *shares fell on the market today; gold shares fell 10% or fell 45 cents on the Stock Exchange; the price of gold fell for the second day running; the pound fell against other European currencies*

(b) to happen *or* to take place **fallen, liegen;** *the public holiday falls on a Tuesday;* **payments which fall due** = payments which are now due to be made **fällige Zahlungen**

◇ **fall away** *verb* to become less **zurückgehen, abnehmen, sinken;** *hotel bookings have fallen away since the tourist season ended*

◇ **fall back** *verb* to become lower or cheaper after rising in price **erneut sinken;** *shares fell back in light trading*

◇ **fall back on** *verb* to have to use money kept for emergencies **zurückgreifen auf;** *to fall back on cash reserves*

◇ **fall-back price** *noun* lowest price which a seller will accept **Mindest-, Vorbehaltspreis;** *the buyer tries to guess the seller's fall-back price; the fall-back price must not be any lower or there won't be any profit in the deal*

◇ **fall behind** *verb* to be late in doing something **in Rückstand/Verzug geraten;** *he fell behind with his mortgage repayments*

◇ **fall guy** *noun (US)* person who tends to be deceived in business deals **(der) Hereingefallene, leichte Beute; Sündenbock;** *he was the fall guy in a complicated Stock Exchange swindle*

◇ **falling** *adjective* which is growing smaller *or* dropping in price **fallend, sinkend, abnehmend; a falling market** = market where prices are coming down **Baissemarkt; the falling pound** = the pound which is losing its value against other currencies **das an Wert verlierende Pfund**

◇ **fall off** *verb* to become lower *or* cheaper *or* less **zurückgehen, abnehmen, fallen;** *sales have fallen off since the tourist season ended*

◇ **fall out** *verb* **the bottom has fallen out of the market** = sales have fallen below what previously seemed to be their lowest point **die Preise sind ins Bodenlose gesunken**

◇ **fall through** *verb* not to happen *or* not to take place **fehlschlagen, mißlingen, scheitern;** *the plan fell through at the last moment*

> QUOTE market analysts described the falls in the second half of last week as a technical correction to the market
>
> *Australian Financial Review*
>
> QUOTE for the first time since mortgage rates began falling in March a financial institution has raised charges on homeowner loans
>
> *Globe and Mail (Toronto)*
>
> QUOTE falling profitability means falling share prices
>
> *Investors Chronicle*

false *adjective* not true *or* not correct **falsch, unrichtig;** *to make a false entry in the balance sheet;* **false claim** = untrue or exaggerated claim made in the advertising of a product **falsche Angabe;** *a voluntary control body was set up to discourage false claims in the advertising business;* **false pretences** = doing or saying something to cheat someone **Vorspiegelung falscher Tatsachen;** *he was sent to prison for obtaining money by false pretences;* **false weight** = weight on shop scales which is wrong and so cheats customers **falsches Gewicht**

◇ **falsify** *verb* to change something to make it wrong **fälschen;** *to falsify the accounts*

◇ **falsification** *noun* action of making false entries in accounts **Verfälschung, Fälschung**

family *noun*

(a) group of products which are linked by a brand name or by their packaging **Markenfamilie; family branding** = selling a variety of different products under the same brand name **Markenfamilienverkauf; family packaging** = selling a whole range of products in similar packaging **Produktgruppenverpackung;** *we hope that family packaging will make for a clear company image*

(b) group of people, formed of parents and children **Familie; family life cycle** = stages through which a consumer passes in his or her life, such as "young marrieds", or "retired", which correspond to different types of buying behaviour **Familien-Lebenszyklus**

fancy *adjective*
(a) fancy goods = small attractive items **Modeartikel**
(b) fancy prices = high prices **Phantasiepreise;** *I don't want to pay the fancy prices they ask in London shops*

fascia *noun* (i) board over a shop on which the name of the shop is written; (ii) board above an exhibition stand on which the name of the company represented can be put **(i) Ladenschild; (ii) Firmenschild**

fast *adjective & adverb* quick *or* quickly **schnell;** *the train is the fastest way of getting to our supplier's factory; home computers sell fast in the pre-Christmas period;* **fast food** = food that can be cooked and sold quickly to customers, often the subject of franchises (such as hamburgers and hot dogs) **Schnellimbiß**
◇ **fast-moving** *or* **fast-selling** *adjective* **fast-selling items** = items which sell fast **schnellverkäufliche Artikel, Artikel mit reißendem Absatz, Selbstläufer;** *dictionaries are not fast-moving stock;* **fast-moving consumer goods (FMCG)** = essential low-price goods which get repeat sales **schnellverkäufliche Konsumgüter;** *he couldn't work in FMCG because his only experience was in industrial selling*

fax
1 *noun* facsimile copy, send via the telephone lines **Fax, Telefax;** *we have received a fax of the design from our advertising agent*
2 *verb* to send a facsimile copy via the telephone **faxen, telefaxen;** *ask the agent to fax us the details of the product launch*

feasibility study *noun* careful investigation of a project to see whether it is worth undertaking **Durchführbarkeitsstudie;** *we will carry out a feasibility study to decide whether it is worth setting up an agency in North America*

feature *noun* article in a newspaper *or* magazine that deals with one subject in depth **Sonderbericht; Feuilletonartikel;** *there is a feature in the next issue describing the history of our company*

feed *verb* to give information *or* tips to another salesman, regarding promising customers or areas for sales **(Material) zuführen;** *I can feed you some interesting sales leads*
◇ **feedback** *noun* information about the results of an activity or a product, that is received by the originator from the sales force or from customers' reactions **Reaktion, Resonanz, Feedback;** *we are getting plenty of negative feedback about our after-sales service; it would be useful to have some feedback from people who had a test drive but didn't buy the car; are we getting any feedback on customer reaction to our new product from the salesmen in the field? have you any feedback from the sales force about customers' reactions to the new model?*

> QUOTE the service is particularly useful when we are working in a crisis management area and we need fast feedback from consumers
> *PR Week*

field *noun* **in the field** = outside the office *or* among the customers **im Außendienst;** *we have sixteen reps in the field;* **to be first in the field** = first company to bring out a product *or* to start a service **etwas als Erster auf den Markt bringen, führend sein;** *Smith Ltd has a great advantage in being first in the field with a reliable electric car;* **field research** *or* **fieldwork** = looking for information that is not yet published and must be obtained in surveys **Feldforschung;** *they had to do a lot of fieldwork before they found the right market for the product; field research is carried out to gauge potential demand;* **field sales force** = salesmen working outside the company's offices, in the field **Außendienstverkaufspersonal;** *the field sales force operates in three main areas; after working for a year in the field sales force, he became field sales manager;* **field sales manager** = manager in charge of a group of salesmen **Außendienstleiter;**

filler *noun*
(a) something which fills a space **Füller, Lückenfüller; stocking filler** = small item which can be used to put into a Christmas stocking **kleines Geschenk für den Weihnachtsstrumpf;** *see also* SHELF FILLER
(b) advertisement used by an editor to fill space in a publication **Füller, Füllanzeige**

filter question *noun* question in a questionnaire designed to separate respondents who are worth questioning further from those who are not **Filterfrage**

finance
1 *noun*
(a) money used by a company, provided by the shareholders or by loans **finanzielle Mittel, Kapital;** *where will they get the necessary finance for the project?;* **finance company** *or* **finance corporation** *or* **finance house** = company which provides money for hire-purchase **Finanzierungsgesellschaft; finance market** = place where large sums of money can be lent or borrowed **Finanzmarkt; high finance** = lending, investing and

borrowing of very large sums of money, organized by financiers **Hochfinanz**
(b) **finance department** *or* **finance committee** = department *or* committee which manages the money used in an organization **Finanzabteilung; Finanzausschuß**
(c) **finances** = money *or* cash which is available **Finanzenmittel;** *the company's finances are in a bad way*
2 *verb* to provide money to pay for something **finanzieren;** *to finance an operation*

◇ **Finance Act** *noun (GB)* annual Act of Parliament which gives the government the power to obtain money from taxes as proposed in the Budget **Finanzgesetz**

◇ **financial** *adjective* concerning money **finanziell, Finanz-; financial advertising** = advertising by companies in the field of financial investment **Finanzwerbung; financial adviser** = person *or* company which gives advice on financial matters for a fee **Finanzberater; financial assistance** = help in the form of money **Finanzhilfe; financial correspondent** = journalist who writes articles on money matters for a newspaper **Wirtschaftskorrespondent; financial position** = state of a company's *or* person's bank balance (assets and debts) **Finanzlage;** *he must think of his financial position;* **financial resources** = money which is available for investment **finanzielle Mittel;** *a company with strong financial resources;* **financial risk** = possibility of losing money **finanzielles Risiko;** *there is no financial risk in selling to East European countries on credit;* **financial statement** = document which shows the financial situation of a company **Finanzbericht;** *the accounts department has prepared a financial statement for the shareholders;* **Financial Times (Ordinary) index** = index published by the "Financial Times", giving share prices on the London Stock Exchange based on a group of major companies **Aktienindex der Financial Times; financial year** = the twelve months' period for a firm's accounts **Rechnungs-, Geschäftsjahr**

◇ **financially** *adverb* regarding money **finanziell, finanz-; company which is financially sound** = company which is profitable and has strong assets **die Firma ist finanziell gesund/finanzkräftig**

◇ **financier** *noun* person who lends large amounts of money to companies **Financier, Geldgeber**

◇ **financing** *noun* providing money **Finanzierung;** *the financing of the project was done by two international banks;* **deficit financing** = planning by a government to borrow money to cover the shortfall between expenditure and income from taxation **Defizitwirtschaft**

fire-fight *verb* to fight bad publicity (for a client) **schlechte Publicity bekämpfen;** *the agency has done fire-fighting work for the egg producers*

firm
1 *noun* business *or* partnership **Firma; Unternehmen;** *he is a partner in a law firm; a manufacturing firm; an important publishing firm*
2 *adjective*
(a) which cannot be changed **stabil, fest, beständig, verbindlich;** *to make a firm offer for something; to place a firm offer for two aircraft; they are quoting a firm price of £1.22 per unit*
(b) not dropping in price, and possibly going to rise **stabil, fest, beständig;** *sterling was firmer on the foreign exchange markets; shares remained firm*
3 *verb* to remain at a price and seem likely to go up **sich festigen;** *the shares firmed at £1.50*

first-hand *adjective*
(a) coming directly from the original source **aus erster Hand; first-hand information** = information from an original source **Information aus erster Hand;** *we had a first-hand account of what happened at the sales meeting from one of the salesmen who was there*
(b) new *or* unused **aus erster Hand, nagelneu;** *I actually bought the TV first-hand, but at a second-hand price*

first-line management *noun* the managers who have immediate contact with the workers **unterste Leitungsebene**

fishy-back freight *noun (US)* transportation of trucks or freight train cars on ferries or barges **Straßen-Wasser-Transport; Trajektfracht**

fix *verb*
(a) to arrange *or* to agree **beschließen; festlegen, festsetzen;** *to fix a budget; to fix a meeting for 3 p.m.; the date has still to be fixed; the price of gold was fixed at $300; the mortgage rate has been fixed at 11%*
(b) to mend **in Ordnung bringen, reparieren;** *the technicians are coming to fix the telephone switchboard; can you fix the photocopier?*
◇ **fixed** *adjective* permanent *or* which cannot be removed **fest, Fest-, gebunden; fixed assets** = property *or* machinery which a company owns and uses **Anlagevermögen;**

fixed break = insistence by an advertiser on having a television or radio advertisement placed in a specific commercial break on a specific day **feste Werbesendungplazierung; fixed costs** = costs paid to produce a product which do not increase with the amount of product made (such as rent) **Fixkosten; Gemeinkosten; fixed expenses** = money which is spent regularly (such as rent, electricity, telephone, etc.) **Fixkosten; fixed position** = placing of an advertisement in a specific location in a publication, or running a commercial at a fixed time of day, at the advertiser's insistence **feste Anzeigenplazierung; feste Werbesendungplazierung; fixed-price agreement** = agreement where a company provides a service *or* a product at a price which stays the same for the whole period of the agreement **Festpreisvereinbarung; fixed scale of charges** = rate of charging which cannot be altered **verbindliche Gebührenordnung; fixed spot** = insistence by an advertiser on having a TV or radio commercial placed in a specific position **feste Werbesendungplazierung**

◇ **fixing** *noun*
(a) arranging **Festsetzung, Festlegung;** *fixing of charges; fixing of a mortgage rate*
(b) price fixing = illegal agreement between companies to charge the same price for competing products **Preisabsprache**
(c) the London gold fixing = system where the world price for gold is set each day in London **London Gold Fixing**

> QUOTE coupons are fixed by reference to interest rates at the time a gilt is first issued
> *Investors Chronicle*
>
> QUOTE you must offer shippers and importers fixed rates over a reasonable period of time
> *Lloyd's List*

flagship *noun* key product in a range, the product on which the reputation of the producer most depends **Flagschiff, Verkaufsschlager**

flash pack *noun* pack or package which shows a price reduction very clearly in order to attract customers **Sonderpreisverpackung, Eyecatcher;** *flash packs are displayed at eye-level on the supermarket shelves to attract the attention of passing customers*

flat rate *noun*
(a) charge which always remains the same **Pauschalpreis, Einheitssatz;** *we pay a flat rate for electricity each quarter; he is paid a flat rate of $2.50 per thousand*
(b) normal charge for advertising space, without allowing for discounts **Grundpreis, Einzelwerbepreis**

flea market *noun* market for secondhand goods (often held outdoors) **Flohmarkt**

flier *noun* promotional leaflet **Flugblatt, Werbezettel, Flyer**

flood
1 *noun* large quantity **Flut, Strom;** *we received a flood of orders; floods of tourists filled the hotels*
2 *verb* to fill with a large quantity of something **überschwemmen;** *the market was flooded with cheap imitations; the sales department is flooded with orders or with complaints*

floor *noun*
(a) part of the room which you walk on **Fußboden, Boden; floor space** = area of floor in an office *or* warehouse **Grund-, Bodenfläche;** *we have 3,500 square metres of floor space to let;* **floor stand** = display stand which stands on the floor, as opposed to one which stands on a table or counter **Bodenverkaufsständer**
(b) all rooms on one level in a building **Stockwerk, Etage;** *the shoe department is on the first floor; her office is on the 26th floor; (US)* **floor manager** = person in charge of the sales staff in a department store **Abteilungsleiter**

◇ **floorwalker** *noun* employee of a department store who advises the customers, and supervises the shop assistants in a department **Ladenaufsicht**

flop
1 *noun* failure *or* thing which has not been successful **Reinfall, Flop, Pleite;** *the new model was a flop*
2 *verb* to fail *or* not to be a success **ein Reinfall/Flop/eine Pleite sein;** *the launch of the new shampoo flopped badly*

flow chart *or* **flow diagram** *noun* diagram which shows the sequence of steps in a procedure *or* production process **Arbeitsablauf-, Flußdiagramm**

fluidity *noun* being able to move easily **Beweglichkeit, Mobilität; fluidity of labour** = extent to which workers move from one place to another to work or from one occupation to another **Freizügigkeit von Arbeitskräften**

fly poster *noun* poster which is pasted to a site without permission and without making any payment **wilder Anschlag, unerlaubter Plakatanschlag**

◇ **fly-posting** *noun* sticking posters up illegally, without permission of the site owner and without making any payment **Wildanschlag, wilde Plakatierung**

FMCG = FAST-MOVING CONSUMER GOODS

FOB *or* **f.o.b.** = FREE ON BOARD

focus group survey *noun* survey method in which a sample of people are asked to discuss some issue freely among themselves **Gruppendiskussion**

fold-out *noun* folded page in a publication, which opens out to show a much larger advertisement **Faltseite, Faltanzeige**

follow *verb* to come behind *or* to come afterwards **folgen;** *the samples will follow by surface mail; we'll pay £10,000 down, with the balance to follow in six months*

◇ **follower** *noun* company which follows others into a market **Marktfolger; market follower strategy** = strategy of a company which does not directly challenge the market leaders, but benefits from their innovations and gains a profitable corner of the market **Marktfolgerstrategie**

◇ **following reading matter** *adjective* good position for an advertisement, which follows an interesting article in a newspaper *or* magazine **textanschließend**

◇ **follow up** *verb* to examine something further **nachgehen; nachfassen;** *I'll follow up your idea of putting our address list on to the computer;* **to follow up an initiative** = to take action once someone else has decided to do something **eine Initiative aufgreifen**

◇ **follow-up letter** *noun* letter sent to someone who has not acted on the instructions in a previous letter, or to discuss in more detail points which were raised earlier **Nachfaß-, Folgeschreiben**

force

1 *noun*

(a) strength **Kraft; to be in force** = to be operating *or* working **in Kraft sein;** *the rules have been in force since 1946;* **to come into force** = to start to operate *or* work **in Kraft treten;** *the new regulations will come into force on January 1st*

(b) labour force *or* **workforce** = all the workers in a company *or* in an area **Belegschaft; Arbeitskräfte, Arbeiterschaft;** *the management has made an increased offer to the labour force; we are opening a new factory in the Far East because of the cheap local labour force;* **sales force** = group of salesmen **Verkaufspersonal, Verkäuferstab**

(c) force majeure = something which happens which is out of the control of the parties who have signed a contract (such as a strike, war, storm, etc.) **höhere Gewalt**

2 *verb* to make someone do something **zwingen;** *competition has forced the company to lower its prices*

◇ **forced** *adjective* **forced consumption** = attempt to impose a rate or type of consumption on consumers **Konsumzwang; forced sale** = sale which takes place because a court orders it *or* because it is the only way to avoid a financial crisis **Zwangs-, Notverkauf**

◇ **force down** *verb* to make something become lower **drücken; to force prices down** = to make prices come down **die Preise drücken;** *competition has forced prices down*

◇ **force up** *verb* to make something become higher **hochtreiben; to force prices up** = to make prices go up **die Preise hochtreiben;** *the war forced up the price of oil*

forecast

1 *noun* description *or* calculation of what will probably happen in the future **Prognose, Voraussage, Vorausberechnung;** *the chairman did not believe the sales director's forecast of higher turnover; we based our calculations on the forecast turnover;* **cash flow forecast** = forecast of when cash will be received or paid out **Cashflow-Prognose; population forecast** = calculation of how many people will be living in a country *or* in a town at some point in the future **Prognose über die Bevölkerungszahlen; sales forecast** = calculation of future sales **Absatzprognose**

2 *verb* to calculate *or* to say what will probably happen in the future **voraussagen, prognostizieren;** *he is forecasting sales of £2m; economists have forecast a fall in the exchange rate*

◇ **forecasting** *noun* calculating what will probably happen in the future **Voraussage, Prognose; judgement forecasting** = forecasting which is done on judgement, rather than by following any scientific technique **intuitive Prognoseverfahren; manpower forecasting** = calculating how many workers will be needed in the future, and how many will actually be available **Personalbestandsprognose**

foreign *adjective* not belonging to one's own country **ausländisch, Auslands-;** *foreign cars have flooded our market; we are increasing our trade with foreign countries;* **foreign currency** = money of another country **Devisen, Fremdwährung; foreign goods** = goods manufactured in other countries **Auslandswaren; foreign**

investments = money invested in other countries **Auslandsinvestitionen; foreign money order** = money order in a foreign currency which is payable to someone living in a foreign country **Auslandszahlungsanweisung; foreign trade** = trade with other countries **Außenhandel**

◇ **foreign exchange** *noun* (i) exchanging the money of one country for that of another; (ii) money of another country **(i) Devisenhandel; (ii) Devisen; foreign exchange broker** *or* **dealer** = person who deals on the foreign exchange market **Devisenhändler, Devisenmakler; foreign exchange dealing** = buying and selling foreign currencies **Devisenhandel; the foreign exchange market** = market where people buy and sell foreign currencies **der Devisenmarkt; foreign exchange reserves** = foreign money held by a government to support its own currency and pay its debts **Devisenreserven; foreign exchange transfer** = sending of money from one country to another **Devisentransfer**

◇ **foreigner** *noun* person from another country **Ausländer/-in**

> QUOTE the dollar recovered a little lost ground on the foreign exchanges yesterday
> *Financial Times*
>
> QUOTE a sharp setback in foreign trade accounted for most of the winter slowdown
> *Fortune*
>
> QUOTE the treasury says it needs the cash to rebuild its foreign reserves which have fallen from $19 billion when the government took office to $7 billion in August
> *Economist*

forex *or* Forex = FOREIGN EXCHANGE

> QUOTE the amount of reserves sold by the authorities were not sufficient to move the $200 billion Forex market permanently
> *Duns Business Month*

forfeit

1 *noun* taking something away as a punishment **Verfall, Verwirkung; forfeit clause** = clause in a contract which says that goods *or* deposit will be taken away if the contract is not obeyed **Verfallsklausel; the goods were declared forfeit** = the court said that the goods had to be taken away from their owner **die Waren wurden für verlustig erklärt**

2 *verb* to have something taken away as a punishment **verwirken; konfiszieren; to forfeit a patent** = to lose a patent because payments have not been made **ein Patent verfallen lassen; to forfeit a deposit** = to lose a deposit which was left for an item because you have decided not to buy that item **eine Anzahlung verwirken/einbüßen**

◇ **forfeiture** *noun* act of forfeiting a property **Konfiskation; Verwirkung**

fork-lift truck

noun type of small tractor, with two metal arms in front, used for lifting and moving pallets **Gabelstapler**

form *noun*

(a) form of words = words correctly laid out for a legal document **Form; Formulierung; receipt in due form** = correctly written receipt **ordnungsgemäße Quittung**

(b) official printed paper with blank spaces which have to be filled in with information **Formular, Vordruck;** *the reps carry pads of order forms;* **application form** = form which has to be filled in to apply for something **Antragsformular; Bewerbungsformular; claim form** = form which has to be filled in when making an insurance claim **Schadensformular**

◇ **form utility** *noun* use for a product created by the introduction of the product **Gebrauchsnutzen**

forma *see* PRO FORMA

format

noun general page design of a publication; the page size of a publication **Format**

forty-eight sheet

noun large poster-sized sheet of paper **Achtundvierzigerformat**

forward

1 *adjective* in advance *or* to be paid at a later date **im voraus, Voraus-; forward buying** *or* **buying forward** = buying shares *or* currency *or* commodities at today's price for delivery at a later date **Terminkauf; forward contract** = agreement to buy foreign currency *or* shares *or* commodities for delivery at a later date at a certain price **Abschluß auf Termin; forward integration** = expansion of a business by becoming its own distributor (as opposed to backward integration, where the company expands by becoming its own supplier) **Vorwärtsintegration;** *forward integration will give the company greater control over its selling; forward integration has brought the company closer to its consumers and has made it aware of their buying habits;* **forward market** = market for purchasing foreign currency *or* oil *or* commodities for delivery at a later date **Terminmarkt; forward price** = price of goods which are to be delivered in the future **Terminkurs; forward (exchange) rate** = rate for purchase of foreign currency at a fixed price for delivery at a later date **Devisenterminkurs;** *what are the forward rates for the pound?;* **forward sales** = sales for delivery at a later date **Terminverkäufe**

2 *adverb*

(a) to date a cheque forward = to put a later

date than the present one on a cheque **einen Scheck vordatieren; carriage forward** *or* **freight forward** = deal where the customer pays for transporting the goods **Frachtnachnahme; charges forward** = charges which will be paid by the customer **Gebühr bezahlt Empfänger**
(b) to buy forward = to buy foreign currency before you need it, in order to be certain of the exchange rate **auf Termin kaufen; to sell forward** = to sell foreign currency for delivery at a later date **auf Termin verkaufen**
(c) balance brought forward *or* **carried forward** = balance which is entered in an account at the end of a period and is then taken to be the starting point of the next period **Saldovortrag**
3 *verb* **to forward something to someone** = to send something to someone **jdm etwas nachsenden;** *to forward a consignment to Nigeria;* **please forward** *or* **to be forwarded** = words written on an envelope, asking the person receiving it to send it on to the person whose name is written on it **bitte nachsenden**

◇ **(freight) forwarder** *noun* person *or* company which arranges shipping and customs documents for several shipments from different companies, putting them together to form one large shipment **Spediteur; Spedition**

◇ **forwarding** *noun*
(a) arranging shipping and customs documents **Spedition; Abfertigung; air forwarding** = arranging for goods to be shipped by air **Luftfrachtspedition; forwarding agent** = FORWARDER; **forwarding instructions** *or* **instructions for forwarding** = instructions showing how the goods are to be shipped and delivered **Versandanweisungen**
(b) forwarding address = address to which a person's mail can be sent on **Nachsendeadresse**

foul *adjective* **foul bill of lading** = bill of lading which says that the goods were in bad condition when received by the shipper **unreines Konnossement**

four four-colour process = printing process where the three primary colours and black are used to create a wide range of shades **Vierfarbendruck; four O's** = simple compact way of summarizing the essentials of a marketing operation, which are objects, objectives, organization and operations **Gedächtnisstütze für das Wichtigste einer Marketingoperation;** *business school students learn the four O's as a simple way of remembering key points in strategy;* **four P's** = simple compact way of summarizing the essentials of the marketing mix, which are product, price, promotion and place; *(entspricht)* **die vier Elemente des Marketing-Mix; four-plus cover** = situation where consumers in the target audience will have seen an advertisement at least four times on average **mehr als vier Kontakte**

fraction *noun* part of a whole **Bruchteil; sampling fraction** = the proportion of a population that is chosen as a sample **Stichprobenumfang**

fragile *adjective* which can be easily broken **zerbrechlich;** *there is an extra premium for insuring fragile goods in shipment*

fragment *verb* to split into sections **auf-, zersplittern; fragmentieren; fragmented market** = market which is split into many small segments, which are more difficult to sell into **Marktsegmentierung**

◇ **fragmentation** *noun* using a variety of media for a publicity campaign **Zersplitterung der Werbekampagne**

> QUOTE the consumer market is fragmenting, which means that brand advertising to the whole market is no longer enough
> *Financial Times*

frame *see* SAMPLING FRAME

franchise
1 *noun* licence to trade using a brand name and paying a royalty for it **Franchise;** *he's bought a printing franchise or a hot dog franchise*
2 *verb* to sell licences for people to trade using a brand name and paying a royalty **auf Franchise-Basis vergeben;** *his sandwich bar was so successful that he decided to franchise it*

◇ **franchisee** *noun* person who runs a franchise **Franchise-Nehmer**

◇ **franchiser** *noun* person who licenses a franchise **Franchise-Geber**

◇ **franchising** *noun* act of selling a licence to trade as a franchise **Franchising;** *he runs his sandwich chain as a franchising operation*

◇ **franchisor** *noun* = FRANCHISER

> QUOTE a quarter of a million Britons are seeking to become their own bosses by purchasing franchises
> *Marketing Week*
> QUOTE feelings are already running high over the question of how to allocate the next TV franchises
> *Marketing*

franco *adverb* free **frei**

fraudulent misrepresentation *noun* making a false statement with the intention of tricking a customer **arglistige Täuschung**

free
1 *adjective & adverb*
(a) not costing any money **kostenlos, gratis, Frei-;** *to be given a free ticket to the exhibition; the price includes free delivery; goods are delivered free; catalogue sent free on request;* **carriage free** = the customer does not pay for the shipping **frachtfrei; free alongside ship** = price that includes all costs up to delivery of goods next to the ship on the quay **frei Längsseite See-, Binnenschiff; free advertisement** = advertisement shown without any charge to the advertiser **Gratisanzeige;** *the newspaper agreed to place a free advertisement for the charity on the back page;* **free delivery area** = area within which a seller will deliver purchases free **Freihauslieferungszone;** *the total price will be low as the goods are being delivered in a free delivery area;* **free docks** = price that includes all costs up to delivery of goods to the docks **frei Dock; free gift** = present received by a customer, either attached to a product bought or given to him by the retailer or producer on proof of purchase of a minimum quantity of goods **Werbegeschenk;** *there is a free gift worth £25 to any customer buying a washing machine;* **free sample** = sample given free in order to advertise a product **Gratisprobe; free trial** = testing of a machine with no payment involved **kostenlos zur Probe;** *to send a piece of equipment for two weeks' free trial;* **free of charge** = with no payment to be made **kostenlos; free on board (f.o.b.)** = (i) price including all the seller's costs until the goods are on the ship for transportation; (ii); *US* price includes all the seller's costs until the goods are delivered to a certain place **(i) f.o.b., frei an Bord; (ii) f.o.b. einschließlich Fracht; free on quay** = price that includes all costs up to delivery of goods next to the ship on the quay **frei Kai; free on rail** = price including all the seller's costs until the goods are delivered to the railway for shipment **frei Bahn; free overboard** *or* **free overside** = price that includes all costs up to arrival of the ship at a port **frei Überbord**
(b) with no restrictions **frei, unabhängig; free competition** = being free to compete without government interference **freier Wettbewerb, Wettbewerbsfreiheit; free currency** = currency which is allowed by the government to be bought and sold without restriction **frei konvertierbare Währung; free enterprise** = system of business with no interference from the government **freies Unternehmertum; free market economy** = system where the government does not interfere in business activity in any way **freie Marktwirtschaft; free port** *or* **free trade zone** = port *or* area where there are no customs duties **Freihafen; Freihandelszone; free of tax** *or* **tax-free** = with no tax having to be paid **steuerfrei;** *he was given a tax-free sum of £25,000 when he was made redundant; interest free of tax or tax-free interest;* **interest-free credit** *or* **loan** = credit *or* loan where no interest is paid by the borrower **zinsloses Darlehen; free of duty** *or* **duty-free** = with no duty to be paid **zollfrei;** *to import wine free of duty or duty-free;* **free trade** = system where goods can go from one country to another without any restrictions **Freihandel;** *the government adopted a free trade policy;* **free trade area** = group of countries practising free trade **Freihandelszone; free trader** = person who is in favour of free trade **Befürworter des Freihandels**
(c) not busy *or* not occupied **frei; unbesetzt;** *are there any free tables in the restaurant? I shall be free in a few minutes; the chairman always keeps Friday afternoon free for a game of bridge*
2 *verb* to make something available *or* easy **flüssigmachen;** *the government's decision has freed millions of pounds for investment*

> QUOTE American business as a whole is increasingly free from heavy dependence on manufacturing
> *Sunday Times*
>
> QUOTE can free trade be reconciled with a strong dollar resulting from floating exchange rates?
> *Duns Business Month*
>
> QUOTE free traders hold that the strong dollar is the primary cause of the nation's trade problems
> *Duns Business Month*

freebie *noun (informal)* product *or* service supplied free of charge (especially a gift to an agent or journalist) **Gratisprobe, Gratisangebot**

freefone *or* **freephone** *noun (GB)* system where one can telephone to reply to an advertisement *or* to place an order *or* to ask for information and the seller pays for the call; *(entspricht)* **SERVICE 130;** *the company included their Freefone number in the advertisement*

◇ **freepost** *noun (GB)* system where one can write to an advertiser to place an order *or* to ask for information to be sent, without paying for a stamp, the company paying for the postage on receipt of the envelope **Gebühr bezahlt Empfänger**

freesheet *noun* local weekly newspaper or magazine which is distributed free of charge and which contains a lot of advertising (which is the source of its revenue) **Anzeigenblatt, Stadtteilzeitung;** *we can use the freesheet and the local evening paper to advertise the shop in the area*

freeze

1 *noun* **credit freeze** = period when lending by banks is restricted by the government **Einfrieren von Krediten; wages and prices freeze** *or* **a freeze on wages and prices** = period when wages and prices are not allowed to be increased **Lohn- und Preisstopp**
2 *verb* to keep money *or* costs, etc. at their present levels and not allow them to rise **einfrieren;** *we have frozen expenditure at last year's level; to freeze wages and prices; to freeze credits; to freeze company dividends*

◇ **freeze out** *verb* **to freeze out competition** = to trade successfully and cheaply and so prevent competitors from operating **Konkurrenz verdrängen**

freight

1 *noun*
(a) cost of transporting goods by air, sea or land **Frachtgebühren;** *at an auction, the buyer pays the freight;* **freight charges** *or* **freight rates** = money charged for transporting goods **Frachtgebühren;** *freight charges have gone up sharply this year; (US)* **freight collect** *or* **freight forward** = arrangement whereby the customer pays for transporting the goods **Frachtnachnahme; freight costs** = money paid to transport goods **Transport-, Frachtkosten;**
(b) air freight = shipping of goods in an aircraft **Luftfracht;** *to send a shipment by air freight;* **air freight charges** *or* **rates** = money charged for sending goods by air **Luftfrachtgebühren**
(c) goods which are transported **Frachtgut to take on freight** = to load goods onto a ship, train or truck **Fracht aufnehmen/aufladen;** *(US)* **freight car** = railway wagon for carrying goods **Güterwagen, Waggon; freight depot** = central point where goods are collected before being shipped **Güterdepot; freight elevator** = strong lift for carrying goods **Warenaufzug; freight plane** = aircraft which carries goods, not passengers **Transportflugzeug; freight train** = train used for carrying goods **Güterzug**
2 *verb* **to freight goods** = to send goods **verfrachten;** *we freight goods to all parts of the USA*

◇ **freightage** *noun* cost of transporting goods **Frachtkosten**

◇ **freighter** *noun*
(a) aircraft or ship which carries goods **Transportflugzeug; Frachter**
(b) person *or* company which organizes the transport of goods **Befrachter**

◇ **freightliner** *noun* train which carries goods in containers **Containerzug;** *the shipment has to be delivered to the freightliner depot*

frequency

noun (i) number of times an advertisement appears in a specific period; (ii) number of times a person sees an advertisement during a campaign (as opposed to the reach, which is the number of people who see the advertisement once) **(i) Insertionshäufigkeit; (ii) Kontakthäufigkeit;** *the plan is to have larger advertisements but less frequency; we feel that a frequency of two showings per night is enough for the first week of the campaign;* **call frequency** = the number of times a salesman visits a particular customer during a certain period **Besuchshäufigkeit**

◇ **frequent** *adjective* which comes *or* goes *or* takes place often **häufig;** *there is a frequent ferry service to France; we send frequent telexes to New York; how frequent are the planes to Birmingham?*

◇ **frequently** *adverb* often **oft, häufig;** *the photocopier is frequently out of order; we telex our New York office very frequently - at least four times a day*

fringe accounts

noun accounts *or* customers that are not very profitable for the supplier **Sekundärkunden;** *the salesmen are not giving priority to these fringe accounts; it is hoped that some of these fringe accounts will soon start buying in larger quantities*

◇ **fringe benefits** *plural noun* extra items given by a company to workers in addition to a salary (such as company cars, private health insurance) **Leistungsanreize für Arbeitnehmer**

front

noun
(a) part of something which faces away from the back **Fassade, Vorderseite;** *the front of the office building is on the High Street; there is a photograph of the managing director on the front page of the company report; our ad appeared on the front page of the newspaper;* **front of book** = the first few pages of a magazine **Titelei; Anzeigenposition im Heftanfang; front cover** = front outside page of a publication (as opposed to the back cover) **Umschlagseite eins; inside front cover** = the advertising page on the inside of the front cover of a magazine **Umschlagseite zwei;** *even advertising on the front covers of national newspapers seems to have no effect on sales of this product*

(b) business or person used to hide an illegal trade **Tarnung; Strohmann;** *his restaurant is a front for a drugs organization*
(c) money up front = payment in advance **Vorauszahlung;** *they are asking for £10,000 up front before they will consider the deal; he had to put money up front before he could clinch the deal*

◊ **frontload** *verb* to plan a publicity campaign where most costs are incurred in the early stages (as opposed to backload, where the costs are mainly incurred in the later stages of the campaign) **Werbebudget in der ersten Hälfte/am Anfang eine Werbeperiode ganz oder zum größeren Teil ausgeben**

◊ **front-line** *adjective* **front-line management** = managers who have immediate contact with the workers **Management, das direkten Kontakt zu den Arbeitern hat; unterste Leitungsebene**

◊ **front man** *noun* person who seems honest but is hiding an illegal trade **Strohmann**

fudge *noun* mistake made in an advertisement **Anzeigenfehler**

fulfil *or* *(US)* **fulfill** *verb* to complete something in a satisfactory way **erfüllen, ausführen;** *the clause regarding payments has not been fulfilled;* **to fulfil an order** = to supply the items which have been ordered **eine Bestellung ausführen;** *we are so understaffed that we can't fulfil any more orders before Christmas*

◊ **fulfilment** *noun* carrying something out in a satisfactory way **Erfüllung, Ausführung; order fulfilment** = supplying items which have been ordered **Auftragserfüllung**

full *adjective*
(a) complete *or* including everything **völlig, vollständig; we are working at full capacity** = we are doing as much work as possible **wir sind voll ausgelastet; full costs** = all the costs of manufacturing a product, including both fixed and variable costs **Vollkosten; full cost pricing** = pricing method based on assessing the full production cost of each product unit and adding a profit margin **Vollkostenpreiskalkulation; full cover** = insurance cover against all risks **voller Versicherungsschutz; in full discharge of a debt** = paying a debt completely **Schuldentilgung in voller Höhe; full employment** = situation where all the people able to work have jobs **Vollbeschäftigung; full price** = price with no discount **voller Preis; full rate** = advertising rate with no discount **Grundpreis; full service agency** = advertising agency offering a broader range of services than ordinary agencies, such as advice on sales promotion, public relations and market research **Full-Service-(Werbe)agentur;** *we have so little marketing expertise, we'll need a full service agency*
(b) in full = completely **voll, ganz, vollständig;** *give your full name and address or your name and address in full; he accepted all our conditions in full; full refund or refund paid in full; he got a full refund when he complained about the service;* **full payment** *or* **payment in full** = paying all money owed **Zahlung in voller Höhe**

◊ **full-function wholesaler** *noun* distributor performing all the normal functions of a wholesaler, such as storage and transport **Großhandelsunternehmen;** *we use the services of one full-function wholesaler in each of our main areas; there is room for only one full-function wholesaler dealing with this product in the Southampton area*

◊ **full-line forcing** *noun* situation where a supplier pressures a customer to buy a complete range of products, rather than just one item **Zwang zur Abnahme eines ganzen Sortiments;** *if the supplier succeeds in full-line forcing, he will probably raise prices*

◊ **full-scale** *adjective* complete *or* very thorough **total, umfassend;** *the MD ordered a full-scale review of credit terms*

◊ **full-time** *adjective & adverb* working all the normal working time (i.e. about eight hours a day, five days a week) **ganztägig, Ganztags-, hauptberuflich;** *she's in full-time work or she works full-time or she's in full-time employment; he is one of our full-time staff*

◊ **full-timer** *noun* person who works full-time **ganztägig Beschäftigte(r)**

function
1 *noun*
(a) duty *or* job **Funktion, Aufgabe; management function** *or* **function of management** = the duties of being a manager **Aufgaben der Betriebsleitung, Führungsfunktion**
(b) figure which can vary, depending on another figure **Funktion; response function** = figure which represents the value of a particular quantity of advertising impressions on a person **Reaktionsfunktion; Kontaktbewertungsfunktion**
2 *verb* to work **funktionieren;** *the advertising campaign is functioning smoothly; the new management structure does not seem to be functioning very well*

◊ **functional** *adjective* referring to a function **funktional; functional discount** =

discount offered on goods sold to distributors **Funktionsrabatt; Händler-, Wiederverkäuferrabatt; functional product differentiation** = ensuring that a product has some functional features that distinguish it from competing ones **funktionale Produktdifferenzierung**

future
1 *adjective* referring to time to come *or* to something which has not yet happened **zukünftig, Zukunfts-; future delivery** = delivery at a later date **Terminlieferung**
2 *noun* time which has not yet happened **Zukunft;** *try to be more careful in future; in future all reports must be sent to Australia by air*

◇ **futurology** *noun* prediction and study of future trends **Futurologie, Zukunftsforschung**

Gg

gable end *noun* end of a building which is used as a poster site **Giebel(spitze)**

gain
1 *noun*
(a) increase *or* becoming larger **Zuwachs, Zunahme; gain in experience** = becoming more experienced **Gewinn an Erfahrung; gain in profitability** = becoming more profitable **Rentabilitätssteigerung**
(b) increase in profit *or* price *or* value **Gewinn;** *oil shares showed gains on the Stock Exchange; as property values rose, speculators in the real-estate market made substantial gains;* **capital gains** = money made by selling a fixed asset **Veräußerungsgewinne; capital gains tax** = tax paid on capital gains **Veräußerungsgewinnsteuer; short-term gains** = gains made over a short period (less than 12 months) **rasch zu erzielende Gewinne**
2 *verb*
(a) to get *or* to obtain **erwerben, erlangen;** *he gained some useful experience working in a bank;* **to gain control of a business** = to buy more than 50% of the shares so that one can direct the business **die Aktienmehrheit an einem Unternehmen erlangen**
(b) to rise in value **steigen, an Wert gewinnen;** *the dollar gained six points on the foreign exchange markets*

galley *or* **galley proof** *noun* first proofs of typesetting, before the text is made up into pages **Druckfahne**

game theory *noun* principles, developed from business games, which relate to making the best choice from a number of possible strategies in various hypothetical situations where conflicting interests are involved **(handelsthematische) Spieltheorie**

gap *noun* empty space **Lücke; gap in the market** = opportunity to make a product which is needed but which no one has sold before **Marktlücke;** *to look for or to find a gap in the market; this computer has filled a real gap in the market;* **gap analysis** = analysis of a market to try to find a gap, or a particular area that is not at present being satisfied **Lückenanalyse;** *gap analysis showed that there was a whole area of the market we were not exploiting; the computer performed a gap analysis and came up with suggestions for a medium-priced machine suitable for the small business market;* **dollar gap** = situation where the supply of dollars is not enough to satisfy the demand for them from overseas buyers **Dollarlücke; trade gap** = difference in value between a country's imports and exports **Außenhandelsdefizit**

> QUOTE these savings are still not great enough to overcome the price gap between American products and those of other nations
> *Duns Business Month*

gatefold *noun* double page spread in which both pages are folded over, and which open out like a gate to give a spread of almost four pages **Fensterfalz, Altarfalz**

GATT = GENERAL AGREEMENT ON TARIFFS AND TRADE

GDP = GROSS DOMESTIC PRODUCT

general *adjective*
(a) the General Agreement on Tariffs and Trade = international organization which aims to try to reduce restrictions in trade between countries **Allgemeines Zoll- und Handelsabkommen**
(b) general cargo = cargo made up of various types of goods **gemischte Fracht, Stückgut;** *the ship left the port with a general cargo bound for various destinations;* *(US)* **general delivery** = post office service which receives parcels and letters for people and keeps them until they are claimed **Ausgabe postlagernder Sendungen;** *he received the mail-order items via general delivery; they use the general delivery since they do not have a business mailing address;* **general trading** = dealing in all types of goods **allgemeiner Handel; general store** = small

shop which sells a large range of goods **Gemischtwarenhandlung; general wholesaler** = wholesaler selling a variety of goods **allgemeiner Großhändler**

generation *noun* stage in the development of a product (each new generation is a new version of the product with certain technical improvements on the preceding version) **Entwicklungsstufe**

generic *noun* former brand name, now given to product rather than a particular brand (such as hoover or thermos) **generische Marke; Gattungsname; generic product** = product with no brand name **generisches Produkt, Gattungsmarke;** *generic products are cheap since they have no name to advertise; next to the brightly packaged branded goods the generic products on display were easily overlooked;* **generic term** = brand name which becomes the name of a type of product (such as Hoover for vacuum cleaner) **generische Marke; Gattungsbegriff**

geocentric stage *noun (US)* advanced stage in a company's international marketing when there is great co-ordination of overseas marketing activities **geozentrische Phase**

geographical *adjective* referring to a certain area **geographisch; geographical concentration** = degree to which consumers in a market are concentrated *or* dispersed in a country or area **geographische Konzentration;** *the number of salesmen needed will depend on the geographical concentration of the market; we only need one wholesaler because of the geographical concentration of the market;* **geographical segmentation** = dividing of a market according to areas or regions **geographische Marktsegmentierung**

gestation period *noun* period of time between the initial inquiry about a product and the placing of an order **Entstehungsperiode;** *the long gestation period is due to inefficient decision-making procedures in the buying company*

ghosting *or* **ghost view** *noun* showing a little of the product itself by removing a small part of the packaging **Innenansicht eines Produktes**

giant retailer *noun* very large retailing group like a department store or chain store **Warenkette, Warenkonzern**

gift token *or* **gift voucher** *noun* card that can be used to buy specified goods up to the value printed on it (often issued by chain stores, the person receiving the voucher being able to redeem it in any store in the chain) **Geschenkgutschein;** *the children each had a £10 gift voucher for Christmas*

gimmick *noun* clever idea *or* trick **Gimmick, Gag;** *a publicity gimmick; the PR men thought up this new advertising gimmick*

giro *noun* **bank giro** *or* **the giro system** = banking system in which money can be transferred from one account to another without writing a cheque **das Girosystem;** *(GB)* **National Giro** = banking system, run by the Post Office, which allows account holders to move money from one account to another free of cost; *(entspricht)* **Postgirodienst;** *a giro cheque; giro account; giro account number; she put £25 into her giro account; to pay by bank giro transfer*

◊ **Girobank** *noun* bank in a giro system **Girobank;** *a National Girobank account*

give away *verb* to give something as a free present **verschenken, vergeben;** *we are giving away a pocket calculator with each £10 of purchases*

◊ **giveaway**

1 *adjective* **to sell at giveaway prices** = to sell at very cheap prices **zu Schleuderpreisen verkaufen**

2 *noun* thing which is given as a free gift when another item is bought **Werbegeschenk**

glut

1 *noun* **a glut of produce** = too much produce, which is then difficult to sell **Produktüberangebot;** *a coffee glut or a glut of coffee;* **glut of money** = situation where there is too much money available to borrowers **Geldschwemme**

2 *verb* to fill the market with something which is then difficult to sell **überschwemmen;** *the market is glutted with cheap cameras*

GNP = GROSS NATIONAL PRODUCT

goal *noun* aim *or* something which you try to do **Ziel;** *our goal is to break even within twelve months; the company achieved all its goals*

going rate *noun* the current price for a product or service **üblicher Satz;** *he cannot* *afford to buy a house at the going rate; the going rate for cleaners is £5.00 per hour*

gondola *noun* display in a supermarket on either side of which shoppers can pass **Gondelaufsatz, Auslageregal**

goods *plural noun*
(a) **goods and chattels** = movable personal possessions **bewegliches Eigentum, Mobiliar**
(b) items which can be moved and are for sale **Waren; goods in bond** = imported goods held by the customs until duty is paid **Waren unter Zollverschluß; capital goods** = machinery, buildings and raw materials which are used to make other goods **Anlagegüter; consumer goods** *or* **consumable goods** = goods bought by the general public and not by businesses **Konsum-, Verbrauchsgüter; dry goods** = cloth and clothes **Textilwaren; finished goods** = manufactured goods which are ready to be sold **Fertigwaren; household goods** = items which are used in the home **Haushaltswaren; luxury goods** = expensive items which are not basic necessities **Luxusartikel; manufactured goods** = items which are made by machine **Fabrik-, Fertig-, Manufakturwaren; Industriegüter; goods in progress** = goods being manufactured which are not complete at the end of an accounting period **Halbfabrikate;** *our current assets are made up of stock, goods in progress, and cash;* **goods in transit** = goods which are in the process of being transported **Transitgüter; goods on consignment** = goods kept for another company to be sold on their behalf for a commission **Konsignationsgüter**
(c) **goods depot** = central warehouse where goods can be stored until they are moved **Güterdepot; goods train** = train for carrying freight **Güterzug**

◇ **goodwill** *noun* good reputation of a business, considered as an intangible asset **Firmenansehen; Goodwill;** *he paid £10,000 for the goodwill of the shop and £4,000 for the stock*

> QUOTE profit margins in the industries most exposed to foreign competition - machinery, transportation equipment and electrical goods
> *Sunday Times*
>
> QUOTE the minister wants people buying goods ranging from washing machines to houses to demand facts on energy costs
> *Times*

GOTS = GROSS OPPORTUNITY TO SEE

grade
1 *noun* level *or* rank **Rang, Stufe; grade level** = classification of a product's quality written on a label attached to the product **Qualitätsbezeichnung;** *many consumers do not properly understand the grade levels;* **high-grade** = of very good quality **hochwertig, erstklassig, Qualitäts-;** *high-grade petrol;* **a high-grade trade delegation** = a delegation made up of important people **eine hochrangige/hochgestellte Handelsdelegation; low-grade** = not very important *or* not of very good quality **untergeordnet; minderwertig;** *a low-grade official from the Ministry of Commerce; the car runs well on low-grade petrol;* **top-grade** = most important *or* of the best quality **hoher, Spitzen-;** *top-grade petrol*
2 *verb*
(a) to sort something into different levels of quality **in Güteklassen einteilen, klassifizieren, einstufen;** *to grade coal*
(b) to make something rise in steps according to quantity **abstufen, staffeln; graded advertising rates** = rates which become cheaper as you take more advertising space **degressive Werbesätze, Malstaffel; graded tax** = tax which rises according to income **Steuern, die der Progression unterliegen**
(c) **graded hotel** = good quality hotel **Sterne-Hotel**

grand
1 *adjective* important **großartig, bedeutend; grand plan** *or* **grand strategy** = major plan **großer/großartiger Plan;** *the grand strategy consisted of opening stores in most of the European capitals; he explained his grand plan for redeveloping the factory site;* **grand total** = final total made by adding together several subtotals **Gesamtsumme, Endbetrag**
2 *noun (informal)* one thousand pounds *or* dollars **tausend Pfund; tausend Dollar;** *they offered him fifty grand for the information*

graph *noun* diagram which shows the relationship between two sets of quantities or values, each of which is represented on an axis **Schaubild, Diagramm;** *to set out the results in a graph; to draw a graph showing rising profitability; the sales graph shows a steady rise;* **graph paper** = special paper with many little squares, used for drawing graphs **Millimeterpapier**

graphics *noun* designs and illustrations in printed work, especially designs which are generated by computers **Graphik;** *in this series of advertisements the graphics do not do justice to the copy*

gratis *adverb* free *or* not costing anything **gratis, umsonst;** *we got into the exhibition gratis*

grey market *noun* legal buying and selling of scarce highly priced goods **grauer Markt;** *if the government puts a ceiling on prices for these products the grey market will become a black market; if new supplies reach this part of the country, there will no longer be a grey market*

grid *noun* graph with lines crossing at right angles and items written in the boxes, used for comparison **Gitter(diagramm); buy grid** = method used for objective assessment of competing products **Gitterkarte(methode);** *see also* REPERTORY GRID TECHNIQUE

gross *adjective*
(a) total *or* with no deductions **brutto, Brutto-; gross audience** *or* **gross impressions** = total number of people who have seen an advertisement, multiplied by the the number of times it has been run **Bruttokontaktsumme; gross circulation** = total sales of a publication before adjusting for error or discounting unsold copies **Druckauflage; gross cover** = the number of times a television *or* radio spot has been seen based on television ratings **Bruttoreichweite; gross earnings** = total earnings before tax and other deductions **Bruttoeinkommen; gross income** *or* **gross salary** = salary before tax is deducted **Bruttoverdienst; gross margin** = gross profit shown as a percentage of sales **Bruttomarge; gross opportunity to see (GOTS)** = number of opportunities that an average member of the target audience will have to see the advertisements in an advertising campaign **Bruttokontaktwahrscheinlichkeit; gross profit** = profit calculated as sales income less the cost of sales **Bruttogewinn;** *(US)* **gross rating point (GRP)** = way of calculating the effectiveness of outdoor advertising, where each point represents one per cent of the population in a certain market **Bruttoreichweite; gross reach** = total number of opportunities for people to see a company's advertisements in a campaign (i.e. the total number of publications sold multiplied by the number of advertisements appearing in each) **Bruttokontaktwahrscheinlichkeit; gross receipts** = total amount of money received before expenses are deducted **Bruttoeinnahmen; gross sales** = money received from sales before deductions for goods returned, special discounts, etc. **Bruttoumsatz;** *gross sales are impressive since many buyers seem to be ordering more than they will eventually need;* **gross yield** = profit from investments before the deduction of tax **Bruttoertrag**
(b) gross domestic product (GDP) = annual value of goods sold and services paid for within a country **Bruttoinlandsprodukt; gross national product (GNP)** = annual value of goods and services in a country including income from other countries **Bruttosozialprodukt**
3 *adverb* with no deductions **brutto;** *his salary is paid gross*
4 *verb* to make a gross profit **brutto verdienen; brutto einnehmen;** *the group grossed £25m in 1985*

> QUOTE news that gross national product increased only 1.3% in the first quarter of the year sent the dollar down on foreign exchange markets
> *Fortune*

group
1 *noun*
(a) several things or people together **Gruppe;** *a group of the staff got together to send a memo to the chairman complaining about noise in the office; the respondents were interviewed in groups of three or four, and then singly;* **group discussion** = survey method in which a sample of people are asked to discuss some issue freely among themselves **Gruppendiskussion, Gruppengespräch;** *the group discussion was taken over by one or two strong personalities; a sample of housewives took part in a group discussion on the new washing powder;* **group interview** = interview with a group of respondents in order to discover the views of the group as a whole, such as a family **Gruppeninterview;** *there were group interviews with all the classes in the school in order to gauge reactions to the new educational programme*
(b) several companies linked together in the same organization **Konzern, Firmengruppe;** *the group chairman or the chairman of the group; group turnover or turnover for the group; the BPCC Group;* **group results** = results of a group of companies taken together **Konzernergebnisse**
2 *verb* **to group together** = to put several items together **zusammenfassen;** *sales from six different agencies are grouped together under the heading "European sales"*

growth *noun* (i) increase in size; (ii) second stage in a product life-cycle, following the launch, when demand for the product increases rapidly **(i) Wachstum, Zunahme; (ii) Wachstumsphase; the company is aiming for growth** = is aiming to expand rapidly **das Unternehmen strebt Expansion an; economic growth** = rate at which a country's national income grows **Wirtschaftswachstum; growth area** = area where sales are increasing rapidly

Wachstumsbereich; growth industry = industry which is expanding rapidly **expandierender Industriezweig; Wachstumsindustrie; growth market** = market where sales are increasing rapidly **wachsender Absatzmarkt;** *we plan to build a factory in the Far East which is a growth market for our products;* **growth rate** = speed at which something grows **Wachstumsrate; growth share matrix** = model for a marketing strategy with various categories of product based on present performance and growth rate **,Growth-Share-Matrix';** *the growth share matrix helped to decide what products needed extra marketing efforts;* **growth vector matrix** = model for a marketing strategy with various choices and combinations of strategy based on product and market development **,Growth-Vector-Matrix'**

> QUOTE a general price freeze succeeded in slowing the growth in consumer prices
> *Financial Times*
>
> QUOTE the thrift had grown from $4.7 million in assets in 1980 to $1.5 billion
> *Barrons*
>
> QUOTE growth in demand is still coming from the private rather than the public sector
> *Lloyd's List*

GRP = GROSS RATING POINT

guarantee

1 *noun*
(a) legal document, in which the producer agrees to compensate the buyer if the product is faulty or becomes faulty before a certain date after purchase **Garantie;** *certificate of guarantee or guarantee certificate; the guarantee lasts for two years; it is sold with a twelve-month guarantee;* **the car is still under guarantee** = is still covered by the maker's guarantee **das Auto hat noch Garantie; extended guarantee** = guarantee offered by a dealer on a product such as a dish-washer, which goes beyond the time specified in the manufacturer's guarantee **verlängerte Garantie**
(b) promise that someone will pay another person's debts **Bürgschaft; to go guarantee for someone** = to act as security for someone's debts **für jdn bürgen/haften**
(c) thing given as a security **Sicherheit;** *to leave share certificates as a guarantee*
2 *verb* to give a promise that something will happen **garantieren; sich verbürgen; to guarantee a debt** = to promise that you will pay a debt incurred by someone else **sich für eine Schuld verbürgen; to guarantee an associate company** = to promise that an associate company will pay its debts **sich für ein Konzernunternehmen verbürgen; to guarantee a bill of exchange** = to promise that the bill will be paid **eine Wechselbürgschaft leisten; the product is guaranteed for twelve months** = the manufacturer says that the product will work well for twelve months, and will mend it free of charge if it breaks down **die Ware hat zwölf Monate Garantie; guaranteed circulation** = the audited circulation of a magazine which is used as a basis for calculating advertising rates **Mindestauflage, garantierte Auflage, Auflagengarantie; guaranteed homes impressions** *or* **guaranteed homes ratings** = advertising package offered by television companies which guarantees the advertisers that their advertising will reach a specified number of people, but leaves it to the TV company to choose the number and timing of the spots **garantierte Einschaltquote, Mindesteinschaltquote; guaranteed prices** = minimum prices guaranteed to an industry by government, with the payment of a subsidy to make up for market prices that fall below this level **garantierte Mindestpreise;** *guaranteed prices help bring some security to a notoriously unstable industry;* **guaranteed wage** = wage which a company promises will not fall below a certain figure **garantierter Mindestlohn, Garantielohn**

◇ **guarantor** *noun* person who promises to pay someone's debts **Bürge/-in;** *he stood guarantor for his brother*

guesstimate

guesstimate *noun (informal)* rough calculation **grobe Schätzung**

gutter

gutter *noun* area where the two pages meet in book or magazine (it can be left blank as a centre margin, or can be printed across to form a double-page spread) **Bundsteg**

Hh

haberdasher

haberdasher *noun* dealer *or* shopkeeper selling small miscellaneous articles related to dress (buttons, thread, etc.) **Kurzwarenhändler**

habit

habit *noun* doing something regularly **Gewohnheit;** *most consumers continue to buy the same brands from force of habit;* **habit buying** = buying a particular product again and again by force of habit, without making any conscious decision to buy **Gewohnheitskauf**

haggle *verb* to discuss prices and terms and try to make them more favourable **feilschen, handeln;** *to haggle about or over the details of a contract; after two days' haggling the contract was signed*

hallmark
1 *noun* mark put on gold or silver items to show that the metal is of the correct quality **Feingehaltsstempel; hallmark of excellence =** reputation that a brand name has for high quality **Gütersiegel**
2 *verb* to put a hallmark on a piece of gold or silver **mit einem Feingehaltsstempel versehen;** *a hallmarked spoon*

hall test *noun* market research test where respondents are asked to go into a public building or central place to answer questions or to test new products **Klassenzimmerbefragung;** *the hall test was conducted in the town's main school*

halo effect *noun* series of positive impressions of a product which consumers retain and which can be revealed by a respondent when questioned in a survey **Ausstrahlungseffekt;** *in some cases, the halo effect can mean little useful criticism being generated*

hand *noun*
(a) to shake hands = to hold someone's hand when meeting to show you are pleased to meet him, or to show that an agreement has been reached **sich die Hand geben;** *the two negotiating teams shook hands and sat down at the conference table;* **to shake hands on a deal =** to shake hands to show that a deal has been agreed **einen Abschluß mit Handschlag besiegeln**
(b) in hand = kept in reserve **vorrätig, zur Verfügung; balance in hand** *or* **cash in hand =** cash held to pay small debts and running costs **Kassen-, Barbestand; Bargeld;** *we have £10,000 in hand;* **work in hand =** work which is in progress but not finished **noch nicht fertiggestellte Arbeit**

◊ **handbill** *noun* sheet of printed paper handed out to members of the public as an advertisement **Reklame-, Handzettel**

◊ **handbook** *noun* book which gives instructions on how to use something **Handbuch, Bedienungsanleitung;** *the handbook doesn't say how you open the photocopier; look in the handbook to see if it tells you how to clean the typewriter;* **service handbook =** book which shows how to service a machine **Wartungsbuch**

◊ **handout** *noun*
(a) publicity handout = information sheet which is given to members of the public **Werbeprospekt, Reklamezettel; Flugblatt**
(b) gift of money **Zuwendung;** *the company exists on handouts from the government*

handle *verb*
(a) to deal with something *or* to organize something **bearbeiten, sich befassen mit, erledigen;** *the accounts department handles all the cash; we can handle orders for up to 15,000 units; they handle all our overseas orders*
(b) to sell *or* to trade in (a sort of product) **führen, handeln mit;** *we do not handle foreign cars; they will not handle goods produced by other firms*

◊ **account handler** *noun* person who works in an advertising agency, and who is responsible for a particular client **Kontakter, Kundenbetreuer**

◊ **handling** *noun* receiving, storing and sending off goods **Beförderung, Umschlag; Bearbeitung, Erledigung, Handhabung; handling charges =** money to be paid for packing and invoicing *or* for dealing with something in general *or* for moving goods from one place to another **Bearbeitungsgebühr; Umschlagspesen;** *if our handling costs rise any further our prices will have to go up; distributing over such a wide area will create enormous handling problems for the company;* **materials handling =** moving materials from one part of a factory to another in an efficient way **innerbetriebliches Transportwesen, Materialfluß**

hardening *noun* **a hardening of prices =** becoming settled at a higher level **das Anziehen der Preise**

◊ **hardness** *noun* **hardness of the market =** being strong *or* not being likely to fall **Festigung des Marktes**

◊ **hard sell** *noun* **to give a product the hard sell =** to make great efforts to persuade people to buy it **für ein Produkt aggressive Verkaufsmethoden anwenden; he tried to give me the hard sell =** he put a lot of effort into trying to make me buy **er versuchte mit allen Mitteln, mich zum Kauf zu überreden**

◊ **hard selling** *noun* act of selling by using great efforts **aggressive Verkaufspolitik;** *a lot of hard selling went into that deal*

◊ **hardware** *noun*
(a) computer hardware = machines used in data processing, including the computers and printers, but not the programs **Computer-Hardware;** *the company offers a hardware maintenance service as part of the deal*

(b) military hardware = guns *or* rockets *or* tanks, etc. **Wehrmaterial**
(c) solid goods for use in the house (such as frying pans or hammers) **Haushaltswaren, Eisenwaren;**

> QUOTE few of the paper millionaires sold out and transformed themselves into hard cash millionaires
> *Investors Chronicle*

harvesting *noun* cutting down investment on a particular product or part of a business for the sake of economy **Abernten; Investitionskürzung; Rationalisierung**

haulage *noun*
(a) road haulage = moving of goods by road **Güterkraftverkehr; road haulage depot** = centre for goods being moved by road, and the lorries which carry them **Güterkraftverkehrsdepot; haulage contractor** = company which arranges for goods to be moved by road or rail under contract **Transport-, Fuhrunternehmer; Spediteur; haulage costs** *or* **haulage rates** = cost *or* rates of transporting goods by road **Transportkosten; haulage firm** *or* **company** = company which transports goods by road **Spedition**
(b) cost of transporting goods by road **Transport-, Beförderungskosten;** *haulage is increasing by 5% per annum*

◊ **haulier** *noun* **road haulier** = company which transports goods by road **Spediteur, Fernspediteur**

hawk *verb* to sell goods from door-to-door or in the street **hausieren; to hawk something round** = to take a product *or* an idea *or* a project to various companies to see if one will accept it **mit etwas hausieren;** *he hawked his idea for a plastic car body round all the major car manufacturers*

◊ **hawker** *noun* person who sells goods from door-to-door or in the street **Hausierer/-in**

headhunt *verb* to look for managers and offer them jobs in other companies **nach Führungskräften suchen; he was headhunted** = he was approached by a headhunter and offered a new job **er wurde abgeworben**

◊ **headhunter** *noun* person *or* company which looks for top managers and offers them jobs in other companies **Headhunter, Talentsucher**

◊ **headline** *noun* heading of an article or advertisement, which is set in much larger type than the rest **Schlagzeile, Überschrift, Headline**

◊ **head-on position** *noun* poster site directly facing traffic **Verkehrsfluß gerichtete Anschlagflächenposition;** *let's try to obtain a head-on position in the central part of town*

heavy *adjective* large *or* in large quantities **hoch, groß, bedeutend, umfangreich;** *a programme of heavy investment overseas; he suffered heavy losses on the Stock Exchange; the company is a heavy user of steel or a heavy consumer of electricity; the government imposed a heavy tax on luxury goods;* **heavy costs** *or* **heavy expenditure** = spending large sums of money **hohe Ausgaben; heavy half** = situation where a small number of customers make up more than half of the total demand for a product **gewichtige Hälfte; heavy user** = consumer who buys more of a product than average **Großverbraucher;** *heavy users will be particularly affected by the price rise;* **heavy viewer** = person who watches a lot of television, and is part of the target audience for commercials **Dauer-, Vielseher;** *heavy viewers gave us the most interesting comments on our advertising*

heterogeneous *adjective* varied **heterogen, verschiedenartig; heterogeneous shopping goods** = goods which vary in quality and style from brand to brand and which consumers spend time in choosing **heterogene Güter;** *compare* HOMOGENEOUS

hierarchy of effects *noun* model showing stages in the effects of advertising on a consumer (awareness, knowledge, liking, preference, conviction and purchase) **Hierarchy-of-effects-Modell (Stufenmodell einer hierarchischen Abfolge von Werbewirkungen: Bekanntheitsgrad, Kenntnis, Schätzen, Präferenz, Überzeugung, Kauf)**

high
1 *adjective*
(a) tall **hoch, hoher;** *the shelves are 30 cm high; they are planning a 30-storey high office block*
(b) large *or* not low **hoher;** *high overhead costs increase the unit price; high prices put customers off; they are budgeting for a high level of expenditure; investments which bring in a high rate of return; high interest rates are crippling small businesses;* **high finance** = lending, investing and borrowing of very large sums of money organized by financiers **Hochfinanz; high flier** = (i) person who is very successful *or* who is likely to get a very important job; (ii) share whose market price is rising rapidly **(i) Senkrechtstarter; (ii) schnell steigende Aktie; high sales** = large amount of revenue

produced by sales **hoher Absatz; high taxation** = taxation which imposes large taxes on incomes *or* profits **hohe Besteuerung; highest tax bracket** = the group which pays the most tax **höchste Steuerklasse; high volume (of sales)** = large number of items sold **hoher Absatz**
(c) highest bidder = person who offers the most money at an auction **Meistbietende(r);** *the property was sold to the highest bidder;* **a decision taken at the highest level** = decision taken by the most important person or group **eine auf höchster Ebene getroffene Entscheidung**
2 *adverb* **prices are running high** = prices are above their usual level **die Preise sind gestiegen**
3 *noun* point where prices *or* sales are very large **Höchststand;** *share prices have dropped by 10% since the January 2nd high; the highs and lows on the Stock Exchange;* **sales volume has reached an all-time high** = has reached its highest point ever **das Umsatzvolumen hat einen absoluten Höchststand erreicht**

◇ **high-grade** *adjective* of very good quality **hochwertig, erstklassig;** *high-grade petrol;* **a high-grade trade delegation** = a delegation made up of very important people **eine hochrangige/hochgestellte Handelsdelegation**

◇ **high-involvement product** *noun* high-priced product that is carefully considered by a consumer before being bought **High-involvement-Produkt**

◇ **high pressure** *noun* strong force by other people to do something **großer Druck; working under high pressure** = working with a manager telling you what to do and to do it quickly *or* with customers asking for supplies urgently **unter großem Druck arbeiten; high-pressure salesman** = salesman who tries to force the customer to buy something he or she does not really need **aggressiver Verkäufer; high-pressure sales techniques** *or* **high-pressure selling** = trying to force a customer to buy something he or she does not really want **aggressive Verkaufsmethoden**

◇ **high-quality** *adjective* of very good quality **Qualitäts-, hochwertig;** *high-quality goods; high-quality steel*

◇ **high season** *noun* period of the year when there are more travellers *or* tourists **Hochsaison;** *the hotels are booked up right through the high season; high-season air fares are 10% higher than in the low season*

hire purchase *noun* system of buying something by paying a sum regularly each month **Raten-, Teilzahlungskauf;** *to buy a refrigerator on hire purchase;* **to sign a hire-purchase agreement** = to sign a contract to pay for something by instalments **einen Teilzahlungskaufvertrag unterschreiben; hire-purchase company** = company which provides money for hire purchase **Teilzahlungsfinanzierungsgesellschaft**

histogram *noun* chart where values or quantities are shown as thick columns of different heights **Histogramm**

historic *or* **historical** *adjective* which goes back over a period of time **historisch; historic(al) cost** = actual cost of something which was purchased some time ago **ursprüngliche Anschaffungskosten; ursprüngliche Herstellungskosten; historical figures** = figures which were current in the past **historische Beträge; historical trend** = trend detected in the past on the basis of historical data **historischer Trend;** *historical trends may help us to predict how the economy will develop in the future; it is difficult to detect any clear historical trends in consumer reaction to our past product launches*

hit rate *noun* rate at which a target is reached (such as the number of mail shots needed before a customer makes an order for a product advertised on them) **Erfolgsquote**

hive off *verb* to split off part of a large company to form a smaller subsidiary **abspalten, ausgliedern;** *the new managing director hived off the retail sections of the company*

hoard *verb* to buy and store food in case of need *or* to keep cash instead of investing it **horten, ansammeln;** *(umg)* **hamstern**

◇ **hoarder** *noun* person who buys and stores food in case of need **Hamsterer**

◇ **hoarding** *noun*
(a) hoarding of supplies = buying large quantities of money *or* food to keep in case of need **Horten von Vorräten** NOTE: the opposite is **dishoarding**
(b) large wooden board for posters **Anschlag-, Plakat-, Reklamewand;** *advertising hoardings have been taken down in that town since the council banned posters; giant hoardings were placed in fields on either side of the road*

> QUOTE as a result of hoarding, rice has become scarce with prices shooting up
> *Business Times (Lagos)*

home *noun*
(a) house *or* place where a consumer lives **Wohnung, Zuhause; home audit** = survey method whereby a panel of householders

keeps records of purchases so that these can be regularly checked for quantity and brand **Haushaltsbuchforschung;** *the home audit showed that although wholesalers were buying the product in large quantities, consumers were not; the home audit suggested that there is little brand loyalty for this type of product;* **home shopping** = buying items direct from the customer's house, using a computer linked to the telephone which is linked to the store's ordering department **Home-Shopping, Teleshopping**

(b) home country = country where a company is based **Heimatland; home industry** = productive work carried out by people at home **Heimindustrie;** *in third world countries there are still many home industries; home industries are disappearing as mass production takes over;* **home market** = market in a producer's own country **Inlandsmarkt;** *let's hope we do as well overseas as in the home market; the home market is fairly safe since demand there is both ample and stable;* **home sales** *or* **sales in the home market** = sales in the country where a company is based **Inlandsabsatz; home-produced products** = products manufactured in the country where the company is based **einheimische Erzeugnisse**

◊ **homegrown** *adjective* which has been developed in a local area *or* in a country where the company is based **einheimisch;** *a homegrown computer industry; India's homegrown car industry*

◊ **homeward** *adjective* going towards the home country **Heim-;** *homeward freight; homeward journey*

◊ **homewards** *adverb* towards the home country **heim, nach Hause;** *cargo homewards*

homogeneous *adjective* uniform *or* unvaried **homogen; homogeneous shopping goods** = goods which vary little in style and quality from brand to brand and which consumers spend little time choosing **homogene Güter;** *compare* HETEROGENEOUS

horizontal *adjective* flat *or* going from side to side, not up and down **horizontal, waagerecht; horizontal communication** = communication between workers at the same level **horizontale Kommunikation; horizontal industrial market** = market in which a product is used by many industries **horizontaler Industriemarkt; horizontal integration** = joining similar companies *or* taking over a company in the same line of business **horizontale Integration; horizontal marketing system** = cooperation between *or* merger of two or more companies whose assets are complementary and who therefore all gain from coming together **horizontales Marketingsystem, horizontale Kooperation; horizontal publication** = publication which is aimed at people in many types and levels of occupation in different industries **Fachzeitschrift, Berufsfachorgan**

horse trading *noun* hard bargaining which ends with someone giving something in return for a concession from the other side **Kuhhandel**

hostess party selling *noun* method of selling certain items (such as household goods) directly by the manufacturer's agent at a party to which potential customers are invited **Partyverkauf**

house *noun*

(a) building in which someone lives **Haus; house property** = private houses, not shops, offices or factories **Hausbesitz; house agent** = estate agent who deals in buying or selling houses **Häuser-, Immobilienmakler**

(b) company **Haus, Firma;** *a French business house; the largest London finance house; he works for a broking house or a publishing house;* **export house** = company which specializes in the export of goods manufactured by other companies **Exportfirma; house advertisement** *or* **house ad** = advertisement in a publication which is placed by the publication itself (offering a readers' inquiry service, special items for sale, etc.) **Eigenanzeige, Eigeninserat; house agency** = advertising agency owned and used by a large company, and which other companies may also use **hauseigene Werbeagentur, Hausagentur; house brand** = brand owned by a distributor rather than by the producer **Hausmarke; house journal** *or* **house magazine** *or* *(US)* **house organ** = magazine produced for the workers or shareholders in a company to give them news about the company **Betriebszeitung, Hausnachrichten; house style** = company's own design which is used in all areas of its activities, such as packaging, stationery and office decoration **Hausstil;** *changing our house style is part of an effort to up-date the company's image; the house style needs a face-lift to suit our international market;* **house telephone** = internal telephone for calling from one office to another **Haustelefon**

◊ **household** *noun* a term for a unit formed of all people living together in a single house or flat, whether it is a single person living alone, a married couple, or a large family **Haushalt; household appliances** = appliances (such as dishwashers and refrigerators) which are used in carrying out day-to-day work in the house **Haushaltsgeräte; household name =** brand name which is recognized by a large number of people **alltägliche Markenname**

◇ **house-to-house** *adjective* going from one house to the next **(von) Haus zu Haus;** *house-to-house canvassing; house-to-house salesman; house-to-house selling; see also* DOOR-TO-DOOR

> QUOTE the extent of single women households has implications for marketing
> *Precision Marketing*

HP = HIRE PURCHASE

human resources *noun* manpower *or* workforce that an organization has available **Arbeitskräfte** *we do not have sufficient human resources either to produce or market the product*

hype
1 *noun* excessive claims made in advertising **übertriebene/reißerische Werbung;** *many consumers were actually put off by all the media hype surrounding the launch of the new magazine*
2 *verb* to make excessive claims in advertising **übertriebene Werbung machen**

hypermarket *noun* very large supermarket, usually outside a large town **Hypermarkt, Verbrauchergroßmarkt, SB-Warenhaus**

hypothesis *noun* assumption *or* theory which must be tested to be confirmed or proved correct **Hypothese;** *let us assume, as a working hypothesis, that we can win a 5% market share within two years of the launch; surveys proved that our original hypothesis about likely consumer behaviour was by and large correct*

Ii

iceberg principle *noun* principle that strong needs and desires lie deep in the human personality and that advertising must work at this level if it is to be effective **Eisberg-Prinzip**

image *noun* general idea that the public has of a product *or* a company **Image;** *they are spending a lot of advertising money to improve the company's image; the company has adopted a down-market image;* **brand image =** qualities which people tend to associate with a particular brand name or branded product **Markenimage, Markenprofil; corporate image =** idea which a company would like the public to have of it **Firmenimage; to promote a corporate image =** to publicize a company so that its reputation is improved **das Firmenimage pflegen; product image =** general idea which the public has of a product **Produktimage**

> QUOTE charities are also ready to buy air time to promote their corporate image
> *Marketing Week*

IMF = INTERNATIONAL MONETARY FUND

imitate *verb* to do what someone else does **nachmachen, kopieren, imitieren;** *they imitate all our sales gimmicks*

◇ **imitation** *noun* thing which is a copy of an original **Nachahmung, Kopie, Imitation; beware of imitations =** be careful not to buy low quality goods which are made to look like other more expensive items **vor Imitationen wird gewarnt**

immediate *adjective*
(a) happening at once **umgehend, prompt, sofort;** *he wrote an immediate letter of complaint; your order will receive immediate attention*
(b) close at hand **unmittelbar, nächstgelegen; immediate environment =** elements *or* factors outside a business organization which directly affect its work, such as the supply of raw materials and demand for its products **Aufgabenumwelt, Mikro-Umwelt;** *the unreliability of our suppliers is one of the worst features of our immediate environment*

impact *noun* shock *or* strong effect **Wirkung, Auswirkung, Druck;** *the impact of new technology on the cotton trade; the new design has made little impact on the buying public;* **impact scheduling =** running advertisements for the same product close together so as to make a strong impression on the target audience **Wuchtplanung;** *impact scheduling can achieve rapid brand awareness*

◇ **impactaplan** *noun* extensive poster advertising campaign **intensive Plakatanschlagkampagne**

imperfect *adjective* not perfect *or* having defects **fehlerhaft;** *sale of imperfect items; to check a batch for imperfect products;* **imperfect competition =** degree of competition in a market which is somewhere between a monopoly at one extreme and perfect competition at the other **unvollkommene Konkurrenz**

◇ **imperfection** *noun* part of an item which is not perfect **Mangel, Fehler;** *to check a batch for imperfections*

import

1 *noun*

(a) imports = goods brought into a country from abroad for sale **Importe, Einfuhren;** *imports from Poland have risen to $1m a year;* **invisible imports** = services (such as banking, tourism, etc.) which are paid for in foreign currency **unsichtbare Importe; visible imports** = real goods which are imported **sichtbare Importe**

(b) import ban = government measure to stop imports **Einfuhrverbot, Einfuhrstopp;** *the government has imposed an import ban on arms;* **import duty** = tax on goods imported into a country **Einfuhrzoll; import levy** = tax on imports, especially a tax imposed by the EC on imports of farm produce from outside the EC **Einfuhrzoll;** *(EG)* **Abschöpfung; import licence** *or* **import permit** = government licence *or* permit which allows goods to be imported **Importlizenz, Importgenehmigung; import quota** = fixed quantity of a particular type of goods which the government allows to be imported **Einfuhrkontingent, Importquote;** *the government has imposed an import quota on cars;* **import surcharge** = extra duty charged on imported goods, to try to prevent them from being imported and to encourage local manufacture **Importabgabe**

2 *verb* to bring goods from abroad into a country for sale **importieren, einführen;** *the company imports television sets from Japan; this car was imported from France; the union organized a boycott of imported cars*

> QUOTE European manufacturers rely heavily on imported raw materials which are mostly priced in dollars
>
> *Duns Business Month*

importation

noun act of importing **Import, Einfuhr;** *the importation of livestock is subject to very strict controls*

◇ **importer** *noun* person *or* company which imports goods **Importeur, Importfirma;** *a cigar importer; the company is a big importer of foreign cars*

◇ **import-export** *adjective* dealing with both bringing foreign goods into a country and sending locally made goods abroad **Import/Export-;** *import-export trade; he's in import-export*

◇ **importing**

1 *adjective* which imports **Import-, Einfuhr-;** *oil-importing countries; an importing company*

2 *noun* act of bringing foreign goods into a country for sale **Import, Einfuhr;** *the level of importing is bound to affect domestic industries*

impression

noun one person's single exposure to an advertisement **Kontakt;** *one impression can be enough to induce a consumer to buy; too many impressions can put consumers off;* **impression cover** = amount of advertising necessary to ensure the required number of impressions **Reichweite; gross impressions** = total number of people who have seen an advertisement, multiplied by the number of times it has been run **Bruttokontaktsumme;** *see also* GUARANTEED

impulse

noun sudden decision **Impuls; impulse buying** = buying things which you have just seen, and which you had not planned to buy **Impuls-, Spontankaufen; impulse buyer** = person who buys something on impulse, not because he intended to buy it **Impuls-, Spontankäufer;** *the store puts racks of chocolates by the checkout to attract the impulse buyer;* **impulse purchase** = thing bought as soon as it is seen **Impulskauf; to do something on impulse** = to do something because you have just thought of it, not because it was planned **etwas spontan/impulsiv tun**

incentive

noun thing which encourages a customer to buy *or* staff to work better **Anreiz, Incentive; incentive bonus** *or* **incentive payment** = extra pay offered to a worker to make him or her work better **Leistungszulage, Prämie; incentive marketing** = additional incentives to buy apart from advertising, such as free gifts **Anreiz-Marketing;** *we will have to use incentive marketing to break down sales resistance;* **incentive scheme** = plan to encourage better work by paying higher commission or bonuses **leistungsabhängiges System, Anreizsystem**

income

noun

(a) money which a person receives as salary or dividends **Einkommen, Einkünfte; annual income** = money received during a calendar year **Jahreseinkommen; disposable income** = income left after tax and national insurance have been deducted **verfügbares Einkommen (nach Steuerabzug), Nettoeinkommen; lower** *or* **upper income bracket** = people who earn low or high salaries categorized for tax purposes **niedrige Einkommensstufe; hohe Einkommensstufe; he comes into the higher income bracket** = he is a person earning a high income and therefore paying more tax

er gehört einer hohen Einkommensstufe an; income distribution = way in which the national income is distributed among the various classes and occupations in a country **Verteilung des Volkseinkommens; income effect** = effect that a change in a person's income has on his or her spending **Einkommensveränderungseffekt**
(b) the government's incomes policy = the government's ideas on how incomes should be controlled **die Lohn-/Einkommenspolitik der Regierung**
(c) *US* **income statement** = accounts for a company which show expenditure and sales balanced to give a final profit or loss **Gewinn- und Verlustrechnung, Aufwands- und Ertragsrechnung**

> QUOTE there is no risk-free way of taking regular income from your money much higher than the rate of inflation
> *Guardian*

indemnity

noun compensation for a loss or wrong **Entschädigung, Vergütung; letter of indemnity** = letter promising payment of compensation for a loss **(schriftliche) Schadloshaltungs-, Ausfallbürgschaftserklärung**

indent

1 *noun*
(a) order placed by an importer for goods from overseas **Auslandsauftrag, Warenbestellung (aus dem Ausland), Indentgeschäft;** *he put in an indent for a new stock of soap*
(b) line of typing which starts several spaces from the left-hand margin **Einrückung, Einzug**
2 *verb*
(a) to indent for something = to put in an order for something **einen Auslandsauftrag erteilen, etwas aus dem Ausland bestellen;** *the department has indented for a new computer*
(b) to start a line of typing several spaces from the left-hand margin **einrücken, einziehen;** *indent the first line three spaces*

independent

1 *adjective* free *or* not controlled by anyone **unabhängig, ungebunden; independent company** = company which is not controlled by another company **unabhängiges Unternehmen; independent trader** *or* **independent shop** = shop which is owned by an individual proprietor, not by a chain **selbständiger Händler; unabhängiges Geschäft; independent variable** = a factor, a change in whose value influences one or more other variables called "dependent variables" **unabhängige Variable;** *in this model personal income is the independent variable and expenditure the dependent variable*
2 *noun* **the independents** = shops or companies which are owned by private individuals **unabhängige Unternehmen; media independent** = business offering other businesses a media buying service, but without the creative services usually offered by advertising agencies **selbständige Media-Agentur**

◇ **Independent Television Commission (ITC)** British statutory body which operates transmitting stations and oversees commercial television and radio **(britische) Rundfunkbehörde**

index

noun regular statistical report which shows rises and falls in prices, etc. **Index; growth index** = index showing how something has grown **Wachstumsindex; cost-of-living index** = way of measuring the cost of living, shown as a percentage increase on the figure for the previous year **Lebenshaltungskostenindex; retail price index** *or (US)* **consumer price index** = index showing how prices of consumer goods have risen over a period of time, used as a way of measuring inflation and the cost of living **Verbraucherpreisindex; wholesale price index** = index showing rises and falls of prices of manufactured goods as they leave the factory **Großhandelspreisindex; the Financial Times Index** = index which shows percentage rises or falls in share prices on the London Stock Exchange based on a small group of major companies **Aktienindex der Financial Times; index number** = number which shows the percentage rise of something over a period of time **Indexzahl, Indexziffer**
NOTE: plural is **indexes** or **indices**

◇ **indexation** *noun* linking of something to an index **Indexbindung, Indexierung; indexation of wage increases** = linking of wage increases to the percentage rise in the cost of living **Indexierung von Gehaltserhöhungen**

◇ **indexing** *noun* method of showing changes in a value over time by starting with a simple base point such as 100, which then serves as a reference point for future years **Indexierung;** *indexing is used to show the rise in the cost of living over a ten-year period*

◇ **index-linked** *adjective* which rises automatically by the percentage increase in the cost of living **indexgebunden, der Inflationsrate angeglichen;** *index-linked pensions; his pension is index-linked; index-linked government bonds*

> QUOTE the index of industrial production sank 0.2 per cent for the latest month after rising 0.3 per cent in March
> *Financial Times*

indicate *verb* to show **(an)zeigen, hinweisen auf;** *the latest figures indicate a fall in the inflation rate; our sales for 1985 indicate a move from the home market to exports*
◊ **indicator** *noun* thing which indicates **Indikator; government economic indicators** = statistics which show how the country's economy is going to perform in the short or long term **staatliche Konjunkturindikatoren**

> QUOTE it reduces this month's growth in the key M3 indicator from about 19% to 12%
> *Sunday Times*
> QUOTE we may expect the US leading economic indicators for April to show faster economic growth
> *Australian Financial Review*
> QUOTE other indicators, such as high real interest rates, suggest that monetary conditions are extremely tight
> *Economist*

indifference curve *noun* line on a graph that joins various points, each point representing a certain combination of two commodities, each combination giving the customer equal satisfaction **Indifferenzkurve**

indigenous *adjective* native *or* belonging to a particular country or area **eingeboren, einheimisch;** *cocoa is not indigenous to the area, but has been grown there for some years*

indirect *adjective* not direct **indirekt, mittelbar; indirect expenses** *or* **costs** = costs which are not directly attached to the making of a product (such as cleaning, rent, administration, etc.) **Fertigungsgemeinkosten; indirect exporting** = selling products to a customer overseas through a middleman in one's own country **indirekter Export;** *there is no need for indirect exporting as we can sell directly to the major department stores in Spain; indirect exporting saved the company from having to worry about export documentation and transportation;* **indirect labour costs** = costs of paying workers who are not directly involved in making a product (such as secretaries, cleaners, etc.) **Lohngemeinkosten; indirect taxation** = taxes (such as sales tax) which are not paid direct to the government **indirekte Besteuerung;** *the government raises more money by indirect taxation than by direct*

individual
1 *noun* one single person **Einzelperson, Individuum;** *savings plan made to suit the requirements of the private individual*
2 *adjective* single *or* belonging to one person **einzeln, individuell;** *a pension plan designed to meet each person's individual requirements; we sell individual portions of ice cream;* **individual demand** = demand from one single consumer **Individualnachfrage**

industry *noun*
(a) all factories *or* companies *or* processes involved in the manufacturing of products **Industrie;** *all sectors of industry have shown rises in output;* **basic industry** = most important industry of a country (such as coal, steel, agriculture, etc.) **Schlüssel-, Grundstoffindustrie; boom industry** *or* **growth industry** = industry which is expanding rapidly **Wachstumsbranche; heavy industry** = industry which deals in heavy raw materials (such as coal) or makes large products (such as ships or engines) **Schwerindustrie; light industry** = industry making small products (such as clothes, books, calculators) **Leichtindustrie; primary industry** = industry concerned with the production or extraction of basic raw materials (such as coal, wood, farm produce) **Rohstoffindustrie; secondary industry** = industry which uses basic raw materials to produce manufactured goods **verarbeitende Industrie; service industry** *or* **tertiary industry** = industry which does not produce raw materials or manufacture products but offers a service (such as banking, retailing, accountancy, etc.) **Dienstleistungsbranche**
(b) group of companies making the same type of product **Branche, Wirtschaftszweig;** *the aircraft industry; the building industry; the car industry; the food processing industry; the mining industry; the petroleum industry*

◊ **industrial**
1 *adjective* referring to manufacturing work **Industrie-, industriell; industrial accident** = accident which takes place at work **Betriebs-, Arbeitsunfall; to take industrial action** = to go on strike or go-slow **Arbeitskampfmaßnahmen ergreifen, in den Ausstand treten; industrial capacity** = amount of work which can be done in a factory or several factories **Fertigungskapazität; industrial centre** = large town with many industries **Industriezentrum;** *(GB)* **industrial court** *or* **industrial tribunal** = court which can decide in industrial disputes if both parties agree to ask it to judge between them **Schiedsgericht; industrial design** = design of products made by machines (such as cars,

refrigerators) **Industriedesign; industrial disputes** = arguments between management and workers **Arbeitskampf; industrial espionage** = trying to find out the secrets of a competitor's work or products, usually by illegal means **Werks-, Wirtschaftsspionage; industrial estate** *or* **industrial park** = area of land near a town specially for factories and warehouses **Industriegebiet, Industriegelände; industrial expansion** = growth of industries in a country *or* a region **industrielle Expansion; industrial goods** *or* **industrial products** = goods or products bought by producers to be used in production **Industriegüter;** *our industrial products are advertised in the specialized press; he is an engineer by profession and sells industrial goods to factories;* **industrial injuries** = injuries which happen to workers at work **Berufsschäden; industrial market** = customers who buy goods to be used in production **Industriegütermarkt; industrial marketing** = marketing of industrial products **Industriemarketing;** *after doing a course in industrial marketing, he got a job selling machinery to aircraft manufacturers;* **industrial processes** = processes involved in manufacturing products in factories **Herstellungsprozesse; industrial relations** = relations between management and workers **Arbeitgeber-Arbeitnehmer-Beziehungen; good industrial relations** = situation where management and workers understand each others' problems and work together for the good of the company **gute Beziehungen zwischen Arbeitgebern und Arbeitnehmern; industrial training** = training of new workers to work in an industry **betriebliche Ausbildung; land zoned for light industrial use** = land where planning permission has been given to build small factories for light industry **für Leichtindustrie vorgesehenes Land; industrial user** = customer who buys industrial products to use in production **industrieller Einkäufer**

2 *noun* **industrials** = shares in manufacturing companies **Industriepapiere, Industriewerte**

◇ **industrialist** *noun* owner *or* director of a factory **Industrieller**

◇ **industrialization** *noun* process of change by which an economy becomes based on industrial production rather than on agriculture **Industrialisierung**

◇ **industrialize** *verb* to set up industries in a country which had none before **industrialisieren; industrialized societies** = countries which have many industries **Industriegesellschaften**

QUOTE indications of renewed weakness in the US economy were contained in figures on industrial production for April

Financial Times

QUOTE central bank and finance ministry officials of the industrialized countries will continue work on the report

Wall Street Journal

QUOTE with the present overcapacity in the airline industry, discounting of tickets is widespread

Business Traveller

inelastic demand *noun* demand which experiences a comparatively small percentage change in response to a percentage change in price **unelastische Nachfrage;** *where a product is a household necessity, you almost always find an inelastic demand;* **inelastic supply** = supply which experiences a comparatively small percentage change in response to a percentage change in price **unelastisches Angebot**

inertia *noun* laziness *or* state of not being able to move or act **Trägheit; inertia selling** = method of selling items by sending them when they have not been ordered and assuming that if the items are not returned, the person who has received them is willing to buy them **negative Option, Trägheitsverkauf;** *see also* LAW OF INERTIA OF LARGE NUMBERS

inferior *adjective* not as good as others **minderwertig, zweitklassig;** *inferior products or products of inferior quality;* **inferior product** = product which consumers buy less of as their incomes rise **minderwertiges Produkt;** *margarine was clearly an inferior product before it came to be considered healthier than butter; as the recession hit, sales of inferior products soared*

inflation *noun* situation where prices rise to keep up with increased production costs **Inflation; we have 15% inflation** *or* **inflation is running at 15%** = prices are 15% higher than at the same time last year **die Inflation beträgt 15%;** *to take measures to reduce inflation; high interest rates tend to increase inflation;* **rate of inflation** *or* **inflation rate** = percentage increase in prices over a twelve-month period **Inflationsrate; demand-led inflation** = inflation caused by a rising demand for goods which cannot be met **Nachfrageinflation; galloping inflation** *or* **runaway inflation** = very rapid inflation which it is almost impossible to reduce **galoppierende Inflation; spiralling inflation** = inflation where price rises make workers ask for higher wages which then increase prices again **eine sich spiralartig entwickelnde Inflation**

◇ **inflationary** *adjective* which tends to increase inflation **Inflations-, inflatorisch, inflationsbedingt;** *inflationary trends in the economy;* **the economy is in an inflationary spiral** = in a situation where price rises encourage higher wage demands which in turn make prices rise **die Wirtschaft befindet sich in einer Inflationsspirale; anti-inflationary measures** = measures to reduce inflation **Maßnahmen zur Inflationsbekämpfung**

> QUOTE the decision by the government to tighten monetary policy will push the annual inflation rate above the year's previous high
> *Financial Times*
>
> QUOTE when you invest to get a return, you want a "real" return -above the inflation rate
> *Investors Chronicle*

inform *verb* to tell someone officially **informieren, mitteilen, benachrichtigen, unterrichten, in Kenntnis setzen;** *I regret to inform you that your tender was not acceptable; we are pleased to inform you that your offer has been accepted; we have been informed by the Department of Trade that new tariffs are coming into force*

◇ **informant** *noun* respondent *or* person who answers questions in a survey **Befragte(r);** *so far only two informants have said that they never buy the product; are most informants reluctant to be questioned?*

◇ **information** *noun*

(a) details which explain something **Information, Informationsmaterial, Unterlagen;** *please send me information on or about holidays in the USA; have you any information on or about deposit accounts? I enclose this leaflet for your information; to disclose a piece of information; to answer a request for information; for further information, please write to Department 27;* **disclosure of confidential information** = telling someone information which should be secret **Enthüllung/Offenlegung vertraulicher Informationen**

(b) information technology = working with computer data **Informationstechnik; information retrieval** = storing and then finding data in a computer **Datenabruf, Wiederauffinden von Information**

(c) information bureau *or* **information office** = office which gives information to tourists *or* visitors **Fremdenverkehrsamt; Auskunft, Information; information officer** = person whose job is to give information about a company *or* an organization *or* a government department to the public; person whose job is to give information to other departments in the same organization **Pressereferent**

inherent vice *noun* tendency of certain goods to spoil during transportation **Verderblichkeit;** *inherent vice discouraged us from importing tropical fruit; inherent vice and pilfering are both problems in the export of medicines to Africa*

in-home selling *noun* selling to a customer in his or her home, either by direct contact or by telephone **Zuhauseverkauf;** *in-home selling is the national strategy for our products; in-home selling is useful when housewives are the target market*

in-house *adjective & adverb* done inside a company's offices, not by an outside contractor **betriebsintern, innerbetrieblich;** *all our advertising material is produced in-house; our in-house design team is preparing dummies for the exhibition*

initial *adjective* first *or* starting **anfänglich, Anfangs-; initial capital** = capital which is used to start a business **Start-, Gründungskapital;** *he started the business with an initial expenditure or initial investment of £500;* **initial sales** = first sales of a new product **Anfangsverkauf;** *the initial response to the TV advertising has been very good*

innovate *verb* to bring in new ideas *or* new methods **Neuerungen einführen**

◇ **innovation** *noun* new idea *or* new method *or* new product **Neueinführung, Neuheit**

◇ **innovative** *adjective* (person or thing) which is new and makes changes **innovatorisch, progressiv**

◇ **innovator** *noun* person or company that brings in new ideas and methods; adopter who buys a new product first **Neuerer**

> QUOTE small innovative companies in IT have been hampered for lack of funds
> *Sunday Times*
>
> QUOTE if innovation equates with daring, then "who dares wins" will be a marketing commandment
> *Marketing Workshop*

input tax *noun* VAT which is paid by a company on goods or services bought **Vorsteuer**

inquiry *noun* request for information about a product **An-, Nachfrage; letter of inquiry** = letter from a prospective customer to a supplier inquiring about products and their prices **briefliche Anfrage;** *we receive ten letters of inquiry a week* *concerning our range of electronic typewriters*

insert *or* **inset**
1 *noun* thing which is put inside something **Beilage; an insert in a magazine mailing** *or* **a magazine insert** = advertising sheet put into a magazine when it is mailed **Werbebeilage; loose insert** = advertising sheet slipped between the pages of a magazine, not bound into it **lose Beilage**
2 *verb* to put something in **beilegen, hineinstecken; einfügen;** *to insert a clause in a contract; to insert a publicity piece in a magazine mailing*

inside front cover *noun* page on the inside of the front cover of a magazine, used for advertisements **Umschlagseite zwei; inside back cover** = similar page on the inside of the back cover **Umschlagseite drei**

instability *noun* being unstable *or* moving up and down **Unbeständigkeit, Veränderlichkeit, Instabilität; period of instability in the money markets** = period when currencies fluctuate rapidly **Zeit der Unsicherheit auf dem Geldmarkt**

install *verb* to put (a machine) into an office *or* into a factory **installieren, aufstellen;** *to install new machinery; to install a new data processing system*

◇ **installation** *noun*
(a) machines, equipment and buildings **Anlage;** *harbour installations; the fire seriously damaged the oil installations*
(b) putting new machines into an office *or* a factory **Installation, Aufstellen, Einbau;** *to supervise the installation of new equipment*

◇ **instalment** *or* *(US)* **installment** *noun* part of a sum owed which is paid regularly until the total amount is paid **Rate;** *the first instalment is payable on signature of the agreement;* **the final instalment is now due** = the last of a series of payments should be paid now **die letzte Rate ist fällig; to pay £25 down and monthly instalments of £20** = to pay a first payment of £25 and the rest in payments of £20 each month **£25 anbezahlen und den Rest in Monatsraten von £20 bezahlen; to miss an instalment** = not to pay an instalment at the right time **mit einer Rate in Rückstand geraten**

◇ **installment plan** *noun (US)* system of buying something by paying a sum regularly each month **Ratenzahlung, Teilzahlungssystem;** *to buy a car on the installment plan*
NOTE: GB English is **hire purchase**

institution *noun* organization *or* society set up for a particular purpose **Institut, Gesellschaft; financial institution** = bank *or* investment trust *or* insurance company whose work involves lending or investing large sums of money **Finanz-, Kreditinstitut**
◇ **institutional** *adjective* referring to a financial institution **institutionell, Instituts-; institutional buying** *or* **selling** = buying or selling shares by financial institutions **Effektenkauf od Effektenverkauf von Finanzinstituten; institutional advertising** = advertising an organization rather than a product **Unternehmens-, Firmenwerbung; institutional investors** = financial institutions who invest money in securities **Kapitalsammelstellen**

> QUOTE during the 1970s commercial property was regarded by big institutional investors as an alternative to equities
> *Investors Chronicle*

in-store promotion *noun* promotion of a product inside a shop, by demonstrations, special gift counters, etc. **Verkaufsförderung in einem Einzelhandelsgeschäft/Warenhaus**

> QUOTE dissatisfied with traditional media advertising, manufacturers in the USA are shifting their money into in-store promotion. The reason why marketers in the US put more effort into in-store marketing is the greater penetration of EPOS
> *Marketing Week*

instrument *noun* legal document **Urkunde, Dokument; negotiable instrument** = document (such as a bill of exchange, or cheque) which can be exchanged for cash **übertragbares/begebbares Wertpapier**

integrate *verb* to link things together to form one whole group **zusammenfassen, zusammenschließen, integrieren;** *(US)* **integrated communications concept** = concept *or* principle that a company should communicate a consistent image of itself and its products on several different levels **integriertes Kommunikationskonzept; integrated marketing** = co-ordination of all of a company's marketing activities in establishing marketing strategies (such as packaging, media promotion, POS material, after-sales service) **integriertes Marketing;** *the separation of departments makes integrated marketing difficult to achieve*
◇ **integration** *noun* bringing several businesses together under a central control **Zusammenfassung, Zusammenschluß, Integration; backward integration** = process of expansion in which a business becomes its own supplier **Rückwärtsintegration;**

forward integration = process of expansion in which a company becomes its own distributor **Vorwärtsintegration; horizontal integration** *or* **lateral integration** = joining similar companies *or* taking over a company in the same line of business as oneself **horizontale** *or* **seitliche Integration; vertical integration** = joining together businesses which deal with different stages in the production or sale of a product **vertikale Integration**

intensive *adjective* **intensive distribution** = use by a producer of as wide a network of distributors as possible to sell products **Intensivvertrieb;** *without intensive distribution we cannot hope to achieve these ambitious sales targets; intensive distribution makes us rely on too many retailers and wholesalers;* **capital-intensive industry** = industry which needs a large amount of capital investment in plant to make it work **kapitalintensiver Industriezweig; labour-intensive industry** = industry which needs large numbers of workers *or* where labour costs are high in relation to turnover **arbeitsintensiver Industriezweig**

intercompany *or* **interfirm comparison** *noun* comparison of different companies to see how much they spend on promotion, what their return on investment is, etc. **zwischenbetrieblicher Vergleich**

◇ **intermedia comparison** *noun* comparison of different media as vehicles for advertising **Intermediavergleich;** *we will carry out intermedia comparisons before deciding on our promotional strategy; compare* INTRAMEDIA COMPARISON

internal *adjective*

(a) inside a company **intern, innerbetrieblich; we decided to make an internal appointment** = we decided to appoint an existing member of staff to the post, and not bring someone in from outside the company **wir beschlossen, die Stelle intern zu besetzen; internal audit** = audit carried out by a department within the company **interne Revision; internal audit department** *or* **internal auditor** = department *or* member of staff who audits the accounts of the company he works for **betriebsinterne Revision; betriebsinterner Revisor; internal telephone** = telephone which is linked to other phones in an office **Haustelefon**

(b) inside a country **Inlands-, Binnen-, Innen-; internal flight** = flight to a town inside the same country **Inlandsflug;** *(US)* **Internal Revenue Service** = government department which deals with tax **Finanzamt, Finanzverwaltung; internal trade** = trade between various parts of a country **Binnenhandel**

◇ **internally** *adverb* inside a company **intern, innerbetrieblich;** *the job was advertised internally*

international *adjective* working between countries **international; international law** = laws governing relations between countries **internationales Recht, Völkerrecht; international marketing** = marketing of a company's products abroad **Internationales Marketing;** *our international marketing so far consists of exporting to three countries; the next stage in the company's international marketing was the setting up of factories overseas;* **the International Monetary Fund** = (part of the United Nations) a type of bank which helps member states in financial difficulties, gives financial advice to members and encourages world trade **Internationaler Währungsfonds, Weltwährungsfonds; international trade** = trade between different countries **Welthandel**

interpolation *noun* method of estimating a value between two established values **Interpolation**

interstate commerce *noun (US)* commerce between different states which is therefore subject to federal government control **zwischenstaatlicher Handel**

interview

1 *noun*

(a) talk with a person who is applying for a job **Vorstellungsgespräch;** *we called six people for interview; I have an interview next week or I am going for an interview next week; during the interview the candidate for the marketing job suggested some business strategies for the company*

(b) contact between a person looking for information or opinions and a person giving them, either through a meeting or by telephone or by post **Befragung, Interview;** *the respondent in the interview would give no opinions about the brand; For various types of interview see also* DEPTH, DIRECTIVE, GROUP, MAIL, PATTERNED, STRUCTURED

(c) sales interview = meeting between a salesman and prospective customer in which the latter may find out relevant information about a product or service in order to make a buying decision **Verkaufsgespräch**

2 *verb*

(a) to talk to a person applying for a job to see if he or she is suitable **ein**

Vorstellungsgespräch führen; *we interviewed ten candidates, but found no one suitable*
(b) to try to get information or opinions from someone, either through a meeting or by telephone or post **interviewen, befragen;** *we interviewed people in the street about their smoking habits*
◇ **interviewee** *noun* person who is being interviewed **Kandidat/-in, Befragte(r), Interviewte(r)**
◇ **interviewer** *noun* person who is conducting the interview **Gesprächsleiter; Interviewer**

intramedia comparison *adjective* comparison of different advertising options within the same medium **Intramediavergleich;** *after extensive intramedia comparison we now know all the possibilities of TV advertising; compare* INTERMEDIA COMPARISON

intransient *adjective* (advertisement) which the target audience can keep and look at again, such as one in a newspaper *or* magazine, as opposed to a transient advertisement on TV or radio **nicht vorübergehend**

in transit *adverb* **goods in transit** = goods being transported **Transitgüter**

intrinsic value *noun* material value of something **Eigenwert;** *these objects have sentimental value, but no intrinsic value at all; the intrinsic value of jewellery makes it a good investment*

introduce *verb* to make a new person or thing known to someone **vorstellen, einführen; to introduce a client** = to bring in a new client and make him known to someone **einen Kunden/Klienten einführen; to introduce a new product on the market** = to produce a new product and launch it on the market **ein neues Produkt auf den Markt bringen**
◇ **introductory** *adjective* **introductory offer** = special price offered on a new product to attract customers **Einführungspreis**

inventory
1 *noun*
(a) stock *or* goods in a warehouse or shop **Lagerbestände, Warenbestände;** *to carry a high inventory; to aim to reduce inventory;* **inventory control** = system of checking that there is not too much stock in a warehouse, but just enough to meet requirements **Bestandskontrolle**
(b) list of the contents of a house for sale, of an office for rent, etc. **Inventarverzeichnis, Inventarliste;** *to draw up an inventory of fixtures ;* **to agree the inventory** = to agree that the inventory is correct **die Inventarliste bestätigen**
2 *verb* to make a list of stock or contents **inventarisieren, Inventar/Bestände aufnehmen**

> QUOTE a warehouse needs to tie up less capital in inventory and with its huge volume spreads out costs over bigger sales
> *Duns Business Month*

investment *noun* placing money in such a way that it will increase in value **Investition, Kapital-, Vermögensanlage; investment advertising** = large expenditure on advertising to achieve long-term objectives **Investitionswerbung**

invisible
1 *adjective* **invisible assets** = assets which have a value but which cannot be seen (such as goodwill or patents) **unsichtbare Vermögenswerte; invisible earnings** = foreign currency earned by a country by providing services, not selling goods **unsichtbare Einkünfte, Einkünfte aus unsichtbaren Leistungen; invisible imports** *or* **exports** = services which are paid for in foreign currency or earn foreign currency without actually selling a product (such as banking or tourism) **unsichtbare Einfuhren; unsichtbare Ausfuhren**
2 *plural noun* **invisibles** = invisible imports and exports **unsichtbare Ein- und Ausfuhren**

invoice
1 *noun*
(a) note asking for payment for goods or services supplied **Rechnung;** *your invoice dated November 10th; they sent in their invoice six weeks late; to make out an invoice for £250; to settle or to pay an invoice;* **the total is payable within thirty days of invoice** = the total sum has to be paid within thirty days of the date on the invoice **der volle Betrag ist innerhalb von dreißig Tagen nach Rechnungsdatum zahlbar; VAT invoice** = invoice which includes VAT **Mehrwertsteuerrechnung**
(b) invoice clerk = office worker who deals with invoices **Fakturist/-in; invoice price** = price as given on an invoice (including discount and VAT) **Rechnungspreis; total invoice value** = total amount on an invoice, including transport, VAT, etc. **voller Rechnungsbetrag**
2 *verb* to send an invoice to someone **Rechnung ausstellen, fakturieren;** *to invoice a customer;* **we invoiced you on November 10th** = we sent you the invoice on November 10th **wir stellten Ihre Rechnung zum 10. November aus**

◇ **invoicing** *noun* sending of an invoice **Abrechnung, Rechnungsausstellung;** *our invoicing is done by computer;* **invoicing department** = department in a company which prepares and sends invoices **Rechnungsabteilung; invoicing in triplicate** = preparing three copies of invoices **Rechnungsausstellung in dreifacher Ausfertigung; VAT invoicing** = sending of an invoice including VAT **Rechnungsausstellung inklusive Mehrwertsteuer**

inward *adjective* towards the home country **Binnen-, Inlands-; inward bill** = bill of lading for goods arriving in a country **Importkonnossement; inward mission** = visit to one's home country by a group of foreign businessmen **Auslandsdelegation**

irrevocable *adjective* which cannot be changed **unwiderruflich; irrevocable acceptance** = acceptance which cannot be withdrawn **unwiderrufliche Annahme; irrevocable letter of credit** = letter of credit which cannot be cancelled or changed **unwiderrufliches Akkreditiv;** *the sellers insisted on being paid by irrevocable letter of credit*

island *noun* **island position** = advertising space separated from other advertising space in a newspaper *or* magazine **Alleinstellung, Inselposition;** *an island position is expensive but will attract great attention;* **island site** *or* **island display** = exhibition stand separated from others **alleinstehende Warenauslage;** *there are only two island sites at the exhibition and we have one of them; an island site means that visitors can approach the stand from several directions*

issue
1 *noun* number of a newspaper *or* magazine **Nummer, Ausgabe; issue life** = time between one issue of a publication and another **Erscheinungsintervall; Lebensdauer der Ausgabe eines Druckmediums;** *the reason the magazine's advertising rates are so expensive is because it has an issue life of three months*
2 *verb* to put out *or* to give out **ausstellen, herausgeben, veröffentlichen, ausgeben, emittieren;** *to issue a letter of credit; to issue shares in a new company; to issue a writ against someone; the government issued a report on London's traffic*

ITC = INDEPENDENT TELEVISION COMMISSION

item *noun*
(a) thing for sale **Artikel, Gegenstand; cash items** = goods sold for cash **Barposten; we are holding orders for out-of-stock items** = for goods which are not in stock **wir haben Bestellungen für Artikel, die nicht am Lager sind;** *please find enclosed an order for the following items from your catalogue*
(b) piece of information **Posten;** *items on a balance sheet;* **extraordinary items** = items in accounts which do not appear each year and need to be noted **Sonderposten; item of expenditure** = goods or services which have been paid for and appear in the accounts **Ausgabeposten**
(c) point on a list **Punkt; we will now take item four on the agenda** = we will now discuss the fourth point on the agenda **wir gehen jetzt zu Punkt vier der Tagesordnung über**
◇ **itemize** *verb* to make a detailed list of things **einzeln aufführen, spezifizieren;** *itemizing the sales figures will take about two days;* **itemized account** = detailed record of money paid or owed **spezifizierte Abrechnung; itemized invoice** = invoice which lists each item separately **aufgegliederte Rechnung**

itinerary *noun* list of places to be visited on one journey **(Vertreter-)Reiseroute;** *a salesman's itinerary*

Jj

jingle *noun* **advertising jingle** *or* **publicity jingle** = short and easily remembered tune to advertise a product on television, etc. **Werbemelodie, Jingle**

job *noun*
(a) piece of work *or* order being worked on **Arbeit, Aufgabe;** *we are working on six jobs at the moment; the shipyard has a big job starting in August*
(b) job lot = group of miscellaneous items sold together **Warenposten;** *he sold the household furniture as a job lot*
◇ **jobber** *noun (US)* wholesaler **Großhändler; rack jobber** = wholesaler who sells goods by putting them on racks in retail shops **Regalgroßhändler**
◇ **jobbing** *noun* doing small pieces of work **Jobben, Gelegenheitsarbeiten verrichten; jobbing gardener** *or* **jobbing printer** = person who does odd jobs in the garden *or* who does small printing jobs **Lohngärtner; Akzidenzdrucker; jobbing production** =

production of several different articles, each to individual requirements **Akkordarbeit**

journal *noun*
(a) book with the account of sales and purchases made each day **Journal**
(b) magazine **Zeitschrift; house journal** = magazine produced for the workers in a company to give them news about the company **Hauszeitschrift, Werkszeitung; trade journal** = magazine produced for people or companies in a certain trade **Branchen-, Fachblatt**

◇ **journalist** *noun* person who writes for a newspaper **Journalist/-in**

journey *noun* long trip, especially a trip made by a salesman **Reise;** *he planned his journey so that he could visit all his accounts in two days;* **journey mapping** = method of calculating how many people pass a poster site **Passantenzählung;** *journey mapping allows us to pinpoint the ten key sites we will be renting for the next three months;* **journey order** = order given by the shopkeeper to a salesman when he calls **Auftrag an Vertreter; journey planning** = planning what calls a salesperson will make and how he or she will reach them most efficiently, giving priority to the more profitable accounts **(Vertreter-)Routenplanung;** *the sales manager will stress how good journey planning will save precious time; inefficient journey planning means miles of unnecessary travelling for the sales force every day*

judgement *or* **judgment** *noun* assessment *or* evaluation of the quality of someone or something **Ansicht, Urteil; judgement forecasting** = forecasting based on judgement rather than on any scientific techniques **intuitive Prognoseverfahren;** *we need more precise information so that we can extrapolate rather than use judgement forecasting; market research departments find judgement forecasting too subjective and unreliable;* **judgement sampling** = choosing a sample for a survey based on judgement of what units would be especially significant rather than applying any scientific techniques **intuitive Stichprobenbildung;** *judgement sampling can produce an insufficiently representative sample*

jumble sale *noun* sale of odd secondhand items organized by a club or organization to raise money; *(entspricht)* **Wohltätigkeitsbasar**

jumpy *adjective* nervous *or* excited **nervös, schreckhaft; the market is jumpy** = the stock market is nervous and share prices are likely to fluctuate **die Börse ist unsicher**

junk mail *noun* unsolicited advertising material which is mailed and thrown away immediately by the people who receive it **(unerwünschte) Reklamesendungen, Wegwerfpost, Papierkorb-Werbung**

jury of executive opinion *noun* using a panel of executives to contribute to forecasting; *(entspricht)* **Expertenpanel**

Kk

KD = KNOCK DOWN

keen *adjective*
(a) eager *or* active **eifrig, aktiv; keen competition** = strong competition **scharfer Wettbewerb;** *we are facing some keen competition from European manufacturers;* **keen demand** = wide demand **große Nachfrage;** *there is a keen demand for home computers*
(b) keen prices = prices which are kept low so as to be competitive **günstige Preise;** *our prices are the keenest on the market*

kerbside conference *noun* discussion of selling techniques between a trainee salesman and the person training him after making a sales call **Besprechung am Straßenrand;** *in the kerbside conference, the sales trainer described a number of different approaches that might have been made to a particular customer*

key *adjective* important **Schlüssel-;** *key factor; key industry; key personnel; key post; key staff;* **key account** = important account or client of an advertising agency **Hauptauftraggeber, Hauptklient, Hauptkunde; key number** = number used in a keyed advertisement **Kennziffer, Chiffre; key prospects** = promising *or* hopeful potential customers **potentielle Kunden;** *in this sales campaign we will be concentrating on key prospects; this is bad journey planning since it does not allow sufficient time to visit all the key prospects*

◇ **keyed advertisement** *noun* advertisement which asks people to write to a specially coded address which will indicate where they saw it, thus helping the advertisers to evaluate the effectiveness of advertising in that particular newspaper *or* magazine **Kennzifferanzeige**

◇ **keypad** *noun* set of keys on a computer **Kleintastatur; numeric keypad** = set of programmable numbered keys on a computer **Zehnertastatur, numerische Tastatur**

kickback *noun* illegal commission paid to someone (especially a government official) who helps in a business deal **Schmiergeld**

king-size *adjective* (i) extra large container of a product (usually comparatively economical to buy); (ii) very large size of poster **(i) großformatig; (ii) King-Size-(Plakat)** *the cash-and-carry only sells king-size packs; the king-size carton contains twice as much as the regular size, but is less than twice as expensive*

kiosk *noun* small wooden shelter, for selling goods out of doors **Kiosk;** *a newspaper kiosk;* **telephone kiosk** = shelter with a public telephone in it **Telefonzelle**

kite *noun (GB)* **kite mark** = mark on goods to show they meet official standards **Gütezeichen**

knock *verb* **to knock the competition** = to hit competing firms hard by vigorous selling **die Konkurrenz schlagen; knocking copy** = advertising material which criticizes competing products **herabsetzende Werbung**

◇ **knock down** *verb* **to knock something down to a bidder** = to sell something at an auction **jdm etwas zuschlagen, jdm den Zuschlag erteilen;** *the stock was knocked down to him for £10,000*

◇ **knockdown** *noun*
(a) knockdown (KD) goods = goods sold in parts, which must be assembled by the buyer **in Einzelteile zerlegte Güter, Selbstbauprodukte;** *many do-it-yourself enthusiasts are buying our knock-down goods; compare* CKD
(b) knockdown prices = very low prices **Spottpreise;** *he sold me the car at a knockdown price*

◇ **knock off** *verb* to reduce a price by a certain amount **nachlassen;** *he knocked £10 off the price as I was paying cash*

> QUOTE for some years butter advertising tended to knock other fats such as margarine
> *Marketing Week*

know-how *noun* knowledge about how something works *or* how something is made **Know-how, Fachkenntnisse;** *electronic know-how; to acquire computer know-how*

Ll

label
1 *noun*
(a) piece of paper *or* card attached to something to show its price *or* an address *or* instructions for use **Etikett, Anhängeschild; gummed label** = label which you wet to make it stick on the item **Aufkleber; self-sticking label** = sticky label, ready to stick on an item **Selbstklebeetikett; tie-on label** = label with a piece of string attached so that it can be tied on to an item **Anhänger**
(b) address label = label with an address on it **Adressenaufkleber; Adressenanhänger; price label** = label showing a price **Preisschild; quality label** = label which states the quality of something **Gütezeichen**
(c) own label goods = goods specially produced for a store with the store's name on them **Eigenmarkenwaren**
2 *verb* to attach a label to something **etikettieren; mit einem Anhänger od Aufkleber versehen; incorrectly labelled parcel** = parcel with the wrong information on the label **falsch beschriftetes Paket**

◇ **labelling** *noun* putting a label on something **Etikettierung; Anbringen eines Anhängers od Aufklebers; labelling department** = section of a factory where labels are attached to the product **Etikettierungsabteilung**

lading *noun* loading *or* putting goods on a ship **Verladen; bill of lading** = list of goods being shipped, which the transporter gives to the person sending the goods to show that they have been loaded **Konnossement**

laggards *noun* category of adopters of a product who are the last to buy it or use it **Nachzügler, Zauderer**

laissez-faire economy *noun* economy where the government does not interfere because it believes it is right to let the economy run itself **Laisser-faire-Wirtschaftspolitik**

land *verb* to put goods *or* passengers on land after a voyage by sea *or* by air **ab-, ausladen; von Bord gehen lassen; löschen;** *to* *land goods at a port; to land passengers at an airport;* **landed costs** = costs of goods which have been delivered to a port, unloaded and passed through customs **Fracht- und Löschungskosten**

◇ **landing** *noun* **landing card** = card given to passengers who have passed customs and can land from a ship *or* an aircraft **Einreisekarte; landing charges** = payment for putting goods on land and the customs duties **Löschungskosten und Löschungszölle; landing order** = permit which allows goods to be unloaded into a bonded warehouse without paying customs duty **Löscherlaubnis**

landscape *noun* illustration or page or a book whose width is greater than its height **querformatige Seite;** *compare* PORTRAIT

late

1 *adjective*

(a) after the time stated or agreed **spät, verspätet;** *we apologize for the late arrival of the plane from Amsterdam;* **there is a penalty for late delivery** = if delivery is later than the agreed date, the supplier has to pay a fine **verspätete Lieferungen werden mit einer Strafe belegt; late majority** = category of adopters of a product who buy or use it after the early majority but before the laggards **späte Mehrheit**

(b) at the end of a period of time **letzter; latest date for signature of the contract** = the last acceptable date for signing the contract **der letzte Termin für die Vertragsunterzeichnung**

(c) latest = most recent **letzter, jüngster;** *he always drives the latest model of car; here are the latest sales figures*

2 *adverb* after the time stated or agreed **spät, verspätet;** *the shipment was landed late; the plane was two hours late*

latent demand *noun* situation where there is demand for a product but potential customers are unable to pay for it **latenter Bedarf;** *we will have to wait for the economy to improve in countries where there is latent demand; situation analysis has shown that there is only latent demand*

lateral *adjective* moving to the side; referring to the side **seitlich, Seiten-; lateral diversification** = adding another quite different type of business to a firm's existing trade **seitliche Diversifikation;** *lateral diversification means bringing in new expertise; lateral diversification brought the company into unknown territory;* **lateral integration** = joining similar companies or taking over a company in the same line of business as oneself **seitliche Integration;** *lateral integration will allow a pooling of resources; lateral integration in the form of a merger will improve the efficiency of both businesses involved;* **lateral thinking** = imaginative approach to problem-solving which involves changing established patterns of thinking to help make a breakthrough **Querdenken, unorthodoxe Denkweise;** *lateral thinking resulted in finding a completely new use for an existing product; brainstorming sessions encourage lateral thinking and originality*

launch

1 *verb* to put a new product on the market (usually spending money on advertising it) **herausbringen, auf den Markt bringen;** *they launched their new car model at the motor show; the company is spending thousands of pounds on launching a new brand of soap*

2 *noun* act of putting a new product on the market **Einführung;** *the launch of the new model has been put back three months; the company is geared up for the launch of its first microcomputer; the management has decided on a September launch date;* **rolling launch** = the gradual launch of a product, by releasing it in selected areas over a period **stufenweise Einführung**

◇ **launching** *noun* act of putting a new product on the market **Einführung; launching costs** = costs of publicity for a new product **Anlaufkosten; launching date** = date when a new product is officially shown to the public for the first time **Einführungstermin; launching party** = party held to advertise the launching of a new product **Einführungsparty für ein neues Produkt**

law *noun* general rule **Gesetz; law of supply and demand** = general rule that the amount of a product which is available is related to the needs of potential customers **Gesetz von Angebot und Nachfrage; law of diminishing returns** = the general rule that beyond a certain point, an increase in one factor of production (land, capital or labour) while the other factors remain constant, will not produce an equal increase in output or profit **Gesetzmäßigkeit vom abnehmenden Ertragszuwachs; law of inertia of large numbers** = principle that larger samples are more likely to be representative of the population than small ones **Gesetz der großen Zahl(en); law of statistical regularity** = principle that a group of people or objects taken from a larger group of people or objects will tend to resemble the larger group **Repräsentativstatistik**

layout *noun* arrangement of words and pictures **Layout;** *I like the illustration and* *the copy but not the layout; the layout needs to be changed so that other features are highlighted*

L/C = LETTER OF CREDIT

lead
1 *noun* information which may lead to a sale **Hinweis;** *it has been difficult starting selling in this territory with no leads to follow up; I was given some useful leads by the salesman who used to cover this territory*
2 *verb*
(a) to be the first *or* to be in front **(an)führen, an der Spitze stehen;** *the company leads the market in cheap computers*
(b) to be the main person in a group **leiten, (an)führen;** *she will lead the trade mission to Nigeria; the tour of American factories will be led by the minister*
◇ **leader** *noun*
(a) person who manages *or* directs others **Leiter/-in, Vorsitzender/Vorsitzende;** *the leader of the construction workers' union or the construction workers' leader; she is the leader of the trade mission to Nigeria; the leader of the trade delegation was invited to meet the President*
(b) product which sells best **Spitzenreiter, führender Artikel; a market leader** = product which sells most in a market *or* company which has the largest share of a market **ein Marktführer; leader pricing** = cutting prices on some goods in the hope that they attract customers to the shop where more profitable sales can be made **Lockpreisstrategie;** *I didn't realize leader pricing was being used until I saw the loss-leaders in the window;* **loss-leader** = article which is sold very cheaply to attract customers **Lockartikel**
(c) main article in a newspaper *or* magazine **Leitartikel;** *we got some welcome publicity in this morning's leader; the leader was very critical of the government's policy*
◇ **leading question** *noun* question in a questionnaire which, by its phrasing, suggests a certain answer **Suggestivfrage;** *interviewers were trained to avoid bias and leading questions; the leading question pressurized the respondent into answering untruthfully*
◇ **lead time** *noun* time between deciding to place an order and receiving the product **Lieferzeit;** *the lead time on this item is more than six weeks*

leaflet *noun* sheet of paper giving information, used to advertise something **Hand-, Reklamezettel;** *to mail leaflets advertising a new hair-dressing salon; they are handing out leaflets describing the financial services they offer; we made a leaflet mailing to 20,000 addresses;* **leave leaflet** = promotional leaflet left by a salesman with a prospective customer **Werbezettel**

leakage *noun* amount of goods lost in storage (by going bad *or* by being stolen *or* by leaking from the container) **Schwund, Verlust**

learning curve *noun* line on a graph which shows the relationship between experience in doing something and competence at carrying it out **Lernkurve**

ledger *noun* book in which accounts are written **Hauptbuch; bought ledger** *or* **purchase ledger** = book in which expenditure is noted **Einkaufsbuch; bought ledger clerk** *or* **sales ledger clerk** = office worker who deals with the bought ledger *or* the sales ledger **Einkaufsbuchhalter; nominal ledger** = book which records a company's income and expenditure in general **Hauptbuch; payroll ledger** = list of staff and their salaries **Lohn- und Gehaltsliste; sales ledger** = book in which sales are noted **Warenausgangsbuch**

legal *adjective*
(a) according to the law *or* allowed by the law **legal, rechtmäßig;** *the company's action was completely legal*
(b) referring to the law **juristisch, rechtlich, Rechts-; to take legal action** = to sue someone *or* to take someone to court **gerichtlich (gegen jdn) vorgehen; to take legal advice** = to ask a lawyer to advise about a legal problem **sich juristisch beraten lassen; legal adviser** = person who advises clients about the law **Rechtsberater; legal currency** = money which is legally used in a country **gesetzliches Zahlungsmittel; legal department** *or* **legal section** = section of a company dealing with legal matters **Rechtsabteilung; legal tender** = coins or notes which can be legally used in making a payment (small denominations cannot be used to pay large debts) **gesetzliches Zahlungsmittel**
◇ **legality** *noun* being allowed by law **Legalität, Gesetzmäßigkeit;** *there is doubt about the legality of the company's action in dismissing him*
◇ **legalize** *verb* to make something legal **legalisieren**
◇ **legalization** *noun* making something legal **Legalisierung**
◇ **legally** *adverb* according to the law **rechtlich; gesetzlich; juristisch; the contract is legally binding** = according to the law, the contract has to be obeyed **der Vertrag ist**

rechtsverbindlich; the directors are legally responsible = the law says that the directors are responsible **die Direktoren sind vor dem Gesetz juristisch verantwortlich**

legend *noun* short note printed underneath an illustration to explain it **Bildunterschrift**

legislation *noun* laws **Gesetzgebung; labour legislation** = laws concerning the employment of workers **Arbeitsgesetzgebung; Arbeitsgesetze**

letter *noun*
(a) piece of writing sent from one person *or* company to another to give information **Brief; business letter** = letter which deals with business matters **Geschäftsbrief; circular letter** = letter sent to many people **Rundschreiben; Umlauf; covering letter** = letter sent with documents to say why they are being sent **Begleitschreiben; follow-up letter** = letter sent to someone who has not acted on the instructions in a previous letter, or to discuss in more detail points which were raised earlier **Nachfaß-, Folgeschreiben; standard letter** = letter which is sent without change to various correspondents **Standard-, Formbrief**
(b) letter of acknowledgement = letter which says that something has been received **Bestätigungsschreiben; letters of administration** = letter given by a court to allow someone to deal with the estate of someone who has died **Bestallungsurkunde zum Nachlaßverwalter; letter of advice** = letter to a customer giving details of goods ordered and shipped but not yet delivered **Avis, Versandanzeige;** *the letter of advice stated that the goods would be at Southampton on the morning of the 6th; the letter of advice reminded the customer of the agreed payment terms;* **letter of complaint** = letter in which someone complains **Beschwerdebrief; letter of credit (L/C)** = letter from a bank allowing someone credit and promising to repay at a later date **Akkreditiv; letter of indemnity** = letter promising payment of compensation for a loss **(schriftliche) Schadloshaltungs-, Ausfallbürgschaftserklärung; letter of inquiry** = letter from a prospective buyer to a supplier inquiring about products and their prices **Anfragebrief;** *the letter of inquiry requested us to send our catalogues and price lists; we received a letter of inquiry concerning possible trade discounts;* **letter of intent** = letter which states what a company intends to do if something happens **Absichtserklärung; letters patent** = official document which gives someone the exclusive right to make and sell something which he has invented **Patenturkunde;**
◇ **letterhead** *noun* name and address of a company printed at the top of a piece of notepaper **Briefkopf**

level *noun* position of something compared to others **Stand, Niveau, Ebene; stock level** = quantity of goods kept in stock **Lagerbestandshöhe; reorder level** = minimum amount of stock of an item, which must be reordered when stock reaches this point **Mindestnachbestellung**

levy
1 *noun* money which is demanded and collected by the government **Steuer; Abgabe; capital levy** = tax on the value of a person's property and possessions **Vermögenssteuer; import levy** = tax on imports, especially, a tax imposed by the EC on imports of farm produce from outside the EC **Einfuhrzoll;** *(EG)* **Abschöpfung; levies on luxury items** = taxes on luxury items **Luxussteuer; training levy** = tax to be paid by companies to fund the government's training schemes **Ausbildungsabgabe**
2 *verb* to demand payment of a tax *or* an extra sum and to collect it **erheben; einziehen;** *the government has decided to levy a tax on imported cars; to levy a duty on the import of luxury items*

> QUOTE royalties have been levied at a rate of 12.5% of full production
> *Lloyd's List*

liability *noun*
(a) being legally responsible for damage *or* loss, etc. **Haftung; to accept liability for something** = to agree that you are responsible for something **für etwas Haftung übernehmen; to refuse liability for something** = to refuse to agree that you are responsible for something **es ablehnen, für etwas zu haften; contractual liability** = legal responsibility for something as stated in a contract **Vertragshaftung; employers' liability insurance** = insurance to cover accidents which may happen at work, and for which the company may be responsible **Unfallhaftpflichtversicherung der Arbeitgeber; limited liability** = situation where someone's liability for debt is limited by law **beschränkte Haftung; limited liability company** = company where a shareholder is responsible for repaying the company's debts only to the face value of the shares he owns **Gesellschaft mit beschränkter Haftung**
(b) liabilities = debts of a business **Verbindlichkeiten, Schulden;** *the balance sheet shows the company's assets and liabilities;* **current liabilities** = debts which

a company should pay within the next accounting period **kurzfristige Verbindlichkeiten; long-term liabilities** = debts which are not due to be paid for some time **langfristige Verbindlichkeiten; he was not able to meet his liabilities** = he could not pay his debts **er konnte seinen Zahlungsverpflichtungen nicht nachkommen; to discharge one's liabilities in full** = to pay everything which one owes **seinen Verbindlichkeiten in voller Höhe nachkommen**

◇ **liable** *adjective*
(a) liable for = legally responsible for **haftbar für;** *the customer is liable for breakages; the chairman was personally liable for the company's debts*
(b) liable to = for which a certain type of payment will have to be made **unterliegen, unterworfen;** *goods which are liable to stamp duty*

licence *or* *(US)* **license** *noun*
(a) official document which allows someone to do something **Genehmigung; Konzession; Lizenz; driving licence** = document which allows someone to drive a car *or* a truck, etc. **Führerschein;** *applicants should hold a valid driving licence;* **import licence** *or* **export licence** = documents which allow goods to be exported or imported **Einfuhrlizenz; Ausfuhrlizenz; liquor licence** = government document allowing someone to sell alcohol **Schankkonzession; off licence** = licence to sell alcohol to be drunk away from the place where it is bought; shop which sells alcohol for drinking at home **Konzession zum Alkoholverkauf; Wein- und Spirituosenhandlung**
(b) goods manufactured under licence = goods made with the permission of the owner of the copyright or patent **in Lizenz hergestellte Waren**

◇ **license**
1 *noun (US)* = LICENCE
2 *verb* to give someone official permission to do something, as when a company allows another to manufacture its products abroad **eine Erlaubnis od Lizenz od Konzession erteilen, genehmigen;** *licensed to sell beers, wines and spirits; to license a company to manufacture spare parts; she is licensed to run an employment agency*

◇ **licensee** *noun* person who has a licence, especially a licence to sell alcohol *or* to manufacture something **Konzessionsinhaber; Lizenzinhaber**

◇ **licensing** *noun* which refers to licences **Schank-; Lizenz-; Konzessions-;** *a licensing agreement; licensing laws; (GB)* **licensing hours** = hours of the day when alcohol can be sold **Ausschankzeiten**

lien *noun* legal right to hold someone's goods and keep them until a debt has been paid **Sicherungspfandrecht**

life *noun* period of time for which something or someone exists **Leben;** *the life of a loan; during the life of the agreement;* **life annuity** *or* **annuity for life** = annual payments made to someone as long as he or she is alive **Leibrente; life assurance** *or* **life insurance** = insurance which pays a sum of money when someone dies, or at a certain date if he or she is still alive **Lebensversicherung; the life assured** *or* **the life insured** = the person whose life has been covered by the life assurance **der Versicherte (in einer Lebensversicherung); life expectancy** = number of years a person is likely to live **Lebenserwartung; shelf life of a product** = length of time during which a product can stay in the shop and still be good to use **Haltbarkeit/Lagerfähigkeit eines Produktes**

◇ **life cycle** *noun* concept used for charting the different stages in the life of people, animals or products **Lebenszyklus; product life cycle** = stages in the life of a product in terms of sales and profitability, from its launch to its decline **Produktlebenszyklus;** *growth is the first stage in the product life cycle*

◇ **life style** *noun* way of living of a particular section of society **Lebensstil;** *these up-market products appeal to people with an extravagant life style; the magazine ran a series of articles on the life styles of some successful businessmen;* **life-style segmentation** = dividing a market into segments according to the way in which customers live **Marktsegmentierung aufgrund des Lebensstils der Kunden;** *see also* VALS

light *adjective*
(a) not heavy **leicht; shares fell back in light trading** = shares lost value on a day when there was little business done on the Stock Exchange **die Aktienwerte fielen bei schwachen Umsätzen; light industry** = industry which makes small products (such as clothes, books, calculators, etc.) **Leichtindustrie light viewer** = person who watches little television **seltener Fernsehzuschauer;** *if too many of the target audience are light viewers, the impact of the commercials will be wasted*
(b) light pen = type of pen which, when passed over a bar code, can read it and pass information in it back to a central computer **Lichtstift**

limit
1 *noun* point at which something ends *or* point where you can go no further **Grenze,**

Limit; to set limits on imports *or* **to impose import limits** = to allow only a certain quantity of imports **Importbeschränkungen einführen; age limit** = top age at which you are allowed to do a job **Altersgrenze;** *there is an age limit of thirty-five on the post of buyer;* **credit limit** = largest amount of money which a customer can borrow **Kreditlinie, Kreditlimit; he has exceeded his credit limit** = he has borrowed more money than he is allowed **er hat seine Kreditlinie überzogen; lending limit** = restriction on the amount of money a bank can lend **Kreditlimit; time limit** = maximum time which can be taken to do something **Frist;** *to set a time limit for acceptance of the offer;* **weight limit** = maximum weight **Höchstgewicht**
2 *verb* to stop something from going beyond a certain point **begrenzen, be-, einschränken; the banks have limited their credit** = the banks have allowed their customers only a certain amount of credit **die Banken haben ihre Kreditvergabe begrenzt; each agent is limited to twenty-five units** = each agent is allowed only twenty-five units to sell **jeder Vertreter bekommt nur fünfundzwanzig Einheiten**

◇ **limitation** *noun*
(a) act of allowing only a certain quantity of something **Be-, Einschränkung, Begrenzung; limitation of liability** = making someone liable for only a part of the damage or loss **Haftungsbeschränkung; time limitation** = limiting the amount of time available **zeitliche Begrenzung;** *the contract imposes limitations on the number of cars which can be imported*
(b) statute of limitations = law which allows only a certain amount of time (a few years) for someone to claim damages or property **Verjährungsausschlußfrist**

◇ **limited** *adjective* restricted *or* not open **beschränkt, begrenzt; limited function wholesaler** = distributor performing only some of the functions of a wholesaler **Streckengroßhändler;** *as a limited function wholesaler the dealer did not provide a delivery service to retailers;* **limited liability** = situation where someone's liability for debt is limited by law **beschränkte Haftung; limited liability company** = company where a shareholder is responsible for the company's debts only to the face value of his shares **Gesellschaft mit beschränkter Haftung; limited market** = market which can take only a certain quantity of goods **begrenzter Absatzmarkt; private limited company** = company with a small number of shareholders, whose shares are not traded on the Stock Exchange; *(entspricht)* **Gesellschaft mit beschränkter Haftung; Public Limited Company** = company whose shares can be bought on the Stock Exchange; *(entspricht)* **Aktiengesellschaft;**

◇ **limiting** *adjective* which limits **be-, einschränkend;** *a limiting clause in a contract; the short holiday season is a limiting factor on the hotel trade*

line *noun*
(a) long mark printed or written on paper **Linie;** *he drew a thick line across the bottom of the column to show which figure was the total;* **line block** = printing block for line drawings **Strichätzung; line drawing** *or* **line illustration** = drawing or illustration consisting only of lines and no tones (shades are shown by lines drawn close together) **Strichzeichnung, Federzeichnung**
(b) shipping line *or* **airline** = large shipping or aircraft company which carries passengers or cargo **Reederei; Fluggesellschaft;** *the profits of major airlines have been affected by the rise in fuel prices*
(c) line of business *or* **line of work** = type of business or work **Branche, Sparte; line of product** *or* **product line** = series of different products which form a group, all made by the same company **Produktlinie, Produktgruppe;** *we do not stock that line; computers are not one of our best-selling lines; they produce an interesting line in garden tools;* **line divestment** = dropping or selling an entire product line so as to concentrate on other products **Eliminierung einer Produktgruppe; line simplification** = removing some products from a product line to make the whole line more easily manageable **Rationalisierung einer Produktlinie**
(d) row of letters *or* figures on a page **Zeile; bottom line** = (i) the last line in accounts, showing the net profit; (ii) final result **Saldo;** *the boss is only interested in the bottom line;* **to open a line of credit** *or* **a credit line** = to make credit available to someone **eine Kreditlinie einräumen**
(e) assembly line *or* **production line** = production system where the product (such as a car) moves slowly through a factory with new sections being added to it as it goes along **Montage-, Fließband, Fertigungsstraße;** *he works on the production line or he's a production line worker in the car factory*
(f) line chart *or* **line graph** = chart or graph using lines to indicate values **Linien-, Strichdiagramm; line printer** = machine which prints information from a computer one line at a time **Zeilendrucker**
(g) line of command *or* **line management** *or* **line organization** = way of organizing a business so that each manager is responsible for doing what his superior tells him to do **Linienorganisation**

lineage *noun* method of measuring a classified advertisement by counting the lines, used for charging purposes **Anzeigenraum, Zeilenzahl**

list
1 *noun*
(a) several items written one after the other **Liste;** *list of products or product list; stock list; to add an item to a list; to cross an item off a list;* **address list** *or* **mailing list** = list of names and addresses of people and companies **Adressenliste; black list** = list of goods *or* companies *or* countries which are banned for trade **schwarze Liste; no direct mail list** = list of people who do not wish to receive any direct mail **Robinsonliste; picking list** = list of items in an order, but listed according to where they can be found in the warehouse **Entnahmeliste**
(b) catalogue **Verzeichnis, Liste; list price** = price as given in a catalogue **Listenpreis; price list** = sheet giving prices of goods for sale **Preisliste**
2 *verb* to write a series of items one after the other **auflisten;** *to list products by category; to list representatives by area; to list products in a catalogue; the catalogue lists twenty-three models of washing machines*
◇ **listing** *noun* **computer listing** = printout of a list of items taken from the data stored in a computer **Computerausdruck; listing paper** = paper made as a long sheet, used in computer printers **Tabellierpapier**

literature *noun* written information about something **Literatur; Prospekte;** *please send me literature about your new product range*

lithography *noun* printing process using a flat surface rather than a raised or relief surface, which works on the principle that ink will be retained on the printing areas of a specially treated surface but not on other areas which have not been treated **Lithographie**

livery *noun* a company's own special design, used on uniforms, office decoration, vehicles, etc. **Firmenzeichen**

living *noun* **cost of living** = money which a person has to pay for rent, food, heating, etc. **Lebenshaltungskosten; cost-of-living index** = way of measuring the cost of living which is shown as a percentage increase on the figure for the previous year **Lebenshaltungskostenindex; he doesn't earn a living wage** = he doesn't earn enough to pay for essentials (food, heat, rent, etc.) **er verdient nicht genug zum Leben; standard of living** *or* **living standards** = quality of personal home life (amount of food, number of clothes bought, size of the family car, etc.) **Lebensstandard;** *living standards fell as unemployment rose*

load
1 *noun*
(a) goods which are transported **Ladung; load of a lorry** *or* **of a container** = goods carried by a lorry or container **Lastwagenladung; Containerladung; lorry-load** *or* **container-load** = amount of goods carried on a lorry or container **Lastwagenladung; Containerladung;** *a container-load of spare parts is missing; they delivered six lorry-loads of coal;* **commercial load** = amount of goods *or* number of passengers which a bus *or* train *or* plane has to carry to make a profit **wirtschaftliche Auslastung; maximum load** = largest weight of goods which a lorry *or* plane can carry **Beladungsgrenze; load-carrying capacity** = amount of goods which a lorry is capable of carrying **Ladefähigkeit; load factor** = number of seats in a bus *or* train *or* plane which are occupied by passengers who have paid the full fare **Auslastungs-, Kapazitätsfaktor**
(b) workload = amount of work which a person has to do **Arbeitsbelastung;** *the sales manager has difficulty coping with his heavy workload*
2 *verb*
(a) to load a lorry *or* **a ship** = to put goods into a lorry *or* a ship for transporting **einen Lastwagen beladen; ein Schiff beladen;** *to load cargo onto a ship; a truck loaded with boxes; a ship loaded with iron;* **a fully loaded ship** = a ship which is full of cargo **ein voll beladenes Schiff**
(b) *(Schiff)* to take on cargo **beladen;** *the ship is loading a cargo of wood*
(c) to put a program into a computer **laden;** *load the word-processing program before you start keyboarding*
(d) loaded price = price which includes an unusually large extra payment for some service **hochgeschraubter Preis;** *that company is notorious for its loaded prices*
◇ **loading** *noun* **loading bay** = section of a warehouse where lorries can drive in to be loaded **Ladeplatz; loading dock** = part of a harbour where ships can load or unload **Verladedock; loading ramp** = raised platform which makes it easier to load goods onto a lorry **Laderampe**

local *adjective* referring to a small area of a country or part of a large town **örtlich, Orts-, lokal; local newspapers** *or* **the local press** = newspapers which are sold in a small area of the country **Lokalblätter; die**

Lokalpresse; local radio station = radio station which broadcasts over a small area of the country **Lokal-, Regionalsender;** *the product was only advertised in the local press as it was only being distributed in that area of the country*

location *noun* place, especially a site where still photographs or films are made **Lage, Standort;** *we still have to decide on locations for the advertisements*

logical models *noun* models of buyer decision-making which assume that purchasing is the result of a set of rational decisions made by the purchaser **logische Modelle;** *logical models do not allow for the unpredictable side of buying behaviour*

logo *or* **logotype** *noun* symbol *or* design *or* group of letters used by a company as a distinguishing mark on its products and in advertising **Firmenzeichen, Logo**

long-dated *adjective* **long-dated bills** = bills which are payable in more than three months' time **langfristige Wechsel**

◇ **long-range** *adjective* for a long period of time in the future **langfristig; long-range economic forecast** = forecast which covers a period of several years **langfristige Konjunkturprognose**

◇ **long-standing** *adjective* which has been arranged for a long time **schon lange bestehend, alt;** *long-standing agreement;* **long-standing customer** *or* **customer of long standing** = person who has been a customer for many years **Stammkunde**

◇ **long-term** *adjective* **on a long-term basis** = for a long period of time **langfristig; long-term debts** = debts which will be repaid many years later *or* over a period of many years **langfristige Verbindlichkeiten; long-term forecast** = forecast for a period of over three years **langfristige Prognose; long-term loan** = loan to be repaid many years later *or* over a period of many years **langfristiges Darlehen; long-term objectives** = aims which will take years to achieve **langfristige Ziele**

> QUOTE land held under long-term leases is not amortized
>
> *Hongkong Standard*
>
> QUOTE the company began to experience a demand for longer-term mortgages when the flow of money used to finance these loans diminished
>
> *Globe and Mail (Toronto)*

loose *adjective* not attached **lose, unverpackt; goods sold loose** = goods sold by weight, not prepacked in bags **lose Waren; loose insert** = advertising material slipped between the pages of a publication **lose Beilage**

lose *verb* not to have something any more **verlieren; to lose an order** = not to get an order which one was hoping to get **einen Auftrag verlieren;** *during the strike, the company lost six orders to American competitors;* **to lose customers** = to have fewer customers **Kunden verlieren;** *they've been losing customers because their service is so slow;* **the company is losing sales** *or* **is losing market share** = the company has fewer sales *or* a smaller share of the market than before **das Unternehmen hat Absatzrückgang/rückläufige Verkäufe od verliert Marktanteile**

◇ **lose out** *verb* to be put in a bad position **Verluste hinnehmen müssen; den kürzeren ziehen;** *the company has lost out in the rush to make cheap computers; we lost out to a Japanese company who put in a lower tender for the job*

loss *noun*
(a) loss of customers = not keeping customers because of bad service *or* high prices, etc. **Kundenabgänge; loss of an order** = not getting an order which was expected **Auftragsverlust; the company suffered a loss of market penetration** = the company found it had a smaller share of the market **das Unternehmen verlor Absatzgebiete;**
(b) having less money than before *or* not making a profit **Verlust, Einbuße; the company suffered a loss** = the company did not make a profit **die Firma mußte Verluste hinnehmen; to report a loss** = not to show a profit in the accounts at the end of the year **Verluste ausweisen;** *the company reported a loss of £1m on the first year's trading ;* **capital loss** = loss made by selling assets **Kapitalverlust; the car was written off as a dead loss** *or* **a total loss** = the car was so badly damaged that the insurers said it had no value **das Auto wurde als Totalschaden abgeschrieben; paper loss** = loss made when an asset has fallen in value but has not been sold **nicht realisierter Verlust; trading loss** = situation where the company's receipts are less than its expenditure **Geschäftsverlust; at a loss** = making a loss *or* not making any profit **mit Verlust;** *the company is trading at a loss; he sold the shop at a loss;* **to cut one's losses** = to stop doing something which was losing money **seine Verluste verringern**
(c) being worth less *or* having a lower value **Verlust;** *shares showed losses of up to 5% on the Stock Exchange*
(d) loss in weight = goods which weigh less than when they were packed **Gewichtsverlust, Gewichtsschwund; loss in transport** = amount of weight which is lost

while goods are being transported **Transportverlust, Transportschaden**

◊ **loss-leader** *noun* article which is sold at a loss to attract customers **Lockartikel;** *we use these cheap films as a loss-leader*

> QUOTE against losses of FFr 7.7m in 1983, the company made a net profit of FFr 300,000 last year
>
> *Financial Times*

low-grade *adjective* not very important *or* not of very good quality **untergeordnet; minderwertig;** *a low-grade official from the Ministry of Commerce; the car runs best on low-grade petrol*

◊ **low-involvement product** *noun* low-priced product for everyday use that is bought by consumers without giving much thought to brands **Low-involvement-Produkt**

◊ **low-pressure** *adjective* **low-pressure selling** = where the salesman does not try to force someone to buy, but only encourages him or her to do so **nicht aggressive Verkaufsmethoden**

◊ **low-quality** *adjective* not of good quality **minderwertig;** *they tried to sell us some low-quality steel*

◊ **low season** *noun* period of the year when there are few travellers *or* tourists **Nachsaison**

loyalty *noun* **brand loyalty** = inclination of a customer to keep buying the same brand of product **Markentreue; customer loyalty** = inclination of a customer to keep shopping at the same shop **Kundentreue; reader loyalty** = inclination of a person to keep reading (and buying) the same publication **Leser-Blatt-Bindung**

> QUOTE the company which knows its own customers, their names, addresses, ages, occupations and buying habits, can better satisfy their needs and retain their loyalty
>
> *Financial Times*
>
> QUOTE though a difficult market to get into, China nevertheless offers a high degree of customer loyalty once successfully entered
>
> *Economist*

lull *noun* quiet period **Flaute;** *after last week's hectic trading, this week there was a welcome lull*

lump *noun* **lump sum** = money paid in one single amount, not in several small sums **Pauschalbetrag;** *when he retired he was given a lump-sum bonus; she sold her house and invested the money as a lump sum*

luxury *noun* expensive thing which is not necessary but which is good to have **Luxus;** *luxury items or luxury goods; a black market in luxury articles;* **luxury product** = product which people buy more of as their incomes rise **Luxusprodukt;** *luxury products such as caviare are selling poorly since the slump; the company has gone up-market and is now selling luxury products*

Mm

macro- *prefix* very large, covering a wide area **makro-, Makro-; macro-economics** = study of the economics of a whole area *or* whole industry *or* whole group of the population *or* whole country, in order to help in economic planning **Makroökonomie; macro-environment** = general environmental factors *or* elements that affect an organization, such as legislation or the country's economy **Makro-Umwelt;** *we must develop a flexible planning system to allow for major changes in the macro-environment;* **macro-marketing** = study of trading activity within a country and its political, economic and social implications **Makromarketing**

magazine *noun* (i) paper, usually with pictures, and printed on glossy paper, which comes out regularly, every month or every week; (ii) special colour supplement published with a newspaper **(i) Zeitschrift, Magazin; (ii) illustrierte Beilage, farbiges Supplement; computer magazine** = magazine with articles on computers and programs **Computerzeitschrift; do-it-yourself magazine** = magazine with articles on work which the average person can do to repair or improve the house **Heimwerkermagazin; house magazine** = magazine produced for the workers in a company to give them news of the company's affairs **Werkszeitung; trade magazine** = magazine produced for people or companies in certain trades **Fachzeitschrift; travel magazine** = magazine with articles on holidays and travel **Reisemagazin; women's magazine** = magazine aimed at the women's market **Frauenzeitschrift; magazine insert** = advertising sheet put into a magazine when it is mailed or sold **Werbebeilage; to insert a leaflet in a specialist magazine** = to put an advertising leaflet into a magazine before it is mailed or sold **einen Anzeigenteil in eine Fachzeitschrift einlegen; magazine mailing** = sending of copies of a magazine by post to subscribers **Zeitschriftenzustellung per Post**

mail

1 *noun*

(a) system of sending letters and parcels

from one place to another **Post;** *to put a letter in the mail; the cheque was lost in the mail; the invoice was put in the mail yesterday; mail to some of the islands in the Pacific can take six weeks;* **by mail** = using the postal services, not sending something by hand or by messenger **per Post; to send a package by surface mail** = to send a package by land or sea, not by air **ein Paket mit gewöhnlicher Post (auf dem Land- od Seeweg) schicken; by sea mail** = sent by post abroad, using a ship **auf dem Seeweg; to receive a sample by air mail** = by post using a plane **ein Muster per Luftpost erhalten; we sent the order by first-class mail** = by the most expensive mail service, designed to be faster **wir schickten die Bestellung per Post erster Klasse; electronic mail** = system of sending messages from one computer to another, using the telephone lines **elektronische Post, E-Mail;** *(US)* **mail interview** *or* **mail survey** = sending a questionnaire to respondents by post for a survey **postalische Befragung;** *not enough consumers responded to the mail interview; to encourage people to cooperate in the mail survey we'll include a free sample with the questionnaire*

(b) letters sent or received **Post;** *has the mail arrived yet? to open the mail; your cheque arrived in yesterday's mail; my secretary opens my mail as soon as it arrives; the receipt was in this morning's mail;* **incoming mail** = mail which arrives **Posteingang; outgoing mail** = mail which is sent out **Postausgang; mail room** = room in an office where incoming letters are sorted and sent to each department, and where outgoing mail is collected for sending **Poststelle**

(c) direct mail = selling a product by sending publicity material to possible buyers through the post **Direktversand; Direktwerbung;** *the company runs a successful direct-mail operation; these calculators are sold only by direct mail;* **direct-mail advertising** = advertising by sending leaflets to people by post **Briefwerbung; mail shot** = single mailing of direct-mail advertising literature **Rundschreiben, Briefwerbeaktion; no direct mail list** = list of people who do not wish to receive any direct mail **Robinsonliste**

2 *verb* to send something by post **(mit der Post) schicken, aufgeben;** *they mailed their catalogue to three thousand customers in Europe; we mailed our order last Wednesday*

◇ **mailer** *noun* printed item specially designed for sending by post **Briefwerbematerial; self-mailer** = promotional material sent through the post, which includes a postage-paid reply section that can be sent back without an envelope and on which customers can make an order **Selfmailer**

◇ **mailing** *noun* sending in the post **Verschicken, Versenden;** *the mailing of publicity material;* **direct mailing** = sending of publicity material by post to possible buyers **Direktversand; Direktwerbung; mailing list** = list of names and addresses of people who might be interested in a product *or* list of names and addresses of members of a society **Adressenliste;** *his name is on our mailing list; to build up a mailing list;* **to buy a mailing list** = to pay a society, etc. money to buy their list of members in order to mail publicity material to them **eine Adressenliste kaufen; mailing piece** = leaflet suitable for sending by direct mail **Postwurfsendung; mailing shot** = leaflets sent by mail to possible customers **Rundschreiben, Briefwerbeaktion**

◇ **mail-order** *noun* system of buying and selling from a catalogue, by placing orders and sending goods by mail **Postversand; mail-order business** *or* **mail-order firm** *or* **mail-order house** = company which sells a product by mail **Versandhaus; mail-order catalogue** = catalogue from which a customer can order items to be sent by mail **Versandhauskatalog**

◇ **mail out** *verb* to send promotional material by mail **(Werbematerial) mit der Post schicken**

◇ **mail-out** *noun* promotional material sent by direct mail, usually accompanied by a letter which may be personalized **Werbeversand**

> QUOTE the building of media lists, the mailing out of releases tailored to the reader interests of newspapers and periodicals, and the follow-up phone calls all have their parallel in direct marketing
>
> *PR Week*

majority *noun* larger group than all other; more than half of a group **Mehrheit, Majorität; early majority** = category of buyers of a product, who buy it later than the early adopters **frühe Mehrheit; late majority** = category of buyers of a product, who buy it later than the early majority but before the laggards **späte Mehrheit**

make
1 *noun* brand *or* type of product manufactured **Marke, Fabrikat;** *Japanese makes of cars; a standard make of equipment; what make is the new computer system or what's the make of the new computer system?*
2 *verb* to produce *or* to manufacture **herstellen, produzieren;** *to make a car or to make a computer; the workmen spent ten*

weeks making the table; the factory makes three hundred cars a day

◇ **makegood** *noun* advertisement placed again in a magazine *or* newspaper free of charge, because a mistake was made in it when it was previously published **Ersatzanzeige**

◇ **make out** *verb* to write **ausstellen;** *to make out an invoice; the bill is made out to Smith & Co.;* **to make out a cheque to someone** = to write someone's name on a cheque **jdm einen Scheck ausstellen**

◇ **make-up** *noun* arrangement of material into pages in a publication **Umbruch**

mall *noun (US)* **shopping mall** = enclosed covered area for shopping, with shops, restaurants, banks and other facilities **Einkaufspassage, Einkaufszentrum, Mall**

manage *verb*

(a) to direct *or* to be in charge of **leiten, führen;** *to manage a department; to manage a branch office*

(b) to manage property = to look after rented property for the owner **Immobilienbesitz verwalten**

(c) to manage to = to be able to do something **es schaffen, es fertigbringen;** *did you manage to see the head buyer? she managed to write six orders and take three phone calls all in two minutes*

◇ **manageable** *adjective* which can be dealt with easily **zu bewältigen;** *difficulties which are still manageable; the problems which the company faces are too large to be manageable by one person*

◇ **management** *noun*

(a) directing *or* running a business **Unternehmensführung, Management;** *to study management; good management or efficient management; bad management or inefficient management; a management graduate or a graduate in management;* **line management** = way of organizing a business where each manager is responsible for doing what his superior tells him to do **Linienmanagement; portfolio management** = buying and selling shares by a specialist on behalf of a client **Effekten-, Portfoliomanagement; product management** = directing the making and selling of a product as an independent item **Produkt-Management; management accountant** = accountant who prepares specialized information for managers so that they can make decisions **Finanzbuchhalter; management accounts** = financial information (on sales, costs, credit, profitability, etc.) prepared for a manager **Rechnungsbericht für die besonderen Zwecke der Unternehmensleitung; Geschäftsbilanz; management committee** = committee which manages a club, a pension fund, etc. **geschäftsführender Ausschuß; Vorstandsgremium; management consultant** = person who gives advice on how to manage a business **Unternehmensberater; management course** = training course for managers **Managerkurs; management development** = selection and training of potential managers **Management-Entwicklung; management by exception** = management system whereby deviations from plans are located and corrected **Management nach Ausnahmeprinzipien; management by objectives** = way of managing a business where the managers work according to a plan and checks are made periodically to see whether their work is completed correctly and on time **Management nach Zielvorgaben; management team** = a group of managers working together **Management-Team; management techniques** = ways of managing a business **Managementmethoden; management training** = training managers by making them study problems and work out ways of solving them **Management-Ausbildung; management trainee** = young person being trained to be a manager **Führungsnachwuchs**

(b) group of managers or directors **Unternehmensleitung, Management;** *the management has decided to give everyone a pay increase;* **top management** = the main directors of a company **Unternehmensspitze, Top-Management; middle management** = the department managers of a company who carry out the policy set by the directors and organize the work of a group of workers **mittleres Management**

◇ **manager** *noun*

(a) head of a department in a company **Abteilungsleiter;** *a department manager; personnel manager; production manager; sales manager;* **accounts manager** = head of the accounts department **Leiter/-in der Buchhaltung; area manager** = manager who is responsible for the company's work (usually sales) in an area **Bezirks-, Gebietsleiter; brand manager** = manager responsible for the marketing of a particular brand **Markenproduktmanager; general manager** = manager in charge of the administration in a large company **geschäftsführender Direktor**

(b) person in charge of a branch or shop **Geschäftsleiter;** *Mr Smith is the manager of our local Lloyds Bank; the manager of our Lagos branch is in London for a series of meetings;* **bank manager** = person in charge of a branch of a bank **Bankdirektor; branch manager** = person in charge of a branch of a company **Filialleiter**

◇ **manageress** *noun* woman who runs a shop, or a department **Geschäftsleiterin; Abteilungsleiterin; Managerin**

◇ **managerial** *adjective* referring to managers **Management-, Führungs-;** *managerial staff;* **to be appointed to a managerial position** = to be appointed a manager **auf eine Manager-Position berufen werden; decisions taken at managerial level** = decisions taken by managers **auf der oberen Geschäftsebene getroffene Entscheidungen**

◇ **managership** *noun* job of being a manager **Managertätigkeit;** *after six years, he was offered the managership of a branch in Scotland*

◇ **managing** *adjective* **managing director** = director who is in charge of a whole company **geschäftsführender Direktor, Geschäftsführer; chairman and managing director** = managing director who is also chairman of the board of directors **Vorsitzender und Geschäftsführer**

> QUOTE the management says that the rate of loss-making has come down and it expects further improvement in the next few years
> *Financial Times*
>
> QUOTE the research director will manage and direct a team of graduate business analysts reporting on consumer behaviour throughout the UK
> *Times*
>
> QUOTE the No. 1 managerial productivity problem in America is managers who are out of touch with their people and out of touch with their customers
> *Fortune*

mandatory *adjective* which is required by law *or* which is stipulated in a contract **obligatorisch; mandatory blurb** = certain words which are required by law to be included in an advertisement (such as a health warning on cigarette advertisements) **rechtsverbindlicher Text/Warnhinweis**

manifest *noun* list of goods in a shipment **Ladeliste; passenger manifest** = list of passengers on a ship or plane **Passagierliste**

manpower *noun* number of workers **Personalbestand; manpower forecasting** = forecasting how many workers will be needed, and how many will be available **Personalbestandsprognose; manpower planning** = planning to obtain the right number of workers for each job **Personalplanung; manpower requirements** = number of workers needed **Bedarf an Arbeitskräften; manpower shortage** *or* **shortage of manpower** = lack of workers **Arbeitskräftemangel**

manufacture
1 *verb* to make a product for sale, using machines **(maschinell) herstellen/fertigen;** *manufactured goods; the company manufactures spare parts for cars*
2 *noun* making a product for sale, using machines **Herstellung, Fertigung; products of foreign manufacture** = products made in foreign countries **ausländische Fabrikate**

◇ **manufacturer** *noun* person *or* company which produces machine-made products **Hersteller;** *foreign manufacturers; cotton manufacturer; sports car manufacturer;* **manufacturer's agent** = person who sells on behalf of a manufacturer and earns a commission **Kommissionsagent; manufacturer's recommended price (MRP)** = price at which the manufacturer suggests the product should be sold on the retail market, though often reduced by the retailer **empfohlener Herstellerpreis;** *all typewriters - 20% off the manufacturer's recommended price*

◇ **manufacturing** *noun* referring to the production of machine-made products for sale **Herstellung, Fertigung; manufacturing capacity** = amount of a product which a factory is capable of making **Fertigungskapazität; manufacturing costs** = costs of making a product **Herstellungskosten; manufacturing industries** = industries which take raw materials and make them into finished products **verarbeitende Industrie**

map *noun* chart which shows a geographical area **Karte; market map** = chart showing the structure of a market in terms of the number and type of consumers and the activity of competitors **graphische Darstellung einer Marktstruktur; Kaufkraftkarte;** *see also* PERCEPTUAL MAP

◇ **mapping** *noun* drawing up a map of an area **Kartenzeichen, Kartographie; journey mapping** = method of calculating how many people pass a poster site **Passantenzählung**

margin *noun*
(a) difference between the money received when selling a product and the money paid for it **Gewinnspanne, Marge; gross margin** = percentage difference between the unit manufacturing cost and the received price **Bruttomarge; net margin** = percentage difference between received price and all costs, including overheads **Nettomarge; we are cutting our margins very fine** = we are reducing our margins as much as possible in order to be more competitive **wir haben unsere Gewinnspannen sehr eng bemessen; our margins have been squeezed** = profits have been reduced because our margins have to be smaller to stay competitive **unsere Gewinnspannen sind gedrückt worden**

(b) extra space *or* time allowed **Spielraum; margin of error** = number of mistakes which are accepted in a document *or* in a calculation **Fehlerspielraum; safety margin** = time *or* space allowed to make something safe **Sicherheitsspielraum; margin of safety** = sales which are above the breakeven point **Sicherheitsmarge**

◇ **marginal** *adjective*
(a) marginal cost = cost of making a single extra unit above the number already planned **Grenzkosten; marginal cost pricing** = pricing method that involves fixing a price per unit that covers marginal costs and makes an acceptable contribution to fixed costs **Grenzkostenpreiskalkulation; marginal pricing** = making the selling price the same as the marginal cost **Grenzpreiskalkulation; marginal productivity** = extra productivity achieved by the use of one more factor of production **Grenzproduktivität; marginal rate of tax** = percentage of tax which a taxpayer pays at the top rate **Grenzsteuersatz; marginal revenue** = income from selling a single extra unit above the number already sold **Grenzertrag; marginal utility** = satisfaction gained from using one more unit of a product **Grenznutzen**
(b) not very profitable *or* hardly worth the money paid **marginal, knapp, gering;** *marginal return on investment;* **marginal land** = land which is almost not worth farming **marginaler Boden; marginal purchase** = thing which a buyer feels is only just worth buying **Grenzkauf, gerade noch vertretbarer Kauf**

marine

1 *adjective* referring to the sea **Meeres-, See-; marine insurance** = insurance of ships and their cargoes **See(transport)versicherung; marine underwriter** = person who insures ships and their cargoes **Seeversicherer**
2 *noun* **the merchant marine** = all the commercial ships of a country **die Handelsmarine**

◇ **maritime** *adjective* referring to the sea **See-, Schiffahrts-; maritime law** = laws referring to ships, ports, etc. **Seerecht; maritime lawyer** = lawyer who specializes in legal matters concerning ships and cargoes **ein auf Seerecht spezialisierter Jurist; maritime trade** = transporting commercial goods by sea **Seehandel**

mark

1 *noun*
(a) sign put on an item to show something **Markierung, Zeichen; assay mark** = hallmark *or* mark put on gold or silver items to show that the metal is of the correct quality **Feingehaltsstempel;** *(GB)* **kite mark** = mark on goods to show that they meet official standards **(dreieckiges) Gütezeichen**
(b) money used in Germany **(D-)Mark;** *the price is twenty-five marks; the mark rose against the dollar* NOTE: usually written **DM** after a figure: **25DM.** Also called **Deutschmark, D-Mark**
2 *verb* to put a sign on something **markieren, bezeichnen;** *to mark a product "for export only"; article marked at £1.50; to mark the price on something;* **marked price** = price which is marked on or attached to an article for sale **markierter Preis**

◇ **mark down** *verb* to make the price of something lower **einen Preis heruntersetzen;** *this range has been marked down to $24.99; we have marked all prices down by 30% for the sale*

◇ **mark-down** *noun*
(a) reduction of the price of something to less than its usual price **Preissenkung**
(b) percentage amount by which a price has been lowered **Preisnachlaß, Rabatt;** *there has been a 30% mark-down on all goods in the sale*

◇ **mark up** *verb* to increase the price of something **erhöhen, heraufsetzen;** *these prices have been marked up by 10%*

◇ **mark-up** *noun*
(a) increase in price **Preiserhöhung, Preisaufschlag;** *since I was last in the store they have put at least a 10% mark-up on the whole range of items*
(b) amount added to the cost price to give the selling price **Handelsspanne; we work to a 3.5 times mark-up** *or* **to a 350% mark-up** = we take the unit cost and multiply by 3.5 to give the selling price **wir haben eine 350%ige Gewinnspanne; mark-up percentage** = mark-up expressed as a percentage either of the cost price or of the selling price **Handelsspanne in Prozent;** *what's the mark-up percentage on these items?*

market

1 *noun*
(a) place (often in the open air) where farm produce and household goods are sold **Markt;** *the fish market is held every Thursday; the open-air market is held in the central square; here are this week's market prices for sheep;* **flea market** = market for secondhand goods **Flohmarkt; market day** = day when a market is regularly held **Markttag;** *Tuesday is market day, so the streets are closed to traffic;* **market dues** = rent for a stall in a market **Standmiete**
(b) the Common Market = the European Economic Community **der Gemeinsame Markt;** *the Common Market agricultural policy or the Common Market ministers*
(c) place where a product might be sold *or* group of people who might buy a product

Markt, Absatzgebiet; home *or* **domestic market** = market in the country where the selling company is based **Binnen-, Inlandsmarkt;** *sales in the home market rose by 22%*

(d) possible sales of a certain type of product *or* demand for a certain type of product **Markt, Absatzmarkt;** *the market for home computers has fallen sharply; we have 20% of the British car market; there's no market for electric typewriters;* **captive market** = market where one supplier has the monopoly and the buyer has no choice **monopolistischer Absatzmarkt; a growth market** = market where sales are likely to rise rapidly **ein Wachstumsmarkt; the labour market** = number of workers available for work **der Arbeitsmarkt; 25,000 graduates have come onto the labour market** = they have become available for work after leaving college **25.000 Hochschulabgänger stehen dem Arbeitsmarkt zur Verfügung; the property market** = sales of houses **der Immobilien- und Grundstücksmarkt**

(e) the black market = buying and selling goods in a way which is not allowed by law **der Schwarzmarkt;** *there is a flourishing black market in spare parts for cars;* **to pay black market prices** = to pay high prices to get items which are not easily available **Schwarzmarktpreise bezahlen;** *see also* GREY MARKET

(f) buyer's market = market where goods are sold cheaply because there is little demand **Käufermarkt; seller's market** = market where the seller can ask high prices because there is a large demand for the product **Verkäufermarkt**

(g) closed market = market where a supplier deals with only one agent or distributor and does not supply any others direct **geschlossener Markt; free market economy** = system where the government does not interfere in business activity in any way **freie Marktwirtschaft; open market** = market where anyone can buy and sell **offener Markt**

(h) market analysis = detailed examination and report on a market **Marktanalyse; market build-up method** = method of assessing the sales potential of a product by adding up the number of potential buyers in each market segment **Marktaufbaumethode; market challenger strategy** = strategy of a company which is challenging the market leaders through pricing, promotion or product design **Marktherausfordererstrategie;** *it's a new aggressive company adopting a market challenger strategy;* **market coverage** = market share *or* measurement of what proportion of the sales of an article is accounted for by a particular brand **Marktanteil;** *the marketing director's brief was to increase market coverage by at least ten per cent;* **market demand** = total demand for a product in the market **Marktnachfrage;** *market demand for this product is falling, as fashions have changed;* **market development** = strategy involving the search for and exploitation of new markets for a product **Marktentwicklung;** *market development for our tractors is part of the company's growth strategy;* **market economist** = person who specializes in the study of financial structures and the return on investments in the stock market **Börsenanalytiker; market factor analysis** = forecasting method which concentrates on certain key market factors that are believed to affect demand **Marktfaktoranalyse; market follower strategy** = strategy of a company which does not directly challenge the market leaders, but attempts to benefit from their innovations and gain a profitable corner of the market **Marktfolgerstrategie;** *adopting a market follower strategy greatly reduces expenditure on research and development;* **market forces** = influences on the sales of a product **Marktkräfte; market forecast** = forecast of prices on the stock market **Marktprognose; market leader** = company with the largest market share **Marktführer;** *we are the market leader in home computers;* **market leader strategy** = strategy of a company which is a market leader and wants to maintain a dominant market share, or to keep its reputation as an innovator **Marktführerstrategie; market map** = chart showing the structure of a market in terms of the number and type of consumers and the activity of competitors **graphische Darstellung einer Marktstruktur;** *one look at the market map shows we are aiming at the wrong target market;* **market niche** = particular segment or specialized area of a market **Marktnische;** *in producing this unusual product, the company has found itself a market niche;* **market opportunities** = possibility of finding new sales in a market **neue Absatzmöglichkeiten; market penetration** = the selling of more products into a market segment, shown as a percentage of the total market **Marktdurchdringung;** *we hope our new product range will increase our market share;* **market potential** = sales of a product that should be achieved with the right kind of marketing effort **Marktpotential;** *the product is promising but has not yet achieved its market potential;* **market price** = price at which a product can be sold **Marktpreis; market profile** = basic characteristics of a particular market **Marktprofil; market rate** = normal price in the market **Marktpreis, üblicher Tarif;** *we pay the market rate for secretaries* or *we pay* *secretaries the market rate;* **market research** = examining the possible sales of a product before it is put on the market or the reasons for its performance after it has been launched **Marktforschung; market segment** = category of consumers in a market definable by their particular needs **Marktsegment; market segmentation** = division of the market or consumers into certain categories according to their buying habits **Marktsegmentierung;** *our strategy is based on satisfying the demands of many different types of buyers and therefore requires thorough market segmentation;* **market share** = percentage of a total market which the sales of a company's product cover **Marktanteil; market survey** = survey *or* general report on market conditions **Marktbefragung, Marktumfrage;** *the market survey suggests that there is no longer much demand for this type of product;* **market trends** = gradual changes taking place in a market **Marktentwicklung, Markttendenzen; market value** = value of a product *or* of a company if sold today **Marktwert**

(i) up market *or* **down market** = more expensive *or* less expensive market **exklusiver/anspruchsvoller Markt; Massenmarkt; to go up-market** *or* **to go down-market** = to make products which appeal to a wealthier section of the market *or* to a wider, less wealthy, section of the market **sich an einen exklusiven Kundenkreis wenden; sich dem Massenmarkt zuwenden**

(j) to be in the market for secondhand cars = to look for secondhand cars to buy **in der Gebrauchtwagenbranche sein; to come on to the market** = to become available for sale **auf den Markt kommen;** *this soap has just come on to the market;* **to put something on the market** = to start to offer something for sale **etwas auf den Markt bringen;** *they put their house on the market; I hear the company has been put on the market;* **the company has priced itself out of the market** = the company has raised its prices so high that its products do not sell **das Unternehmen hat sich durch überhöhte Preise wettbewerbsunfähig gemacht**

2 *verb* to sell (products) **vertreiben, auf den Markt bringen;** *this product is being marketed in all European countries*

◇ **marketable** *adjective* which can be sold easily **absatz-, marktfähig**

◇ **marketer** *noun* person or company that carries out marketing activities **Marketing-Fachmann; Marketing-Unternehmen;** *the company has been in manufacturing for ten years, and is now becoming a marketer of its own products as well; most direct marketers support the Post Office, which is almost the sole channel for their services*

marketing *noun* the process of identifying needs and satisfying these with suitable goods or services, through product design, distribution and promotion, either as a business or as a non-profit-making organization **Marketing;** *the firm's products were good but they had difficulty in selling them because of bad marketing; experience in selling and market research gave him a good background for a career in marketing; see also* DIRECT MARKETING, EXTENSIVE MARKETING, INTEGRATED MARKETING; **marketing agreement** = contract by which one company undertakes to market another company's products **Vertriebsvereinbarung; marketing board** = organization set up by the government *or* by a group of producers to help producers market a certain type of product **Marketing-Verband;** *the Milk Marketing Board assures farmers of a fair price for their milk;* **marketing budget** = money set aside by an organization for its marketing activities **Marketingetat; marketing communications** = all methods of communicating used in marketing, such as television, radio and sales literature **Marketingkommunikation; marketing concept** = business idea or philosophy based on the importance of profit, consumer satisfaction and the welfare of the general public **Marketingkonzept; marketing department** = department in a company which specializes in using marketing techniques to sell a product, and which is responsible for taking marketing initiatives such as advertising and public relations **Marketingabteilung; marketing intelligence** = information about a market that can help a marketing effort **Marketinginformation; marketing manager** = person in charge of a marketing department **Marketingmanager;** *the marketing manager has decided to fire the sales manager for not developing an effective sales force;* **marketing mix** = combination of all the elements that make up marketing, such as price and distribution and advertising **Marketing-Mix;** *(compare* FOUR P'S) *personal selling is a vital part of the company's marketing mix;* **marketing model** = overview of the entire marketing process which can be shown graphically, possibly using as computer, and used to solve problems **Marketingmodell; marketing plan** = plan, usually annual, for a company's marketing activities, specifying expenditure and expected revenue and profits **Marketingplan;** *has this year's marketing plan been drawn up yet? the marketing plan is flexible enough to allow for an increase in advertising costs;* **marketing policy** = basic attitudes underlying a company's marketing activities **Absatzpolitik;**

marketing research = all research carried out in the interests of successful marketing, including market research, media research and product research **Marketingforschung; marketing services** = marketing functions other than selling, such as market research and advertising **Marketingdienstleistungen;** *our sales drive is supported by well-developed and effective marketing services;* **marketing strategy** = strategy *or* planning for marketing activities **Marketingstrategie;** *what marketing strategy should be adopted to reach these long-term objectives? the marketing strategy was one of expansion through diversification and market development*

◇ **marketplace** *noun*
(a) open space in the middle of a town where a market is held **Marktplatz**
(b) situation and environment in which goods are sold **Markt;** *our salesmen find life difficult in the marketplace; what's the reaction to the new car in the marketplace? or what's the marketplace reaction to the new car?*

> QUOTE over the past 15 months there has been a dramatic loss of confidence among marketers across the whole of British industry
> *Marketing Week*
>
> QUOTE our scheme has been running for 12 years, but we've only really had a true marketing strategy since 1984
> *Marketing*
>
> QUOTE long-term marketing involves making a serious effort to identify what the company's customers will need in the future
> *Management Today*
>
> QUOTE the next decade will see major changes in the marketing mix
> *Marketing Workshop*
>
> QUOTE direct marketing is one of the faster growing elements of the marketing mix
> *Marketing*
>
> QUOTE reporting to the marketing director, the successful applicant will be responsible for the development of a training programme for the new sales force
> *Times*
>
> QUOTE most discounted fares are sold by bucket shops but in today's competitive marketplace any agent can supply them
> *Business Traveller*

mart *noun* market *or* place where things are sold **Markt; car mart** = secondhand car salesroom **Gebrauchtwagenverkaufsraum; auction mart** = auction rooms **Auktionsräume**

mass *noun*
(a) large group of people **Menge; mass marketing** = marketing which aims at reaching large numbers of people **Massenabsatzstrategie; mass media** = means of communication which reach large numbers of people (such as radio, television, newspapers) **Massenmedien; mass unemployment** = unemployment of large numbers of workers **Massenarbeitslosigkeit**
(b) large number **Masse, Menge;** *we have a mass of letters or masses of letters to write; they received a mass of orders or masses of orders after the TV commercials*

◇ **mass-produce** *verb* to manufacture identical products in large quantities **in Massen produzieren;**

◇ **mass production** *noun* manufacturing large quantities of identical products **Massenproduktion, serienmäßige Herstellung**

master *adjective* main *or* original **Original; master copy of a file** = main copy of a computer file, kept for security purposes **Stamm-, Bestandsdatei; master sample** = collection of basic sampling units (such as parliamentary constituencies) compiled by research organizations to help a company's market research **Ausgangsstichprobe**

matched sample *noun* the use of two samples of people with the same characteristics to compare reactions to different products in tests **Parallelisierung**

material *noun*
(a) substance which can be used to make a finished product **Material; building materials** = bricks, cement, etc. used in building **Baustoffe; raw materials** = substances which have not been manufactured (such as wool, wood, sand, etc.) **Rohstoffe; synthetic materials** = substances made as products of a chemical process **Kunststoffe; materials control** = system to check that a company has enough materials in stock to do its work **Materialsteuerung; materials handling** = moving materials from one part of a factory to another in an efficient way **innerbetriebliches Transport- und Lagerwesen, Materialfluß**
(b) display material = posters, photographs, etc., which can be used to attract attention to goods which are for sale **Dekorationsmaterial**

matrix *noun* arrangement of data in horizontal and vertical columns **Matrize**

matter *noun*
(a) printed matter = printed books, newspapers, publicity sheets, etc. **Drucksache; publicity matter** = sheets *or* posters *or* leaflets used for publicity **Werbematerial**
(b) editorial matter = text of a magazine which is written by journalists, and not

part of an advertisement **redaktioneller Text; next matter** = placing of an advertisement in a magazine, so that it is next to editorial text **neben Text, textanschließend**

mature

1 *adjective* **mature economy** = fully developed economy **entwickelte Volkswirtschaft**
2 *verb* **bills which mature in three weeks' time** = bills which will be due for payment in three weeks **Wechsel, die in drei Wochen fällig werden**

◇ **maturity** *noun* third stage in a product life cycle when a product is well established in the market, though no longer enjoying increasing sales, after which sooner or later it will start to decline **Reifephase**

maximal awareness

noun advertising point at which a consumer is convinced enough by a product's advertising to buy the product **höchster Bekanntheitsgrad;** *the marketing director considered the advertisement's message too weak to achieve maximal awareness*

maximization

noun making as large as possible **Maximierung; profit maximization** *or* **maximization of profit** business strategy based on achieving as high a profit as possible **Gewinnmaximierung**

◇ **maximize** *verb* to make as large as possible **maximieren;** *the management's aim is to maximize profits*

maximum

1 *noun* largest possible number *or* price *or* quantity **Maximum; up to a maximum of £10** = no more than £10 **bis zu maximal £10; to increase exports to the maximum** = as much as possible **Exporte auf das Maximum erhöhen;** *it's the maximum the insurance company will pay* NOTE: plural is **maxima**
2 *adjective* largest possible **maximal, Höchst-;** *maximum income tax rate or maximum rate of income tax; maximum load; maximum production levels; maximum price;* **to increase production to the maximum level** = as much as possible **die Produktion auf das Maximum erhöhen; maximum price** = highest legal price for a product **Höchstpreis;** *the government insists on such a low maximum price that we'll never break even; demand for the product is so low that no company is charging the maximum price*

mean

1 *adjective* average **mittlerer, durchschnittlich, Mittel-;** *mean annual increase;* **mean price** = average price of a share in a day's trading **Mittelkurs**
2 *noun* average *or* number calculated by adding several quantities together and dividing by the number of quantities added **Mittelwert, Durchschnitt;** *unit sales are over the mean for the first quarter or above the first quarter mean*

◇ **means** *plural noun*
(a) way of doing something **Mittel;** *air freight is the fastest means of getting stock to South America; do we have any means of copying all these documents quickly?*
(b) money *or* resources **Mittel;** *the company has the means to launch the new product; such a level of investment is beyond the means of a small private company;* **means test** = inquiry into how much money someone earns to see if he or she is eligible for state benefits **Bedürftigkeitsüberprüfung; he has private means** = he has income from dividends *or* interest *or* rent which is not part of his salary **ihm stehen private Mittel zur Verfügung**

mechanical

adjective worked by a machine **mechanisch; mechanical data** = information regarding the printing of newspapers *or* magazines (such as format, column width, etc.) **technische Daten/Einzelheiten**

media

noun means of communicating a message (about a product or service) to the audienc **Medien; the mass media** = means of communicating information to the general public (such as television, radio, newspapers) **die Massenmedien;** *the product attracted a lot of interest in the media or a lot of media interest;* **advertising media** = types of media used as a vehicle for advertising **Werbemedien, Werbeträger; electronic media** = advertising media such as television, radio and teletext services **elektronische Medien; mixed media** = various types of media used together in a promotional campaign **Mediakombination; printed media** = advertising media such as magazines and newspapers **Druckmedien; media analysis** *or* **media research** = examining different types of media and their audiences (such as the readers of newspapers, television viewers) to see which is best for promoting a certain type of product **Mediaanalyse; Medienforschung; media broker** = business which offers organizations a media buying service and possibly additional services such as media planning **Media-Agentur; media buyer** = person in an advertising agency or in the advertising department of a company who places advertisements in the media on behalf of an organization **Streuplaner,**

Streufachmann; media buying = placing advertisements in the media on behalf of an organization **Streuplanung;** *efficient media buying is impossible without a good knowledge of comparative media costs;* **media class** = basic type of medium, such as TV, radio or the press **Medienkategorie; media coverage** = reports about something in the media **Berichterstattung durch die Medien;** *we got good media coverage for the launch of the new model;* **media data form** = document giving basic data or information about a publication, such as circulation, readership and geographical distribution **Medieninformationskarte; media event** = happening which is staged by, or organized so as to attract the attention of, the mass media **Medienveranstaltung; media independent** *or* **media shop** = business which offers organizations a media buying service, but without the creative services usually offered by advertising agencies **Streuagentur; media option** = single unit of advertising space or time **einzelne/r Werbefläche/Werbespot; media owner** = person or company that owns a magazine or newspaper, or radio or TV station **Medieneigentümer; media planning** = strategy concerned with what type of media should be used and how much advertising should be done and when **Mediaplanung;** *the marketing manager and media buyer are having a media planning session; proper media planning avoids overexpenditure on promotion;* **media research** = study or investigation of a target audience in order to improve an organization's promotional activities **Media-, Werbeträgerforschung; media schedule** = all the details of advertising to be used in a promotional campaign, such as the timing and positioning of advertisements **Mediaplan; media selection** = choosing the right type of media for a promotional campaign **Mediaselektion;** *the agency will give us guidance on media selection;* **media shop** = media independent (a business which offers organizations a media buying service but without the creative services usually offered by an advertising agency) **Streuagentur;** (NOTE: **media** can be followed by a singular or plural verb, though the singular form is **medium**)

> QUOTE both advertisers and agencies agree that the media owners do their bit to keep advertisers well informed
>
> *Marketing Workshop*
>
> QUOTE media costs represent a major expense for advertisers
>
> *Marketing*

median *noun* middle number in a list of numbers **Zentralwert, Median**

medium *noun* one particular means of communicating information to the public **Mittel; advertising medium** = type of advertisement (such as a TV commercial) **Werbeträger;** *the product was advertised through the medium of the trade press*

◇ **medium-term** *adjective* referring to a point between short-term and long-term **mittelfristig; medium-term forecast** = forecast for two or three years **mittelfristige Prognose**

megastore *noun* very large store **Megaladen**

mercantile *adjective* commercial **handeltreibend, Handels-; mercantile agent** = person who sells for a business or another person and earns a commission **Handelsvertreter; mercantile country** = country which earns income from trade **Handelsnation; mercantile law** = laws relating to business **Handelsrecht (Teil des Wirtschaftrechts); mercantile marine** = all the commercial ships of a country **Handelsmarine; mercantile paper** = negotiable document used in commerce **Warenpapier**

merchandise

1 *noun* goods which are for sale *or* which have been sold **Ware;** *the merchandise is shipped through two ports;* **distress merchandise** = goods sold off cheaply to pay a company's debts **im Notverkauf abgesetzte Waren**

2 *verb* to sell goods by a wide variety of means, including display, advertising, sending samples, etc. **Absatzförderung betreiben;** *to merchandise a product*

◇ **merchandiser** *noun* person *or* company which organizes the display and promotion of goods **Experte für Absatzpolitik/Merchandising**

◇ **merchandising** *noun* organizing the display and promotion of goods in retail outlets **Merchandising, Absatzpolitik;** *merchandising of a product; merchandising department*

merchant *noun*

(a) businessman who buys and sells, especially one who buys imported goods in bulk for retail sale **Händler;** *coal merchant; tobacco merchant; wine merchant*

(b) merchant bank = bank which lends money to companies and deals in international finance; *(entspricht)* **Investmentbank; merchant banker** = person who has a high position in a merchant bank; *(entspricht)* **Bankier in einer Investmentbank; merchant navy** *or* **merchant**

marine = all the commercial ships of a country **Handelsmarine; merchant ship** *or* **merchant vessel** = commercial ship *or* ship which carries a cargo **Handelsschiff**

◇ **merchantable** *adjective* of good enough quality for sale and use **zum Verkauf geeignet, verkäuflich**

◇ **merchanting** *noun* action of buying and selling **Handeltreiben**

◇ **merchantman** *noun* commercial ship **Handelsschiff**

merge *verb* to join together **fusionieren, zusammenschließen;** *the two companies have merged; the firm merged with its main competitor*

◇ **merger** *noun* joining together of two or more companies **Fusion;** *as a result of the merger, the company is now the largest in the field*

message *noun*
(a) piece of news which is sent to someone **Mitteilung, Nachricht;** *I'll leave a message with his secretary; can you give the director a message from his wife? he claims he never received the message*
(b) idea that is communicated by promotion **Botschaft;** *the agency was given clear instructions as to what message the advertisement should convey; few people interviewed in the survey knew what the advertisement's message was supposed to be; the message on the poster was conveyed in only three words;* **message effect** = effect of an advertisement's message on the target audience **Werbewirkung;** *the message effect was lost because too many people didn't understand the joke used in the advertisement; after the campaign we'll try to assess what the message effect has been*

metamarketing *noun (US)* marketing applied to all kinds of organizations, such as hospitals, churches and religions as well as to profit-making concerns **Metamarketing**

micro- *prefix* very small **mikro-, Mikro-; micro-economics** = study of the economics of persons or single companies **Mikroökonomie; micro-environment** = elements *or* factors outside a business organization which directly affect it, such as supply of raw materials, demand for its products and rival companies **Aufgabenumwelt, Mikro-Umwelt;** *unreliability of suppliers is one the greatest problems in our micro-environment;* **micro-marketing** = study of the marketing strategy of the individual business **Mikromarketing**

middleman *noun* businessman who buys from the manufacturer and sells to retailers or to the public **Zwischenhändler;** *we sell direct from the factory to the customer and cut out the middleman*

milk *verb* to make as much profit for as long as possible out of a particular product or service **melken;** *we intend to milk the product hard for the next two years, before it becomes obsolete*

minicontainer *noun* small container **Minicontainer**

◇ **minimarket** *noun* very small self-service store **Minimarkt, kleiner Selbstbedienungsladen**

misc = MISCELLANEOUS

miscellaneous *adjective* various *or* mixed *or* not all of the same sort **verschieden; gemischt;** *miscellaneous items; a box of miscellaneous pieces of equipment; miscellaneous expenditure*

misrepresentation *noun* making a wrong statement in order to persuade someone to enter into a contract (such as to buy a product or service) **falsche Darstellung; fraudulent misrepresentation** = false statement made wilfully to trick someone **Vorspiegelung falscher Tatsachen, arglistige Täuschung**

mission *noun*
(a) the long-term objectives of an organization **Auftrag;** *our mission is to be the market leader in selling fixatives in southern Europe*
(b) group of people going on a journey for a special purpose **Gesandtschaft, Delegation; trade mission** = visit by a group of businessmen to discuss trade **Handelsdelegation;** *he led a trade mission to China;* **inward mission** = visit to one's home country by a group of foreign businessmen **Delegation aus dem Ausland; outward mission** = visit by a group of businessmen to a foreign country **Auslandsbesuch einer Delegation; a fact-finding mission** = visit to an area to search for information about a problem **ein Erkundigungsbesuch**

◇ **missionary selling** *noun* approaching new customers with a product **Verkauf an neue Kunden, propagieren;** *we have never sold there before, so be prepared for missionary selling; some salesmen are not aggressive enough for missionary selling*

mix *noun* arrangement of different things together **Mischung; marketing mix** = combination of all the elements that make up marketing, such as price, distribution and promotion **Marketing-Mix; product mix** = combination of products made or sold by the same company **Produktmix, Produktpalette; promotional mix** = different elements used in a company's promotion **Verkaufsförderungsmix**

◊ **mixed** *adjective* made up of different sorts *or* of different types of things together **gemischt; mixed economy** = system which contains both nationalized industries and private enterprise **Mischwirtschaft; mixed farm** = farm which has both animals and crops **gemischte Landwirtschaft; mixed media** = various types of media, used together in a promotional package **Verwendung mehrerer Medien**

MMC = MONOPOLIES AND MERGERS COMMISSION

mobile *adjective* which can move about **beweglich, mobil; mobile shop** = van fitted out like a small shop which travels around selling groceries or vegetables **Verkaufswagen**

mock-up *noun* model of a new product for testing or to show to possible buyers **Attrappe**

mode *noun*
(a) way of doing something **Art (und Weise), Form; mode of payment** = way in which payment is made (such as cash or cheque) **Zahlungsweise**
(b) most common result found in a sample **Modus**

model
1 *noun*
(a) small copy of something to show what it will look like when finished **Modell;** *he showed us a model of the new office building*
(b) style *or* type *or* version of a product **Modell;** *this is the latest model; the model on display is last year's; he drives a 1985 model Ford;* **demonstration model** = piece of equipment used in demonstrations and then sold cheaply **Vorführmodell**
(c) person whose job is to wear new clothes to show them to possible buyers **Mannequin, Model(l);** *(männlich)* **Dressman**
(d) description in the form of mathematical data **Modell; economic model** = computerized plan of a country's economic system, used for forecasting economic trends **(EDV-)Modell zur Wirtschaftsprognose; marketing model** = description of an entire marketing process, shown graphically and on computer, used to solve marketing problems **Marketingmodell;** *see also* VEBLENIAN MODEL
2 *adjective* which is a perfect example to be copied **vorbildlich, mustergültig, Muster-, Modell-;** *a model agreement*
3 *verb* to wear new clothes to show them to possible buyers **als Mannequin arbeiten; als Dressman arbeiten**

modem *noun* device which links a computer to the telephone line, allowing data to be sent from one computer to another by telephone **Modem**

modify *verb* to change *or* to make something fit a different use **modifizieren, ändern;** *the management modified its proposals; this is the new modified agreement; the car will have to be modified to pass government tests; the refrigerator was considerably modified before it went into production;* **modified rebuy** = type of organizational buying decision where either the product or the supplier has changed in some way from the previous purchase **modifizierter Wiederholungskauf**

◊ **modification** *noun* change **Modifizierung, Änderung;** *to make or to carry out modifications to the plan; the new model has had several important modifications; we asked for modifications to the contract*

modular *adjective* made of various sections **modular, aus Elementen zusammengesetzt**

monadic test *noun* product test involving only one product **monadischer Test, Einzeltest**

monetary *adjective* referring to money or currency **monetär; währungspolitisch, Währungs-; the government's monetary policy** = the government's policy relating to finance (bank interest rates, taxes, government expenditure and borrowing) **die Geldmengenpolitik der Regierung; monetary standard** = fixing of a fixed exchange rate for a currency **Währungseinheit; the international monetary system** = methods of controlling and exchanging currencies between countries **das internationale Währungssystem; the European Monetary System (EMS)** = system of controlled exchange rates between some member countries of the Common Market **das Europäische Währungssystem; the International Monetary Fund (IMF)** = (part of the United Nations) a type of bank which helps member states in financial difficulties, gives financial advice to members and encourages world trade **Internationaler Währungsfonds, Weltwährungsfonds; monetary unit** = standard currency in a country (the pound, the dollar, the franc, etc.) **Währungseinheit**

> QUOTE the decision by the government to tighten monetary policy will push the annual inflation rate above the year's previous high
> *Financial Times*
>
> QUOTE it is not surprising that the Fed started to ease monetary policy some months ago
> *Sunday Times*
>
> QUOTE a draft report on changes in the international monetary system
> *Wall Street Journal*

money *noun*
(a) coins and notes used for buying and selling **Geld; to earn money** = to have a salary *or* wages **Geld verdienen; to earn good money** = to have a large salary *or* high wages **gut verdienen; to lose money** = to make a loss *or* not to make a profit **Geld verlieren/einbüßen; the company has been losing money for months** = the company has been working at a loss **das Unternehmen hat seit Monaten Geldeinbußen zu verzeichnen; to get your money back** = to earn enough to cover your original investment **sein Geld wieder herausbekommen; to make money** = to make a profit **Geld verdienen; to put money into the bank** = to deposit money into a bank account **Geld auf die Bank bringen; to put money into a business** = to invest money in a business **Geld in ein Geschäft investieren;** *he put all his redundancy money into a shop;* **to put money down** = to pay cash, especially as a deposit **eine Anzahlung leisten;** *he put £25 down and paid the rest in instalments;* **cheap money** = money which can be borrowed at a low rate of interest **billiges Geld; danger money** = extra salary paid to workers in dangerous jobs **Gefahrenzulage; dear money** = money which has to be borrowed at a high rate of interest **teures Geld; easy money** = money which can be earned with no difficulty **leicht verdientes Geld;** *selling insurance is easy money;* **hot money** = money which is moved from country to country to get the best returns **heißes Geld; paper money** = money in notes, not coins **Papiergeld; ready money** = cash *or* money which is immediately available **Bargeld, flüssige Mittel; money lying idle** = money not being used to produce interest **totes Kapital**
(b) money supply = amount of money which exists in a country **Geldreserve, Geldvolumen; money markets** = markets for buying and selling short-term loans **Geldmärkte;** *the international money markets are nervous;* **money rates** = rates of interest for borrowers or lenders **Geldmarktsätze**
(c) money order = document which can be bought for sending money through the post **Postanweisung; foreign money order** *or* **international money order** *or* **overseas money order** = money order in a foreign currency which is payable to someone living in a foreign country **Auslandszahlungsanweisung**
(d) monies = sums of money **Gelder;** *monies owing to the company; to collect monies due*
◇ **money-back guarantee** *noun* a guarantee that money will be paid back to customers who are not satisfied with their purchases **bei Nichtgefallen Geld zurück, Rückgaberecht mit Gelderstattung**
◇ **money-making** *adjective* which makes money **einträglich, gewinnbringend;** *a money-making plan*
◇ **money-off coupon** *noun* coupon in a newspaper or on a package, which can be cut off and used to claim a discount on the next purchase **Preisnachlaßgutschein**
◇ **money-spinner** *noun* item which sells very well *or* which is very profitable **Kassenschlager**

monopoly *noun* situation where one person or company is the only supplier of a particular product or service **Monopol;** *to have the monopoly of alcohol sales or to have the alcohol monopoly; to be in a monopoly situation; the company has the absolute monopoly of imports of French wine; the factory has the absolute monopoly of jobs in the town;* **monopoly profit** = profit earned by a business through having a monopoly **Monopolprofit; public monopoly** *or* **state monopoly** = situation where the state is the only suppliers of a product or service (such as the Post Office, the coal industry,etc.) **staatliches Monopol;** *(GB)* **the Monopolies and Mergers Commission (MMC)** = organization which examines takeovers and mergers to make sure that a monopoly is not being created **das Kartellamt;** NOTE: **trust** is used more often in US English
◇ **monopolist** *noun* business which is the sole seller in a market **Monopolist**
◇ **monopolistic competition** *noun* situation where there are only a few producers who therefore control the market between them **monopolistischer Wettbewerb;** *with only three suppliers of cotton in the country it was a clear case of monopolistic competition*
◇ **monopolize** *verb* to create a monopoly *or* to get control of all the supply of a product **monopolisieren, beherrschen**
◇ **monopolization** *noun* making a monopoly **Monopolisierung**

monopsony *noun* situation where there is only one buyer for a particular product **Monopson;** *monopsony gives the buyer leverage in demanding a low price*

◊ **monopsonist** *noun* sole buyer of a particular product **Monopsonist**

morphological analysis *noun* method of identifying the most profitable market segments by exploring various dimensions, such as countries, market types, etc. **morphologische Analyse**

motivated *adjective* **highly motivated sales staff** = sales staff who are very eager to sell **hochmotiviertes Verkaufspersonal**

◊ **motivation** *noun* encouragement *or* being eager to sell **Motivation; the sales staff lack motivation** = the sales staff are not motivated enough **dem Verkaufspersonal mangelt es an Motivation**

◊ **motivational research** *noun* research into the psychological reasons behind buying behaviour **Motivforschung;** *our motivational research failed to tell us why the product is so popular*

move *verb* to be sold *or* to sell **umziehen; verlegen;** *the stock is starting to move; the salesmen will have to work hard if they want to move all that stock by the end of the month*

◊ **moving average** *noun* method for working out averages while allowing for seasonal variations, by moving the period under consideration forward at regular intervals **gleitender Durchschnitt**

MRP = MANUFACTURER'S RECOMMENDED PRICE

multi- *prefix* referring to many things **multi-, Multi-; multi-channel system** = distribution system used by a producer which makes use of more than one distribution channel **mehrkanäliges Vertriebssystem; multi-pack offer** = special promotional offer, where an extra pack is offered free, or at a reduced price, for each pack bought at full price **Mehrfachpackungsangebot**

◊ **multilateral** *adjective* between several parties **multilateral;** *a multilateral agreement;* **multilateral trade** = trade between several countries **multilateraler Handel**

◊ **multimedia** *adjective* referring to several media used in a project **unter Verwendung mehrerer Medien;** *we are going for an all-out multimedia advertising campaign*

◊ **multinational** *noun* company which has branches *or* subsidiary companies in several countries **multinationaler Konzern;** *the company has been bought by one of the big multinationals*

multiple

1 *adjective* many **mehr-, vielfach; multiple choice question** = type of question used in a survey which allows the respondent to choose a single answer from several possible ones **Auswahlfrage;** *the questionnaire had eight multiple choice questions, two dichotomous questions and one open question;* **multiple correlation** = method for measuring the effect of several independent variables on one dependent variable **Mehrfachkorrelation; multiple discriminant analysis** = method for assessing products by separating out their various attributes, and estimating the relative values of these attributes to different market segments, the whole process producing an assessment of the general potential of a product **multiple Diskriminanzanalyse; multiple pricing** = fixing the same price for several different products **gemeinsamer Preis; multiple regression analysis** = method for discovering the relationship between several independent variables and one dependent variable **Mehrfachregressionsanalyse; multiple store** = one store in a chain of stores **Filiale**

2 *noun* company with stores in several different towns **Einzelhandelskette**

multi-stage sample *noun* sample selected by ensuring equal proportions of various categories existing in the population and then using random sampling to select respondents within these categories **mehrstufige Auswahl**

Nn

name *noun* word used to call a thing *or* a person by **Name;** *I can't remember the name of the managing director of Smith's Ltd; his first name is John, but I'm not sure what his surname is;* **brand name** = name of a particular make of product **Markenname; corporate name** = name of a large corporation **Firmenname; under the name of** = using a particular name **unter dem Namen; trading under the name of "Best Foods"** = using the name "Best Foods" as a commercial name, though it is not the official legal name of the company **ein Produkt unter dem Namen "Best Foods" verkaufen**

◇ **named** *adjective* **person named in the policy** = person whose name is given on an insurance policy as the person insured **der (in der Police benannte) Versicherte**

narrowcasting *noun* reaching only a small, special audience through an electronic medium such as cable television **Senden im geschlossenen System/Kreislauf**

nation *noun* country and the people living in it **Nation; Volk; most favoured nation** = country which has the best trade terms **meistbegünstigtes Land; most-favoured-nation clause** = agreement between two countries that each will give the other the best possible trade terms in commercial contracts **Meistbegünstigungsklausel; the United Nations** = organization linking almost all the countries in the world **die Vereinten Nationen**

◇ **national** *adjective* referring to the whole of a particular country **national, National-; national account** = customer with branches or locations all over the country **überregionaler Kunde/Auftraggeber; national advertising** = advertising in every part of a country, not just in the capital **landesweite/überregionale Werbung;** *we took national advertising to promote our new 24-hour delivery service;* **national campaign** = sales or publicity campaign in every part of a country **landesweite/überregionale Kampagne; national income** = value of income from the sales of goods and services in a country **Volkseinkommen; national newspapers** *or* **the national press** = newspapers which sell in all parts of a country **überregionale Presse; gross national product (GNP)** = annual value of goods and services in a country including income from other countries **Bruttosozialprodukt;**

◇ **nationalization** *noun* taking over of private industry by the state **Verstaatlichung**

◇ **nationwide** *adjective* all over a country **landesweit;** *the union called for a nationwide strike; we offer a nationwide delivery service; the new car is being launched with a nationwide sales campaign*

natural *adjective*

(a) found in the earth **natürlich, Natur-;** *natural gas;* **natural resources** = raw materials (such as coal, gas, iron, etc.) which are found in the earth **Bodenschätze**
(b) not made by people **Natur-;** *natural fibres*
(c) normal **natürlich;** *it was only natural that the shopkeeper should feel annoyed when the hypermarket was built close to his shop;* **natural break** = convenient or reasonable point in a TV programme for a commercial break **natürliche Sendeunterbrechung**

NBA = NET BOOK AGREEMENT

necessity *noun* thing which is vitally important, without which nothing can be done or one cannot survive **Notwendigkeit; das Notwendigste; the basic necessities** = the very least that people need to live, such as food and clothing **die Lebensbedürfnisse;** *being unemployed makes it difficult to afford even the basic necessities;* **necessity products** = ordinary everyday products of which consumers tend not to buy much more as their incomes rise **Verbrauchsgüter des täglichen Bedarfs;** *consumers find shopping for necessity products boring; fancy packaging will not increase sales of necessity products*

negative *adjective* meaning "no" **negativ, verneinend; the answer was in the negative** = the answer was "no" **der Bescheid war negativ; negative cash flow** = situation where a company is spending more money than it receives **negativer Cashflow; negative demand** = firm decisions by consumers not to buy a particular product **negative Nachfrage;** *negative demand was due to offensive advertising;* **negative variance** = difference between a financial plan and its outcome that means a less favourable profit than expected **negative Abweichung;** *the unexpected increase in raw material prices meant a negative variance of $5000; a sudden fall in revenue resulted in a negative variance for the year as a whole*

negotiable *adjective* which can be transferred from one person to another or exchanged for cash **begebbar; not negotiable** = which cannot be exchanged for cash **unverkäuflich; "not negotiable"** = words written on a cheque to show that it can be paid only to a certain person **nicht übertragbar; negotiable cheque** = cheque made payable to bearer (i.e. to anyone who holds it) **Inhaberscheck; negotiable instrument** = document (such as a bill of exchange, or cheque) which can be exchanged for cash **begebbares Wertpapier**

◇ **negotiate** *verb* **to negotiate with someone** = to discuss a problem formally with someone, so as to reach an agreement **mit jdm verhandeln;** *the management refused to negotiate with the union;* **to negotiate terms and conditions** *or* **to negotiate a contract** = to discuss and agree terms of a contract **Bestimmungen und Bedingungen aushandeln; einen Vertrag aushandeln; he negotiated a £250,000 loan with the bank** = he came to an agreement with the bank for a loan of £250,000 **er handelte ein Darlehen in Höhe von £250.000 mit der Bank aus; negotiating committee** = group of representatives of management or unions who negotiate a wage settlement **Verhandlungsausschuß**

◇ **negotiation** *noun* discussion of terms and conditions to reach an agreement **Verhandlung; contract under negotiation** = contract which is being discussed **Vertrag wird verhandelt; a matter for negotiation** = something which must be discussed before a decision is reached **eine Verhandlungssache; to enter into negotiations** *or* **to start negotiations** = to start discussing a problem **Verhandlungen aufnehmen; to resume negotiations** = to start discussing a problem again, after talks have stopped for a time **Verhandlungen wiederaufnehmen; to break off negotiations** = to refuse to go on discussing a problem **Verhandlungen abbrechen; to conduct negotiations** = to negotiate **Verhandlungen führen; negotiations broke down after six hours** = discussions stopped because no agreement was possible **die Verhandlungen scheiterten nach sechs Stunden; pay negotiations** *or* **wage negotiations** = discussions between management and workers about pay **Lohnverhandlungen**

◇ **negotiator** *noun*
(a) person who discusses a problem with the aim of reaching an agreement **Verhandlungsführer, Unterhändler; an experienced union negotiator** = member of a union who has a lot of experience of discussing terms of employment with management **ein erfahrener Gewerkschaftsunterhändler**
(b) *GB* person who works in an estate agency **Makler**

> QUOTE initial salary is negotiable around $45,000 per annum
> *Australian Financial Review*
>
> QUOTE after three days of tough negotiations, the company reached agreement with its 1,200 unionized workers
> *Toronto Star*
>
> QUOTE many of the large travel agency chains are able to negotiate even greater discounts
> *Duns Business Month*

net

1 *adjective* price *or* weight *or* pay, etc. after all deductions have been made **netto, Netto-; net assets** *or* **net worth** = value of all the property of a company after taking away what the company owes **Reinvermögen; net cash flow** = difference between money coming in and money going out of a firm **Netto-Cashflow; net circulation** = total sales figure of a publication after adjusting for error and discounting unsold copies **effektive Nettoauflage; net cover** = percentage of target audience exposed at least once to an advertisement on TV or radio **Nettoreichweite; net earnings** *or* **net income** = total earnings of a business after tax and other deductions **Netto-, Reingewinn; net income** *or* **net salary** = the amount of a person's income which is left after deducting tax, etc. **Nettoverdienst, Nettogehalt; net loss** = actual loss, after deducting overheads **Nettoverlust; net margin** = percentage difference between received price and all costs, including overheads **Nettomarge; net national product** = gross national product less investment on capital goods and depreciation **Nettosozialprodukt; net price** = price which cannot be reduced by a discount **Nettopreis; net profit** = profit calculated as sales income less all expenditure **Netto-, Reingewinn; net reach** = total number of people who have seen a press advertisement at least once **Nettoreichweite; net receipts** = receipts after deducting commission *or* tax *or* discounts, etc. **Nettoeinnahmen; net sales** = sales less damaged or returned items **Nettoumsatz; net weight** = weight of goods after deducting the weight of packaging material and container **Nettogewicht; net yield** = profit from investments after deduction of tax **Nettoertrag**
2 *verb* to make a true profit **netto einnehmen/verdienen, Reingewinn erzielen;** *to net a profit of £10,000*

◇ **Net Book Agreement (NBA)** *noun (GB)* agreement in the bookselling business that all books will be sold by booksellers at retail prices fixed by the publishers **Vereinbarung zur Preisbindung bei Büchern**

> QUOTE out of its earnings a company will pay a dividend. When shareholders receive this it will be net, that is it will have had tax deducted at 30 per cent
> *Investors Chronicle*

network

1 *noun*
(a) system which links different points together **Netz(werk); a network of distributors** *or* **a distribution network** = series of points *or* warehouses from which goods are sent all over a country **Verteiler-, Vertriebsnetz; computer network** = computer system where several micros are linked so that they all draw on the same database **Computernetz(werk), Rechnerverbund; network analysis** = analysis of a project by charting the individual activities involved, each with the time needed for its completion, so that the timing of the whole can be planned and controlled **Netzplantechnik**

(b) television network = system of linked television stations covering the whole country **Sendernetz; network programming** = scheduling TV programmes over the whole network **Sendernetzprogrammgestaltung**
2 *verb* to link together in a network **vernetzen; to network a television programme** = to send out the same television programme through several TV stations **ein Fernsehprogramm im ganzen Netzbereich senden; networked system** = computer system where several micros are linked together so that they all draw on the same database **Mehrplatzsystem, Rechnerverbund**

never-never *noun (informal)* buying on credit **‚Stottern'**; *he bought his car on the never-never*

new *adjective* recent *or* not old **neu; new buy** = type of organizational buying where a completely new type of product is bought **Neuproduktaufnahme; new product committee** = group of people from different departments in a company who work together on a new product development project; *(entspricht)* **die Produktmanager;** *the new product committee met regularly to monitor the progress in the product's development;* **new product development (NPD)** = improving existing products or developing completely new ones **Produktentwicklung;** *the company fell behind because it failed to invest enough in new product development;* **new technology** = electronic instruments which have recently been invented **neue Technologie**

◇ **news** *noun* information about things which have happened **Nachricht(en);** *business news; financial news; financial markets were shocked by the news of the devaluation;* **news agency** = office which distributes news to newspapers and television companies **Nachrichtenagentur, Nachrichtendienst; news release** = sheet giving information about a new event which is sent to newspapers and TV and radio stations so that they can use it **Pressenotiz;** *the company sent out a news release about the new managing director*

◇ **newsletter** *noun* **company newsletter** = printed sheet or small newspaper giving news about a company **Firmenmitteilungsblatt**

◇ **newspaper** *noun* regular publication (usually daily or weekly) which gives items of general news, sold to the general public **Zeitung; national newspaper** = newspaper which is sold throughout a whole country and carries national and international news **überregionale Zeitung; local newspaper** = newspaper which is sold only in a restricted area, and mainly carries news about that area **Lokalzeitung**

next matter *or* **next-to-reading matter** *noun* placing of an advertisement in a publication, right beside editorial matter **neben Text, textanschließend**

niche *noun* special place in a market, occupied by one company **Nische, Platz**

Nielsen Index publication of a number of different retail and wholesale audit services corresponding to type of outlet and area of the country **Nielsen-Index**

no-change discount *noun* reduction in the price of an advertisement which uses the same artwork as a previous one **Mal-, Wiederholungsrabatt**

no direct mail list *noun* list of people who do not wish to receive any direct mail **Robinsonliste**

non- *prefix* not **nicht-, Nicht-**

◇ **non-acceptance** *noun* situation in which the person who is to pay a bill of exchange does not accept it **Akzeptverweigerung**

◇ **non-business organization** *noun (US)* organization (such as a club) which is not allowed by law to make a profit **gemeinnütziges/nichtkommerzielles Unternehmen;** *though only a non-business organization, the charity used highly sophisticated marketing techniques; he became a fundraiser for a non-business organization*

◇ **non-delivery** *noun* failure to deliver goods ordered **Nichtlieferung**

◇ **non-directive interview** *noun* interview using no preset questions and following no fixed pattern **nichtdirektive Befragung**

◇ **non-durables** *plural noun* goods which are used up soon after they have been bought (such as food, newspapers, etc.) **kurzlebige Konsumgüter**

◇ **non-negotiable** *adjective* **non-negotiable instrument** = document (such as a crossed cheque) which cannot be exchanged for cash **Rektapapier**

◇ **non-payment** *noun* **non-payment of a debt** = not paying a debt due **Nichtzahlung einer Verpflichtung**

◇ **non-price competition** *noun* attempt to compete in a market through other means than price, such as quality of product and promotion **preisunabhängiger Wettbewerb**

non-profit-making organization *or* *(US)* **non-profit organization** *noun* organization (such as a club or charity) which does not exist to make a profit, but to provide some sort of service to people **gemeinnütziges/nichtkommerzielles Unternehmen;** *non-profit-making organizations are exempted from tax*

> QUOTE situations can and inevitably do occur in non-profit organizations when no monetary charge can be made for products and services
> *Quarterly Review of Marketing*

non-refundable *adjective* which will not be refunded **nicht erstattungsfähig;** *non-refundable deposit*

◊ **non-returnable** *adjective* which cannot be returned **Einweg-; non-returnable packing** = packing which is to be thrown away and not returned to the sender once it has been used **Einweg(ver)packung**

◊ **non-statistical error** *noun* distortion of the results of a survey owing to bias and mistakes made in conducting the survey **systematischer Fehler**

normal *adjective* usual *or* which happens regularly **normal, üblich;** *now that the strike is over we hope to resume normal service as soon as possible;* **under normal conditions** = if things work in the usual way **unter normalen Bedingungen;** *under normal conditions a package takes two days to get to Copenhagen;* **normal distribution** = term used in sampling theory, referring to the results of a sample and meaning a symmetrical distribution of values around a mean or average, so that one can be confident that the sample is properly representative of the population or universe **Normalverteilung; normal price** = price that can be expected for a product under normal market conditions **marktüblicher Preis, Normalpreis; normal profit** = minimum profit that can motivate a business to carry on a certain type of production *or* selling **Deckungsbeitrag**

note *noun*
(a) short document *or* short piece of information **Mitteilung; Bescheid; advice note** = written notice to a customer giving details of goods ordered and shipped but not yet delivered **Versandanzeige, Avis; contract note** = note showing that shares have been bought or sold but not yet paid for **Ausführungsanzeige; cover note** = letter from an insurance company giving details of an insurance policy and confirming that the policy exists **vorläufiger Versicherungsschein, Deckungszusage; covering note** = letter sent with documents to explain why you are sending them **Begleitschreiben; credit note** = note showing that money is owed to a customer **Gutschriftsanzeige; debit note** = note showing that a customer owes money **Lastschriftanzeige;** *we undercharged Mr Smith and had to send him a debit note for the extra amount;* **delivery note** = list of goods being delivered, given to the customer with the goods **Lieferschein; dispatch note** = note saying that goods have been sent **Versandschein; note of hand** *or* **promissory note** = document stating that someone promises to pay an amount of money on a certain date **Schuldschein**
(b) short letter *or* short piece of information **Notiz, Nachricht;** *to send someone a note; I left a note on his desk; she left a note for the managing director with his secretary*
(c) bank note *or* **currency note** = piece of printed paper money **Banknote;** *a £5 note; he pulled out a pile of used notes*

◊ **noting** *noun* noticing (though not necessarily reading and understanding) an advertisement in a publication **Beachtung; noting score** = percentage of total readers who note an advertisement **Beachtungswert;** *the amount of advertising we will need to do depends on the anticipated noting score*

notice *noun*
(a) official warning that a contract is going to end *or* that terms are going to be changed **Bescheid; until further notice** = until different instructions are given **bis auf weiteres;** *you must pay £200 on the 30th of each month until further notice*
(b) time allowed before something takes place **Frist; at short notice** = with very little warning **kurzfristig;** *the bank manager will not see anyone at short notice;* **you must give seven days' notice of withdrawal** = you must ask to take money out of the account seven days before you want it **Sie haben sieben Tage Kündigungsfrist**

◊ **noticeboard** *noun* board fixed to a wall where notices can be put up **Schwarzes Brett, Anschlagbrett;** *did you see the new list of prices on the noticeboard?*

novelty *noun* original amusing article which is often bought as a gift **Scherzartikel;** *a novelty shop provided paper hats for parties*

NPD = NEW PRODUCT DEVELOPMENT

null *adjective* with no meaning *or* which cannot legally be enforced **nichtig, ungültig; the contract was declared null and void** = the contract was said to be invalid **der Vertrag wurde für ungültig erklärt; to render a**

decision null = to make a decision useless *or* to cancel a decision **eine Entscheidung für nichtig erklären/aufheben**

◊ **nullification** *noun* act of making something invalid **Annullierung, Aufhebung**

◊ **nullify** *verb* to make something invalid *or* to cancel something **annullieren, für nichtig erklären**

numeric *or* **numerical** *adjective* referring to numbers **numerisch, zahlenmäßig; in numerical order** = in the order of figures (such as 1 before 2, 33 before 34) **in zahlenmäßiger Folge;** *file these invoices in numerical order;* **numeric data** = data in the form of figures **numerische Daten; numeric keypad** = part of a computer keyboard which is a programmable set of numbered keys **Zehnertastatur, numerische Tastatur**

Oo

the four O's simple compact way of summarizing the essentials of a marketing operation, which are objects, objectives, organization and operations **eine Gedächtnisstütze für das Wichtigste einer Marketingoperation;** *business school students learn the four O's as a simple way of remembering key points in strategy*

objective
1 *noun* something which you hope to achieve **Ziel;** *the company has achieved its objectives; we set the sales forces certain objectives;* **long-term objective** *or* **short-term objective** = aim which you hope to achieve within a few years or a few months **langfristige Zielsetzung; kurzfristige Zielsetzung; management by objectives** = way of managing a business where the managers work according to a plan and checks are made periodically to see whether their work is completed correctly and on time **Management nach Zielvorgaben; objective-and-task method** = method of calculating an advertising appropriation by basing it on the actual amount needed to achieve the objectives **Ziel-Aufgaben-Methode**
2 *adjective* considered from a general point of view not from that of the person involved **objektiv, sachlich;** *they have been asked to carry out an objective survey of the market*

obligation *noun*
(a) duty to do something **Verpflichtung; to be under an obligation to do something** = to feel it is your duty to do something **sich verpflichtet fühlen, etwas zu tun;** *there is no obligation to buy; to be under no obligation to do something;* **he is under no contractual obligation to buy** = he has signed no contract which forces him to buy **er ist nicht vertraglich zum Kauf verpflichtet; to fulfil one's contractual obligations** = to do what is stated in a contract **seine Vertragspflicht erfüllen; two weeks' free trial without obligation** = the customer can try the item at home for two weeks without having to buy it at the end of the test **zwei Wochen Probezeit ohne Kaufzwang**
(b) debt **Verbindlichkeit; to meet one's obligations** = to pay one's debts **seinen Verbindlichkeiten nachkommen**

observation method *noun* market research method of obtaining information by observation, rather than interviews **Beobachtungsmethode;** *the observation method does not tell you anything about the consumers' attitudes to the product*

obsolescence *noun* act of going out of date because of advances in design or technology, and therefore becoming less useful and valuable **Obsoleszenz, Veralten; artificial obsolescence** = deliberately making old models seem out-of-date by bringing out new ones with changes and additional features which will attract the customer **künstliche Obsoleszenz, geplante Veralterung; built-in obsolescence** *or* **planned obsolescence** = method of ensuring continuing sales of a product by making it in such a way that it will soon become obsolete **eingebaute/qualitative Obsoleszenz; geplante Veralterung; dynamic obsolescence** = redesigning a company's product to make other products in the market obsolete **geplante/funktionelle Obsoleszenz**
◊ **obsolescent** *adjective* becoming out of date **veraltend**
◊ **obsolete** *adjective* no longer used **überholt, veraltet;** *when the office was equipped with word-processors the typewriters became obsolete*

odd *adjective*
(a) odd numbers = numbers (like 17 or 33) which cannot be divided by two **ungerade Zahlen;** *odd-numbered buildings or buildings with odd numbers are on the south side of the street;* **odd-even pricing** = using either odd or even numbers in pricing, according to what seems most psychologically effective in persuading customers to buy **Odd-Even Pricing (Endzifferneffekt);** *students*

can study the psychological bases of odd-even pricing
(b) one of a group **einzeln; an odd shoe** = one shoe of a pair **ein einzelner Schuh; we have a few odd boxes left** = we have a few boxes left out of the total shipment **wir haben einige wenige Kisten übrig; odd lot** = group of miscellaneous items for sale at an auction **Auktionsposten; to do odd jobs** = to do various pieces of work **Gelegenheitsarbeiten verrichten**
(c) odd sizes = strange sizes which are not usual **keine gängigen Größen; Übergrößen; Untergrößen**

◇ **odd-job-man** *noun* person who does various pieces of work **Gelegenheitsarbeiter**

◇ **oddments** *plural noun* items left over; pieces of large items sold separately **Restposten, Rest-, Einzelbestände**

off

1 *adverb*
(a) not working *or* not in operation **abgesagt, ausgefallen, nicht mehr geltend;** *the agreement is off; they called the strike off*
(b) taken away from a price **ermäßigt, mit Ermäßigung;** *these carpets are sold at £25 off the marked price; we give 5% off for quick settlement*
2 *preposition* subtracted from **von;** *to take £25 off the price; we give 10% off our normal prices*

◇ **off-card rate** *noun* specially arranged price for advertising space or time **Sonderpreis;** *the newspaper offered us an off-card rate for space which was still empty the day before publication*

offer

1 *noun*
(a) statement that you are willing to pay a certain amount of money to buy something **Angebot;** *to make an offer for a company; he made an offer of £10 a share; we made a written offer for the house; £1,000 is the best offer I can make; to accept an offer of £1,000 for the car;* **the house is under offer** = someone has made an offer to buy the house and the offer has been provisionally accepted **für das Haus liegt ein Kaufangebot vor; we are open to offers** = we are ready to discuss the price which we are asking **Angebote werden entgegengenommen; cash offer** = being ready to pay in cash **Barangebot; or near offer** = or an offer of a price which is slightly less than the price asked **oder gegen Höchstgebot; Verhandlungsbasis, VB;** *the car is for sale at £2,000 or near offer* (NOTE: often shortened to **o.n.o.)**
(b) statement that you are willing to sell something **Verkaufsangebot; offer for sale** = situation where a company advertises new shares for sale **Zeichnungsangebot, Angebot; offer price** = price at which new shares are put on sale **Emissionskurs**
(c) he received six offers of jobs *or* **six job offers** = six companies told him he could have a job with them **ihm wurden sechs Stellen angeboten**
(d) banded offer = type of sales promotion involving the offer of an additional item along with the main one **Combipack-Angebot; bargain offer** = sale of a particular type of goods at a cheap price **Sonderangebot;** *this week's bargain offer - 30% off all carpet prices;* **introductory offer** = special price offered on a new product to attract customers **Einführungspreis; premium offer** = present given to a customer, either attached to the product bought, or given by the retailer on proof of purchase of a minimum quantity of goods **Zugabenangebot, Werbegeschenk; special offer** = goods put on sale at a specially low price **Sonderangebot;** *we have a range of men's shirts on special offer;* **total offer** = complete package offered to the customer (including the product or service itself, its price, availability and promotion) **Gesamtangebot**
2 *verb*
(a) to say that you are willing to pay a certain amount of money for something **bieten;** *to offer someone £100,000 for his house; he offered £10 a share*
(b) to say that you are willing to sell something **anbieten;** *we offered the house for sale*

Office of Fair Trading (OFT)

government organization which protects both traders and consumers from unfair practices in the market **Amt für Verbraucherschutz**

offload

verb to pass something which is not wanted on to someone else **abstoßen, abschieben; to offload excess stock** = to try to sell excess stock **Überbestand abstoßen; to offload costs onto a subsidiary company** = to try to get a subsidiary company to pay some charges so as to reduce tax **Kosten auf eine Tochtergesellschaft umlegen**

off-peak

adjective not during the most busy time **außerhalb der Stoßzeit/Hauptbelastungszeit/Hauptverkehrszeit; during the off-peak period** = at the time when business is less busy **außerhalb der Stoßzeit; off-peak tariff** *or* **rate** = lower charges used when the service is not busy **verbilligter Tarif (außerhalb der Stoßzeit)**

off-price label *noun* label on a product which shows a reduced price **‚Jetzt-Früher'-Preisschild**

off-season
1 *adjective* **off-season tariff** *or* **rate** = cheap fares which are charged in a season when there is less business **Tarif außerhalb der Saison**
2 *noun* less busy season for travel (usually during the winter) **Nebensaison;** *to travel in the off-season; air fares are cheaper in the off-season*

off-the-page buying *noun* buying items which have been advertised in magazines or newspapers **Ankaufen durch die Druckmedien**

OFT = OFFICE OF FAIR TRADING

oligopoly *noun* situation where only a few sellers control the market **Oligopol;** *an oligopoly means that prices can be kept high*
◇ **oligopsony** *noun* situation where only a few buyers control the market **Oligopson**

omnibus *noun* **omnibus advertisement** = advertisement which covers several different products **Anzeigenkollektiv; omnibus agreement** = agreement which covers many different items **Globalabkommen; omnibus survey** = survey to which several companies subscribe, each adding specific questions of its own **Omnibusumfrage**

oncosts *plural noun* fixed costs *or* money spent in producing a product which does not rise with the quantity of the product made **Fixkosten**

one-stop shopping centre *noun* shopping centre with a comprehensive choice of shops and supermarkets, designed to cover all of a person's shopping needs **One-Stop-Einkaufszentrum, Regionalzentrum**
◇ **one-time rate** *noun* special rate for an advertisement that is only placed once **Einmaltarif**

on-pack promotion *noun* advertising material on the outside of packaged goods **Packungswerbung;** *we use on-pack promotion to stimulate buying at the point-of-sale; our on-pack promotion is designed to complement the TV advertising campaign*

o.n.o. = OR NEAR OFFER

open
1 *adjective*
(a) at work *or* not closed **geöffnet;** *the store is open on Sunday mornings; our offices are open from 9 to 6; they are open for business every day of the week*
(b) ready to accept something **offen, offenstehend; the job is open to all applicants** = anyone can apply for the job **die Stelle steht allen Bewerbern offen; open to offers** = ready to accept a reasonable offer **Angebote werden entgegengenommen; the company is open to offers for the empty factory** = the company is ready to discuss an offer which is lower than the suggested price **die Firma zieht Angebote für die leerstehende Fabrik in Betracht**
(c) open account = unsecured credit *or* amount owed with no security **Kontokorrentkonto mit Kreditlinie; open cheque** = cheque which is not crossed and can be cashed anywhere **Barscheck; open credit** = bank credit given to good customers without security up to a certain maximum sum **Blankokredit; open market** = market where anyone can buy or sell **freier Markt;**
2 *verb*
(a) to start a new business working **eröffnen, aufmachen;** *she has opened a shop in the High Street; we have opened an office in London*
(b) to start work *or* to be at work **aufmachen, öffnen, geöffnet sein;** *the office opens at 9 a.m.; we open for business on Sundays*

◇ **open-dating** *noun* putting the sell-by date on a packet in an uncoded form which can be understood by the consumers **nicht kodierte Datierung;** *open-dating is considered by many to be an important feature of consumer protection in food products*

◇ **open-door policy** *noun* policy of a country to accept imports from all other countries on equal terms **(Handels)politik der offenen Tür**

◇ **open-ended** *or (US)* **open-end** *adjective* with no fixed limit *or* with some items not specified **offen, unbeschränkt, unbefristet; Blanko-;** *open-ended agreement;* **open-ended question** = question in a questionnaire which allows a respondent to answer as he or she likes without having to choose from pre-set answers **offene Frage;** *open-ended questions elicit answers that are original but hard to evaluate; an open-ended question is needed here, since the question involves the respondent's personal feelings*

◇ **opening**
1 *noun*
(a) act of starting a new business **Eröffnung;** *the opening of a new branch; the opening of a new market or of a new distribution network*

(b) opening hours = hours when a shop *or* business is open **Öffnungs-, Geschäftszeit**
(c) opportunity to do something **Gelegenheit, Möglichkeit; job openings** = jobs which are empty and need filling **freie Stellen;** *we have openings for office staff;* **market opening** = possibility of starting to do business in a new market **Markterschließung**
2 *adjective* at the beginning *or* first **Eröffnungs-, einleitend; opening balance** = balance at the beginning of an accounting period **Eröffnungsbetrag; opening bid** = first bid at an auction **Eröffnungsgebot; opening entry** = first entry in an account **Eröffnungsbuchung; opening price** = price at the start of the day's trading **Eröffnungs-, Anfangskurs; opening stock** = stock at the beginning of the accounting period **Eröffnungsbestand**

◊ **open pricing** *noun* attempt by companies to achieve some cooperation and conformity in pricing **offene Preispolitik;** *representatives from the major companies in the industry are meeting to establish an open-pricing policy*

◊ **open up** *verb* **to open up new markets** = to work to start business in markets where such business has not previously existed **neue Märkte erschließen**

operate *verb*
(a) to work *or* to be in force **gelten, wirksam werden;** *the new terms of service will operate from January 1st; the rules operate on inland postal services only*
(b) to operate a machine = to make a machine work **eine Maschine bedienen;** *he is learning to operate the new telephone switchboard*

◊ **operating** *noun* general running of a business *or* of a machine **Betrieb; operating budget** = forecast of income and expenditure over a period of time **Betriebswirtschaftsplan; operating costs** *or* **operating expenses** = costs of the day-to-day organization of a company **Betriebskosten, betriebliche Aufwendungen; operating manual** = book which shows how to work a machine **Benutzerhandbuch, Bedienungsanleitung; operating profit** *or* **operating loss** = profit or loss made by a company in its usual business **Betriebsgewinn; Betriebsverlust; operating statement** = financial statement which shows a company's expenditure and income and consequently its final profit or loss **Betriebsabrechnung;** *the operating statement shows unexpected electricity costs; let's look at the operating statement to find last month's expenditure;* **operating supplies** = low-priced industrial products that are normally bought by producers **Betriebsstoffe;** *production came to a standstill for lack of operating supplies; we are now ordering operating supplies for next month's production;* **operating system** = the main program which operates a computer **Betriebssystem**

◊ **operation** *noun* business organization and work **Geschäft, Tätigkeit, Bereich;** *the company's operations in West Africa; he heads up the operations in Northern Europe;* **operations review** = examining the way in which a company or department works to see how it can be made more efficient and profitable **Betriebsanalyse; a franchising operation** = selling licences to trade as a franchise **eine Franchisevergabe**

◊ **operational** *adjective*
(a) referring to how something works **betrieblich, Betriebs-, Funktions-; operational budget** = forecast of expenditure in running a business **Betriebsbudget; operational costs** = costs of running a business **Betriebskosten; operational planning** = planning how a business is to be run **Betriebsplanung; operational research** = study of a company's way of working to see if it can be made more efficient and profitable **Unternehmensforschung, Operational-Research**
(b) working *or* in operation **einsatzbereit;** *it will be another six months before the plant is fully operational*

opinion *noun* **public opinion** = what people think about something **öffentliche Meinung; opinion poll** *or* **opinion research** = asking a sample group of people what their opinion is, so as to work out the probable opinion of the whole population **Meinungsumfrage; Meinungsforschung;** *opinion polls showed that the public preferred butter to margarine; before starting the new service, the company carried out nationwide opinion polls;* **opinion-formers** *or* **opinion-leaders** = people whose opinions influence others in society **Meinungsführer;** *a pop-star is the ideal opinion-leader if we are aiming at the teenage market; the celebrity used in the sales promotion campaign was not respected enough to be a true opinion-former*

opportunity *noun* chance to do something successfully **Gelegenheit, Chance, Möglichkeit; investment opportunities** *or* **sales opportunities** = possibilities for making investments or sales which will be profitable **Investitionsmöglichkeiten; Verkaufsmöglichkeiten; market opportunity** = possibility of going into a market for the first time **neue Absatzmöglichkeit(en); opportunities to see (OTS)** = number of opportunities an average member of the target audience will have to see an advertisement **Kontaktchancen, Kontaktwahrscheinlichkeiten; employment opportunities** *or* **job opportunities** = jobs which are available **Beschäftigungsmöglichkeiten;** *the increase in export orders has created hundreds of job opportunities;* **purchasing opportunity** = possibility for a customer to make a purchase **Kaufgelegenheit; opportunity and threat analysis** = company's analysis of both the advantages and disadvantages in its environment in order to ensure sound strategic planning **Marketing-Umwelt-Analyse; opportunity cost** = cost of a business initiative in terms of profits that could have been gained through an alternative plan **Gelegenheitskosten;** *it's a good investment plan and we will not be deterred by the opportunity cost*

optimal *adjective* best **optimal; optimal balance** = best combination of elements or activities that can be achieved in a marketing mix **optimales Gleichgewicht;** *if it achieves optimal balance the company will soon be a market leader*

option *noun* **option to purchase** *or* **to sell** = giving someone the possibility of buying or selling something within a period of time at a specified price **Optionsrecht auf Kauf, Kaufoption; Optionsrecht auf Verkauf, Verkaufsoption; first option** = allowing someone to be the first to have the possibility of deciding something **Vorhand; to grant someone a six-month option on a product** = to allow someone six months to decide if he wants to be the agent for the product or if he wants to manufacture it **jdm für ein Produkt ein sechsmonatiges Optionsrecht einräumen; to take up an option** *or* **to exercise an option** = to accept the option which has been offered and to put it into action **sein Optionsrecht ausüben;** *he exercised his option or he took up his option to acquire sole marketing rights to the product;* **I want to leave my options open** = I want to be able to decide what to do when the time is right **ich will mich nicht festlegen; ich will mir alle Möglichkeiten offenhalten; to take the soft option** = to decide to do something which involves the least risk, effort or problems **den Weg des geringsten Widerstandes wählen**

◇ **optional** *adjective* which can be added if the customer wants **auf Wunsch erhältlich;** *the insurance cover is optional;* **optional extras** = items (such as a radio) which can be added (to a car) if wanted **Extras, Sonderzubehör**

Oracle teletext service broadcast by the IBA **(britische) Bildschirmzeitung**

order
1 *noun*
(a) pay to Mr Smith or order = pay money to Mr Smith or as he orders **zahlbar an Herrn Smith oder dessen Order; pay to the order of Mr Smith** = pay money directly into Mr Smith's account **zahlbar an Herrn Smith, auf Order Smith lautend**
(b) official request for goods to be supplied **Bestellung, Auftrag;** *to give someone an order or to place an order with someone for twenty filing cabinets;* **to fill** *or* **to fulfil an order** = to supply items which have been ordered **einer Bestellung nachkommen;** *we are so understaffed we can't fulfil any more orders before Christmas; to fill an order for twenty filing cabinets;* **purchase order** = official paper which places an order for something **Auftrag, Bestellung; repeat order** = order for something which has been ordered before **Nachbestellung; order fulfilment** = supplying items which have been ordered **Auftragsausführung, Ausführung der Bestellung; terms: cash with order** = the goods will be supplied only if payment in cash is made at the same time as the order is placed **Zahlungsbedingungen: Barzahlung bei Bestellung; items available to order only** = items which will be manufactured only if someone orders them **nur auf Bestellung erhältliche Waren; on order** = ordered but not delivered **bestellt;** *this item is out of stock, but is on order;* **unfulfilled orders** *or* **back orders** *or* **outstanding orders** = orders received in the past and not yet supplied **noch ausstehende Lieferungen, Auftragsrückstände, unerledigte Aufträge; order book** = record of orders **Bestellbuch; Auftragsbuch; the company has a full order book** = it has enough orders to work at full capacity **das Unternehmen hat volle Auftragsbücher; telephone orders** = orders received over the telephone **telefonische Bestellungen;** *since we mailed the catalogue we have had a large number of telephone orders;* **a pad of order forms** = a pad of blank forms for orders to be written on **ein Block Bestellformulare**
(c) item which has been ordered **Bestellung;** *the order is to be delivered to our warehouse;* **order picking** = collecting various items in a warehouse to make up an order to be sent to a customer **Zusammenstellung einer Bestellung**
(d) instruction **Anweisung, Anordnung; delivery order** = instructions given by the customer to the person holding his goods, telling him to deliver them **Lieferauftrag**
(e) document which allows money to be paid to someone **Zahlungsanweisung, Order;**

he sent us an order on the Chartered Bank; **banker's order** *or* **standing order** = order written by a customer asking a bank to make a regular payment **Dauerauftrag;** *he pays his subscription by banker's order;* **money order** = document which can be bought for sending money through the post **Postanweisung**
2 *verb* to ask for goods to be supplied **bestellen;** *to order twenty filing cabinets to be delivered to the warehouse; they ordered a new Rolls Royce for the managing director*

organization *noun*
(a) arranging something so that it works efficiently **Organisation, Planung, Aufbau, Einteilung;** *the chairman handles the organization of the AGM; the group's organization is too centralized to be efficient; the organization of the head office into departments has led to increased efficiency;* **organization and methods** = examining how an office works, and suggesting how it can be made more efficient **Organisation und Durchführung; organization chart** = list of people working in various departments, showing how a company *or* office is organized **Stellenbesetzungsplan; Diagramm der Unternehmensstruktur, Organigramm; line organization** = way of organizing a business in which each manager is responsible for doing what his superior tells him to do **Linienorganisation**
(b) group or institution which is arranged for efficient work **Organisation; the Organization of Petroleum Exporting Countries** = group of major countries who are producers and exporters of oil **Organisation erdölexportierender Länder, OPEC; a government organization** = official body, run by the government **eine staatliche Organisation, Regierungsstelle; travel organization** = body representing companies in the travel business **Verband der Reiseveranstalter; employers' organization** = group of employers with similar interests **Arbeitgeberverband**

◊ **organizational buying** *noun* buying by a large organization, such as a company or government department, as opposed to purchases by individual consumers **(Firmen)einkauf**

◊ **organize** *verb* to arrange something so that it works efficiently **organisieren, planen, aufbauen, einteilen;** *the company is organized into six profit centres; the group is organized by areas of sales;* **organized labour** = workers who are members of trade unions **gewerkschaftlich organisierte Arbeiter; organized market** = market controlled by regulations set down by government or an official organization **organisierter Markt;** *the government feels that an organized market is not conducive to business initiative*

orientation *noun* main interest *or* type of activity **Orientierung;** *the company's orientation is towards production and it has little marketing experience*

◊ **oriented** *adjective* interested in *or* involved with **ausgerichtet, orientiert;** *our strategy is oriented towards achieving further growth in the export market; the promotion is entirely product-oriented*

origin *noun* where something comes from **Herkunft, Provenienz;** *spare parts of European origin;* **certificate of origin** = document showing where goods were made **Provenienz-, Herkunftszertifikat; country of origin** = country where a product is manufactured **Herkunftsland**

◊ **original**
1 *adjective* which was used or made first **original, Original-;** *they sent a copy of the original invoice; he kept the original receipt for reference;* **original purchase** = copy of a magazine or newspaper which is actually bought by the reader, rather than simply read by him or her **tatsächlicher Kauf**
2 *noun* first copy made **Original;** *send the original and file two copies*

◊ **originally** *adverb* first *or* at the beginning **ursprünglich**

OTS = OPPORTUNITIES TO SEE

outbid *verb* to offer a better price than someone else **überbieten;** *we offered £100,000 for the warehouse, but another company outbid us*

◊ **outdoor advertising** *noun* advertising on the outside of a building or in the open air, using posters on hoardings or neon signs **Außenwerbung**

◊ **outer pack** *noun* container which holds a number of smaller packaged units **Sammel-, Umpackung;** *the goods are sold in outer packs, each containing twenty packets;* **display outer** = container for goods in transit which can also be used as a display container for goods in a shop **Auslage-, Ausstellungskarton;**

◊ **outlet** *noun* place where something can be sold **Verkaufsstelle, Geschäft; retail outlets** = shops which sell to the general public **Einzelhandelsgeschäfte**

◊ **out of date** *adjective & adverb* old-fashioned *or* no longer modern **veraltet, altmodisch, unzeitgemäß;** *their computer system is years out of date; they're still using out-of-date equipment*

◇ **out of stock** *adjective & adverb* with no stock left **nicht vorrätig;** *those records are temporarily out of stock; several out-of-stock items have been on order for weeks*

◇ **output** *noun* amount which a company or a person or a machine produces **Produktion, Ausstoß, Output;** *output has increased by 10%; 25% of our output is exported;* **output per hour** = amount produced in one hour **Produktionsleistung pro Stunde, Stundenleistung; output bonus** = extra payment for increased production **Produktionsprämie; output tax** = VAT charged by a company on goods or services sold **Bruttomehrwertsteuer**

◇ **outsell** *verb* to sell more than someone **höhere Verkaufszahlen haben, mehr verkaufen;** *the company is easily outselling its competitors*

◇ **outsize** *noun* size which is larger than usual; *(von Kleidung)* **Übergröße; an outsize order** = a very large order **eine Riesenbestellung**

◇ **outstanding** *adjective* not yet paid or completed **ausstehend, unbezahlt; outstanding debts** = debts which are waiting to be paid **Außenstände; outstanding orders** = orders received but not yet supplied **ausstehende Lieferungen, Auftragsrückstände, unerledigte Aufträge; what is the amount outstanding?** = how much money is still owed? **wie hoch ist der noch ausstehende Betrag?; matters outstanding from the previous meeting** = questions which were not settled at the previous meeting **von der vorhergehenden Besprechung noch offenstehende Punkte**

◇ **outward mission** *noun* visit by a group of businessmen to a foreign country **Delegation ins Ausland**

over- *prefix* more than **über-; shop which caters to the over-60s** = shop which has goods which appeal to people who are more than sixty years old **Laden, der auf Kunden über sechzig ausgerichtet ist**

◇ **overall** *adjective* covering *or* including everything **gesamt, umfassend, Gesamt-; although some divisions traded profitably, the company reported an overall fall in profits** = the company reported a general fall in profits **obwohl einige Unternehmensbereiche einen Gewinn erzielten, meldete das Unternehmen insgesamt einen Gewinnverlust; overall plan** = plan which covers everything **Gesamtplan**

◇ **overcharge**
1 *noun* charge which is higher than it should be **zuviel berechneter Betrag;** *to pay back an overcharge*
2 *verb* to ask too much money **zuviel berechnen;** *they overcharged us for our meals; we asked for a refund because we'd been overcharged*

◇ **overhead**
1 *adjective* **overhead costs** *or* **expenses** = money spent on the day-to-day cost of a business **Betriebskosten, allgemeine Unkosten, Festkosten; overhead budget** = plan of probable overhead costs **Festkostenbudget**
2 *noun* **overheads** *or (US)* **overhead** = costs of the day-to-day running of a business **allgemeine Unkosten, Festkosten, Gemeinkosten;** *the sales revenue covers the manufacturing costs but not the overheads*

◇ **overlay** *noun* transparent plastic sheet placed over artwork with instructions for changing it or used to show how the artwork is to be printed **Transparentauflage, Auflegemaske**

◇ **overmatter** *or* **oversetting** *noun* text which when typeset is too long for the space available **Übersatz**

◇ **overpayment** *noun* paying too much **Überbezahlung**

◇ **overprice** *verb* to charge a higher price than is justified by demand **zu hohe Preise setzen;** *overpricing led to the producer being priced out of the market*

◇ **overprint** *verb* to print text on paper which already contains printed matter **überdrucken, eindrucken;** *the retailer's name and address is overprinted on the catalogue*

◇ **overproduce** *verb* to produce too much **überproduzieren**

◇ **overproduction** *noun* manufacturing too much of a product **Überproduktion**

◇ **overseas**
1 *adjective* across the sea *or* to foreign countries **überseeisch, Übersee-; ausländisch, Auslands-; an overseas call** = phone call to another country **ein Auslandsgespräch; the overseas division** = section of a company dealing with trade with other countries **die Auslandsabteilung; overseas markets** = markets in foreign countries **Überseemärkte; Märkte im Ausland; overseas trade** = trade with foreign countries **Überseehandel; Handel mit dem Ausland**
2 *noun* foreign countries **Ausland;** *the profits from overseas are far higher than those of the home division*

◇ **oversell** *verb* to sell more than you can produce **zu große Mengen verkaufen; he is oversold** = he has taken orders for more of a product than he can produce **er hat mehr verkauft, als er liefern kann; the market is oversold** = stock market prices are too low, because there have been too many sellers **die Kurse fallen aufgrund einer Überzahl an Verkäufern**

◇ **overstock**
1 *verb* to have more stock than is needed **sich übermäßig mit Waren eindecken, zu große Lagerbestände haben; to be overstocked with spare parts** = to have too many spare parts in stock **zu viele Ersatzteile auf Lager haben**
2 *plural noun (US)* **overstocks** = more stock than is needed to supply orders **Überbestand;** *we will have to sell off the overstocks to make room in the warehouse*
◇ **overweight** *adjective* **the package is sixty grams overweight** = the package weighs sixty grams too much **das Paket hat sechzig Gramm Übergewicht**

> QUOTE Cash paid for your stock: any quantity, any products, overstocked lines, factory seconds
> *Australian Financial Review*
> QUOTE it ties up less capital in inventory and with its huge volume spreads out costs over bigger sales; add in low overhead (i.e. minimum staff, no deliveries, no credit cards) and a warehouse club can offer bargain prices
> *Duns Business Month*

own brand goods *noun* products specially packed for a store with the store's name on them **Eigenmarkenwaren**

owner *noun* person who owns something **Eigentümer/-in; media owner** = person or company that owns a magazine or newspaper or radio or TV station **Medieneigentümer; sole owner** = person who owns something on his or her own, without any partners **Alleineigentümer; owner-occupier** = person who owns and lives in a house **Bewohner des eigenen Grundbesitzes; at owner's risk** = situation where goods shipped or stored are insured by the owner, not by the transport company or the storage company **auf eigene Gefahr; goods sent at owner's risk** = situation where the owner has to insure the goods while they are being transported **Warensendung mit Gefahr beim Absender**
◇ **own label goods** *noun* goods specially produced for a store with the store's name on them **Eigenmarkenwaren, Hausmarkenwaren**

Pp

the four P's simple compact way of summarizing the essentials of the marketing mix, which are product, price, promotion and place; *(entspricht)* **die vier Elemente des Marketing-Mix**

pack
1 *noun* **pack of items** = items put together in a container for selling **eine Packung Waren;** *pack of cigarettes; pack of biscuits; pack of envelopes;* **items sold in packs of 200** = sold in boxes containing 200 items **Waren in 200-Stück-Packungen; Waren, die in Packungen zu 200 Stück verkauft werden; banded pack** = pack which includes an additional item along with the main one **Verbundpackung; blister pack** *or* **bubble pack** = type of packing where the item for sale is covered with a stiff plastic cover sealed to a card backing **Schrumpffolienverpackung; display pack** = specially attractive box for showing goods for sale **Schaupackung, Präsentationspackung; dummy pack** = empty pack for display in a shop **Attrappe, Schaupackung, Leerpackung; six-pack** = box containing six items (often bottles or cans) **Sechserpack; in pack** = placed inside the packaging with the product **eingepackt;** *in pack promotion may include information on other products in the same line*
2 *verb* to put things into a container for selling *or* sending **ver-, einpacken;** *to pack goods into cartons; the biscuits are packed in plastic wrappers; the computer is packed in expanded polystyrene before being shipped*

package
1 *noun*
(a) goods packed and wrapped for sending by mail **Paket;** *the Post Office does not accept bulky packages; the goods are to be sent in airtight packages*
(b) group of different items joined together in one deal **Paket; pay package** *or* **salary package** *or* *(US)* **compensation package** = salary and other benefits offered with a job **Gesamtvergütung;** *the job carries an attractive salary package;* **package deal** = agreement which covers several different items **Verhandlungspaket; Pauschalarrangement;** *we are offering a package deal which includes the whole office computer system, staff training and hardware maintenance;* **package holiday** *or* **package tour** = holiday *or* tour where the hotel, travel and meals are all included in the price **Pauschalreise;** *the travel company is arranging a package trip to the international computer exhibition*
2 *verb*
(a) to package goods = to wrap and pack goods in an attractive way **Waren (attraktiv) verpacken**
(b) to package holidays = to sell a holiday package including travel, hotels and food **Pauschalreisen anbieten**

◇ **packaging** *noun*
(a) the action of putting things into packages **Packen, Verpacken**

(b) material used to protect goods which are being packed **Verpackungsmaterial;** *airtight packaging; packaging material*
(c) attractive material used to wrap goods for display **dekoratives Verpackungsmaterial; family packaging** = selling a whole range of products in similar packaging **Produktgruppenverpackung**

> QUOTE the consumer wants to be challenged by more individual products and more innovative packaging
> *Marketing*
> QUOTE promotional packaging can mean rethinking more than just the pack graphics
> *Marketing*
> QUOTE airlines will book not only tickets but also hotels and car hire to provide a complete package
> *Business Traveller*
> QUOTE in today's fast-growing packaged goods area many companies are discovering that a well-recognized brand name can be a priceless asset
> *Duns Business Month*

packer *noun* person who packs goods **Packer/-in**

◇ **packet** *noun* small box of goods for selling **Päckchen;** *packet of cigarettes; packet of biscuits; packet of filing cards;* **item sold in packets of 20** = sold in boxes containing 20 items each **Ware, die in 20-Stück-Packungen verkauft wird; postal packet** = small container of goods sent by post **Postpaket**

◇ **packing** *noun*
(a) action of putting goods into boxes and wrapping them for shipping **Verpacken;** *what's the cost of the packing? is packing included in the price?;* **packing case** = large wooden box for carrying easily broken items **Kiste; packing charges** = money charged for putting goods into boxes **Verpackungskosten; packing list** *or* **packing slip** = list of goods which have been packed, sent with the goods to show they have been checked **Packzettel; packing station** = place where goods are packed for transport **Packstelle;** *from the production line the goods are taken directly to the packing station; the company has three packing stations, each one dealing with goods for a particular part of the world*
(b) material used to protect goods **Verpackungsmaterial;** *packed in airtight packing;* **non-returnable packing** = packing which is to be thrown away when it has been used and not returned to the sender **Einwegpackung**

page *noun* one side of a sheet of printed paper in a book *or* newspaper *or* magazine **Seite; full page** = size of advertisement taking up one complete page **ganzseitig; half page** *or* **quarter page** = sizes of advertisement which take up half or a quarter of a page **halbseitig; viertelseitig;** *a full page advertisement costs $600; we'll take a quarter page in the July issue;* **page proof** = proof after the text has been made up into pages, ready for checking before printing **Bogenkorrektur; page rate** = cost of a whole page of advertising space **Seitenpreis;** *what's the page rate in that paper? the page rate is lower in August when circulation is at its lowest;* **page traffic** = proportion of readers of a publication who read a particular page **Lesegeschehen pro Seite;** *let's find out the page traffic before we decide to advertise on page two*

paired comparison *noun* test in which respondents compare two brands on the basis of certain attributes which are common to both **Paarvergleich**

pallet *noun* flat wooden base on which goods can be stacked for easy handling by a fork-lift truck, and on which they remain for the whole of their transportation **Palette**

◇ **palletize** *verb* to put goods on pallets **palettieren;** *palletized cartons*

pamphlet *noun* small booklet of advertising material or of information **Prospekt, Broschüre**

panel *noun*
(a) flat surface standing upright **Tafel, Brett; display panel** = flat area for displaying goods in a shop window **Auslage-, Anschlagfläche; advertisement panel** = specially designed large advertising space in a newspaper **Kasten**
(b) panel of experts = group of people who give advice on a problem **Expertenpanel, Sachverständigenausschuß; consumer panel** = group of consumers who report on goods they have used so that the manufacturer can improve the goods, or use the consumers' reports in his advertising **Verbraucherpanel, Verbrauchertestgruppe**

panic buying *noun* rush to buy something at any price because stocks may run out or because the price may rise **Angst-, Panikkäufe;** *panic buying of sugar or of dollars*

pantry check *noun* survey method whereby a panel or sample of householders keep records of purchases so that these can be regularly checked for quantity and brand **Speisekammertest;** *the pantry check suggests that there is little brand loyalty for that type of product*

paper *noun*
(a) documents which can represent money (bills of exchange, promissory notes, etc.) **Geldmarktpapiere; bankable paper** = document which a bank will accept as security for a loan **bankfähiges Papier; negotiable paper** = document which can be transferred from one owner to another for money **begebbares Wertpapier**
(b) paper money *or* **paper currency** = banknotes **Papiergeld**
(c) newspaper **Zeitung; trade paper** = newspaper aimed at people working in a certain industry **Fachzeitschrift; free paper** *or* **giveaway paper** = newspaper which is given away free, and which relies for its income on its advertising **Werbe-, Anzeigenblatt**

parallel billboard *noun* billboard which is parallel to a main road **Anschlagbrett parallel zum Verkehrsfluß**

parcel
1 *noun* goods wrapped up in paper *or* plastic, etc. to be sent by post **Paket; to tie up a parcel** = to fasten a parcel with string **ein Paket verschnüren; parcel delivery service** = private company which delivers parcels within a certain area **Kurierdienst; parcels office** = office where parcels can be handed in for sending by mail **Paketannahme; parcel post** = mail service for sending parcels **Paketpost;** *send the order by parcel post;* **parcel rates** = charges for sending parcels by post **Paketgebühren, Pakettarife**
2 *verb* to wrap and tie up in a parcel **(als Paket) verpacken;** *to parcel up a consignment of books*

Pareto effect *or* **Pareto's law** *noun* situation where a small percentage of customers may account for a large percentage of the value of a company's sales or of a company's profits (also called the eighty-twenty rule) **Pareto-Effekt**

part *noun*
(a) spare part = small piece of machinery to replace a part of a machine which is broken **Ersatzteil;** *the photocopier won't work - we need to replace a part or a part needs replacing*
(b) to offer *or* **take something in part exchange** = giving *or* taking an old product as part of the payment for a new one **etwas in Zahlung geben od nehmen;** *they refused to take my old car in part exchange for the new one;* **part payment** = paying part of a whole payment **Teilzahlung, Abschlagzahlung;** *I gave him £250 as part payment for the car;* **part delivery** *or* **part order** *or* **part shipment** = delivering *or* shipping only some of the items in an order **Teillieferung, Teilsendung**

party *noun*
(a) company *or* person involved in a legal dispute *or* legal agreement **Partei;** *one of the parties to the suit has died; the company is not a party to the agreement;* **third party** = any third person, in addition to the two main people involved in a contract **Dritter, dritte Person;**
(b) group of people who meet to celebrate something or to enjoy themselves **Party; party plan selling** = selling by salesmen who present their products at parties organized in their homes **Partyverkauf;** *party plan selling provides a relaxed atmosphere in which people are more inclined to buy the products being shown*

pass off *verb* **to pass something off as something else** = to pretend that it is another thing in order to cheat a customer **etwas für/als etwas anderes ausgeben;** *he tried to pass off the wine as French, when in fact it came from outside the Common Market*

◇ **pass-on readership** *noun* evidence that there is more than one reader for a single copy of a publication **Folgeleserschaft;** *we know the magazine's circulation, but will have to estimate the level of pass-on readership*

patent
1 *noun*
(a) official document showing that a person has the exclusive right to make and sell an invention **Patenturkunde, Patent;** *to take out a patent for a new type of light bulb; to apply for a patent for a new invention;* **letters patent** = official term for a patent **Patenturkunde; patent applied for** *or* **patent pending** = words on a product showing that the inventor has applied for a patent **Patent angemeldet, angemeldetes Patent; to forfeit a patent** = to lose a patent because payments have not been made **ein Patent verfallen lassen/verwirken; to infringe a patent** = to make and sell a product which works in the same way as a patented product and not pay a royalty for it **ein Patent verletzen; infringement of patent** *or* **patent infringement** = act of illegally making or selling a product which is patented **Patentverletzung**
(b) patent agent = person who advises on patents and applies for patents on behalf of clients **Patentanwalt; to file a patent application** = to apply for a patent **ein Patent anmelden, eine Patentanmeldung einreichen; patent medicine** = medicine which is registered as a patent **patentrechtlich geschütztes Arzneimittel; patent office** = government office which grants patents and supervises them

Patentamt; patent rights = rights which an inventor holds under a patent **Patentrecht**
2 *verb* **to patent an invention** = to register an invention with the patent office to prevent other people from copying it **eine Erfindung patentieren lassen**

◇ **patented** *adjective* which is protected by a patent **gesetzlich/patentrechtlich geschützt**

◇ **patentee** *noun* person *or* business that has acquired a patent **Patentinhaber/-in;** *we shall have to obtain the patentee's permission to manufacture the product*

patron *noun*
(a) regular customer **Stammgast; Stammkunde;** *there is a special offer for regular patrons of the restaurant; to judge by its wealthy patrons, the store is clearly aimed at an up-market clientele*
(b) person who gives an organization or charity his or her financial support **Schirmherr, Gönner, Förderer;** *the chairman is a patron of several leading charities*

◇ **patronage** *noun* being a regular customer **Kundschaft**

◇ **patronize** *verb* to be a regular customer **(regelmäßig) besuchen;** *I stopped patronizing that restaurant on the day I found a cigarette in my soup*

pattern *noun*
(a) pattern book = book showing examples of design **Musterbuch**
(b) general way in which something usually happens **Struktur, übliches Schema;** *pattern of prices or price pattern; pattern of sales or sales pattern;* **pattern of trade** *or* **trading pattern** = general way in which trade is carried on **Handelsstruktur;** *the company's trading pattern shows high export sales in the first quarter and high home sales in the third quarter*

◇ **patterned interview** *noun* interview using pre-set questions following a fixed pattern **strukturiertes Interview**

pay *verb*
(a) to give money to buy an item or a service **(be)zahlen;** *to pay £1,000 for a car; how much did you pay to have the office cleaned?;* **to pay in advance** = to give money before you receive the item bought *or* before the service has been completed **im voraus bezahlen;** *we had to pay in advance to have the new telephone system installed;* **to pay in instalments** = to give small amounts of money regularly over an agreed period of time **in Raten zahlen;** *we are paying for the computer by monthly instalments of £50;* **to pay cash** = to pay the complete sum in cash **bar bezahlen; "pay cash"** = words written on a crossed cheque to show that it can be paid in cash if necessary; *(GB)* **Barauszahlung; to pay by cheque** = to pay by giving a cheque, not by using cash or credit card **mit (einem) Scheck bezahlen; to pay by credit card** = to pay, using a credit card and not a cheque or cash **mit Kreditkarte bezahlen; pay television** *or* **pay TV** = television service that is paid for by regular subscriptions **Münzfernsehen; Pay TV**
(b) to give money **(be)zahlen; to pay on demand** = to pay money when it is asked for, not after a period of credit **auf Anforderung bezahlen; please pay the sum of £10** = please give £10 in cash or by cheque **bitte bezahlen Sie den Betrag von £10;**
(c) to give money which is owed *or* which has to be paid **(be)zahlen, begleichen;** *to pay a bill; to pay an invoice; to pay duty on imports; to pay tax*

◇ **payable** *adjective* which is due to be paid **zahlbar, fällig; payable in advance** = which has to be paid before the goods are delivered **im voraus zahlbar; payable on delivery** = which has to be paid when the goods are delivered **zahlbar bei Lieferung; payable on demand** = which must be paid when payment is asked for **zahlbar bei Sicht/auf Verlangen; payable at sixty days** = which has to be paid by sixty days after the date of invoice **zahlbar innerhalb von sechzig Tagen; cheque made payable to bearer** = cheque which will be paid to the person who has it, not to any particular name written on it **Überbringer-, Inhaberscheck; shares payable on application** = shares which must be paid for when you apply to buy them **bei Antragstellung zahlbare Wertpapiere; accounts payable** = money owed by a company **Verbindlichkeiten; bills payable** = bills which a debtor will have to pay **Wechselverbindlichkeiten; electricity charges are payable by the tenant** = the tenant (and not the landlord) must pay for the electricity **Elektrizitätskosten sind vom Mieter zu tragen**

◇ **pay down** *verb* **to pay money down** = to make a deposit **Geld anzahlen;** *he paid £50 down and the rest in monthly instalments*

◇ **payee** *noun* person who receives money from someone *or* person whose name is on a cheque **Zahlungsempfänger**

◇ **payer** *noun* person who gives money to someone **Zahler; slow payer** = person *or* company which does not pay debts on time **säumiger Schuldner;** *he's known to be a slow payer*

◇ **payload** *noun* cargo *or* passengers carried by a ship *or* train *or* plane for which payment is made **Nutzlast**

◇ **payment** *noun*
(a) giving money **Zahlung, Bezahlung, Begleichung;** *payment in cash or cash payment; payment by cheque; payment of*

interest or *interest payment;* **payment after delivery** = paying for goods at an agreed date after delivery **Zahlung nach Lieferung;** *there is a 10% discount for payment on delivery, but none for payment after delivery;* **payment on account** = paying part of the money owed **Abschlagszahlung, Akontozahlung; payment on delivery** = paying for goods when they are delivered **Zahlung gegen Nachnahme;** *some customers won't agree to payment on delivery and want more time to settle up;* **full payment** or **payment in full** = paying all money owed **Zahlung in voller Höhe; payment on invoice** = paying money as soon as an invoice is received **Zahlung bei Erhalt der Rechnung; payment in kind** = paying by giving goods or food, but not money **Sachleistung, Bezahlung in Naturalien; payment by results** = money given which increases with the amount of work done or goods produced **Leistungslohn; payment supra protest** = payment of a bill of exchange by a third party to protect the debtor's honour **Ehrenzahlung**
(b) money paid **Zahlung; back payment** = paying money which is owed **Nach-, Rückzahlung; deferred payments** = money paid later than the agreed date **aufgeschobene Zahlung;** *the company agreed to defer payments for three months;* **down payment** = part of a total payment made in advance **Anzahlung; repayable in easy payments** = repayable with regular small sums **zahlbar in bequemen Raten; incentive payments** = extra pay offered to a worker to make him work better **Leistungszulage, Prämie; balance of payments** = the international financial position of a country including visible and invisible trade **Zahlungsbilanz**

PD = PHYSICAL DISTRIBUTION

P/E ratio = PRICE/EARNINGS RATIO

peak
1 *noun* highest point **Höhepunkt, Höchststand; peak period** = time of the day when most commuters are travelling or when most electricity is being used, etc. **Hauptverkehrszeit, Stoßzeit; Hauptbelastungszeit; time of peak demand** = time when something is being used most **Spitzenbedarfszeit; peak output** = highest output **Höchstproduktion; peak time** = time during the day when the greatest number of people are watching television **Hauptsendezeit;** *for the price of a 30-second spot at peak time we can get two minutes in mid-morning;* **peak year** = best year or year when the largest quantity of products was produced or when sales were highest **Spitzenjahr;** *the shares reached their peak in January; the share index has fallen 10% since the peak in January*
2 *verb* to reach the highest point **den Höchststand erreichen;** *productivity peaked in January; shares have peaked and are beginning to slip back*

peddle *verb* to sell goods from door to door or in the street **hausieren; Wandergewerbe betreiben**
◊ **pedlar** *noun* person who sells goods from door to door or in the street **Hausierer, ambulanter Händler**

peer group *noun* class of people that a person can respect or identify with, because they belong to the same age group, social class or have the same opinions **seinesgleichen;** *consumers are found to be especially influenced by the tastes and opinions of those in their peer groups*

peg
1 *noun* hook to hang clothes on **Kleiderhaken; off-the-peg clothes** = clothes which are made ready to wear in certain standard sizes **Kleider von der Stange**
2 *verb* to maintain prices at a certain level **Preise stützen/stabilisieren;**

pen *noun* **light pen** = type of pen which when passed over a bar code can read it and send information back to a computer **Lichtstift, Lesepistole;**

penalty clause *noun* clause in a contract that lays down how much must be paid by a party who does not fulfil his or her part of that contract **Strafklausel, Bestimmung der Vertragsstrafe;**

penetrate *verb* **to penetrate a market** = to get into a market and capture a share of it **in einen Markt vordringen, sich auf einem Markt durchsetzen**
◊ **penetration** *noun* (i) percentage of a target market that accepts a product; (ii) percentage of a target audience reached by an advertisement **(i) Penetration(sgrad); (ii) Reichweite;** *our promotion will have to be far more effective if we are to achieve penetration;* **market penetration** = the selling of more of a company's products into a market segment, shown as a percentage of the total market **Marktdurchdringung; penetration pricing** = pricing a product low enough to achieve market penetration **Penetrationspreispolitik;** *penetration pricing is helping us acquire a bigger market share at the expense of short-term profits*

per annum *adverb* in a year **im/pro Jahr;** *what is their turnover per annum?*

◊ **per capita** *adjective & adverb* for each person **pro Person/Kopf; average income per capita** *or* **per capita income** = average income of one person **Durchschnittseinkommen pro Person, Pro-Kopf-Einkommen; per capita expenditure** = total money spent divided by the number of people involved **Pro-Kopf-Ausgaben**

perceptual map *noun* map *or* diagram which represents how consumers view various comparative products on the basis of certain factors or attributes **Wahrnehmungslandkarte;** *thorough analysis of perceptual maps was followed by decisions on changes in product design and marketing strategy*

perfect
1 *adjective* completely correct *or* with no mistakes **perfekt, fehlerlos, vollkommen;** *we check each batch to make sure it is perfect; she did a perfect typing test;* **perfect competition** = hypothetical model of a market where all products of a particular type are identical, where there is complete information about market conditions available to buyers and sellers and complete freedom for sellers to enter or to leave the market **vollkommene Konkurrenz; perfect market** = hypothetical market where there is perfect competition **bilaterales Polypol**
2 *verb* to develop *or* improve something until it is as good as it can be **vervollkommnen, perfektionieren;** *he perfected the process for making high-grade steel*

periodical *noun* magazine which comes out regularly (usually once a month or once a week) **Zeitschrift, Magazin, Periodikum;** *we have not yet decided in which periodicals we should run the advertisement*

perishable
1 *adjective* which can go bad *or* become rotten easily **leicht verderblich;** *perishable goods or items or cargo*
2 *plural noun* **perishables** = goods which can go bad easily **(leicht) verderbliche Ware**

permanent *adjective* which will last for a very long time *or* for ever **dauerhaft, fest, unbefristet;** *he has found a permanent job; she is in permanent employment; the permanent staff and the part-timers;* **permanent income hypothesis** = theory that people spend in line with the average income they expect to receive in their lifetime **Einkommenshypothese**

permit
1 *noun* official document which allows someone to do something **Genehmigung, Erlaubnis; building permit** = official document which allows someone to build on a piece of land **Baugenehmigung; export permit** *or* **import permit** = official document which allows goods to be exported *or* imported **Exportgenehmigung; Importgenehmigung; work permit** = official document which allows someone who is not a citizen to work in a country **Arbeitserlaubnis**
2 *verb* to allow someone to do something **genehmigen, erlauben, gestatten;** *will we be permitted to use her name in the advertising copy? smoking is not permitted in the design studio*

persistent demand *noun* continuous *or* stable demand for a product **laufender/ständiger Bedarf;** *persistent demand for the product means that there is very little pressure to adapt it; the product is so useful that it is not surprising there is a persistent demand for it*

personal *adjective* referring to one person **persönlich; personal call** = (i) telephone call where you ask the operator to connect you with a particular person; (ii) telephone call not related to business **(i) Gespräch mit Voranmeldung; (ii) Privatgespräch; personal interview** = questioning respondents in a survey directly, by meeting them **persönliches Interview;** *the advantage of a personal interview is that we have the chance to explain the questions; it's possible that interviewers' bias may influence results in a personal interview;* **personal selling** = selling to a customer by personal contact, either face to face or by telephone **persönlicher Verkauf;** *personal selling allows any doubts the prospective customer may have to be cleared up by the salesman*

◊ **personality** *noun* famous person (usually connected with television or sport) **Persönlichkeit; personality promotion** = promotion which makes use of famous people to endorse a product **Prominentenwerbung;** *personality promotion is a tried and tested method of promoting beauty products; a famous pop star was chosen for the personality promotion because of his widespread popularity among the target audience*

◊ **personalized** *adjective* with the name of a particular person written on it **mit dem Namen oder den Initialien versehen;** *he has a personalized briefcase;* **personalized mailing** = mailing of letters addressed to particular people by name **personalisierte Mailing**

persuade *verb* to talk to someone and get him or her to do what you want **überreden, dazubringen;** *after ten hours of discussion, they persuaded the MD to resign; we could not persuade the French company to sign the contract*

◇ **persuasibility** *noun (US)* degree to which a target audience can be persuaded through advertising that a product has good qualities **Beeinflußbarkeit, Persuasibilität;** *persuasibility will depend on consumer's experience with products similar to the ones we are promoting*

photoengraving *noun* process of producing a metal plate for printing, by photographing on the plate which is then etched in such a way that prints can be taken from it **Chemigraphie**

◇ **photogravure** *noun* type of photoengraving where the design is etched into the metal rather than in relief **Heliogravüre, Photogravüre**

◇ **phototypesetting** *noun* typesetting by photographic means rather than by using metal type **Photosatz**

physical distribution (PD) *noun* the process of moving goods from the producer to the end user **physische Distribution;** *physical distribution is always a problem because of high transportation costs*

picking *noun*
(a) selecting a product according to its packaging or place on the shelf, rather than by making a conscious decision to buy **oberflächige Kaufentscheidung, Schnappkauf**
(b) order picking = collecting various items in a warehouse to make up an order to be sent to a customer **Zusammenstellung einer Bestellung; picking list** = list of items in an order, listed according to where they can be found in the warehouse **Entnahmeliste**

◇ **pick up** *verb* to get better *or* to improve **sich erholen;** *business or trade is picking up*

◇ **pickup** *noun* **pickup (truck)** = type of small van for transporting goods **offener Kleintransporter; pickup and delivery service** = service which takes goods from the warehouse and delivers them to the customer **Abhol- und Zustelldienst**

pie chart *noun* diagram where information is shown as a circle cut up into sections of different sizes **Kreisdiagramm**

piggy-back freight *noun (US)* transport of loaded trucks on freight trains **Huckepacktransport, Huckepackverkehr;** *compare* FISHY-BACK

◇ **piggy-back promotion** *noun* sales promotion for one product which accompanies promotion for another product **Huckepackwerbung, Huckepackverkaufsförderung**

pilferage *or* **pilfering** *noun* stealing small amounts of money *or* small items from an office *or* shop **geringfügiger Diebstahl;** *(umg)* **Mauserei**

pilot *adjective* used as a test, which, if successful, will then be expanded into a full operation **Pilot-;** *the company set up a pilot project to see if the proposed manufacturing system was efficient; the pilot factory has been built to test the new production processes; he is directing a pilot scheme for training unemployed young people*

pioneer
1 *noun* first person *or* company to do something **Pionier, Wegbereiter, Vorreiter;** *Smith, Inc. were pioneers in the field of market research;* **pioneer project** *or* **pioneer development** = project or development which is new and has never been tried before **Pionierprojekt; bahnbrechende Entwicklung pioneer selling** = hard, intensive selling in new markets **(intensiver) Initialverkauf;** *a campaign of pioneer selling was organized to educate the public in the use of the new product; there was a lot of consumer resistance to pioneer selling, since few customers had heard of the product or thought they needed it*
2 *verb* to be the first to do something **Pionierarbeit leisten, initiieren, den Weg bahnen;** *the company pioneered developments in the field of electronics*

pipeline *noun* distribution channel (from manufacturer through wholesalers and retailers to the customer) **Absatzweg;** *how many different businesses are involved in the product's pipeline?*

pirate
1 *noun* person who copies a patented invention or a copyright work and sells it **Plagiator, Markenpirat; Hersteller von Raubdrucken;** *a pirate copy of a book*
2 *verb* to copy a copyright work **unerlaubt nachahmen/nachbauen, plagiieren; einen Raubdruck herstellen;** *a pirated book or a pirated design; the designs for the new dress collection were pirated in the Far East*

◇ **piracy** *noun* copying of patented inventions or copyright works **Patentverletzung, unerlaubte Nachahmung; Raubdruck; Markenpiraterie**

pitch *noun* **sales pitch** = talk by a salesman to persuade someone to buy **Verkaufsrede, Verkaufspräsentation**

pix *plural noun (informal)* pictures (used in advertising or design) **Bilder**

placard *noun* poster of double crown size (i.e. 30 inches deep by 20 inches wide) **Anschlagzettel, kleines Plakat**

placement test *noun* test where different versions of a new product are tested in different places and with different types of consumer (as opposed to market tests, where the new product is actually sold through normal distribution channels in the test areas) **Store-Test**

◇ **placement testing** *noun* sending a product to different places for trial and then interviewing the users on its performance **Durchführung von Store-Tests;** *placement testing revealed that the product was too easily breakable*

◇ **place utility** *noun* usefulness to a customer of receiving a product at a particular place **örtlich gebundener Nutzen; Plazierungsfestlegung**

plain cover *noun* **to send something under plain cover** = to send something in an ordinary envelope with no company name printed on it **etwas in einem neutralen Umschlag schicken**

plan *noun* way of doing something which has been decided on and organized in advance **Plan; business plan** = plan of a company's anticipated expenditure, sales and profits, drawn up to discuss with a potential backer (such as the bank manager) **Geschäftsplan; contingency plan** = plan which will be put into action if something unexpected happens **Krisenplan; marketing plan** = plan, usually drawn up once a year, of a company's marketing activities, with details of proposed expenditure and expected revenue and profits **Marketingplan; plans board** = group of senior managers that meets to discuss campaign strategy **Planungsausschuß;** *the plans board will meet on Monday to discuss the latest sales figures; the plans board has decided to concentrate the campaign in those areas where there are most sales representatives*

◇ **planned** *adjective* **planned obsolescence** = built-in obsolescence *or* method of ensuring continuing sales of a product by making it in such a way that it will soon become obsolete **geplante Obsoleszenz;** *planned obsolescence was condemned by the consumer organization as a cynical marketing ploy*

◇ **planning** *noun* organizing how something should be done, especially how a company should be run to make increased profits **Planung;** *long-term planning or short-term planning;* **corporate planning** = planning the future financial state of a group of companies **langfristige Unternehmensplanung; economic planning** = planning the future financial state of the country for the government **Wirtschaftsplanung; journey** *or* **territorial planning** = planning the calls which a salesperson will make, and how he or she will reach them most efficiently **(Vertreter-)Routenplanung; manpower planning** = planning to get the right number of workers for each job **Personalplanung; media planning** = deciding what media should be used in a promotional campaign **Mediaplanung**

plateau *noun* level point (as when sales or costs stop increasing) **Sättigungsniveau; plateau pricing** = setting a medium price for a product where the raw materials used in making it are subject to wide price fluctuations **Durchschnittspreiskalkulation**

platform *noun* **copy platform** = the main theme of the text of an advertisement **Copy-Plattform, Grundthema eines Werbetexts**

PLC = PUBLIC LIMITED COMPANY

ploy *noun* trick *or* gimmick, used to attract customers **Werbetrick, Gimmick**

plug
1 *noun* **to give a plug to a new product** = to publicize a new product **für ein neues Produkt Reklame machen**
2 *verb* to publicize *or* to advertise **anpreisen, Reklame machen für;** *they ran six commercials plugging holidays in Spain*

point *noun* place *or* position **Stelle, Ort; point of purchase (POP)** = place where a product is bought (which is usually the same as point of sale, though not always, as in the case of mail order purchases) **Einkaufsstelle, Einkaufsort; point of purchase advertising (POPA)** = advertising (such as posters or dump bins) at the place where the products are bought **POP-Werbung; point of sale (POS)** = place where a product is sold (such as a shop) **Verkaufsstelle, Verkaufsort; point of sale material** = display material (such as posters, dump bins) to advertise a product where it is being sold **Werbematerial für den Verkaufsort, POS-**

Werbematerial; breakeven point = position at which sales cover costs but do not show a profit **Kostendeckungspunkt, Break-Even-Punkt; customs entry point** = place at a border between two countries where goods are declared to customs **Zollanmeldungsstelle, Grenzübergangsstelle; sampling point** = place where sampling is carried out **Samplepoint; starting point** = place where something starts **Ausgangspunkt**

policy *noun*
(a) decisions on the general way of doing something **Kurs, Politik, Linie, Taktik, Verfahrensweise;** *government policy on wages or government wages policy; the government's prices policy or incomes policy; the country's economic policy; a company's trading policy;* **the government made a policy statement** *or* **made a statement of policy** = the government made its plans public **die Regierung gab eine Grundsatzerklärung ab; budgetary policy** = policy of expected income and expenditure **Budgetpolitik**
(b) company policy = the company's agreed plan of action *or* the company's way of doing things **Unternehmenspolitik;** *what is the company policy on credit? it's against company policy to give more than thirty days' credit; our policy is to submit all contracts to the legal department*

poll
1 *noun* **opinion poll** = asking a sample group of people, taken at random, what they feel about something, so as to guess the opinion of the whole population **Meinungsumfrage;** *opinion polls showed the public preferred butter to margarine; before starting the service the company carried out a nationwide opinion poll*
2 *verb* **to poll a sample of the population** = to ask a sample group of people what they feel about something **eine repräsentative Bevölkerungsgruppe befragen**

polycentric stage *noun (US)* stage in a company's international marketing when there is a separate marketing planning unit for each country **mehrzentrische Phase;** *it's an expanding multinational in its polycentric stage*

POP = POINT OF PURCHASE
◇ **POPA** = POINT OF PURCHASE ADVERTISING

popular *adjective* liked by many people **beliebt, populär;** *this is our most popular model; the South Coast is the most popular area for holidays;* **popular prices** = prices which are low and therefore liked by most customers **populäre Preise; popular pricing** = pricing method which tries to fix prices that will be popular with customers **populäre Preispolitik;** *our competitor's popular pricing strategy is a serious threat to our sales*

population *noun*
(a) number of people who live in a country *or* in a town **Bevölkerung;** *it is a city with a population of over one million; the working population of the country is getting older;* **floating population** = people who move from place to place **nicht seßhafte Bevölkerung**
(b) total number of people in a group under study in a survey, from which a sample is chosen **Grundgesamtheit**

port *noun* harbour *or* place where ships come to load *or* unload **Hafen;** *the port of Rotterdam;* **inland port** = port on a river *or* canal **Binnenhafen; to call at a port** = to stop at a port to load or unload cargo **einen Hafen anlaufen; port authority** = organization which runs a port **Hafenbehörde; port of call** = port at which a ship often stops **Anlaufhafen; port charges** *or* **port dues** = payment which a ship makes to the port authority for the right to use the port **Hafengebühren; port of embarkation** = port at which passengers get on a ship **Einschiffungshafen; port installations** = buildings and equipment of a port **Hafenanlagen; commercial port** = port which has only goods traffic **Handelshafen; fishing port** = port which is used mainly by fishing boats **Fischereihafen; free port** = port where there are no customs duties to be paid **Freihafen**

portfolio *noun*
(a) folder containing a selection of samples **Mappe;** *the student brought a portfolio of designs to show the design department manager*
(b) collection of investments made by a person or company **Aktienportefeuille;**
(c) product portfolio = collection of products made by the same company **Produktportfolio**

> QUOTE the Italian manufacturer has shaken up its drinks portfolio with a new launch and two relaunches
> *Marketing Week*

portrait *noun* illustration, page or book, where the height is greater than the width **hochformatige Seite;** *compare* LANDSCAPE

POS *or* **p.o.s.** = POINT OF SALE

position *noun*
(a) situation *or* state of affairs **Lage, Situation; what's the cash position?** = what's the state of the company's current account? **wieviel Geld haben wir flüssig?; bargaining position** = statement of position by one group during negotiations **Verhandlungsposition**
(b) place where something is **Position, Stellung; preferred position** = place in a publication where an advertiser asks for his or her advertisement to be put **Vorzugsplatz**
◇ **positioning** *noun*
(a) creating an image for a product in the minds of consumers **Positionierung; brand positioning** *or* **product positioning** = placing a brand *or* product in the market, so that it is recognizable to the public **Markenpositionierung; Produktpositionierung;** *see also* REPOSITIONING
(b) placing an advertisement on a page of a magazine **Positionieren**

positive *adjective* meaning "yes" **bejahend, positiv, zustimmend; positive cash flow** = situation where more money is coming in than is being spent **positiver Cashflow; positive variance** = difference between a financial plan and its outcome, that means a more favourable profit than expected **positive Abweichung;** *the managing director is pleased because costs this year show a £60,000 positive variance*

post
1 *noun*
(a) system of sending letters and parcels from one place to another **Post;** *to send an invoice by post; he put the letter in the post; the cheque was lost in the post;* **to send a reply by return of post** = to reply to a letter immediately **postwendend antworten; letter post** *or* **parcel post** = service for sending letters or parcels **Briefpost; Paketpost; post room** = room in an office where the post is sorted and sent to each department or collected from each department for sending **Poststelle**
(b) letters sent or received **Post;** *has the post arrived yet? my secretary opens the post as soon as it arrives; the receipt was in this morning's post; the letter didn't arrive by the first post this morning*
2 *verb* to send something by post **abschicken, mit der Post schicken;** *to post a letter or to post a parcel*
◇ **post code** *noun* series of numbers and letters which forms part of an address, indicating the street and the town in a way which can be read by a scanner **Postleitzahl** (NOTE: US English is **zip code)**

post- *prefix* later **nach-, Nach-, post-, Post-; post purchase** = after a purchase has been made **nach dem Kauf; post-purchase advertising** = advertising designed to minimize post-purchase anxiety **Nachkaufwerbung; post-purchase anxiety** = feelings of doubt about a purchase after it has been made **Kaufreue; post-purchase assessment** = assessment of a product by the purchaser after it has been bought and used **Nachkaufbewertung; post-test** = evaluation of an advertising campaign after it has taken place, or of a product after it has been launched **Posttest;** *the post-test showed that an unnecessary amount of money had been spent ;* **post-testing** = evaluating an advertising campaign after it has been run or a product after it has been launched **Durchführung von Posttests**

postage *noun* payment for sending a letter or parcel by post **Porto, Postgebühren;** *what is the postage to Nigeria?;* **postage paid** = words printed on an envelope to show that the sender has paid the postage even though there is no stamp on it **Gebühr/Porto bezahlt, gebührenfrei; postage stamp** = small piece of paper attached to a letter or parcel to show that you have paid for it to be sent through the post **Briefmarke**

postal *adjective* referring to the post **Post-; postal charges** *or* **postal rates** = money to be paid for sending letters or parcels by post **Postgebühren, Posttarife;** *postal charges are going up by 10% in September;* **postal interview** = POSTAL SURVEY; **postal order** = document bought at a post office, as a method of sending small amounts of money by post **Postanweisung; postal sales** = sales of products by post, through advertisements in the press **Verkauf durch die Post;** *the company carried out postal sales from a big warehouse in the north;* **postal survey** = sending questionnaires for a survey by post for respondents to fill in and send back **postalische Befragung;** *not enough consumers responded to the postal survey*

poster *noun* large notice *or* advertisement to be stuck up outdoors **Plakat, Poster; poster site** = place reserved for posters **Anschlagstelle, Plakatanschlagstellenstandort;** *we want a poster site in a busy street; I wish we could afford a prime poster site for our fund-raising campaign*

post free *adverb* without having to pay any postage **portofrei;** *the game is obtainable post free from the manufacturer*

postpaid *adjective* with the postage already paid **Gebühr bezahlt;** *the price is £5.95 postpaid*

potential
1 *adjective* possible **potentiell; potential customers** = people who could be customers **potentielle Kunden, Interessenten; potential demand** = situation where there is no demand as yet for a product but there is money to buy it **potentielle Nachfrage;** *though there is no interest in our product in Saudi Arabia as yet, there is considerable potential demand;* **potential market** = market which could be exploited **potentieller Markt; the product has potential sales of 100,000 units** = the product will possibly sell 100,000 units **das Produkt hat ein Umsatzpotential von 100 000 Einheiten; he's a potential managing director** = he's the sort of man who could become managing director **er kommt als Generaldirektor in Frage**
2 *noun* possibility of becoming something **Potential; sales potential** = maximum market share that can be achieved by a product **Absatzpotential; product with considerable sales potential** = product which is likely to have very large sales **Produkt mit beträchtlichen Absatzchancen;** *the product has enormous sales potential being both cheaper and longer-lasting than any of its rivals on the market;* **to analyze the market potential** = to examine the market for a market to see how large it possibly is **die Absatzmöglichkeiten analysieren; earning potential** = amount of money which someone should be able to earn *or* amount of dividend which a share is capable of earning **Erwerbsfähigkeit; Ertragsfähigkeit**

> QUOTE career prospects are excellent for someone with growth potential
> *Australian Financial Review*
> QUOTE for sale: established general cleaning business; has potential to be increased to over 1 million dollar turnover
> *Australian Financial Review*

PR = PUBLIC RELATIONS *a PR firm is handling all our publicity; he works in PR; the PR people gave away 100,000 balloons*

preapproach *noun (US)* stage in a salesman's training devoted to planning actual meetings with customers **Besuchsplanung;** *preapproach sessions cover techniques in assessing customers and their needs*

precinct *noun* separate area **Bereich, Gebiet, Bezirk; pedestrian precinct** = area of streets, where no cars are allowed and shoppers can walk freely **Fußgängerzone; shopping precinct** = separate area of shops, usually with the streets closed to traffic **(verkehrsfreies) Einkaufsviertel**

pre-coding *noun* assigning codes to items on questionnaires in order to facilitate reference and evaluation **Verschlüsselung;** *much time was lost in the survey through a confusing pre-coding system; freelance interviewers should be given a complete explanation of the pre-coding of questionnaires*

pre-empt *verb* to get an advantage by doing something quickly before anyone else **zuvorkommen;** *they staged a management buyout to pre-empt a takeover bid;* **pre-empt selling** = selling television advertising time at a lower rate with the proviso that another advertiser can take it over if he offers the full rate **absetzbarer Verkauf von Werbesendungen;** *as we're on a tight advertising budget we'll have to go for pre-empt selling*

premium *noun* amount added to a normal price or rate for a product or service **Prämie; premium offer** = present which is given to the customer, either attached to the product bought or given by a retailer on proof of purchase of a minimum quantity of goods **Zugabeangebot, Werbegeschenk**

prepack *or* **prepackage** *verb* to pack something before putting it on sale **im voraus verpacken;** *the fruit are prepacked or prepackaged in plastic trays; the watches are prepacked in attractive display boxes*

prepaid *adjective* paid in advance **vorausbezahlt; carriage prepaid** = note showing that the transport costs have been paid in advance **frachtfrei; prepaid reply card** = stamped addressed card which is sent to someone so that he can reply without paying the postage **frankierte/freigemachte Antwortkarte**
◇ **prepay** *verb* to pay in advance **im voraus bezahlen**
◇ **prepayment** *noun* payment in advance **Vorauszahlung; to ask for prepayment of a fee** = to ask for the fee to be paid before the work is done **Vorauszahlung des Honorars verlangen**

preparatory set *noun* principle that people have preconceived ideas about brands which influence their buying decisions **Vorstellungsbild**

presence *noun* measurement of an advertisement's real audience as opposed to its potential audience **Präsenz;** *with an impressive presence our advertisement should have considerable effect*

presentation *noun*
(a) showing a document **Vorlage; cheque payable on presentation** = cheque which will be paid when it is presented **Scheck bei Vorlage zahlbar; free admission on presentation of this card** = you do not pay to go in if you show this card **Eintritt kostenlos bei Vorlage der Karte**
(b) demonstration *or* exhibition of a proposed plan **Präsentation, Vorführung;** *we were not very impressed with the presentation, and will have to think again about investing in the scheme; the distribution company made a presentation of the services they could offer; we have asked two PR firms to make presentations of proposed publicity campaigns*
(c) demonstration by a salesman of a product **Vorführung;** *the manufacturer made a presentation of his new product line to possible customers; we have some slides of the product which we use in presentations;* **canned presentation** = standard sales presentation which some salesmen use all the time instead of adapting their presentation technique to different customers **routinemäßige/stereotype Vorführung**

press *noun* newspapers and magazines **Presse; the local press** = newspapers which are sold in a small area of the country **die Lokalpresse; the national press** = newspapers which sell in all parts of the country **die überregionale Presse;** *the new car has been advertised in the national press; we plan to give the product a lot of press publicity; there was no mention of the new product in the press;* **press conference** = meeting where reporters from newspapers are invited to hear news of a new product *or* of a court case *or* of a takeover bid, etc. **Pressekonferenz; press coverage** = reports about something in the press **Presseberichte, Berichterstattung durch die Presse;** *we were very disappointed by the press coverage of the new car;* **press cutting** = (i) cutting out pieces in newspapers and magazines which refer to items of particular interest; (ii) piece cut out of a newspaper *or* magazine, which refers to an item of particular interest **(i) Presseausschneiden; (ii) Zeitungs-, Zeitschriftenausschnitt;** *we've kept a file of press cuttings about the new car;* **press date** = date on which a publication is printed **(Zeitpunkt der) Drucklegung; press relations** = part of the public relations activity of an organization, aimed at building up good relations with the press **Pressearbeit, Pflege der Beziehung zur Presse;** *if the company image is to improve we must first improve our press relations;* **press release** = sheet sent to newspapers and TV and radio stations giving news about something **Pressemitteilung;** *the company sent out a press release about the launch of the new car*

pressure *noun* **high pressure** = strong force by other people to do something **großer Druck; working under high pressure** = working with a manager telling you what to do and to do it quickly *or* with customers asking for supplies urgently **unter Druck/Streß arbeiten; high-pressure salesman** = salesman who tries to force the customer to buy something he or she does not really need **aggressiver Verkäufer; high-pressure sales techniques** *or* **high-pressure selling** = trying to force a customer to buy something he or she does not really want **aggressive Verkaufsmethoden; low-pressure selling** = sales where the salesman does not try to force someone to buy, but only encourages him or her to do so **nicht aggressive Verkaufsmethoden; pressure group** = group of people who try to influence the government *or* the local town council, etc. **Interessengruppe;** *the institute which represented the advertising profession, rapidly became a powerful pressure group*

prestige *noun* status *or* reputation achieved because of being successful *or* wealthy *or* powerful **Prestige; prestige advertising** = advertising in high quality magazines to increase a company's reputation **Prestigewerbung, Repräsentationswerbung; prestige product** = expensive luxury product **Luxus-, Prestigeartikel; prestige offices** = expensive offices in a good area of the town **Repräsentationsbüro**

pre-testing *noun* testing or evaluating a product or advertising campaign before it is launched or run **Pretesten, Durchführung von Pretests;** *pre-testing has shown that the product would do well in the country as a whole; the area chosen for pre-testing may not be representative enough of the whole country*

preview *noun* showing of a film, television commercial or an exhibition to a specially invited audience before the general public sees it **Vorschau**

price
1 *noun* money which has to be paid to buy something **Preis; agreed price** = price which

has been accepted by both the buyer and seller **vereinbarter Preis; all-in price** = price which covers all items in a purchase (goods, insurance, delivery, etc.) **Pauschalpreis, Gesamtpreis; asking price** = price which the seller is hoping to be paid for the item when it is sold **geforderter Preis; Verhandlungsbasis; bargain price** = very cheap price **Sonder-, Spottpreis; catalogue price** *or* **list price** = price as marked in a catalogue or list **Katalog-, Listenpreis; competitive price** = low price aimed at competing with a rival product **wettbewerbsfähiger Preis; cost price** = selling price which is the same as that which the seller paid for the item (either the manufacturing price or the wholesale price) **Selbstkostenpreis; cut price** = very cheap price **Niedrigpreis; discount price** = full price less a discount **Diskontpreis, Preis nach Abzug des Rabatts; factory price** *or* **price ex factory** = price not including transport from the maker's factory **Preis ab Werk; fair price** = good price for both buyer and seller **fairer/angemessener Preis; firm price** = price which will not change **Festpreis;** *they are quoting a firm price of $1.23 a unit;* **going price** *or* **current price** *or* **usual price** = the price which is being charged now **gängiger/jetziger/üblicher Preis; to sell goods off at half price** = to sell goods at half the price at which they were being sold before **Waren zum halben Preis losschlagen; market price** = price at which a product can be sold **Marktpreis; net price** = price which cannot be reduced by a discount **Nettopreis; retail price** = price at which the retailer sells to the final customer **Einzelhandels-, Laden-, Endpreis; retail price index** = index which shows how prices of consumer goods have increased or decreased over a period of time **Index der Einzelhandelspreise; spot price** = price for immediate delivery of a commodity **Lokopreis;** *the spot price of oil on the commodity markets*

(b) price ceiling = highest price which can be reached **oberste Preisgrenze; price competition** = attempt to compete in a market through skilful pricing **Preiswettbewerb; price control** = legal measures to stop prices rising too fast **Preiskontrolle; Preisüberwachung; price cutting** = sudden lowering of prices **plötzliche Preissenkung; price-cutting war** = competition between companies to get a larger market share by cutting prices **Preiskrieg; price differential** = difference in price between products in a range **Preisgefälle, Preisunterschied; price discrimination** = charging different prices in different markets or to different types of customer **Preisdifferenzierung;** *price discrimination has caused some ill-feeling among customers;* **price effect** = result of a change in price on a person's buying habits **Preisänderungseffekt;** *before fixing the price, we'll have to carry out a survey to determine the price effect;* **price fixing** = illegal agreement between companies to charge the same price for competing products **Preisabsprache; price label** *or* **price tag** = label which shows a price **Preisschild;** *the takeover bid put a $2m price tag on the company;* **price leadership** = situation where the producers model their prices on those of one leading producer **Preisführerschaft; price level** = average price of a particular product in a country at a particular time **Preisniveau; price list** = sheet giving prices of goods for sale **Preisliste; price maintenance** = agreement between producers or distributors on a minimum price for a product **Preisbindung der zweiten Hand; price-off label** = label on a product showing a reduced price **Nachlaß zeigendes Preisschild; price pegging** = maintaining prices at a certain level **Preisstützen; price point** = exact price which is most profitable for sellers because it maximizes revenue **Gewinnmaximierungspreis;** *we must have a meeting to determine price points for our products;* **price range** = series of prices for similar products from different suppliers **Preisklasse; cars in the £6-7,000 price range** = cars of different makes, selling for between £6,000 and £7,000 **Wagen in der Preisklase von £6000 bis £7000; price ring** = group of producers or distributors who agree to control prices and market conditions in their industry **Kartell; price-sensitive product** = product which will not sell if the price is increased **preisempfindliches Produkt; price war** = reduction of prices by competing firms in order to maintain or increase their market shares **Preiskrieg;** *a full-scale price war will mean lower prices for consumers*

(c) to increase in price = to become more expensive **teurer werden;** *petrol has increased in price or the price of petrol has increased;* **to increase prices** *or* **to raise prices** = to make items more expensive **Preise erhöhen; we will try to meet your price** = we will try to offer a price which is acceptable to you **wir werden versuchen, ihrer Preisvorstellung zu entsprechen; to cut prices** = to reduce prices suddenly **Preise plötzlich senken; to lower prices** *or* **to reduce prices** = to make items cheaper **Preise senken/herabsetzen/reduzieren, mit dem Preis heruntergehen**

2 *verb* to give a price to a product **einen Preis festsetzen;** *car priced at £5,000;* **competitively priced** = sold at a low price which competes with that of similar goods from other companies **zu einem wettbewerbsfähigen Preis; the company has priced itself out of the market** = the company has raised its prices so high that its products do not sell **das Unternehmen ist durch seine überhöhten Preise wettbewerbsunfähig geworden**

◇ **price/earnings ratio (P/E ratio)** *noun* comparison between the market price of a share and the current dividend it produces **Kurs-Gewinn-Verhältnis**

◇ **pricing** *noun* giving a price to a product **Preisfestsetzung, Preiskalkulation, Preisbildung; pricing policy** = a company's policy in giving prices to its products **Preispolitik;** *our pricing policy aims at producing a 35% gross margin;* **common pricing** = illegal fixing of prices by several businesses so that they all charge the same price **Preisabsprache; competitive pricing** = putting a low price on a product so that it competes with similar products from other companies **wettbewerbsfähige Auspreisung; contribution pricing** = setting a price for a product so as to maximize its contribution to fixed costs **Deckungsbeitragsrechnung; marginal pricing** = making the selling price the same as the cost of a single extra unit above the number already planned **Grenzkostenpreiskalkulation; penetration pricing** = setting a low price for a product to try to penetrate the market **Penetrationspreispolitik; plateau pricing** = setting a medium price for a product where the raw materials used in making it are subject to wide price fluctuations **Durchschnittspreiskalkulation**

> QUOTE in today's circumstances, price-cutting is inevitable in an attempt to build up market share
> *Marketing Week*
>
> QUOTE that British goods will price themselves back into world markets is doubtful as long as sterling labour costs continue to rise
> *Sunday Times*
>
> QUOTE the average price per kilogram for this season has been 300c
> *Australian Financial Review*
>
> QUOTE European manufacturers rely heavily on imported raw materials which are mostly priced in dollars
> *Duns Business Month*

primary *adjective* basic **grundlegend; primary brand** = brand owned by a distributor rather than by a producer **Erstmarke; primary commodities** = raw materials or food **Grundstoffe; primary data** = data or information which has not yet been compiled and published and must therefore be found by field research **Primärdaten;** *the company's market research proved very expensive since it needed so much primary data;* **primary demand** = demand for a product in general, as opposed to demand for a particular brand **Grundbedarf, Primärnachfrage;** *the main producer companies are cooperating to create primary demand since this type of product is quite new to the public;* **primary industry** = industry dealing with basic raw materials (such as coal, wood, farm produce, etc.) **Rohstoffindustrie; primary products** = products (such as wood, milk, fish, etc.) which are basic raw materials **Primärprodukte**

prime *adjective* most important **Haupt-, wesentlich; prime cost** = cost involved in producing a product, excluding overheads **Selbstkosten, Gestehungskosten; prime rate** *or* **prime** = best rate of interest at which a bank lends to its customers **Prime Rate, Leitzins (für erste Adressen); prime time** = most expensive advertising time for TV commercials, usually in the evenings, from 6 p.m. to 10.30 p.m. **Hauptsendezeit;** *we are putting out a series of prime-time commercials*

◇ **priming** *noun see* PUMP PRIMING

> QUOTE the base lending rate, or prime rate, is the rate at which banks lend to their top corporate borrowers
> *Wall Street Journal*

principal
1 *noun* person *or* company which is represented by an agent **Auftraggeber/-in;** *the agent has come to London to see his principals*
2 *adjective* most important **Haupt-, wichtigste(r,s);** *the principal shareholders asked for a meeting; the country's principal products are paper and wood*

> QUOTE the company was set up with funds totalling 145m with the principal aim of making capital gains on the secondhand market
> *Lloyd's List*

print run *noun* the number of copies of a publication or piece of advertising material which are printed **Druckauflage;** *the company has ordered a print run of 100,000 for their new catalogue*

private *adjective*
(a) belonging to a single person, not a company *or* the state **privat, Privat-; letter marked "private and confidential"** = letter which must not be opened by anyone other than the person it is addressed to **ein Brief mit der Aufschrift ‚streng vertraulich'; private client** *or* **private customer** = client who has dealings with a company as an individual, not as the representative of another company **Privatkunde; private income** = income from dividends *or* interest *or* rents

which is not part of a salary **Privateinkommen; private investor** = ordinary person with money to invest **Privatanleger; private property** = property which belongs to a private person *or* company, not to the state or to a local authority **Privatbesitz; Privatgrundstück**
(b) private brand = brand owned by a distributor rather than by a producer **Hausmarke, Händlermarke**
(c) private limited company = company with a small number of shareholders whose shares are not traded on the Stock Exchange; *(entspricht)* **Gesellschaft mit beschränkter Haftung**
(d) private enterprise = businesses which are owned by private shareholders, not by the state **Privatunternehmen;** *the project is funded by private enterprise;* **the private sector** = all companies which are owned by private shareholders, not by the state **Privatsektor**

◇ **privately** *adverb* away from other people **unter vier Augen;** *the deal was negotiated privately*

◇ **privatization** *noun* selling a nationalized industry to private owners **Privatisierung, Zurückführung in Privateigentum**

◇ **privatize** *verb* to sell a nationalized industry to private owners **privatisieren**

> QUOTE in the private sector the total number of new house starts was 3 per cent higher than in the corresponding period last year, while public sector starts were 23 per cent lower
> *Financial Times*
>
> QUOTE even without privatization, water charges would probably have to rise to pay for meeting EC water-quality rules
> *Economist*
>
> QUOTE management had offered to take the company private through a leveraged buyout for $825 million
> *Fortune*

PRO = PUBLIC RELATIONS OFFICER

probable *adjective* likely to happen **wahrscheinlich, zu erwarten;** *it is probable that the company will collapse if a rescue package is not organized before the end of the month*

◇ **probability** *noun* likelihood that something will happen, expressed mathematically **Wahrscheinlichkeit; probability sampling** = choosing samples for testing without any special selection method **Wahrscheinlichkeitsauswahl**

probing *noun* attempt by an interviewer to get the interviewee to develop an answer **Eindringen;** *no amount of probing would induce the housewife to say why she did not like the new washing powder*

problem children *noun* in the Boston matrix, products which are not very profitable, and have a low market share and a high growth rate **Sorgenkinder;** *the problem children in our range make very little contribution to the company profits* (NOTE: also called **question marks** and **wild cats)**

procurement *noun* the activity of buying **Beschaffung;** *procurement of raw materials is becoming very complicated with the entry of so many new suppliers into the market*

produce *verb* to make *or* to manufacture **herstellen, produzieren, erzeugen, fertigen;** *to produce cars or engines or books;* **to mass-produce** = to make large quantities of a product **in Massenanfertigung/serienweise herstellen**

◇ **producer** *noun* person *or* company *or* country which manufactures **Hersteller, Erzeuger, Produzent;** *country which is a producer of high quality watches; the company is a major car producer;* **producer market** = customers who buy goods to be used in production **Produzentenmarkt; producer's surplus** = amount by which the actual price of a product is more than the minimum which the producer would accept for it **Produzentenrente;** *there is a considerable producer's surplus because the product is in short supply; if our customer knew the producer's surplus she would have offered much less than the asking price*

product *noun*
(a) thing which is made *or* manufactured **Produkt, Erzeugnis; basic product** = main product made from a raw material **Grundprodukt; by-product** = secondary product made as a raw material is being processed **Nebenprodukt; end product** *or* **final product** *or* **finished product** = manufactured product, made at the end of a production process **Endprodukt; generic product** = product with no brand name (such as electricity or gas) **Gattungsmarke**
(b) manufactured item for sale **Produkt, Artikel, Ware; product acceptance** = degree to which a product is selling well **Produktakzeptanz;** *we do not know what product acceptance will be in such an unknown market;* **product advertising** = advertising a particular named product, not the company which makes it **Produktwerbung; product analysis** = examining each separate product in a company's range to see why it sells *or* who buys it, etc. **Produktanalyse; product concept** = concept for a totally new product or an adaptation of an existing one **Produktkonzept; product deletion** *or* **product**

elimination = discontinuing of products as news ones are added to a company's product range **Produktelimination;** *product deletion was caused by poor sales; if production costs continue to rise then product deletion will be the only answer;* **product design** = design of consumer products **Produktgestaltung;** **product development** = improving an existing product line to meet the needs of the market **Produktentwicklung;** **product differentiation** = ensuring that a product has some unique features that distinguish it from competing ones **Produktdifferenzierung;** *we are adding some extra features to our watches in the interest of product differentiation;* **product engineer** = engineer in charge of the equipment for making a product **Fertigungsingenieur;** **product idea** = idea for a totally new product or an adaptation of an existing one **Produktidee;** **product idea testing** = evaluating a new product idea, usually by consulting representatives from all main departments in a company and interviewing a sample of consumers **Produktideenbewertung;** **product image** = general idea which the public has of a product **Produktimage;** *we need a huge promotional campaign to create the desired product image; the product functions well but has the wrong image;* **product life cycle** = course of a product's life in terms of sales and profitability from its development to its decline **Produktlebenszyklus;** *the machine has reached a point in its product life cycle where we should be thinking about a replacement for it; what stage is this product at in its product life cycle?;* **product line** *or* **product range** = series of different products made by the same company which form a group (such as different models of cars, pens in different colours, etc.) **Produktlinie, Produktgruppe;** **product management** = directing the making and selling of a product as an independent item **Produkt-Management;** **product manager** = manager or executive responsible for the marketing of a particular product **Produktmanager;** *to co-ordinate the selling of our entire range we need more consultation between product managers;* **product-market strategies** = basic marketing strategies consisting of either market penetration, market development, product development or diversification **Produkt/Markt-Strategien;** **product mix** = the particular combination of products made by the same company **Produkt-Mix, Produktpalette;** **product-plus** = features of a product which make it particularly attractive **überlegene Produkteigenschaften;** **product portfolio** = collection of products made by the same company **Produktportfolio;** **product portfolio analysis** = model for marketing strategy with various categories of product based on present performance and growth rate, which can help a business to plan its product development and strategy **Produktportfolio-Analyse;** *product portfolio analysis showed that some products were neither performing well nor showing any signs of increasing their market share;* **product positioning** = placing a product in the market so that it is recognizable to the public **Produktpositionierung;** **product range** = (i) series of products from which the customer can choose; (ii) series of different products made by the same company which form a group **(i) Sortiment, Angebot, Auswahl; (ii) Produktlinie, Produktgruppe;** **product strategy** = various elements (such as price, design and availability) which a company has to take into account when developing a product **Produkt(entwicklungs)strategie;** **product testing** = testing a product by allowing a sample of consumers to use it without knowing which brand it is **Durchführung von Produkttests;** *product testing showed that unfortunately consumers preferred two other brands to this one*

> QUOTE today new marketing is about new products based on consumer understanding and technology
>
> *Marketing Week*
>
> QUOTE consistency of product is probably essential for successful branding
>
> *Marketing Workshop*
>
> QUOTE any expansion or change in market share is most likely to come from the development and improvement of existing products
>
> *Marketing*

production *noun* making *or* manufacturing of goods for sale **Herstellung, Produktion, Erzeugung, Fertigung;** *production will probably be held up by industrial action; we are hoping to speed up production by installing new machinery;* **batch production** = production in batches **Serienfertigung;** **domestic production** = production of goods in the home market **Inlandsproduktion;** **mass production** = manufacturing of large quantities of goods **Massenproduktion, serienmäßige Herstellung;** *mass production of cars or of calculators;* **rate of production** *or* **production rate** = speed at which items are made **Produktionsleistung;** **production cost** = cost of making a product **Produktionskosten;** **production department** = section of a company which deals with the making of the company's products **Fertigungsabteilung;** **production line** = system of making a product, where each item (such as a car) moves slowly through the factory with new sections added to it as it goes along **Fertigungsstraße, Fließband;** *he works on the production line; she is a production line worker;* **production manager** = person in charge of the production department **Produktionsleiter, Leiter der Fertigung; production unit** = separate small group of workers producing a certain product **Produktionseinheit**

◇ **productive** *adjective* which produces **produktiv; productive capital** = capital which is invested to give interest **arbeitendes/gewinnbringendes Kapital; productive discussions** = useful discussions which lead to an agreement *or* decision **produktive Gespräche**

◇ **productivity** *noun* rate of output per worker *or* per machine in a factory **Produktivität;** *bonus payments are linked to productivity; the company is aiming to increase productivity; productivity has fallen or risen since the company was taken over;* **productivity agreement** = agreement to pay a productivity bonus **Produktivitätsabkommen; productivity bonus** = extra payments made to workers because of increased production **Produktivitätsprämie, Leistungszulage; productivity drive** = extra effort to increase productivity **Produktivitätskampagne**

> QUOTE though there has been productivity growth, the absolute productivity gap between many British firms and their foreign rivals remains
>
> *Sunday Times*
>
> QUOTE if growth does slow down in 1989, as it is likely to do, productivity will slow down with it
>
> *Management Today*

profile *noun* description of the characteristics of something **Kurzübersicht, Profil; customer profile** = description of an average customer for a product or service **Kundenprofil; market profile** = basic characteristics of a particular market **Marktprofil**

> QUOTE the audience profile does vary greatly by daypart: 41.6% of the adult audience is aged 16 to 34 during the morning period, but this figure drops to 24% during peak viewing time
>
> *Marketing Week*

profit *noun* money gained from a sale which is more than the money spent on making the item sold or on providing the service offered **Gewinn, Profit, Erlös; clear profit** = profit after all expenses have been paid **Rein-, Nettogewinn;** *we made $6,000 clear profit on the deal;* **gross profit** = profit calculated as sales income less the cost of the goods sold **Bruttogewinn; net profit** = amount by which income from sales is larger than all expenditure **Nettogewinn; operating profit** = result where sales from normal business activities are higher than the costs **Betriebsgewinn; trading profit** = result where the company's receipts are higher than its expenditure **Geschäftsgewinn; profit and loss account** = accounts for a company which show expenditure and income balanced to show a final profit *or* loss **Gewinn- und Verlustrechnung; profit margin** = percentage difference between sales income and the cost of sales **Gewinnspanne; profit maximization** = business strategy or policy based on achieving as high a profit as possible **Gewinnmaximierung;** *the company considers profit maximization a socially irresponsible policy;* **profits tax** *or* **tax on profits** = tax to be paid on profits **Gewinnsteuer; profit before tax** *or* **pretax profit** = profit before any tax has been paid **Gewinn vor (Abzug der) Steuern; profit after tax** = profit after tax has been paid **Gewinn nach Steuern; to take one's profit** = to sell shares at a higher price than was paid for them, rather than keep them as an investment **seinen Gewinn mitnehmen; to show a profit** = to make a profit and state it in the company accounts **einen Gewinn aufweisen;** *we are showing a small profit for the first quarter;* **to make a profit** = to have more money as the result of a deal **einen Gewinn machen; to move into profit** = to start to make a profit **in die schwarzen Zahlen kommen;** *the company is breaking even now, and expects to move into profit within the next two months;* **to sell at a profit** = to sell at a price which gives you a profit **mit Gewinn verkaufen; excess profit** = profit which is higher than is thought to be normal **Mehrgewinn; excess profits tax** = tax on excess profits **Steuer zur Abschöpfung von Höchstgewinnen; healthy profit** = quite a large profit **stattlicher Gewinn; paper profit** = profit on an asset which has increased in price but has not been sold **Buchgewinn;** *he is showing a paper profit of £25,000 on his investment*

◇ **profitability** *noun*
(a) ability to make a profit **Rentabilität**
(b) amount of profit made as a percentage of costs **Profitabilität; measurement of profitability** = way of calculating how profitable something is **Rentabilitätsberechnung**

◇ **profitable** *adjective* which makes a profit **rentabel, gewinnbringend, ertragreich, einträglich**

◇ **profit centre** *noun* person *or* department which is considered separately for the purposes of calculating a profit **Ertragszentrum, Profit-Center**

◇ **profiteer** *noun* person who makes too much profit, especially when goods are rationed *or* in short supply **Profit-, Geschäftemacher, Wucherer**

◊ **profiteering** *noun* making too much profit **Geschäftemacherei, Preistreiberei, Wuchergeschäfte**

◊ **profit-making** *adjective* which makes a profit **gewinnbringend, rentabel;** *it is hoped to make it into a profit-making concern; the whole project was expected to be profit-making by 1988;* **non-profit-making** = (organization, such as a club) which is not allowed by law to make a profit **gemeinnützig, nicht auf Erwerbszwecke ausgerichtet;** *non-profit-making organizations are exempt from tax*

> QUOTE because capital gains are not taxed and money taken out in profits and dividends is taxed, owners of businesses will be using accountants and tax experts to find loopholes in the law
> *Toronto Star*
>
> QUOTE the bank transferred $5 million to general reserve compared with $10 million in 1983 which made the consolidated profit and loss account look healthier
> *Hongkong Standard*
>
> QUOTE some profit-taking was seen yesterday as investors continued to lack fresh incentives to renew buying activity
> *Financial Times*

pro forma *noun* **pro forma (invoice)** = invoice sent to a buyer before the goods are sent, so that payment can be made or business documents produced **Proforma-Rechnung;** *they sent us a pro forma*

project *noun*
(a) plan **Plan;** *he has drawn up a project for developing new markets in Europe*
(b) particular job of work which follows a plan **Projekt, Vorhaben;** *we are just completing an engineering project in North Africa; the company will start work on the project next month;* **project analysis** = examining all the costs *or* problems generated by a project before starting work on it **Projektanalyse; project engineer** = engineer in charge of a project **Projektingenieur; project manager** = manager in charge of a project **Projektleiter**

◊ **projected** *adjective* planned *or* expected **geplant, erwartet; projected sales** = forecast of sales **erwarteter Absatz, Verkaufsprognose;** *projected sales in Europe next year should be over £1m*

◊ **projection** *noun* forecast of something which will happen in the future **Vorhersage, Prognose;** *projection of profits for the next three years; the sales manager was asked to draw up sales projections for the next three years*

promissory note *noun* document stating that someone promises to pay an amount of money on a certain date **Schuldschein**

promote *verb* to advertise **werben, Reklame machen; to promote a new product** = to increase the sales of a new product by a sales campaign *or* TV commercials *or* free gifts **durch Werbung den Verkauf eines neuen Produktes fördern**

◊ **promotion** *noun* all means of conveying the message about a product *or* service to potential customers (by publicity *or* sales campaign *or* TV commercials *or* free gifts, etc.) **Werbekampagne für ein Produkt, Verkaufsförderungsmaßnahmen;** *our promotion budget has been doubled; the promotion team has put forward plans for the launch; we are offering free holidays in France as part of our special in-store promotion;* **personality promotion** = promotion which makes use of famous people to endorse a product **Prominentenwerbung;** *a famous football star was chosen for the personality promotion because of his widespread popularity among the target audience*

◊ **promotional** *adjective* used in an advertising campaign **Werbe-;** *the admen are using balloons as part of their promotional material;* **promotional allowance** = discount which is offered to a buyer in return for some promotional activity in connection with the product sold **Werberabatt; promotional budget** = forecast cost of promoting a new product **Werbeetat; promotional mix** = combination of all the elements that make up a company's promotion **Verkaufsförderungsmix;** *our promotional mix consists of an extended TV and radio advertising campaign; the exact promotional mix will depend on the costs of the various media available;* **promotional price** = reduced price offered in order to maximize sales (often when a product is launched) **Werbepreis; promotional tools** = material used in promotion, such as display material and sales literature **Verkaufsförderungsmittel;** *a draw for a free holiday on the exhibition stand is one of the best promotional tools I know; the salesmen are armed with a full range of promotional tools*

◊ **promotools** *noun* *(informal)* = PROMOTIONAL TOOLS

> QUOTE the simplest way to boost sales at the expense of regional newspapers is by a heavyweight promotional campaign
> *Marketing Week*
>
> QUOTE finding the right promotion to appeal to children is no easy task
> *Marketing*
>
> QUOTE you have to study the profiles and people involved very carefully and tailor the promotion to fill those needs
> *Marketing Week*

prompt
1 *adjective* rapid *or* done immediately **prompt, sofortig;** *prompt service; prompt reply to a letter;* **prompt payment** = payment made rapidly **pünktliche Zahlung; prompt supplier** = supplier who delivers orders rapidly **Lieferant, der sofort liefert**
2 *noun* information *or* idea offered to a person to help him or her answer a question in a survey **Gedächtnisstütze, Erinnerungshilfe**
3 *verb* to give someone help in answering a question **vorsagen;** *in order to avoid influencing the answers, the interviewer must prompt the respondent only when it is really necessary;* **prompted recall** = test to see how well someone can remember an advertisement in which the respondent is given some help such as a picture which he or she might associate with the advertisement **gestützte Erinnerung;** *after a prompted recall test, the company and its advertising agency decided to change the advertisement*

proof *noun*
(a) proof of purchase = evidence (such as a sales slip) to show that an article has been purchased, in order, for example, to claim some benefit such as a free gift, or in order to claim reimbursement **Kaufnachweis**
(b) typeset text which has to be checked for errors before it is finally printed **Korrekturbogen**

propaganda *noun* attempt to spread an idea through clever use of the media and other forms of communication **Propaganda;** *the charity has been criticized for spreading political propaganda; the government is using propaganda to discourage people from buying our products*

propensity *noun* tendency **Neigung; propensity to consume** = relationship between consumers' needs and their expenditure on goods **Konsumneigung; propensity to import** = relationship between changes in the national income and changes in expenditure on imports **Importneigung; propensity to invest** = tendency of producers to invest in capital goods **Investitionsneigung; propensity to save** = tendency of consumers to save instead of spending on consumer goods **Sparneigung**

proprietary goods *noun* products (such as medicines) that are owned by the company which makes them **gesetzlich geschützte Waren, Markenartikel**

prospect *noun*
(a) prospects = possibilities for the future **Aussichten; prospects for the market** *or* **market prospects are worse than they were last year** = sales in the market are likely to be lower than they were last year **die Markterwartungen sind schlechter als letztes Jahr**
(b) person who may become a customer **Interessent/-in;** *the salesmen were looking out for possible prospects;* **key prospects** = potential customers who are very likely to buy **potentielle Kunden**
◊ **prospective** *adjective* which may happen in the future **voraussichtlich; a prospective buyer** = someone who may buy in the future **ein potentieller Käufer;** *there is no shortage of prospective buyers for the computer*
◊ **prospectus** *noun* document which gives information to attract buyers *or* customers **Prospekt;** *the restaurant has young women handing out prospectuses in the street*

protectionism *noun* protecting producers in the home country against foreign competitors by banning or taxing imports or by imposing import quotas **Protektionismus**

protest
1 *noun* official document which proves that a bill of exchange has not been paid **Wechselprotest**
2 *verb* **to protest a bill** = to draw up a document to prove that a bill of exchange has not been paid **Wechselprotest einlegen**

prototype *noun* first model of a new product before it goes into production **Prototyp;** *prototype car or prototype plane; the company is showing the prototype of the new model at the exhibition*

provisional *adjective* temporary *or* not final or permanent **vorläufig, provisorisch, Interims-;** *provisional forecast of sales; provisional budget; they telexed their provisional acceptance of the contract*

prune *verb* to reduce a product range by deleting old products **eliminieren, streichen, rationalisieren;** *the new marketing director* *insisted on pruning the product line to streamline the company's functions*

psychogalvanometer *noun* instrument used to measure emotional reactions to advertising by checking the degree of sweating on palms **Psychogalvanometer;** *the results of the psychogalvanometer test suggested that the ad was so dull it had no effect whatever on the public*

◇ **psychographics** *noun* study of the life style of different sectors of society for marketing purposes **psychographische Merkmalsanalyse; Psychogramm;** *psychographics can help define the market segment we should be aiming for with our product;* **psychographic segmentation** = dividing a market into segments according to the life styles of the customers **psychographische Marktsegmentierung**

public

1 *adjective* referring to all the people in general **öffentlich; public image** = idea which the people have of a company *or* a person **Image;** *the minister is trying to improve his public image;* **public sector** = nationalized industries and public services **öffentlicher Bereich, staatlicher Sektor; public service advertising** = advertising a public service or cause such as famine relief **Veröffentlichung von Werbemitteln zur Information der Öffentlichkeit;** *because it was a public service advertisement, the newspaper charged a specially low rate;* **public transport** = transport (such as buses, trains, etc.) used by members of the public **öffentliche Verkehrsmittel; public warehouse** = warehouse which stores goods awaiting shipment or which have just been landed **öffentliches Warenlager**

2 *noun*

(a) the public *or* **the general public** = the people **die Öffentlichkeit**

(b) publics = groups of people that are identified for marketing purposes **Publikum;** *what publics is this product likely to appeal to? different marketing messages need to be aimed at different publics*

◇ **public relations (PR)** *plural noun* keeping good relations between a company *or* a group and the public so that people know what the company is doing and approve of it **PR-Arbeit, Public Relations, Öffentlichkeitsarbeit;** *a public relations man; he works in public relations; a public relations firm handles all our publicity;* **a public relations exercise** = a campaign to improve public relations **eine PR-Kampagne, eine Kampagne zur Verbesserung der Public Relations; public relations officer (PRO)** = person in an organization who is responsible for public relations activities **Leiter der PR-Abteilung**

publication *noun*

(a) act of making something public by publishing it **Veröffentlichung, Bekanntgabe, Bekanntmachung;** *the publication of the government report has provoked complaints from the advertising industry*

(b) thing which has been published, such as a book, newspaper, magazine, etc. **Publikation, Veröffentlichung; a business publication** = a magazine aimed at business people **eine Wirtschaftspublikation**

publicity *noun* attracting the attention of the public to products or services by mentioning them in the media **Werbung, Reklame; Publicity; publicity agency** *or* **publicity bureau** = office which organizes publicity for companies who do not have publicity departments **Werbeagentur; publicity budget** = money allowed for expenditure on publicity **Werbeetat; publicity campaign** = organized operation to publicize something over a period of time **Werbeaktion, Werbekampagne; publicity copy** = text of an advertisement before it is printed **Werbetextentwurf; publicity department** = section of a company which organizes the company's publicity **Werbeabteilung; publicity expenditure** = money spent on publicity **Werbekosten; publicity manager** = person in charge of a publicity department **Werbeleiter; publicity matter** = sheets *or* posters *or* leaflets used for publicity **Werbematerial**

◇ **publicize** *verb* to attract people's attention to a product for sale *or* a service *or* an entertainment **werben, Werbung/Reklame machen;** *the campaign is intended to publicize the services of the tourist board; we are using advertisements on buses to publicize our products; audiences were small because the play had not been publicized properly*

puff *noun* claim made for a product *or* an organization in order to promote it **marktschreierische Anpreisung, Schleichwerbung;** *the magazine article was supposed to about telecommunications, but was just a puff for a new modem*

pull strategy *noun* attempt by a producer to persuade final users to buy a product and so "pull" the product through the distribution channel to the point-of-sale **Pull-Strategie;** *we must develop a better pull strategy to allow retailers to sell off their excess stocks;* **pull-push strategy** = combination of both pull and push strategies **Pull-Push-Strategie**

pump priming *noun* investment by the government in new projects, which it is hoped will benefit the economy **Ankurbelung durch staatliche Investitionen**

pup *noun (informal)* worthless item **Schund;** *that street trader sold me a pup*

purchase
1 *noun* thing which has been bought **Kauf; to make a purchase** = to buy something **einen Kauf tätigen, eine Anschaffung machen; purchase book** = records of purchases **Wareneingangsbuch; purchase ledger** = book in which expenditure is noted **Einkaufsbuch; purchase order** = official order made out by a purchasing department for goods which a company wants to buy **Auftrag, Bestellung;** *we cannot supply you without a purchase order number;* **purchase price** = price paid for something **Kaufpreis; purchase tax** = tax paid on things which are bought **Kaufsteuer;** *(entspricht)* **Verbrauchssteuer; bulk purchase** *or* **quantity purchase** = buying of large quantities of goods at low prices **Mengen-, Posteneinkauf; cash purchase** = purchase made in cash **Barkauf; hire purchase** = system of buying something by paying a sum regularly each month **Raten-, Teilzahlungskauf;** *he is buying a refrigerator on hire purchase;* **hire purchase agreement** = contract to pay for something by instalments **Teilzahlungskaufvertrag; impulse purchase** = thing bought as soon as it is seen **Impulskauf**
2 *verb* to buy **kaufen, erwerben, erstehen, einkaufen, ankaufen; to purchase something for cash** = to pay cash for something **etwas bar kaufen**

◊ **purchaser** *noun* person *or* company which purchases **Käufer/-in, Erwerber/-in; the company is looking for a purchaser** = the company is trying to find someone who will buy it **für das Unternehmen wird ein Käufer gesucht;** *the company has found a purchaser for its warehouse*

◊ **purchasing** *noun* buying **Einkauf, Warenbeschaffung; purchasing department** = section of a company which deals with buying stock, raw materials, equipment, etc. **Abteilung Einkauf; purchasing manager** = head of a purchasing department **Einkaufsleiter; purchasing officer** = person in a company *or* organization who is responsible for buying stock, raw materials, equipment, etc. **Einkäufer; purchasing opportunity** = possibility for a customer to make a purchase **Kaufgelegenheit; purchasing power** = quantity of goods which can be bought by a group of people *or* with a certain amount of money **Kaufkraft;** *the decline in the purchasing power of the pound;* **central purchasing** = purchasing organized by the main office for all departments or branches **zentraler Einkauf; repeat purchasing** = frequent buying of a low-price product for household use **Wieder(holungs)kauf**

pure competition *noun* hypothetical model of a market where all products of a particular type are identical, where there is complete information about market conditions available to buyers and sellers, and complete freedom for sellers to enter or leave the market **vollkommene Konkurrenz**

push strategy *noun* (i) attempt by a manufacturer to push the product towards the customer; (ii) attempt by a producer to persuade distributors to take part in the marketing of a product, so "pushing" it through the distribution channel **(i) & (ii) Push-Strategie; push-pull strategy** = combination of both push and pull strategies **Push-Pull-Strategie**

put down *verb* to make a deposit **anzahlen;** *to put down money on a house*

◊ **put in** *verb* **to put an ad in a paper** = to have an ad printed in a newspaper **ein Inserat aufgeben; to put in a bid for something** = to offer (usually in writing) to buy something **für etwas ein Angebot machen; to put in an estimate for something** = to give someone a written calculation of the probable costs of carrying out a job **für etwas einen Kostenvoranschlag machen; to put in a claim for damage** = to ask an insurance company to pay for damage **einen Schadensersatzanspruch stellen;**

pyramid selling *noun* method of selling based on selling franchises to distributors at various levels in the distribution channel, each of whom buys goods from another distributor at a higher level **Verkaufspyramide**

Qq

quad crown *noun* poster size corresponding to twice a double crown **Papierformat von 30 x 40 Zoll**

quality *noun*
(a) what something is like *or* how good or bad something is **Qualität; we sell only quality farm produce** = we sell only farm produce of the best quality **wir verkaufen nur**

Agrarprodukte bester Qualität; *there is a market for good quality secondhand computers;* **high quality** *or* **top quality** = very best quality **Spitzenqualität, erstklassige Qualität;** *the store specializes in high quality imported items;* **quality press** = newspapers aiming at the upper end of the market **Prestigezeitungen;** *we advertise in the quality Sundays*
(b) quality control = checking that the quality of a product is good **Qualitätskontrolle; quality controller** = person who checks the quality of a product **Qualitätskontrolleur**

◇ **qualitative** *adjective* referring to quality **qualitativ; qualitative data** = data found in qualitative research **qualitative Daten; qualitative research** = survey based on finding the opinions of respondents rather than any scientifically measurable data **qualitative Analyse;** *qualitative research can be used to ascertain consumers' attitudes to a new advertising campaign; qualitative research will not give objective information*

quantity *noun*
(a) amount *or* number of items **Menge, Quantität, Anzahl;** *a small quantity of illegal drugs; he bought a large quantity of spare parts*
(b) large amount **große Stückzahl;** *the company offers a discount for quantity purchase;* **quantity discount** = discount based on quantity bought or on the value of total purchases **Mengenrabatt;** *there is a quantity discount of 15% on purchases of more than 100 units of any product; we offer a quantity discount on purchases of more than 500 items*

◇ **quantitative** *adjective* referring to quantity **quantitativ; quantitative data** = information gathered in quantitative research **quantitative Daten; quantitative research** = survey based on measurable data **quantitative Analyse;** *quantitative research will provide a firm basis for strategy decisions*

> QUOTE the collection of consumer behaviour data in the book covers both qualitative and quantitative techniques
> *Quarterly Review of Marketing*

quarterly *noun* newspaper or magazine which appears four times a year **Vierteljahrespublikation;** *we're advertising in a medical quarterly*

quasi- *prefix* almost *or* which seems like **Quasi, quasi-; quasi-retailing** = retailing relating to the provision of services, as in restaurants or hairdressers **Quasi-Einzelhandel**

quay *noun* place in a port where ships can tie up **Kai; free on quay** = price which includes all costs up to delivery of the goods to the quay, ready to be loaded **frei Kai; price ex quay** = price that includes all costs up to delivery of the goods on land at a port, including customs duties and unloading costs **Preis ab Kai**

question marks *noun* in the Boston matrix, products which are not very profitable, having a low market share, but a high growth rate **Fragezeichen;** (same as **problem children** or **wild cats)**

questionnaire *noun* printed list of questions, especially used in market research **Fragebogen;** *to send out a questionnaire to test the opinions of users of the system; to answer* or *to fill in a questionnaire about holidays abroad*

quota *noun* limited amount of something which is allowed to be produced or imported, etc. **Kontingent, Quote; import quota** = fixed quantity of a particular type of goods which the government allows to be imported **Einfuhrkontingent, Importquote;** *the government has imposed a quota on the importation of cars; the quota on imported cars has been lifted;* **quota sample** = sample which is preselected on the basis of specific criteria so as best to represent the universe **Quota-Auswahl;** *the quota sample was used to represent the various racial groupings in their correct proportions;* **quota system** = system where imports *or* supplies are regulated by fixing maximum amounts **Kontingentierungssystem, Quotensystem; to arrange distribution through a quota system** = to arrange distribution by allowing each distributor only a certain number of items **den Vertrieb durch ein Quotensystem regeln**

quote
1 *verb*
(a) to repeat words used by someone else; to repeat a reference number **zitieren, anführen; angeben;** *he quoted figures from the annual report; in reply please quote this number; when making a complaint please quote the batch number printed on the box; he replied, quoting the invoice number*
(b) to estimate *or* to say what costs may be **(einen Preis) angeben/nennen;** *to quote a price for supplying stationery; their prices are always quoted in dollars; he quoted me a price of £1,026; can you quote for supplying 20,000 envelopes?*
2 *noun (informal)* estimate of how much something will cost **Angebot;** *to give someone a quote for supplying computers; we have asked for quotes for refitting the*

shop; his quote was the lowest of three; we accepted the lowest quote

◇ **quotation** *noun* estimate of how much something will cost **Kostenvoranschlag;** *they sent in their quotation for the job; to ask for quotations for refitting the shop; his quotation was much lower than all the others; we accepted the lowest quotation*

Rr

R&D = RESEARCH AND DEVELOPMENT *the R&D department; the company spends millions on R&D*

rack *noun* frame to hold items for display **Ständer, Gestell, Regal;** *card rack; display rack; magazine rack;* **rack board** = board on which items can be displayed, showing the names and prices of products **Präsentationsgestell; rack jobber** = wholesaler who sells goods by putting them on racks in retail shops **Regalgroßhändler**

racket *noun* illegal deal which makes a lot of money **betrügerisches Geschäft, Betrügerei, Gaunerei;** *he runs a cut-price ticket racket*

◇ **racketeer** *noun* person who runs a racket **Betrüger/-in, Gauner/-in**

rail *noun* using a railway **Bahn;** *six million commuters travel to work by rail each day; we ship all our goods by rail; rail travellers are complaining about rising fares; rail travel is cheaper than air travel;* **free on rail** = price including all the seller's costs until the goods are delivered to the railway for shipment **frei Waggon**

◇ **railhead** *noun* end of a railway line **Endbahnhof;** *the goods will be sent to the railhead by lorry*

◇ **railway** *or (US)* **railroad** *noun* system using trains to carry passengers and goods **Bahn;** *a railway station; a railway line; the British railway network*

rake-off *noun* a person's share of profits from a deal, especially if obtained illegally **Provision;** *I have a contact in government who can help us to get the contract, but he will expect at least a 10% rake-off; the group gets a rake-off on all the company's sales; he got a £100,000 rake-off for introducing new business; he didn't agree to the plan because his rake-off would be too small to make taking such a risk worthwhile*

random *adjective* done without making any special choice **Zufalls-, zufällig, willkürlich; random check** = check on items taken from a group without any special choice **Stichprobe; random error** = computer error which has no special reason **Zufallsfehler; random fluctuation** = unforeseeable deviation from an expected trend **zufällige Abweichung; random sample** = sample for testing, chosen without any special method of selection **zufällige Stichprobe; random sampling** = choosing samples for testing without any special method of selection **Stichprobenauswahl; random walk** = sampling technique which allows for random selection within certain parameters set up by a non-random technique **Random-Route-Verfahren; at random** = without special choice **wahllos, aufs Geratewohl;** *the chairman picked out two salesmen's reports at random*

range

1 *noun*

(a) series of items from which the customer can choose **Sortiment, Angebot, Auswahl;** *we offer a wide range of sizes or range of styles; their range of products or product range is too narrow; we have the most modern range of models or model range on the market*

(b) variation from small to large or from a top to a bottom figure **(Preis)lage, (Preis)klasse; (Gehalts)spanne; Größe;** *I am looking for something in the £2 - £3 price range; we make shoes in a wide range of prices*

(c) type or variety of things which someone can do **Bereich, Gebiet, Feld;** *this falls within the company's range of activities*

2 *verb* to vary *or* to be different **reichen/gehen von ... bis, variieren;** *the company sells products ranging from cheap down-market pens to imported luxury items; the company's salary scale ranges from £5,000 for a trainee to £50,000 for the managing director; our activities range from mining in the USA to computer servicing in Scotland*

> QUOTE the latest addition to the range features two hotplates, a storage cupboard, a refrigerator and a microwave oven
> *Sales & Marketing Management*
>
> QUOTE the range has been extended to nine products
> *Marketing Week*

rapport *noun* good communication and understanding between two people **Beziehung, Verhältnis;** *the interviewer managed to establish a good rapport with the interviewees; co-ordination is difficult owing to lack of rapport between the* *marketing manager and the managing director*

rate *noun*
(a) money charged for time worked *or* work completed **Satz, Gebühr, Preis; all-in rate** = price which covers all items in a purchase (such as delivery, tax and insurance, as well as the goods themselves) **Inklusivpreis; card rate** = charge for advertising which is laid out in the rate card **Listenpreis; fixed rate** = charge which cannot be changed **fester Satz/Preis; flat rate** = (i) charge which always stays the same or which applies to anybody; (ii) normal charge for advertising space or time, without allowing for discounts **(i) Pauschale; Grundgebühr; Einheitstarif; (ii) Grund-, Listenpreis; Einzelwerbepreis;** *a flat-rate increase of 10%; we pay a flat rate for electricity each quarter; he's paid a flat rate of £2 per thousand;* **full rate** = full charge, with no reductions **voller Satz/Preis; the going rate** = the usual *or* the current rate of payment **der übliche Satz; the market rate** = normal price in the market **der Marktpreis, üblicher Preis;** *we pay the going rate or the market rate for typists; the going rate for offices is £10 per square foot;* **page rate** = charge for taking a full page advertisement in a publication **Seitenpreis; reduced rate** = specially cheap charge **ermäßigter Tarif**
(b) discount rate = percentage taken by a bank when it buys bills **Diskontsatz; insurance rates** = amount of premium which has to be paid per £1000 of insurance **Versicherungsprämiensatz; interest rate** *or* **rate of interest** = percentage charge for borrowing money **Zinssatz; rate of return** = amount of interest *or* dividend which comes from an investment, shown as a percentage of the money invested **Rendite**
(c) bank base rates = basic rate of interest which a bank uses to calculate the actual rate of interest on loans to customers **Eckzins, Bankleitzinssatz; cross rate** = exchange rate between two currencies expressed in a third currency **Kreuzkurs; exchange rate** *or* **rate of exchange** = rate at which one currency is exchanged for another **Wechselkurs;** *what is today's rate or the current rate for the dollar?;* **to calculate costs on a fixed exchange rate** = to calculate costs on an exchange rate which does not change **die Kosten berechnen anhand eines festen Wechselkurses; forward rate** = rate for purchase of foreign currency at a fixed price for delivery at a later date **Devisenterminkurs; freight rates** = charges for transporting goods **Frachtgebühren; letter rate** *or* **parcel rate** = postage (calculated by weight) for sending a letter *or* a parcel **Briefgebühr; Paketgebühr;** *it's more expensive to send a packet letter rate but it will get there more quickly;* **night rate** = cheap telephone calls at night **Nachttarif, Mondschein-Tarif**
(d) amount *or* number *or* speed compared with something else **Rate;** *the rate of increase in redundancies; the rate of absenteeism or the absenteeism rate always increases in fine weather;* **birth rate** = number of children born per 1,000 of the population **Geburtenrate; call rate** = number of calls (per day *or* per week) which a salesman makes on customers **Besuchsrate; depreciation rate** = rate at which an asset is depreciated each year in the company accounts **Abschreibungssatz; error rate** = number of mistakes per thousand entries *or* per page **Fehlerquote; rate of sales** = speed at which units are sold **Absatzgeschwindigkeit; rate of turnover** = length of time taken from the purchase of an item of stock to its replacement after being sold **Umsatzgeschwindigkeit;** *the rate of turnover is so low that some articles have been in the shop for more than a year*

◇ **rate card** *noun* list of charges for advertising issued by a media owner (such as a magazine) **Anzeigenpreisliste;** *if you look at the rate card you will find the various charges for display advertising*

rating *noun*
(a) action of giving something a value **Schätzung, Bewertung; exempt rating** = right of a business not to add VAT to the price of goods or services **Steuerfreieinschätzung; vendor rating** = the assessment of a vendor by a buyer **Verkäuferschätzung**
(b) ratings = lists of TV or radio programmes based on the estimated number of people who watch or listen to them **Einschaltquote;** *the show is high in the ratings, which means it will attract good publicity*

ratio *noun* proportion *or* quantity of something compared to something else **Verhältnis;** *the ratio of successes to failures; our product outsells theirs by a ratio of two to one;* **price/earnings ratio (P/E ratio)** = comparison between the market price of a share and the current dividend it produces **Kurs-Gewinn-Verhältnis;** *the shares sell at a P/E ratio of 7*

rationalization *noun* streamlining *or* making more efficient **Rationalisierung**

◇ **rationalize** *verb* to streamline *or* to make more efficient **rationalisieren;** *the rail company is trying to rationalize its freight services*

raw *adjective* in the original state *or* not processed **roh, unverarbeitet; raw data** = data as it is put into a computer, without being analysed **Ausgangsdaten, Urdaten; raw materials** = substances which have not been manufactured (such as wool, wood, sand, etc.) **Rohstoffe**

> QUOTE it makes sense for them to produce goods for sale back home in the US from plants in Britain where raw materials are relatively cheap
> *Duns Business Month*

reach
1 *noun* the actual number of people who see an advertisement once (as opposed to the frequency, which is the number of times one person sees an advertisement over a given period of time) **Reichweite;** *the success of an advertisement depends on its reach;* **cumulative reach** = the number of people who have seen an advertisement at least once over a period of time **kumulative Reichweite; gross reach** = total number of opportunities for people to see a company's advertisements in a publication **Bruttoreichweite; net reach** = total number of people who have seen an advertisement at least once **Nettoreichweite**
2 *verb* to get to an audience **erreichen; ansprechen;** *what percentage of the target audience did the advertisement reach?*

reader *noun* person who reads a newspaper or magazine **Leser/-in; reader advertisement** = advertisement in the form of editorial matter **Textanzeige; reader loyalty** = the inclination of a person to keep reading the same publication **Leser-Blatt-Bindung, Leserloyalität; reader's inquiry card** *or* **reader's service card** = card bound into a magazine which contains a matrix of numbers and letters on which readers can mark codes for products they wish to have further information about; the card is returned to the publisher, who gets the advertiser to send the relevant information to the reader **Kennzifferndienstkarte, Leserservicekarte**

◇ **readership** *noun* all the people who read a particular publication **Leserschaft;** *our readership has increased since we included more feature articles in the magazine;* **pass-on readership** = the number of people who read a publication who have not bought it, but borrowed it from a purchaser **Folgeleserschaft**

◇ **reading and noting** *noun* research statistic showing the proportion of the readership of the publication who actually read a given advertisement **Lesen und Sehen**

readvertise *verb* to advertise again **nochmals inserieren; to readvertise a post** = to put in a second advertisement for a vacant post **eine Stelle nochmals inserieren;** *all the candidates failed the test, so we will just have to readvertise*

◇ **readvertisement** *noun* second advertisement for a vacant post **Zweitinserat**

ready *adjective*
(a) fit to be used *or* to be sold **fertig, bereit;** *the order will be ready for delivery next week; the driver had to wait because the shipment was not ready*
(b) ready cash = money which is immediately available for payment **Bargeld; these items find a ready sale in the Middle East** = these items sell rapidly *or* easily in the Middle East **diese Waren finden im Nahen Osten schnellen/reißenden Absatz; ready market** = market with a high turnover of goods **aufnahmefähiger Markt;** *distribution has to be good in such a ready market;* **ready sale** = sale that is easily achieved **schneller Verkauf;** *lengthy negotiations are a trial for salesmen used to ready sales*

◇ **ready-made** *or* **ready-to-wear** *adjective* (clothes) which are mass-produced, not made for each customer personally **Fertig-, fertig, gebrauchsfertig; Konfektions-, von der Stange;** *the ready-to-wear trade has suffered from foreign competition*

real *adjective* true *or* not an imitation **echt;** *his case is made of real leather or he has a real leather case; that car is a real bargain at £300;* **real income** *or* **real wages** = income which is available for spending after tax, etc. has been deducted **Realeinkommen; Reallohn; in real terms** = actually *or* really **Real-, in reeller Kaufkraft;** *prices have gone up by 3% but with inflation running at 5% that is a fall in real terms;* **real time** = time when a computer is working on the processing of data **Echtzeit, Real-time;**

rebate *noun*
(a) reduction in the amount of money to be paid **Rabatt, Preisnachlaß;** *to offer a 10% rebate on selected goods*
(b) money returned to someone because he has paid too much **Rückzahlung, Rückvergütung, Rückerstattung;** *he got a tax rebate at the end of the year*

◇ **rebating** *noun* offering a rebate **Rabattgewähren; commission rebating** = advertising agency's discounting of invoices for media costs sent to clients, in effect taking them out of its own commission or profit margin **Kommissionsrabatt**

rebound *verb* to go back up again quickly **wieder ansteigen;** *the market rebounded when the government lowered interest rates again*

rebuy *noun* act of buying a product again **Anschluß-, Wieder(holungs)kauf; modified rebuy** = buying decision where either the product or the supplier has changed from the time of the previous purchase **modifizierter Wiederholungskauf; straight rebuy** = buying decision where the same product is bought again from the same supplier **direkter Anschlußkauf**

recall *noun* ability to remember an advertisement **Erinnerung; aided** *or* **prompted recall** = test to see how well someone can remember an advertisement in which the respondent is given some help, such as a picture which he or she might associate with the advertisement **gestützte Erinnerung; unprompted recall** = recall test where the respondent is given no help in remembering the advertisement **ungestützte Erinnerung; recall test** = advertising research test to see how well someone can remember an advertisement **Erinnerungs-, Gedächtnistest;** *a disappointing number of respondents in the recall text failed to remember the advertisement*

receipt
1 *noun*
(a) paper showing that money has been paid *or* that something has been received **Quittung, Beleg, Empfangsbestätigung;** *customs receipt; rent receipt; receipt for items purchased; please produce your receipt if you want to exchange items;* **receipt book** *or* **book of receipts** = book of blank receipts to be filled in when purchases are made **Quittungsblock**
(b) receipts = money earned from sales **Einnahmen, Einkünfte;** *to itemize receipts and expenditure; receipts are down against the same period last year*
2 *verb* to stamp *or* to sign a document to show that it has been received *or* to stamp an invoice to show that it has been paid **Empfang bestätigen, quittieren**

recession *noun* fall in trade *or* in the economy **Rezession, Konjunkturrückgang;** *the recession has reduced profits in many companies; several firms have closed factories because of the recession*

recipient *noun* person who receives **Empfänger/-in;** *the recipient of the award for salesman of the year; a registered letter must be signed for by the recipient*

reciprocal *adjective* done by one country *or* person *or* company to another which does the same thing in return **wechsel-, gegenseitig;** *they signed a reciprocal trade agreement;* **reciprocal holdings** = situation where two companies own shares in each other to prevent takeover bids **gegenseitige Beteiligung; reciprocal trade** = trade between two countries **zweiseitiger Handel**

◇ **reciprocate** *verb* to do the same thing to someone as he has done to you **etwas im Gegenzug/als Gegenleistung tun; mitziehen, sich revanchieren;** *they offered us an exclusive agency for their cars and we reciprocated with an offer of the agency for our buses*

> QUOTE in 1934 Congress authorized President Roosevelt to seek lower tariffs with any country willing to reciprocate
> *Duns Business Month*

recognize *verb*
(a) to know someone *or* something because you have seen *or* heard them before **erkennen, wiedererkennen;** *I recognized his voice before he said who he was; do you recognize the handwriting on the letter?*
(b) to recognize a union = to accept that a union can act on behalf of staff **eine Gewerkschaft anerkennen;** *although all the staff had joined the union, the management refused to recognize it;* **recognized agent** = agent who is approved by the company for which he acts **zugelassener Vertreter**

◇ **recognition** *noun*
(a) act of recognizing **Anerkennung, Zulassung; brand recognition** = ability of the consumer to recognize a brand on sight **Markenwiedererkennung; recognition test** = advertising research test to see how well someone can remember an advertisement either with or without prompting or aided recall **Wiedererkennungstest**
(b) official approval given by the controlling media organizations to an advertising agency, so that the agency can receive commissions from media owners **Anerkennung einer Werbeagentur durch ein Medium**

recommended retail price (RRP) *noun* price at which the manufacturer suggests the product should be sold on the retail market, though this may be reduced by the retailer **empfohlener Herstellerpreis, empfohlener Einzelhandelspreis, unverbindliche Preisempfehlung;**

record
1 *noun*
(a) records = documents which give information **Unterlagen, Aufzeichnungen,**

Akten; *the names of customers are kept in the company's records; we find from our records that our invoice No. 1234 has not been paid*
(b) description of what has happened in the past **Vergangenheit;** *the salesman's record of service or service record; the company's record in industrial relations;* **track record** = what is known about a company's or a salesman's successes or failures in the past **Erfolgs- und Leistungsnachweis;** *he has a good track record as a salesman; the company has no track record in the computer market*
(c) success which is better than anything before **Rekord; record sales** *or* **record losses** *or* **record profits** = sales *or* losses *or* profits which are higher than ever before **Spitzenumsätze; Rekordverluste; Höchstgewinne;** *1985 was a record year for the company; sales for 1983 equalled the record of 1980; our top salesman has set a new record for sales per call;* **we broke our record for June** = we sold more than we have ever sold before in June **wir haben unseren Rekord für Juni gebrochen**
2 *verb* to note *or* to report **aufzeichnen, protokollieren; registrieren, verzeichnen;** *the company has recorded another year of increased sales; your complaint has been recorded and will be investigated;* **recorded delivery** = mail service where the letters are signed for by the person receiving them **Einschreiben**

◊ **record-breaking** *adjective* which is better (or worse) than anything which has happened before **Rekord-;** *we are proud of our record-breaking profits in 1984*

◊ **recording** *noun* making of a note **Aufzeichnung, Eintragung; Registrierung;** *the recording of an order or of a complaint*

recruit *verb* **to recruit new staff** = to get new staff to join a company **weiteres Personal einstellen;** *we are recruiting staff for our new store*

◊ **recruitment** *or* **recruiting** *noun* **the recruitment of new staff** = looking for new staff to join a company **Personalbeschaffung; recruitment advertising** = advertising of jobs **Stellenanzeigen;** *a sudden need for labour has led to a huge demand for recruitment advertising*

recycle *verb* to take waste material and process it so that it can be used again **recyceln, recyclieren, wiederaufbereiten; recycled paper** = paper made from waste paper **Recyclingpapier, Umweltschutzpapier**

redeem *verb* to trade in vouchers or stamps for a special free gift or a reduction in price **einlösen**

◊ **redemption** *noun* trading in of vouchers, coupons or stamps for a gift or a price reduction **Einlösung**

reduction *noun* lowering (of prices, etc.) **Reduzierung, Ermäßigung, Herabsetzung, Verringerung, Senkung;** *price reductions; tax reductions; staff reductions; reduction of expenditure; reduction in demand; the company was forced to make reductions in its advertising budget*

re-export
1 *noun* exporting of goods which have been imported **Wiederausfuhr;** *re-export trade; we import wool for re-export; the value of re-exports has increased*
2 *verb* to export something which has been imported **wiederausführen**

◊ **re-exportation** *noun* exporting goods which have been imported **Wiederausfuhr**

reference group *noun* group of people who share some interest or purpose and regularly interact **Bezugsgruppe**

refund
1 *noun* money paid back **Rückerstattung;** *to ask for a refund; she got a refund after complaining to the manager;* **full refund** *or* **refund in full** = refund of all the money paid **Rückerstattung in voller Höhe;** *he got a full refund when he complained about the service*
2 *verb* to pay back money **erstatten, rückerstatten, zurückzahlen;** *to refund the cost of postage; all money will be refunded if the goods are not satisfactory*

◊ **refundable** *adjective* which can be paid back **zurückerstattbar;** *refundable deposit; the entrance fee is refundable if you purchase £5 worth of goods*

regiocentre stage *noun (US)* stage in a company's international marketing when a region consisting of several countries is treated as one market **regiozentrische Phase**

register *noun* **cash register** = machine with a drawer for keeping the cash received which shows and adds the prices of items bought in a shop **Registrierkasse**

◊ **registered** *adjective*
(a) which has been noted on an official list **eingetragen, registriert, angemeldet; the company's registered office** = the head office of the company as noted in the register of companies **der eingetragene Sitz**

der Gesellschaft; registered design = design which is legally registered to protect the owner against unauthorized use of it by others **Gebrauchsmuster**
(b) registered letter *or* **registered parcel** = letter *or* parcel which is noted by the post office before it is sent, so that compensation can be claimed if it is lost **Einschreibebrief; eingeschriebenes Päckchen;** *to send documents by registered mail or registered post*

◇ **registration** *noun* act of having something noted on an official list **Eintragung, Registrierung, Anmeldung, Erfassung;** *registration of a trademark;* **certificate of registration** *or* **registration certificate** = document showing that an item has been registered **Eintragungsbescheinigung, Meldeschein;** *(für Kraftfahrzeuge)* **Zulassungspapiere; registration fee** = money paid to have something registered **Anmeldegebühr; registration number** = official number (such as the number of a car) **Eintragungsnummer; Kraftfahrzeugkennzeichen**

regression analysis *noun* method of discovering the relationship between one dependent variable and one or more independent variables **Regressionsanalyse**

regular *adjective*
(a) which happens *or* comes at the same time each day *or* each week *or* each month *or* each year **regelmäßig, regulär; regular customer** = customer who always buys from the same shop **Stammkunde; regular staff** = full-time staff **ständiges/festangestelltes Personal**
(b) ordinary *or* standard **normal, regulär;** *the regular price is $1.25, but we're selling them at 99c;* **regular model** = main product in a company's product range **Standardmodell;** *we estimate that 65% of the customers interested in our product range will buy the regular model;* **regular size** = ordinary size (smaller than economy size, family size, etc.) **Normalformat, Standardgröße**

◇ **regulate** *verb*
(a) to adjust something so that it works well *or* is correct **regulieren, einstellen, ordnen**
(b) to change *or* maintain something by law **regeln; prices are regulated by supply and demand** = prices are increased or lowered according to supply and demand **Preise werden durch Angebot und Nachfrage bestimmt; government-regulated price** = price which is imposed by the government **staatlich vorgeschriebener Preis**

◇ **regulation** *noun*
(a) making sure that something will work well or correctly **Regelung, Regulierung;** *the regulation of trading practices*
(b) regulations = laws *or* rules **Vorschriften, Satzung, Statuten;** *the new government regulations on housing standards; fire regulations or safety regulations; regulations concerning imports and exports*
NOTE: no plural for (a)

> QUOTE EEC regulations which came into effect in July insist that customers can buy cars anywhere in the EEC at the local pre-tax price
> *Financial Times*
>
> QUOTE a unit trust is established under the regulations of the Department of Trade, with a trustee, a management company and a stock of units
> *Investors Chronicle*

reimport
1 *noun* importing of goods which have been exported from the same country **Wiedereinfuhr**
2 *verb* to import goods which have been exported **wiedereinführen**

◇ **reimportation** *noun* importing goods which have been exported **Wiedereinfuhr**

reinforcement advertising *noun* advertising aimed at making the positive features of a product stronger in order to reassure people who have already purchased it **Festigungs-, Verstärkungswerbung**

reject *noun* thing which has been thrown out because it is not of the usual standard **Ausschußware; zweite Wahl, B-Sortiment;** *sale of rejects or of reject items; to sell off reject stock;* **reject shop** = shop which specializes in the sale of rejects **Laden für Partiewaren/Waren zweiter Wahl**

relation *noun*
(a) in relation to = referring to *or* connected with **in Zusammenhang mit, in bezug auf;** *I am phoning in relation to our conversation yesterday*
(b) public relations (PR) = keeping good links between a company *or* a group and the public so that people know what the company is doing and approve of it **PR-Arbeit, Public Relations, Öffentlichkeitsarbeit; public relations department** = section of a company which deals with relations with the public **PR-Abteilung, Abteilung für Öffentlichkeitsarbeit; public relations officer** = official who deals with relations with the public **Leiter der PR-Abteilung**

relaunch
1 *noun* putting a product back on the market again **Relaunch, Wiedereinführung;** *the relaunch is scheduled for August*
2 *verb* to put a product on the market again **wiedereinführen;** *the product will be relaunched with some minor modifications next autumn*

release
1 *noun*
(a) setting free **Freistellung, Freigabe, Entbindung; Entlassung;** *release from a contract; release of goods from customs*
(b) press release *or* **news release** = sheet giving news about something, which is sent to newspapers and TV and radio stations so that they can use the information **Pressemitteilung;** *the company sent out or issued a press release about the launch of their new car*
(c) new releases = new records put on the market **Neuerscheinungen auf dem Plattenmarkt**
2 *verb* to put on the market **herausbringen, veröffentlichen;** *to release a new record;* **to release dues** = to send off orders which had been piling up while a product was out of stock **überfällige Bestellungen abwickeln**

remainder
1 *noun* **remainders** = new books sold cheaply **Restauflagen; remainder merchant** = book dealer who buys unsold new books from publishers at a very low price **auf Restauflagen spezialisierter Buchhändler**
2 *verb* **to remainder books** = to sell new books off cheaply **Restauflagen billig verkaufen;** *the shop was full of piles of remaindered books*

reminder *noun* letter to remind a customer that he has not paid an invoice **Mahnung;** *to send someone a reminder;* **reminder advertising** = advertising designed to remind consumers of a product already advertised **Erinnerungswerbung;** *reminder advertising is particularly important in a highly competitive market*

remnant *noun* odd piece of a large item sold separately **Rest;** *remnant sale or sale of remnants*

render *verb* **to render an account** = to send in an account **eine Rechnung vorlegen;** *payment for account rendered; please find enclosed payment per account rendered*

reorder
1 *noun* further order for something which has been ordered before **Nachbestellung;** *the product has only been on the market ten days and we're already getting reorders;* **reorder level** = fixed amount of an item in stock; when stock falls to this level it must be reordered from the supplier **Mindestnachbestellung**
2 *verb* to place a new order for something **nachbestellen;** *we must reorder these items because stock is getting low*

rep
1 *noun* = REPRESENTATIVE *to hold a reps' meeting; our reps make on average six calls a day;* **commission rep** = representative who is not paid a salary but receives a commission on sales **Provisionsvertreter**
2 *verb (informal)* to act as a sales representative for **vertreten;** *he reps for two firms on commission*

repack *verb* to pack again **umpacken, wieder verpacken**
◊ **repacking** *noun* packing again **Umpacken**

repeat *verb* **to repeat an order** = to order something again **eine Nachbestellung aufgeben, etwas nachbestellen; repeat order** = new order for something which has been ordered before **Nachbestellung;** *the product has only been on the market ten days and we're already flooded with repeat orders;* **repeat purchasing** = frequent buying of a low-priced item that is for everyday use (such as soap or bread) **Wieder(holungs)kauf;** *see also* ATR

repertory grid technique *noun* market research technique in which a test is first run to discover what the respondents' main criteria are in judging product brands, followed by another test in which the respondents evaluate brands on the basis of these established criteria **Repertoire-Verfahren, Repertory-Grid-Verfahren**

reply
1 *noun* answer **Antwort, Erwiderung;** *there was no reply to my letter or to my phone call; I am writing in reply to your letter of the 24th; the company's reply to the takeover bid;* **reply card** *or* **reply coupon** = form attached to a coupon ad which has to be filled in and returned to the advertiser **Antwortkarte, Coupon; international postal reply coupon** = coupon which can be used in another country to pay the postage of replying to a letter **internationaler Antwortschein;** *he enclosed an international reply coupon with his letter ;* **reply paid card** *or* **letter** = card or letter to be sent back to the sender with a reply, the sender having

already paid for the return postage **freigemachte/frankierte Antwortkarte**
2 *verb* to answer **antworten, erwidern;** *to reply to a letter; the company has replied to the takeover bid by offering the shareholders higher dividends*

report
1 *noun*
(a) statement describing what has happened *or* describing a state of affairs **Bericht;** *to draft a report; to make a report or to present a report or to send in a report; the sales manager reads all the reports from the sales team; the chairman has received a report from the insurance company;* **the company's annual report** *or* **the chairman's report** *or* **the directors' report** = document sent each year by the chairman of a company or the directors to the shareholders, explaining what the company has done during the year **Geschäftsbericht; Jahresbericht des Aufsichtsratsvorsitzenden; feasibility report** = document which says if something can be done **Durchführbarkeitsstudie; progress report** = document which describes what progress has been made **Fortschrittsbericht**
(b) a report in a newspaper *or* **a newspaper report** = article *or* news item **Zeitungsbericht, Meldung in der Zeitung;** *can you confirm the report that the company is planning to close the factory?*
(c) official document from a government committee **Untersuchungsbericht;** *the government has issued a report on the credit problems of exporters*
2 *verb*
(a) to make a statement describing something **berichten, melden;** *the salesmen reported an increased demand for the product; he reported the damage to the insurance company; we asked the bank to report on his financial status; he reported seeing the absentee in a shop*
(b) to report to someone = to be responsible to *or* to be under someone **jdm unterstehen;** *he reports direct to the managing director; the salesmen report to the sales director*

> QUOTE a draft report on changes in the international monetary system
> *Wall Street Journal*
>
> QUOTE responsibilities include the production of premium quality business reports
> *Times*
>
> QUOTE the research director will manage a team of business analysts monitoring and reporting on the latest developments in retail distribution
> *Times*
>
> QUOTE the successful candidate will report to the area director for profit responsibility for sales of leading brands
> *Times*

repositioning *noun* changing or adjusting the consumers' idea of a product by a change in its advertising **Neu-, Umpositionierung;** *if this spring's promotional campaign doesn't achieve a repositioning of the product, sales will continue to fall*

> QUOTE it is thought that the company will reposition the range in the mass market or relaunch it
> *Marketing Week*

repossess *verb* to take back an item which someone is buying under a hire-purchase agreement, because the purchaser cannot continue the payments **wieder in Besitz nehmen**

represent *verb* to work for a company, showing goods or services to possible buyers **vertreten;** *he represents an American car firm in Europe; our French distributor represents several other competing firms*
◊ **representation** *noun* act of selling goods for a company **Vertretung;** *we offered them exclusive representation in Europe; they have no representation in the USA*
◊ **representative**
1 *adjective* which is an example of what all others are like **repräsentativ, typisch;** *we displayed a representative selection of our product range; the sample chosen was not representative of the whole batch*
2 *noun*
(a) sales representative = person who works for a company *or* companies, selling goods or services to customers **Reisende(r), Handelsvertreter(in);** *we have six representatives in Europe; they have vacancies for representatives to call on accounts in the north of the country*
(b) company which works for another company, selling their goods **Agent, Repräsentant, Vertretung;** *we have appointed Smith & Co our exclusive representatives in Europe*

resale *noun* selling goods which have been bought **Wieder-, Weiterverkauf;** *to purchase something for resale; the contract forbids resale of the goods to the USA*
◊ **resale price maintenance (RPM)** *noun* system where the price for an item is fixed by the manufacturer and the retailer is not allowed to sell it at a lower price **Preisbindung zweiter Hand, vertikale Preisbindung**

research
1 *noun* trying to find out facts *or* information **Forschung; consumer research** = research into why consumers buy goods

and what goods they may want to buy **Konsumforschung; armchair research** *or* **desk research** = looking for information that has already been compiled **Sekundärforschung; field research** = research to find information which has not been published and has to be found through surveys **Feldforschung; market research** = (i) examining the possible sales of a product and the possible customers for it before it is put on the market; (ii) examining the reasons for the good or bad sales of a product after it has been launched **(i) prospektive Marktforschung; (ii) retrospektive Marktforschung; marketing research** = research carried out in the interests of successful marketing, including market research, media research and product research **Marketingforschung; media research** = study or evaluation of a target audience in order to improve an organization's promotional activities **Mediaforschung; product research** = research carried out to examine various competing products in a market and the potential market for such products **Produktforschung; research and development (R&D)** = scientific investigation which leads to making new products or improving existing products **Forschung und Entwicklung;** *the company spends millions on research and development;* **scientific research** = study to try to find out information **wissenschaftliche Forschung;** *he is engaged in research into the packaging of the new product line; the company is carrying out research into finding a cure for the common cold;* **research department** = section of a company which does research **Forschungsabteilung; research institute** *or* **organization** = place which exists only to carry out research **Forschungsinstitut, Forschungsanstalt; research unit** = separate small group of research workers **Forschungsgruppe; research worker** = person who works in a research department **Angestellte(r) in einer Forschungsanstalt**

2 *verb* to study *or* to try to find out information about something **forschen, Forschung betreiben;** *to research the market for a product*

◇ **researcher** *noun* person who carries out research **Forscher/-in;** *government statistics are a useful source of information for the desk researcher*

> QUOTE drug companies must make a massive investment in research and development if they are to ensure their future, according to a recently published report
>
> *Marketing*

resell

verb to sell something which has been bought **weiter-, wiederverkaufen**

◇ **reseller market** *noun* customers who buy products in order to resell them as wholesalers or retailers **Wiederverkäufermarkt;** *fewer and fewer consumers are buying the product, so prices are falling in the reseller market*

reserve

1 *noun* **reserve price** = lowest price which a seller will accept at an auction **Vorbehaltspreis;** *the painting was withdrawn when it failed to reach its reserve price*

2 *verb* **reserved market** *or* **restricted market** = market in which producers agree not to sell more than a certain amount in order to control competition **beschränkter Markt**

resistance

noun **consumer resistance** *or* **sales resistance** = lack of enthusiasm for a product on the part of consumers **Kaufunlust;**

resources

noun

(a) source of supply of something **Mittel, Ressourcen; natural resources** = supplies of gas, oil, coal, etc., which are available in the ground **Bodenschätze;** *the country is rich in natural resources;* **we are looking for a site with good water resources** = a site with plenty of water available **wir suchen ein Gelände mit guter Wasserversorgung**

(b) financial resources = supply of money for something **finanzielle Mittel;** *the costs of the London office are a drain on the company's financial resources; the company's financial resources are not strong enough to support the cost of the research programme;* **the cost of the new project is easily within our resources** = we have enough money to pay for the new project **die Kosten für das neue Projekt liegen durchaus im Rahmen unserer finanziellen Möglichkeiten**

respond

verb to reply (to a question) **antworten**

◇ **respondent** *noun* person who answers questions in a survey **Befragte(r);** *some of the respondents' answers were influenced by the way the questions were asked*

◇ **response** *noun* way of responding to a question **Antwort; response function** = number which represents the value of a particular quantity of impressions on a person **Reaktionsfunktion; response rate** = proportion of people approached in a survey who agree to answer questions **Rücklaufrate;** *the response rate has been very disappointing*

> QUOTE forecasting consumer response is one problem which will never be finally solved
>
> *Marketing Week*

restock *verb* to order more stock **Lager auffüllen;** *to restock after the Christmas sales*

◇ **restocking** *noun* ordering more stock **Lagerauffüllung**

restraint *noun* control **Be-, Einschränkung; pay restraint** *or* **wage restraint** = keeping increases in wages under control **Politik der Lohnkontrolle; restraint of trade** = (i) situation where a worker is not allowed to use his knowledge in another company if he changes jobs; (ii) attempt by companies to fix prices *or* create monopolies *or* reduce competition, which could affect free trade **(i) Geheimhaltungspflicht; (ii) Wettbewerbs-, Handelsbeschränkung**

restrict *verb* to limit *or* to impose controls on **be-, einschränken;** *to restrict credit; we are restricted to twenty staff by the size of our offices; to restrict the flow of trade or to restrict imports;* **to sell into a restricted market** = to sell goods into a market where the supplier has agreed to limit sales to avoid competition **Waren auf einem beschränkten Markt absetzen**

◇ **restriction** *noun* limit *or* controlling **Be-, Einschränkung;** *import restrictions or restrictions on imports;* **to impose restrictions on imports** *or* **on credit** = to start limiting imports *or* credit **Importbeschränkungen od Kreditrestriktionen einführen; to lift credit restrictions** = to allow credit to be given freely **Kreditrestriktionen aufheben**

◇ **restrictive** *adjective* which limits **einschränkend, restriktiv; restrictive trade practices** = arrangement between companies to fix prices *or* to share the market, etc. **wettbewerbsbeschränkende Geschäftspraktiken**

retail
1 *noun* sale of small quantities of goods to ordinary customers **Einzelhandel; retail audit** = market research method by which a research company regularly checks a sample of retailers for unit sales and stock levels of different brands **Einzelhandelsbestandsaufnahme;** *since subscribing to the retail audit we've been able to compare our performance with that of our competitors;* **retail dealer** = person who sells to the general public **Einzelhändler; retail price** = full price paid by a customer in a shop **Einzelhandels-, Laden-, Endpreis; retail price index** = index showing how prices of retail goods have increased or fallen over a period of time **Index der Einzelhandelspreise; retail shop** *or* **retail outlet** = shop which sells goods to the general public **Einzelhandelsgeschäft; the retail trade** = all people *or* businesses selling goods retail **der Einzelhandel; the goods in stock have a retail value of £1m** = the value of the goods if sold to the public is £1m before discounts, etc. are taken into account **der Wiederverkaufswert der Waren auf Lager beträgt £1 Mio**
2 *adverb* **he sells retail and buys wholesale** = he buys goods in bulk at a wholesale discount and sells in small quantities to the public **er verkauft im Einzelhandel und kauft im Großhandel**
3 *verb*
(a) to retail goods = to sell goods direct to the public **Waren im Einzelhandel verkaufen**
(b) to sell for a price **wiederverkauft werden für; these items retail at** *or* **for 25p** = the retail price of these items is 25p **diese Waren kosten im Einzelhandel 25 Pence**

◇ **retailer** *noun* person who runs a retail business, selling goods direct to the public **Einzelhändler; retailer cooperative** = group of retailers who buy together from suppliers so as to be able to enjoy quantity discounts **Einzelhandelsgenossenschaft**

◇ **retailing** *noun* selling of full price goods to the public **Einzelhandel;** *from car retailing the company branched out into car leasing*

QUOTE provisional figures show retail sales dropped 1.5% in January but wholesale prices released this week reveal a 1% increase last month

Marketing

QUOTE voucher schemes are very attractive from the retailers' point of view

Marketing Week

retire *verb* **to retire a bill** = to pay a bill of exchange when it is due **einen Wechsel einlösen**

retrenchment *noun* reduction of a company's expenditure or expansion plans **Kürzung, Senkung, Abbau, Einschränkung;** *the company is in for a period of retrenchment*

return
1 *noun*
(a) sending back **Rückgabe, Rücksendung; he replied by return of post** = he replied by the next post service **er antwortete postwendend; return address** = address to send something back **Absender; sale or return** = system whereby the retailer sends back goods if they are not sold, and pays the wholesaler only for those goods which have been sold **auf/in Kommission;** *these goods are all on sale or return*
(b) filling in an official form **Erklärung;** *he has completed his VAT return for the quarter*
(c) return on investment (ROI) = amount of sales *or* profit which can be calculated as a

direct result of an expenditure (such as a promotion campaign) **Ertrag aus investiertem Kapital, Kapitalrendite, Investitionsrentabilität;**
2 *verb* to send back **zurückgeben, zurückschicken, zurücksenden;** *to return unsold stock to the wholesaler; to return a letter to sender;* **returned empties** = empty bottles *or* containers which are sent back to a supplier **Leergut**

◇ **returnable** *adjective* which can be returned **Mehrweg-;** *these bottles are non-returnable*

◇ **returns** *plural noun* unsold goods, especially books *or* newspapers *or* magazines sent back to the supplier **Retourwaren, Rücksendungen; Remittenden**

revenue *noun* money received **Einnahmen, Einkünfte, Einkommen;** *revenue from advertising or advertising revenue; oil revenues have risen with the rise in the dollar;* **revenue accounts** = accounts of a business which record money received as sales, commission, etc. **Ertragskonto**

reverse *adjective* opposite *or* in the opposite direction **umgekehrt, entgegengesetzt; reverse takeover** = takeover of a large company by a small company **gegenläufige Fusion; reverse charge call** = telephone call which the person receiving the call agrees to pay for **R-Gespräch**

revoke *verb* to cancel **aufheben, rückgängig machen, annullieren;** *to revoke a clause in an agreement; the quota on luxury items has been revoked*

◇ **revocable** *adjective* **revocable letter of credit** = letter of credit that can be cancelled **widerrufliches Akkreditiv**

risk *noun*
(a) possible harm *or* chance of danger **Risiko; to run a risk** = to be likely to suffer harm **Gefahr laufen; to take a risk** = to do something which may make you lose money or suffer harm **ein Risiko eingehen; financial risk** = possibility of losing money **finanzielles Risiko;** *there is no financial risk in selling to East European countries on credit; he is running the risk of overspending his promotion budget; the company is taking a considerable risk in manufacturing 25m units without doing any market research*
(b) risk analysis = analysis of how much can be lost and gained through various marketing strategies **Risikoanalyse;** *after protracted risk analysis a very ambitious strategy was adopted; our risk analysis must concentrate on competitor activity;* **risk capital** = capital for investment which may easily be lost in risky projects, but which can also provide high returns **Risiko-, Wagniskapital**
(c) carrier's risk = situation where the carrier is responsible for loss or damage to goods being transported **Spediteursrisiko; at owner's risk** = situation where goods shipped *or* stored are insured by the owner, not by the transport company or the storage company **auf Gefahr des Eigentümers;** *goods left here are at owner's risk; the shipment was sent at owner's risk*
(d) loss *or* damage against which you are insured **Risiko, Gefahr, Gefährdung; fire risk** = situation *or* goods which could start a fire **Feuergefahr;**
(e) he is a good *or* **bad risk** = it is not likely *or* it is very likely that the insurance company will have to pay out against claims where he is concerned **bei ihm besteht ein geringes od hohes Schadensrisiko**

◇ **risk-free** *adjective* with no risk involved **risikolos, wenig riskant;** *a risk-free investment*

◇ **risky** *adjective* dangerous *or* which may cause harm **gewagt, riskant;** *he lost all his money in some risky ventures in South America*

> QUOTE there is no risk-free way of taking regular income from your money higher than the rate of inflation and still preserving its value
> *Guardian*

rival *noun* person *or* company which competes in the same market **Konkurrent/-in; Konkurrenz;** *a rival company; to undercut a rival; we are analysing the rival brands on the market;* **rival brands** *or* **rival products** = brands or products that are competing for sales **Konkurrenzmarken; Konkurrenzprodukte**

road *noun*
(a) way used by cars *or* lorries, etc. to move from one place to another **Straße;** *to send or to ship goods by road; road transport costs have risen; the main office is in London Road; use the Park Road entrance to get to the buying department*
(b) on the road = travelling **unterwegs;** *the salesmen are on the road thirty weeks a year; we have twenty salesmen on the road*

ROB = RUN OF BOOK

rock bottom *noun* **rock-bottom prices** = the lowest prices possible **Tiefst-, Niedrigst-, Schleuderpreise; sales have reached rock bottom** = sales have reached the lowest point possible **der Absatz hat einen Tiefpunkt erreicht**

> QUOTE investment companies took the view that secondhand prices had reached rock bottom and that levels could only go up
>
> *Lloyd's List*

rocket *verb* to rise fast **emporschnellen, sprunghaft ansteigen;** *rocketing prices; prices have rocketed*

ROI = RETURN ON INVESTMENT

roll over *verb* **to roll over credit** *or* **a debt** = to make credit available over a continuing period *or* to allow a debt to stand after the repayment date **bei Fälligkeit einen Kredit erneuern/umschulden**

◇ **rolling** *adjective* continuing with no break **rollend, Roll-; rolling launch** = gradual launch of a new product onto the market (by launching it in certain areas over a period) **stufenweise Einführung; rolling plan** = plan which runs for a period of time and is updated regularly during that time **revolvierende Planung**

◇ **roll out** *verb* to extend a company's marketing of a product from its original area to cover a wider one **ausrollen, ausbreiten**

ROP = RUN OF PAPER

rough *noun* outline plan of an illustration for an advertisement **Rohentwurf, Skizze;** *the agency sent the rough to the advertisers for approval; the advertising department will consider the rough carefully before telling the agency to go ahead and run the advertisement*

◇ **rough out** *verb* to make a draft *or* a general design **grob entwerfen;**

ROW = RUN OF WEEK

royalty *noun* money (usually a certain percentage of the sales, or a certain amount per sale) paid to (i) an inventor; (ii) a writer; (iii) the owner of land, for the right to use a property **(i) Lizenz-, Patentgebühr; (ii) Tantiemen, Autorenhonorar; (iii) Nutzungsgebühr;** *he is receiving royalties from his invention*

RPM = RESALE PRICE MAINTENANCE

RRP = RECOMMENDED RETAIL PRICE

run
1 *noun*
(a) making a machine work **Durchlauf, Maschinenlauf; a cheque run** = series of cheques processed through a computer **Verbuchung von Schecks mittels Computer; a computer run** = period of work of a computer **Arbeitsgang/Durchlauf eines Computers; test run** = trial made on a machine **Probelauf**
(b) number of copies of a particular publication which have been printed **Auflage; split run** = printing of the same issue of a publication in several production runs, allowing different advertisements to be placed in different printings **Auflagengabelung, Auflagensplit; run of book (ROB)** *or* **run of paper (ROP)** = advertiser's order to the advertising department of a publication buying advertising space at the basic rate and not specifying the position of the advertisement in the publication **ohne Plazierungsvereinbarung, freie Plazierung; run of week (ROW)** = advertiser's order to the advertising department of a publication buying advertising space at the basic rate and not specifying the issue it will appear in **im Laufe der Woche**
2 *verb*
(a) to be in force **gelten, gültig sein;** *the lease runs for twenty years; the lease has only six months to run*
(b) to amount to **sich belaufen auf, gehen;** *the costs ran into thousands of pounds*
(c) to manage *or* to organize **betreiben, leiten, führen;** *she runs a mail-order business from home; they run a staff sports club; he is running a multimillion-pound company*
(d) to operate a machine **bedienen, betreiben;** *do not run the photocopier for more than four hours at a time; the computer was running invoices all night*

◇ **run down** *verb*
(a) to reduce a quantity gradually **abbauen;** *to run down stocks or to let stocks run down*
(b) to slow down the business activities of a company before it is closed **nach und nach auflösen;** *the company is being run down*

◇ **running** *noun*
(a) running total = total carried from one column of figures to the next **laufende Summe**
(b) running costs *or* **running expenses** *or* **costs of running a business** = money spent on the day-to-day cost of keeping a business going **Betriebskosten, allgemeine Unkosten, Festkosten**

◇ **run-on** *noun* copies of a publication printed in addition to the original print order, as in the case of a leaflet whose setting-up costs have been covered and more copies of which can be printed at a relatively cheap unit cost **zusätzlich zur Auflage gedruckte Bogen**

Ss

sachet *noun* small package or envelope containing a liquid or powder product **Sachet;** *if you are travelling, buy a sachet of shampoo; the magazine came with a free sachet of skin cream attached*

sack *noun* large bag made of strong cloth or plastic **Sack;** *a sack of potatoes; we sell onions by the sack*

safe *adjective* **see-safe** = agreement where a supplier will give credit for unsold goods at the end of a period **Kauf mit Rückgaberecht/auf Kommission; Remission**

sale *noun*
(a) act of selling *or* of giving an item in exchange for money **Verkauf; cash sale** = selling something for cash **Barverkauf; credit card sale** = selling something for credit, using a credit card **Verkauf auf Kreditkarte; forced sale** = selling something because a court orders it *or* because it is the only thing to do to avoid a financial crisis **Zwangsverkauf; sale as seen** = sale with no guarantee of quality **Verkauf ohne Gewähr;** *if the equipment if for sale as seen, we shall have no comeback if it breaks down;* **sale by description** = sale on condition that the goods match the description of them given by the seller **Verkauf nach Beschreibung; sale or return** = system where the retailer sends goods back if they are not sold, and pays the supplier only for goods sold **Verkauf auf Kommission, Kauf mit Rückgaberecht;** *we have taken 4,000 items on sale or return;* **bill of sale** = document which the seller gives to the buyer to show that a sale has taken place **Kaufvertrag; conditions of sale** = agreed ways in which a sale takes place (such as discounts and credit terms) **Verkaufsbedingungen**
(b) for sale = ready to be sold **zu verkaufen; to offer something for sale** *or* **to put something up for sale** = to announce that something is ready to be sold **etwas zum Verkauf anbieten;** *they put the factory up for sale; his shop is for sale; these items are not for sale to the general public*
(c) on sale = being sold in a shop **verkäuflich;** *these items are on sale in most chemists*
(d) sales = money received for selling something *or* number of items sold **Umsatz, Absatz;** *sales have risen over the first quarter;* **sales agent** = person who sells for a business or another person and earns a commission **Kommissionsagent;** *how many sales agents do we have in this area? he's a competent sales agent representing several non-competing companies;* **sales aids** = various tools used for selling, such as samples, display cases and sales literature **Instrumente der Verkaufsförderung, Werbehilfen;** *the sales manager gave a talk on new sales aids which had just become available; an exhibition of sales aids was held at the salesmen's conference;* **sales analysis** = examining the reports of sales to see why items have or have not sold well **Umsatz-, Absatzanalyse; sales appeal** = quality which makes customers want to buy **Kaufanreiz; sales audit** = analysis of a company's sales in terms of such factors as product, revenue and area **Absatzrevision; sales book** = record of sales **Verkaufsbuch, Warenausgangsjournal; book sales** = sales as recorded in the sales book **Absatz laut Verkaufsbuch; sales budget** = plan of probable sales **Absatzplanung; sales call** = visit to a prospective customer in order to make a sale **Verkaufsbesuch;** *how many sales calls does the manager expect us to make each day? he kept reports on all his sales calls;* **sales campaign** = planned work to achieve higher sales **Verkaufsaktion; sales conference** *or* **sales meeting** = meeting of sales managers, representatives, publicity staff, etc. to discuss results and future sales plans **Konferenz zur Absatzplanung; sales contest** = scheme that rewards salesmen with the best results and so encourages effort and initiative **Verkaufswettbewerb; sales contract** = contract between a buyer and a seller, whereby the former agrees to pay money to the latter in return for goods **Kaufvertrag;** *the sales contract was signed after lengthy negotiations over price and delivery; the sales contract commits us to the purchase;* **cost of sales** = all the costs of a product sold, including manufacturing costs and the staff costs of the production department **Absatz-, Vertriebskosten; sales department** = section of a company which deals with selling the company's products or services **Verkaufsabteilung, Abteilung Verkauf; domestic sales** *or* **home sales** = sales in the home market **Inlandsabsatz; sales drive** = vigorous work to increase sales **Verkaufskampagne; sales executive** = person in a company in charge of sales **Verkaufsleiter; sales figures** = total sales, or sales broken down by category **Verkaufs-, Absatzzahlen; sales force** = group of salesmen **Verkäuferstab, Verkaufspersonal; sales forecast** = calculation of future sales **Absatzprognose; forward sales** = sales (of shares, commodities, foreign exchange, etc.) for delivery at a later date **Terminverkäufe; sales interview** = meeting between a salesman and a prospective

customer in which the latter obtains all information about a product necessary for him to be able to make a buying decision **Verkaufsgespräch;** *at the beginning of the sales interview, the salesman established exactly what the prospective customer's needs were;* **sales lead** = information which may lead to a sale **Verkaufshinweis;** *it has been difficult approaching this territory with no sales leads to follow up; I was given some useful sales leads by the salesman who used to operate here;* **sales ledger** = book in which income from sales is recorded **Warenausgangsbuch; sales ledger clerk** = office worker who deals with the sales ledger **für das Warenausgangsbuch zuständige(r) Angestellte(r); sales literature** = printed information (such as leaflets, prospectuses) which helps sales **Werbematerial, Verkaufsprospekte; sales manager** = person in charge of a sales department **Verkaufsleiter; sales mix** = different elements used in selling a company's products **Absatz-Mix;** *what sort of sales mix works best with secondhand cars? sales aids are not part of our sales mix;* **sales pitch** = talk by a salesman to persuade someone to buy **Verkaufsrede, Verkaufspräsentation;** *salesmen can put off a lot of customers with their high-pressure sales pitch;* **sales promotion** = promotional and sales techniques aimed at short-term increases in sales, such as free gifts, competitions, and price discounts **Absatz-, Verkaufsförderung;** *we need some good sales promotion to complement our advertising campaign; let's hope this sales promotion will help us sell off our stock;* **sales quotas** = sales targets given to salesmen which are based on either unit sales or revenue **Absatz-, Verkaufsquoten;** *the sales manager intends to introduce sales quotas, in order to put extra pressure on salesmen;* **monthly sales report** = report made every month showing the number of items *or* amount of money received for selling stock **monatlicher Absatzbericht;** *in the sales reports all the European countries are bracketed together; detailed sales reports help the sales manager work out an effective sales strategy;* **sales representative** = person who works for a company *or* companies, selling products or services to customers **Reisende(r); Handelsvertreter(in); sales resistance** = lack of willingness by the public to buy a product **Kaufunlust; sales response** = degree to which customers buy a product in response to the promotion of it **Verkaufswirkung (der Werbung);** *there was very poor sales response to the advertising campaign; although the product was not spectacular, the sales response was enormous;* **sales revenue** = money received from sales **Verkaufserlös; sales tax** = tax to be paid on each item sold **Warenumsatzsteuer; sales techniques** = methods used by a salesman to persuade customers to buy, such as presentation of goods, demonstrations and closing of sales **Verkaufstechniken; sales volume** *or* **volume of sales** = number of units sold **Absatz-, Umsatzvolumen, Absatz**

(e) selling of goods at specially low prices **Ausverkauf;** *the shop is having a sale to clear old stock; the sale price is 50% of the normal price;* **bargain sale** = sale of all goods in a store at cheap prices **Ausverkauf; clearance sale** = sale of items at low prices to get rid of the stock **Räumungsverkauf; half-price sale** = sale of items at half the usual price **Verkauf zum halben Preis; jumble sale** = sale of old used household goods; *(entspricht)* **Wohltätigkeitsbasar; the sales** = period when major stores sell many items at specially low prices **Schlußverkauf;** *I bought this in the sales or at the sales or in the January sales*

◇ **saleability** *noun* quality of an item which makes it easy to sell **Absatzfähigkeit**

◇ **saleable** *adjective* which can easily be sold **gut verkäuflich, absatzfähig**

◇ **saleroom** *noun* room where an auction takes place **Auktionsraum**

◇ **salesclerk** *noun (US)* person who sells goods to customers in a store **Verkäufer/-in**

◇ **salesgirl** *noun* girl who sells goods to customers in a store **Verkäuferin**

◇ **saleslady** *noun* woman who sells goods to customers in a store **Verkäuferin**

◇ **salesman** *noun*

(a) man who sells goods or services to members of the public **Verkäufer;** *he is the head salesman in the carpet department; a used car salesman ;* **door-to-door salesman** = man who goes from one house to the next, asking people to buy something **Hausierer; Vertreter; insurance salesman** = man who encourages clients to take out insurance policies **Versicherungsvertreter**

(b) person who represents a company *or* companies, selling products or services to retail shops **Reisender;** *we have six salesmen calling on accounts in central London*

◇ **salesmanship** *noun* art of selling *or* of persuading customers to buy **Gewandtheit beim Verkaufen, Verkaufstechnik**

◇ **salesperson** *noun* person who sells goods or services to members of the public **Verkäufer/-in**

◇ **saleswoman** *noun* woman in a shop who sells goods to customers **Verkäuferin**

> QUOTE the novelty in the £1m sales promotion is that the consumer will know immediately if he or she has won a bottle of champagne
> *Marketing Week*
>
> QUOTE many on Wall Street are suspicious of the recent sales and production gains posted by American Industry
> *Management Today*
>
> QUOTE the latest car sales for April show a 1.8 per cent dip from last year's total
> *Investors Chronicle*
>
> QUOTE the wage agreement includes sales clerks and commission sales people in stores in Toronto
> *Toronto Star*

sample

1 *noun*

(a) specimen *or* a small part of an item which is used to show what the whole item is like **Muster, Probe, Warenprobe;** *a sample of the cloth or a cloth sample;* **check sample** = sample to be used to see if a whole consignment is acceptable **Prüfmuster; free sample** = sample given free to advertise a product **Gratisprobe; sample book** *or* **book of samples** = book showing samples of different types of cloth *or* paper, etc. **Musterbuch**

(b) small group taken to show what a larger group is like **Auswahl;** *we interviewed a sample of potential customers;* **random sample** = a sample chosen without any special selection method **Stichprobe;** *see also* MASTER SAMPLE, MATCHED SAMPLE, QUOTA SAMPLE

2 *verb*

(a) to test *or* to try something by taking a small amount **probieren, testen, kosten;** *to sample a product before buying it*

(b) to ask a representative group of people questions to find out what the reactions of a much larger group would be **eine Repräsentativerhebung durchführen;** *they sampled 2,000 people at random to test the new drink*

◊ **sampling** *noun*

(a) testing a product by taking a small amount **Probeentnahme;** *sampling of Common Market produce;* **acceptance sampling** = testing a small sample of a batch to see if the whole batch is good enough to be accepted **Qualitätskontrolle mittels Stichproben**

(b) testing the reactions of a small group of people to find out the reactions of a larger group of consumers **Stichprobenverfahren, Befragung eines repräsentativen Querschnitts; random sampling** = choosing samples for testing without any special selection method **Stichprobenauswahl; sampling error** = difference between the results achieved in a survey using a sample and what the results would be using the entire population or universe **Zufallsfehler; sampling fraction** = proportion of a population or universe that is chosen as a sample **Stichprobenumfang;** *the sampling fraction will have to be small since we cannot afford many interviews with respondents;* **sampling frame** = definition of the population or universe out of which a sample is to be taken **Grundgesamtheit; sampling point** = place where sampling is carried out **Samplepoint;** *the sampling point was just outside the main railway station*

> QUOTE all firms in the sample received the same questionnaire along with a covering letter explaining the objectives of the study
> *International Journal of Advertising*

sandwich boards

sandwich boards *noun* boards with advertisements on them carried in front of and behind a person **Sandwich-Plakate, von Plakatträger getragene Werbetafel**

◊ **sandwich man** *noun* man who carries sandwich boards **Sandwichman, Plakatträger**

satisfaction

satisfaction *noun* feeling of being happy *or* good feeling **Zufriedenheit, Befriedigung, Zufriedenstellung; customer satisfaction** = making a customer pleased with what he has bought **Zufriedenstellung des Kunden; job satisfaction** = a worker's feeling that he is happy in his place of work and pleased with the work he does **Zufriedenheit am Arbeitsplatz**

◊ **satisfy** *verb*

(a) to satisfy a client = to make a client pleased with what he has purchased **einen Kunden zufriedenstellen; a satisfied customer** = a customer who has got what he wanted **ein zufriedener Kunde**

(b) to satisfy a demand = to fill a demand **Nachfrage stillen/befriedigen;** *we cannot produce enough to satisfy the demand for the product*

◊ **satisfying** *noun* making satisfactory profits and maintaining an acceptable market share rather than maximizing profits at all costs **Satisfizierung**

saturation

saturation *noun* filling completely; fourth stage in a product's life-style where sales level off **Sättigung; saturation of the market** *or* **market saturation** = situation where the market has taken as much of the product as it can buy **Marktsättigung; the market has reached saturation point** = the market is at a point where it cannot buy any more of a product **der Markt hat den Sättigungsgrad erreicht; saturation advertising** = highly intensive advertising campaign **Sättigungswerbung;** *saturation advertising is needed when there are large numbers of rival products on the market*

◇ **saturate** *verb* to fill something completely **sättigen;** *to saturate the market; the market for home computers is saturated*

SBU = STRATEGIC BUSINESS UNIT

scale
1 *noun*
(a) system which is graded into various levels **Skala, Tabelle; scale of charges** *or* **scale of prices** = list showing various prices **Preisliste, Gebührenordnung, Tarife; fixed scale of charges** = rate of charging which does not change **verbindliche Gebührenordnung;**
(b) scales = machine for weighing **Waage**
2 *verb* **to scale down** *or* **to scale up** = to lower *or* to increase proportionally **verringern, herabsetzen; erhöhen, heraufsetzen; scaling technique** = use of scales in questionnaires to facilitate interpretation of results **Skalierungsverfahren;** *the scaling technique was so complicated that the respondents did not understand the questions*

scarce *adjective* not easily found *or* not common **rar, selten, knapp;** *scarce raw materials; reliable trained staff are scarce*
◇ **scarceness** *or* **scarcity** *noun* lack *or* being scarce **Knappheit, Seltenheit, Mangel;** *the scarceness of trained staff; there is a scarcity of trained staff;* **scarcity value** = value of something because it is rare and there is a large demand for it **Seltenheitswert**

scattered markets *noun* markets which are spread around a wide area, and therefore can only be reached by a company with an efficient distribution system **verstreute Märkte**

scenario *noun* possible future sequence of events **Szenario, (Szenarium);** *before we decide on any plan let's look at the various scenarios open to us; what scenario do you envisage if our main rival in the market tries to take us over?*

schedule *noun*
(a) list (especially additional documents attached to a contract) **Verzeichnis, Liste, Aufstellung; Anhang;** *please find enclosed our schedule of charges; schedule of territories to which a contract applies; see the attached schedule or as per the attached schedule*
(b) list of things in the order in which they should be done **(Arbeits-, Lehr-, Stunden-, Termin-, Zeit)plan;** *the chairman has a very full schedule of appointments; according to the schedule the campaign should start next month;* **on schedule** = at the time *or* stage set down in the schedule **fahrplanmäßig, pünktlich;** *the launch took place on schedule; the agency is way behind schedule with the promotional material*

science *noun* study *or* knowledge based on observing and testing **Wissenschaft; business science** *or* **management science** = the study of business *or* management techniques **Wirtschaftswissenschaft; Managementlehre;** *he has a master's degree in business science;* **science park** = area near a town or university set aside for technological industries **Technologiezentrum**
◇ **scientific** *adjective* referring to science **(natur)wissenschaftlich; scientific management** = school of management that believes in maximizing production through scientific or technical means **wissenschaftliche Betriebsführung;** *while scientific management has improved our efficiency and profits, it has been at the expense of human considerations*

scope *noun* opportunity *or* possibility **Möglichkeiten; there is scope for improvement in our sales performance** = the sales performance could be improved **unsere Verkaufsleistung könnte verbessert werden;** *there is considerable scope for expansion into the export market*

scrambled merchandising *noun* displaying and selling products which are unrelated to most of the others in the store **gemischtes Merchandising**

screen *verb* to examine something carefully to evaluate or assess it **durchleuchten; to screen candidates** = to examine candidates to see if they are suitable **Bewerber sieben/aussondern**
◇ **screening** *noun*
(a) evaluating *or* estimating new product ideas **Screening;** *representatives from each department concerned will take part in the screening process; screening showed the product idea to be unrealistic for our production capacity*
(b) the screening of candidates = examining candidates to see if they are suitable **das Aussondern geeigneter Bewerber**

sea *noun* area of salt water **Meer, See;** *to send a shipment by sea;* **by sea mail** = sent by post abroad, using a ship, not by air **Postsendung auf dem Seeweg**
◇ **seaport** *noun* port by the sea **Seehafen**

seal
1 *noun*
(a) common seal *or* **company's seal** = metal stamp for stamping documents with the

name of the company to show they have been officially approved **Firmensiegel;** *to attach the company's seal to a document;* **contract under seal** = contract which has been legally approved with the seal of the company **beurkundeter/besiegelter Vertrag**
(b) piece of paper *or* metal *or* wax attached to close something, so that it can be opened only if the paper *or* metal *or* wax is removed or broken **Versiegelung; customs seal** = seal attached by customs office to a box, to show that the contents have not passed through customs **Plombe, Zollverschluß**
2 *verb*
(a) to close something tightly **fest verschließen, zukleben;** *the computer disks were sent in a sealed container;* **sealed envelope** = envelope where the back has been stuck down to close it **verschlossener Briefumschlag;** *the information was sent in a sealed envelope;* **sealed bid price** = price of goods or a service for which suppliers are invited to submit bids which are then considered together by the buyer who then chooses the lowest bidder **Ausschreibungspreis; sealed tenders** = tenders sent in sealed envelopes, which will all be opened at a certain time **versiegelte Submissionsofferten;** *the company has asked for sealed bids for the warehouse*
(b) to attach a seal *or* to stamp something with a seal **versiegeln; plombieren;** *the customs sealed the shipment*

season *noun*

(a) one of four parts which a year is divided into (spring, summer, autumn, winter) **Jahreszeit**
(b) a period of time when something usually takes place **Saison; low season** *or* **high season** = period when there are few travellers *or* lots of travellers **Nachsaison; Haupt-, Hochsaison;** *air fares are cheaper in the low season;* **tourist season** *or* **holiday season** = period when there are many people on holiday **Urlaubszeit; busy season** *or* **slack season** = period when a company is busy *or* not very busy **umsatzstarke/belebte Jahreszeit; umsatzschwache Jahreszeit, Zeit der Flaute; dead season** = time of year when there is a slump in the tourist industry **Nebensaison, tote Jahreszeit; end of season sale** = selling goods cheaply when the season in which they would be used is over (such as summer clothes sold cheaply in the autumn) **Saisonschlußverkauf**

◇ **seasonal** *adjective* which lasts for a season *or* which only happens during a particular season **Saison-, saisonbedingt, jahreszeitlich bedingt;** *the demand for this item is very seasonal; seasonal variations in sales patterns;* **seasonal adjustments** = changes made to figures to take account of seasonal variations **Saisonbereinigungen; seasonal demand** = demand which exists only during the high season **saisonbedingte Nachfrage; seasonal discount** = discount offered by media owners to advertisers at certain times of the year **Saisonrabatt; seasonal unemployment** = unemployment which rises and falls according to the season **saisonbedingte Arbeitslosigkeit**

◇ **seasonally** *adverb* **seasonally adjusted figures** = statistics which are adjusted to take account of seasonal variations **saisonbereinigte Beträge**

second *adjective*

(thing) which comes after the first **zweite(r,s); second generation product** = product which has been developed from another **Produkt der zweiten Generation; second half-year** = six month period from July to the end of December **zweites Halbjahr; second quarter** = three month period from April to the end of June **zweites Quartal**

◇ **secondary** *adjective* second in importance **sekundär, Sekundär-, Neben-, zweitrangig; secondary audience** = people who read a publication after the original purchaser has finished with it **Sekundär-, Folgeleser; secondary banks** = companies which provide money for hire-purchase deals **Teilzahlungsinstitute; secondary data** = data or information which has already been compiled and is therefore found through desk research **Sekundärdaten;** *all this secondary data can be found in our files; we found the secondary data in the embassy library;* **secondary industry** = industry which uses basic raw materials to make manufactured goods **verarbeitende Industrie; secondary meaning** = nickname given to a brand deliberately by the producer or by the consumer **Zweit-, Spitzname**

◇ **second-class** *adjective & adverb* less expensive *or* less comfortable way of travelling **zweite Klasse;** *to travel second-class; the price of a second-class ticket is half that of a first class; I find second-class hotels are just as comfortable as the best ones;* **second-class mail** = (i); *GB* less expensive, slower, mail service; (ii); *US* mail service for sending newspapers and magazines **(i) Postsendungen zweiter Klasse; (ii)** *(entspricht)* **Drucksache;** *a second-class letter is slower than a first-class; send it second-class if it isn't urgent*

◇ **secondhand** *adjective & adverb* used *or* not new *or* which has been owned by someone before **gebraucht, Gebraucht-;** *a secondhand car salesman; the secondhand computer market or the market in secondhand computers; to buy something secondhand; look at the prices of secondhand cars or look at secondhand car* *prices;* **secondhand dealer** = dealer who buys and sells secondhand items **Gebrauchtwarenhändler**

◇ **secondment** *noun* being seconded to another job for a period **(vorübergehende) Versetzung;** *he is on three years' secondment to an Australian college*

◇ **seconds** *plural noun* items which have been turned down by the quality controller as not being top quality **zweite Wahl, B-Sortiment;** *the shop has a sale of seconds*

sector *noun* part of the economy *or* the business organization of a country **Sektor, Bereich;** *all sectors of the economy suffered from the fall in the exchange rate; technology is a booming sector of the economy;* **public sector** = nationalized industries and public services **öffentlicher Bereich, staatlicher Sektor; public sector borrowing requirement** = amount of money which a government has to borrow to pay for its own spending **Kreditbedarf der öffentlichen Hand; private sector** = all companies which are owned by private shareholders, not by the state **Privatsektor;** *the expansion is completely funded by the private sector; salaries in the private sector have increased faster than in the public sector*

> QUOTE government services form a large part of the tertiary or service sector
> *Sydney Morning Herald*
>
> QUOTE in the dry cargo sector, a total of 956 dry cargo vessels are laid up - 3% of world dry cargo tonnage
> *Lloyd's List*

see-safe *noun* agreement where a supplier will give credit for unsold goods at the end of a period **Kauf mit Rückgaberecht/auf Kommission; Remission;** *we bought the stock see-safe*

segment
1 *noun* a section of a market defined by certain criteria **Marktsegment**
2 *verb* to divide a potential market into different segments **segmentieren**

◇ **segmentation** *noun* division of the market or consumers into certain categories according to their buying habits **Marktsegmentierung;** *market segmentation will show us ways of getting more variety into our product line; see also* BEHAVIOURAL, DEMOGRAPHIC, GEOGRAPHICAL, LIFE-STYLE, USAGE, VOLUME

> QUOTE like direct mail, telemarketing has assumed greater importance as consumer markets have become segmented
> *Financial Times*
>
> QUOTE different market segments and, ultimately, individual consumers, must be addressed separately
> *Financial Times*

select
1 *adjective* of top quality *or* specially chosen **exklusiv, auserwählt, auserlesen;** *our customers are very select; a select range of merchandise*
2 *verb* to choose **auswählen, aussuchen; selected items are reduced by 25%** = some items have been reduced by 25% **einige ausgewählte Artikel sind um 25% herabgesetzt**

◇ **selection** *noun* choice; thing which has been chosen **Auswahl;** *a selection of our product line;* **selection board** *or* **selection committee** = committee which chooses a candidate for a job **Auswahlkomitee, Bewerbungsausschuß; selection procedure** = general method of choosing a candidate for a job **Auswahlverfahren**

◇ **selective** *adjective* choosing carefully **selektiv, gezielt; selective demand** = demand for a particular brand **selektive Nachfrage; selective distribution** = use by a producer of a limited number of wholesalers and retailers in a particular area **selektiver Vertrieb;** *this specialized product will need selective distribution; selective distribution may not enable the goods to reach consumers in sufficient quantities;* **selective mailing** = mailing out of promotional material to a selected address list **selektiver Werbeversand; selective perception** = an individual's tendency unconsciously to select what he or she wants from an advertisement **selektive Wahrnehmung;** *we must take selective perception into account when deciding what to stress in the advertising*

self- *prefix* referring to oneself **Selbst-**

◇ **self-completion** *noun* type of questionnaire that can be filled in without an interviewer being present **schriftlicher Fragebogen;** *these self-completion questionnaires can be sent out through the post; self-completion is not a good idea if the respondents don't understand the questions*

◇ **self-image** *noun* idea that a person has about himself or herself **Selbstimage**

◇ **self-liquidating offer** *noun* offer of a free gift, in order to encourage the customer to adopt the brand, made with a product whose sale is intended both to cover the cost of the offer and reduce overall promotional costs for the product **Self-liquidating offer (SLO), Zugabeartikel zum**

Selbstkostenpreis; *even with the self-liquidating offer our sales have not gone up very much*

◇ **self-made man** *noun* man who has become rich and successful through his own efforts, not because he inherited money or position **Selfmademan**

◇ **self-mailer** *noun* promotional material sent through the post, which includes a postage-paid reply section that can be sent back without an envelope and on which customers can make an order **Selfmailer;** *only 10% of the self-mailers we sent out have elicited any response*

◇ **self-reference criterion** *noun* assumption that a product can successfully be sold abroad on the basis of its success in the home market **selbstbezogene Erfolgsannahme, selbstwerbendes Kriterium**

◇ **self-regulation** *noun* control of its own members by a body (such as a trade association or the Stock Exchange) **Selbstverwaltung**

◇ **self-regulatory** *adjective* (group) which regulates itself **selbstverwaltend**

◇ **self-service** *adjective* **a self-service store** = shop where customers take goods from the shelves and pay for them at the checkout **ein Selbstbedienungsgeschäft; self-service petrol station** = petrol station where the customers put the petrol in their cars themselves **Tankstelle mit Selbstbedienung**

sell

1 *noun* act of selling **Verkauf, Verkaufstaktik, Verkaufsstrategie; to give a product the hard sell** = to make great efforts to persuade customers to buy it **ein Produkt aggressiv verkaufen; he tried to give me the hard sell** = he put a lot of effort into trying to persuade me to buy his product **er versuchte auf aggressive Art, mich zum Kauf zu bewegen; soft sell** = persuading people to buy by encouraging and not trying to force them to do so **diskreter/zurückhaltender Verkauf**

2 *verb*

(a) to give goods in exchange for money **verkaufen;** *to sell cars or to sell refrigerators; they have decided to sell their house; they tried to sell their house for £100,000; to sell something on credit; her house is difficult to sell; their products are easy to sell;* **to sell forward** = to sell foreign currency, commodities, etc. for delivery at a later date **auf Termin verkaufen**

(b) to be bought **sich verkaufen, Absatz finden, verkauft werden;** *these items sell well in the pre-Christmas period; those packs sell for £25 a dozen*

◇ **sell-by date** *noun* date on a food packet which is the last date on which the food is guaranteed to be good **Mindesthaltbarkeitsdatum**

◇ **seller** *noun*

(a) person who sells **Verkäufer/-in;** *there were few sellers in the market, so prices remained high;* **seller's market** = market where the seller can ask high prices because there is a large demand for the product **Verkäufermarkt**

(b) thing which sells **gängiger Artikel;** *this book is a steady seller;* **best-seller** = item (especially a book) which sells very well **Bestseller**

◇ **selling**

1 *noun* **direct selling** = selling a product direct to the customer without going through a shop **Direktverkauf; mail-order selling** = selling by taking orders and supplying a product by post **Versandhandel; selling agent** = person who sells for a business or another person and earns a commission **Kommissionär; selling costs** = amount of money to be paid for advertising, reps' commissions, etc., involved in selling something **Vertriebskosten; selling price** = price at which someone is willing to sell **Verkaufspreis**

2 *suffix* **fast-selling items** = items which sell quickly **leichtverkäufliche Artikel, Artikel mit reißendem Absatz, Selbstläufer; best-selling car** = car which sells better than other models **meistverkauftes Automodell**

◇ **sell off** *verb* to sell goods quickly to get rid of them **abstoßen**

◇ **sell out** *verb*

(a) to sell all stock **ausverkaufen;** *to sell out of a product line; we've sold out of electronic typewriters; this item has sold out*

(b) to sell out = to sell one's business **seine Firma verkaufen;** *he sold out and retired to the seaside*

◇ **sellout** *noun* **this item has been a sellout** = all the stock of the item has been sold **dieser Artikel ist ausverkauft**

semantic differential

semantic differential *noun* scaling technique which provides a range of possible answers between two opposite descriptive words **semantisches Differential**

semi-

semi- *prefix* half **halb, Halb-**

◇ **semi-display advertisement** *noun* advertisement that has some of the features of a display advertisement (such as a border and its own typeface or illustrations), but which is printed on the classified advertisement page **rubrizierte Großanzeige**

◇ **semi-finished products** *noun* products which are partly finished **Halbfabrikate**

◇ **semi-solus** *noun* advertisement that shares a page with other advertisements, but is not immediately next to any of them

alleinstehende Anzeige im Anzeigenteil einer Publikation

◇ **semi-structured interview** *noun* interview using some pre-set questions but allowing some questions of the interviewer's choice as well **halbstrukturiertes Interview;** *part of a semi-structured interview consists in respondents describing their first reactions to the advertisement*

◇ **semi-variable costs** *noun* money paid to produce a product which increases, though less than proportionally, with the quantity of the product made **halbvariable Kosten; Sprungkosten;** *stepping up production will mean an increase in semi-variable costs*

semiotics *noun* use of such promotional tools as package design, logos and slogans in marketing **Semiotik**

send away for *verb* to write asking for something to be sent to you **etwas bestellen/anfordern;** *we sent away for the new catalogue*

◇ **sender** *noun* person who sends **Absender; "return to sender"** = words on an envelope *or* parcel to show that it is to be sent back to the person who sent it **zurück an Absender**

◇ **send off for** *verb* to write asking for something to be sent to you **etwas bestellen/anfordern;** *we sent off for the new catalogue*

sensitive *adjective* able to feel something sharply **empfindlich, sensibel;** *the market is very sensitive to the result of the elections;* **price-sensitive product** = product which will sell less if the price is increased **preisempfindliches Produkt**

sequential sampling *noun* carrying on the process of sampling until enough respondents have been interviewed to provide the necessary information **Sequentialanalyse**

serial number *noun* number in a series **Fabrikationsnummer; Seriennummer;** *this batch of shoes has the serial number 25-02*

service

1 *noun*

(a) the work of dealing with customers *or* payment for this work **Bedienung;** *the service in that restaurant is extremely slow; to add on 10% for service;* **the bill includes service** = includes a charge added for the work involved **die Rechnung ist einschließlich Bedienung; service charge** = charge added to the bill in a restaurant to pay for service *or* amount paid by tenants in a block of flats for general cleaning **Bedienung(szuschlag); Reinigungskosten**

(b) keeping a machine in good working order **Wartung;** *the machine has been sent in for service; the routine service of equipment;* **service contract** = contract by which a company keeps a piece of equipment in good working order **Wartungsvertrag; after-sales service** = service of a machine carried out by the seller for the buyer **Kundendienst; service centre** = office *or* workshop which specializes in keeping machines in good working order **Kundendienstvertragswerkstatt; service department** = section of a company which takes responsibility for after-sales service **technischer Kundendienst; service engineer** = engineer who specializes in keeping machines in good working order **Kundendienstmechaniker; service handbook** *or* **service manual** = book which shows how to service a machine **Wartungshandbuch; service station** = garage where you can buy petrol and have small repairs done to a car **Tankstelle mit Reparaturwerkstatt**

(c) business *or* office which gives help when it is needed **Dienst, Service; answering service** = office which answers the telephone and takes messages for a company **Fernsprechauftragsdienst; full-service agency** = advertising agency which offers a broader range of services, such as advice on sales promotion, public relations and market research **Full-Service-Werbeagentur; 24-hour service** = help which is available for the whole day **Tag- und Nachtdienst; service bureau** = office which specializes in helping other offices **Büro-Service; service department** = department of a company which does not deal with production or sales (accounts, personnel, etc.) **allgemeine Kostenstelle; service level** = measurement of how efficient a producer is in distributing goods, such as minimum number of backorders at any one time or delivery frequency to an area **Servicegrad;** *service levels must be improved to fight competition; the product is competitive in itself, but sales are affected by a low service level*

(d) services = benefits which are sold to customers or clients such as transport or education **Dienste, Betriebe;** *we give advice to companies on the marketing of services; we must improve the exports of both goods and services;* **service industry** = industry which does not make products, but offers a service (such as banking, insurance, transport, etc.) **Dienstleistungsbranche**

2 *verb*

(a) to keep a machine in good working order **warten;** *the car needs to be serviced*

every six months; the computer has gone back to the manufacturer for servicing
(b) to pay the interest on a debt **Schuldzinsen bezahlen**

set

1 *noun* group of items which go together *or* which are used together *or* which are sold together **Set, Satz, Sortiment;** *set of tools or set of equipment;* **boxed set** = set of items sold together in a box **in einer Schachtel verpacktes Set**
2 *adjective* fixed *or* which cannot be changed **fest, festgelegt, Fix-;** *set price;* **set menu** = cheaper menu in a restaurant where there are only a few choices **Tagesmenü**
3 *verb* to fix *or* to arrange **festlegen, festsetzen;** *we have to set a price for the new computer; the price of the calculator has been set low, so as to achieve maximum unit sales;* **the auction set a record for high prices** = the prices at the auction were the highest ever reached **bei der Auktion wurden Rekordpreise erzielt**

◊ **set up** *verb*
(a) to begin (something) *or* to organize (something) new **eröffnen, gründen; veranlassen, einsetzen;** *to set up an inquiry or a working party;* **to set up a company** = to start a company legally **eine Firma gründen**
(b) to set up in business = to start a new business **sich niederlassen;** *he set up in business as an insurance broker; he set himself up as a freelance engineer*

◊ **setting up costs** *or* **setup costs** *plural noun* costs of getting a machine *or* a factory ready to make a new product after finishing work on a previous one **Rüstkosten**

settle

settle *verb* **to settle an account** = to pay what is owed **eine Rechnung bezahlen; ein Konto be-, ausgleichen**

◊ **settlement** *noun* payment of an account **Abrechnung, Bezahlung; settlement day** = day when accounts have to be settled **Abrechnungstag, Stichtag; our basic discount is 20% but we offer an extra 5% for rapid settlement** = we take a further 5% off the price if the customer pays quickly **wir geben normalerweise 20% Rabatt, aber wir bieten weitere 5% für prompte Bezahlung; settlement in cash** *or* **cash settlement** = payment of an invoice in cash, not by cheque **Barzahlung**

share

1 *noun* **market share** *or* **share of the market** = percentage of a total market covered by the sales of a company or product **Marktanteil;** *the company hopes to boost its market share; their share of the market has gone up by 10%*
2 *verb* to divide something up among several people **sich teilen, auf-, verteilen;** *three companies share the market; to share computer time; to share the profits among the senior executives;* **to share information** *or* **to share data** = to give someone information which you have **Information/Daten zugänglich machen**

shelf

shelf *noun* flat surface attached to a wall *or* in a cupboard on which items for sale are displayed **Regal;** *the shelves in the supermarket were full in readiness for the Christmas rush;* **shelf filler** = person whose job it is to make sure that the shelves in a shop are kept full of items for sale **Regalauffüller; shelf life of a product** = number of days or weeks when the product will stay on the shelf in the shop and still be good to use **Haltbarkeit/Lagerfähigkeit eines Produktes; shelf space** = amount of space on shelves in a shop **Regalfläche, Regalplatz; shelf talker** *or* **shelf wobbler** = card placed on the shelf in a shop to promote a product **Regalsprecher, Regalschild**

shelving

shelving *noun* rows of shelves *or* space on shelves **Regale;** *we installed metal shelving in the household goods department*

shift

1 *noun* movement *or* change **Änderung, Wandel, Trend, Verlagerung;** *a shift in the company's marketing strategy; the company is taking advantage of a shift in the market towards higher priced goods*
2 *verb* to move *or* to sell **verkaufen;** *(umg)* **loswerden;** *we shifted 20,000 items in one week*

ship

1 *noun* large boat for carrying passengers and cargo on the sea **Schiff; cargo ship** = ship which carries cargo, not passengers **Frachter, Fracht-, Transportschiff; container ship** = ship made specially to carry containers **Containerschiff; ship chandler** = person who supplies goods (such as food) to ships **Schiffsausrüster; to jump ship** = to leave the ship on which you are working and not come back **ohne Erlaubnis abheuern**
2 *verb* to send (goods), but not always on a ship **versenden, befördern, transportieren; verschiffen;** *to ship goods to the USA; we ship all our goods by rail; the consignment of cars was shipped abroad last week;* **to drop ship** = to deliver a large order direct to a customer's shop or warehouse, without going through an agent **direkt liefern**

◊ **ship broker** *noun* person who arranges shipping *or* transport of goods for customers on behalf of ship owners **Schiffsmakler**

◊ **shipment** *noun* goods sent **Sendung, Ladung;** *two shipments were lost in the fire; a shipment of computers was damaged; we make two shipments a week to France;* **bulk shipment** = shipment of a large quantity of goods **Massengütertransport; consolidated shipment** = goods from different companies grouped together into a single shipment **Sammelladung; drop shipment** = delivery of a large order from a manufacturer direct to a customer's shop or warehouse, without going through an agent **Direktlieferung**

◊ **shipper** *noun* person who sends goods *or* who organizes the sending of goods for other customers **Spediteur;** *(Überseefrachtverkehr)* **Ablader**

◊ **shipping** *noun* sending of goods **Versand, Transport; Verschiffung;** *shipping charges or shipping costs;* **shipping agent** = company which specializes in the sending of goods **Spediteur, Speditionsfirma; shipping clerk** = clerk who deals with shipping documents **Expedient; Reedereiangestellte(r); shipping company** *or* **shipping line** = company which owns ships **Reederei; shipping instructions** = details of how goods are to be shipped and delivered **Versandanweisungen; shipping note** = note which gives details of goods being shipped **Frachtbrief, Versandanzeige**

NOTE: that **shipping** does not always mean using a ship

shop

1 *noun*

(a) place where goods are stored and sold **Laden, Geschäft;** (NOTE: US English usually uses **store)** *bookshop; computer shop; electrical goods shop; he has bought a shoe shop in the centre of town; she opened a women's clothes shop; all the shops in the centre of town close on Sundays;* **corner shop** = small privately owned general store **Tante-Emma-Laden; retail shop** = shop where goods are sold only to the public **Einzelhandelsgeschäft; shop assistant** = person who serves customers in a shop **Verkäufer/-in; shop audit** = market research method by which a research company regularly checks a sample of retailers for unit sales and stock levels of different brands **Einzelhandelsbestandsaufnahme;** *since subscribing to the shop audit we have seen how much better we're doing than our competitors;* **shop front** = part of a shop which faces the street, including the entrance and windows **Ladenfront; shop window** = window in a shop where goods are displayed so that customers can see them *or* place where goods or services can be exhibited **Schaufenster;** *the Trade Fair is a shop window for British goods*

(b) advertising agency **Werbeagentur; media shop** = business which offers organizations a media buying service, but without the creative services offered by full agencies **Streuagentur**

(c) place where goods are made *or* workshop **Werkstatt; machine shop** = place where working machines are kept **Maschinensaal; repair shop** = small factory where machines are repaired **Reparaturwerkstatt; on the shop floor** = in the factory *or* in the works *or* among the ordinary workers **im Betrieb;** *the feeling on the shop floor is that the manager doesn't know his job*

2 *verb* **to shop (for)** = to look for things in shops **einkaufen**

◊ **shop around** *verb* to go to various shops or offices and compare prices before making a purchase *or* before placing an order **sich umsehen;** *you should shop around before getting your car serviced; he's shopping around for a new computer; it pays to shop around when you are planning to get a mortgage*

◊ **shopkeeper** *noun* person who owns or runs a shop **Laden-, Geschäftsinhaber**

◊ **shoplifter** *noun* person who steals goods from shops **Ladendieb**

◊ **shoplifting** *noun* stealing goods from shops **Ladendiebstahl**

◊ **shopper** *noun* person who buys goods in a shop **Käufer/-in;** *the store stays open to midnight to cater for late-night shoppers;* **shoppers' charter** = law which protects the rights of shoppers against shopkeepers who are not honest **Verbraucherschutzgesetz**

◊ **shopping** *noun*

(a) buying goods in a shop; goods bought in a shop **Einkaufen; Einkäufe;** *he goes shopping on Saturday mornings; they do all their shopping in the local supermarket*

(b) shopping basket = basket for carrying shopping **Einkaufskorb;** *(US)* **shopping cart** = trolley *or* small metal cart used by customers in a supermarket to carry their purchases **Einkaufswagen; shopping centre** = group of shops linked together with car parks and restaurants **Einkaufszentrum; shopping goods** = high-priced goods whose purchase has to be considered carefully by customers, who compare the merits of competing brands **Shopping Goods (Güter des gehobenen Bedarfs);** *(US)* **shopping mall** = enclosed covered area for shopping, with shops, restaurants, banks and other facilities **Einkaufspassage, Mall; shopping precinct** = part of town which is usually closed to traffic so that people can walk about and shop **(verkehrsfreies) Einkaufsviertel; window shopping** = looking at goods in shop windows, without buying anything **Schaufensterbummel; shopping**

around = looking at prices in various shops before buying what you want **preisbewußter Einkauf**

◇ **shop-soiled** *adjective* dirty because of having been on display in a shop **angeschmutzt**

◇ **shopwalker** *noun* employee of a department store who advises the customers and supervises the shop assistants in a department **Abteilungsleiter**

short *adjective*
(a) for a small period of time **kurz, Kurz-; short credit** = terms which allow the customer only a little time to pay **kurzfristiger Kredit; in the short term** = in the near future *or* quite soon **in kurzer Zeit, in Kürze, kurzfristig**
(b) not as much as should be **zu wenig;** *the shipment was three items short;* **when we cashed up we were £10 short** = we had £10 less than we should have had **als wir Kasse machten, fehlten £10; to give short weight** = to sell something which is lighter than it should be **etwas zu knapp abwiegen**
(c) short of = having less than needed *or* with not enough of **knapp an;** *we are short of staff or short of money; the company is short of new ideas*
(d) to sell short = to agree to sell something (such as shares) which you do not possess, but which you think you will be able to buy for less than the selling price you have agreed **leerverkaufen; short selling** *or* **selling short** = arranging to sell something in the future which you think you can buy for less than the agreed selling price **Fixgeschäft, Leerverkauf; to borrow short** = to borrow for a short period **kurzfristig aufnehmen**

◇ **shortage** *noun* lack *or* not having enough **Mangel, Verknappung, Engpaß;** *a chronic shortage of skilled staff; we employ part-timers to make up for staff shortages; the import controls have resulted in the shortage of spare parts;* **manpower shortage** *or* **shortage of manpower** = lack of workers **Arbeitskräftemangel; there is no shortage of investment advice** = there are plenty of people who want to give advice on investments **es herrscht kein Mangel an Kapitalanlageberatern/Tips zur Kapitalanlage**

◇ **short-change** *verb* to give a customer less change than is right, hoping that he or she will not notice **zu wenig herausgeben**

◇ **short-dated** *adjective* **short-dated bills** = bills which are payable within a few days **kurzfristige Wechsel; short-dated securities** = government stocks which mature in less than five years time **Papiere mit kurzer/bis zu fünfjähriger Laufzeit**

◇ **shorthanded** *adjective* without enough staff **unterbesetzt, knapp an Personal;** *we're rather shorthanded at the moment*

◇ **short-range** *adjective* **short-range forecast** = forecast which covers a period of a few months **kurzfristige Prognose**

◇ **short-staffed** *adjective* with not enough staff **unterbesetzt, knapp an Personal;** *we're rather short-staffed at the moment*

◇ **short-term** *adjective* for a short period **kurzfristig;** *to place money on short-term deposit; short-term contract;* **on a short-term basis** = for a short period **kurzfristig, auf kurze Sicht; short-term debts** = debts which have to be repaid within a few weeks **kurzfristige Schulden; short-term forecast** = forecast which covers a period of a few months **kurzfristige Prognose; short-term gains** = gains made over a short period (less than 12 months) **rasch zu erzielende Gewinne; short-term loan** = loan which has to be repaid within a few weeks **kurzfristiger Kredit; short-term planning** = planning for the immediate future **kurzfristige Planung**

shot *noun* **mail shot** *or* **mailing shot** = leaflets sent by post to possible customers **Briefwerbeaktion, Rundschreiben**

shout *noun* bold statement promoting a book, either printed on the cover or on posters and leaflets **kurzer Werbeslogan;** *the author disliked the shout on the cover suggested by the publisher's promotional manager*

show *noun* exhibition *or* display of goods or services for sale **Ausstellung, Messe;** *motor show; computer show;* **show house** *or* **show flat** = house *or* flat built and furnished so that possible buyers can see what similar houses could be like **Musterhaus; Musterwohnung**

◇ **showcard** *noun* piece of cardboard with advertising material, put near an item for sale **Schaufensterschild, Schaufensterplakat**

◇ **showcase** *noun* cupboard with a glass front or top to display items **Schaukasten, Vitrine**

◇ **showroom** *noun* room where goods are displayed for sale **Ausstellungsraum;** *car showroom*

shrink *verb* to get smaller **schrumpfen, zurückgehen;** *the market has shrunk by 20%; the company is having difficulty selling into a shrinking market*

◇ **shrinkage** *noun*
(a) amount by which something gets smaller **Schwund, Einbußen, Minderung;** *to allow for shrinkage*
(b) *(informal)* losses of stock through theft (especially by the shop's own staff) **Ladendiebstahl**

◇ **shrink-wrapped** *adjective* covered in tight plastic protective cover **eingeschweißt**
◇ **shrink-wrapping** *noun* act of covering (a book, fruit, a record, etc.) in a tight plastic cover **Schrumpfpackung**

SIC = STANDARD INDUSTRIAL CLASSIFICATION

sideline *noun* business which is extra to your normal work **Nebenbeschäftigung;** *he runs a profitable sideline selling postcards to tourists*

sight *noun* seeing **Sicht, Anblick; bill payable at sight =** bill which must be paid when it is presented **Wechsel zahlbar bei Sicht; sight bill** *or* **sight draft =** bill of exchange which is payable at sight **Sichtwechsel, Sichttratte; to buy something sight unseen =** to buy something without having inspected it **etwas unbesehen kaufen**

sign *noun* advertising board *or* notice which advertises something **Schild, Ladenschild;** *they've asked for planning permission to put up a large red shop sign; advertising signs cover most of the buildings in the centre of the town*

single column centimetre *noun* unit of measurement for newspaper and magazine advertisements, representing one column which is one centimetre in depth **Zeilenzentimeter**
◇ **single sourcing** *noun* obtaining all of a company's supplies from one source or supplier **Single-Sourcing;** *the buying department believes that single sourcing will lead to higher raw material costs; single sourcing has simplified our purchasing plans*

situation *noun* state of affairs **Lage, Situation;** *financial situation of a company; the general situation of the economy;* **situation analysis** *or* **situation audit =** stage in marketing planning concerned with investigating the organization's strengths and weaknesses **unternehmungsinterne Analyse;** *in the situation analysis particular attention was paid to existing production capacity; it is clear from the situation analysis that distribution is our biggest problem*

skimming *noun* fixing a high price on a product in order to achieve high short-term profits (the high price reflects the customer's appreciation of the added value of the new product, and will be reduced in due course as the product becomes established on the market) **Skimming(-Politik);** *we are skimming the market with a product that will soon be obsolete*

skip scheduling *noun* arranging for an advertisement to appear in every other issue of a publication **Anzeigenplazierung in jeder zweiten Auflage**

slash *verb* to cut *or* to reduce sharply **radikal herabsetzen, stark reduzieren;** *to slash prices or credit terms; prices have been slashed in all departments; the bank has been forced to slash interest rates*

sleeper *noun* product which does not sell well for some time, then suddenly becomes very popular **Spätzünder**

slogan *noun* **publicity slogan =** catch phrase (words which can be easily remembered) which is used in publicity for a product **Slogan, Werbespruch;** *we are using the slogan "Smiths can make it" on all our publicity*

slot *noun* period of time available for a TV or radio commercial **Werbesendezeit;** *the company took six 60-second slots at peak viewing time;* **slot machine =** machine which provides drinks *or* cigarettes, plays music, etc. when a coin is put in it **Automat**

slump
1 *noun*
(a) rapid fall **Sturz, Fall, plötzlicher Rückgang; Baisse;** *slump in sales; slump in profits; slump in the value of the pound; the pound's slump on the foreign exchange markets*
(b) period of economic collapse with high unemployment and loss of trade **Depression, starker Konjunkturrückgang;** *we are experiencing slump conditions;* **the Slump =** the world economic crisis of 1929-33 **die Weltwirtschaftskrise**
2 *verb* to fall fast **stürzen, plötzlich fallen;** *profits have slumped; the pound slumped on the foreign exchange markets*

smuggle *verb* to take goods into a country without declaring them to the customs **schmuggeln;** *they had to smuggle the spare parts into the country*
◇ **smuggler** *noun* person who smuggles **Schmuggler/-in**
◇ **smuggling** *noun* taking goods illegally into a country **Schmuggel;** *he made his money in arms smuggling*

snap up *verb* to buy something quickly **aufkaufen, wegschnappen;** *to snap up a* *bargain; he snapped up 15% of the company's shares*

snip *noun (informal)* bargain **Schnäppchen;** *these typewriters are a snip at £50*

social *adjective* referring to society in general **Sozial-, gesellschaftlich; social audit** = analysis of the social consequences of a particular marketing strategy **Überprüfung der Sozialfolgen;** *the social audit focussed on the effects of pollution in the area; the social audit showed that the factory could provide jobs for five per cent of the unemployed in the small town nearby;* **social cost** = negative effect of a type of production on society **negative Einwirkung auf das Sozialwesen; social costs** = ways in which something will affect people **gesellschaftliche Kosten;** *the report examines the social costs of building the factory in the middle of the town; the industry's representative denied that any social cost was involved in the new development;* **social marketing** = marketing with the purpose of contributing to society rather than just making a profit **Sozio-Marketing; social security** = money from contributions paid to the National Insurance provided by the government to people who need it **Sozialunterstützung;** *he gets weekly social security payments;* **the social system** = the way society is organized **Gesellschaftsordnung**

◊ **societal** *adjective* referring to society **gesellschaftlich, Gesellschafts-; societal marketing** = social marketing *or* marketing with the purpose of contributing to society rather than just making a profit **Sozio-Marketing**

◊ **society** *noun*
(a) way in which the people in a country are organized **Gesellschaft; consumer society** = type of society in which consumers are encouraged to buy goods **Konsumgesellschaft; affluent society** = type of society in which most people are quite rich **Wohlstandsgesellschaft**
(b) club *or* group of people with the same interests **Verein, Gesellschaft;** *he has joined a computer society;* **building society** = financial institution which accepts and pays interest on deposits, and lends money to people who are buying property **Bausparkasse; cooperative society** = organization where customers and workers are partners and share the profits **Genossenschaft; friendly society** = group of people who pay regular subscriptions to a fund which is used to help members who are ill or in financial trouble **Versicherungsverein auf Gegenseitigkeit**

◊ **socio-economic** *adjective* referring to social and economic conditions, social classes and income groups **sozio-ökonomisch, sozialökonomisch;** *we have commissioned a thorough socio-economic analysis of our potential market;* **socio-economic groups** = groups in society divided according to income and position **sozialökonomische Gruppierungen**

soft *adjective* not hard **weich; soft currency** = currency of a country with a weak economy, which is cheap to buy and difficult to exchange for other currencies **weiche Währung; soft sell** = persuading people to buy by encouragement and suggestion, rather than by applying strong sales pressure **diskreter/zurückhaltender Verkauf**

◊ **software** *noun* computer programs (as opposed to machines) **Software**

sole *adjective* only **Allein-, alleinig; sole agency** = agreement to be the only person to represent a company *or* to sell a product in a certain area **Alleinvertretung; Alleinvertrieb;** *he has the sole agency for Ford cars;* **sole agent** = person who has the sole agency for a product in an area **Alleinvertreter; sole distributor** = retailer who is the only one in an area who is allowed to sell a certain product **Alleinvertrieb; sole owner** = person who owns a business on his or her own, with no partners **Alleineigentümer; sole trader** = person who runs a business by himself or herself but has not registered it as a company **Einzelkaufmann**

solicit *verb* **to solicit orders** = to ask for orders *or* to try to get people to order goods **sich um Aufträge bemühen**

solus (advertisement) *noun* advertisement which does not appear near other advertisements for similar products **alleinstehende Anzeige, Inselanzeige; semi-solus** = advertisement that shares a page with other advertisements, but is not immediately next to any of them **Inzelanzeige im Anzeigenteil einer Publikation**

source *noun* place where something comes from **Quelle, Ursprung;** *source of income; you must declare income from all sources to the tax office;* **income which is taxed at source** = where the tax is removed before the income is paid **Einkommen mit Quellenbesteuerung; source credibility** = image people have of a persuader which will determine his or her credibility **Kommunikatorglaubwürdigkeit**

◊ **sourcing** *noun* **single sourcing** = obtaining all of a company's supplies from one source or supplier **Single-Sourcing;** *the buying department believes that single sourcing will lead to higher raw material costs; single sourcing has simplified our purchasing plans*

space *noun* empty place *or* empty area **Platz, Raum; advertising space** = space in a newspaper set aside for advertisements **Anzeigenraum; to take advertising space in a newspaper** = to place a large advertisement in a newspaper **Anzeigenraum in einer Zeitung belegen**

spatial segmentation *noun* segmentation or division of a market according to areas or regions **geographische Marktsegmentierung**

spec *noun* **to buy something on spec** = to buy something as a speculation, without being sure of its value **etwas auf gut Glück kaufen**

◊ **specs** *plural noun* = SPECIFICATIONS

special *adjective* different *or* not normal *or* referring to one particular thing **besonder, speziell, Sonder-;** *he offered us special terms; the car is being offered at a special price;* **special position** = especially good place in a publication for advertising **Vorzugsplatz;** *if we are prepared to invest the money we could choose a special position for the advertisement*

◊ **specialist** *noun* person *or* company which deals with one particular type of product or one subject **Fachmann, Experte/Expertin, Spezialist/-in; Fachhandel;** *you should go to a specialist in computers or to a computer specialist for advice*

◊ **speciality** *or* **specialty** *noun* particular interest *or* special type of product which a company deals in **Spezialität, Spezialgebiet, Fachgebiet;** *their speciality is computer programs; we only deal in specialty goods; these specialty goods require expert personal selling; there's a high profit margin on specialty goods;* **specialty store** = shop selling a limited range of items of good quality **Spezialgeschäft**

◊ **specialization** *noun* study of one particular thing *or* dealing with one particular type of product **Spezialisierung;** *the company's area of specialization is accounts packages for small businesses*

◊ **specialize** *verb* to trade in one particular type of product or service **(sich) spezialisieren;** *the company specializes in electronic components; they have a specialized product line; he sells very specialized equipment for the electronics industry*

> QUOTE the group specializes in the sale, lease and rental of new and second-user hardware
> *Financial Times*
>
> QUOTE airlines offer special stopover rates and hotel packages to attract customers to certain routes
> *Business Traveller*

specify *verb* to state clearly what is needed **angeben, einzeln aufführen, spezifizieren;** *to specify full details of the goods ordered; do not include VAT on the invoice unless specified*

◊ **specification** *noun* detailed information about what is needed *or* about a product to be supplied **Beschreibung, Spezifikation;** *to detail the specifications of a computer system;* **job specification** = very detailed description of what is involved in a job **Stellen-, Arbeitsplatzbeschreibung; to work to standard specifications** = to work to specifications which are acceptable anywhere in the industry **nach Norm arbeiten; the work is not up to specification** *or* **does not meet our specifications** = the product is not made in the way which was detailed **die Arbeit wurde nicht den Spezifikationen nach ausgeführt**

specimen *noun* thing which is given as a sample **Muster, Probe, Probeexemplar; to give specimen signatures on a bank mandate** = to write the signatures of all the people who can sign cheques for an account so that the bank can recognize them **auf einer Kontovollmacht Unterschriftproben geben**

spend *verb*

(a) to pay money **ausgeben;** *they spent all their savings on buying the shop; the company spends thousands of pounds on research*

(b) to use time **verbringen;** *the company spends hundreds of man-hours in meetings; the chairman spent yesterday afternoon with the auditors*

◊ **spending** *noun* paying money **Ausgaben;** *cash spending or credit card spending;* **consumer spending** = spending by consumers **Ausgaben der Privathaushalte; spending money** = money for ordinary personal expenses **Taschengeld; spending power** = having money to spend on goods; amount of goods which can be bought for a certain sum of money **Kaufkraft;** *the spending power of the pound has fallen over the last ten years; the spending power of the student market*

sphere *noun* area **Bereich, Gebiet;** *sphere of activity; sphere of influence*

spinner *noun* revolving stand on which goods are displayed in a shop **drehbarer Warenständer;** *there was a spinner with different types of confectionery at each checkout*

spinoff *noun* useful product developed as a secondary product from a main item **Nebenprodukt;** *one of the spinoffs of the research programme has been the development of the electric car*

split run *noun* printing of the same issue of a publication in several production runs, so that different advertisements may be placed in different printings, allowing the effect of the different advertising to be compared **Auflagengabelung, Auflagensplit**

sponsor
1 *noun*
(a) person who pays money to help research *or* to pay for a business venture; company which pays to help a sport *or* exhibition *or* concert, etc., in return for advertising rights **Sponsor**
(b) company which pays for the making of a TV programme by taking advertising time on the programme **Fernsehwerbungtreibender, Sponsor**
2 *verb* to pay money to help research *or* business development **als Sponsor finanzieren, sponsoren;** *to sponsor a television programme; the company has sponsored the football match; government-sponsored trade exhibition*

◇ **sponsorship** *noun* act of sponsoring **finanzielle Förderung, Sponsoring;** *government sponsorship of overseas selling missions*

spot *noun*
(a) spot cash = cash paid for something bought immediately **sofortige Bezahlung, Sofortliquidität; the spot market in oil** = the market for buying oil for immediate delivery **der Kassamarkt für Öl; spot price** *or* **spot rate** = price *or* rate for something which is delivered immediately **Lokopreis**
(b) place **Ort, Platz, Stelle; to be on the spot** = to be at a certain place **an Ort und Stelle sein;** *we have a man on the spot to deal with any problems which occur on the building site*
(c) TV spot = period on TV which is used for commercials **Fernsehspot, Werbesendezeit;** *we are running a series of TV spots over the next three weeks*

> QUOTE with most of the world's oil now traded on spot markets, Opec's official prices are much less significant than they once were
> *Economist*

spread *noun* two facing pages in a magazine or newspaper used by an advertiser for a single advertisement running across the two pages **Doppelseite; doppelseitige Anzeige; centre spread** = two facing pages in the centre of a publication, which are used by an advertiser for one advertisement **Doppelseite/doppelseitige Anzeige in der Heftmitte**

stability *noun* being steady *or* not moving up or down **Stabilität, Beständigkeit;** *price stability; a period of economic stability; the stability of the currency markets*

◇ **stabilization** *noun* making stable *or* preventing sudden changes in prices, etc. **Stabilisierung, Festigung; stabilization of the economy** = keeping the economy stable by preventing inflation from rising, cutting high interest rates and excess money supply **Stabilisierung der Wirtschaft**

◇ **stabilize** *verb* to make steady **(sich) stabilisieren, festigen; prices have stabilized** = prices have stopped moving up or down **die Preise haben sich stabilisiert; to have a stabilizing effect on the economy** = to make the economy more stable **eine stabilisierende Wirkung auf die Wirtschaft haben**

◇ **stable** *adjective* steady *or* not moving up or down **stabil, beständig, gleichbleibend;** *stable prices; stable exchange rate; stable currency; stable economy;* **stable market** = market where sales do not change much in response to changes in price (and where demand is therefore inelastic) **stabiler Markt**

stagflation *noun* inflation and stagnation of an economy **Stagflation, realer Stillstand bei steigenden Preisen**

stagnation *noun* not increasing *or* not making any progress **Stagnation, Stillstand;** *the country entered a period of stagnation;* **economic stagnation** = lack of expansion in the economy **Wirtschaftsstagnation**

stake
1 *noun* money invested **Beteiligung, Einlage; to have a stake in a business** = to have money invested in a business **einen Anteil an einem Unternehmen haben; to acquire a stake in a business** = to buy shares in a business **einen Anteil an einem Unternehmen erwerben;** *he acquired a 25% stake in the business*
2 *verb* **to stake money on something** = to risk money on something **Geld setzen auf**

◇ **stakeholder theory** *noun* theory that a business organization should base its policies on the interests of elements outside it such as suppliers, consumers, and the general public, as well as on its own profit-making objectives **Stakeholder-Theorie, profitunabhängige Kriterien**

> QUOTE other investments include a large stake in a Chicago-based insurance company, as well as interests in tobacco products and hotels
> *Lloyd's List*

stamp trading *noun* giving out stamps or vouchers to customers according to the value of their purchases, the stamps being exchangeable for more goods or for cash **Rabattmarkenverteilung;** *compare* TRADING STAMP

stand *noun* arrangement of shelves *or* tables, etc. at an exhibition for showing a company's products **Stand; display stand** = special stand for displaying goods for sale **Auslagenstand, Vollsichtregal; exhibition stand** = separate section of an exhibition where a company exhibits its products or services **Messestand; news stand** = small wooden shop on a pavement, for selling newspapers **Zeitungsstand**

standard
1 *noun* normal quality *or* normal conditions which other things are judged against **Norm, Standard, Niveau; standard of living** *or* **living standards** = a person's material well-being and quality of home life **Lebensstandard; production standards** = quality of production **Produktionsstandard; up to standard** = of acceptable quality **den Anforderungen genügend;** *this batch is not up to standard or does not meet our standards;* **gold standard** = linking of the value of a currency to value of a quantity of gold **Goldwährung**
2 *adjective* normal *or* usual **Standard-, üblich, handelsüblich, normal;** *a standard model car; we have a standard charge of £25 for a thirty-minute session;* **standard agreement** *or* **standard contract** = normal printed contract form **Mustervertrag; standard costs** = planned costs for the period ahead **Normalkosten; standard costing** = planning costs for the period ahead and, at the end of the period, comparing these figures with actual costs in order to make necessary adjustments in planning **Normalkostenrechnung; standard deviation** = way in which the results of a sample deviate from the mean or average **Standardabweichung; standard error** = extent to which chance affects the accuracy of a sample **Standardfehler; Standard Industrial Classification (SIC)** = the official listing and coding of industries and products (in the USA) **Standard Klassifikation der Industrie; standard letter** = letter which is sent without any change to various correspondents **Standard-, Formbrief; standard rate** = basic rate of income tax which is paid by most taxpayers **Standardsteuersatz**

◇ **standardization** *noun* making sure that everything fits a standard *or* is produced in the same way **Normung, Standardisierung, Typung;** *standardization of design; standardization of measurements;* **standardization of products** = reducing a large number of different products to a series which have the same measurements *or* design *or* packaging, etc. **Produkttypung**

◇ **standardize** *verb* to make sure that everything fits a standard *or* is produced in the same way **normen, standardisieren, vereinheitlichen**

◇ **Standard Rate & Data Service (SRDS)** American publication listing advertising rates, circulation and other details of major American magazines, newspapers and other advertising media **amerikanische Werbeinformationszeitschrift**

NOTE: the comparable British publication is **British Rate and Data (BRAD)**

standing
1 *adjective* **standing order** = order written by a customer asking a bank to pay money regularly into an account **Dauerauftrag;** *I pay my subscription by standing order*
2 *noun*
(a) long-standing customer *or* **customer of long standing** = person who has been a customer for many years **ein treuer/langjähriger Kunde**
(b) good reputation **Ansehen, Ruf; Bonität;** *the financial standing of a company;* **company of good standing** = very reputable company **eine angesehene Firma**

stand out test *noun* test designed to assess how well a package stands out or catches the eye on a shelf **Augenfälligkeitstest;** *stand out tests were carried out to evaluate how effective the colour of the new product packaging was*

staple *adjective* **staple commodity** = basic food or raw material **Haupterzeugnis; staple industry** = main industry in a country **Hauptindustriezweig; staple product** = basic product **Hauptprodukt**

star *noun* in the Boston matrix, product which has a high market share and a high growth rate; it will need cash to finance its growth, but eventually should become a cash cow **Star;** *we have only one star product but it's put our company on the map; they're hoping that at least two of their new product range will turn out to be stars*

starch ratings *noun (US)* method of assessing the effectiveness of an organization's advertising **Starch-Bewertungen**

start *noun* beginning **Beginn, Anfang, Start; cold start =** starting up a new company where there was none before **ein völliger Neubeginn**

◇ **start-up** *noun* beginning of a new company *or* new product **Neugründung; Anlauf;** *start-up costs*

state-of-the-art *adjective* as technically advanced as possible **technisch auf dem neuesten Stand**

statement *noun* **statement of account =** list of invoices and credits and debits sent by a supplier to a customer at the end of each month **Abrechnung**

static market *noun* a market which does not increase or decrease significantly over a period of time **statischer Markt;** *technology is changing so fast that we can't rely on the market remaining static*

statistics *plural noun* study of facts in the form of figures **Statistik; Statistiken, statistische Unterlagen;** *to examine the sales statistics for the previous six months; government trade statistics show an increase in imports*

◇ **statistical** *adjective* based on figures **statistisch;** *statistical analysis; statistical information;* **statistical discrepancy =** amount by which sets of figures differ **statistische Abweichung; statistical error =** difference between results achieved in a survey using a sample and what results would be using the entire population or universe **statistischer Fehler**

steady demand *noun* demand for a product which continues in a regular way **gleichbleibende Nachfrage**

sterling *noun* standard currency used in the United Kingdom **Sterling;** *to quote prices in sterling or to quote sterling prices;* **pound sterling =** official term for the British currency **Pfund Sterling; sterling area =** area of the world where the pound sterling is the main trading currency **Sterlingzone; sterling balances =** a country's trade balances expressed in pounds sterling **Außenhandelsbilanz in Pfund Sterling; sterling crisis =** fall in the exchange rate of the pound sterling **Sterlingkrise**

> QUOTE it is doubtful that British goods will price themselves back into world markets as long as sterling labour costs continue to rise faster than in competitor countries
> *Sunday Times*

sticker
1 *noun* small piece of gummed paper or plastic to be stuck on something as an advertisement *or* to indicate a price **Aufkleber, Etikett**
2 *verb* to put a price sticker on an article for sale **auszeichnen, mit Preisschildern versehen;** *we had to sticker all the stock;* **to re-sticker stock =** to put new stickers on stock (as when increasing the price) **Waren neu auszeichnen**

stock
1 *noun*
(a) supply of raw materials **Vorrat;** *we have large stocks of oil or coal; the country's stocks of butter or sugar*
(b) quantity of goods for sale **Lager-, Warenbestand; opening stock =** details of stock at the beginning of an accounting period **Eröffnungsbestand; closing stock =** details of stock at the end of an accounting period **Schlußbestand; stock code =** number and letters which indicate an item of stock **Warencode; stock control =** making sure that enough stock is kept and that quantities and movements of stock are noted **Lagersteuerung; stock depreciation =** reduction in the value of stock which is held in a warehouse for some time **Lagerbestandsabschreibung; stock figures =** details of how many goods are in the warehouse *or* store, etc. **Lagerbestandsverzeichnis; stock level =** quantity of goods kept in stock **Lagerbestandshöhe;** *we try to keep stock levels low during the summer;* **stock turn** *or* **stock turnround** *or* **stock turnover =** total value of stock sold in a year divided by the average value of goods in stock **Lagerumschlag; stock valuation =** estimating the value of stock at the end of an accounting period **Bewertung des Lagerbestandes; to buy a shop with stock at valuation =** to pay the same amount for the stock as its value as estimated by the valuer **ein Geschäft inklusive des Warenbestandes zum Schätzpreis kaufen; stock in hand =** stock held in a shop *or* warehouse **Waren auf Lager; to purchase stock at valuation =** to pay the price fixed by a valuer for stock **den Warenbestand zum Schätzpreis kaufen**
(c) **in stock** *or* **out of stock =** available *or* not available in the warehouse *or* store **vorrätig sein; nicht vorrätig/ausverkauft sein;** *to hold 2,000 lines in stock; the item went out of stock just before Christmas but came back into stock in the first week of January; we're*

out of stock of this item or this item is out of stock; **to take stock** = to count the items in a warehouse **Inventur machen**
2 *adjective* normal *or* usually kept in stock **Standard-; Lager-;** *butter is a stock item for any good grocer;* **stock size** = normal size **gängige Größe;** *we only carry stock sizes of shoes*
3 *verb* to hold goods for sale in a warehouse *or* store **führen, auf Lager halten;** *to stock 200 lines;* **stocking agent** = wholesaler who sells for a producer and earns a commission **Kommissionär**

◇ **stock controller** *noun* person who notes movements of stock **Lagerverwalter**

◇ **stock-in-trade** *noun* goods held by a business for sale **Bestände, Sortiment**

◇ **stockist** *noun* person *or* shop which stocks a certain item **Fachhändler, Fachgeschäft**

◇ **stocklist** *noun* list of items carried in stock **Warenverzeichnis, Lagerbestandsverzeichnis**

◇ **stockpile**
1 *noun* supplies kept by a country *or* a company in case of need **Vorrat, Reserve;** *a stockpile of raw materials*
2 *verb* to buy items and keep them in case of need **Vorräte anlegen, horten;** *to stockpile raw materials*

◇ **stockroom** *noun* room where stores are kept **Lager**

◇ **stocktaking** *noun* counting of goods in stock at the end of an accounting period **Inventur, Bestandsaufnahme;** *the warehouse is closed for the annual stocktaking;* **stocktaking sale** = sale of goods at cheap prices to clear a warehouse before stocktaking **Ausverkauf wegen Inventur**

◇ **stock up** *verb* to buy supplies of something which you will need in the future **einen Vorrat anlegen, Lager auffüllen;** *they stocked up with computer paper*

stop

1 *noun* stopping supplies *or* payments **Einstellung; Sperrung; account on stop** = account which is not supplied because it has not paid its latest invoices **gesperrtes Konto;** *to put an account on stop;* **to put a stop on a cheque** = to tell the bank not to pay a cheque which you have written **einen Scheck sperren lassen**
2 *verb* **to stop an account** = not to supply an account on credit any more because bills have not been paid **ein Konto sperren; to stop a cheque** = to ask a bank not to pay a cheque you have written **einen Scheck sperren lassen; to stop payments** = not to make any further payments **Zahlungen einstellen**

◇ **stoppage** *noun* act of stopping **Unterbrechung, Stillstand;** *stoppage of deliveries; stoppage of payments; deliveries will be late because of stoppages on the production line;* **stoppage in transit** = legal right of a seller to stop delivery of goods that are in transit if he has reason to believe the customer will not pay for them owing to insolvency **Anhalten von bereits abgeschickten Waren seitens des Absenders**

storage *noun*

(a) keeping in store *or* in a warehouse **Lagerung, Aufbewahrung;** *we put our furniture into storage;* **storage capacity** = space available for storage **Lagerkapazität; storage company** = company which keeps items for customers **Lagerungsfirma, Lagerhaus; storage facilities** = equipment and buildings suitable for storage **Lagereinrichtungen; storage unit** = device attached to a computer for storing information on disk or tape **Speichergerät; cold storage** = keeping food, etc. in a cold store to prevent it going bad **Kaltlagerung, Kühlhauslagerung; to put a plan into cold storage** = to postpone work on a plan, usually for a very long time **einen Plan auf Eis legen**
(b) cost of keeping goods in store **Lagerkosten, Lagergeld;** *storage was 10% of value, so we scrapped the stock*
(c) facility for storing data in a computer **Speicher, Speicherung;** *disk with a storage capacity of 10Mb*

store

1 *noun*
(a) place where goods are kept **Lager(halle), Lagerhaus, Magazin; cold store** = warehouse *or* room where food can be kept cold **Kühlhaus**
(b) quantity of items *or* materials kept because they will be needed **Vorrat, Bestände;** *I always keep a store of envelopes ready in my desk*
(c) large shop **Geschäft;** *a furniture store; a big clothing store;* **chain store** = one store in a number of stores **Filiale, Kettenladen; department store** = large store with sections for different types of goods **Kaufhaus, Warenhaus; discount store** = shop which specializes in cheap goods sold at a high discount **Diskont-, Billigladen; general store** *or* **stores** = small shop which sells a wide range of products **Gemischtwarenhandlung; store audit** = market research method by which a research company regularly checks a sample of stores for unit sales and stock levels of different brands **Einzelhandelsbestandsaufnahme; store card** = plastic card allowing the holder to charge

purchases to a credit account with a store **Kunden(kredit)karte, Membercard**
2 *verb*
(a) to keep in a warehouse **(ein)lagern;** *to store goods for six months*
(b) to keep for future use **aufbewahren, speichern;** *we store our pay records on computer*
◇ **storekeeper** *or* **storeman** *noun* person in charge of a storeroom **Lagerverwalter, Lagerist**
◇ **storeroom** *noun* room *or* small warehouse attached to a factory where stock can be kept **Lager, Lagerraum**

storyboard *noun* series of drawings which give the outline of a film or TV advertisement **Storyboard;** *if the advertiser likes the storyboard, the agency will go ahead with the idea*

straight rebuy *noun* type of organizational buying decision where the same product is bought as before from the same supplier **direkter Anschlußkauf**

strategy *noun* plan of future action **Strategie;** *business strategy; sales strategy; marketing strategy; pricing strategy*
◇ **strategic** *adjective* based on a plan of action **strategisch; strategic business unit (SBU)** = part or division of a large company which forms its own business strategy **Strategischer Geschäftsbereich (SGB); strategic planning** = planning the future work of a company **strategische Planung**

stratification *noun*
(a) structure of a questionnaire which should help to ensure reliable answers and facilitate the evaluation of results **Schichtung;** *the results of the survey are hard to interpret owing to poor questionnaire stratification; good stratification will streamline the whole process*
(b) framework for the selection of a sample that ensures that it adequately represents the population or universe **geschichtete Auswahl**

streamline *verb* to make (something) more efficient *or* more simple **rationalisieren;** *to streamline the accounting system; to streamline distribution services*
◇ **streamlined** *adjective* efficient *or* rapid **rationalisiert;** *streamlined production; the company introduced a streamlined system of distribution*
◇ **streamlining** *noun* making efficient **Rationalisierung, Straffung**

structure
1 *noun* way in which something is organized **Struktur, Aufbau, Gefüge;** *the paper gives a diagram of the company's organizational structure; the price structure in the small car market; the career structure within a corporation; the company is reorganizing its discount structure;* **capital structure of a company** = way in which a company's capital is set up **die Kapitalstruktur einer Firma; the company's salary structure** = organization of salaries in a company with different rates of pay for different types of job **die Gehaltsstruktur eines Unternehmens**
2 *verb* to arrange in a certain way **aufbauen, gestalten, strukturieren;** *to structure a meeting;* **structured interview** = interview using preset questions and following a fixed pattern **strukturiertes Interview**

stuff *verb* to put papers, etc. into envelopes **stecken;** *we pay casual workers £2 an hour for stuffing envelopes or for envelope stuffing*
◇ **stuffer** *noun (US)* advertising material that is put in an envelope for mailing **Stuffer, Anzeigen-, Werbebeilage**

style *noun* way of doing *or* making something **Stil, Art;** *a new style of product; old-style management techniques;* **style obsolescence** = redesign of a product in order to make previous models obsolete and therefore encourage buying of the latest one **stylistische/modische Obsoleszenz; house style** = a company's own particular design, used in all areas of its activities, such as on packaging, stationery and office decoration **Hausstil**

suasionetics *noun (US)* techniques used to persuade people to adopt certain ideas or behaviour patterns **Überredungstechnik**

sub- *prefix* under *or* less important **Unter-, unter-, Sub-, sub-**
◇ **sub-agency** *noun* small agency which is part of a large agency **Untervertretung**
◇ **sub-agent** *noun* person who is in charge of a sub-agency **Untervertreter**
◇ **subcontract**
1 *noun* contract between the main contractor for a whole project and another firm who will do part of the work **Unterauftrag, Untervertrag;** *they have been awarded the subcontract for all the electrical work in the new building; we'll put the electrical work out to subcontract*
2 *verb* to agree with a company that they will do part of the work for a project

Unteraufträge vergeben/weitervergeben; *the electrical work has been subcontracted to Smith Ltd*

◇ **subcontractor** *noun* company which has a contract to do work for a main contractor **Subunternehmer**

◇ **subculture** *noun* part or sector of society identifiable by factors such as life-style, religion and race **Subkultur;** *studies were made of spending in the student subculture; different subcultures have different buying priorities*

subliminal advertising *noun* advertising that attempts to leave certain impressions on the subconscious mind of the person who sees it or hears it (without that person realising that this is being done) **unterschwellige Werbung;** *the government is thinking of banning subliminal advertising*

subsample *noun* subdivision of a sample **Teilstichprobe**

subscribe *verb* **to subscribe to a magazine** = to pay in advance for a series of issues of a magazine **eine Zeitschrift abonnieren; subscribed circulation** = circulation of a publication that is paid for in advance **Abonnementsauflage**

◇ **subscriber** *noun* **subscriber to a magazine** *or* **magazine subscriber** = person who has paid in advance for a series of issues of a magazine **Zeitschriftenabonnent;** *the extra issue is sent free to subscribers*

◇ **subscription** *noun* money paid in advance for a series of issues of a magazine *or* for membership of a society **Abonnement; Mitgliedsbeitrag;** *did you remember to pay the subscription to the computer magazine? he forgot to renew his club subscription;* **to take out a subscription to a magazine** = to start paying for a series of issues of a magazine **eine Zeitschrift abonnieren; to cancel a subscription to a magazine** = to stop paying for a magazine **eine Zeitschrift abbestellen, ein Zeitschriftenabonnement kündigen; subscription rate** = amount of money to be paid for a series of issues of a magazine **Abonnementspreis**

subsidiary
1 *adjective* (thing) which is less important **nebensächlich, Neben-;** *they agreed to most of the conditions in the contract but queried one or two subsidiary items;* **subsidiary company** = company which is owned by a parent company **Tochtergesellschaft**
2 *noun* company which is owned by a parent company **Tochtergesellschaft;** *most of the group profit was contributed by the subsidiaries in the Far East*

subsidize *verb* to help by giving money **subventionieren;** *the government has refused to subsidize the car industry;* **subsidized accommodation** = cheap accommodation which is partly paid for by an employer or a local authority, etc. **subventionierte Wohnung**

◇ **subsidy** *noun*
(a) money given to help something which is not profitable **Subvention;** *the industry exists on government subsidies; the government has increased its subsidy to the car industry*
(b) money given by a government to make something cheaper **Subvention;** *the subsidy on butter or the butter subsidy*

> QUOTE a serious threat lies in the estimated 400,000 tonnes of subsidized beef in EEC cold stores
> *Australian Financial Review*

substitute
1 *noun* person *or* thing which takes the place of someone *or* something else **Vertreter/-in, Vertretung, Stellvertreter; Ersatz; substitute product** = product which may be bought instead of another when the price of the latter changes or if it becomes unavailable **Substitutionsgut;** *we must match our competitors since they produce substitute products to ours; as the price of substitute products falls, they will be much in demand*
2 *verb* to take the place of something else **ersetzen, austauschen**

◇ **substitution effect** *noun* extent to which consumers will change from one product to another when the price of the former rises **Substitutionseffekt**

suggestion *noun* proposal *or* idea which is put forward **Vorschlag, Empfehlung, Anregung; suggestion box** = place in a company where members of staff can put forward their ideas for making the company more efficient and profitable **Kasten für Verbesserungsvorschläge; suggestion selling** = selling in such a way that the customer believes he or she really wants the product **Suggestion;** *trainee salesmen learn the application of psychology to suggestion selling*

supermarket *noun* large store, usually selling food, where customers serve themselves and pay at a checkout **Supermarkt;** *sales in supermarkets or supermarket sales account for half the company's turnover;* **supermarket trolley** =

small metal cart used by shoppers to put their purchases in **Einkaufswagen**

supernormal profit *noun* profit earned by a business through having a monopoly **außergewöhnlicher (Monopol)gewinn;** *this company has survived the recession owing to supernormal profits*

supersite *noun* particularly large poster site **Groß-, Mammutanschlagfläche;** *if we cannot afford a supersite we will have to settle for a site on an underground station; there are some key supersites at the side of the motorway*

superstore *noun* very large self-service store which sells a wide range of goods **Einkaufs-, Verbrauchermarkt; SB-Warenhaus**

supplement *noun* special addition to a magazine or newspaper which is given free to customers **Supplement;** *the colour supplement is mostly full of advertising; the supplement contains special articles on recent marketing strategies; what are the advertising rates in that paper's supplement?*

supply
1 *noun*
(a) providing something which is needed **Versorgung, Angebot, Lieferung; elastic supply** = supply which experiences quite a large percentage change in response to a change in price **elastisches Angebot; money supply** = amount of money which exists in a country **Geldreserve, Geldvolumen; supply price** = price at which something is provided **Angebotspreis; supply and demand** = amount of a product which is available and the amount which is wanted by customers **Angebot und Nachfrage; the law of supply and demand** = general rule that the amount of a product which is available is related to the needs of potential customers **das Gesetz von Angebot und Nachfrage**
(b) in short supply = not available in large enough quantities to meet the demand **knapp sein;** *spare parts are in short supply because of the strike*
(c) stock of something which is needed **Vorrat, Bestand;** *the factory is running short of supplies of coal; supplies of stationery have been reduced;* **office supplies** = goods needed to run an office (such as paper, pens, typewriters) **Bürobedarf**
(d) exempt supplies = products *or* services on which the business supplying them does not have to charge VAT **steuerfreie Produkte**
2 *verb* to provide something which is needed **liefern, beliefern, versorgen;** *to supply a factory with spare parts; the finance department supplied the committee with the figures; details of staff addresses and phone numbers can be supplied by the personnel department*
◇ **supply-side economics** *noun* economic theory that governments should encourage producers and suppliers of goods by cutting taxes, rather than encourage demand by making more money available in the economy **angebotsorientierte Wirtschaftspolitik**
◇ **supplier** *noun* person *or* company which supplies *or* sells goods or services **Lieferant, Zulieferer;** *office equipment supplier; they are major suppliers of spare parts to the car industry*

surcharge *noun* extra charge **Zuschlag, Aufschlag, Aufpreis; import surcharge** = extra duty charged on imported goods, to discourage their importation and encourage local manufacture **Importabgabe**

surplus *noun* extra stock *or* something of which there is more than is needed **Überschuß;** *surplus government equipment; surplus butter is on sale in the shops; we are holding a sale of surplus stock; governments are trying to find ways of reducing the agricultural surpluses in the Common Market; we are trying to let surplus capacity in the warehouse;* **budget surplus** = more revenue than was planned for in the budget **Etatüberschuß; these items are surplus to our requirements** = we do not need these items **diese Waren sind überschüssig; to absorb a surplus** = to take a surplus into a larger amount **einen Mehrbetrag verrechnen**
◇ **buyer's surplus** *noun* difference between what a buyer *or* consumer is willing to pay for something and what he or she actually does pay for it **Käuferrente; Konsumentenrente**

survey *noun* detailed report on a problem or particular subject **Studie, Untersuchungsbericht;** *the government has published a survey of population trends; we've asked the sales department to produce a survey of competing products;* **postal survey** = survey carried out by sending questionnaires to respondents by post **postalische Befragung**

swatch *noun* small sample **Muster(streifen); colour swatch** = small sample of colour which the finished product must look like **Farbmuster**

switch *verb* to change from one thing to another **wechseln, übertragen;** *to switch* *funds from one investment to another; the job was switched from our British factory to the States;* **switch selling** = selling technique which involves offering an apparently good bargain as bait in order to gain the attention of a prospective customer then approaching him or her with a different offer which is more profitable to the seller **Lock(vogel)angebot (Verkaufstechnik);** *trainee salesmen are coached in switch selling*

SWOT analysis method of developing a marketing strategy based on an assessment of the Strengths and Weaknesses of the company and the Opportunities and Threats in the market **SWOT-Analyse (Stärken, Schwächen des Unternehmens und Gelegenheiten, Gefahren des Marktes);** *SWOT analysis would allow us to plan ahead in line with developments in the environment; the company used SWOT analysis to make the best use of their assets in the existing circumstances*

symbol *noun* sign *or* picture *or* object which represents something **Symbol;** *they use a bear as their advertising symbol;* **symbol group** = group to which symbol retailers belong; *(entspricht)* **Einkaufsgenossenschaft; symbol retailer** = retailer that is a member of an independent group which secures favourable prices from suppliers through buying in bulk and has its own symbol or logo; *(entspricht)* **Mitglied (Einzelhändler) einer Einkaufsgenossenschaft**

synchro marketing *noun* finding ways to use spare resources during periods of low demand **Synchro-Marketing;** *synchro marketing will stop wastage of our production and storage capacity in the off-season*

syndicated research *noun* market research carried out by agencies and sold to several different companies **agenturverbreitete Forschung**

synectics *noun* brainstorming *or* group discussions designed to elicit creative solutions to problems **Synektik;** *we are beginning to apply synectics to our strategy formulation; synectics is being encouraged as a method of approaching case-studies in business school*

synergy *noun* producing greater effects by joining forces rather than by acting separately **Synergismus**

system *noun*
(a) arrangement *or* organization of things which work together **System;** *our accounting system has worked well in spite of the large increase in orders;* **decimal system** = system of mathematics based on the number 10 **Dezimalsystem; filing system** = way of putting documents in order for easy reference **Ablagesystem; to operate a quota system** = to regulate supplies by fixing certain allowed quantities **ein Quotensystem anwenden;** *we arrange our distribution using a quota system - each agent is allowed only a certain number of units*
(b) computer system = set of programs, commands, etc. which run a computer **Computersystem**
(c) systems analysis = using a computer to suggest how a company could work more efficiently, by analysing the way in which it works at present **Systemanalyse; systems analyst** = person who specializes in systems analysis **Systemanalytiker, Systemberater; systems management** = directing and controlling all the elements in an organization to achieve its basic objectives **systemorientiertes Management; systems selling** = selling products plus related services such as needs assessment and installation **Systemverkauf**

Tt

table *noun* list of figures *or* facts set out in columns **Tabelle, Übersicht; table of random numbers** = table of numbers in no particular order or pattern, which is used for selecting samples in market research **Zufallszahlentabelle**

◇ **tabloid** *noun* small size of newspaper, as opposed to the broadsheet **kleinformatige(s) Zeitung(sblatt);** *we're advertising in three tabloids concurrently*

tachistoscope *or* **T-scope** *noun* device used to measure the threshold of involvement when a person is exposed to an advertisement **Tachistokop**

tactic *noun* step or move involved in carrying out strategy **Taktik;** *concentrating our sales force in that area could be a good tactic; securing a key position at an exhibition is an old tactic which always produces good results*

tag *noun* label **Schild, Etikett;** *price tag; name tag*

tailor *verb* to design something for a specific purpose **zuschneiden;** *we mail out press releases tailored to the reader interests of each particular newspaper or periodical*

take
1 *noun* money received in a shop **Einnahme**
2 *verb* to receive *or* to get **nehmen; einnehmen; bekommen; the shop takes £2,000 a week** = the shop receives £2,000 a week in cash sales **das Geschäft nimmt £2.000 pro Woche ein; he takes home £250 a week** = after deductions for tax, etc., his salary is £250 a week **er verdient pro Woche £250 netto**
◇ **takeaway** *noun* shop which sells food to be eaten at some other place **Imbißstube, Restaurant mit Straßenverkauf;** *a takeaway meal; a Chinese takeaway*
◇ **takeover** *noun* buying a business **Übernahme; takeover bid** = offer to buy all or most of the shares in a company so as to control it **Übernahmeangebot; to make a takeover bid for a company** = to offer to buy most of the shares in a company **ein Übernahmeangebot für ein Unternehmen machen; to withdraw a takeover bid** = to say that you no longer offer to buy the shares in a company **ein Übernahmeangebot zurückziehen; the company rejected the takeover bid** = the directors recommended that the shareholders should not accept the offer **das Unternehmen wies das Übernahmeangebot zurück;** *the disclosure of the takeover bid raised share prices;* **contested takeover** = takeover which the board of the company being bought do not recommend, and try to fight **angefochtene Übernahme**
◇ **taker** *noun* buyer *or* person who wants to buy **Abnehmer/-in;** *there were no takers for the new shares*
◇ **takings** *plural noun* money received in a shop *or* a business **Einnahmen;** *the week's takings were stolen from the cash desk*

target
1 *noun* thing to aim for **Ziel; production target** = amount of units a factory is expected to produce **Produktionsziel; sales target** = amount of sales a representative is expected to achieve **Verkaufsziel; target audience** = consumers at whom an advertisement is aimed **Zielpublikum;** *what is the best media to reach our target audience? the style of the advertisement will depend on the target audience;* **target market** = market in which a company is planning to sell its goods **Zielmarkt, Zielgruppe; to set targets** = to fix amounts *or* quantities which workers have to produce *or* reach **Ziele setzen; to meet a target** = to produce the quantity of goods *or* sales which are expected **ein (gestecktes) Ziel erreichen; to miss a target** = not to produce the amount of goods *or* sales which are expected **ein (gestecktes) Ziel nicht erreichen;** *they missed the target figure of £2m turnover*
2 *verb* to aim at *or* to aim to sell to **anstreben, abzielen auf; to target a market** = to plan to sell goods in a certain market **auf einen Markt abzielen;** *many people working in PR are using direct marketing as a precise means of targeting the market*

> QUOTE in a normal leveraged buyout the acquirer raises money by borrowing against the assets of the target company
> *Fortune*
>
> QUOTE the minister is persuading the oil, gas, electricity and coal industries to target their advertising towards energy efficiency
> *Times*
>
> QUOTE direct marketing is all about targeting the audience, individualising the message and getting a response
> *PR Week*

tariff *noun*
(a) customs tariffs = tax to be paid for importing *or* exporting goods **Zolltarife; tariff barriers** = customs duty intended to make imports more difficult **Zollschranken;** *to impose tariff barriers on or to lift tariff barriers from a product;* **differential tariffs** = different duties for different types of goods **Staffeltarife, Differentialzölle; General Agreement on Tariffs and Trade** = international agreement to try to reduce restrictions on trade between countries **Allgemeines Zoll- und Handelsabkommen**
(b) rate of charging for electricity, hotel rooms, train tickets, etc. **Tarif, Preis**

task *noun* work which has to be done **Aufgabe; to list task processes** = to make a list of various parts of a job which have to be done **Arbeitsabläufe auflisten; objective-and-task method** = way of calculating an advertising appropriation by basing it on the actual amount needed to achieve the objectives **Ziel-Aufgaben-Methode**

TAT = THEMATIC APPERCEPTION TEST

TC = TILL COUNTERMANDED

team *noun* group of people who work together **Team, Mannschaft; management team** = group of all the managers working in the same company **Management-Team; sales team** = all the representatives, salesmen and sales managers working in a company **Verkaufsteam**

tear sheet *noun* page taken from a published magazine or newspaper, sent to an advertiser as proof that his advertisement has been run **Belegseite, Einzelbeleg**

teaser *noun* advertisement that gives little information about a product in order to attract customers by making them curious to know more **Neugier weckende Werbung, Teaser**

technical *adjective* referring to a particular machine *or* process **technisch;** *the document gives all the technical details on the new computer;* **technical press** = newspapers and magazines on scientific or technical subjects **technische Presse, Fachpresse;** *we need to advertise this product in the technical press*

◇ **technique** *noun* skilled way of doing a job **Technik, Verfahren;** *the company has developed a new technique for processing steel; he has a special technique for answering complaints from customers;* **management techniques** = skill in managing a business **Managementmethoden; marketing techniques** = skill in marketing a product **Marketing-Methoden**

telemarketing *noun* selling a product *or* service over the telephone **Telefonmarketing;** *telemarketing is unsatisfactory for products which require demonstrating*

◇ **telemarketer** *noun* person who sells by telephone **Telefonmarketing-Fachmann, Telefonmarketer**

telephone *noun* **telephone interview** = TELEPHONE SURVEY; **telephone orders** = orders received by telephone **telefonische Bestellungen;** *since we mailed the catalogue we have received a large number of telephone orders;* **telephone survey** = interviewing respondents by telephone for a survey **telefonische Befragung;** *how many people in the sample hung up before replying to the telephone survey?*

◇ **telesales** *plural noun* selling by telephone *or* sales made by telephone **Telefonverkauf; Telefonverkäufe**

◇ **teleshopping** *noun* shopping from home by means of a television screen and a home computer **Teleshopping**

◇ **teletext** *noun* videotext broadcast by a TV company (such as Ceefax on BBC or Oracle on ITV) **Bildschirmtext, Teletext**

television (TV) *noun* broadcasting of moving images **Fernsehen; cable television** = television service which a viewer receives via a cable from a particular station, and pays for on a subscription basis **Kabelfernsehen; satellite television** = television service which is broadcast from a satellite, and which the viewer receives using a special aerial **Satellitenfernsehen; television consumer audit** = questioning a sample of television viewers on their viewing and impressions **Werbeträger-Panelanalyse (von Fernsehhaushalten); television network** = system of linked television stations covering the whole country **Sendernetz; television ratings (TVR)** = statistics showing size and type of television audiences at different times of day for various channels and programmes **Fernseheinschaltquoten;** *we will have to consult the TV ratings before buying a spot;* **television station** = (i) the place from which a television broadcast is transmitted; (ii) the wavelength on which it is transmitted **(i) Sendestation; (ii) Sender**

tender

1 *noun* offer to work for a certain price **Submission, Angebot;** *a successful tender or an unsuccessful tender;* **to put a project out to tender** *or* **to ask for** *or* **to invite tenders for a project** = to ask contractors to give written estimates for a job **Angebote für ein Projekt einholen; ein Projekt ausschreiben; to put in a tender** *or* **to submit a tender** = to make an estimate for a job **ein Angebot machen; to sell shares by tender** = to ask people to offer in writing a price for shares **Aktien auf dem Angebotsweg verkaufen; sealed tenders** = tenders sent in sealed envelopes which will all be opened together at a certain time **versiegelte Submissionsofferten**

2 *verb* **to tender for a contract** = to put forward an estimate of cost for work to be carried out under contract **sich (im Ausschreibungsweg) um einen Auftrag bewerben;** *to tender for the construction of a hospital*

◇ **tenderer** *noun* person *or* company which tenders for work **Submittent;** *the company was the successful tenderer for the project*

◇ **tendering** *noun* act of putting forward an estimate of cost **Angebot(sabgabe);** *to be successful, you must follow the tendering procedure as laid out in the documents*

terms *noun* conditions *or* duties which have to be carried out as part of a contract *or* arrangements which have to be agreed before a contract is valid **Bedingungen;** *he refused to agree to some of the terms of the contract; by or under the terms of the* *contract, the company is responsible for all damage to the property; to negotiate for better terms;* **terms of payment** *or* **payment terms** = conditions for paying something **Zahlungsbedingungen; terms of sale** = conditions attached to a sale **Verkaufsbedingungen; terms of trade** = ratio of a country's import prices to export prices **Austauschverhältnisse; cash terms** = lower terms which apply if the customer pays cash **Barzahlungsbedingungen; "terms: cash with order"** = terms of sale showing that payment has to be made in cash when the order is placed **'Bedingungen: Barzahlung bei Bestellung'; easy terms** = arrangement by which a purchaser pays for the purchases in several small payments over a period of time, rather than in one large payment **günstige Bedingungen; Zahlungserleichterungen; on favourable terms** = on especially good terms **sehr günstige Bedingungen;** *the shop is let on very favourable terms;* **trade terms** = special discount for people in the same trade **Händlerrabatt**

territory *noun* area visited by a salesman **Bezirk, Gebiet;** *we have added more salesmen to our team, and so the reps' territories are smaller; his territory covers the whole of the north of the country*

◇ **territorial planning** *noun* planning of a salesman's calls, taking into account the best use of time in travelling and the priority of important customers **(Vertreter-)Routenplanung;** *the sales manager is giving the sales team some guidelines on territorial planning; bad territorial planning means time wasted in travelling;* **territorial rights** = rights of a distributor, granted by the producer or supplier, to sell a product in a certain geographical area, possibly on condition that certain methods are used in the selling **gebietsgebundene Vertretungsrechte**

tertiary *adjective* **tertiary industry** = service industry *or* industry which does not produce or manufacture but offers a service (such as banking, retailing or accountancy) **Dienstleistungsbranche; tertiary readership** = people who do not buy a newspaper or magazine but come across it as a result of another activity, such as waiting for an appointment with the dentist **Drittleserschaft, tertiäre Leserschaft;** *many glossy magazines have a relatively small circulation but a high tertiary readership;* **tertiary sector** = section of the economy containing the service industries **Dienstleistungssektor, tertiärer Sektor**

test
1 *noun*
(a) examination to see if something works well
or is possible **Test, Prüfung; test certificate** = certificate to show that something has passed a test **Abnahme-, Zulassungsbescheinigung; feasibility test** = test to see if something is possible **Durchführbarkeitstest; market test** = examination to see if a sample of a product will sell in a market by selling it through the normal retail channels **Markttest**
(b) test close = trying to obtain at least one immediate order from a buyer to see how promising a customer he or she is **Testende**
2 *verb* to examine something to see if it is working well **testen, prüfen; to test the market for a product** *or* **to test-market a product** = to show samples of a product in a market to see if it will sell well **den Markt für ein Produkt testen;** *we are test-marketing the toothpaste in Scotland*
◇ **test-drive** *verb* **to test-drive a car** = to drive a car (before buying it) to see if it works well **ein Auto probefahren**
◇ **testing** *noun* examining something to see if it works well **Erprobung, Prüfung;** *during the testing of the system several defects were corrected*

testimonial *noun* written report about someone's character *or* ability **Zeugnis, Referenz;** *to write someone a testimonial;* **unsolicited testimonial** = letter praising someone *or* a product, without the writer having been asked to write it **ohne Aufforderung gegebene Empfehlung; testimonial advertising** = advertising which makes use of testimonials from famous or qualified people, or from satisfied customers, to endorse a product **Testimonialwerbung, Leitbildwerbung**

T-group *noun* group of trainees following a training method, often used in training sales staff, which uses group discussion and activities to develop social skills and general self-awareness **Fortbildungsgruppe**

thematic apperception test (TAT) *noun* test used to ascertain attitudes or reactions to a brand, which consists in showing pictures to the subject who then constructs a story round them **Thematischer Apperzeptionstest (TAT)**

tie *verb* to attach *or* to fasten (with string, wire, etc.) **binden, befestigen;** *he tied the parcel with thick string; she tied two labels onto the parcel*
◇ **tied shop** *noun* business which has agreed to sell only a particular supplier's products **Einzellieferantgeschäft;** *the store*

felt constrained by the tied shop agreement and wanted to offer a wider range of brands
◇ **tie-on label** *noun* label with a piece of string attached so that it can be tied onto an item **Anhänger**
◇ **tie-up** *noun* link *or* connection **Verbindung;** *the company has a tie-up with a German distributor*

till *noun* drawer for keeping cash in a shop **Ladenkasse; cash till** = cash register *or* machine with a drawer for keeping the cash received, which shows and adds prices of items bought **Kasse;** *there wasn't much money in the till at the end of the day*

till countermanded (TC) *noun* clause in a contract which states that an advertisement will run until stopped by the advertiser **bis auf weiteres**

time *noun*
(a) period over which something takes place (such as one hour, two days, fifty minutes, etc.) **Zeit; computer time** = time when a computer is being used (paid for at an hourly rate) **Rechen-, Rechnerzeit; Betriebszeit; real time** = time when a computer is working on the processing of data while it is on-line to the source of that data **Echtzeit, Real-time; time and duty study** = study to see how effectively salesmen are using their time **Zeit- und Aufgabenstudie** *(entspricht)* **REFA-Studie;** *the time and duty study showed that 30% of time is wasted; the aim of the time and duty study was to streamline our sales activities;* **time and motion study** = study in an office *or* factory of how long it takes to do certain jobs and the movements workers have to make to do them **Zeit- und Bewegungsstudie** *(entspricht)* **REFA-Studie; time and motion expert** = person who analyses time and motion studies and suggests changes in the way work is done; *(entspricht)* **REFA-Fachmann; time segment** = period set aside for advertisements on television **(Sense)zeitsegment; time series analysis** = method of assessing the effect of a variable on events over a period of time, by first examining a period of time without the variable, and then one with it **Zeitreihenanalyse**
(b) period before something happens **Zeitspanne; Frist; delivery time** = number of days before something will be delivered **Lieferzeit; lead time** = time between placing an order and receiving the goods **Lieferzeit; time limit** = period during which something should be done **Frist; to keep within the time limits** *or* **within the time schedule** = to complete work by the time stated **die Fristen einhalten; time utility** = usefulness to a customer of receiving a product at a particular time **zeitlich gebundener Nutzen;** *time utility has meant avoiding unreliable suppliers; some customers put time utility before place utility*

◇ **timelength** *noun* length of a cinema, television or radio advertisement **Zeitdauer einer Werbesendung;** *find out the rates for the various timelengths before placing the commercial*

tip
1 *noun*
(a) money given to someone who has helped you **Trinkgeld;** *I gave the taxi driver a 10 cent tip; the staff are not allowed to accept tips*
(b) advice on buying or doing something which could be profitable **Tip;** *a stock market tip; he gave me a tip about a share which was likely to rise because of a takeover bid;* **tip sheet** = newspaper which gives information about shares which should be bought or sold **Börsenratgeber**
2 *verb*
(a) to give money to someone who has helped you **Trinkgeld geben;** *he tipped the receptionist £5*
(b) to say that something is likely to happen *or* that something might be profitable **einen Tip geben;** *two shares were tipped in the business section of the paper; he is tipped to become the next chairman*

TIR = TRANSPORT INTERNATIONAL ROUTIER

token *noun*
(a) thing which acts as a sign *or* symbol **Zeichen; Symbol; token charge** = small charge which does not cover the real costs **symbolische Gebühr;** *a token charge is made for heating;* **token payment** = small payment to show that something is not being given away free **symbolische Zahlung; token rent** = very low rent payment to show that a rent is being asked for **geringe/symbolische Miete; token strike** = short strike to show that workers have a grievance **Warnstreik**
(b) book token *or* **flower token** *or* **gift token** = card bought in a store which is given as a present and which must be exchanged in that store for goods **Büchergutschein; Blumengutschein; Geschenkgutschein;** *we gave her a gift token for her birthday*

top-selling *adjective* which sells better than all other products **meistverkauft;** *top-selling brands of toothpaste*

torture testing *noun* pushing products to their limits during product testing **Bruchproben;** *torture testing will show up any product deficiencies while changes can still be made*

total
1 *adjective* complete *or* with everything added together **gesamt, ganz; völlig, absolut;** *total amount; total assets; total cost; total expenditure; total income; total output; total revenue;* **total audience package** = media owner's arrangement or scheduling of advertisements across time segments on television and radio **Gesamtzuschauerschafts-, Gesamthörerschaftspaket; total distribution system** = system where all distribution decisions (including the purchasing of raw materials and parts, as well as the movement of finished products) are taken globally **Gesamtvertriebssystem; total offer** = complete package offered to the customer (including the product or service itself, its price, availability and promotion) **Gesamtangebot**

track record *noun* what is known about a company *or* salesman's good or bad performance in the past **Erfolgs- und Leistungsnachweis;** *he has a good track record as a secondhand car salesman; the company has no track record in the computer market*

trade
1 *noun*
(a) business of buying and selling **Handel; Gewerbe; export trade** *or* **import trade** = the business of selling to other countries *or* buying from other countries **Exporthandel; Importhandel; foreign trade** *or* **overseas trade** *or* **external trade** = trade with other countries **Außenhandel; Überseehandel; home trade** = trade in the country where a company is based **Binnenhandel; trade cycle** = period during which trade expands, then slows down, then expands again **Konjunkturzyklus; balance of trade** *or* **trade balance** = international trading position of a country, excluding invisible trade **Handelsbilanz;** *the country had an adverse balance of trade for the second month running;* **favourable balance of trade** = situation where a country's exports are larger than its imports **aktive Handelsbilanz**
(b) to do a good trade in a range of products = to sell a large number of a range of products **mit einer Produktenserie guten Absatz erzielen; fair trade** = international business system where countries agree not to charge import duties on certain items imported from their trading partners **Nichtdiskriminierung im Außenhandel; free trade** = system where goods can go from one country to another without any restrictions **Freihandel; free trade area** = group of countries practising free trade **Freihandelszone; trade agreement** = international agreement between countries over general terms of trade **Handelsabkommen; trade bureau** = office which specializes in commercial enquiries **Handels-, Wirtschaftsbüro; to impose trade barriers on** = to restrict the import of certain goods by charging high duty **mit Importrestriktionen belegen; trade deficit** *or* **trade gap** = difference in value between a country's high imports and low exports **Außenhandelsdefizit; trade description** = description of a product to intended to attract customers **Warenkennzeichnung;** *(GB)* **Trade Descriptions Act** = act which limits the way in which products can be described so as to protect customers from misleading descriptions made by manufacturers **Warenkennzeichnungsgesetz; trade directory** = book which lists all the businesses and business people in a town **Branchenadreßbuch; trade mission** = visit to a country by a group of foreign businessmen to discuss trade **Handelsmission; to ask a company to supply trade references** = to ask a company to give names of traders who can report on the company's financial situation and reputation **ein Unternehmen um Handelsauskünfte ersuchen**

(c) people *or* companies dealing in the same type of product **Branche, Gewerbe;** *he's in the secondhand car trade; she's very well known in the clothing trade;* **trade association** = group which links together companies in the same trade **Wirtschafts-, Handelsverband; trade counter** = shop in a factory *or* warehouse where goods are sold to retailers **Warenausgabe für den Einzelhandel, Großhandelsverkauf; trade discount** *or* **trade terms** = discount offered on products sold to distributors **Händlerrabatt;** *the generous trade discount will mean lower prices for the consumer as well; the shop enjoys a 50% trade discount on items bought from the wholesaler;* **trade fair** = large exhibition and meeting for advertising and selling a certain type of product **Handelsmesse;** *there were two trade fairs running in London at the same time; to organize or to run a trade fair;* **trade journal** *or* **trade magazine** *or* **trade paper** *or* **trade publication** = magazine or newspaper produced for people and companies in a certain trade **Fachzeitschrift; (Branchen-, Industrie-, Handels-, Gewerbe-); trade press** = all the magazines produced for people working in a certain trade **Fachpresse; trade price** = special wholesale price paid by a

retailer to the manufacturer or wholesaler **Großhandelspreis; trade promotion** = promotion of products to distributors **Verkaufs-, Absatzförderung;** *the new trade promotion campaign is designed to attract wholesalers in all our areas of distribution;* **trade route** = route along which goods are transported for trade **Handelsstraße, Handelsweg;** *the main trade routes were studied to see which areas of the country were most accessible; when the Suez Canal was closed some vital trade routes were affected*
2 *verb* to buy and sell *or* to carry on a business **handeln, Handel treiben;** *to trade with another country; to trade on the Stock Exchange; the company has stopped trading; the company trades under the name "Eeziphitt"*

◊ **trade in** *verb*
(a) to buy and sell certain items **handeln mit, Handel treiben mit;** *the company trades in imported goods; he trades in French wine*
(b) to give in an old item as part of the payment for a new one **in Zahlung geben;** *the chairman traded in his old Rolls Royce for a new model*

◊ **trade-in** *noun* old item (such as a car *or* washing machine) given as part of the payment for a new one **in Zahlung gegebener Gegenstand;** *to give the old car as a trade-in;* **trade-in price** = amount allowed by the seller for an old item being traded in for a new one **Preis bei Inzahlungnahme**

◊ **trademark** *or* **trade name** *noun* particular name, design, etc. which has been registered by the manufacturer and which cannot be used by other manufacturers **Warenzeichen, Handelsmarke;** *you can't call your beds "Softn'kumfi" - it is a registered trademark*

◊ **trade-off** *noun* exchanging one thing for another as part of a business deal **Austausch**

◊ **trader** *noun* person who does business **Händler/-in, Kaufmann/Kauffrau; commodity trader** = person whose business is buying and selling commodities **Warenterminhändler; free trader** = person who is in favour of free trade **Befürworter des Freihandels; sole trader** = person who runs a business, usually by himself or herself, but has not registered it as a company **Einzelkaufmann**

◊ **tradesman** *or* **tradeswoman** *noun* shopkeeper *or* person who runs a shop **Einzelhändler, Kaufmann/Kauffrau**

◊ **tradespeople** *noun* shopkeepers **Geschäftsleute**

> QUOTE trade between Britain and other countries which comprise the Economic Community has risen steadily from 33% of exports in 1972 to 50% in 1987
>
> *Sales & Marketing Management*
>
> QUOTE Brazil's trade surplus is vulnerable both to a slowdown in the American economy and a pick-up in its own
>
> *Economist*

trading *noun* business of buying and selling **Handel; trading account** = account of a company's gross profit **Erfolgskonto; trading area** = group of countries which trade with each other **Handelszone, Absatzgebiet; trading channel** = series of purchases and sales from company to company which are made until the finished product is purchased by the customer **Absatzweg; trading company** = company which specializes in buying and selling goods **Handelsgesellschaft; adverse trading conditions** = bad conditions for trade **erschwerte Handelsbedingungen; trading down** = selling at lower prices to increase sales volume **Trading-down;** *trading down has become necessary because too many customers are put off by our high prices;* **trading estate** = area of land near a town specially for factories and warehouses **Industrie-, Gewerbegebiet; trading loss** = situation where a company's receipts are less than its expenditure **Geschäftsverlust; trading partner** = company *or* country which trades with another **Handelspartner; trading profit** = situation where a company's gross receipts are more than its gross expenditure **Geschäftsgewinn; trading stamp** = special type of stamp given away by a shop, which the customer can collect and later exchange for free goods **Rabattmarke; trading stock** = goods held by a business for sale **Warenbestand;** *we'll have to offer large discounts if we want to sell off all this trading stock;* **trading up** = selling products at higher prices to raise their prestige and achieve a higher profit margin **Trading-up;** *trading up is part of our strategy to go up market;* **fair trading** = way of doing business which is reasonable and does not harm the customer **lauterer Wettbewerb;** *(GB)* **Office of Fair Trading (OFT)** = government department which protects consumers against unfair or illegal business **Amt für Verbraucherschutz; insider trading** = illegal buying or selling of shares by staff of a company who have secret information about the company's plans **Insiderhandel**

traffic *noun*
(a) number of customers who enter a store **Besucherfluß, Kundenverkehr; page traffic** = the proportion of readers of a paper who

see a particular page **Lesegeschehen pro Seite**
(b) progress or flow of advertising work in an agency **Traffic, Arbeitsfluß, Auftragsabwicklung (in einer Werbeagentur)**
(c) movement of cars *or* lorries *or* trains *or* planes; movement of people *or* goods in vehicles **Verkehr;**
(d) illegal trade **Dealen, Handel;** *drugs traffic or traffic in drugs*

tramp ship *noun* ship with no fixed schedule or itinerary that can be chartered by a company to transport goods **Trampschiff**

transaction *noun* **business transaction =** piece of business *or* buying or selling **geschäftliche Transaktion; cash transaction =** transaction paid for in cash **Bar-, Kassegeschäft; a transaction on the Stock Exchange =** purchase *or* sale of shares on the Stock Exchange **eine Börsentransaktion;** *the paper publishes a daily list of Stock Exchange transactions;* **exchange transaction =** purchase *or* sale of foreign currency **Devisengeschäft; fraudulent transaction =** transaction which aims to cheat someone **Schwindelgeschäft**

transfer *noun* moving someone *or* something to a new place **Transfer; Versetzung; Verlegung; Übertragung;** *he applied for a transfer to our branch in Scotland;* **transfer of property** *or* **transfer of shares =** moving the ownership of property *or* shares from one person to another **Eigentumsüberschreibung; Aktienübertragung; airmail transfer =** sending money from one bank to another by airmail **Luftpostüberweisung; bank transfer =** moving money from a bank account to an account in another country **Banküberweisung; credit transfer** *or* **transfer of funds =** moving money from one account to another **Kredittransfer; Geldtransfer; electronic funds transfer at point of sale (eftpos) =** system where money is immediately debited from the customer's bank account to the store's account as the purchase is registered at the cash desk **elektronische Kasse; stock transfer form =** form to be signed by the person transferring shares **Aktienübertragungsformular**

tranship *verb* to move cargo from one ship to another **umladen, umschlagen**

transient *adjective* (advertisement) which the target audience cannot keep to look at again, such as a cinema advertisement, as opposed to an intransient one in a newspaper or magazine **vorübergehend**

transit *noun* movement of passengers *or* goods on the way to a destination **Transit; Transport;** *to pay compensation for damage suffered in transit or for loss in transit; some of the goods were damaged in transit;* **goods in transit =** goods being transported from warehouse to customer **Transitgüter**

transport
1 *noun* moving of goods or people **Transport, Beförderung;** *air transport or transport by air; rail transport or transport by rail; road transport or transport by road; passenger transport or the transport of passengers; the passenger transport services of British Rail; what means of transport will you use to get to the factory?;* **the visitors will be using public transport** *or* **private transport =** the visitors will be coming by bus *or* train, etc., or in their own cars **die Besucher werden öffentliche od private Verkehrsmittel benutzen; public transport system =** system of trains, buses, etc. used by the general public **öffentliches Verkehrsnetz; transport advertising =** advertising appearing on or in forms of transportation such as buses or trains **Verkehrsmittelwerbung;** *transport advertising will reach too broad a public for our product; is your transport advertising on the sides of buses or in underground trains?*
2 *verb* to move goods *or* people from one place to another in a vehicle **transportieren, befördern;** *the company transports millions of tons of goods by rail each year; the visitors will be transported to the factory by air or by helicopter or by taxi*

◇ **transportation** *noun*
(a) moving goods *or* people from one place to another **Transport, Beförderung**
(b) vehicles used to move goods *or* people from one place to another **Beförderungs-, Verkehrsmittel;** *the company will provide transportation to the airport;* **ground transportation =** buses, taxis, etc. available to take passengers from an airport to the town **Bodentransport**

◇ **transporter** *noun* company which transports goods **Transportunternehmen**

◇ **Transport International Routier (TIR)** *noun* system with international documents which allows dutiable goods to cross several European countries by road without paying duty until they reach their final destination **TIR**

travel *verb* to go from one place to another, showing a company's goods to buyers and taking orders from them

Vertreter sein; bereisen; *he travels in the North for an insurance company*

◇ **traveller** *or (US)* **traveler** *noun* **commercial traveller** = salesman who travels round an area visiting customers on behalf of his company *or* several companies; *(old-fashioned)* **Reisende(r); Handelsvertreter(in)**

◇ **travelling** *noun* **travelling expenses** = money spent on travelling and hotels for business purposes **Reisespesen; travelling salesman** = salesman who travels around an area visiting customers on behalf of his company *or* several companies; *(old-fashioned)* **Reisender; Handelsvertreter;** *we have ten travelling salesmen presently working in the field; travelling salesmen must make regular contact with company headquarters by phone*

treaty *noun*
(a) agreement between countries **Staatsvertrag; Abkommen;** *commercial treaty*
(b) agreement between individual persons **Vertrag; to sell a house by private treaty** = to sell a home to another person not by auction **ein Haus privat verkaufen**

trend *noun* general way things are going **Trend, Tendenz;** *there is a trend away from old-established food stores; a downward trend in investment; we notice a general trend towards selling to the student market; the report points to inflationary trends in the economy; we have noticed an upward trend in sales;* **economic trends** = way in which a country's economy is moving **ökonomische Entwicklungen; market trends** = gradual changes taking place in a market **Marktentwicklungen, Markttendenzen; trend analysis** = analysis of particular statistics over a period of time in order to identify trends **Trendanalyse;** *trend analysis has shown how soon major competitors begin to copy innovations*

trial *noun* test to see if something is good **Probe; Erprobung; Prüfung; on trial** = being tested **getestet werden; zur Prüfung/Probe;** *the product is on trial in our laboratories;* **trial period** = time when a customer can test a product before buying it **Probezeit; trial sample** = small piece of a product used for testing **Muster, Probestück; free trial** = use of a machine *or* product for a certain period of time in order to test it, without having to pay **kostenlos zur Probe**

trolley *noun* small metal cart which is used by customers in supermarkets to carry their shopping **Einkaufswagen**

truck *noun*
(a) large motor vehicle for carrying goods **Last(kraft)wagen; fork-lift truck** = type of small tractor with two metal arms in front, used for lifting and moving pallets **Gabelstapler;** *(US)* **truck distributor** *or* **truck jobber** = limited function wholesaler, who usually only delivers goods directly by truck to retailers **Großhändler, der per LKW liefert**
(b) open railway wagon for carrying goods **(offener) Güterwagen**

◇ **truckage** *noun* carriage of goods in trucks **Lastwagentransport;** *what will the truckage costs be for these goods?*

◇ **trucking** *noun* carrying goods in trucks **Güter(kraft)verkehr, Spedition;** *trucking firm*

trust *noun (US)* small group of companies which control the supply of a product **Syndikat**

◇ **trustbusting** *noun (US)* breaking up monopolies to encourage competition **Monopol-, Trustzerschlagung**

tube cards *noun* cards with advertisements on them which are either on the walls of underground stations or inside underground trains **U-Bahn-Plakate;** *half the tube cards in one carriage were advertising the same product; the underground railway system uses tube cards to advertise its own services*

turn *noun* **stock turn** = total value of stocks sold in a year divided by the average value of goods in stock **Lagerumschlag;** *the company has a stock turn of 6.7*

◇ **turn over** *verb* to have a certain amount of sales **umsetzen;** *we turn over £2,000 a week*

◇ **turnover** *noun*
(a) *GB* amount of sales **Umsatz;** *the company's turnover has increased by 235%; we based our calculations on the forecast turnover;* **stock turnover** = total value of stock sold in a year divided by the average value of goods held in stock **Lagerumschlag**
(b) *US* number of times something is used *or* sold in a period (usually one year), expressed as a percentage of a total **Umschlaggeschwindigkeit**

◇ **turn round** *verb* to make a previously loss-making company profitable **sanieren; he turned the company round in less than a year** = he made the company profitable in less than a year **in weniger als einem Jahr sanierte er das Unternehmen**

◇ **turnround** *noun*
(a) value of goods sold during a year divided by the average value of goods held in stock **mittlerer Lagerumschlag**

(b) action of emptying a ship, plane, etc. and getting it ready for another commercial journey **Entladung und Wiederfahrbereitmachung**
(c) making a company profitable again **Sanierung**

> QUOTE a 100,000 square foot warehouse can turn its inventory over 18 times a year, more than triple a discounter's turnover
> *Duns Business Month*
>
> QUOTE combined turnover for building and engineering was £692 million in 1986, up just 1.3% on the previous year
> *Management Today*
>
> QUOTE the US now accounts for more than half our world-wide sales; it has made a huge contribution to our earnings turnround
> *Duns Business Month*

TVR = TELEVISION RATINGS

tying contract *noun* contract under which a producer sells a product to a distributor on condition that the latter also buys another product **Kopplungsvertrag;** *tying contracts are used to get wholesalers acquainted with lesser known products*

typological analysis *noun* categorization of households based on socio-economic factors and buying habits **typologische Analyse;** *typological analysis helped the company clarify what market segments the new product should be aimed at*

Uu

ultimate *adjective* last *or* final **letzter, End-; ultimate consumer** = person who buys the product for personal rather than industrial use **Endverbraucher;** *the high distribution costs of the product will be paid for by the ultimate consumer*

umbrella *noun* **umbrella advertising** = advertising an organization or an association of companies rather than a single product **Schirmwerbung; umbrella organization** = large organization which includes several smaller ones **Dachorganisation**

unaided recall *see* UNPROMPTED RECALL

unavailable *adjective* not available **nicht erhältlich, nicht verfügbar;** *the following items on your order are temporarily unavailable*
◇ **unavailability** *noun* not being available **Nichtverfügbarkeit**

uncontrollable *adjective* which cannot be controlled **nicht unter Kontrolle zu bringen, unkontrollierbar; uncontrollable variable** = variable *or* factor that cannot be controlled in marketing, such as legislation or the state of the country's economy **unkontrollierbare Variable;** *there are too many uncontrollable variables for any real planning; changes in fashion constitute a dangerous uncontrollable variable for a clothes shop*

under- *prefix* less important than *or* lower than **Unter-**
◇ **underbid** *verb* to bid less than someone **unterbieten**
◇ **underbidder** *noun* person who bids less than the person who buys at an auction **Mitbieter**
◇ **undercharge** *verb* to ask for too little money **zu wenig berechnen;** *he undercharged us by £25*
◇ **undercut** *verb* to offer something at a lower price than someone else **unterbieten**
◇ **underdeveloped** *adjective* which has not been developed **unterentwickelt;** *Japan is an underdeveloped market for our products;* **underdeveloped countries** = countries which are not fully industrialized **Entwicklungsländer**
◇ **underline** *noun* short description printed underneath an illustration **Bildunterschrift**
◇ **underprice** *verb* to charge a lower price than is justified by demand **zu niedrige Preise setzen;** *the company underpriced its products due to ignorance of the growing market; underpricing can be used as a strategy to increase market share*
◇ **undersell** *verb* to sell more cheaply than **unterbieten; unter Preis verkaufen;** *to undersell a competitor;* **the company is never undersold** = no other company sells goods as cheaply as this one **diese Firma wird nie unterboten/ist der billigste Anbieter**
◇ **undervalued** *adjective* not valued highly enough **unterbewertet, zu niedrig geschätzt;** *the properties are undervalued on the balance sheet; the dollar is undervalued on the foreign exchanges*
◇ **undervaluation** *noun* being valued at less than the true worth **Unterbewertung, zu niedrige Schätzung**
◇ **underweight** *adjective* **the pack is twenty grams underweight** = the pack weighs

twenty grams less than it should **das Gewicht der Packung liegt zwanzig Gramm unter dem Normalgewicht**

undifferentiated *adjective* that which has no unique feature **undifferenziert; undifferentiated marketing strategy** = marketing strategy which seeks to present a product to the public without stressing any unique feature of the product, thus appealing to all segments of the market **undifferenzierte Marketingstrategie; undifferentiated product** = product which has no unique feature to set it apart from others on the market **undifferenziertes Produkt;** *only an extra-low price will sell an undifferentiated product in a market where there is already a wide choice of brands*

undue influence *noun* unfair pressure put on someone to sign a contract **unzulässiger Einfluß;** *the salesmen were discouraged from exerting undue influence on prospective buyers*

unfair *adjective* **unfair competition** = trying to do better than another company by using techniques such as importing foreign goods at very low prices or by wrongly criticizing a competitor's products **unlauterer Wettbewerb; unfair dismissal** = removing someone from a job for reasons which are not fair **ungerechtfertigte Entlassung**

unfavourable *adjective* not favourable **ungünstig, negativ; unfavourable balance of trade** = situation where a country imports more than it exports **passive Handelsbilanz; unfavourable exchange rate** = exchange rate which gives an amount of foreign currency for the home currency which is not good for trade **ungünstiger Wechselkurs;** *the unfavourable exchange rate hit the country's exports*

unfulfilled *adjective* (order) which has not yet been supplied **unerfüllt, nicht ausgeführt**

unilateral *adjective* on one side only *or* done by one party only **unilateral, einseitig;** *they took a unilateral decision to cancel the contract*

◇ **unilaterally** *adverb* by one party only **unilateral, einseitig;** *the decision was taken to cancel the contract unilaterally*

unique *adjective* special *or* unlike anything else **einmalig, einzigartig; unique selling proposition (USP)** = special quality of a product which makes it different from other goods and is used as a key theme in advertising **einzigartiges Verkaufsargument, USP;** *a five-year guarantee makes this product a unique selling proposition*

unit *noun*

(a) single product for sale **Einheit, Stück; unit cost** = the cost of one item (i.e total product costs divided by the number of units produced) **Einheits-, Stückkosten; unit pack** = pack containing only one unit of a product **Einzelpackung;** *will the product be sold in unit packs, or in packs of ten or twenty units?;* **unit price** = the price of one item **Einheits-, Stückpreis; unit pricing** = pricing items by showing how much each costs per unit of measurement (i.e. per metre or per kilo, etc.) **Festlegen des Einheitspreises**

(b) separate piece of equipment or furniture **Element; display unit** = special stand for showing goods for sale **Auslagenstand; visual display unit** = screen attached to a computer which shows the information stored in the computer **Bildschirm-, Bildsichtgerät**

(c) factory unit = single building on an industrial estate **Fabrikgebäude**

(d) production unit = separate small group of workers who produce a certain product **Produktionseinheit; research unit** = separate small group of research workers **Forschungsgruppe**

universe *noun* total population which is under study in a survey and out of which a sample is selected **Grundgesamtheit;** *is this sample really representative of the universe? in the survey, the universe is all British men between the ages of forty and fifty; from a universe of two million, a sample of two hundred was chosen by random selection*

unladen *adjective* empty *or* without a cargo **unbeladen**

unlimited *adjective* with no limits **unbegrenzt;** *the bank offered him unlimited credit;* **unlimited liability** = situation where a sole trader or each partner is responsible for all the firm's debts with no limit on the amount each may have to pay **unbeschränkte Haftung**

unload *verb*

(a) to take goods off (a ship, etc.) **ent-, ausladen; löschen;** *the ship is unloading at Hamburg; we need a fork-lift truck to unload the lorry; we unloaded the spare parts at Lagos; there are no unloading facilities for container ships*

(b) to sell stock which is no longer needed at a lower price than usual **abstoßen;** *they tried to unload some unsellable items onto the Far Eastern market*

◇ **unloading** *noun* selling off goods at a lower price than usual, often when they are no longer being produced and the producers merely want to get rid of remaining stock **Abstoßung;** *many customers are taking advantage of our unloading and are buying in bulk*

unprofitable *adjective* not profitable **unrentabel**

> QUOTE the airline has already eliminated a number of unprofitable flights
> *Duns Business Month*

unprompted recall *noun* recall test, an advertising research test to see how well someone can remember an advertisement where the respondent is given no help in remembering the advertisement **ungestützte Erinnerung;** *a disappointing number of respondents did not remember the advertisement at all in an unprompted recall; compare* PROMPTED RECALL

unseen *adverb* not seen **unsichtbar; unbesehen; ungesehen; to buy something sight unseen** = to buy something without having inspected it **etwas unbesehen kaufen**

unsold *adjective* not sold **unverkauft;** *unsold items will be scrapped*

unsolicited *adjective* which has not been asked for **unverlangt;** *an unsolicited gift;* **unsolicited testimonial** = letter praising someone *or* a product without the writer having been asked to write it **ohne Aufforderung gegebene Empfehlung**

unstructured interview *noun* interview using no preset questions and following no fixed pattern **unstrukturiertes Interview;** *unstructured interviews are found to be very effective in eliciting original suggestions for product improvement; shy respondents open up well in unstructured interviews where they have more freedom of expression*

unsubsidized *adjective* with no subsidy **nicht subventioniert**

unused *adjective* which has not been used **ungebraucht, unbenutzt;** *we are trying to sell off six unused typewriters*

up to date *adjective & adverb* current *or* recent *or* modern **aktuell, auf dem neuesten Stand;** *an up-to-date computer system;* **to bring something up to date** = to add the latest information or equipment to something **etwas auf den neuesten Stand bringen; to keep something up to date** = to keep adding information to something so that it always has the latest information in it **etwas auf dem laufenden halten, etwas aktualisieren;** *we spend a lot of time keeping our mailing list up to date*

update
1 *noun* information added to something to make it up to date **Aktualisierung**
2 *verb* to revise something so that it is always up to date **aktualisieren, auf den neuesten Stand bringen;** *the figures are updated annually*

up front *adverb* in advance **im voraus; money up front** = payment in advance **Vorauszahlung;** *they are asking for £100,000 up front before they will consider the deal; he had to put money up front before he could clinch the deal*

uplift *noun* increase **Anhebung;** *the contract provides for an annual uplift of charges*

up-market *adverb & adjective* more expensive *or* appealing to a wealthier section of the population **anspruchsvoll, exklusiv; the company has decided to move up-market** = the company has decided to start to produce more luxury items **die Firma entschied sich, anspruchsvollere Produkte/mehr Produkte des gehobenen Bedarfs anzubieten**

> QUOTE up-market companies which are doing well need a conference venue to reflect this
> *Marketing Week*
> QUOTE prices of up-market homes (costing $350,000 or more) are falling in many areas
> *Economist*

upset price *noun* lowest price which the seller will accept, and which is therefore the starting price at an auction **Mindest-, Vorbehaltspreis**

upturn *noun* movement towards higher sales or profits **Aufschwung;** *an upturn in the economy; an upturn in the market*

usage *noun* how something is used **Gebrauch, Anwendung;** *(US)* **usage pull** = degree to which those who see or hear advertisements for a product buy more of it than those who do not **verkaufsfördernde Wirkung der Werbung;** *we're only able to* *assess usage pull some time after the advertising campaign;* **usage segmentation** = dividing a market into segments according to the type of use which customers will make of the product **Marktsegmentierung aufgrund des Gebrauchsnutzens des Produkts**

user *noun* person who uses something **Benutzer/-in, Anwender/-in; end user** = person who actually uses a product (as opposed to the purchaser, who may not actually use it himself) **Endverbraucher; user's guide** *or* **handbook** = book showing someone how to use something **Benutzerhandbuch**

◇ **user-friendly** *adjective* which a user finds easy to work **benutzerfreundlich;** *these programs are really user-friendly*

USP = UNIQUE SELLING PROPOSITION

utility *noun* usefulness or satisfaction that a consumer gets from a product **Nutzen;** *the price charged depends on the product's utility;* **utility goods** = basic goods that are necessary for everyday life **Gebrauchsgüter;** *even some utility goods can be considered luxuries during a depression; consumers say that shopping for utility goods is routine and boring; see also* FORM, MARGINAL, PLACE, TIME UTILITY

Vv

valorem *see* AD VALOREM

VALS (acronym for Values And Life-Styles) system of dividing people into segments according to their life-styles **Marktsegmentierung aufgrund von Werten und Lebensstilen**

value
1 *noun* amount of money which something is worth **Wert;** *he imported goods to the value of £250; the fall in the value of sterling; the valuer put the value of the stock at £25,000;* **good value (for money)** = a bargain *or* something which is worth the price paid for it **preiswert, preisgünstig;** *that restaurant gives value for money; buy that computer now - it is very good value; holidays in Italy are good value because of the exchange rate;* **to rise in value** *or* **to fall in value** = to be worth more *or* less **im Wert steigen; im Wert fallen; asset value** = value of a company calculated by adding together all its assets **Vermögenswert; book value** = value as recorded in the company's accounts **Buch-, Bilanzwert; "sample only - of no commercial value"** = not worth anything if sold **‚unentgeltliche Werbeprobe'; declared value** = value of goods entered on a customs declaration form **angemeldeter/angegebener Wert; discounted value** = difference between the face value of a share and its lower market price **Diskontwert; face value** = value written on a coin *or* banknote *or* share **Nominal-, Nennwert; market value** = value of an asset *or* of a product *or* of a company, if sold today **Marktwert; par value** = value written on a share certificate **Nennwert; scarcity value** = value of something which is worth a lot because it is rare and there is a large demand for it **Seltenheitswert; surrender value** = money which an insurer will pay if an insurance policy is given up before maturity date **Rückkaufswert; value added** = value which is added to a product as it is distributed, owing to the costs incurred and profits taken by distributors **Mehrwert; value analysis** = analysis by a producer of all aspects of a finished product to determine how it could be made at minimum cost **Produktbewertungsanalyse;** *value analysis showed an excessive amount of rubber was used in manufacturing the product;* **value engineering** = analysis by a producer of all aspects of a product at the design stage to determine how it could be made at minimum cost **Produktbewertung in der Entwicklungsphase;** *value engineering allows very economical production and competitive prices at every stage in the distribution channel*
2 *verb* to estimate how much money something is worth **schätzen;** *he valued the stock at £25,000; we're having the jewellery valued for insurance;* **valued impression per pound (VIP)** = method of showing how many readers are reached by advertising for a given sum of money; *(entspricht)* **Tausenderpreis**

◇ **Value Added Tax (VAT)** *noun* tax imposed as a percentage of the invoice value of goods and services (a company pays the government the tax on goods or services sold - the output tax - and claims back from the government the tax on goods or services which it has bought - the input tax) **Mehrwertsteuer**

◇ **valuation** *noun* estimation of how much something is worth **Schätzung, Bewertung; stock valuation** = estimating the value of stock at the end of an accounting period **Bewertung des Lagerbestandes; to buy a shop with stock at valuation** = to pay the same amount for the stock as its value as estimated by the valuer **ein Geschäft**

inklusive des Warenbestandes zum Schätzpreis kaufen

◇ **valuer** *noun* person who estimates how much money something is worth **Schätzer**

van *noun* small goods vehicle **kleiner, geschlossener Lastwagen; Lieferwagen; delivery van** = van for delivering goods to customers **Lieferwagen; van ship** = ship designed to carry goods in containers **Containerschiff**

variable
1 *adjective* which changes **variabel, veränderlich, schwankend; variable costs** = production costs which increase with the quantity made (such as wages, raw materials, etc.) **variable Kosten**
2 *noun* thing which changes **Variable; controllable variables** = factors that can be controlled such as a company's marketing mix **kontrollierbare Variablen;** *because there were so few controllable variables the outcome of the marketing plan was very uncertain; although our advertising expenditure is a controllable variable, our main competitor's is not;* **dependent variables** = factors which change as a result of changes in others **abhängige Variablen**

◇ **variance** *noun* difference **Diskrepanz, Abweichung, Unterschied; budget variance** = difference between the cost as estimated for the budget, and the actual cost **Budgetabweichung; negative** *or* **positive variance** = difference between a budget and the outcome, which may mean a smaller *or* larger profit than expected **negative od positive Abweichung; at variance with** = which does not agree with **unvereinbar mit;** *the actual sales are at variance with the sales reported by the reps*

◇ **variation** *noun* amount by which something changes **Abweichung; seasonal variations** = changes which take place because of the seasons **saisonbedingte Abweichungen;** *seasonal variations in buying patterns*

variety *noun* different types of things **Auswahl, Vielfalt, Anzahl;** *the shop stocks a variety of goods; we had a variety of visitors at the office today; (US)* **variety store** = shop selling a wide range of usually cheap items **Gemischtwarenladen; variety chain store** = chain store which sells a large range of goods **Gemischtwarenkettenladen;** *the variety chain stores sell everything from jewellery to electrical products; variety chain stores are setting up their own factories to produce at least some of their own stock*

VAT = VALUE ADDED TAX *the invoice includes VAT at 15%; the government is proposing to increase VAT to 17.5%; some items (such as books) are zero-rated for VAT; he doesn't charge VAT because he asks for payment in cash;* **VAT declaration** = statement declaring VAT income to the VAT office **Mehrwertsteuererklärung; VAT invoicing** = sending of an invoice including VAT **Mehrwertsteuerabrechnung; VAT invoice** = invoice which shows VAT separately **Mehrwertsteuerrechnung; VAT inspector** = government official who examines VAT returns and checks that VAT is being paid **Finanzbeamter (zuständig für Mehrwertsteuer); VAT office** = government office dealing with the collection of VAT in a particular area; *(entspricht)* **Umsatzsteuerstelle**

◇ **VATman** *or* **vatman** *noun* VAT inspector **Finanzbeamter (zuständig für Mehrwertsteuer)**

Veblenian model *noun* a theory of buying behaviour proposed by Veblen, which explains much of consumption in terms of social influences or pressures rather than economic ones **Veblen-Modell;** *a Veblenian model helps to illustrate the non-rational side of consumer behaviour*

vehicle *noun*
(a) machine with wheels, used to carry goods *or* passengers on a road **Fahrzeug; commercial vehicle** *or* **goods vehicle** = van *or* truck used for business purposes **Nutzfahrzeug; heavy goods vehicle** = very large lorry **Schwerfahrzeug;** *goods vehicles can park in the loading bay*
(b) specific newspaper, magazine, TV programme or radio programme used to carry an advertisement **Werbeträger;** *the media planner had two days to decide which vehicle to use for the press advertising*

vending *noun* selling **Verkauf; (automatic) vending machine** = machine which provides drinks, cigarettes, etc. when a coin is put in **Automat**

◇ **vendor** *noun*
(a) person who sells (a property) **Grundstücksverkäufer;** *the solicitor acting on behalf of the vendor*
(b) person who sells goods **Verkäufer/-in; street vendor** = person who sells food or small items in the street **Straßenhändler; vendor rating** = assessment of a vendor by a buyer on the basis of the vendor's reliability and the quality and price of the goods on offer **Verkäuferschätzung;** *vendor rating has already disqualified three suppliers on the grounds of price; a good reputation for quick delivery is a key factor in the buying department's vendor ratings*

venture
1 *noun* business *or* commercial deal which involves a risk **gewagtes Unternehmen;** *he lost money on several import ventures; she's started a new venture - a computer shop;* **joint venture** = very large business project in which two or more companies, often from different countries, join together **Joint-venture, Gemeinschaftsunternehmen; venture capital** = capital for investment which may easily be lost in risky projects, but can also provide high returns **Risiko-, Wagniskapital; venture team** = group of people from different departments in a company who work together on a new product development project **Unternehmensgruppe, Innovationsteam, Produktgruppenmanagement;** *the venture team met regularly to monitor progress in the product's development*
2 *verb* to risk (money) **riskieren, aufs Spiel setzen**

venue *noun* place where something is organized **Tagungsort, Ort;** *the venue for the exhibition has been changed from the town hall to the conference centre*

vertical *adjective* upright *or* straight up or down **senkrecht, vertikal; vertical communication** = communication between senior managers via the middle management to the workers **vertikale Kommunikation; vertical industrial market** = market in which a product is used by only one industry **vertikaler Industriemarkt; vertical integration** = joining two businesses together which deal with different stages in the production or sale of a product **vertikale Integration; vertical marketing system** = distribution system that is a co-ordinated integrated unit involving the manufacturer, the wholesaler and the retailer, where marketing decisions are taken globally **vertikales Marketing, vertikale Kooperation; vertical publication** = publication for people working at different levels in the same industry **Vertikalpublikation;** *compare* HORIZONTAL

vessel *noun* ship **Schiff; merchant vessel** = commercial ship which carries a cargo **Handelsschiff**

video tape
1 *noun* magnetic tape for recording sound and vision, used for making original recordings or taping existing television material **Magnetbildband, Videoband;** *the advertiser studied the video tape of the advertisement and sent his comments to the agency*
2 *verb* to record something on video tape **auf Magnetbildband aufnehmen;** *the reactions of respondents trying the product for the first time were videotaped*

viewer *noun* person who watches television **Zuschauer/-in; heavy viewer** = person who watches television frequently, and is part of the target audience for commercials **Dauer-, Vielseher**

VIP = VALUED IMPRESSION PER POUND

visible *adjective* which can be seen **sichtbar; visible imports** *or* **exports** = real products which are imported *or* exported **sichtbare Importe; sichtbare Exporte**

visual *adjective* which can be seen **sichtbar, visuell, Anschauungs-; visual display terminal** *or* **visual display unit (VDU)** = screen attached to a computer which shows the information stored in the computer **Monitor, Bildschirmgerät, (Bild)sichtgerät**

◊ **visualizer** *noun* person who produces visual ideas for advertisements or advertising campaigns **Visualiser, (graphischer) Ideengestalter**

voice-over *noun* commentary for a TV or cinema advertisement, spoken by an actor who does not appear in the advertisement **Off-Kommentar, Sprechertext**

volume *noun* quantity of items **Menge, Umfang, Volumen; volume discount** = discount given to customer who buys a large quantity of goods **Mengenrabatt; volume of output** = number of items produced **Produktionsvolumen; volume of sales** *or* **sales volume** = number of items sold **Absatz(volumen); low** *or* **high volume of sales** = small *or* large number of items sold **geringer Absatz; hoher Absatz; volume of trade** *or* **volume of business** = number of items sold *or* number of shares sold on the Stock Exchange during a day's trading **Umsatzvolumen;** *the company has maintained the same volume of business in spite of the recession;* **volume segmentation** = segmentation *or* division of a market on the basis of the quantity of the product bought **Marktsegmentierung aufgrund von Absatzvolumen**

◊ **volumetrics** *noun* analysis of the relative influence of various media by considering the number of people who are exposed to them, and their importance as buyers; *(entspricht)* **Maßstäbe für Kontaktqualität;** *volumetrics has been our most useful tool in media buying; the marketing department* *consulted an expert in volumetrics to help plan the advertising campaign*

voluntary *adjective*
(a) done freely *or* without anyone forcing you to act **freiwillig; voluntary control** = system adopted by the advertising industry for controlling possible abuses which involves following certain guidelines laid down for the industry as a whole **freiwillige Kontrolle;** *if voluntary controls are not effective, the government will have to bring in legislation*
(b) done without being paid **freiwillig; voluntary chain** *or* **voluntary group** = distributors who join together to buy from suppliers so as to enjoy quantity discounts **freiwillige Kette; freiwillige Gruppe;** *after joining the voluntary chain the shop saved up to 20% in buying;* **voluntary organization** = organization which has no paid staff **Wohltätigkeitsorganisation**

◇ **voluntarily** *adverb* without being forced or paid **freiwillig**

voucher *noun*
(a) paper which is given instead of money **Gutschein; cash voucher** = paper which can be exchanged for cash **Bargeldgutschein;** *the customer gets a cash voucher to the value of £2 with every £20 of purchases ;* **gift voucher** = card, bought in a store, which is given as a present and which must be exchanged for goods in that store **Geschenkgutschein; luncheon voucher** = ticket, given by an employer to a worker, which can be exchanged in a restaurant for food **Essensmarke**
(b) written document from an auditor to show that the accounts are correct *or* that money has really been paid **Buchungsbeleg; Beleg, Quittung**

Ww

wagon *or* **waggon** *noun* goods truck used on the railway **Güterwagen, Waggon;** *(US)* **waggon jobber** = limited function wholesaler, usually one who delivers goods by truck to retailers **Großhändler, der per LKW liefert;** *compare* TRUCK JOBBER

warehouse
1 *noun* large building where goods are stored **Lager(haus); bonded warehouse** = warehouse where goods are stored until excise duty has been paid **Zollager; warehouse capacity** = space available in a warehouse **Lagerhauskapazität; price ex warehouse** = price for a product which is to be collected from the manufacturer's or agent's warehouse and so excludes delivery **Preis ab Lager**
2 *verb* to store (goods) in a warehouse **lagern**

◇ **warehousing** *noun* act of storing goods **Lagerung;** *warehousing costs are rising rapidly*

◇ **warehouseman** *noun* person who works in a warehouse **Lagerarbeiter**

warranty *noun* legal document which promises that a machine will work properly and in which the producer agrees to compensate the buyer if the product is faulty or becomes faulty before a certain date **Garantie;** *the car is sold with a twelve-month warranty; the warranty covers spare parts but not labour costs*

waybill *noun* list of goods carried, made out by the carrier **Frachtbrief**

wear and tear *noun* damage to a product through use over a period of time **Abnutzungs- und Verschleißerscheinungen**

weekly *noun* newspaper *or* magazine which is published each week **Wochenzeitung; Wochenzeitschrift;** *the clothes were advertised in the fashion weeklies*

weight *noun* measurement of how heavy something is **Gewicht; to sell fruit by weight** = the price is per pound *or* per kilo of the fruit **Obst nach Gewicht verkaufen; false weight** = weight on a shop scales which is wrong and so cheats customers **falsches Gewicht; gross weight** = weight of both the container and its contents **Bruttogewicht; net weight** = weight of goods after deducting the packing material and container **Nettogewicht; to give short weight** = to give less than you should **zu knapp abwiegen; inspector of weights and measures** = government official who inspects goods sold in shops to see if the quantities and weights are correct **Eichmeister**

◇ **weighted** *adjective* **weighted average** = average which is calculated taking several factors into account, giving some more value than others **Bewertungsdurchschnitt; weighted index** = index where some important items are given more value than less important ones **Bewertungsindex**

◇ **weighting** *noun* statistical process which gives more importance to some figures or results than others in the process of reaching a final figure or result **Gewichtung**

wet goods *noun* goods that are sold in liquid form **Flüssigware;** *special plastic containers have to be used for wet goods; inflammable wet goods are the most dangerous type of product to transport*

wheel of retailing *noun* model which explains changes in the evolution of the retailing trade **Dynamik der Betriebsformen**

white goods *plural noun*
(a) machines (such as refrigerators, washing machines, etc.) used in the kitchen **elektrische Haushaltsgeräte**
(b) sheets *or* towels, etc. **Bett- und Tischwäsche**

wholesale *noun & adverb* buying goods from manufacturers and selling in large quantities to traders who then sell in smaller quantities to the general public **(im) Großhandel;** *wholesale discount; wholesale shop;* **wholesale dealer** = person who buys in bulk from manufacturers and sells to retailers **Großhändler; wholesale price index** = index showing the rises and falls of prices of manufactured goods as they leave the factory **Großhandelspreisindex; he buys wholesale and sells retail** = he buys goods in bulk at a wholesale discount and then sells in small quantities to the public **er kauft im Großhandel und verkauft im Einzelhandel**

◊ **wholesaler** *noun* person who buys goods in bulk from manufacturers and sells them to retailers **Großhändler**

wild cats *noun* in the Boston matrix, products which are not very profitable, having a low market share but which have a high growth rate **Wildkatzen**
NOTE: also called **problem children** or **question marks**

win *verb* to be successful **gewinnen; to win a contract** = to be successful in tendering for a contract **einen Vertrag bekommen;** *the company announced that it had won a contract worth £25m to supply buses and trucks*

window *noun* **shop window** = large window in a shop front, where customers can see goods displayed **Schaufenster; window display** = display of goods in a shop window **Auslage, Schaufensterdekoration; window shopping** = looking at goods in shop windows, without buying anything **Schaufensterbummel**

◊ **window dressing** *noun* putting goods on display in a shop window, so that they attract customers **Dekoration**

wobbler *noun* **shelf wobbler** = card placed on the shelf in a shop to promote a product **Regalschild**

work-in-progress *noun* value of goods being manufactured which are not complete at the end of an accounting period **Halbfabrikate;** *our current assets are made up of stock, goodwill and work-in-progress*

◊ **works** *noun* factory **Werk, Fabrik;** *an industrial works; an engineering works; the steel works is expanding;* **price ex works** = price excluding transport from the manufacturer's factory **Preis ab Werk**

◊ **workshop** *noun* small factory **Werkstatt**

world *noun*
(a) the earth **Welt; the world market for steel** = the possible sales of steel in the whole world **der Weltmarkt für Stahl; world enterprise** = advanced form of international marketing **Globalmarketing; to have world rights to a product** = to have the right to sell the product anywhere in the world **die weltweiten Rechte für ein Produkt haben**
(b) people in a particular business *or* people with a special interest **Welt, Berufssphäre;** *the world of big business; the world of publishing or the publishing world; the world of lawyers or the legal world*

◊ **worldwide** *adjective & adverb* everywhere in the world **weltweit;** *the company has a worldwide network of distributors; worldwide sales or sales worldwide have topped two million units; this make of computer is available worldwide*

wrap (up) *verb* to cover something all over (in paper) **einwickeln, einpacken;** *he wrapped (up) the parcel in green paper;* **to gift-wrap a present** = to wrap a present in special coloured paper **ein Geschenk verpacken; shrink-wrapped** = covered in tight plastic protective cover **eingeschweißt**

◊ **wrapper** *noun* material which wraps something **Verpackung;** *the biscuits are packed in plastic wrappers*

◊ **wrapping** *noun* **wrapping paper** = special coloured paper for wrapping presents **Geschenkpapier; gift-wrapping** = (i) service in a store for wrapping presents for customers; (ii) coloured paper for wrapping presents **(i) Geschenkverpackungsdienst; (ii) Geschenkpapier; shrink-wrapping** = act of covering (a book, fruit, a record, etc.) in a tight plastic cover **Schrumpfpackung**

Xx Yy Zz

brand X the anonymous brand which is used on TV commercials as a comparison to the named brand being advertised **Marke X**

yard *noun* measure of length (= 0.91 metres) **Yard**

yearbook *noun* reference book which is published each year with updated or new information **Jahrbuch;** *look up the trade statistics in the latest Government Yearbook*

yellow pages *plural noun* section of a telephone directory (printed on yellow paper) which lists businesses under various headings (such as computer shops or newsagents, etc.) **Gelbe Seiten, Branchenverzeichnis**

yen *noun* money used in Japan **Yen**
NOTE: usually written as **Y** before a figure: **Y2,700** (say "two thousand seven hundred yen")

yuppies *noun* young professional people with relatively high incomes **Yuppies;** (Short for **Young Upwardly-mobile** *or* **Urban Professionals)**

zero-rated *adjective* (item) which has a VAT rate of 0% **mehrwertsteuerfrei**

◇ **zero-rating** *noun* rating of an item at 0% VAT; **Mehrwertsteuerbefreiung**

zip code *noun (US)* numbers used to indicate a postal delivery area in an address on an envelope **Postleitzahl;** (NOTE: GB English is **postcode)**

zone
1 *noun* area of a town *or* country (for administrative purposes) **Zone, Gebiet; development zone** *or* **enterprise zone** = area which has been given special help from the government to encourage businesses and factories to set up there **Förderungsgebiet; free trade zone** = area where there are no customs duties **Freihandelszone**
2 *verb* to divide (a town) into different areas for planning purposes **in Zonen aufteilen; land zoned for light industrial use** = land where planning permission has been given to build small factories for light industry **für Leichtindustrie vorgesehenes Land**

Deutsch-Englisches Register

Aa

Abbau: *retrenchment*
Abbau einschränkender Bestimmungen: *deregulation*
abbauen: *run down*
Abbaurecht: *mining concession*
ABC-Methode: *ABC method*
Abernten: *harvesting*
Abfallprodukt: *by-product*
Abfertigung: *forwarding*
Abflauen: *downturn*
Abgabe: *levy*
Abgabe von Angeboten: *bidding*
abgemacht: *agreed*
abgeworben: **er wurde ~** *he was headhunted*
abhängig: *dependent*
abhängig von: *depending on*
abheben: *draw*
abholen: *collect*
Abholmarkt: *box store (US); cash and carry*
Abhol- und Zustelldienst: *pickup and delivery service*
Abkommen: *agreement; deal; treaty*
abladen: *land*
Ablader: *shipper*
Ablagesystem: *filing system*
Ablehnung: **allgemeine ~** *blanket refusal*
Abmachung: *agreement* **faire ~** *fair deal*
Abnahme: *decline*
Abnahmebescheinigung: *test certificate*
abnehmen: *decline; fall away; fall off*
Abnehmer: *taker*
Abnutzungs- und Verschleißerscheinungen: *wear and tear*
Abonnement: *subscription*
Abonnementsauflage: *subscribed circulation*
Abonnementspreis: *subscription rate*
Abrechnung: *invoicing; settlement; (statement of) account* **spezifizierte ~** *itemized account*
Abrechnungstag: *account day; settlement day*
Abrechnungszeitraum: *accounting period*
Absahnungspolitik: *creaming*
Absatz: *article; clause; disposal; sales* **erwarteter ~** *projected sales* **geringer ~** *low volume of sales* **hoher ~** *high (volume of) sales*
Absatzanalyse: *sales analysis*
Absatzbericht: **monatlicher ~** *monthly sales report*
Absatzdiagramm: *sales chart*
absatzfähig: *marketable; saleable*
Absatzfähigkeit: *saleability*
Absatz finden: *sell*
Absatzförderung: *sales promotion; trade promotion*
Absatzförderung betreiben: *merchandise*
Absatzgebiet: *market; trading area*
Absatzgeschwindigkeit: *rate of sales*
Absatzkanäle: *channels of distribution* or *distribution channels*
Absatzkosten: *cost of sales*
Absatz laut Verkaufsbuch: *book sales*
Absatzmarkt: **begrenzter ~** *limited market* **monopolistischer ~** *captive market* **wachsender ~** *growth market*
Absatz-Mix: *sales mix*
Absatzmöglichkeiten: **die ~ analysieren** *to analyze the market potential* **neue ~** *market opportunities*
Absatzplanung: *sales budget*
Absatzpolitik: *marketing policy; merchandising*
Absatzpotential: *sales potential*
Absatzprognose: *sales forecast*
Absatzquoten: *sales quotas*
Absatzrevision: *sales audit*
Absatzvolumen: *sales volume* or *volume of sales*
Absatzweg: *trading channel; pipeline*
Absatzwegkapitän: *channel captain (US)*
Absatzwegkapitänseinfluß: *channel power*
Absatzzahlen: *sales figures*
abschicken: *post*
abschieben: *offload*
Abschlagszahlung: *payment on account; part payment*
abschließen: *close*
abschließend: *closing*
Abschluß: *bargain; close; deal*
Abschluß auf Termin: *forward contract*
Abschluß eines Verkaufs: *closing a sale*
Abschlußrabatt: *concession close*
Abschlußtechnik: *closing technique*
Abschöpfung: *import levy*
Abschöpfungsstrategie: *creaming*
Abschreibungssatz: *depreciation rate*
Absender: *consignor; dispatcher; return address; sender* **zurück an ~** *"return to sender"*
Absichtserklärung: *letter of intent*
absolut: *absolute; total*
absorbieren: *absorb*
abspalten: *hive off*
abstoßen: *offload; sell off; unload*
Abstoßung: *unloading*
abstufen: *grade*
Abteilung: *department; division*
Abteilung Einkauf: *purchasing department*
Abteilung für Öffentlichkeitsarbeit: *public relations department*
Abteilungs-: *divisional*
Abteilungsleiter: *head of department* or *department head* or *department manager; floor manager (US); shopwalker*
Abteilungsleiterin: *manageress*
Abteilung Verkauf: *sales department*
abverkaufen: *clear*
Abweichung: *deviation; variance; variation* **negative ~** *negative variance* **positive ~** *positive variance* **statistische ~** *statistical discrepancy* **zufällige ~** *random fluctuation*

Abweichungen: **saisonbedingte** ~ *seasonal variations*

abwerten: *devalue*

Abwertung: *devaluation*

Abzahlungskredit: *consumer credit*

Abzahlungsrabatt: *deferred rebate*

abzielen auf: *target*

Achtundvierzigerformat: *forty-eight sheet*

ad hoc: *ad hoc*

administrativ: *administrative*

Adoption: *adoption*

Adoptionskurve: *adoption curve*

Adreßbuch: *directory*

Adressenanhänger *or* **Adressenaufkleber:** *address label*

Adressenliste: *address list or mailing list*

Agate(-Zeile): *agate (US)*

Agent: *agent; representative*

Agentur: *agency*

Agio: *exchange premium*

AIDA-Modell: *AIDA*

Airline: *airline*

Akkordarbeit: *jobbing production*

Akkreditiv: *letter of credit (L/C)* **unwiderrufliches** ~ *irrevocable letter of credit* **widerrufliches** ~ *revocable letter of credit*

Akontozahlung: *payment on account*

Akronym: *acronym*

Akte: *document*

Akten: *records*

Aktie: **eine schnell steigende** ~ *a boom share; a high flier*

Aktiengesellschaft: *corporation (US); Public Limited Company*

Aktienkapital: *share capital*

Aktienportefeuille: *portfolio*

Aktienübertragung: *transfer of shares*

Aktienübertragungsformular: *stock transfer form*

Aktion: *campaign*

Aktionswerbung: *direct-action advertising*

Aktiva: *asset*

Aktivsaldo: *credit balance*

aktualisieren: *to update* **etwas** ~ *to keep something up to date*

Aktualisierung: *update*

aktuell: *up to date*

Akzelerationsprinzip: *accelerator*

Akzept: **unwiderrufliches** ~ *irrevocable acceptance* **vorbehaltloses** ~ *clean acceptance*

akzeptabel: *acceptable*

Akzeptant: *acceptor*

Akzeptanz: *adoption*

Akzeptbank: *accepting house*

akzeptieren: *accept; adopt*

Akzeptierende: **früh** ~ *early adopters*

Akzeptleistung gegen Dokumente: *acceptance against documents*

Akzeptverweigerung: *non-acceptance*

Akzidenzdrucker: *jobbing printer*

Alleineigentümer: *sole owner*

alleinig: *sole*

Alleinstellung: *island position*

Alleinvertreter: *sole agent*

Alleinvertretung: *sole agency*

Alleinvertretungsvereinbarung: *exclusive agreement*

Alleinvertrieb: *sole agency; sole distributor; exclusivity*

allgemein: *common*

Altarfalz: *gatefold*

Altersgrenze: *age limit*

Altersgruppe: *age group*

altmodisch: *out of date*

Amt für Verbraucherschutz: *Office of Fair Trading (OFT) (GB)*

Amtsweg: **den** ~ **beschreiten** *to go through the official channels*

Analyse: **morphologische** ~ *morphological analysis* **qualitative** ~ *qualitative research* **quantitative** ~ *quantitative research* **typologische** ~ *typological analysis* **unternehmungsinterne** ~ *situation analysis* **vergleichende** ~ *comparative analysis*

analysieren: *analyse or analyze*

Analytiker: *analyst*

anbieten: *offer*

Anblick: *sight*

ändern: *modify*

Änderung: *modification; shift*

Andlersche Losgrößenformel: *economic order quantity*

Anerkennung: *recognition*

Anfang: *start*

anfänglich: *initial*

Anfangskurs: *opening price*

Anfangsverkauf: *initial sales*

anfordern: **etwas** ~ *send away for or send off for (something)*

Anforderung: **auf** ~ **bezahlen** *to pay on demand*

Anforderungen: **den** ~ **genügend** *up to standard*

Anfrage: *inquiry* **briefliche** ~ *letter of inquiry*

Anfragebrief: *letter of inquiry*

anführen: *lead; quote*

Angabe: **falsche** ~ *false claim*

angeben: *quote; specify*

Angebot: *bid; offer; quote (informal); range; supply; tender; tendering* **aggregiertes** ~ *aggregate supply* **ein** ~ **abgeben** *to put in a bid or to enter a bid (for something)* **ein** ~ **machen** *to put in a tender or to submit a tender* **elastisches** ~ *elastic supply* **gesamtes** ~ *aggregate supply* **günstiges** ~ *bargain offer* **unelastisches** ~ *inelastic supply*

Angebote werden entgegengenommen: *open to offers*

Angebotsabgabe: *tendering*

Angebotspreis: *supply price*

Angebotsüberschuß: *excess supply*

Angebot und Nachfrage: *supply and demand*

Angelegenheit: *business*
angemeldet: *registered*
angesammelt: *aggregate*
angeschmutzt: *shop-soiled*
angewiesen: *dependent*
angewiesen sein auf: *to depend on*
angleichen: *adjust*
Angstkäufe: *panic buying*
Anhang: *schedule*
Anhänger *or* **Anhängeschild:** *tie-on label*
anhäufend: *cumulative*
Anhebung: *uplift*
ankaufen: *purchase*
Ankäufer: *acquirer*
Anlage: *enclosure; facility (US); installation*
Anlagegüter: *capital goods*
Anlagevermögen: *capital assets or fixed assets; fixed capital*
Anlauf: *start-up*
Anlaufhafen: *port of call*
Anlaufkosten: *launching costs*
anlegen: *berth*
Anmeldegebühr: *registration fee*
Anmeldung: *registration*
Annahme: *acceptance* **unwiderrufliche ~** *irrevocable acceptance*
Annahme eines Angebotes: *acceptance of an offer*
annehmbar: *acceptable*
annehmen: *accept; adopt*
Annonce: *advertisement*
annoncieren: *advertise*
annullieren: *nullify; revoke*
Annullierung: *nullification*
Anordnung: *order*
anpassen: *adapt; adjust*
Anpassung: *adaptation*
anpreisen: *plug*
Anpreisung: **marktschreierische ~** *puff*
anrechenbar: *chargeable*
Anregung: *suggestion*
Anreiz: *incentive*
Anreiz-Marketing: *incentive marketing*
Anreizsystem: *incentive scheme*
anrufen: *call in*
ansammeln: *hoard*
Anschaffung: *acquisition*
Anschaffungskosten: **ursprüngliche ~** *historic(al) cost*
Anschauungs-: *visual*
Anschlag: **wilder ~** *fly poster*
Anschlagbeginn: *date-in-charge*
Anschlagbrett: *billboard; noticeboard*
Anschlagfläche: *display panel*
Anschlagstelle: *poster site*
Anschlagwand: *hoarding*
Anschlagwerbewarenzeichen: *adshel*
Anschlagzettel: *bill; placard*
Anschlußkauf: *rebuy* **direkter ~** *straight rebuy*
anschneiden: *bleed*
Ansehen: *standing*
Ansicht: *judgement or judgment*
ansprechen: *reach*
anspruchsvoll: *up-market*
ansteigen: *escalate* **wieder ~** *rebound*
anstreben: *target*
Antitrust-: *anti-trust*
Antragsformular: *application form*
Antwort: *reply; response*
Antwortcoupon: *reply coupon*
antworten: *reply; respond*
antwortete: **er ~ postwendend** *he replied by return of post*
Antwortkarte: *reply card* **frankierte** *or* **freigemachte ~** *prepaid reply card; reply paid card*
Antwortschein: **internationaler ~** *international postal reply coupon*
Anwaltskosten: *legal expenses*
Anweisung: *order*
Anwender: *user*
Anwendung: *usage*
Anzahl: *quantity; variety*
Anzahl der Abschlüsse *or* **Anzahl der Börsengeschäfte:** *bargains done*
anzahlen: *put down*
Anzahlung: *advance; deposit; down payment* **eine ~ einbüßen** *or* **verwirken** *to forfeit a deposit* **eine ~ leisten** *to pay money on account; to put money down*
Anzeige: *advertisement* **alleinstehende ~** *solus (advertisement)* **doppelseitige ~** *(double page) spread* **redaktionell aufgezogene** *or* **redaktionell gestaltete ~** *editorial advertisement* **textanschließende ~** *backup ad*
anzeigen: *indicate*
Anzeigenbeilage: *stuffer (US)*
Anzeigenblatt: *freesheet; free paper or giveaway paper*
Anzeigenfehler: *fudge*
Anzeigenkollektiv: *omnibus advertisement*
Anzeigenkosten: *advertising rates*
Anzeigenkunde: *advertiser*
Anzeigenleiter: *advertisement manager*
Anzeigenplazierung: **feste ~** *fixed position*
Anzeigenposition im Heftanfang: *front of book*
Anzeigenpreisliste: *rate card*
Anzeigenraum: *advertising space; lineage*
Anzeigenraum belegen: *to take advertising space*
Anzeigenschluß: *closing; copy date*
Anzeigen(ver)mittler: *space buyer*
anziehen: *advance*
Anziehungskraft: *appeal*
Appell: **emotionaler ~** *emotional appeal*
Arbeit: **die ~ niederlegen** *to down tools*
Arbeiter: **gewerkschaftlich organisierte ~** *organized labour*

Arbeiterschaft: *labour force or workforce*
Arbeitgeber-Arbeitnehmer-Beziehungen: *industrial relations*
Arbeitgeberverband: *employers' organization*
Arbeitsablaufdiagramm: *flow chart; flow diagram*
Arbeitsabläufe auflisten: *to list task processes*
Arbeitsbelastung: *workload*
Arbeitserlaubnis: *work permit*
Arbeitsfluß: *traffic*
Arbeitsgang eines Computers: *a computer run*
Arbeitsgesetze or **Arbeitsgesetzgebung:** *labour legislation*
Arbeitskampf: *industrial dispute*
Arbeitskampfmaßnahmen ergreifen: *to take industrial or direct action*
Arbeitskräfte: *labour force or workforce; human resources* **direkte ~** *direct labour*
Arbeitskräftemangel: *manpower shortage or shortage of manpower*
Arbeitslosigkeit: saisonbedingte ~ *seasonal unemployment*
Arbeitsmarkt: der ~ *the labour market*
Arbeitsplan: *schedule*
Arbeitsplatzbeschreibung: *job specification*
Arbeitstage: drei ~ *three clear days*
Arbeitsunfall: *industrial accident*
Arbeitsvertragsbedingungen: *conditions of employment or conditions of service*
Armer Hund: *dog*
Art: *mode; style*
Art-Direktor: *art director*
Artikel: *article; item; product* **führender ~** *leader* **gängiger ~** *seller* **leichtverkäufliche** or **schnellverkäufliche ~** *fast-selling items*
Arzneimittel: patentrechtlich geschütztes ~ *patent medicine*
Aspekt: ökonomischer ~ *economics*
Atmosphäre: *atmosphere*
Atrium: *atrium*
ATR-Modell: *ATR*
Attrappe: *dummy pack; mock-up*
audiovisuell: *audio-visual*
Aufbau: *organization; structure*
aufbauen: *organize; structure*
aufbewahren: *store*
Aufbewahrung: *storage*
Aufforderung: *demand*
aufführen: einzeln ~ *itemize; specify*
Auffülladung: *berth cargo*
Aufgabe: *function; job; task*
Aufgaben der Betriebsleitung: *management function or function of management*
Aufgabenumwelt: *business environment; immediate environment; micro-environment*
aufgeben: *mail*
Aufgeld: *exchange premium*
aufgeschoben: *deferred*
aufgrund: *due*
aufhalten: *delay*
aufheben: *revoke*
Aufhebung: *nullification*
aufkaufen: *snap up*
Aufkleber: *gummed label; sticker*
Auflage: *batch; circulation; condition; run* **garantierte ~** *guaranteed circulation*
Auflagen: mit ~ *conditional*
Auflagengabelung: *split run*
Auflagengarantie: *guaranteed circulation*
Auflagenhöhe: *circulation*
Auflagennummer: *batch number*
Auflagensplit: *split run*
Auflegemaske: *overlay*
auflisten: *list*
auflösen: *close*
Auflösungswert: *break-up value*
aufmachen: *open*
Aufmachungsmuster: *dummy*
Aufmerksamkeit: *attention*
Aufmöbelung: *face-lift*
Aufnahme von Aktion: *action shot*
aufnehmen: *absorb*
Aufpreis: *surcharge*
aufrufen: *access*
aufschieben: *defer*
Aufschlag: *surcharge*
Aufschub: *deferment*
Aufschwung: *boom; upturn*
Aufsicht: *control* **unter staatlicher ~** *government-controlled*
Aufsichtsrat: *directorate*
Aufsichtsratsmitglied: *director; non-executive director*
aufsplittern: *fragment*
Aufstellen: *installation*
aufstellen: *install*
Aufstellung: *schedule*
aufteilen: *break up; share*
Aufteilen der Menge: *bulk-breaking or breaking bulk*
Auftrag: *mission; order* **einen ~ stornieren** *to countermand an order* **einen ~ verlieren** *to lose an order*
Auftrag an Vertreter: *journey order*
Aufträge: unerledigte ~ *back orders; outstanding orders; unfulfilled orders*
Auftraggeber: *client; principal* **überregionaler ~** *national account*
Auftragnehmer: *contractor*
Auftragsabwicklung: *traffic*
Auftragsarbeit: *contract work*
Auftragsarbeit vergeben: *to put work out to contract*
Auftragsausführung: *order fulfilment*
Auftragsbestätigungsunternehmen: *confirming house*
Auftragsbuch: *order book*
Auftragserfüllung: *order fulfilment*

Auftragsrückstände: *back orders; outstanding orders; unfulfilled orders*
Auftragsverlust: *loss of an order*
Aufwands- und Ertragsrechnung: *income statement (US)*
Aufwendungen: **außerordentliche ~** *below-the-line expenditure* **betriebliche ~** *operating costs or operating expenses*
aufzeichnen: *record*
Aufzeichnung: *recording*
Aufzeichnungen: *records*
Augen: **unter vier ~** *privately*
Augenbewegungstest: *eye-movement test*
Augenfälligkeitstest: *stand out test*
Auktion: *auction*
Auktionator: *auctioneer*
Auktionsposten: *odd lot*
Auktionsraum: *saleroom*
Auktionsräume: *auction mart*
Ausbau: *expansion*
ausbauen: *expand*
ausbeuten: *exploit*
Ausbildung: **betriebliche ~** *industrial training*
Ausbildungsabgabe: *training levy*
ausbreiten: *roll out*
auserlesen or **auserwählt:** *select*
Ausfallbürgschaftserklärung: *letter of indemnity*
Ausfuhr: *export; exportation*
Ausfuhren: **unsichtbare ~** *invisible exports*
ausführen: *describe; effect; export; fulfil or fulfill (US)*
Ausfuhrlizenz: *export licence*
Ausfuhrprämie: *export bounty*
Ausführung: *fulfilment*
Ausführung der Bestellung: *order fulfilment*
Ausführungsanzeige: *contract note*
Ausfuhrzoll: *export duty*
Ausgabe: *edition; expense; issue*
Ausgaben: *spending* **abzugsfähige ~** *allowable expenses* **hohe ~** *heavy costs or heavy expenditure*
Ausgaben der Privathaushalte: *consumer spending*
Ausgabeposten: *item of expenditure*
Ausgabe postlagernder Sendungen: *general delivery (US)*
Ausgangsdaten: *raw data*
Ausgangspunkt: *base; starting point*
Ausgangsstichprobe: *master sample*
ausgeben: *issue; spend*
ausgedehnt: *extensive*
ausgeführt: **nicht ~** *unfulfilled*
ausgenommen: *exempt*
ausgerichtet: *oriented*
ausgerichtet sein auf: *cater for*
ausgliedern: *hive off*
aushandeln: *bargain*
Ausklarierungsschein: *clearance certificate*
Auskunft: *information bureau or information office*
ausladen: *land; unload*
Auslage: *display*
Auslagefläche: *display panel*
Auslagekarton: *display outer*
Auslagekasten: *dump bin*
Auslagenstand: *display stand or display unit*
Auslageregal: *gondola*
Ausland: *overseas*
Ausländer: *foreigner*
ausländisch: *external; foreign; overseas*
Auslandsabteilung: **die ~** *the overseas division*
Auslandsauftrag: *indent* **einen ~ erteilen** *to indent for something*
Auslandsdelegation: *inward mission*
Auslandsgespräch: **ein ~** *an overseas call*
Auslandsinvestitionen: *foreign investments*
Auslandskonto: *external account*
Auslandswaren: *foreign goods*
Auslandszahlungsanweisung: *foreign or international or overseas money order*
Auslastung: **wirtschaftliche ~** *commercial load*
Auslastungsfaktor: *load factor*
ausnutzen: *exploit*
Auspreisung: **konkurrenzfähige** or **wettbewerbsfähige ~** *competitive pricing*
ausrollen: *roll out*
Ausschankzeiten: *licensing hours (GB)*
ausschließlich: *exclusive of*
Ausschluß der Gewährleistung: *caveat emptor*
Ausschlußklausel: *exclusion clause*
Ausschneiden: *clipping*
Ausschnitt: *cutting*
Ausschnittdienst: *press cutting agency*
Ausschreibungspreis: *sealed bid price*
Ausschreibungsschluß: *closing; closing date*
Ausschuß: **geschäftsführender ~** *management committee*
Ausschußware: *reject*
ausschütten: *distribute*
Außendienst: **im ~** *in the field*
Außendienstleiter: *field sales manager*
Außendienstverkaufspersonal: *field sales force*
Außenhandel: *external or foreign or overseas trade*
Außenhandelsdefizit: *trade deficit or trade gap*
Außenplakatwand: **großformatige ~** *billboard (US)*
Außenstände: *accounts receivable; outstanding debts* **nicht einziehbare ~** *bad debt*
Außenwerbung: *outdoor advertising*
außerbetrieblich: *external*
Aussichten: *prospects*
ausstehend: *outstanding*
ausstellen: *display; draw; issue; make out*
Ausstellen von Rechnungen: *billing (US)*
Aussteller: *drawer; exhibitor*
Ausstellung: *exhibition; show*

Ausstellungsbehälter: *dump bin*
Ausstellungskarton: *display outer*
Ausstellungsraum: *exhibition room* or *hall; showroom*
Ausstellungsstück: *exhibit*
Ausstoß: *output*
Ausstrahlungseffekt: *halo effect*
aussuchen: *select*
Austausch: *exchange; trade-off*
austauschbar: *exchangeable*
austauschen: *substitute*
Austauschverhältnisse: *terms of trade*
Ausverkauf: *bargain sale; sale*
ausverkaufen: *clear; sell out*
Ausverkauf wegen Inventur: *stocktaking sale*
Auswahl: *depth; range; sample; selection; variety* **geschichtete ~** *stratification* **mehrstufige ~** *multi-stage sample*
auswählen: *select*
Auswahlfrage: *multiple choice question*
Auswahlkomitee: *selection board* or *selection committee*
Auswahlverfahren: *selection procedure*
ausweiten: *expand*
Ausweitung: *expansion*
auswerten: *analyse* or *analyze*
Auswertung: *analysis*
Auswirkung: *effect; impact*
auszeichnen: *sticker*
Auto: ein ~ probefahren *to test-drive a car*
Automat: *(automatic) vending machine; dispenser; slot machine*
Automatenvertrieb: *automatic selling* or *automatic vending*
automatisch: *automatic*
Automatisierung: *automation*
Automodell: meistverkauftes ~ *best-selling car*
Auto-Montagewerk: *car assembly plant*
Autorenhonorar: *royalty*
Avis: *advice of dispatch; letter of advice; advice note* **laut ~** *as per advice*

Bb

Babyboomer: *baby boomer*
Bahn: *rail; railway* or *railroad (US)* **frei ~** *free on rail*
Baisse: *slump*
Baissemarkt: *a falling market*
baldmöglichst: *at your earliest convenience*
Balkendiagramm: *bar chart*
Bankakzept: *bank bill*
Bankdirektor: *bank manager*
Banker: *banker*
Bankgebühren: *bank charges*
Bankgiro: *bank giro (GB)*
Bankier: *banker*
Bankkonto: *bank account* or *banking account (US)*
Bankkredit: *bank credit*
Bankleitzinssatz: *bank base rates*
Banknote: *(bank) bill (US); bank note* or *currency note*
Banktratte: *(bank) draft*
Banküberweisung: *bank transfer*
Bankwechsel: *bank draft; banker's bill* or *bank bill (GB)*
Banner: *banner*
bar: etwas ~ kaufen *to purchase something for cash*
Barangebot: *cash offer*
Barauszahlung: *"pay cash" (GB)*
Barbestand: *cash balance; balance in hand*
bar bezahlen: *to pay cash*
Bar-Code: *bar code*
Bargebot: ein ~ machen *to make a cash bid*
Bargeld: *cash; cash in hand; hard cash; ready cash; ready money*
Bargeldgutschein: *cash voucher*
Bargeschäft: *cash sale* or *cash transaction*
Barkasse: *petty cash*
Barkauf: *cash purchase*
Barposten: *cash items*
Barpreis: *cash price*
Barreserven: *cash reserves*
Barscheck: *open* or *uncrossed cheque*
Barverkauf: *cash deal; cash sale*
Barvorschuß: *cash advance*
bar zahlen: *to pay cash down*
Barzahlung: *cash (payment); cash settlement* or *settlement in cash*
Barzahlungsangebot: *cash offer*
Barzahlungsbedingungen: *cash terms*
Barzahlungspreis: *cash price*
Barzahlungsrabatt: *cash discount* or *discount for cash*
Basis: *base; basis*
Basisjahr: *base year*
Baugenehmigung: *building permit*
Bausparkasse: *building society*
Baustoffe: *building materials*
Bauunternehmer: *property developer*
Bayes(sches)-Theorem: *Bayesian decision theory*
Beachtung: *attention; noting*
Beachtungswert: *noting score*
Bearbeiten: *editing*
bearbeiten: *handle*
Bearbeitung: *handling*
Bearbeitungsgebühr: *handling charge*
Bedarf: *demand* **den ~ decken** *to meet a demand* or *to fill a demand* **latenter ~** *latent demand* **laufender ~** *persistent demand* **ständiger ~** *persistent demand*
Bedarf an Arbeitskräften: *manpower requirements*
bedeutend: *grand; heavy*

bedienen: *run*
Bedienung: *service; service charge*
Bedienungsanleitung: *handbook; operating manual*
Bedienungszuschlag: *service charge*
bedingt: *conditional*
Bedingung: *condition* **unter der ~** *on condition*
Bedingungen: *terms* **günstige ~** *easy or favourable terms* **harte ~ stellen** *to drive a hard bargain* **unter normalen ~** *under normal conditions*
Bedürftigkeitsüberprüfung: *means test*
Beeinflußbarkeit: *persuasibility (US)*
Beeinflussungsmöglichkeiten: *channels of influence*
beenden: *close*
Beendigung: *end*
befassen: sich ~ mit *deal with; handle*
befestigen: *tie*
befördern: *carry; ship; transport*
Beförderung: *carrying; handling; transport; transportation*
Beförderungskosten: *haulage*
Beförderungsmitttel: *transportation*
Befrachter: *freighter*
befragen: *canvass; interview*
Befragte(r): *informant; interviewee; respondent*
Befragung: *interview* **direktive ~** *directive interview* **nichtdirektive ~** *non-directive interview* **postalische ~** *mail interview or mail survey (US); postal survey* **telefonische ~** *telephone survey*
befreien: *to exempt*
befreit: *exempt*
Befriedigung: *satisfaction*
Befürworter des Freihandels: *free trader*
begebbar: *negotiable*
Beginn: *start*
begleichen: *pay*
Begleichung: *payment*
Begleitschreiben: *covering letter; covering note*
begrenzen: *limit*
Begrenzung: *limitation* **zeitliche ~** *time limitation*
Behälter: *bin; container*
beherrschen: *monopolize*
beifügen: *enclose*
Beilage: *enclosure; insert or inset* **bunte or illustrierte ~** *colour supplement* **lose ~** *loose insert*
beilegen: *enclose; insert or inset*
beisteuern: *to contribute*
Beitrag: *contribution* **einen ~ leisten** *to contribute*
Beitragsanalyse: *contribution analysis*
Beitragspreiskalkulation: *contribution pricing*
bejahend: *positive*
Bekanntgabe: *publication*
Bekanntheit: *awareness*
Bekanntheitsgrad: höchster ~ *maximal awareness*
Bekanntmachung: *publication*
bekommen: *take*
bekräftigen: *confirm*
Bekräftigung: *confirmation*
beladen: *load*
Beladungsgrenze: *maximum load*
belastbar: *debitable*
Belastung: *charge*
belaufen: sich ~ auf *run*
Beleg: *receipt; voucher*
Belegschaft: *labour force or workforce*
Belegseite: *tear sheet*
beliebig: *discretionary*
beliebt: *popular*
beliefern: *supply*
benachrichtigen: *inform*
Benachrichtigung: *advice* **laut ~** *as per advice*
Benutzer: *user*
benutzerfreundlich: *user-friendly*
Benutzerhandbuch: *operating manual; user's guide or handbook*
Beobachtungsmethode: *observation method*
beratend: *consulting*
Berater: *consultant*
Beratung: *consultancy*
berechnen: *bill; charge* **zu ~** *chargeable*
Berechnung: grobe ~ *rough estimate*
Bereich: *operation; precinct; range; sector; sphere* **öffentlicher ~** *public sector*
bereisen: *travel*
bereit: *ready*
Bereitstellung: *appropriation*
Bergbaukonzession: *mining concession*
Bericht: *report*
berichten: *to report*
Berücksichtigung: *account*
Berufsfachorgan: *horizontal publication*
Berufsschäden: *industrial injuries*
Beschaffung: *procurement*
Beschäftigte(r): ganztägig ~ *full-timer*
Beschäftigungsmöglichkeiten: *employment or job opportunities*
Bescheid: *note; notice*
beschließen: *decide; fix*
Beschluß: *decision*
Beschlußfassung: *decision-making*
beschränken: *limit; restrict*
Beschränkung: *limitation; restraint; restriction*
beschreiben: *describe*
Beschreibung: *description; specification* **korrekte ~** *accurate description*
Beschwerdeabteilung: *complaints department*
Beschwerdebrief: *letter of complaint*
besonder: *ad hoc; special*
Besprechung: *conference*
Besprechung am Straßenrand: *kerbside conference*
Besprechungszimmer: *conference room*

Bestallungsurkunde zum Nachlaßverwalter: *letters of administration*
Bestand: *supply*
Bestände: *stock-in-trade; store*
Bestände aufnehmen: *to inventory*
beständig: *firm; stable*
Beständigkeit: *stability*
Bestandsaufnahme: *stocktaking*
Bestandsdatei: *master copy of a file*
Bestandskontrolle: *inventory control*
Bestandteil: *component*
bestätigen: *acknowledge; confirm*
Bestätigung: *acknowledgement; confirmation*
Bestätigungsschreiben: *confirmation; letter of acknowledgement*
Bestellbuch: *order book*
bestellen: *order* **etwas ~** *send away for or send off for (something)*
Bestellmenge: **optimale ~** *economic order quantity*
bestellt: *on order*
Bestellung: *order; purchase order* **auf ~ anfertigen** *customize* **eine ~ ausführen** *to deal with an order* **einer ~ nachkommen** *to fill or to fulfil an order*
Bestellungen: **telefonische ~** *telephone orders* **überfällige ~ abwickeln** *to release dues*
Besteuerung: **hohe ~** *high taxation* **indirekte ~** *indirect taxation*
Bestimmung der Vertragsstrafe: *penalty clause*
Bestrebung: *aim*
Bestseller: *best-seller*
Besuch: *call* **unangemeldeter ~** *cold call*
besuchen: *patronize* **jdn ~** *to call on someone*
Besucherfluß: *traffic*
Besuchsbericht: *call report*
Besuchshäufigkeit: *call frequency*
Besuchsplanung: *preapproach (US)*
Besuchsrate: *call rate*
Besuchszyklus: *call cycle*
Beteiligung: *stake* **gegenseitige ~** *reciprocal holdings*
Betrachtungsweise: *approach*
Betrag: **zuviel berechneter ~** *overcharge*
Beträge: **historische ~** *historical figures* **saisonbereinigte ~** *seasonally adjusted figures*
betreiben: *run*
Betreuung: **gastronomische ~** *catering*
Betrieb: *business; operating* **im ~** *on the shop floor*
Betriebe: *services*
betrieblich: *operational*
Betriebsabrechnung: *operating statement*
Betriebsanalyse: *operations review*
Betriebsanlage: *facility (US)*
Betriebsbudget: *operational budget*
Betriebsführung: **wissenschaftliche ~** *scientific management*
Betriebsgewinn: *operating profit*
betriebsintern: *in-house*
Betriebskosten: *operating or operational or overhead or running costs; costs of running a business; business or general or operating or overhead or running expenses*
Betriebsplanung: *operational planning*
Betriebsstoffe: *operating supplies*
Betriebssystem: *operating system*
Betriebsunfall: *industrial accident*
Betriebsverlust: *operating loss*
Betriebswirtschaftsplan: *operating budget*
Betriebszeit: *computer time*
Betriebszeitung: *house journal or house magazine or house organ (US)*
Betrüger: *racketeer*
Betrügerei: *racket*
Bett- und Tischwäsche: *white goods*
Beute: **leichte ~** *fall guy (US)*
Bevölkerung: *population* **nicht seßhafte ~** *floating population*
Bevollmächtigte(r): *accredited agent*
bewältigen: **zu ~** *manageable*
beweglich: *mobile*
Beweglichkeit: *fluidity*
Bewegungsaufnahme: *action shot*
Bewerber aussondern *or* **sieben:** *to screen candidates*
Bewerbungsausschuß: *selection board or selection committee*
Bewerbungsformular: *application form*
Bewertung: *rating; valuation*
Bewertung des Lagerbestandes: *stock valuation*
Bewertungsdurchschnitt: *weighted average*
Bewertungsindex: *weighted index*
Bewirtungsspesen: *entertainment expenses*
Bewußtheit: *awareness*
bezahlen: *pay*
Bezahlung: *payment; settlement* **sofortige ~** *spot cash*
Bezahlung in Naturalien: *payment in kind*
bezeichnen: *mark*
Beziehung: *rapport*
Bezirk: *precinct; territory*
Bezirksleiter: *area manager*
Bezogener: *drawee*
bezug: **in ~ auf** *in relation to*
Bezugsgruppe: *reference group*
Bezugsquellennachweis: *dealer tie-in*
Bieten: *bidding*
bieten: *offer* **auf etwas ~** *to bid for something*
Bieter: *bidder*
Bilanzwert: *book value*
bilateral: *bilateral*
Bilder: *pix (informal)*
Bildschirmgerät: *visual display terminal or visual display unit (VDU)*
Bildschirmtext: *teletext*
Bildschirmzeitung: *Ceefax; Oracle*
Bildsichtgerät: *visual display terminal or visual display unit (VDU)*

Bildüberschrift: *caption*
Bildunterschrift: *caption; legend; underline*
billigen: *to approve of*
Billigladen: *cut-price store; discount store*
binden: *tie*
Bingo-Karte: *Bingo card*
Binnenhafen: *inland port*
Binnenhandel: *internal trade; home trade*
Binnenmarkt: *home or domestic market*
bitte nachsenden: *please forward or to be forwarded*
Blanko-: *open-ended or open-end (US)*
Blankokredit: *open credit*
Blankoscheck: *blank cheque*
Blickregistrierungsverfahren *or* **Blickverlaufstest:** *eye-movement test*
Blindband: *dummy*
Blindtesten: *blind testing*
Block: ein ~ Bestellformulare *a pad of order forms*
blühend: *booming*
Blumengutschein: *flower token*
Blüte: *dud (informal)*
Boden: *floor* **marginaler ~** *marginal land*
Bodenfläche: *floor space*
Bodenschätze: *natural resources*
Bodentransport: *ground transportation*
Bodenverkaufsständer: *floor stand*
Body Copy: *body copy*
Bogenkorrektur: *page proof*
Bonität: *creditworthiness; standing*
Bonitätsbeurteilung: *credit rating*
Bonus aus Kapitalerträgen: *capital bonus*
Boom: *boom*
Bord: frei an ~ *free on board (f.o.b.)*
Börse: *Stock Exchange*
Börsenanalytiker: *market economist*
Börsengeschäft: *bargain*
Börsenmakler: *(stock)broker*
Börsenratgeber: *tip sheet*
Börsentransaktion: eine ~ *a transaction on the Stock Exchange*
Botschaft: *message*
Boutique: *boutique*
Boykott: *boycott*
boykottieren: *to black; to boycott*
Brainstorming: *brainstorming*
Branche: *industry; line of business or line of work; trade*
Branchenadreßbuch: *commercial or trade directory*
Branchenblatt: *trade journal*
Branchenverzeichnis: *classified directory*
Branchenzeitschrift: *trade journal or magazine or paper or publication*
Break-Even-Analyse: *breakeven analysis*
Break-Even-Punkt: *breakeven point*
Brett: *panel*
briefen: *brief*
Briefgebühr: *letter rate*
Briefing: *briefing*
Briefkopf: *letterhead*
Briefmarke: *postage stamp*
Briefpost: *letter post*
Briefumschlag: verschlossener ~ *sealed envelope*
Briefwerbeaktion: *mail shot or mailing shot*
Briefwerbematerial: *mailer*
Briefwerbung: *direct-mail advertising*
Broschüre: *brochure; pamphlet*
Bruchproben: *torture testing*
Bruchteil: *fraction*
brutto: *gross*
Bruttoeinkommen: *gross earnings*
Bruttoeinnahmen: *gross receipts*
brutto einnehmen: *to gross*
Bruttoertrag: *gross yield*
Bruttogewicht: *gross weight*
Bruttogewinn: *gross profit*
Bruttoinlandsprodukt: *gross domestic product (GDP)*
Bruttokontaktsumme: *gross audience; gross impressions*
Bruttokontaktwahrscheinlichkeit: *gross opportunity to see (GOTS)*
Bruttomarge: *gross margin*
Bruttomehrwertsteuer: *output tax*
Bruttoreichweite: *gross cover; gross reach*
Bruttosozialprodukt: *gross national product (GNP)*
Bruttoumsatz: *gross sales*
brutto verdienen: *to gross*
Bruttoverdienst: *gross income or gross salary*
B-Sortiment: *rejects; seconds*
Bücher: die ~ führen *to keep the accounts*
Büchergutschein: *book token*
Buchgewinn: *paper profit*
Buchhalter: *accountant*
Buchhaltung: *accountancy; accounting; accounts department*
Buchungsbeleg: *voucher*
Buchungsbestätigung: *confirmation of a booking*
Buchwert: *book value*
Budget: *budget*
Budgetabweichung: *budget variance*
Budgetbedarf: *budgetary requirements*
budgetieren: *to budget*
Budgetierung: *budgeting*
Budget-Konto: *budget account*
Budgetkontrolle: *budgetary control*
Budgetpolitik: *budgetary policy*
Bulldoggenausgabe: *bulldog*
Bulletin: *bulletin*
Bundsteg: *gutter*
Bups: *buppies (US)*
Bürge: *guarantor*
bürgen: für jdn ~ *to go guarantee for someone*
Bürgschaft: *guarantee*

Büroausstattung *or* **Büroeinrichtung:** *business equipment*
Bürobedarf: *office supplies*
Büro-Service: *service bureau*
Bürovorsteher: *administrator*
Bus: gemieteter ~ *chartered bus*
Business Class: *business class*

Cc

Carnet: *carnet*
Carryover-Effekt: *carry-over effect*
Cashflow: diskontierter ~ *discounted cash flow* **negativer ~** *negative cash flow* **positiver ~** *positive cash flow*
Cashflow-Bericht: *cash flow statement*
Cashflow-Prognose: *cash flow forecast*
Chance: *opportunity*
Chartepartie: *charter party*
Charterer: *charterer*
Charterflug: *charter flight*
Charterflugzeug: *charter plane*
Chartern: *chartering*
chartern: *to charter*
Charterung: *charter*
Checkliste: *checklist*
Chemigraphie: *photoengraving*
Chiffre: *code; key number*
cif: *c.i.f.; cost, insurance and freight*
Clusteranalyse: *cluster analysis*
Code: *code*
Combipack-Angebot: *banded offer*
Computer: *computer* **auf ~ umstellen** *computerize*
Computerausdruck: *computer listing*
Computerdatei: *computer file*
Computerfehler: *computer error*
Computer-Hardware: *computer hardware*
computerisieren: *computerize*
computerisiert: *computerized*
computerlesbar: *computer-readable*
Computernetz(werk): *computer network*
Computerprogramm: *computer program*
Computerprogrammierer: *computer programmer*
Computerspiele: handelsthematische ~ *business games*
Computersprache: *computer language*
Computersystem: *computer system*
Computerzeitschrift: *computer magazine*
Computing: *computing*
Container: *container* **auf ~ umstellen** *containerize*
Containerladung: *container load or load of a container*
Containerschiff: *container ship; van ship*
Containerzug: *freightliner*
Convenience Goods: *convenience goods*
Copy: *(publicity) copy*
Copy-Einweisung: *copy brief*
Copy-Plattform: *copy platform*
Copytesten: *copy testing*
Coupon: *coupon* **mit ~ versehen** *couponed*
Couponanzeige: *coupon ad*
Courtage: *brokerage or broker's commission*
Couvert: *cover charge*
Critical-Path-Analyse: *critical path analysis*

Dd

Dachorganisation: *umbrella organization*
DAGMAR-Modell: *DAGMAR*
Darlehen: *advance; credit* **langfristiges ~** *long-term loan* **zinsloses ~** *interest-free credit or loan*
Darstellung: falsche ~ *misrepresentation* **graphische ~** *diagram*
Daten: empirische ~ *empirical data* **numerische ~** *numeric data* **qualitative ~** *qualitative data* **quantitative ~** *quantitative data* **technische ~** *mechanical data*
Datenabruf: *information retrieval*
Datenbank: *data bank or bank of data; database*
Datenblatt: *data sheet*
Datenerfassung: *data acquisition or acquisition of data*
Datenkasse: *electronic point of sale (epos)*
Datenverarbeitung: *data processing* **elektronische ~** *electronic data processing*
Daten zugänglich machen: *to share data*
Datum: *date*
Datum(s)stempel: *date stamp*
Dauerauftrag: *banker's order; standing order*
Dauereffekte: *durable effects*
dauerhaft: *permanent*
Dauerseher: *heavy viewer*
dazubringen: *persuade*
Dealen: *traffic*
Debet: *debit*
Debetseite: *debit side*
Debetspalte: *debit column; debtor side*
Deck: *deck*
Deckladung: *deck cargo*
Deckungsbeitrag: *contribution pricing*
Deckungszusage: *cover note*
Defizit: *deficit* **ein ~ ausgleichen** *to make good a deficit*
Defizitwirtschaft: *deficit financing*
Deflation: *deflation*
deflationär: *deflationary*
Degeneration(sphase): *decline*
Dekoration: *window dressing*
Dekorationsmaterial: *display material*
Delegation: *mission*
Delegation ins Ausland: *outward mission*
Delkredereagent: *del credere agent*

Delphi-Methode: *delphi method*
Demarketing: *demarketing*
Demographie: *demography*
demographisch: *demographic*
Denkweise: unorthodoxe ~ *lateral thinking*
Deport: *backwardation*
Depot: *depot*
Depression: *depression; slump*
Deregulation: *deregulation*
derzeitig: *current*
Design: *design*
Design-Abteilung: *design department*
Designer: *designer*
Designerprodukte: *designer products*
Design-Faktor: *design factor*
Design-Studio: *design studio*
Desk Researcher: *desk researcher*
Devisen: *foreign currency; foreign exchange*
Devisengeschäft: *exchange transaction*
Devisenhandel: *(foreign) exchange dealings*
Devisenhändler: *(foreign) exchange dealer; exchanger*
Devisenkonto: *foreign currency account*
Devisenkontrollen: *exchange controls*
Devisenmakler: *foreign exchange broker*
Devisenmarkt: *foreign exchange market*
Devisenreserven: *foreign currency reserves; foreign exchange reserves*
Devisenterminkurs: *forward (exchange) rate*
Devisentransfer: *foreign exchange transfer*
Devisenverkehr: *foreign exchange*
Dezimalsystem: *decimal system*
Diagramm: *chart; diagram; graph* **in einem** ~ *diagrammatically*
Diagramm der Unternehmensstruktur: *organization chart*
Diebstahl: geringfügiger ~ *pilferage or pilfering*
Dienst: *service*
Dienstleistungen: *direct services*
Dienstleistungsbranche: *service industry; tertiary industry*
Dienstleistungssektor: *tertiary sector*
Dienstleistungsvertrag: *service contract*
dienstlich: *on business*
Dienstreise: *business trip*
Dienstweg: den ~ **beschreiten** *to go through the official channels*
Differential: semantisches ~ *semantic differential*
Differentialtarife *or* **Differentialzölle:** *differential tariffs*
Differenzierung: *differentiation*
Diffusion: *diffusion*
Diffusionskurve: *diffusion curve*
DINKs: *Dinkies*
Direct-Response-Werbung: *direct response advertising*
Direkmarketing-Verband: europäischer ~ *European Direct Marketing Association (EDMA)*
Direktabbuchung: *direct debit*
Direktexport: *direct export*
Direktion: *directorate*
direkt liefern: *to drop ship*
Direktlieferung: *drop shipment*
Direktmarketing: *direct marketing (DM)*
Direktor: *director* **geschäftsführender** ~ *managing director; executive director; general manager* **unternehmensfremder** ~ *outside director*
Direktorenstelle: *directorship*
Direktorium: *directorate*
Direktverkauf: *direct selling; door-to-door canvassing; face-to-face selling*
Direktversand *or* **Direktwerbung:** *direct mail; direct mailing*
Diskont: *cash discount or discount for cash*
Diskontbank: *discount house*
Diskonter: *discount house; discounter*
diskontfähig: *discountable*
Diskonthaus: *discount house; discounter*
Diskontladen: *discount house; discount store; discounter*
Diskontpreis: *discount price*
Diskontsatz: *discount rate*
Diskonttabelle: *table of discounts or discount table*
Diskontwert: *discounted value*
Diskrepanz: *variance*
Diskriminanzanalyse: multiple ~ *multiple discriminant analysis*
Diskriminierung: *discrimination*
Diskussionssitzung: *brainstorming*
Dispersion: *dispersion*
Dissonanz: kognitive ~ *cognitive dissonance*
Dissonanzreduktion: *dissonance reduction*
Distribution: physische ~ *physical distribution (PD)*
Diversifikation: *diversification* **seitliche** ~ *lateral diversification*
diversifizieren: *diversify*
D-I-Y-Geschäft: *do-it-yourself store*
D-Mark: *mark*
Dock: frei ~ *free docks*
Do-it-yourself Magazin: *do-it-yourself magazine*
Dokument: *document; instrument*
Dokumentarfilm: *documentary*
dokumentarisch: *documentary*
Dokumentation: *documentation*
Dokumente gegen Akzept: *documents against acceptance*
Dokumente gegen Bezahlung *or* **Wechsel:** *documents against cash or presentation*
Dollar: *dollar* **tausend** ~ *grand (informal)*
Dollarkrise: *dollar crisis*
Dollarlücke: *dollar gap or dollar shortage*
Dollarzone: *dollar area*
Doppeldeckerplakat: *double-decker*
Doppelkrone: *double crown*
Doppelpreisauszeichnung: *double-pricing*
Doppelseite: *spread*

Doppelspalte: *double column*
doppelt: *double*
Doppelte: das ~ verdienen *to be on double time*
Doppelverdiener: kinderlose ~ *Dinkies*
Double Crown: *double crown*
Draufgeld: *earnest*
Drehbuchannahme: *copy clearance*
Dressman: *model* **als ~ arbeiten** *to model*
Dritter: *third party*
Drittleserschaft: *tertiary readership*
Druck: *impact* **großer ~** *high pressure*
Druckauflage: *gross circulation; print run*
drücken: *depress; force down*
Druckfahne: *galley or galley proof*
Drucklegung: *press date*
Druckmedien: *printed media*
Drucksache: *printed matter*
Drucksachenbeilage: *envelope stuffer*
Dummy: *dummy*
Dumping: *dumping*
Durchführbarkeitsstudie: *feasibility study or feasibility report*
Durchführbarkeitstest: *feasibility test*
durchführen: *effect*
Durchführung von Konzepttests: *concept testing*
Durchführung von Posttests: *post-testing*
Durchführung von Pretests: *pre-testing*
Durchführung von Produkttests: *product testing*
Durchlauf: *run*
durchleuchten: *screen*
durchmachen: *experience*
Durchschnitt: *average; mean* **gewogener ~** *weighted average* **gleitender ~** *moving average* **im ~** *on (an) average*
durchschnittlich: *average; mean*
durchschnittlich betragen: *average; average out*
Durchschnittseinkommen pro Person: *average income per capita or per capita income*
Durchschnittspreiskalkulation: *plateau pricing*
durchwählen: *to dial direct*
Duty-Free-Shop: *duty-free shop*
Dynamik der Betriebsformen: *wheel of retailing*
Dyopol: *duopoly*

Ee

Ebene: *level*
echt: *real*
Echtzeit: *real time*
Eckzins: *bank base rate*
EDV-Abteilung: *computer department*
EDV-Modell zur Wirtschaftsprognose: *economic model*
EDV-Service: *computer services*
EDV-Servicebüro: *computer bureau*
Effekt: *effect*
Effektenhandel: geordneter ~ *fair dealing*
Effektenmanagement: *portfolio management*
effektiv: *effective*
Ego: *ego*
ehemalig: *ex-*
Ehrenzahlung: *payment supra protest*
Eichmeister: *inspector of weights and measures*
eifrig: *keen*
Eigenanzeige *or* **Eigeninserat:** *house advertisement or house ad*
Eigenkapital: *equity capital*
Eigenmarke: *own brand*
Eigenmarkenwaren: *own brand goods; own label goods*
eigentlich: *basic*
Eigentum: bewegliches ~ *goods and chattels*
Eigentümer: *owner*
Eigentumsüberschreibung: *transfer of property*
Eigenwert: *intrinsic value*
Eil-: *express*
Eilzustellung: *express delivery*
Einband: *cover*
Einbanddeckel: hinterer ~ *(back) cover page* **vorderer ~** *(front) cover page*
Einbau: *installation*
Einbuße: *loss*
Einbußen: *shrinkage*
Eindringen: *probing*
eindrucken: *overprint*
Einfluß: unzulässiger ~ *undue influence*
Einflußwege: *channels of influence*
einfrieren: *freeze*
Einfrieren von Krediten: *credit freeze*
einfügen: *insert or inset*
Einfuhr: *importation; importing*
Einfuhren: *imports* **unsichtbare ~** *invisible imports*
einführen: *import; introduce*
Einfuhrkontingent: *import quota*
Einfuhrlizenz: *import licence*
Einfuhrstopp: *import ban*
Einführung: *launch; launching* **stufenweise ~** *rolling launch*
Einführungspreis: *introductory offer*
Einführungsprobleme: *barriers to entry into a market*
Einführungstermin: *launching date*
Einfuhrverbot: *import ban*
Einfuhrzoll: *customs duty; import duty; import levy*
Eingangsdatum: *date of receipt*
eingebaut: *built-in*
eingeboren: *indigenous*
eingepackt: *in pack*
eingeschweißt: *shrink-wrapped*
eingetragen: *registered*
einheimisch: *domestic; homegrown; indigenous*
Einheit: *unit*

Einheitskosten: *unit cost*
Einheitspreis: *unit price*
Einheitssatz *or* **Einheitstarif:** *flat rate*
Einkauf: *purchasing* **preisbewußter** ~ *shopping around* **zentraler** ~ *central purchasing*
Einkäufe: *shopping*
Einkaufen: *buying; shopping*
einkaufen: *buy; purchase; to shop (for)*
Einkäufer: *buyer; purchasing officer* **industrieller** ~ *industrial user*
Einkaufsabteilung: *buying department*
Einkaufsbuch: *bought ledger; purchase ledger*
Einkaufsbuchhalter: *bought ledger clerk*
Einkaufskorb: *shopping basket*
Einkaufsleiter: *head buyer; purchasing manager*
Einkaufsmarkt: *superstore*
Einkaufsort *or* **Einkaufsstelle:** *point of purchase (POP)*
Einkaufspassage: *shopping mall*
Einkaufsviertel: *shopping precinct*
Einkaufswagen: *shopping cart (US); (supermarket) trolley*
Einkaufszentrum: *shopping mall (US); shopping centre*
Einkommen: *income; revenue* **verfügbares** ~ *discretionary income; disposable income*
Einkommen mit Quellenbesteuerung: *income which is taxed at source*
Einkommenshypothese: *permanent income hypothesis*
Einkommensstufe: hohe ~ *upper income bracket* **niedrige** ~ *lower income bracket*
Einkommensveränderungseffekt: *income effect*
Einkünfte: *income; receipts; revenue* **unsichtbare** ~ *invisible earnings*
Einlage: *stake*
einlagern: *store*
einleitend: *opening*
einlösbar: *cashable*
einlösen: *redeem*
Einlösen eines Schecks: *clearance of a cheque*
Einlösung: *redemption*
einmalig: *unique*
Einmaltarif: *one-time rate*
Einnahme: *take*
Einnahmen: *receipts; revenue; takings*
Einnahmen- und Ausgabenplanung: *cash budget*
einnehmen: *capture; take*
einpacken: *pack; wrap (up)*
Einreisekarte: *landing card*
einrichten: ein Konto ~ *to open an account*
Einrichtungen: *facilities*
einrücken: *to indent*
Einrückung: *indent*
einsatzbereit: *operational*
Einschaltquote: *ratings* **garantierte** ~ *guaranteed homes impressions or guaranteed homes ratings*
Einschiffungshafen: *port of embarkation*
einschränken: *limit; restrict*
einschränkend: *limiting; restrictive*
Einschränkung: *limitation; restraint; restriction; retrenchment*
Einschreibebrief: *registered letter*
Einschreiben: *recorded delivery*
einseitig: *unilateral; unilaterally*
einsetzen: *set up*
einstellen: *drop; regulate*
Einstellung: *attitude; stop*
Einstellungsforschung: *attitude research*
Einstellungsmessung: *attitude measurement*
Einstellungsskala: *attitude scale*
Einstellungstesten: *attitude testing*
einstufen: *classify; grade*
einteilen: *organize*
Einteilung: *organization*
Eintrag: einen ~ **zurückbuchen** *to contra an entry*
einträglich: *money-making; profitable*
Eintragung: *recording; registration*
Eintragungsbescheinigung: *certificate of registration or registration certificate*
Eintragungsnummer: *registration number*
eintreiben: *collect*
Eintritt(sgebühr): *admission charge or entry charge*
einverstanden sein: *agree*
einwandfrei: *clean*
Einweg-: *disposable; non-returnable*
Einweg(ver)packung: *non-returnable packing*
Einweisung: *brief*
Einweisungs- und Einsatzbesprechung: *briefing*
einwickeln: *wrap (up)*
Einzelbeleg: *tear sheet*
Einzelbestände: *oddments*
Einzelhandel: *retail; retailing* **der** ~ *the retail trade*
Einzelhandelsbestandsaufnahme: *retail audit; shop audit; store audit*
Einzelhandelsgenossenschaft: *retailer cooperative*
Einzelhandelsgeschäft: *retail shop or retail outlet*
Einzelhandelskette: *multiple*
Einzelhandelspreis: *retail price* **empfohlener** ~ *recommended retail price (RRP)*
Einzelhändler: *retail dealer; retailer; tradesman*
Einzelhändlernachweis: *dealer tie-in*
Einzelheiten: technische ~ *mechanical data*
Einzelkaufmann: *sole trader*
einzeln: *individual; odd*
Einzelpackung: *unit pack*
Einzelperson: *individual*
Einzelwerbepreis: *flat rate*
einziehen: *collect; indent; levy*
einzigartig: *unique*
Einzug: *indent*
Eisberg-Prinzip: *iceberg principle*
Eisenwaren: *hardware*
Elan: *drive*

elastisch: *elastic*
Elastizität: *elasticity*
Elektronik: *electronics*
Element: *unit*
elementar: *basic*
Elementen: **aus ~ zusammengesetzt** *modular*
Elimination: *deletion*
eliminieren: *delete; eliminate; prune*
Eliminierung: *elimination*
Eliminierung einer Produktgruppe: *line divestment*
E-Mail: *electronic mail*
Embargo: *embargo* **ein ~ aufheben** *to lift an embargo* **ein ~ verhängen** *to embargo* **einem ~ unterliegen** *to be under an embargo*
Emissionsabteilung: *new issues department*
Emissionskurs: *offer price*
emittieren: *issue*
Empfänger: *consignee; recipient*
Empfangsbestätigung: *receipt*
Empfangsdatum: *date of receipt*
Empfangsschein: *delivery receipt*
Empfehlung: *suggestion*
empfindlich: *sensitive*
emporschnellen: *rocket*
Endbahnhof: *railhead*
Endbetrag: *grand total*
Endlospapier: *continuous stationery*
Endpreis: *retail price*
Endprodukt: *end or final or finished product*
Endverbraucher: *end consumer; end user; ultimate consumer*
Engpaß: *bottleneck; shortage*
en gros: *in bulk*
Entbindung: *release*
entgegengesetzt: *reverse*
enthalten: *contain*
Enthüllung vertraulicher Informationen: *disclosure of confidential information*
entladen: *unload*
Entladung und Wiederfahrbereitmachung: *turnround*
Entlassung: *release* **ungerechtfertigte ~** *unfair dismissal*
Entnahmeliste: *picking list*
Entschädigung: *indemnity*
entscheiden: *decide*
Entscheidung: *decision*
Entscheidungsbaum: *decision tree*
Entscheidungseinheit: *decision-making unit (DMU)*
Entscheidungsfindung: *decision-making*
Entscheidungsfreiheit: *discretion*
Entscheidungsprozeß: *decision-making process*
Entscheidungstheorie: *decision theory*
Entscheidungsträger: *decision-maker*
entschließen: **sich ~** *decide*
Entschluß: *decision*
Entstehungsperiode: *gestation period*
entwerfen: *design*
entwickeln: *develop*
Entwicklung: *development* **bahnbrechende ~** *pioneer development*
Entwicklungen: **ökonomische ~** *economic trends*
Entwicklungsland: *developing country or developing nation*
Entwicklungsländer: *underdeveloped countries*
Entwicklungsstufe: *generation*
Entwurf: *design; dummy*
Erbschaftssteuer: *estate duty or death duty (US)*
erfahren: *to experience; experienced*
Erfahrung: *experience*
Erfahrungseffekt: *experience effect*
Erfahrungskurve: *experience curve*
Erfassung: *registration*
Erfolgskonto: *trading account*
Erfolgsquote: *hit rate*
Erfolgs- und Leistungsnachweis: *track record*
erfüllen: *fulfil or fulfill (US)*
Erfüllung: *fulfilment*
ergänzend: *complementary*
erhältlich: **nicht ~** *unavailable*
erheben: *charge; levy*
erhöhen: *mark up; scale up*
Erhöhung: *advance*
erholen: **sich ~** *pick up*
Erinnerung: *recall* **gestützte ~** *aided or prompted recall* **ungestützte ~** *unprompted recall*
Erinnerungshilfe: *prompt*
Erinnerungstest: *recall test*
Erinnerungswerbung: *reminder advertising*
erkennen: *recognize*
Erklärung: *return*
Erkundigungsbesuch: **ein ~** *a fact-finding mission*
erlangen: *gain*
erlauben: *to permit*
Erlaubnis: *permit* **ohne ~ abheuern** *to jump ship*
erleben: *experience*
erledigen: *handle*
Erledigung: *handling*
Erlös: *profit*
ermäßigt: *off; reduced*
Ermäßigung: *reduction*
Ermessen: *discretion* **nach jds ~** *at the discretion of someone*
erneut sinken: *fall back*
erobern: *capture*
eröffnen: *open; set up*
Eröffnung: *opening*
Eröffnungsbestand: *opening stock*
Eröffnungsbetrag: *opening balance*
Eröffnungsbuchung: *opening entry*
Eröffnungsgebot: *opening bid*
Eröffnungskurs: *opening price*
Erprobung: *testing; trial*

erreichen: *reach*
Ersatz: *substitute*
Ersatzanzeige: *makegood*
Ersatzfahrzeug: *courtesy car*
Ersatzteil: *spare part*
Erscheinungsintervall: *issue life*
erschließen: *develop*
Erschließung: industrielle ~ *industrial development*
ersetzen: *substitute*
erstatten: *refund*
erstattungsfähig: nicht ~ *non-refundable*
erstehen: *purchase*
erstklassig: *high-grade*
Erstmarke: *primary brand*
Ertrag: laufende ~ *current yield*
ertraglos: *dead*
ertragreich: *profitable*
Ertragsfähigkeit: *earning potential*
Ertragskonto: *revenue account*
Ertragszentrum: *profit centre*
erwarten: *expect* **zu** ~ *probable*
erwartet: *due; projected*
erweitern: *diversify; expand*
Erweiterung: *expansion*
Erweiterung des Produktangebots: *product diversification or diversification into new products*
Erwerb: *acquisition*
erwerben: *acquire; gain; purchase*
Erwerber: *acquirer; purchaser*
Erwerbsfähigkeit: *earning potential*
erwidern: *to reply*
Erwiderung: *reply*
erzeugen: *produce*
Erzeuger: *producer*
Erzeugnis: *product*
Erzeugnisse: einheimische ~ *home-produced products*
Erzeugung: *production*
eskalieren: *escalate*
Essensmarke: *luncheon voucher*
Etage: *floor*
Etat: *budget* **den** ~ **ausgleichen** *to balance the budget*
Etat-: *budgetary*
Etatüberschuß: *budget surplus*
Ethik: *ethics*
Etikett: *label; sticker; tag*
etikettieren: *to label*
Etikettierung: *labelling*
Etikettierungsabteilung: *labelling department*
Europäische: die ~ **Gemeinschaft** *the European Economic Community* **das** ~ **Währungssystem** *the European Monetary System (EMS)*
exakt: *accurate; accurately*
exklusiv: *select; up-market*
exklusive: *exclusive of*
Exklusivrecht: *exclusivity*
expandieren: *expand*
Expansion: *expansion* **industrielle** ~ *industrial expansion*
Expedient: *dispatcher; shipping clerk*
Experiment-Methode: *experimental method*
Experte: *expert; specialist*
Experte für Merchandising: *merchandiser*
Expertenpanel: *jury of executive opinion; panel of experts*
Expertin: *expert; specialist*
Expertise: *expert's report; expertise*
Export: *export; exportation* **indirekter** ~ *indirect exporting*
Exportabteilung: *export department*
Exporte: sichtbare ~ *visible exports*
Exporteur: *exporter*
Exportfirma: *export house; exporter*
Exportgenehmigung: *export permit*
Exporthandel: *export trade*
exportieren: *to export*
Exportkreditversicherung: staatliche ~ *Export Credit Guarantee Department (ECGD)*
Exportleiter: *export manager*
Exportlizenz: *export licence*
Exportzoll: *export duty*
Expreß: per ~ *express*
extern: *external*
Extrapolation: *extrapolation*
Extras: *optional extras*
Eyecatcher: *flash pack*

Ff

Fabrik: *works*
Fabrikat: *make*
Fabrikate: ausländische ~ *products of foreign manufacture*
Fabrikationsnummer: *serial number*
Fabrikgebäude: *factory unit*
Fabrikwaren: *manufactured goods*
Fachblatt: *trade journal*
Fachgebiet: *speciality or specialty*
Fachgeschäft or **Fachhändler:** *stockist; specialist*
Fachkenntnisse: *know-how*
Fachmann: *expert; specialist*
Fachmesse: *trade fair*
Fachpresse: *technical press; trade press*
Fachwissen: *expertise*
Fachzeitschrift: *horizontal publication; trade journal or magazine or paper or publication*
Factor: *factor*
Factoring: *factoring*
Factoring-Gebühren: *factoring charges*
fahrplanmäßig: *on schedule*
Fahrzeug: *vehicle*
fair: *fair*

Faksimile: *facsimile*
Faktor: *factor* **ausschlaggebender** *or* **entscheidender** ~ *deciding factor*
Faktoren: zyklische ~ *cyclical factors*
Faktorenanalyse: *factor analysis*
Faktum: *fact*
Faktura: *bill*
Fakturieren: *billing (US)*
fakturieren: *to invoice*
Fakturist: *invoice clerk*
Fall: *slump*
Fallen: *fall*
fallen: *drop; fall; fall off*
fällig: *due; payable*
fällig werden: *to fall due or to become due*
Fallstudie: *case study*
falsch: *false*
fälschen: *falsify*
Fälschung: *falsification*
Faltanzeige: *fold-out*
Faltseite: *fold-out*
Familie: *family*
Familien-Lebenszyklus: *family life cycle*
Farbbeilage: *colour supplement*
Farbmuster: *colour swatch*
Fassade: *front*
Fautfracht: *dead freight*
Fax: *fax*
faxen: *to fax*
Federzeichnung: *line drawing or line illustration*
Feedback: *feedback*
Fehler: *error; imperfection* **statistischer** ~ *statistical error* **systematischer** ~ *non-statistical error; bias*
fehlerfrei: *accurate; accurately*
fehlerhaft: *imperfect*
fehlerlos: *perfect*
Fehlerquote: *error rate*
Fehlerspielraum: *margin of error*
Fehlfracht: *dead freight*
fehlschlagen: *fall through*
feilschen: *haggle*
Feingehaltsstempel: *hallmark; assay mark*
Feld: *range*
Feldforschung: *field research or fieldwork*
Fensterfalz: *gatefold*
Fernlast: *distance freight*
Fernseheinschaltquoten: *television ratings (TVR)*
Fernsehen: *television (TV)*
Fernsehspot: *TV spot*
Fernsehwerbungtreibender: *sponsor*
Fernsehzuschauer: seltener ~ *light viewer*
Fernspediteur: *road haulier*
Fernsprechauftragsdienst: *answering service*
fertig: *ready; ready-made or ready-to-wear*
fertigbringen: es ~ *to manage to*
fertigen: *manufacture; produce*
Fertiggerichte: *convenience foods*
Fertigung: *manufacture; manufacturing; production*
Fertigungsabteilung: *production department*
Fertigungsgemeinkosten: *indirect expenses or costs*
Fertigungsingenieur: *product engineer*
Fertigungskapazität: *industrial or manufacturing capacity*
Fertigungsstraße: *assembly line or production line*
Fertigwaren: *finished goods; manufactured goods*
fest: *firm; fixed; permanent*
festgelegt: *set*
festigen: *stabilize* **sich** ~ *firm*
Festigung: *stabilization*
Festigung des Marktes: *hardness of the market*
Festigungswerbung: *reinforcement advertising*
Festkosten: *overhead costs or overheads or overhead (US); running costs or costs of running a business; general or overhead or running expenses*
Festkostenbudget: *overhead budget*
festlegen: *fix; set*
Festlegen des Einheitspreises: *unit pricing*
Festlegung: *fixing*
Festpreis: *firm price*
Festpreisvereinbarung: *fixed-price agreement*
festsetzen: *fix; set*
Festsetzung: *fixing*
fest verschließen: *seal*
Feuergefahr: *fire risk*
Feuilletonartikel: *feature*
Filiale: *branch; chain store; multiple store*
Filialleiter: *branch manager*
Filmausschnitt: kurzer ~ *clip*
Filterfrage: *filter question*
Financier: *financier*
Finanz-: *budgetary; financial*
Finanzabteilung: *finance department*
Finanzamt: *Internal Revenue Service (US)*
Finanzausschuß: *finance committee*
Finanzbeamter: *VAT inspector; VATman or vatman*
Finanzberater: *financial adviser*
Finanzbericht: *financial statement*
Finanzbuchhalter: *management accountant*
Finanzenmittel: *finances*
Finanzgesetz: *Finance Act (GB)*
Finanzhilfe: *financial assistance*
finanziell: *financial; financially*
finanzieren: *finance*
Finanzierung: *financing*
Finanzierungsgesellschaft: *finance company or finance corporation or finance house*
Finanzinstitut: *financial institution*
Finanzlage: *financial position*
Finanzmarkt: *finance market*

Finanzplanung: *budgeting*
Finanzwerbung: *financial advertising*
Firma: *firm; house* **eine angesehene ~** *a company of good standing* **eine ~ gründen** *to set up a company*
Firmen-: *corporate*
Firmenansehen: *goodwill*
Firmeneinkauf: *organizational buying*
Firmengruppe: *group*
Firmenimage: *corporate image* **das ~ pflegen** *to promote a corporate image*
Firmenmitteilungsblatt: *company newsletter*
Firmenname: *corporate name*
Firmenschild: *fascia*
Firmensiegel: *common seal or company's seal*
Firmenvorstand: *board of directors*
Firmenwerbung: *institutional advertising*
Firmenzeichen: *livery; logo or logotype*
Fischereihafen: *fishing port*
Fixgeschäft: *short selling or selling short*
Fixkosten: *fixed costs; fixed expenses; oncosts*
Flagschiff: *flagship*
Flaschenanhänger: *bottle hanger*
Flaute: *depression; downturn; lull*
Fließband: *assembly line; production line*
Fließbandherstellung: *continuous process production*
Flohmarkt: *flea market*
Flop: *flop*
florierend: *booming*
Flugblatt: *flier; publicity handout*
Fluggesellschaft: *air carrier; airline*
Flußdiagramm: *flow chart; flow diagram*
flüssigmachen: *free*
Flüssigwaren: *wet goods*
Flut: *flood*
Flyer: *flier*
f.o.b.: *free on board (f.o.b.)*
Folge: in zahlenmäßiger ~ *in numerical order*
Folgeleser: *secondary audience*
Folgeleserschaft: *pass-on readership*
folgen: *follow*
Folgeschreiben: *follow-up letter*
Förderer: *patron*
fordern: *to demand*
Forderung: *demand* **uneinbringliche ~** *bad debt*
Förderung: finanzielle ~ *sponsorship*
Forderungen ankaufen: *to factor*
Forderungseinziehung: *debt collection*
Förderungsgebiet: *development area or development zone; enterprise zone*
Form: *mode*
Format: *format*
Formbrief: *standard letter*
Formular: *form*
Formulierung: *form of words*
forschen: *to research*
Forscher: *researcher*
Forschung: *research* **agenturverbreitete ~** *syndicated research* **wissenschaftliche ~** *scientific research*
Forschung betreiben: *to research*
Forschungsabteilung: *research department*
Forschungsanstalt: *research organization*
Forschungsgruppe: *research unit*
Forschungsinstitut: *research institute*
Forschung und Entwicklung: *research and development (R&D)*
Fortschritt: *advance*
Fortschrittsbericht: *progress report*
Fracht: *cargo* **gemischte ~** *general cargo*
Fracht aufladen or aufnehmen: *to take on freight*
Frachtbrief: *consignment note; shipping note; waybill*
Frachter: *freighter; cargo ship*
frachtfrei: *carriage free; carriage paid; carriage prepaid*
Frachtgebühren: *freight charges or freight rates*
Frachtgut: *freight*
Frachtkosten: *freight costs; freightage*
Frachtnachnahme: *carriage forward; carriage forward or freight forward; freight collect (US)*
Frachtschiff: *cargo ship*
Fracht- und Löschungskosten: *landed costs*
Fracht verladen: *to load cargo*
Frachtvertrag: *charter party*
Frage: offene ~ *open-ended question*
Fragebogen: *questionnaire*
Fragezeichen: *question mark(s)*
fragmentieren: *fragment*
Franchise: *franchise*
Franchise-Basis: auf ~ vergeben *to franchise*
Franchise-Geber: *franchiser*
Franchise-Nehmer: *franchisee*
Franchisevergabe: eine ~ *a franchising operation*
Franchising: *franchising*
Frauenzeitschrift: *women's magazine*
frei: *franco; free*
Freigabe: *release*
Freihafen: *free port*
Freihandel: *free trade*
Freihandelszone: *free port or free trade zone; free trade area; free trade zone*
Freihauslieferungszone: *free delivery area*
Freikarte: *complimentary ticket*
Freistellung: *release*
Freiversand or Freivertrieb: *controlled circulation*
freiwillig: *voluntary; voluntarily*
Freizeichnungsklausel: *exclusion clause*
Freizügigkeit von Arbeitskräften: *fluidity of labour*
Fremdenverkehrsamt: *information bureau or information office*
Fremdwährung: *foreign currency*
Fremdwährungskonto: *foreign currency account*
Friedenspflicht: *cooling-off period*

Frist: *notice; time limit* **eine ~ einhalten** *to meet a deadline*
Fristen: die ~ einhalten *to keep within the time limits or within the time schedule*
Frühadopter: *early adopters*
frühzeitig: *early*
führen: *carry; direct; handle; lead; manage; run; stock*
führend sein: *to be first in the field*
Führerschein: *driving licence*
Führung: *administration; direction*
Führungs-: *managerial*
Führungsfunktion: *management function or function of management*
Führungskräften: nach ~ suchen *to headhunt*
Führungsnachwuchs: *management trainee*
Fuhrunternehmer: *carter; haulage contractor*
Füllanzeige: *filler*
Füller: *filler*
Full-Service-(Werbe)agentur: *full service agency; full-service agency*
Fünfdollarschein: *five dollar bill*
Funkmedienkontakter: *time buyer*
Funktion: *function*
funktional: *functional*
funktionieren: *to function*
Funktionsrabatt: *functional discount*
Fusion: *merger* **gegenläufige ~** *reverse takeover*
fusionieren: *merge*
Fußboden: *floor*
Fußgängerzone: *pedestrian precinct*
Futurologie: *futurology*

Gg

Gabelstapler: *fork-lift truck*
Gag: *gimmick*
Gang: *aisle*
ganz: *in full; total*
ganzseitig: *full page*
ganztägig: *full-time*
Garantie: *guarantee; warranty* **verlängerte ~** *extended guarantee*
Garantielohn: *guaranteed wage*
garantieren: *to guarantee*
Garantieverletzung: *breach of warranty*
Gaststättengewerbe: *the catering trade*
Gattungsbegriff: *generic term*
Gattungsmarke: *generic product*
Gattungsname: *generic (name)*
Gauner: *racketeer*
Gaunerei: *racket*
Gebiet: *area; precinct; range; sphere; territory; zone*
Gebietsleiter: *area manager*
Gebot: *bid; bidding*
Gebrauch: *usage*
Gebrauchsanweisung: *directions for use*
gebrauchsfertig: *ready-made or ready-to-wear*
Gebrauchsgüter: *utility goods* **langlebige ~** *consumer durables*
Gebrauchsmuster: *registered design*
Gebrauchsnutzen: *form utility*
gebraucht: *secondhand*
Gebrauchtwagenverkaufsraum: *car mart*
Gebrauchtwarenhändler: *secondhand dealer*
Gebühr: *charge; rate* **symbolische ~** *token charge*
Gebühr bezahlt: *postage paid; postpaid*
Gebühr bezahlt Empfänger: *charges forward; freepost (GB)*
gebührenfrei: *free of charge; postage paid*
Gebührenordnung: *scale of charges or scale of prices* **verbindliche ~** *fixed scale of charges*
gebunden: *fixed*
Geburtenrate: *birth rate*
Gedächtnisstütze: *prompt*
Gedächtnistest: *recall test*
Gedeck: *cover charge*
Gefahr: *risk* **auf eigene ~** *at owner's risk*
Gefährdung: *risk*
Gefahrenzulage: *danger money*
Gefahr laufen: *to run a risk*
Gefälligkeit: aus ~ *ex-gratia*
Gefälligkeitswechsel: *accommodation bill*
gefälscht: *dud (informal)*
Gefüge: *structure*
Gegenbuchung: *contra entry* **als ~** *per contra or as per contra*
Gegengebot: *counterbid; counter-offer*
Gegenkonto or Gegenrechnung: *contra account*
gegenseitig: *reciprocal*
Gegenstand: *item*
gegenüberliegend: *facing*
gegenwärtig: *current*
Gegenwerbung: *counteradvertising*
gegenzeichnen: *countersign*
Gehalt: ein ~ beziehen *to draw a salary*
Gehaltsscheck: *pay cheque or salary cheque*
Gehaltsspanne: *salary range*
Geheimhaltungspflicht: *restraint of trade*
Gelbe Seiten: *yellow pages*
Geld: billiges ~ *cheap money* **heißes ~** *hot money* **leicht verdientes ~** *easy money* **teures ~** *dear money*
Geld anzahlen: *to pay money on account; to pay money down*
Geldautomat: *cash dispenser*
Geldautomatenkarte: *cash card*
Geld einbüßen: *to lose money*
Gelder: *monies*
Geldgeber: *backer; financier*
Geldkassette: *cash box*
Geldmärkte: *money markets*
Geldmarktpapiere: *paper*

Geldmarktsätze: *money rates*
Geldreserve: *money supply*
Geldschwemme: *glut of money*
Geld setzen auf: *to stake money on something*
Geldtransfer: *credit transfer or transfer of funds*
Geld verdienen: *to earn money; to make money*
Geld verlieren: *to lose money*
Geldvolumen: *money supply*
Gelegenheit: *opening; opportunity*
Gelegenheitsarbeiten verrichten: *jobbing; to do odd jobs*
Gelegenheitsarbeiter: *odd-job-man*
Gelegenheitskauf: *bargain*
Gelegenheitskosten: *opportunity cost*
gelten: *operate; run*
Gemeinkosten: *fixed costs; overheads or overhead (US)*
gemeinnützig: *non-profit-making*
gemeinsam: *common*
Gemeinsame: der ~ Markt *the (European) Common Market*
Gemeinschaftskonto: *joint account*
Gemeinschaftsunternehmen: *joint venture*
gemischt: *miscellaneous; mixed*
Gemischtwarenhandlung: *general store*
Gemischtwarenkettenladen: *variety chain store*
Gemischtwarenladen: *variety store (US)*
genau: *accurate; accurately*
genehmigen: *to agree; approve; license; permit*
Genehmigung: *approval; licence or license (US); permit*
Genehmigungszertifikat: *certificate of approval*
Generaldirektor: *managing director*
Genossenschaft: *cooperative society*
Gentleman's Agreement: *gentleman's agreement*
geöffnet: *open*
geographisch: *geographical*
geplant: *projected*
Geratewohl: aufs ~ *at random*
gerecht: *fair*
gerichtlich vorgehen: *to take legal action*
Gerichtskosten tragen: *to pay costs*
gering: *marginal*
geringer werden: *decline*
gesamt: *aggregate; overall; total*
Gesamtangebot: *total offer*
Gesamtgebühr: *inclusive charge*
Gesamthörerschaftspaket: *total audience package*
Gesamtnachfrage: *composite demand*
Gesamtplan: *overall plan*
Gesamtpreis: *all-in price*
Gesamtsumme: *grand total*
Gesamtvereinbarung: *blanket agreement*
Gesamtvergütung: *pay package or salary package or compensation package (US)*
Gesamtvertriebssystem: *total distribution system*
Gesamtwerbezeit: *commercial time*
Gesamtzuladung: *deadweight capacity or deadweight tonnage*
Gesamtzuschauerschaftspaket: *total audience package*
Gesandtschaft: *mission*
Geschäft: *bargain; business; deal; operation; outlet; shop; store* **betrügerisches ~** *racket* **das ~ aufgeben** *to go out of business* **ein ~ abschließen** *to close a sale* **ein ~ gründen** *to go into business* **im ~ sein** *to be in business* **kein gewinnbringendes ~** *not a commercial proposition* **unabhängiges ~** *independent shop*
Geschäftemacher: *profiteer*
Geschäftemacherei: *profiteering*
geschäftlich: *on business; commercial(ly)*
Geschäftsadresse: *business address*
Geschäftsbericht: *the company's annual report or the chairman's report or the directors' report*
Geschäftsbesuch: *business call*
Geschäftsbilanz: *management accounts*
Geschäftsbrief: *business letter*
Geschäftsbücher: *the accounts of a business or a company's accounts; a company's books*
Geschäftsessen: *business lunch/meal*
Geschäftsfrau: *businesswoman*
Geschäftsführer: *managing director*
Geschäftsgewinn: *trading profit*
Geschäftsinhaber: *shopkeeper*
Geschäftsjahr: *financial year*
Geschäftskorrespondenz: *business correspondence*
Geschäftsleiter: *manager*
Geschäftsleiterin: *manageress*
Geschäftsleitung: *directorate*
Geschäftsleute: *tradespeople*
Geschäftsmann: *businessman*
Geschäftsplan: *business plan*
Geschäftspraktiken: wettbewerbsbeschränkende ~ *restrictive trade practices*
Geschäftsreise: *business trip*
Geschäftsschluß: *closing time*
Geschäftsstelle: *branch*
Geschäftsstunden: *business hours*
Geschäftsverlust: *trading loss*
Geschäftsviertel: *business centre*
Geschäftszeit: *business hours; opening hours*
geschätzt: *estimated*
Geschenk: ein ~ verpacken *to gift-wrap a present*
Geschenkgutschein: *gift coupon; gift token; gift voucher*
Geschenkpapier: *wrapping paper; gift-wrapping*
Geschenkverpackungsdienst: *gift-wrapping service*
Geschwätz: leeres ~ *eye-wash*
Gesellschaft: *institution; society*
gesellschaftlich: *social; societal*
Gesellschaftsordnung: *the social system*
Gesetz: *law*

Gesetzentwurf *or* **Gesetzesvorlage:** *bill*
Gesetzgebung: *legislation*
gesetzlich: *legally*
gesetzlich geschützt: *patented*
Gesetzmäßigkeit: *legality*
Gespräche: produktive ~ *productive discussions*
Gespräch mit Voranmeldung: *personal call*
Gesprächsleiter: *interviewer*
gestalten: *structure*
Gestaltung: künstlerische ~ *design*
Gestaltung des Fimenimages: *atmospherics*
gestatten: *permit*
Gestehungskosten: *prime cost*
Gestell: *rack*
gesteuert: *controlled*
gestreut anlegen: *diversify*
getestet werden: *on trial*
gewagt: *risky*
gewähren: *extend*
Gewalt: höhere ~ *force majeure*
Gewandtheit beim Verkaufen: *salesmanship*
Gewäsch: *eye-wash*
Gewerbe: *business; trade*
Gewerbegebiet: *commercial district; trading estate*
Gewerbezeitschrift: *trade journal or magazine or paper or publication*
gewerblich: *commercially*
Gewerkschaft: eine ~ **anerkennen** *to recognize a union*
Gewerkschaftsfunktionär: *(business) agent (US)*
Gewerkschaftsunterhändler: ein erfahrener ~ *an experienced union negotiator*
Gewicht: falsches ~ *false weight*
Gewichtsschwund *or* **Gewichtsverlust:** *loss in weight*
Gewichtung: *weighting*
Gewinn: *gain; profit* **außergewöhnlicher** ~ *supernormal profit* **einen** ~ **aufweisen** *to show a profit* **einen** ~ **machen** *to make a profit* **mit** ~ **verkaufen** *to sell at a profit* **seinen** ~ **mitnehmen** *to take one's profit* **stattlicher** ~ *healthy profit*
Gewinn an Erfahrung: *gain in experience*
gewinnbringend: *commercial; money-making; profitable; profit-making*
gewinnen: *win*
Gewinnmaximierung: *profit maximization or maximization of profit*
Gewinn nach Steuern: *profit after tax*
Gewinnschwelle: *breakeven point*
Gewinnschwellenanalyse: *breakeven analysis*
Gewinnspanne: *margin; profit margin*
Gewinnsteuer: *profits tax or tax on profits*
Gewinn- und Verlustrechnung: *profit and loss account; income statement (US)*
Gewinnverteilungsrechnung: *appropriation account*
Gewinn vor Steuern: *profit before tax or pretax profit*

Gewohnheit: *habit*
Gewohnheitskauf: *habit buying*
gezielt: *selective*
Giebel(spitze): *gable end*
Gimmick: *gimmick; ploy*
Girobank: *Girobank*
Girokonto: *current account; checking account (US); cheque account; drawing account*
Girosystem: das ~ *bank giro or the giro system*
Gitter(diagramm): *grid*
Gitterkarte(methode): *buy grid*
Glaskasten: *display case*
Glättung: exponentielle ~ *exponential smoothing*
Gläubiger: *creditor* **nachrangiger** ~ *deferred creditor*
Gläubigerversammlung: *creditors' meeting*
Glaubwürdigkeitslücke: *credibility gap*
gleich: *directly*
gleichbleibend: *stable*
Gleichgewicht: *equilibrium* **optimales** ~ *optimal balance*
Gleichgewichtsmangel: *disequilibrium*
gleichmäßig: *continuous*
Globalabkommen: *omnibus agreement*
Globalmarketing: *world enterprise*
Goldwährung: *gold standard*
Gondelaufsatz: *gondola*
Gönner: *patron*
Goodwill: *goodwill*
Graphik: *graphics*
graphisch dargestellt: *in diagrammatic form*
gratis: *courtesy; free; gratis*
Gratisangebot: *freebie (informal)*
Gratisanzeige: *free advertisement*
Gratisprobe: *free sample; freebie (informal)*
Gratisversand *or* **Gratisverteilung:** *controlled circulation*
Gratiswerbesendung: *bonus spot*
Grenze: *limit*
Grenzertrag: *marginal revenue*
Grenzkauf: *marginal purchase*
Grenzkosten: *marginal cost*
Grenzpreiskalkulation: *marginal pricing*
Grenzproduktivität: *marginal productivity*
Grenzsteuersatz: *marginal rate of tax*
Grenzübergangsstelle: *customs entry point*
grob entwerfen: *rough out*
Großanschlagfläche: *supersite*
Großanzeige: *display ad; display advertisement* **rubrizierte** ~ *semi-display advertisement*
Großanzeigenwerbung: rubrizierte ~ *classified display advertising*
großartig: *grand*
Größe: gängige ~ *stock size*
Größendegression: *economies of scale*
großformatig: *king-size*
Großhandel: *wholesale*
Großhandelspreis: *trade price*

Großhandelspreisindex: *wholesale price index*
Großhandelsunternehmen: *full-function wholesaler*
Großhandelsverkauf: *trade counter*
Großhändler: *jobber (US); wholesale dealer; wholesaler* **allgemeiner ~** *general wholesaler*
Großindustrie *or* **Großunternehmertum:** *big business*
Großverbraucher: *heavy user*
Grundbedarf: *primary demand*
gründen: *set up*
Grundfläche: *floor space*
Grundgebühr: *flat rate*
Grundgesamtheit: *population; sampling frame; universe*
Grundkapital: genehmigtes ~ *authorized capital*
Grundlage: *base; basis*
Grundlagen: *basics*
grundlegend: *primary*
Grundpreis: *basic price or basic rate; flat rate*
Grundprodukt: *basic product*
Grundrabatt: *basic discount*
Grundsachverhalt: *basics*
Grundstoffe: *basic commodities; primary commodities*
Grundstoffindustrie: *basic industry*
Grundstücks- und Immobilienmakler(büro): *estate agency*
Grundstücksverkäufer: *vendor*
Gründungskapital: *initial capital*
Gruppe: *cluster; group* **freiwillige ~** *voluntary group*
Gruppendiskussion *or* **Gruppengespräch:** *group discussion*
Gruppeninterview: *group interview*
Gruppierungen: sozialökonomische ~ *socio-economic groups*
gültig bleiben: *to remain in effect*
Gummiband: *(rubber) band*
Gutachter: *consultant*
Güteklassen: in ~ einteilen *grade*
Güter: heterogene ~ *heterogeneous shopping goods* **homogene ~** *homogeneous shopping goods* **langlebige ~** *durable goods* **schwere ~** *deadweight* **zu verzollende ~** *goods which are liable to duty*
Güterdepot: *freight depot; goods depot*
Güterkraftverkehr: *road haulage; trucking*
Güterkraftverkehrsdepot: *road haulage depot*
Gütersiegel: *hallmark of excellence*
Güterwagen: *freight car (US); truck; wagon or waggon*
Güterzug: *freight train; goods train*
Gütezeichen: *quality label; kite mark (GB)*
gutheißen: *to approve of*
Gutschein: *coupon; voucher*
gutschreiben: *to credit*
Gutschrift: *credit entry*
Gutschriftsanzeige: *credit note*
Gutschriftszettel: *credit memorandum or credit memo (US)*
Gutsverwalter: *land agent*

Hh

Haben: *credit*
Habenbuchung: *credit entry*
Habenseite: *credit side*
Habenspalte: *credit column*
Hafen: *port* **einen ~ anlaufen** *to call at a port*
Hafenanlagen: *port installations*
Hafenbehörde: *port authority*
Hafengebühren: *dock or port or harbour dues; port charges*
haftbar für: *liable for*
haften: für jdn ~ *to go guarantee for someone*
Haftung: beschränkte ~ *limited liability* **unbeschränkte ~** *unlimited liability*
Haftungsbeschränkung: *limitation of liability*
Halbfabrikate: *goods in progress; semi-finished products; work-in-progress*
Halbjahr: zweites ~ *second half-year*
halbseitig: *half page*
Haltbarkeit eines Produktes: *shelf life of a product*
Haltbarkeitskodierung: *date code*
Haltung: *attitude*
Hamsterer: *hoarder*
hamstern: *hoard*
Hand: aus erster ~ *first-hand*
Handbuch: *handbook*
Handel: *bargain; commerce; deal; trade; trading; traffic* **allgemeiner ~** *general trading* **multilateraler ~** *multilateral trade* **zweiseitiger ~** *reciprocal trade* **zwischenstaatlicher ~** *interstate commerce (US)*
Handeln: *bargaining*
handeln: *to bargain; deal; haggle; trade*
handeln mit: *to handle; trade in*
Handelsabkommen: *trade agreement* **zweiseitiges ~** *bilateralism*
Handelsattach: *commercial attachffi*
Handelsbedingungen: erschwerte ~ *adverse trading conditions*
Handelsberater: *commercial counsellor*
Handelsbeschränkung: *restraint of trade*
Handelsbilanz: *balance of trade or trade balance* **aktive ~** *favourable balance of trade* **passive ~** *unfavourable balance of trade*
Handelsbilanz in Dollar: *dollar balances*
Handelsbrauch: *customs of the trade*
Handelsbüro: *trade bureau*
Handelsdelegation: *trade mission* **eine hochgestellte** *or* **hochrangige ~** *a high-grade trade delegation*
Handelsgesellschaft: *trading company*
Handelshafen: *commercial port*

Handelsinstitut: *commercial college*
Handelskammer: *Chamber of Commerce*
Handelskurs: *commercial course*
Handelsmarine: *mercantile marine; merchant navy or merchant marine*
Handelsmarke: *dealer's brand; distributor's brand; trademark or trade name*
Handelsmesse: *trade fair*
Handelsmission: *trade mission*
Handelsnation: *mercantile country*
Handelspartner: *trading partner*
Handelsrecht: *commercial law; mercantile law*
Handelsreisende(r): *commercial traveller*
Handelsschiff: *merchant ship or merchant vessel; merchantman*
Handelsspanne: *mark-up*
Handelsspanne als Prozentsatz: *mark-up percentage*
Handelsstraße: *trade route*
Handelsstruktur: *pattern of trade or trading pattern*
handelsüblich: *standard*
Handelsverband: *trade association*
Handelsverbot: *embargo*
Handelsverkehr: *commerce*
Handelsvertreter: *commercial agent; commercial traveller; mercantile agent; sales representative; travelling salesman*
Handelsweg: *trade route*
Handelszeitschrift: *trade journal or magazine or paper or publication*
Handelszone: *trading area*
Handeltreiben: *merchanting*
Handel treiben: *to deal; trade*
handeltreibend: *mercantile*
Handel treiben mit: *to trade in*
Handgeld: *earnest*
Handhabung: *handling*
Händler: *broker; dealer; distributor; merchant; trader* **ambulanter ~** *pedlar* **selbständiger ~** *independent trader*
Händlerabsatzförderung: *deal in*
Händlerhilfen: *dealer aids*
Händlermarke: *private brand*
Händlerrabatt: *trade discount; functional discount; trade terms*
Handschuhabteilung: *glove counter*
Handzettel: *handbill; leaflet*
hart verhandeln: *to drive a hard bargain*
häufig: *common; frequent; frequently*
Hauptauftraggeber: *key account*
Hauptbelastungszeit: *peak period*
Hauptbelastungszeit or Hauptverkehrszeit: außerhalb der ~ *off-peak*
Hauptbuch: *ledger; nominal ledger*
Haupterzeugnis: *staple commodity*
Hauptindustriezweig: *staple industry*
Hauptklient or Hauptkunde: *key account*
Hauptprodukt: *staple product*
hauptsächlich: *basic*
Hauptsaison: *high season*
Hauptsendezeit: *peak time; prime time*
Haupttextteil: *body copy*
Hauptverkehrszeit: *peak period*
Hausagentur: *house agency*
Hausbesitz: *house property*
Hause: nach ~ *homewards*
Häusermakler: *house agent*
Haushalt: *budget; household*
Haushaltsbuchforschung: *home audit*
Haushaltsgeräte: *domestic or household appliances* **elektrische ~** *white goods*
Haushaltswaren: *household goods; hardware*
hausieren: *hawk; peddle* **mit etwas ~** *to hawk something round*
Hausierer: *door-to-door salesman; hawker; pedlar*
Hausiergewerbe: *door-to-door selling*
Hauslieferung: *door-to-door service*
Hausmarke: *dealer's brand; distributor's brand; house brand; private brand*
Hausnachrichten: *house journal or house magazine or house organ (US)*
Hausse: *boom*
Hausstil: *house style*
Haustelefon: *house telephone; internal telephone*
Haustürverkauf: *door-to-door canvassing; door-to-door selling*
Hauszeitschrift: *house journal*
Headhunter: *headhunter*
Headline: *headline*
Heimarbeit: *cottage industry*
Heimatland: *home country*
Heimindustrie: *home industry*
Heimverbrauch: *home or domestic consumption*
Heimwerkerladen: *do-it-yourself store*
Heimwerkermagazin: *do-it-yourself magazine*
Heizkostenpauschale: nominelle ~ *token charge for heating*
helfen: *aid; help*
Heliogravüre: *photogravure*
herabsetzen: *depress; disparage; scale down*
Herabsetzung: *reduction*
herangehen or herantreten: *to approach*
Herangehensweise: *approach*
heraufsetzen: *mark up; scale up*
herausbringen: *launch; release*
Herausforderer: *challenger*
herausgeben: *issue*
Hereingefallene(r): *fall guy (US)*
Herkunft: *origin*
Herkunftsland: *country of origin*
Herkunftszertifikat: *certificate of origin*
herstellen: *make; manufacture; produce*
Hersteller: *manufacturer; producer*
Herstellerpreis: empfohlener ~ *manufacturer's recommended price (MRP); recommended retail price (RRP)*

Hersteller von Raubdrucken: *pirate*
Herstellung: *manufacture; manufacturing; production* **serienmäßige ~** *mass production*
Herstellungskosten: *manufacturing costs or production costs* **ursprüngliche ~** *historic(al) cost*
Herstellungsprozesse: *industrial processes*
Herstellung unter Vertrag: *contract manufacturing*
heterogen: *heterogeneous*
Hierarchy-of-effects-Modell: *hierarchy of effects*
High-involvement-Produkt: *high-involvement product*
Hilfsbetriebe des Handels: *aids-to-trade; ancillaries-to-trade; commercial services*
Hilfsmittel: *aid*
hineinstecken: *insert or inset*
Hintermann: *backer*
Hinweis: *lead*
hinweisen auf: *indicate*
hinzuziehen: *call in*
Histogramm: *histogram*
historisch: *historic or historical*
Hochfinanz: *high finance*
Hochkonjunktur: *boom*
Hochsaison: *high season*
Höchstgebot: *closing bid* **oder gegen ~** *or near offer*
Höchstgewicht: *weight limit*
Höchstgewinne: *record profits*
Höchstgrenze: *ceiling*
Höchstpreis: *maximum price*
Höchstproduktion: *peak output*
Höchststand: *high; peak* **den ~ erreichen** *to peak*
hochtreiben: *force up*
hochwertig: *high-grade; high-quality*
Höhepunkt: *peak*
Home-Shopping: *home shopping*
homogen: *homogeneous*
horizontal: *horizontal*
horizontale Integration: *horizontal integration*
horten: *hoard; stockpile*
Horten von Vorräten: *hoarding of supplies*
Huckepacktransport: *piggy-back freight (US)*
Huckepackverkaufsförderung: *piggy-back promotion*
Huckepackwerbung: *piggy-back promotion*
Hypermarkt: *hypermarket*
Hypothese: *hypothesis*

Ii

Ideengestalter: *visualizer*
Illustrationen: *artwork*
Image: *image; public image*
Imbißstube: *takeaway*
Imitation: *imitation*
imitieren: *imitate*
Immobilienbesitz verwalten: *to manage property*
Immobilienmakler: *house agent*
Import: *importation; importing*
Importabgabe: *import surcharge*
Importbeschränkungen einführen: *to set limits on imports or to impose import limits*
Importe: sichtbare ~ *visible imports* **unsichtbare ~** *invisible imports*
Importeur *or* **Importfirma:** *importer*
Importgenehmigung: *import permit*
Importhandel: *import trade*
importieren: *import*
Importkonnossement: *inward bill*
Importlizenz: *import licence*
Importneigung: *propensity to import*
Importquote: *import quota*
Importrestriktionen: mit ~ belegen *to impose trade barriers*
Impuls: *impulse*
impulsiv: etwas ~ tun *to do something on impulse*
Impulskauf: *impulse purchase*
Impulskäufe: *impulse buying*
Impulskäufer: *impulse buyer*
Incentive: *incentive*
Indentgeschäft: *indent*
Index: *index*
Indexbindung: *indexation*
Index der Einzelhandelspreise: *retail price index*
indexgebunden: *index-linked*
Indexierung: *indexation; indexing*
Indexierung von Gehaltserhöhungen: *indexation of wage increases*
Indexzahl *or* **Indexziffer:** *index number*
Indifferenzkurve: *indifference curve*
Indikator: *indicator*
indirekt: *indirect*
Individualnachfrage: *individual demand*
individuell: *individual*
individuell anpassen: *customize*
Individuum: *individual*
Indossament: *endorsement*
Indossant: *endorser*
Indossat: *endorsee*
industrialisieren: *industrialize*
Industrialisierung: *industrialization*
Industrie: *industry* **verarbeitende ~** *secondary industry; manufacturing industry*
Industriedesign: *industrial design*
Industriegebiet: *industrial estate; trading estate*
Industriegelände: *industrial park*
Industriegesellschaften: *industrialized societies*
Industriegüter: *manufactured goods; industrial goods or industrial products*
Industriegütermarkt: *industrial market*
industriell: *industrial*
Industrieller: *industrialist*
Industriemarketing: *industrial marketing*

Industriemarkt: **horizontaler** ~ *horizontal industrial market* **vertikaler** ~ *vertical industrial market*

Industriepapiere *or* **Industriewerte:** *industrials*

Industriezeitschrift: *trade journal or magazine or paper or publication*

Industriezentrum: *industrial centre*

Industriezweig: **arbeitsintensiver** ~ *labour-intensive industry* **expandierender** ~ *growth industry* **kapitalintensiver** ~ *capital-intensive industry*

Inflation: *inflation* **galoppierende** ~ *galloping or runaway inflation*

inflationsbedingt: *inflationary*

Inflationsrate: *rate of inflation or inflation rate* **der ~ angeglichen** *index-linked*

inflatorisch: *inflationary*

Information: *information; information bureau or information office*

Informationsamt der Regierung: *Central Office of Information (COI)*

Informationsblatt: *fact sheet*

Informationsbuch: *fact book*

Informationsmaterial: *information*

Informationsstop: *embargo*

Informationsstop verhängen: *to embargo*

Informationstechnik: *information technology*

Information zugänglich machen: *to share information*

informieren: *advise; brief; inform*

Inhaberscheck: *negotiable cheque; cheque (made payable) to bearer*

Inhaltsbeschreibung: **unkorrekte** ~ *false description of contents*

Initialverkauf: **intensiver** ~ *pioneer selling*

Initialwort: *acronym*

Initiative: **eine ~ aufgreifen** *to follow up an initiative*

initiieren: *pioneer*

Inkassobeauftragter: *debt collector*

Inkassobüro *or* **Inkassofirma:** *debt collection agency; collecting agency*

Inklusivpreis: *all-in price; all-in rate*

Inlandsabsatz: *home sales or sales in the home market; domestic sales*

Inlandsflug: *internal flight*

Inlandsmarkt: *home or domestic market*

Inlandsproduktion: *domestic production*

Inlandsverbrauch: *home or domestic consumption*

Innenansicht eines Produktes: *ghosting or ghost view*

innerbetrieblich: *in-house; internal; internally*

Innovation: *face-lift*

Innovationsteam: *venture team*

innovatorisch: *innovative*

Inselanzeige: *solus (advertisement)*

Inselposition: *island position*

Inserat: **ein ~ aufgeben** *to put an ad in a paper*

Inserent: *advertiser*

Insertionshäufigkeit: *frequency*

Insiderhandel: *insider trading*

Instabilität: *instability*

Installation: *installation*

installieren: *install*

Institut: *institution*

institutionell: *institutional*

instruieren: *brief*

Instrumente der Verkaufsförderung: *sales aids*

Integration: *integration* **horizontale** ~ *horizontal integration* **seitliche** ~ *lateral integration* **vertikale** ~ *vertical integration*

integrieren: *integrate*

Intensivinterview: *depth interview*

Intensivvertrieb: *intensive distribution*

Interessengruppe: *pressure group*

Interessenkonflikt: *conflict of interest*

Interessent: *prospect*

Interessenten: *potential customers*

Interims-: *provisional*

Intermediavergleich: *intermedia comparison*

intern: *internal; internally*

Internationaler Währungsfonds: *The International Monetary Fund (IMF)*

Internationales Marketing: *international marketing*

Interpolation: *interpolation*

Interview: *interview* **halbstrukturiertes** ~ *semi-structured interview* **persönliches** ~ *personal interview* **strukturiertes** ~ *patterned interview; structured interview* **unstrukturiertes** ~ *unstructured interview*

interviewen: *interview*

Interviewer: *interviewer*

Interviewte(r): *interviewee*

Intramediavergleich: *intramedia comparison*

Inventar aufnehmen *or* **inventarisieren:** *to inventory*

Inventarliste *or* **Inventarverzeichnis:** *inventory* **die ~ bestätigen** *to agree the inventory*

Inventur: *stocktaking*

Inventur machen: *to take stock*

Investition: *contribution of capital; investment*

Investitionen: *capital expenditure or investment or outlay*

Investitionskürzung: *harvesting*

Investitionsmöglichkeiten: *investment opportunities*

Investitionsneigung: *propensity to invest*

Investitionsrentabilität: *return on investment (ROI)*

Investitionswerbung: *investment advertising*

Investmentbank: *merchant bank*

Investor: *contributor of capital*

Jj

Jahr: **im** *or* **pro** ~ *per annum*

Jahrbuch: *yearbook*
Jahresabschluß: *annual accounts*
Jahresbericht: *directors' report*
Jahresbericht des Aufsichtsratsvorsitzenden: *the chairman's report*
Jahresbilanz: *annual accounts*
Jahreseinkommen: *annual income*
Jahreszeit: *season* **belebte ~** *busy season* **tote ~** *dead season* **umsatzschwache ~** *slack season* **umsatzstarke ~** *busy season*
jahreszeitlich bedingt: *seasonal*
Ja-Nein-Frage: *dichotomous question*
Jetzt-Früher-Preisschild: *off-price label*
Jingle: *advertising jingle or publicity jingle*
Jobben: *jobbing*
Joint-venture: *joint venture*
Journal: *journal*
Journalist: *journalist*
jüngster: *latest*
juristisch: *legal; legally*

Kk

Kabelfernsehen: *cable television*
Kai: *quay* **frei ~** *free on quay*
Kalkulation: *budgeting*
Kaltlagerung: *cold storage*
Kampagne: *campaign* **landesweite** *or* **überregionale ~** *national campaign*
Kampf: *battle*
Kanal: *channel*
Kandidat: *interviewee*
Kannibalisierungseffekt: *cannibalism*
Kapazitätsfaktor: *load factor*
Kapital: *capital; finance* **arbeitendes ~** *productive capital* **ausgegebenes ~** *issued capital* **einbezahltes ~** *paid-up capital* **gewinnbringendes ~** *productive capital* **totes ~** *money lying idle*
Kapitalanlage: *investment*
Kapitalflucht: *flight of capital*
Kapitalgesellschaft: *corporation*
Kapitalismus: *capitalism*
Kapitalist: *capitalist*
kapitalistisch: *capitalist*
Kapitalkonto: *capital account*
Kapitalmarkt: *capital market*
Kapitalrendite: *return on investment (ROI)*
Kapitalreserven: *capital reserves*
Kapitalsammelstellen: *institutional investors*
Kapital schlagen aus: *capitalize on*
Kapitalstruktur eines Unternehmens: *capital structure of a company*
Kapitaltransfersteuer: *capital transfer tax*
Kapitalverkehr: *movements of capital*
Kapitalverlust: *capital loss*
Kargo: *cargo*
Karte: *card; map* **nach der ~** *à la carte*
Kartell: *cartel; price ring*
Kartellamt: **das ~** *the Monopolies and Mergers Commission (MMC) (GB)*
Kartenschalter: *ticket counter*
Kartenzeichen *or* **Kartographie:** *mapping*
Karton: *carton*
Kassakonto: *cash account*
Kasse: *cash desk; checkout; cash till*
Kassegeschäft: *cash sale or cash transaction*
Kassenbestand: *cash balance*
Kassenbuch: *cash book*
Kassenkonto: *cash account*
Kassenschlager: *money-spinner*
Kassierer: *cashier*
Kasten: *box; advertisement panel*
Kasten für Verbesserungsvorschläge: *suggestion box*
Katalog: *catalogue or catalog (US)*
katalogisieren: *to catalogue or catalog (US)*
Katalogpreis: *catalogue price*
Kauf: *purchase* **einen ~ tätigen** *to make a purchase* **guter ~** *good buy* **nach dem ~** *post purchase* **schlechter ~** *bad buy* **tatsächlicher ~** *original purchase*
Kaufanreiz: *sales appeal*
Kaufen: *buying*
kaufen: *buy; purchase*
Käufer: *buyer; purchaser; shopper* **ein potentieller ~** *a prospective buyer*
Käufermarkt: *buyers' market*
Käuferrente: *buyer's surplus*
Käuferrisiko: *buyer's risk*
Kauffrau: *dealer; trader; tradeswoman*
Kaufgelegenheit: *purchasing opportunity*
Kaufhaus: *department store*
Kaufkategorien: *buy classes*
Kaufkraft: *buying power; purchasing power; spending power*
Kaufmann: *dealer; trader; tradesman*
Kauf mit Rückgaberecht: *sale or return*
Kaufnachweis: *proof of purchase*
Kaufoption: *option to purchase*
Kaufphasen: *buy phases*
Kaufpreis: *purchase price*
Kaufreue: *post-purchase anxiety*
Kaufsteuer: *purchase tax*
Kaufunlust: *consumer resistance; sales resistance*
Kaufvertrag: *bill of sale; sales contract*
Kaufwerbung: *direct-action advertising*
Kaufwunsch: *desire to purchase*
Kenntnis: **in ~ setzen** *advise; inform*
Kennziffer: *key number*
Kennzifferanzeige: *keyed advertisement*
Kennzifferkarte: *Bingo card*
Kennzifferndienstkarte: *reader's inquiry card or reader's service card*
Kette: *chain* **freiwillige ~** *voluntary chain*
Kettenladen: *chain store*

King-Size-(Plakat): *king-size (poster)*
Kiosk: *kiosk*
Kiste: *bin; case; packing case*
Kisten: sechs ~ Wein *six cases of wine*
Klappentext: *blurb*
Klasse: *range* **zweite ~** *second-class*
Klassenzimmerbefragung: *hall test*
klassifizieren: *classify; grade*
Klausel: *article; clause*
Kleiderhaken: *peg*
Kleinanzeigen: *classified ads or small ads or want ads; classified advertisements*
Kleinbetrieb: ein ~ *a small-scale enterprise*
Kleintastatur: *keypad*
Kleintransporter: offener ~ *pickup (truck)*
Kleinunternehmer: *small businessman*
Klientel: *clientele; custom*
Klienten: einen ~ einführen *to introduce a client*
Klumpen: *cluster*
Klumpenauswahl: *cluster sampling*
knapp: *marginal; scarce* **zu ~ abwiegen** *to give short weight*
knapp an: *short of*
Knappheit: *scarceness or scarcity*
knapp sein: *in short supply*
Know-how: *know-how*
Kollektivversicherung: *blanket insurance*
Kolumne: *column*
kommerzialisieren: *commercialize*
Kommerzialisierung: *commercialization*
kommerziell: *commercial; commercially*
Kommission: *commission* **auf ~** *sale or return*
Kommissionär: *accredited agent; buying agent; commission agent; export agent; factor; factoring agent; selling agent; stocking agent*
Kommissionsagent: *commission agent; manufacturer's agent; sales agent*
Kommissionsgebühr: *commission; factorage*
Kommissionshandel: *factoring*
Kommissionsrabatt: *commission rebating*
Kommissionsvorschuß: *drawing account*
Kommunikation: horizontale ~ *horizontal communication* **vertikale ~** *vertical communication*
Kommunikationswege: neue ~ erschließen *to open up new channels of communication*
Kommunikatorglaubwürdigkeit: *source credibility*
komplementär: *complementary*
Komplementärgüterangebot: *complementary supply*
Komplementärgüternachfrage: *complementary demand*
Komplementärprodukt: *complementary product*
Kondition: *condition*
Konfektions-: *ready-made or ready-to-wear*
Konferenz: *conference*
Konferenz zur Absatzförderung *or* **Konferenz zur Absatzplanung:** *sales conference or sales meeting*
Konfiskation: *forfeiture*
konfiszieren: *forfeit*
Konjunkturindikatoren: *economic indicators* **staatliche ~** *government economic indicators*
Konjunkturindustrie: *boom industry*
Konjunkturprognose: langfristige ~ *long-range economic forecast*
Konjunkturrückgang: *recession* **starker ~** *slump*
Konjunkturzyklus: *business or economic or trade cycle*
Konkurrent: *competitor; rival*
Konkurrenz: *competition; rival* **die ~** *the competition* **die ~ schlagen** *to knock the competition* **unvollkommene ~** *imperfect competition* **vollkommene ~** *perfect competition; pure competition*
Konkurrenzartikel: *competitive products*
konkurrenzfähig: *competitive*
Konkurrenzfähigkeit: *competitiveness*
Konkurrenzmarken: *rival brands*
Konkurrenzprodukte: *competing products; competitive products; rival products*
Konkurrenzproduktnachfrage: *competitive demand*
Konkurrenz verdrängen: *to freeze out competition*
konkurrierend: *competing*
Konkursgläubiger: nachrangiger ~ *deferred creditor*
Konnossement: *bill of lading* **reines ~** *clean bill of lading* **unreines ~** *claused bill of lading; dirty bill of lading; foul bill of lading*
Konsignationsgüter: *goods on consignment*
Konsortium: *consortium*
konsultieren: *consult*
Konsum: *consumption* **auffälliger** *or* **demonstrativer ~** *conspicuous consumption*
Konsument: *consumer*
Konsumentenbefragung: *consumer survey*
Konsumentenmarkt: *consumer market*
Konsumentenrente: *consumer's surplus; buyer's surplus*
Konsumentensouveranität: *consumer sovereignty*
Konsumerismus: *consumerism*
Konsumforschung: *consumer research*
Konsumgenossenschaft: *consumer cooperative*
Konsumgesellschaft: *consumer society*
Konsumgüter: *consumable goods; consumer goods* **kurzlebige ~** *non-durables* **langlebige ~** *consumer durables* **schnellverkäufliche ~** *fast-moving consumer goods (FMCG)*
Konsumneigung: *propensity to consume*
Konsumzwang: *forced consumption*
Kontakt: *exposure; impression*
Kontaktbewertungsfunktion: *response function*
Kontaktchancen: *opportunities to see (OTS)*

Kontakter: *account handler*

Kontakthäufigkeit: *frequency* **durchschnittliche ~** *average frequency*

Kontaktwahrscheinlichkeiten: *opportunities to see (OTS)*

Kontingent: *quota*

Kontingentierungssystem: *quota system*

kontinuierlich: *continuous*

Kontinuität: *continuity*

Konto: *account* **ein ~ auflösen** *to close an account* **ein ~ ausgleichen** or **begleichen** *to settle an account* **ein ~ belasten** *to debit an account* **ein ~ einrichten** or **eröffnen** *to open an account* **ein ~ sperren** *to stop an account* **gemeinsames ~** *joint account* **gesperrtes ~** *frozen account; account on stop* **laufendes ~** *current account; cheque account; checking account (US); demand deposit (US); drawing account* **umsatzloses ~** *dead account* **überzogenes ~** *overdrawn account*

Kontokorrentkonto: *current account; demand deposit (US); drawing account*

Kontokorrentkonto mit Kreditlinie: *open account*

Konto mit Habensaldo: *account in credit*

Kontrolle: *control* **außer ~** *out of control* **freiwillige ~** *voluntary control* **unter ~** *under control*

Kontrollfrage: *control question*

Kontrollgruppe: *control group*

kontrollierbar: *controllable*

kontrollieren: *to control*

Kontrolliste: *checklist*

Kontrollmodell: anpassungsfähiges ~ *adaptive control model (US)*

Konzentration: *concentration* **geographische ~** *geographical concentration*

Konzept: *concept*

Konzern: *group* **multinationaler ~** *multinational*

Konzernergebnisse: *group results*

Konzession: *concession; licence* or *license (US)*

Konzessionär: *concessionnaire*

Konzessions-: *licensing*

Konzessionsinhaber: *licensee*

Konzession zum Alkoholverkauf: *off licence*

Kooperation: *co-operation* **horizontale ~** *horizontal marketing system* **vertikale ~** *vertical marketing system*

kooperativ: *co-operative*

Kooperative: *co-operative*

kooperieren: *co-operate*

Kopf: pro ~ *per capita*

Kopie: *imitation*

kopieren: *copy; imitate*

Kopierer: *copier* or *copying machine*

Kopplungsvertrag: *tying contract*

Körperschaftssteuer: *corporation tax; corporation income tax*

Körpersprache: *body language*

Korrekturbogen: *proof*

Korrelation: *correlation*

Korrelationskoeffizient: *coefficient of correlation*

kosmetisch: *cosmetic*

Kosten: *centre* or *center (US); charge; cost; expense* **die ~ decken** *to cover costs* **gesellschaftliche ~** *social costs* **halbvariable ~** *semi-variable costs* **variable ~** *variable costs*

kosten: *to cost; sample*

Kostenanalyse: *cost analysis*

Kostenanschlag: *bid*

Kostenberechnung: *costing*

kostendeckend arbeiten: *break even*

Kostendeckungspunkt: *breakeven point*

Kostenfaktor: *cost factor*

kostenlos: *free; free of charge*

Kosten-Plus-System: *cost plus*

Kostenpreisberechnung: durchschnittliche ~ *average cost pricing*

Kosten pro Anfrage: *cost per inquiry*

Kostenprogression: *diseconomies of scale*

Kostenrechner: *cost accountant*

Kostenrechnung: *cost accounting*

Kostenrentabilität: *cost-effectiveness*

Kostensenkung: *cost cutting*

Kostenstelle: *cost centre* **allgemeine ~** *service department*

Kosten und Fracht: *cost and freight*

Kostenvoranschlag: *bid; estimate; quotation* **einen ~ machen** *to put in an estimate*

kostenwirksam: *cost-effective*

kostspielig: *costly; expensive*

Kraft: *force* **in ~ sein** *to be in force* **in ~ treten** *to come into force*

Kraftfahrzeugkennzeichen: *registration number*

kreativ: *creative*

Kredit: *credit* **auf ~** *on credit* **kurzfristiger ~** *short credit; short-term loan* **langfristiger ~** *extended credit* **offener ~** *open credit* **prolongierter ~** *extended credit* **unwiderruflicher ~** *confirmed credit* **verlängerter ~** *extended credit*

Kreditauskunftei: *credit agency* or *credit bureau (US)*

Kreditbank: *credit bank*

Kreditinstitut: *financial institution*

Kreditkarte: *credit card* **mit ~ bezahlen** *to pay by credit card*

Kreditkontrolle: *credit control*

Kreditkunde: *account*

Kreditlimit: *credit limit; lending limit*

Kreditlinie: eine ~ einräumen *to open a line of credit* or *a credit line*

Kreditmodalitäten: *credit facilities*

Kreditnehmer: *debtor*

Kreditrestriktionen aufheben: *to lift credit restrictions*

Kreditsaldo: *credit balance*

Kreditspalte: *credit column*

Kredittransfer: *credit transfer* or *transfer of funds*

kreditwürdig: *credit-worthy*

Kreditwürdigkeit: *creditworthiness*

Kreisdiagramm: *pie chart*

Kreislauf: *cycle*
Kreuzkurs: *cross rate*
Kreuzpreiselastizität der Nachfrage: *cross elasticity of demand*
Krisenplan: *contingency plan*
Kuhhandel: *horse trading*
Kühlhaus: *cold store*
Kühlhauslagerung: *cold storage*
Kulanzzahlung: *ex-gratia payment*
kumulativ: *cumulative*
Kunde: *client; customer* **ein langjähriger** *or* **treuer ~** *a long-standing customer or customer of long standing* **ein zufriedener ~** *a satisfied customer* **überregionaler ~** *national account*
Kunden: einen ~ einführen *to introduce a client* **einen ~ zufriedenstellen** *to satisfy a client* **potentielle ~** *key prospects; potential customers* **stille ~** *dormant accounts*
Kundenabgänge: *loss of customers*
Kundenattraktivität: *customer appeal*
Kundenbetreuer: *account executive; account handler*
Kundendienst: *after-sales service; customer service* **technischer ~** *service department*
Kundendienstabteilung: *customer service department*
Kundendienstmechaniker: *service engineer*
Kundendienstvertragswerkstatt: *service centre*
Kundenkonto: *account; charge account (US)* **ein ~ einrichten** *or* **eröffnen** *to open an account* **ein ~ sperren** *to close or stop an account*
Kundenkredit: *consumer credit*
Kunden(kredit)karte: *charge card; store card*
Kundenkreditkonto: *account; charge account; credit account*
Kundenkreis: *clientele*
Kundenprofil: *customer profile*
Kundentransportwagen: *courtesy car*
Kundentreue: *customer loyalty*
Kundenverkehr: *traffic*
Kunden verlieren: *to lose customers*
Kundenverlust(rate): *attrition (rate)*
Kündigungsklausel: *termination clause*
Kundin: *client; customer*
Kundschaft: *clientele; custom; patronage*
künstlerisch: *creative*
Kunststoffe: *synthetic materials*
Kupon: cum ~ *cum coupon* **ex ~** *ex coupon* **mit ~** *cum coupon* **ohne ~** *ex coupon*
Kuponanzeige: *coupon ad*
Kurierdienst: *delivery service*
Kurs: *course; policy*
Kurs-Gewinn-Verhältnis: *price/earnings ratio (P/E ratio)*
Kursus: *course*
Kurve: *curve*
Kürze: in ~ *in the short term*
kürzeren: den ~ ziehen *to lose out*
kurzfristig: *at short notice; (in the) short term; on a short-term basis*
kurzfristig aufnehmen: *to borrow short*
Kurzmitteilung: *compliments slip*
Kurzübersicht: *profile*
Kürzung: *retrenchment*
Kurzwarenhändler: *haberdasher*

Ll

Ladefähigkeit: *load-carrying capacity*
Ladeliste: *manifest*
Laden: *shop*
laden: *to load*
Ladenaufsicht: *floorwalker*
Ladendieb: *shoplifter*
Ladendiebstahl: *shoplifting; shrinkage (informal)*
Ladenfront: *shop front*
Ladeninhaber: *shopkeeper*
Ladenkasse: *till*
Ladenpreis: *retail price*
Ladenschild: *fascia; sign*
Ladenschluß: *closing time*
Ladenschwengel: *counter-jumper (informal)*
Ladentisch: *counter*
Ladeplatz: *loading bay*
Laderampe: *loading ramp*
Ladung: *cargo; load; shipment*
Lage: *location; position; range; situation*
Lager: *stockroom; store; storeroom; warehouse* **auf ~ haben** *to carry* **auf ~ halten** *to stock*
Lagerarbeiter: *warehouseman*
Lager auffüllen: *to restock; stock up*
Lagerauffüllung: *restocking*
Lagerbestand: *stock; inventory*
Lagerbestandsabschreibung: *stock depreciation*
Lagerbestandshöhe: *stock level*
Lagerbestandsverzeichnis: *stock figures; stocklist*
Lagereinrichtungen: *storage facilities*
Lagerfähigkeit eines Produktes: *shelf life of a product*
Lagergeld: *storage*
Lagerhalle: *store*
Lagerhaus: *depot; store; warehouse*
Lagerhauskapazität: *warehouse capacity*
Lagerist: *storekeeper or storeman*
Lagerkapazität: *storage capacity*
Lagerkosten: *storage*
lagern: *store; warehouse*
Lagerraum: *storeroom*
Lagersteuerung: *stock control*
Lagerumschlag: *stock turn or stock turnround or stock turnover*
Lagerung: *storage; warehousing*
Lagerungsfirma: *storage company*
Lagerverwalter: *stock controller; storekeeper or storeman*

Laisser-faire-Wirtschaftspolitik: *laissez-faire economy*
Land: meistbegünstigtes ~ *most favoured nation*
Länder: erdölexportierende ~ *oil-exporting countries*
landesweit: *nationwide*
Landwirtschaft: gemischte ~ *mixed farm*
lange: schon ~ bestehend *long-standing*
langfristig: *long-range; on a long-term basis*
Längsseite: frei ~ Binnenschiff *or* **Seeschiff** *free alongside ship*
Lastkraftwagen: *lorry; truck*
Lastschrift: *debit entry*
Lastschriftanzeige: *debit note*
Lastwagen: *lorry; truck*
Lastwagenladung: *load of a lorry; lorry-load*
Lastwagentransport: *truckage*
Layout: *layout*
Lebensbedürfnisse: die ~ *the basic necessities*
Lebenserwartung: *life expectancy*
Lebenshaltungskosten: *cost of living*
Lebenshaltungskostenindex: *cost-of-living index*
Lebenshaltungskostenzuschuß: *cost-of-living allowance*
Lebensmittellieferant: *caterer*
Lebensstandard: *standard of living or living standards*
Lebensstil: *life style*
Lebensversicherung: *life assurance or life insurance*
Lebenszyklus: *life cycle*
Leergut: *returned empties*
Leerpackung: *dummy pack*
Leerverkauf: *short selling or selling short*
leerverkaufen: *to sell short*
legal: *over the counter; legal*
legalisieren: *legalize*
Legalisierung: *legalization*
Legalität: *legality*
Legende: *caption*
Lehrgang: *course* **kaufmännischer ~** *commercial course*
Lehrplan: *schedule*
Leibrente: *life annuity or annuity for life*
Leichtindustrie: *light industry*
leicht verderblich: *perishable*
leihen: *advance*
Leihwagen: kostenloser ~ *courtesy car*
Leistungsanreize für Arbeitnehmer: *fringe benefits*
Leistungslohn: *payment by results*
Leistungszulage: *incentive bonus or incentive payment; productivity bonus*
Leitartikel: *editorial; leader*
Leitbildwerbung: *endorsement advertising; testimonial advertising*
leiten: *direct; lead; manage; run*
Leiter: *director; leader*
Leiter der Buchhaltung: *accounts manager*
Leiter der EDV-Abteilung: *computer manager*
Leiter der Fertigung: *production manager*
Leiter der Grafikabteilung: *art director*
Leiter der PR-Abteilung: *public relations officer (PRO)*
Leitung: *control; direction*
Leitungsebene: unterste ~ *first-line or front-line management*
Leitzins: *prime rate or prime*
Lernkurve: *learning curve*
Lesegeschehen pro Seite: *page traffic*
Lesen und Sehen: *reading and noting*
Lesepistole: *light pen*
Leser: *reader*
Leser-Blatt-Bindung *or* **Leserloyalität:** *reader loyalty*
Leserschaft: *readership* **tertiäre ~** *tertiary readership*
Leserservicekarte: *reader's service card*
Lichtstift: *light pen*
Lieferant: *supplier*
Lieferauftrag: *delivery order*
liefern: *deliver; supply*
Lieferpreis: *delivered price*
Lieferschein: *delivery note*
Lieferung: *consignment; delivery; supply* **eine ~ abnehmen** *or* **übernehmen** *to take delivery of goods* **zahlbar bei ~** *payable on delivery*
Lieferungen: ausstehende ~ *back or outstanding or unfulfilled orders*
Liefervertrag: *(delivery) contract*
Lieferwagen: *delivery van*
Lieferzeit: *delivery time; lead time*
Liegegeld: *demurrage*
Liegeplatz: *berth*
Limit: *limit*
Linie: *line; policy*
Liniendiagramm: *line chart; line graph*
Linienfrachtschiff: *cargo liner*
Linienmanagement: *line management*
Linienorganisation: *line organization*
Liquiditätsreserven: *cash reserves*
Liste: *catalogue or catalog (US); list; schedule* **schwarze ~** *black list*
Listenpreis: *card rate; catalogue price; list price*
Literatur: *literature*
Lithographie: *lithography*
Lizenz: *licence or license (US)*
Lizenzgebühr: *royalty*
Lizenzinhaber: *licensee*
Lockangebot: *bait*
Lockartikel: *loss-leader*
Lockpreisstrategie: *leader pricing*
Lockvogel: *call bird*
Logo: *logo or logotype*
Lohngärtner: *jobbing gardener*
Lohngefälle: *wage differentials*

Lohngefälle abbauen: *to erode wage differentials*
Lohngemeinkosten: *indirect labour costs*
Lohnkosten: *labour costs*
Lohnscheck: *pay cheque or salary cheque*
Lohn- und Gehaltsliste: *payroll ledger*
Lohn- und Preisstopp: *wages and prices freeze or a freeze on wages and prices*
Lohnverhandlungen: *pay negotiations or wage negotiations*
lokal: *local*
Lokalblätter: *local newspapers*
Lokalpresse: **die ~** *the local press*
Lokalsender: *local radio station*
Lokalzeitung: *local newspaper*
Lokopreis: *spot price or spot rate*
London Gold Fixing: *the London gold fixing*
löschen: *close; land; unload*
Löscherlaubnis: *landing order*
Löschungskosten und Löschungszölle: *landing charges*
lose: *loose*
losschlagen: *to dispose of*
loswerden: *to shift*
Low-involvement-Produkt: *low-involvement product*
Lücke: *gap*
Lückenanalyse: *gap analysis*
Lückenfüller: *filler*
luftdicht: *airtight*
Luftfahrtgesellschaft: *air carrier*
Luftfracht: *air cargo; air freight* **per ~ senden** *to airfreight*
Luftfrachtgebühren: *air freight charges or rates*
Luftfrachtspedition: *air forwarding*
Luftpost: *airmail* **per ~ schicken** *to airmail*
Luftpostaufkleber: *airmail sticker*
Luftpostbrief: *air letter*
Luftpostüberweisung: *airmail transfer*
Luftpostumschlag: *airmail envelope*
Luftwerbung: *aerial advertising*
Luxus: *luxury*
Luxusartikel: *luxury goods*
Luxusprodukt: *luxury product; prestige product*
Luxussteuer: *levies on luxury items*

Mm

Macht: *control*
Magazin: *magazine; periodical; store*
Magnetbildband: *video tape* **auf ~ aufnehmen** *to video tape*
Mahnung: *reminder* **letzte ~** *final demand*
Mailing: **personalisierte ~** *personalized mailing*
Majorität: *majority*
Makler: *agent; broker; negotiator (GB)*
Maklergebühr: *brokerage or broker's commission*
Makromarketing: *macro-marketing*
Makroökonomie: *macro-economics*
Makro-Umwelt: *macro-environment*
Mall: *shopping mall (US)*
Malrabatt: *no-change discount*
Malstaffel: *graded advertising rates*
Mammutanschlagfläche: *supersite*
Management: *management* **mittleres ~** *middle management* **systemorientiertes ~** *systems management*
Management-Ausbildung: *management training*
Management-Entwicklung: *management development*
Managementlehre: *business science or management science*
Managementmethoden: *management techniques*
Management nach Ausnahmeprinzipien: *management by exception*
Management nach Zielvorgaben: *management by objectives*
Management-Team: *management team*
Managerin: *manageress*
Managerkurs: *management course*
Managertätigkeit: *managership*
Mangel: *imperfection; scarceness or scarcity; shortage*
Mannequin: *model* **als ~ arbeiten** *to model*
Mannschaft: *team*
Manufakturwaren: *manufactured goods*
Manuskriptannahme: *copy clearance*
Mappe: *portfolio*
Marge: *margin*
marginal: *marginal*
Mark: *mark*
Marke: *brand; make* **generische ~** *generic; generic term*
Markenartikel: *branded goods; proprietary goods*
Markenbekanntheit *or* **Markenbewußtsein:** *brand awareness*
Markenfamilie: *family*
Markenfamilienbranding: *blanket branding; family branding*
Markenführer: *brand leader*
Markengebung: *branding*
Markenimage: *brand image*
Markenkampf: *battle of the brands (US)*
Markenname: *brand name* **alltägliche ~** *household name*
Markenpirat: *pirate*
Markenpiraterie: *piracy*
Markenproduktmanager: *brand manager*
Marken(produkt)positionierung: *brand positioning*
Markenprofil: *brand image*
Markentreue: *brand loyalty* **tief verwurzelte ~** *deep-rooted demand*
Markenwechsel: *brand switching*
Markenwiedererkennung: *brand recognition*

Marketing: *marketing* **flächendeckendes ~** *extensive marketing* **getrenntes ~** *divergent marketing* **gezieltes ~** *concentrated marketing* **integriertes ~** *integrated marketing* **kooperatives ~** *co-operative marketing* **vertikales ~** *vertical marketing*

Marketingabteilung: *marketing department*

Marketingdienstleistungen: *marketing services*

Marketingdirektor: *marketing director*

Marketingetat: *marketing budget*

Marketing-Fachmann: *marketer*

Marketingforschung: *marketing research*

Marketinginformation: *marketing intelligence*

Marketingkommunikation: *marketing communications*

Marketingkonzept: *marketing concept*

Marketingmanager: *marketing manager*

Marketing-Methoden: *marketing techniques*

Marketing-Mix: *marketing mix*

Marketingmodell: *marketing model*

Marketingplan: *marketing plan*

Marketingstrategie: *marketing strategy* **undifferenzierte ~** *undifferentiated marketing strategy*

Marketingsystem: horizontales ~ *horizontal marketing system*

Marketing-Umwelt-Analyse: *opportunity and threat analysis*

Marketing-Unternehmen: *marketer*

Marke X: *brand X*

markieren: *to mark*

Markierung: *mark*

Markt: *market; marketplace; mart* **aufnahmefähiger ~** *ready market* **beschränkter ~** *reserved* or *restricted market* **den ~ beherrschen** *to corner the market* **einen ~ schließen** *to close a market* **flauer ~** *depressed market* **freier ~** *open market* **geschlossener ~** *closed market* **grauer ~** *grey market* **offener ~** *open market* **organisierter ~** *organized market* **potentieller ~** *potential market* **stabiler ~** *stable market* **statischer ~** *static market*

Marktanalyse: *market analysis*

Marktanteil: *market coverage; market share*

Marktaufbaumethode: *market build-up method*

Marktbefragung: *market survey*

Marktdurchdringung: *market penetration*

Märkte: neue ~ erschließen *to open up new markets*

Märkte im Ausland: *overseas markets*

Marktentwicklung: *market development*

Marktentwicklungen: *market trends*

Markterschließung: *market opening*

marktfähig: *marketable*

Marktfaktoranalyse: *market factor analysis*

Marktfolger: *follower*

Marktfolgerstrategie: *market follower strategy*

Marktforschung: *market research* **fortlaufende** or **kontinuierliche ~** *continuous research*

Marktführer: *market leader*

Marktführerstrategie: *market leader strategy*

Marktherausfordererstrategie: *market challenger strategy*

Marktkräfte: *market forces*

Marktlücke: *gap in the market*

Marktnachfrage: *market demand*

Marktnische: *market niche*

Marktplatz: *marketplace*

Marktpotential: *market potential*

Marktpreis: *market price; market rate*

Marktprofil: *market profile*

Marktprognose: *market forecast*

Marktsättigung: *saturation of the market* or *market saturation*

Marktsegment: *market segment*

Marktsegmentierung: *market segmentation; segmentation* **demographische ~** *demographic segmentation* **geographische ~** *geographical* or *spatial segmentation* **psychographische ~** *psychographic segmentation*

Markt-Strategien: *product-market strategies*

Markttag: *market day*

Markttendenzen: *market trends*

Markttest: *market test*

Marktumfrage: *market survey*

Marktwert: *market value*

Marktwirtschaft: freie ~ *free market economy*

Marktzugang: *access to the market*

Marktzugänglichkeit: *accessibility*

Marotte: *fad*

Maschine: eine ~ bedienen *to operate a machine*

Maschinenlauf: *run*

Maschinensaal: *machine shop*

Masse: *bulk; mass*

Massen: in ~ *in bulk* **in ~ produzieren** *mass-produce*

Massenabsatzstrategie: *mass marketing*

Massenanfertigung: in ~ herstellen *to mass-produce*

Massenarbeitslosigkeit: *mass unemployment*

Massengütertransport: *bulk shipment*

Massengutfrachter: *bulk carrier*

Massenmedien: *mass media*

Massenproduktion: *mass production*

Maßnahmen zur Inflationsbekämpfung: *anti-inflationary measures*

Maßstäbe für Kontaktqualität: *volumetrics*

Material: *material*

Materialfluß: *materials handling*

Materialsteuerung: *materials control*

Matrize: *matrix*

Matrose: gemeiner ~ *deck hand*

Mauserei: *pilferage* or *pilfering*

maximal: *maximum*

maximieren: *maximize*

Maximierung: *maximization*

Maximum: *maximum*

mechanisch: *mechanical*

Media-Agentur: *media broker* **selbständige ~** *media independent*
Mediaanalyse: *media analysis*
Mediaforschung: *media research*
Mediakombination: *mixed media*
Median: *median*
Mediaplan: *media schedule*
Mediaplanung: *media planning*
Mediaselektion: *media selection*
Medien: *media* **elektronische ~** *electronic media*
Medieneigentümer: *media owner*
Medieninformationskarte: *media data form*
Medienkategorie: *media class*
Medienveranstaltung: *media event*
Meer: *sea*
Meeres-: *marine*
Megaladen: *megastore*
Mehrbetrag: *excess* **einen ~ verrechnen** *to absorb a surplus*
mehrfach: *multiple*
Mehrfachkorrelation: *multiple correlation*
Mehrfachpackungsangebot: *multi-pack offer*
Mehrfachregressionsanalyse: *multiple regression analysis*
Mehrgewinn: *excess profit*
Mehrheit: *majority* **frühe ~** *early majority* **späte ~** *late majority*
Mehrplatzsystem: *networked system*
Mehrweg-: *returnable*
Mehrwert: *value added*
Mehrwertsteuer: *Value Added Tax (VAT)*
Mehrwertsteuerabrechnung: *VAT invoicing*
Mehrwertsteuerbefreiung: *exempt rating; zero-rating*
Mehrwertsteuererklärung: *VAT declaration*
mehrwertsteuerfrei: *zero-rated*
Mehrwertsteuerrechnung: *VAT invoice*
Meinung: **öffentliche ~** *public opinion*
Meinungsforscher: *canvasser*
Meinungsforschung: *opinion research*
Meinungsführer: *opinion-formers or opinion-leaders*
Meinungsumfrage: *canvassing; opinion poll*
Meistbegünstigungsklausel: *most-favoured-nation clause*
Meistbietende(r): *highest bidder*
meistverkauft: *top-selling*
melden: *report*
Meldeschein: *certificate of registration or registration certificate*
melken: *milk*
Membercard: *store card*
Menge: *bulk; mass; quantity; volume*
Mengen: **in ~** *in bulk*
Mengeneinkauf: *bulk buying or bulk purchase; quantity purchase*
Mengenrabatt: *bulk discount; bulk rate; quantity discount; volume discount* **10% ~** *10% discount for quantity purchases* **kumulativer ~** *cumulative quantity discount*
Merchandising: *merchandising*
Merkmalsanalyse: **psychographische ~** *psychographics*
Messe: *show*
Messehalle: *exhibition room or hall*
Messestand: *exhibition stand*
Metamarketing: *metamarketing (US)*
Miete: **geringe** *or* **symbolische ~** *token rent*
Mieten: *chartering*
mieten: *charter*
Mieter: *charterer*
Mikromarketing: *micro-marketing*
Mikroökonomie: *micro-economics*
Mikro-Umwelt: *business environment; immediate environment; micro-environment*
Milchkuh: *cash cow*
Millimeterpapier: *graph paper*
Minderung: *shrinkage*
minderwertig: *inferior; low-grade; low-quality*
Mindestauflage: *guaranteed circulation*
Mindesteinschaltquote: *guaranteed homes impressions or guaranteed homes ratings*
Mindesthaltbarkeitsdatum: *sell-by date*
Mindestlohn: **garantierter ~** *guaranteed wage*
Mindestnachbestellung: *reorder level*
Mindestpreis: *fall-back price; upset price*
Mindestpreise: **garantierte ~** *guaranteed prices*
Minicontainer: *minicontainer*
Minimarkt: *minimarket*
Ministerium: *department*
Minusbetrag: *deficit*
Mischkonzern: *conglomerate*
Mischung: *mix*
Mischwirtschaft: *mixed economy*
mißlingen: *fall through*
Mitarbeit: *co-operation*
Mitbieter: *underbidder*
Miteigentum: *common ownership*
Mitgliedsbeitrag: *subscription*
Mitläufereffekt: *demonstration effect*
mitteilen: *inform*
Mitteilung: *advice; message; note*
Mittel: *means; medium; resources* **finanzielle ~** *finance; financial resources* **flüssige ~** *liquid assets; ready money*
mittelbar: *indirect*
mittelfristig: *medium-term*
Mittelkurs: *mean price*
Mittelseiten: *centre spread*
Mittelwert: *average; mean*
mittlerer: *mean*
mitziehen: *reciprocate*
mobil: *mobile*
Mobiliar: *goods and chattels*
Mobilität: *fluidity*
Mode: *fad*

Modeartikel: *fancy goods*
Model(l): *model*
Modelle: **logische** ~ *logical models* **zyklische** ~ *cycle models*
Modell zur Wirtschaftsprognose: *economic model*
Modem: *modem*
Modetorheit: *fad*
modifizieren: *modify*
Modifizierung: *modification*
modular: *modular*
Modus: *mode*
Möglichkeit: *opening; opportunity*
Möglichkeiten: *scope*
Mondschein-Tarif: *night rate*
monetär: *monetary*
Monitor: *monitor; visual display terminal*
Monopol: *monopoly* **staatliches** ~ *public monopoly or state monopoly* **unumschränktes** ~ *absolute monopoly*
Monopolgewinn: **außergewöhnlicher** ~ *supernormal profit*
monopolisieren: *monopolize*
Monopolisierung: *monopolization*
Monopolist: *monopolist*
Monopolprofit: *monopoly profit*
Monopolzerschlagung: *trustbusting (US)*
Monopson: *monopsony*
Monopsonist: *monopsonist*
Montage: *assembly*
Montageband: *assembly line or production line*
Motivation: *motivation*
Motivforschung: *motivational research*
Motorrad-Bote: *dispatch rider*
Mülleimerkontrolle: *dustbin check*
multilateral: *multilateral*
Münzfernsehen: *pay television or pay TV*
Muster: *sample; specimen*
Musterbuch: *pattern book; sample book or book of samples*
mustergültig: *model*
Musterhaus: *show house*
Musterstreifen: *swatch*
Mustervertrag: *standard agreement or standard contract*
Musterwohnung: *show flat*

Nn

Nachahmung: *imitation* **unerlaubte** ~ *piracy*
nachbestellen: *reorder* **etwas** ~ *to repeat an order*
Nachbestellung: *reorder; repeat order* **eine** ~ **aufgeben** *to repeat an order*
nachfassen: *follow up*
Nachfaßschreiben: *follow-up letter*
Nachfrage: *demand; inquiry* **abgeleitete** ~ *derived demand* **aggregierte** ~ *aggregate demand* **direkte** ~ *direct demand* **effektive** ~ *effective demand* **elastische** ~ *elastic demand* **gesamte** ~ *aggregate demand* **gleichbleibende** ~ *steady demand* **große** ~ *keen demand* **negative** ~ *negative demand* **potentielle** ~ *potential demand* **saisonbedingte** ~ *seasonal demand* **selektive** ~ *selective demand* **tief verwurzelte** ~ *deep-rooted demand* **unelastische** ~ *inelastic demand*
Nachfrageanalyse: *demand theory*
Nachfrage befriedigen: *to satisfy a demand*
Nachfrageinflation: *demand-led inflation*
Nachfragepreis: *demand price*
Nachfrageprognose: *demand forecasting*
Nachfrage stillen: *to satisfy a demand*
Nachfragetabelle: *demand schedule*
Nachfrageüberschuß: *excess demand*
nachgehen: *follow up*
Nachkaufbewertung: *post-purchase assessment*
Nachkaufwerbung: *post-purchase advertising*
nachlassen: *knock off*
Nachlaßverwalter: *administrator*
Nachlaß zeigendes Preisschild: *price-off label*
nachmachen: *imitate*
Nachnahme: *charges forward* **gegen or per** ~ *cash on delivery; collect on delivery (US)*
Nachricht: *message; note*
Nachrichten: *news*
Nachrichtenagentur: *news agency*
Nachrichtenblatt: *bulletin*
Nachrichtendienst: *news service*
Nachsaison: *low season*
Nachsendeadresse: *forwarding address*
nachsenden: **jdm etwas** ~ *to forward something to someone*
nächstgelegen: *immediate*
Nachteil: *drawback*
Nachttarif: *night rate*
Nachzahlung: *back payment*
Nachzügler: *laggards*
Nachzugsaktien: *deferred stock*
nagelneu: *first-hand*
Namen: **unter dem** ~ *under the name of*
Nation: *nation*
national: *national*
natürlich: *natural*
naturwissenschaftlich: *scientific*
Neben-: *secondary; subsidiary*
Nebenausgaben: *extras*
Nebenbeschäftigung: *sideline*
Nebenkosten: *incidental expenses; extras*
Nebenprodukt: *by-product; spinoff*
nebensächlich: *subsidiary*
Nebensaison: *dead season; off-season*
negativ: *negative; unfavourable*
nehmen: *take*
Neigung: *propensity*
nennen: *quote*
Nennwert: *face value; par value*

nervös: *jumpy*
netto: *net*
Nettoauflage: **effektive ~** *net circulation*
Netto-Cashflow: *net cash flow*
Nettoeinkommen: *disposable income*
Nettoeinnahmen: *net receipts*
netto einnehmen: *to net*
Nettoertrag: *net yield*
Nettogehalt: *net salary*
Nettogewicht: *net weight*
Nettogewinn: *clear profit; net profit*
Nettomarge: *net margin*
Nettopreis: *net price*
Nettoreichweite: *net cover; net reach*
Nettosozialprodukt: *net national product*
Nettoumsatz: *net sales*
netto verdienen: *to net*
Nettoverdienst: *net income or net salary*
Nettoverlust: *net loss*
Netzplantechnik: *network analysis*
Netz(werk): *network*
neu: *new*
Neubeginn: **ein völliger ~** *cold start*
Neueinführung: *innovation*
Neuerer: *innovator*
Neuerungen einführen: *to innovate*
Neugier weckende Werbung: *teaser*
Neugründung: *start-up*
Neuheit: *innovation*
Neupositionierung: *repositioning*
Neuproduktaufnahme: *new buy*
Nichtdiskriminierung im Außenhandel: *fair trade*
nichtig: *null* **für ~ erklären** *nullify*
Nichtlieferung: *non-delivery*
Nichtverfügbarkeit: *unavailability*
Nichtzahlung einer Verpflichtung: *non-payment of a debt*
niederlassen: **sich ~** *to set up in business*
Niederlassung: *branch*
niedrig: **zu ~ geschätzt** *undervalued*
Niedrigpreis: *cut price*
Niedrigpreisgeschäft: *cut-price store*
Niedrigstpreise: *rock-bottom prices*
Nielsen-Index: *Nielsen Index*
Nische: *niche*
Niveau: *level; standard*
nochmals inserieren: *readvertise*
Nominalwert: *face value*
Norm: *standard* **nach ~ arbeiten** *to work to standard specifications*
normal: *common; normal; regular; standard*
Normalformat: *regular size*
Normalkosten: *standard costs*
Normalkostenrechnung: *standard costing*
Normalpreis: *normal price*
Normalprodukt: *normal product*
Normalrabatt: *basic discount*
Normalverteilung: *normal distribution*
normen: *standardize*
Normung: *standardization*
Notiz: *note*
Notverkauf: *distress sale; distress selling; forced sale*
Notwendigkeit: *necessity*
numerisch: *numeric or numerical*
Nummer: *issue*
Nutzen: *utility*
nutzen: *exploit*
Nutzfahrzeug: *commercial vehicle or goods vehicle*
Nutzlast: *payload*
Nutzungsgebühr: *royalty*

Oo

objektiv: *objective*
obligatorisch: *mandatory*
Obsoleszenz: *obsolescence* **eingebaute ~** *built-in obsolescence* **funktionelle ~** *dynamic obsolescence* **geplante ~** *planned obsolescence* **künstliche ~** *artificial obsolescence* **modische** *or* **stylistische ~** *style obsolescence*
Odd-Even Pricing: *odd-even pricing*
offen: *open; open-ended or open-end (US)*
Offenlegung vertraulicher Informationen: *disclosure of confidential information*
offenstehend: *open*
öffentlich: *public*
Öffentlichkeit: **die ~** *the public or the general public*
Öffentlichkeitsarbeit: *public relations (PR)*
Off-Kommentar: *voice-over*
öffnen: *open*
Öffnungszeit: *opening hours*
Ökonometrie: *econometrics*
Ökonomie: *economics*
Oligopol: *oligopoly*
Oligopson: *oligopsony*
Omnibusumfrage: *omnibus survey*
One-Stop-Einkaufszentrum: *one-stop shopping centre*
OPEC: *the Organization of Petroleum Exporting Countries (OPEC)*
Operational-Research: *operational research*
optimal: *optimal*
Option: **negative ~** *inertia selling*
Optionsgeschäfte machen: *to deal in options*
Optionsrecht: **sein ~ ausüben** *to take up an option or to exercise an option*
Optionsrecht auf Kauf: *option to purchase*
Optionsrecht auf Verkauf: *option to sell*
Order: *order*
ordnen: *regulate*
Ordnung: **in ~ bringen** *fix*
Organigramm: *organization chart*

Organisation: *organization* **eine staatliche** ~ *a government organization* **karitative** ~ *charity*
Organisation erdölexportierender Länder: *the Organization of Petroleum Exporting Countries*
Organisation und Durchführung: *organization and methods*
organisieren: *organize*
orientiert: *oriented*
Orientierung: *orientation*
Original: *master; original*
original: *original*
Ort: *point; spot; venue*
örtlich: *local*
Ortsnetzkennzahl: *area code*
Output: *output*

Pp

Paarvergleich: *paired comparison; diadic test*
Päckchen: *packet* **eingeschriebenes** ~ *registered parcel*
Packen: *packaging*
Packer: *packer*
Packstelle: *packing station*
Packung: **eine** ~ **Waren** *a pack of items*
Packungswerbung: *on-pack promotion*
Packzettel: *packing list or packing slip*
Paket: *package; parcel* **ein** ~ **verschnüren** *to tie up a parcel* **falsch beschriftetes** ~ *incorrectly labelled parcel*
Paketannahme: *parcels office*
Paketgebühren *or* **Pakettarife:** *parcel rates*
Paketpost: *parcel post*
Palette: *pallet*
palettieren: *palletize*
Panik-Dumping von Sterling: *panic dumping of sterling*
Panikkäufe: *panic buying*
Papier: **bankfähiges** ~ *bankable paper*
Papiergeld: *paper money or paper currency*
Papierkorb-Werbung: *junk mail*
Papierstreifen: *band*
Pappkarton: *carton*
Paragraph: *article; clause*
Parallelisierung: *matched sample*
Pareto-Effekt: *Pareto effect*
Partei: *party*
Party: *party*
Partyverkauf: *hostess party selling; party plan selling*
Passagierliste: *passenger manifest*
Passantenzählung: *journey mapping*
passend: *convenient*
Patent: *patent* **angemeldetes** ~ *patent applied for or patent pending* **ein** ~ **anmelden** *to file a patent application* **ein** ~ **verletzen** *to infringe a patent*
Patentamt: *patent office*
Patent angemeldet: *patent applied for or patent pending*
Patentanmeldung: **eine** ~ **einreichen** *to file a patent application*
Patentanwalt: *patent agent*
Patentgebühr: *royalty*
Patentinhaber: *patentee*
Patentrecht: *patent rights*
patentrechtlich geschützt: *patented*
Patenturkunde: *letters patent; patent*
Patentverletzung: *infringement of patent or patent infringement; piracy*
Pauschalarrangement: *package deal*
Pauschalbetrag: *lump sum*
Pauschale: *inclusive charge; flat rate*
Pauschalpreis: *flat rate; all-in price*
Pauschalreise: *package holiday or package tour*
Pauschalreisen anbieten: *to package holidays*
Pay TV: *pay television or pay TV*
PC: *personal computer or home computer*
Penetrationspreispolitik: *penetration pricing*
Penetration(sgrad): *penetration*
perfekt: *perfect*
perfektionieren: *to perfect*
Periodikum: *periodical*
Person: **dritte** ~ *third party* **pro** ~ *per capita*
Personal: **festangestelltes** ~ *regular staff* **knapp an** ~ *shorthanded; short-staffed* **ständiges** ~ *regular staff* **weiteres** ~ **einstellen** *to recruit new staff*
Personalbeschaffung: *the recruitment of new staff*
Personalbestand: *manpower*
Personalbestandsprognose: *manpower forecasting*
Personalcomputer: *personal computer or home computer*
Personalplanung: *manpower planning*
persönlich: *personal*
Persönlichkeit: *personality*
Pfund: **tausend** ~ *grand (informal)*
Pfund Sterling: *pound sterling*
Phantasiepreise: *fancy prices*
Phase: **ethnozentrische** ~ *ethnocentric stage* **geozentrische** ~ *geocentric stage* **mehrzentrische** ~ *polycentric stage* **regiozentrische** ~ *regiocentre stage*
Photogravüre: *photogravure*
Photosatz: *phototypesetting*
Pilot-: *pilot*
Pionier: *pioneer*
Pionierarbeit leisten: *to pioneer*
Pionierprojekt: *pioneer project*
Plagiator: *pirate; plagiarist*
plagiieren: *to pirate; plagiarise*
Plakat: *bill; poster* **kleines** ~ *placard*
Plakatanschlag: **unerlaubter** ~ *fly poster*
Plakatanschlagkampagne: **intensive** ~ *impactaplan*

Plakatanschlagstellenstandort: *poster site*
Plakatierung: **wilde** ~ *fly-posting*
Plakatträger: *sandwich man*
Plakatwand: *hoarding*
Plan: *plan; project; schedule* **großartiger** ~ *grand plan or grand strategy*
planen: *organize*
Planobogen: *broadsheet*
Planung: *organization; planning* **kurzfristige** ~ *short-term planning* **revolvierende** ~ *rolling plan* **strategische** ~ *strategic planning*
Planungsausschuß: *plans board*
Planwirtschaft: *planned economy*
Platz: *space; spot*
Plausibilitätskontrolle: *editing*
Plazierung: **freie** ~ *run of book (ROB) or run of paper (ROP)*
Plazierungsvereinbarung: **ohne** ~ *run of book (ROB) or run of paper (ROP)*
Pleite: *flop*
Plombe: *customs seal*
plombieren: *to seal*
plötzlich fallen: *slump*
Politik: *policy*
Politik der Lohnkontrolle: *pay or wage restraint*
Polypol: **bilaterales** ~ *perfect market*
populär: *popular*
POP-Werbung: *point of purchase advertising (POPA)*
Portfoliomanagement: *portfolio management*
Porto: *postage*
Porto bezahlt: *postage paid*
portofrei: *post free*
Portokasse: *petty cash*
Position: *position*
Positionierung: *positioning*
Positionierungstestverfahren: *placement testing*
positiv: *positive*
Post: *mail; post* **elektronische** ~ *electronic mail* **per** ~ *by mail*
Postanweisung: *money order; postal order*
Postausgang: *outgoing mail*
Posteingang: *incoming mail*
Posten: *item*
Posteneinkauf: *bulk buying or bulk purchase; quantity purchase*
Poster: *poster*
Postgebühren: *postage; postal charges*
Postgirodienst: *National Giro (GB)*
Postleitzahl: *post code; zip code (US)*
Postpaket: *postal packet*
Postsendungen zweiter Klasse: *second-class mail*
Poststelle: *mail room; post room*
Posttarife: *postal rates*
Posttest: *post-test*
Postversand: *mail-order*
postwendend antworten: *to send a reply by return of post*
Postwurfsendung: *mailing piece*
POS-Werbematerial: *point of sale material*
Potential: *potential*
potentiell: *potential*
PR-Abteilung: *public relations department*
praktisch: *convenient*
Prämie: *bonus; incentive payment; premium*
PR-Arbeit: *public relations (PR)*
Präsentation: *presentation*
Präsentationspackung: *display pack*
Präsenz: *presence*
Preis: *cost; price; rate; tariff* **angemessener** ~ *fair price* **einen** ~ **festsetzen** *to price* **einen** ~ **heruntersetzen** *to mark down* **erhöhter** ~ *loaded price* **erwarteter** ~ *expected price* **fairer** ~ *fair price* **fester** ~ *fixed rate* **gängiger** ~ *going price* **geforderter** ~ *asking price* **jetziger** ~ *current price* **konkurrenzfähiger** ~ *competitive price* **markierter** ~ *marked price* **marktüblicher** ~ *market rate* **niedrigster** ~ *bottom price* **staatlich vorgeschriebener** ~ *government-regulated price* **unter** ~ **verkaufen** *to undersell* **üblicher** ~ *usual price* **vereinbarter** ~ *agreed price* **voller** ~ *full price; full rate* **wettbewerbsfähiger** ~ *competitive price*
Preis ab Hafen: *price ex dock*
Preis ab Kai: *price ex quay*
Preis ab Lager: *price ex warehouse*
Preis ab Schiff: *price ex ship*
Preisabsprache: *common pricing; price fixing*
Preis ab Werk: *price ex works or ex factory; factory price*
Preisänderungseffekt: *price effect*
Preisanstieg: *escalation of prices*
Preisaufschlag: *mark-up*
Preisausschreiben: *competition; contest*
Preis bei Inzahlungnahme: *trade-in price*
Preisbildung: *pricing*
Preisbindung: *price control(s)* **vertikale** ~ *resale price maintenance (RPM); administered price (US)*
Preisbindung zweiter Hand: *resale price maintenance (RPM); administered price (US)*
Preisdifferenzierung: *price discrimination*
Preise: **die** ~ **drücken** *to force prices down* **die** ~ **hochtreiben** *to force prices up* **günstige** ~ *keen prices* **populäre** ~ *popular prices*
Preise erhöhen: *to increase prices or to raise prices*
Preise herabsetzen *or* **reduzieren:** *to lower or reduce prices*
Preisempfehlung: **unverbindliche** ~ *recommended retail price (RRP)*
Preisen: **mit wettbewerbsfähigen** ~ *competitively priced* **zu herabgesetzten** ~ *cut-price*
Preise plötzlich senken: *to cut prices*
Preiserhöhung: *mark-up*
Preise senken: *to lower or reduce prices*
Preiseskalation: *escalation of prices*
Preise stabilisieren *or* **stützen:** *to peg (prices)*
Preisfestsetzung: *pricing*
Preisführerschaft: *price leadership*

Preisgefälle: *price differential*
Preisgleitklausel: *escalator clause or escalation clause*
Preisgrenze: oberste ~ *ceiling price or price ceiling*
preisgünstig: *good value (for money)*
Preiskalkulation: *pricing*
Preisklasse: *price range*
Preiskontrolle: *price control*
Preiskrieg: *price-cutting war; price war*
Preislage: *range*
Preisliste: *price list; scale of charges or scale of prices*
Preisnachlaß: *discount; mark-down; rebate*
Preisnachlaßgutschein: *money-off coupon*
Preisniveau: *price level*
Preispolitik: *pricing policy* **offene ~** *open pricing* **populäre ~** *popular pricing*
Preisschild: *price label; price tag*
Preisschildern: mit ~ versehen *to sticker*
Preissenkung: *price cutting; mark-down*
Preisstützen: *price pegging*
Preistreiberei: *profiteering*
Preisüberwachung: *price control*
Preisunterschied: *price differential*
preiswert: *good value (for money)*
Preiswettbewerb: *price competition*
Presse: *press* **technische ~** *technical press* **überregionale ~** *national newspapers or the national press*
Pressearbeit: *press relations*
Presseausschneiden: *press cutting*
Presseausschnittdienst: *clipping service; press cutting agency*
Presseberichte: *press coverage*
Pressekonferenz: *press conference*
Pressemitteilung or **Pressenotiz:** *press release or news release*
Pressereferent: *information officer*
Prestige: *prestige*
Prestigeartikel: *prestige product*
Prestigekonsum: *conspicuous consumption*
Prestigewerbung: *prestige advertising*
Prestigezeitungen: *quality press*
Pretesten: *pre-testing*
Primärdaten: *primary data*
Primärnachfrage: *primary demand*
Primärprodukte: *primary products*
Prime Rate: *prime rate or prime*
privat: *private*
Privatanleger: *private investor*
Privatbesitz: *private property*
Privateinkommen: *private income*
Privatgespräch: *personal call*
Privatgrundstück: *private property*
privatisieren: *privatize*
Privatisierung: *privatization*
Privatkunde: *private client or private customer*
Privatsektor: *private sector*
Privatunternehmen: *private enterprise*
Privatvermögen: bewegliches ~ *personal assets*
Privatvertrag: durch ~ *by private contract*
Privatwirtschaft: *private enterprise*
PR-Kampagne: eine ~ *a public relations exercise*
Probe: *sample; specimen; trial* **kostenlos zur ~** *free trial* **zur ~** *on approval; on trial*
Probeentnahme: *sampling*
Probeexemplar: *specimen*
Probelauf: *test run*
Probestück: *trial sample*
Probewerbesendung: *animatic*
Probezeit: *trial period*
probieren: *to sample*
Problemlösung: extensives ~ *extensive problem-solving*
Produkt: *product* **generisches ~** *generic product* **minderwertiges ~** *inferior product* **preisempfindliches ~** *price-sensitive product* **undifferenziertes ~** *undifferentiated product*
Produktakzeptanz: *product acceptance*
Produktanalyse: *product analysis*
Produktbewertungsanalyse: *value analysis*
Produktdifferenzierung: *product differentiation* **funktionale ~** *functional product differentiation*
Produkte: konkurrenzfähige ~ *competitive products* **steuerfreie ~** *exempt supplies*
Produkteigenschaften: überlegene ~ *product-plus*
Produktelimination: *product elimination; product deletion*
Produktentwicklung: *product development*
Produktentwicklungsstrategie: *product strategy*
Produktforschung: *product research*
Produktgestaltung: *product design*
Produktgruppe: *product line or product range*
Produktgruppenmanagement: *venture team*
Produktgruppenverpackung: *family packaging*
Produktidee: *product idea*
Produktideenbewertung: *product idea testing*
Produktimage: *product image*
Produktion: *output; production*
Produktionseinheit: *production unit*
Produktionseinstellung zugunsten Fremdbezugs: *disintegration*
Produktionskosten: *manufacturing or production costs*
Produktionsleistung: *rate of production or production rate*
Produktionsleistung pro Stunde: *output per hour*
Produktionsleiter: *production manager*
Produktionsmittel: *capital equipment*
Produktionsprämie: *output bonus*
Produktionsprozeß: kontinuierlicher ~ *continuous process production*
Produktionsstandard: *production standards*
Produktionsvolumen: *volume of output*
Produktionsziel: *production target*

produktiv: *productive*
Produktivität: *productivity*
Produktivitätsabkommen: *productivity agreement*
Produktivitätskampagne: *productivity drive*
Produktivitätsprämie: *productivity bonus*
Produktkonzept: *product concept*
Produktlebenszyklus: *product life cycle*
Produktlinie: *line of product or product line; product range*
Produkt-Management: *product management*
Produktmanager: *product manager*
Produkt-Mix: *product mix*
Produktpalette: *product mix*
Produktportfolio: *product portfolio*
Produktportfolio-Analyse: *product portfolio analysis*
Produktpositionierung: *product positioning*
Produktpositionierungstest: *placement test*
Produktstrategie: *product strategy*
Produkttypung: *standardization of products*
Produktüberangebot: *a glut of produce*
Produktwerbung: *product advertising*
Produzent: *producer*
Produzentenmarkt: *producer market*
Produzentenrente: *producer's surplus*
produzieren: *make; produce*
Profil: *profile*
Profit: *profit*
Profitabilität: *profitability*
Profit Center: *profit centre*
Profitmacher: *profiteer*
Proforma-Rechnung: *pro forma (invoice)*
Prognose: *forecast; forecasting; projection* **kurzfristige ~** *short-range or short-term forecast* **langfristige ~** *long-term forecast* **mittelfristige ~** *medium-term forecast*
Prognoseverfahren: **intuitive ~** *judgement forecasting*
prognostizieren: *to forecast*
Programmierer: *computer programmer*
Programmunterbrechung für Werbung: *commercial break*
progressiv: *innovative*
Projekt: *project* **ein ~ ausschreiben** *to put a project out to tender or to ask for or to invite tenders for a project*
Projektanalyse: *project analysis*
Projektingenieur: *project engineer*
Projektleiter: *project manager*
Projektstudie: *case study*
Pro-Kopf-Ausgaben: *per capita expenditure*
Pro-Kopf-Einkommen: *income per capita or per capita income*
Prolongation: *extension*
prolongieren: *extend*
Prominentenwerbung: *personality promotion*
prompt: *immediate; prompt*
Propaganda: *propaganda*
Prospekt: *broadside (US); brochure; catalogue or catalog (US); pamphlet; prospectus*
Protektionismus: *protectionism*
protokollieren: *record*
Prototyp: *prototype*
Provenienz: *origin*
Provenienzzertifikat: *certificate of origin*
Provision: *commission; factorage; rake-off*
Provisionsagent: *commercial agent*
Provisionseinkäufer: *buying agent*
Provisionsvertreter: *commission rep*
Provisionsvorschuß: *drawing account*
provisorisch: *provisional*
prüfen: *test*
Prüfmuster: *check sample*
Prüfung: *test; testing; trial* **zur ~** *on trial*
Psychogalvanometer: *psychogalvanometer*
Publicity: *exposure; publicity*
Public Relations: *public relations (PR)*
Publikation: *publication*
Publikum: *audience; publics* **kumuliertes ~** *cumulative audience or cumulative reach* **unfreiwilliges ~** *captive audience*
Publizität: *exposure*
Pull-Push-Strategie: *pull-push strategy*
Pull-Strategie: *pull strategy*
Punkt: *item*
pünktlich: *on schedule*
Push-Pull-Strategie: *push-pull strategy*
Push-Strategie: *push strategy*

Qq

Qualität: *quality* **erstklassige ~** *high quality or top quality*
qualitativ: *qualitative*
Qualitätsbezeichnung: *grade level*
Qualitätskontrolle: *quality control*
Qualitätskontrolle mittels Stichproben: *acceptance sampling*
Qualitätskontrolleur: *quality controller*
Quantität: *quantity*
quantitativ: *quantitative*
Quartal: **zweites ~** *second quarter*
Quasi-Einzelhandel: *quasi-retailing*
Quatsch: *eye-wash*
Quelle: *source*
Querdenken: *lateral thinking*
quittieren: *to receipt*
Quittung: *receipt; voucher* **ordnungsgemäße ~** *receipt in due form*
Quittungsblock: *receipt book or book of receipts*
Quota-Auswahl: *quota sample*
Quote: *quota*
Quotensystem: *quota system* **ein ~ anwenden** *to operate a quota system*

Rr

Rabatt: *discount; mark-down; rebate*
Rabatt gewähren: *to discount*
Rabattmarke: *trading stamp*
Rabattmarkenverteilung: *stamp trading*
radikal herabsetzen: *slash*
Random-Route-Verfahren: *random walk*
Rang: *grade*
rar: *scarce*
Rate: *instalment or installment (US); rate*
Raten: **in ~ zahlen** *to pay in instalments*
Ratenzahlung: *deferred payment; installment plan (US)*
Raten(zahlungs)kauf: *hire purchase*
ratifizieren: *approve*
rationalisieren: *prune; rationalize; streamline*
Rationalisierung: *harvesting; rationalization; streamlining*
Rationalisierung einer Produktlinie: *line simplification*
rationell: *economical*
Raubdruck: *piracy* **einen ~ herstellen** *to pirate*
Raum: *space*
räumen: *to clear*
Räumungsverkauf: *clearance sale; closing-down sale*
Reaktion: *feedback* **verzögerte ~** *delayed response*
Reaktionsfunktion: *response function*
Realeinkommen: *real income*
Reallohn: *real wages*
Real-time: *real time*
Rechengeschwindigkeit: *computing speed*
Rechenschaft ablegen: *to account for*
Rechenzeit: *computer time*
Rechenzentrum: *computer bureau*
Rechner: *computer* **kommerzieller ~** *business computer*
Rechnerverbund: *computer network; networked system*
Rechnerzeit: *computer time*
Rechnung: *bill; invoice* **aufgegliederte ~** *itemized invoice* **die ~ begleichen** *or* **bezahlen** *to foot the bill* **eine ~ bezahlen** *to settle an account* **eine ~ vorlegen** *to render an account* **in ~ stellen** *to bill; to charge*
Rechnung ausstellen: *to invoice*
Rechnungsabteilung: *invoicing department*
Rechnungsausstellung: *invoicing*
Rechnungsausstellung inklusive Mehrwertsteuer: *VAT invoicing*
Rechnungsbetrag: **fälliger ~** *balance due* **voller ~** *total invoice value*
Rechnungsbuch: *account book*
Rechnungsjahr: *financial year*
Rechnungslegung zum Wiederbeschaffungswert: *current cost accounting*
Rechnungspreis: *invoice price*
Rechnungsprüfer: *accountant*
Rechnungsprüfung *or* **Revision:** *audit* **außerbetriebliche ~** *external audit* **unabhängige ~** *external audit*
Rechnungswesen: *accountancy; accounting*
Recht: **internationales ~** *international law*
rechtlich: *legal; legally*
rechtmäßig: *legal*
Rechtsabteilung: *legal department or legal section*
Rechtsberater: *legal adviser*
Rechtsbewilligung: *charter*
rechtsgültig: *in due form*
Rechtstitel: **urkundlicher ~** *document of title*
recyceln *or* **recyclieren:** *recycle*
Recyclingpapier: *recycled paper*
Redaktion: *editorial board*
redaktionell: *editorial*
Redaktionskomitee: *editorial board*
Redigieren: *editing*
Reduktionsmarketing: *demarketing*
Reduzierung: *reduction*
Reederei: *shipping company or shipping line*
Reedereiangestellte(r): *shipping clerk*
REFA-Fachmann: *time and motion expert*
REFA-Studie: *time and motion study*
Referenz: *testimonial*
Regal: *rack; shelf*
Regalauffüller: *shelf filler*
Regale: *shelving*
Regalfläche: *shelf space*
Regalgroßhändler: *rack jobber*
Regalleiste: *channel strip*
Regalplatz: *shelf space*
Regalschild *or* **Regalsprecher:** *shelf talker or shelf wobbler*
regelmäßig: *regular*
regeln: *regulate*
Regelung: *regulation*
Regierungsstelle: *government organization*
Regionalsender: *local radio station*
Regionalzentrum: *one-stop shopping centre*
registrieren: *record*
Registrierkasse: *cash register or cash till*
registriert: *registered*
Registrierung: *recording; registration*
Regressionsanalyse: *regression analysis*
regulär: *regular*
regulieren: *regulate*
Regulierung: *regulation*
Reichweite: *audience; cover; coverage; impression cover; penetration; reach* **kumulative ~** *cumulative reach* **tatsächliche ~** *effective cover* **wirksame ~** *effective cover*
Reifephase: *maturity*
rein: *clean*
Reinfall: *flop*
Reingewinn: *net profit; clear profit*
Reingewinn erzielen: *to net*

Reinigungskosten: *service charge*
Reinvermögen: *net assets or net worth*
Reise: *journey*
Reisebüro: *travel agency*
Reisemagazin: *travel magazine*
Reisende(r): *sales representative; sales(wo)man; commercial traveller; travelling sales(wo)man*
Reiseroute: *itinerary*
Reiseschecks: *traveller's cheques*
Reisespesen: *travelling expenses*
Reiz: *appeal*
Reklamationsabteilung: *complaints department*
Reklame: *advertisement; publicity*
Reklame machen: *promote; publicize; advertise; plug*
Reklamesendungen: *junk mail*
Reklamewand: *hoarding*
Reklamezettel: *handbill; publicity handout; leaflet*
Rekord: *record*
Rekordverluste: *record losses*
Rektapapier: *non-negotiable instrument*
Relaunch: *relaunch*
Remission: *buy-back agreement; see-safe*
Remittenden: *returns*
Rendite: *rate of return*
rentabel: *economic; profitable; profit-making*
Rentabilität: *profitability*
Rentabilitätsanalyse: *breakeven analysis*
Rentabilitätsberechnung: *measurement of profitability*
Rentabilitätsschwelle: *breakeven point*
Rentabilitätssteigerung: *gain in profitability*
Reparaturwerkstatt: *repair shop*
reparieren: *fix*
Repertoire-Verfahren *or* **Repertory-Grid-Verfahren:** *repertory grid technique*
Repräsentant: *representative*
Repräsentationsbüro: *prestige offices*
Repräsentationswerbung: *prestige advertising*
repräsentativ: *representative*
Repräsentativerhebung: **eine ~ durchführen** *to sample*
Reserve: *stockpile*
Resonanz: *feedback*
Ressourcen: *resources*
Rest: *remnant*
Restauflagen: *remainders*
Restauflagen billig verkaufen: *to remainder books*
Restaurant für Außer-Haus-Verkauf: *takeaway*
Restbestände *or* **Restposten:** *oddments*
restriktiv: *restrictive*
Retourwaren: *returns*
revanchieren: **sich ~** *reciprocate*
Revision: **(betriebs)interne ~** *internal audit*
Revisor: **betriebsinterner ~** *internal auditor*
Revitalisierungs-Strategie: *extension strategy*
Rezession: *recession*
R-Gespräch: *collect (US); reverse charge call*
Richtlinien: *code of practice*
Richtpreis: **empfohlener ~** *recommended price*
Riesenbestellung: **eine ~** *an outsize order*
Riesenpackung: *bonus size*
Risiko: *risk* **ein ~ eingehen** *to take a risk* **finanzielles ~** *financial risk*
Risikoanalyse: *risk analysis*
Risikokapital: *risk capital; venture capital*
risikolos: *risk-free*
riskant: *risky*
riskieren: *venture*
Robinsonliste: *asterisk law; no direct mail list*
roh: *raw*
Rohentwurf: *rough*
Rohstoffe: *raw materials*
Rohstoffindustrie: *primary industry*
Rolltreppe: *escalator*
rückerstatten: *to refund*
Rückerstattung: *rebate; refund*
Rückforderung(sanspruch): *comeback*
Rückgabe: *return*
Rückgaberecht mit Gelderstattung: *money-back guarantee*
Rückgang: *decline; downturn; drop* **plötzlicher ~** *slump*
rückgängig machen: *revoke*
rückkaufen: *buy in*
Rückkaufsvertrag: *buy-back agreement*
Rückkaufswert: *surrender value*
Rücklaufrate: *response rate*
Rücknahmevereinbarung: *buy-back agreement*
Rückseite: *back*
Rücksendung: *return*
Rückstand: *backlog* **in ~ geraten** *fall behind*
Rücktrittsfrist: *cooling-off period*
Rücktrittsfristgesetze: *cooling-off laws*
Rückvergütung: *rebate*
Rückwärtsintegration: *backward integration*
Rückzahlung: *back payment; rebate*
Rückzoll: *drawback*
Ruf: *standing*
ruhend: *dormant*
Rundfunkbehörde: *Independent Television Commission (ITC)*
Rundfunkwerbungtreibender: *contracting company*
Rundschreiben: *circular; circular letter; mail shot; mailing shot*
Rundschreiben verschicken: *circularize*
Rüstkosten: *setting up costs or setup costs*

Ss

Sache: *business*

Sachet: *sachet*
Sachkenntnis: *expertise*
sachkundig: *experienced*
Sachleistung: *payment in kind*
sachlich: *objective*
Sachverständigenausschuß: *panel of experts*
Sachverständigengutachten: *expert's report*
Sachverständiger: *expert*
Sachwerte: **bilanzirbare** ~ *tangible assets*
Sack: *sack*
Saison: *season*
saisonbedingt: *seasonal*
Saisonbereinigungen: *seasonal adjustments*
Saisonrabatt: *seasonal discount*
Saisonschlußverkauf: *end of season sale*
Saldo: *bottom line* **einen ~ vortragen** *to carry over a balance*
Saldovortrag: *balance brought forward or carried forward*
Sammelgut *or* **Sammelladung:** *consolidated shipment*
Sammelgutunternehmen: *consolidator*
Samplepoint: *sampling point*
Sandwichman: *sandwich man*
Sandwich-Plakate: *sandwich boards*
sanieren: *to turn round*
Sanierung: *turnround*
Satellitenfernsehen: *satellite television*
Satisfizierung: *satisfying*
sättigen: *saturate*
Sättigung: *saturation*
Sättigungsniveau: *plateau*
Sättigungswerbung: *saturation advertising*
Satz: *rate; set* **fester** ~ *fixed rate* **unvollständiger** ~ *broken lot* **üblicher** ~ *going rate* **voller** ~ *full rate*
Satzumfangsberechnung: *copy fitting*
Satzung: *regulations*
sauber: *clean*
Säulendiagramm: *bar chart*
SB-Warenhaus: *hypermarket; superstore*
Schachtel: *box*
Schadensersatzanspruch: **einen ~ stellen** *to put in a claim for damage*
Schadensformular: *claim form*
Schadloshaltungserklärung: *letter of indemnity*
schaffen: *create* **es** ~ *to manage to*
Schankkonzession: *liquor licence*
Schattenwirtschaft: *black economy*
schätzen: *estimate; value*
Schätzer: *appraiser (US); estimator; valuer*
Schätzung: *estimate; estimation; rating; valuation* **bei vorsichtiger** ~ *at a conservative estimate* **grobe** ~ *rough estimate; guesstimate (informal)* **zu niedrige** ~ *undervaluation*
Schaubild: *diagram; graph* **in einem** ~ *diagrammatically*
Schaufenster: *shop window*
Schaufensterbummel: *window shopping*
Schaufensterdekoration: *window display*
Schaufensterplakat *or* **Schaufensterschild:** *showcard*
Schaukasten: *display cabinet or display case; showcase*
Schaupackung: *display pack; dummy pack*
Scheck: *cheque or check (US)* **einen ~ einlösen** *to cash a cheque* **einen ~ girieren** *to endorse a cheque* **einen ~ unterschreiben** *to sign a cheque* **einen ~ vordatieren** *to date a cheque forward* **mit ~ bezahlen** *to pay by cheque* **nichteingelöster** ~ *dishonoured cheque* **ungedeckter** ~ *dud cheque or bouncing cheque or cheque which bounces or rubber check (US)*
Scheckheft: *cheque book*
Scheckkarte: *cheque guarantee card; debit card*
Schein: *(bank) bill (US); currency note*
Scheinfirma: *dummy*
Scheinkommittent: *dummy*
scheitern: *fall through*
Schema: **übliches** ~ *pattern*
Scherzartikel: *novelty*
Schichtung: *stratification*
schicken: *dispatch; mail*
Schiedsgericht: *industrial court or industrial tribunal (GB)*
Schiff: *ship; vessel* **ein ~ beladen** *to load a ship*
Schiffahrts-: *maritime*
Schiffsausrüster: *ship chandler*
Schiffsmakler: *ship broker*
Schild: *sign; tag*
schildern: *describe*
Schilderung: *description*
Schirmherr: *patron*
Schirmwerbung: *umbrella advertising*
Schlagzeile: *headline*
Schleichwerbung: *puff*
Schleuderausfuhr: *dumping*
Schleuderpreis: *rock-bottom price*
Schleuderpreisen: **zu ~ verkaufen** *to sell at giveaway prices*
schließen: *close; close down*
Schließung: *closing; closure*
Schließungstag: *closing date*
Schlußbestand: *closing stock*
Schlüsselindustrie: *basic industry*
Schlußkurs *or* **Schlußnotierung:** *closing price*
Schlußzeile: *base line*
Schmiergeld: *kickback*
Schmuggel: *smuggling*
schmuggeln: *smuggle*
Schmuggelware: *contraband (goods)*
Schmuggler: *smuggler*
schmutzig: *dirty*
Schnäppchen: *bargain; snip (informal)*
Schneiden: *editing*
Schnellimbiß: *fast food*
schöpferisch: *creative*
Schranke: *barrier*

schreckhaft: *jumpy*
Schreibblock: *desk pad*
Schreibfehler: *clerical error*
Schreibtisch: *desk*
schrumpfen: *shrink*
Schrumpffolienverpackung: *blister pack; bubble card or bubble pack*
Schrumpfpackung: *shrink-wrapping*
Schuld: fundierte ~ *funded debt*
Schulden: *debt; liabilities* **fällige** ~ *debts due* **kurzfristige** ~ *short-term debts*
Schulden begleichen: *to pay off a debt*
Schulden eintreiben: *to collect a debt*
Schuldeneintreiber: *debt collector*
Schuldeneintreibung: *debt collection*
Schulden einziehen: *to collect a debt*
Schulden haben: *to be in debt*
Schulden machen: *to get into debt*
Schulden tilgen: *to pay off a debt*
Schulden zurückzahlen: *to pay back a debt*
Schuldner: *debtor* **säumiger** ~ *slow payer*
Schuldnerland: *debtor nation*
Schuldposten: *debit*
Schuldrecht: *contract law or law of contract*
Schuldschein: *note of hand or promissory note*
Schuldzinsen bezahlen: *to service (a debt)*
Schund: *pup (informal)*
Schundware: *catchpenny*
schwankend: *variable*
Schwarzes Brett: *noticeboard*
Schwarzmarkt: *black market*
Schwarzmarktpreise bezahlen: *to pay black market prices*
Schwerfahrzeug: *heavy goods vehicle*
Schwergut: *deadweight cargo*
Schwerindustrie: *heavy industry*
Schwindelgeschäft: *fraudulent transaction*
Schwund: *leakage; shrinkage*
Schwung: *drive*
Screening: *screening*
Sechserpack: *six-pack*
See: *sea*
Seefahrts-: *maritime*
Seehafen: *seaport*
Seehandel: *maritime trade*
Seerecht: *maritime law*
See(transport)versicherung: *marine insurance*
Seeversicherer: *marine underwriter*
Seeweg: auf dem ~ *by sea mail*
segmentieren: *segment*
seinesgleichen: *peer group*
Seite: *page* **gegenüberliegende** ~ *facing page* **hochformatige** ~ *portrait* **querformatige** ~ *landscape*
Seitenpreis: *page rate*
seitlich: *lateral*
Sektor: *sector* **staatlicher** ~ *public sector* **tertiärer** ~ *tertiary sector*
sekundär: *secondary*
Sekundärdaten: *secondary data*
Sekundärforscher: *desk researcher*
Sekundärforschung: *armchair research; desk research* **außerbetriebliche** ~ *external desk research* **innerbetriebliche** ~ *internal desk research*
Sekundärkunden: *fringe accounts*
Sekundärleser: *secondary audience*
Selbstbauprodukte: *Completely Knocked Down products (CKD products); knockdown (KD) goods*
Selbstbedienungsgeschäft: ein ~ *a self-service store*
Selbstbedienungsladen: kleiner ~ *minimarket*
Selbstimage: *self-image*
Selbstklebeetikett: *self-sticking label*
Selbstkosten: *direct cost; prime cost*
Selbstkostenpreis: *cost price* **zum** ~ **verkaufen** *to sell at cost*
Selbstläufer: *fast-selling items*
selbstverwaltend: *self-regulatory*
Selbstverwaltung: *self-regulation*
selektiv: *selective*
Selfmademan: *self-made man*
Selfmailer: *self-mailer*
selten: *scarce*
Seltenheit: *scarceness or scarcity*
Seltenheitswert: *scarcity value*
Semiotik: *semiotics*
senden: *dispatch*
Sendepause für Werbung: *commercial break*
Sender: *television station*
Senderabkürzung: *call letters (US)*
Sendernetz: *television network*
Sendernetzprogrammgestaltung: *network programming*
Sendestation: *television station*
Sendeunterbrechung: natürliche ~ *natural break*
Sendezeitabstand für Konkurrenten: *commercial protection; competitive separation*
Sendezeitsegment: *time segment*
Sendung: *air; dispatch; shipment*
Sendung durch Paketförderungsgesellschaft: *expressage (US)*
senken: *depress*
senkrecht: *vertical*
Senkrechtstarter: *high flier*
Senkung: *reduction; retrenchment*
sensibel: *sensitive*
Sequentialanalyse: *sequential sampling*
Serie: *batch*
Serienfertigung: *batch production*
Seriennummer: *batch number; serial number*
serienweise: in ~ **herstellen** *to mass-produce*
Service: *service*
SERVICE 130: *freefone or freephone (GB)*
Serviceauto: *courtesy car*
Servicegrad: *service level*

Set: *set*
Shopping Goods: *shopping goods*
Sicherheit: *guarantee*
Sicherheitsmarge *or* **Sicherheitsspielraum:** *safety margin or margin of safety*
Sicherungskopie: *backup copy*
Sicherungspfandrecht: *lien*
Sicht: *sight* **auf kurze ~** *on a short-term basis* **nach ~** *after-sight*
sichtbar: *visible; visual*
Sichteinlage: *demand deposit (US)*
Sichttage: *days of grace*
Sichttratte: *sight draft*
Sichtwechsel: *demand bill; sight bill*
Signifikanzniveau: *confidence level*
Single-Sourcing: *single sourcing*
sinken: *decline; fall; fall away*
sinkend: *falling*
Sinn: *effect*
Situation: *position; situation*
Sitz: *base*
Skala: *scale* **bipolare ~** *bipolar scale*
Skalierungsverfahren: *scaling technique*
Skimming: *skimming*
Skizze: *rough*
Slogan: *publicity slogan*
sofortig: *prompt*
Sofortliquidität: *spot cash*
Software: *software*
Soll: *debit*
Sollbuchung: *debit entry*
Sollsaldo: *debit balance*
Sollspalte: *debtor side*
Soll und Haben: *debit and credit*
Sollzinsen: *interest charges*
Sonderangebot: *bargain offer; special offer*
Sonderangebotsabteilung: *budget department*
Sonderangebotsankaufen: *cherry-picking (US)*
Sonderangebotsstand: *bargain counter*
Sonderausgaben: *extras*
Sonderbericht: *feature*
Sonderposten: *extraordinary items*
Sonderpreis: *bargain price; off-card rate*
Sonderpreisverpackung: *flash pack*
Sondertisch: *bargain counter*
Sonderwarenauslage: *dump display*
Sonderzubehör: *optional extras*
Sonntag: **geschäftsfreier ~** *Sunday closing*
Sorgenkinder: *problem children*
Sortiment: *assortment; product range; range; set*
Sortimentserweiterung: *product diversification*
sozialökonomisch: *socio-economic*
Sozialunterstützung: *social security*
Sozio-Marketing: *social marketing; societal marketing*
sozio-ökonomisch: *socio-economic*
Spalte: *column*
Spannband: *banner*
Spanne: *range*
Sparkampagne: *economy drive*
Sparkonto: *deposit account; savings account*
Sparmaßnahmen einführen: *to introduce economies or economy measures*
Sparneigung: *propensity to save*
Sparpackung: *economy size*
Sparpreise: *budget prices*
sparsam: *economical*
Sparsamkeit: *economy*
Sparte: *line of business or line of work*
Spätzünder: *sleeper*
Spediteur: *forwarding agent; (freight) forwarder; haulage contractor; road haulier; shipper; shipping agent*
Spediteursrisiko: *carrier's risk*
Spedition: *carrier; (freight) forwarder; haulage firm or company*
Speicher: *storage*
Speichergerät: *storage unit*
speichern: *to store*
Speicherung: *storage*
Speisekammertest: *pantry check*
Speisekarte: **nach der ~** *fl la carte*
sperren: *close*
sperrig: *bulky*
Sperrung: *stop*
Sperrung eines Kundenkreditkontos: *closing of an account*
Spesen: *expenses*
Spesenkonto: *expense account*
spezialangefertigt: *custom-built or custom-made*
Spezialgebiet: *speciality or specialty*
Spezialgeschäft: *specialty store*
spezialisieren: *specialize*
Spezialisierung: *specialization*
Spezialist: *specialist*
Spezialität: *speciality or specialty*
speziell: *special*
Spezifikation: *specification*
spezifizieren: *itemize; specify*
Spiel: **aufs ~ setzen** *venture*
Spielraum: *margin*
Spieltheorie: *game theory*
Spitzenbedarfszeit: *time of peak demand*
Spitzenjahr: *peak year*
Spitzenqualität: *high quality or top quality*
Spitzenreiter: *leader*
Spitzenumsätze: *record sales*
Sponsor: *backer; sponsor* **als ~ finanzieren** *to sponsor; to back*
sponsoren: *to sponsor*
Sponsoring: *sponsorship*
spontan: **etwas ~ tun** *to do something on impulse*
Spontankäufe: *impulse buying*
Spontankäufer: *impulse buyer*
Spottpreis: *bargain price; knockdown price*

Sprechertext: *voice-over*
Spruchband: *banner*
sprunghaft ansteigen: *to rocket*
Staatsbetrieb: *state enterprise*
Staatshaushalt: der ~ *the Budget*
Staatsverschuldung: *National Debt*
Staatsvertrag: *treaty*
Stabdiagramm: *bar chart*
stabil: *firm; stable*
stabilisieren: *stabilize*
Stabilisierung: *stabilization*
Stabilisierung der Wirtschaft: *stabilization of the economy*
Stabilität: *stability*
Stadtteilzeitung: *freesheet*
staffeln: *grade*
Staffeltarife: *differential tariffs*
Stagflation: *stagflation*
Stagnation: *stagnation*
Stammaktien: *common stock (US)*
Stammdatei: *master copy of a file*
Stammgast: *patron*
Stammkunde: *long-standing customer or customer of long standing; patron; regular customer*
Stand: *level; stand*
Standard: *standard*
Standardabweichung: *standard deviation*
Standardbrief: *standard letter*
Standardfehler: *standard error*
Standardgröße: *regular size*
standardisieren: *standardize*
Standardisierung: *standardization*
Standardmodell: *regular model*
Standardsteuersatz: *standard rate*
Ständer: *rack*
Standmiete: *market dues*
Standort: *base; location*
Stange: *carton* **von der** ~ *ready-made or ready-to-wear*
stapeln: *to batch*
Star: *star*
Starch-Bewertungen: *starch ratings (US)*
stark reduzieren: *to slash*
Start: *start*
Startkapital: *initial capital*
stationieren: *base*
Stationsabkürzung: *call letters (US)*
Statistik(en): *statistics*
statistisch: *statistical*
Statuten: *regulations*
stecken: *to stuff*
steigen: *to advance; to gain*
Stelle: *point; spot*
Stellen: freie ~ *job openings*
Stellenanzeigen: *recruitment advertising*
Stellenbeschreibung: *job specification*
Stellenbesetzungsplan: *organization chart*
Stellenvermittlung: *employment agency*
Stellung: *position*
Stellvertreter: *substitute*
Stempelgebühr: *stamp duty*
Sterling: *sterling*
Sterlingkrise: *sterling crisis*
Sterlingzone: *sterling area*
Sterne-Hotel: *graded hotel*
stetig: *continuous*
Steuer: *duty; levy*
Steuerberater: *accountant*
steuerfrei: *exempt from tax or tax exempt; free of tax or tax-free*
Steuerfreieinschätzung: *exempt rating*
Steuergutschrift: *tax credit*
Steuerklasse: höchste ~ *highest tax bracket*
steuern: *to control*
Steuerungssysteme: *control systems*
Stichprobe: *check; sample* **zufällige** ~ *random sample*
Stichprobenauswahl: *random sampling*
Stichprobenbildung: intuitive ~ *judgement sampling*
Stichprobenumfang: *sampling fraction*
Stichprobenverfahren: *sampling*
Stichtag: *deadline; effective date; settlement day*
Stiftung: wohltätige ~ *charity*
Stil: *style*
still: *dormant*
stillegen: *close down*
Stillegung: *closure*
Stillstand: *stagnation; stoppage*
Stockwerk: *floor*
Storyboard: *storyboard*
Stoßzeit: *peak period* **außerhalb der** ~ *off-peak; during the off-peak period*
Stottern: *never-never (informal)*
Straffung: *streamlining*
Strafklausel: *penalty clause*
Straßenhändler: *street vendor*
Straßen-Wasser-Transport: *fishy-back freight (US)*
Strategie: *strategy*
strategisch: *strategic*
Strategischer Geschäftsbereich: *strategic business unit (SBU)*
streben nach: *aim*
Streckengroßhändler: *limited function wholesaler*
streichen: *delete; eliminate; prune*
Streichung: *deletion; divestment; elimination*
Streß: unter ~ **arbeiten** *to work under (high) pressure*
Streuagentur: *media independent or media shop*
Streufachmann *or* **Streuplaner:** *media buyer*
Streuplanung: *media buying*
Streuung: *dispersion*
Strich: über dem ~ *above-the-line*

Strichätzung: *line block*
Strichdiagramm: *line chart or line graph*
Strichkodierung: *bar code*
Strichzeichnung: *line drawing or line illustration*
Strohmann: *front; front man*
Strom: *flood*
Struktur: *pattern; structure*
strukturieren: *structure*
Stück: *unit* **angepaßtes** or **überarbeitetes** ~ *adaptation*
Stückgut: *general cargo*
Stückkosten: *unit cost*
Stückpreis: *unit price*
Stückzahl: große ~ *quantity*
Studie: *survey*
Stufe: *grade*
Stuffer: *stuffer (US)*
Stundenleistung: *output per hour*
Stundenplan: *schedule*
Sturz: *drop; slump*
stürzen: *to drop; to slump*
Subkultur: *subculture*
Submissionsofferten: versiegelte ~ *sealed tenders*
Submittent: *tenderer*
Substitutionseffekt: *substitution effect*
Substitutionsgut: *substitute product*
Subunternehmer: *subcontractor*
Subvention: *subsidy*
subventionieren: *subsidize*
subventioniert: nicht ~ *unsubsidized*
Suggestivfrage: *leading question*
Summe: laufende ~ *running total*
Sündenbock: *fall guy (US)*
Supermarkt: *supermarket*
Supplement: *(colour) supplement*
SWOT-Analyse: *SWOT analysis*
Symbol: *symbol; token*
Synchro-Marketing: *synchro marketing*
Syndikat: *trust (US)*
Synektik: *synectics*
Synergismus: *synergy*
System: *system* **leistungsabhängiges** ~ *incentive scheme*
Systemanalyse: *systems analysis*
Systemanalytiker or **Systemberater:** *systems analyst or adviser*
Systemverkauf: *systems selling*
Szenario or **Szenarium:** *scenario*

Tt

Tabelle: *scale; table*
Tabellierpapier: *listing paper*
Tachistokop: *tachistoscope or T-scope*
Tafel: *panel*
Tag des Inkrafttretens: *effective date*
Tagebuch: *diary*
Tagebuchmethode: *diary method*
Tageskurs: *current rate of exchange*
Tagesmenü: *set menu*
Tagespreis: *current price*
Tageszeitsegment: *daypart*
Tag- und Nachtdienst: *24-hour service*
Tagung: *conference*
Tagungsort: *venue*
Taktik: *policy; tactic*
Talentsucher: *headhunter*
Tankstelle mit Reparaturwerkstatt: *service station*
Tankstelle mit Selbstbedienung: *self-service petrol station*
Tante-Emma-Laden: *corner shop*
Tantiemen: *royalty*
Tarif: *tariff* **ermäßigter** ~ *reduced rate* **üblicher** ~ *market rate* **verbilligter** ~ *off-peak tariff or rate*
Tarife: *scale of charges or scale of prices*
Tarifverhandlungen: *(free) collective bargaining*
Tarnung: *front*
Taschengeld: *spending money*
Tastatur: numerische ~ *numeric keypad*
Tätigkeit: *operation*
Tätigkeitsbeschreibung: *job description*
Tatsache: *fact*
tatsächlich: *effective*
Tausch: *exchange*
Tauschabkommen: *barter agreement or barter arrangement or barter deal*
tauschen: *to exchange*
Tauschhandel: *barter; bartering*
Tauschhandel treiben: *to barter*
Täuschung: arglistige ~ *fraudulent misrepresentation*
Tauschwirtschaft: *exchange economy*
Tausenderpreis: *cost per thousand (CPT)*
Team: *team*
Teaser: *teaser*
Technik: *technique*
technisch: *technical*
Technologie: neue ~ *new technology*
Technologiezentrum: *science park*
teilen: sich ~ *share*
Teillieferung or **Teilsendung:** *part delivery or part order or part shipment*
Teilstichprobe: *subsample*
Teilzahlung: *part payment* **als** ~ *on account* **eine** ~ **leisten** *to advance on account*
Teilzahlungsfinanzierungsgesellschaft: *hire-purchase company*
Teilzahlungsinstitute: *secondary banks*
Teilzahlungskauf: *hire purchase*
Teilzahlungskaufvertrag: *hire purchase agreement*
Teilzahlungssystem: *installment plan (US)*

Telefax: *fax*
telefaxen: *to fax*
Telefonbuch: *directory*
Telefonmarketer: *telemarketer*
Telefonmarketing: *telemarketing*
Telefonmarketing-Fachmann: *telemarketer*
Telefonverkauf: *telesales*
Telefonzelle: *telephone kiosk*
Teleshopping: *home shopping; teleshopping*
Teletext: *teletext*
Tendenz: *trend*
Termin: *deadline* **auf ~ kaufen** *to buy forward* **auf ~ verkaufen** *to sell forward*
Terminkalender: *diary*
Terminkauf: *forward buying or buying forward*
Terminkurs: *forward price*
Terminlieferung: *future delivery*
Terminmarkt: *forward market*
Terminplan: *schedule*
Terminverkäufe: *forward sales*
Test: *test* **monadischer ~** *monadic test*
testen: *to sample; to test*
Testende: *test close*
Testimonialwerbung: *endorsement advertising; testimonial advertising*
teuer: *costly; expensive*
Teuerungszulage: *cost-of-living bonus*
teurer werden: *to increase in price*
Text: gegenüber ~ *facing matter or facing text matter* **neben ~** *next matter or next-to-reading matter* **rechtsverbindlicher ~** *mandatory blurb* **redaktioneller ~** *editorial matter*
textanschließend: *next matter or next-to-reading matter*
Textanzeige: *reader advertisement*
Textilwaren: *dry goods*
Thekenaufstellpackung: *counterpack*
Thematischer Apperzeptionstest: *thematic apperception test (TAT)*
Tiefeninterview: *depth interview*
Tiefpunkt: *bottom*
Tiefstand: *depression*
Tiefstpreis: *rock-bottom price*
Tiefststand: *bottom*
Tip: *tip* **einen ~ geben** *to tip*
TIR: *Transport International Routier (TIR)*
Titelbox: *ear*
Titelei: *front of book*
Titelpräsentation: *face out*
Tochtergesellschaft: *subsidiary (company)*
Top-Management: *top management*
Totalausverkauf: *closing-down sale*
Totalverlust: *dead loss*
Touristenklasse: *economy class*
Trading-down: *trading down*
Trading-up: *trading up*
Traffic: *traffic*
Tragfähigkeit: *deadweight capacity or deadweight tonnage*
Trägheit: *inertia*
Trägheitsverkauf: *inertia selling*
Trajektfracht: *fishy-back freight (US)*
Trampschiff: *tramp ship*
Transaktion: geschäftliche ~ *business transaction*
Transfer: *transfer*
Transit: *transit*
Transitgüter: *goods in transit*
Transparent: *banner*
Transparentauflage: *overlay*
Transport: *carriage; carrying; cartage; shipping; transit; transport; transportation*
Transporter: *carrier*
Transportflugzeug: *cargo plane; freight plane*
transportieren: *to ship; to transport*
Transportkosten: *carriage; freight costs; haulage costs or haulage rates; haulage*
Transportschaden: *loss in transport*
Transportschiff: *cargo ship*
Transportunternehmen: *carrier; transporter*
Transportunternehmer: *haulage contractor*
Transportverlust: *loss in transport*
Transportwesen: innerbetriebliches ~ *materials handling*
Trassant: *drawer*
Trassat: *drawee*
Tratte: *bill (of exchange)*
Trend: *shift; trend* **exponentieller ~** *exponential diffusion or exponential growth* **historischer ~** *historical trend*
Trendanalyse: *trend analysis*
Tresen: *counter*
treuhänderisch hinterlegt: *in escrow*
Treuhandkonto: *escrow account (US)*
Trinkgeld: *tip*
Trinkgeld geben: *to tip*
Tröpfelkampagne: *drip*
Trustzerschlagung: *trustbusting (US)*
Tüte: *carton*
typisch: *representative*
Typung: *standardization*

Uu

U1: *front cover*
U2: *inside front cover*
U3: *inside back cover*
U4: *back cover*
U-Bahn-Plakate: *tube cards*
Überbestand: *overstocks (US)*
Überbestand abstoßen: *to offload excess stock*
Überbezahlung: *overpayment*
überbieten: *outbid*
Überbord: frei ~ *free overboard or free overside*

Überbringerscheck: *cheque (made payable) to bearer*
überdrucken: *overprint*
übereinstimmen (mit): *agree (with)*
Übergewicht: *excess baggage*
Übergröße: *outsize*
überholt: *obsolete*
Überkapazität: *excess capacity*
Überlegung: **nach reiflicher ~** *after due consideration*
Überlegungsfrist: *cooling-off period*
übermäßig: *exorbitant*
Übernahme: *absorption; takeover* **angefochtene ~** *contested takeover*
Übernahmeangebot: *takeover bid* **ein ~ zurückziehen** *to withdraw a takeover bid*
Überproduktion: *overproduction*
überproduzieren: *overproduce*
Überprüfung der Sozialfolgen: *social audit*
Überprüfung der Werbung: *advertising control*
überqueren: *cross*
überreden: *persuade*
Übersatz: *overmatter or oversetting*
Überschrift: *headline*
Überschuß: *excess; surplus*
überschwemmen: *flood; glut*
Überseehandel: *overseas trade; foreign trade; external trade*
überseeisch: *overseas*
Überseemärkte: *overseas markets*
Übersicht: *table*
übertragbar: **nicht ~** *"not negotiable"*
übertragen: *switch*
Übertragung: *delivery; transfer*
Übertragungswirkung: *carry-over effect*
übertrieben: *exorbitant*
Überwachung: *control*
Überziehungskredit: *overdraft facility*
üblich: *normal; standard*
Umbruch: *make-up*
Umfang: *depth; volume*
umfangreich: *extensive; heavy*
umfassend: *extensive; full-scale; overall*
Umgebung: *environment*
umgehend: *immediate*
umgekehrt: *reverse*
umladen: *tranship*
Umlauf: *circular (letter)* **in ~ bringen** *circulate*
Umlaufvermögen: *circulating capital; current assets*
umpacken: *repack*
Umpackung: *outer pack*
Umpositionierung: *repositioning*
Umsatz: *billing; sales; turnover*
Umsatzanalyse: *sales analysis*
Umsatzdiagramm: *sales chart*
Umsatzgeschwindigkeit: *rate of turnover*
Umsatzsteuerstelle: *VAT office*
Umsatzvolumen: *sales volume or volume of sales; volume of trade or volume of business*
Umschlag: *cover; handling*
umschlagen: *tranship*
Umschlaggeschwindigkeit: *turnover (US)*
Umschlagseite: **dritte ~** *inside back cover* **erste ~** *front cover* **letzte** or **vierte ~** *back cover* **zweite ~** *inside front cover*
Umschlagseite drei: *inside back cover*
Umschlagseite eins: *cover page; front cover*
Umschlagseite vier: *cover page; back cover*
Umschlagseite zwei: *inside front cover*
Umschlagspesen: *handling charges*
umsehen: **sich ~** *shop around*
umsetzen: *turn over*
umsonst: *gratis*
Umstellung auf Containertransport: *containerization*
umtauschbar: *exchangeable*
Umwelt: *environment*
Umweltsanalyse: *environmental analysis*
Umweltschutzpapier: *recycled paper*
umziehen: *move*
unabhängig: *free; independent*
unbedingt notwendig: *essential*
unbefristet: *open-ended or open-end (US); permanent*
unbegrenzt: *unlimited*
unbeladen: *unladen*
unbenutzt: *unused*
unbeschränkt: *absolute; open-ended or open-end (US)*
unbesehen: *unseen* **etwas ~ kaufen** *to buy something sight unseen*
unbesetzt: *free*
Unbeständigkeit: *instability*
unbezahlt: *outstanding*
undifferenziert: *undifferentiated*
unerfüllt: *unfulfilled*
unerläßlich: *essential*
unerlaubt nachahmen or **unerlaubt nachbauen:** *to pirate*
Unfallhaftpflichtversicherung der Arbeitgeber: *employers' liability insurance*
ungebraucht: *unused*
ungebunden: *independent*
ungültig: *null*
ungünstig: *unfavourable*
unilateral: *unilateral; unilaterally*
unkontrollierbar: *uncontrollable*
Unkosten: *expenses* **allgemeine ~** *overhead expenses or general expenses or running expenses; overhead costs; overheads or overhead (US); running costs or costs of running a business* **die ~ einschränken** *to cut down on expenses*
unmittelbar: *direct; immediate*
unproduktiv: *dead*
unrentabel: *not commercially viable; unprofitable*
unrichtig: *false*

unsichtbar: *unseen*
untätig: *dormant*
Unterauftrag: *subcontract*
Unteraufträge vergeben: *to subcontract*
unterbesetzt: *shorthanded; short-staffed*
unterbewertet: *undervalued*
Unterbewertung: *undervaluation*
unterbieten: *underbid; undercut; undersell*
Unterbrechung: *stoppage*
unterentwickelt: *underdeveloped*
untergeordnet: *low-grade*
Untergeschoß: *basement*
Untergrößen: *odd sizes*
Unterhändler: *negotiator*
Unterlagen: *information; records* **statistische ~** *statistics*
unterliegen: *liable to*
Unternehmen: *business; corporation; enterprise; firm* **ein staatliches ~** *a state enterprise* **gemeinnütziges ~** *non-business organization (US); non-profit organization* **gewagtes ~** *venture* **konkurrierende ~** *competing firms* **nichtkommerzielles ~** *non-business organization (US); non-profit organization* **unabhängige ~** *the independents* **unabhängiges ~** *independent company*
Unternehmen mit Staatsaufträgen: *government contractor*
Unternehmensberater: *management consultant*
Unternehmensbereich: *division*
Unternehmensforschung: *operational research*
Unternehmensführung: *management*
Unternehmensgewinne: *corporate profits*
Unternehmensgruppe: *venture team*
Unternehmensleitung: *management*
Unternehmensplan: **langfristiger ~** *corporate plan*
Unternehmensplanung: **langfristige ~** *corporate planning*
Unternehmenspolitik: *company policy*
Unternehmensspitze: *top management*
Unternehmenswerbung: *corporate advertising; institutional advertising*
Unternehmer: *contractor; entrepreneur*
unternehmerisch: *entrepreneurial*
Unternehmertum: *enterprise* **freies ~** *free enterprise*
unterrichten: *advise; inform*
Unterscheidungskompetenz: *distinctive competence*
Unterscheidungstest: *discrimination test*
Unterscheidungsvorteil: *differential advantage*
Unterschied: *variance*
unterschiedlich: *differential*
unterstehen: **jdm ~** *to report to someone*
unterstützen: **jdn ~** *to back someone*
Unterstützung: **finanzielle ~** *backing*
Untersuchungsbericht: *report; survey*
Untervertrag: *subcontract*
Untervertreter: *sub-agent*
Untervertretung: *sub-agency*
unterwegs: *on the road*
unterworfen: *liable to*
Unterzeichnung des Kaufvertrages: *exchange of contracts*
unverarbeitet: *raw*
unvereinbar mit: *at variance with*
unverkäuflich: *not negotiable*
unverkauft: *unsold*
unverlangt: *unsolicited*
unverpackt: *loose*
unverschämt: *exorbitant*
unvorbereitet: *cold*
unwiderruflich: *irrevocable*
unzeitgemäß: *out of date*
Urdaten: *raw data*
Urkunde: *document; instrument*
urkundlich: *documentary*
Urlaubszeit: *tourist season or holiday season*
Ursprung: *source*
ursprünglich: *originally*
Urteil: *judgement or judgment*
US Aktien: *dollar stocks*
Usance: *the customs of the trade*
USP: *unique selling proposition (USP)*

Vv

variabel: *variable*
Variable: *variable* **abhängige ~** *dependent variable* **unabhängige ~** *independent variable* **(un)kontrollierbare ~** *(un)controllable variable*
variieren: *range*
VB: *o.n.o. (or near offer)*
Veblen-Modell: *Veblenian model*
Veralten: *obsolescence*
veraltend: *obsolescent*
Veralterung: **geplante ~** *artificial or built-in or planned obsolescence*
veraltet: *obsolete; out of date*
veränderlich: *variable*
Veränderlichkeit: *instability*
veranlassen: *set up*
veranschlagt: *estimated*
verantworten: **sich ~** *to account for*
veräußern: *to dispose of*
Veräußerung: *disposal*
Veräußerungsgewinn: *capital gains*
Veräußerungsgewinnsteuer: *capital gains tax*
Verband der Reiseveranstalter: *travel organization*
Verbesserung: *advance*
verbindlich: *firm*
Verbindlichkeit: *obligation*

Verbindlichkeiten: *accounts payable; liabilities* **gesicherte ~** *secured debts* **kurzfristige ~** *current liabilities* **langfristige ~** *long-term liabilities; long-term debts* **seinen ~ nachkommen** *to meet one's obligations* **ungesicherte ~** *unsecured debts*

Verbindung: *tie-up*

Verbrauch: *consumption*

Verbraucher: *consumer*

Verbraucher-Abholmarkt: *box store (US); cash and carry*

Verbraucherabsatzförderung: *deal out*

Verbraucherbefragung: *consumer survey*

Verbraucherberatung: *consumer council*

Verbrauchergroßmarkt: *hypermarket*

Verbrauchermarkt: *consumer market; superstore*

Verbraucherpanel: *consumer panel*

Verbraucherpreisindex: *retail price index or consumer price index (US)*

Verbraucherschutz: *consumer protection*

Verbraucherschutzgesetz: *shoppers' charter*

Verbraucherschutzpolitik: *consumerism*

Verbrauchertestgruppe: *consumer panel*

Verbraucherverband: *Consumers Association (CA)*

Verbrauchsgüter: *consumer goods or consumable goods*

Verbrauchssteuer: *excise duty; purchase tax*

verbringen: *spend*

Verbundpackung: *banded pack*

verbürgen: sich ~ *guarantee*

Verderblichkeit: *inherent vice*

verdienen: gut ~ *to earn good money*

verdoppeln: *double*

Verein: *society*

vereinbaren: *agree*

Vereinbarung: *agreement; contract*

vereinheitlichen: *standardize*

Vereinten: die ~ Nationen *the United Nations*

Verfahren: *technique*

Verfahrensweise: *policy*

Verfall: *forfeit*

Verfallsdatum: *after-date*

Verfallsklausel: *forfeit clause*

Verfälschung: *falsification*

verfrachten: *to freight goods*

verfügbar: nicht ~ *unavailable*

Verfügung: zur ~ *in hand*

Vergangenheit: *record*

vergeben: *give away*

Vergleich: *comparison* **zwischenbetrieblicher ~** *intercompany or interfirm comparison*

vergleichend: *comparative*

Vergleichsjahr: *base year*

Vergleichswerbung: *comparative advertising*

vergrößern: *expand*

Vergrößerung: *expansion*

Vergütung: *indemnity*

Verhältnis: *rapport; ratio*

verhandeln: mit jdm ~ *to negotiate with someone*

Verhandlung: *negotiation*

Verhandlungen abbrechen: *to break off negotiations*

Verhandlungen aufnehmen: *to enter into or start negotiations*

Verhandlungen führen: *to conduct negotiations*

Verhandlungen wiederaufnehmen: *to resume negotiations*

Verhandlungsausschuß: *negotiating committee*

Verhandlungsbasis: *basis for negotiation; or near offer*

Verhandlungsführer: *negotiator*

Verhandlungspaket: *package deal*

Verhandlungsposition: *bargaining position*

Verhandlungssache: eine ~ *a matter for negotiation*

Verhandlungsstärke: *bargaining power*

Verjährungsausschlußfrist: *statute of limitations*

Verkauf: *disposal; sale; sell; vending* **automatischer ~** *automatic selling or automatic vending* **diskreter ~** *soft sell* **persönlicher ~** *face-to-face selling; personal selling* **schneller ~** *ready sale* **zum ~ geeignet** *merchantable* **zurückhaltender ~** *soft sell*

Verkauf auf Kommission: *sale or return*

Verkauf auf Kommissionsbasis: *commission sale or sale on commission*

Verkauf auf Kreditkarte: *credit card sale*

Verkäufe: ungesetzliche ~ *under-the-counter sales*

verkaufen: *sell; shift* **mehr ~** *outsell* **zu ~** *for sale*

Verkäufer: *salesclerk (US); salesman; salesperson; seller; shop assistant; vendor* **aggressiver ~** *high-pressure salesman*

Verkäuferin: *salesgirl; saleslady; saleswoman*

Verkäufermarkt: *seller's market*

Verkäuferschätzung: *vendor rating*

Verkäuferstab: *sales force*

Verkauf im Freiverkehr: *over-the-counter sales*

verkäuflich: *merchantable; on sale* **gut ~** *saleable*

Verkauf nach Beschreibung: *sale by description*

Verkauf ohne Gewähr: *sale as seen*

Verkaufsabteilung: *sales department*

Verkaufsaktion: *sales campaign*

Verkaufsangebot: *offer*

Verkaufsargument: einzigartiges ~ *unique selling proposition (USP)*

Verkaufsauflage: *paid circulation*

Verkaufsbedingungen: *conditions of sale; terms of sale*

Verkaufsbesuch: *sales call*

Verkaufsbuch: *sales book*

Verkaufsdirektor: *sales director*

Verkaufserlös: *sales revenue*

Verkaufsförderung: *sales promotion; trade promotion*

Verkaufsförderungsmaßnahmen: *promotion*

Verkaufsförderungsmittel: *promotional tools*

Verkaufsförderungsmix: *promotional mix*

Verkaufsgespräch: *sales interview*
Verkaufshilfen: *sales aids*
Verkaufshinweis: *sales lead*
Verkaufskampagne: *sales drive*
Verkaufsleiter: *sales executive; sales manager*
Verkaufsmethoden: aggressive ~ *high-pressure sales techniques* or *high-pressure selling* **nicht aggressive** ~ *low-pressure selling*
Verkaufsmöglichkeiten: *sales opportunities*
Verkaufsoption: *option to sell*
Verkaufsort: *point of sale (POS)*
Verkaufspersonal: *sales force* **hochmotiviertes** ~ *highly motivated sales staff*
Verkaufspolitik: aggressive ~ *hard selling*
Verkaufspräsentation: *sales pitch*
Verkaufspreis: *selling price*
Verkaufsprognose: *projected sales*
Verkaufsprospekte: *sales literature*
Verkaufsquoten: *sales quotas*
Verkaufsrecht: *access to the market*
Verkaufsrede: *sales pitch*
Verkaufsschlager: *flagship*
Verkaufsstelle: *outlet; point of sale (POS)*
Verkaufsstrategie or **Verkaufstaktik:** *sell*
Verkaufsteam: *sales team*
Verkaufstechnik: *salesmanship*
Verkaufstechniken: *sales techniques*
Verkaufswagen: *mobile shop*
Verkaufswettbewerb: *sales contest*
Verkaufswirkung: *sales response*
Verkaufszahlen: *sales figures* **höhere** ~ **haben** *outsell*
Verkaufsziel: *sales target*
Verkehr: *traffic*
Verkehrsflugzeug: *commercial aircraft*
Verkehrsfluß gerichtete Anschlagflächenposition: *head-on position*
Verkehrsmittel: *transportation* **öffentliche** ~ *public transport*
Verkehrsmittelanschlag: *car card*
Verkehrsmittelwerbung: *transport advertising*
Verkehrsnetz: öffentliches ~ *public transport system*
Verknappung: *shortage*
Verladedock: *loading dock*
Verladen: *lading*
Verlagerung: *shift*
verlangen: *demand*
verlängern: *extend*
Verlängerung: *extension*
verlegen: *move*
Verlegung: *transfer*
Verletzung: *breach*
Verletzung der Gewährleistungspflicht: *breach of warranty*
verlieren: *lose*
Verlust: *deficit; leakage; loss* **mit** ~ *at a loss* **nicht realisierter** ~ *paper loss*
Verluste: seine ~ **verringern** *to cut one's losses*
Verluste hinnehmen müssen: *lose out*
Verlustfaktor: *downside factor*
Vermarktung des Lagerbestandes: *dishoarding*
vermindern: *depress*
Vermögensanlage: *investment*
Vermögenssteuer: *capital levy*
Vermögenswert: *asset; asset value*
Vermögenswerte: blockierte or **eingefrorene** ~ *frozen assets* **immaterielle** ~ *intangible assets* **materielle** ~ *tangible assets* **unsichtbare** ~ *invisible assets*
verneinend: *negative*
vernetzen: *network*
veröffentlichen: *issue; release*
Veröffentlichung: *publication*
Verpacken: *packaging; packing*
verpacken: *pack; parcel* **wieder** ~ *repack*
Verpackung: *wrapper*
Verpackungskosten: *packing charges*
Verpackungsmaterial: *packaging; packing*
verpflichtet: sich ~ **fühlen** *to be under an obligation (to do something)*
Verpflichtung: *obligation*
verramschen: *dispose*
Verrechnungsscheck: *crossed cheque*
verringern: *depress; scale down*
Verringerung: *reduction*
Versammlung: *assembly*
Versand: *consignation; consignment; dispatch; shipping*
Versandabteilung: *dispatch department*
Versandanweisungen: *forwarding instructions* or *instructions for forwarding; shipping instructions*
Versandanzeige: *advice of dispatch; advice note* or *letter of advice; consignment note; shipping note*
Versandhandel: *mail-order selling*
Versandhaus: *mail-order business* or *mail-order firm* or *mail-order house*
Versandhauskatalog: *mail-order catalogue*
Versandschein: *dispatch note*
verschenken: *give away*
Verschicken: *mailing*
verschieben: *defer*
verschieden: *differential; miscellaneous*
verschiedenartig: *heterogeneous*
Verschiedenes: *any other business*
verschiffen: *ship*
Verschiffung: *shipping*
Verschlüsselung: *pre-coding*
verschulden: sich ~ *to get into debt*
Versenden: *consignation; consignment; mailing*
versenden: *dispatch; ship*
Versender: *consignor*
Versetzung: *secondment; transfer*
Versicherte: der ~ *the life assured* or *the life insured; person named in the policy*
Versicherungsprämiensatz: *insurance rates*

Versicherungsschein: vorläufiger ~ *cover note*
Versicherungsschutz: voller ~ *full cover*
Versicherungsverein auf Gegenseitigkeit: *friendly society*
Versicherungsvertreter: *insurance agent; insurance salesman*
Versicherung und Fracht: *insurance and freight*
versiegeln: *to seal*
Versiegelung: *seal*
versorgen: *to supply*
Versorgung: *supply*
verspäten: sich ~ *to delay*
verspätet: *late*
Verspätung: *delay*
Verstaatlichung: *nationalization*
Verstärkungswerbung: *reinforcement advertising*
versteigern: *to auction*
Versteigerung: *auction* **holländische ~** *Dutch auction*
Verstoß: *breach*
versuchsweise: *on approval*
vertagen: *defer*
Vertagung: *deferment*
verteilen: *share*
Verteiler: *distributor*
Verteilernetz: *distribution network; network of distributors*
Verteilerorganisationen: *distributive trades*
Verteilerzettel: *distribution slip*
verteilt anlegen: *diversify*
vertikal: *vertical*
Vertikalpublikation: *vertical publication*
Vertrag: *contract; treaty* **besiegelter ~** *contract under seal* **durch ~** *contractually* **einen ~ aushandeln** *to negotiate a contract* **einen ~ bekommen** *to win a contract* **unter ~ stehen** *to be under contract*
vertraglich: *contractual; contractually*
Vertragsbedingungen: *terms of a contract*
Vertragsbruch: *breach of contract*
Vertragshaftung: *contractual liability*
Vertragslieferant: *contract carrier*
vertragsmäßig: *contractual*
Vertragspartner: *contracting party*
Vertragspflicht: seine ~ erfüllen *to fulfil one's contractual obligations*
Vertragsrecht: *contract law* or *law of contract*
Vertragsverlängerung: *extension of a contract*
Vertrag wird verhandelt: *contract under negotiation*
Vertrauen: *confidence*
vertreiben: *distribute; market*
vertreten: *rep (informal); represent*
Vertreter: *agent; canvasser; door-to-door salesman; rep (informal)* or *representative; substitute* **zugelassener ~** *recognized agent*
Vertreterbesuch: unangemeldeter ~ *cold call*
Vertreterbesuche: *canvassing*
Vertreterprovision: *agent's commission*
Vertretung: *agency; representation; representative; substitute*
Vertrieb: *distribution; distributorship* **selektiver ~** *selective distribution*
Vertriebskosten: *cost of sales; selling costs*
Vertriebsnetz: *distribution network*
Vertriebssystem: mehrkanäliges ~ *multi-channel system*
Vertriebsvereinbarung: *marketing agreement*
Vertriebsweg: verwalteter ~ *administered channel*
Vertriebswege: *distribution channels* or *channels of distribution*
Vertriebswegmitglieder: *channel members*
Vertriebszählung: *distribution census*
vervollkommnen: *to perfect*
verwalten: *to administer*
Verwalter: *administrator*
Verwaltung: *administration*
Verwaltungskosten: *expenses of the administration* or *administration expenses*
Verwaltungsratsmitglied: außerordentliches ~ *associate director*
verwaltungstechnisch: *administrative*
verwirken: *to forfeit*
Verwirkung: *forfeit; forfeiture*
verzeichnen: *record*
Verzeichnis: *list; schedule*
verzögern: sich ~ *delay*
Verzögerung: *delay*
Verzug: *delay* **in ~ geraten** *fall behind*
Videoband: *video tape*
vielfach: *multiple*
Vielfalt: *variety*
Vielseher: *heavy viewer*
Vierfarbendruck: *four-colour process*
Vierfelder-Portfolio-Matrix: *Boston matrix*
Vierteljahrespublikation: *quarterly*
viertelseitig: *quarter page*
Visitenkarte: *business card*
Visualiser: *visualizer*
visuell: *visual*
Vitrine: *display cabinet* or *display case; showcase*
Volk: *nation*
Völkerrecht: *international law*
Volkseinkommen: *national income*
Volkswirt: *economist*
Volkswirtschaft: *economics* **entwickelte ~** *mature economy*
Volkszählung: *census*
vollautomatisch: *fully automatic*
Vollbeschäftigung: *full employment*
vollkommen: *perfect*
Vollkosten: *full costs*
Vollkostenpreiskalkulation: *full cost pricing*
Vollkostenrechnung: *absorption costing*
Vollsichtregal: *display stand* or *display unit*
vollständig: *full; in full*

Volumen: *volume*
vorab: *in advance; advance*
voraus: **im ~** *in advance; advance; forward; up front* **im ~ bezahlen** *to pay in advance; prepay* **im ~ verpacken** *prepack or prepackage* **im ~ zahlbar** *payable in advance*
Vorausberechnung: *forecast*
vorausbezahlt: *prepaid*
Voraussage: *forecast; forecasting*
voraussagen: *to forecast*
voraussichtlich: *prospective*
Vorauszahlung: *money up front; prepayment*
Vorbehalt: **unter ~** *conditional* **unter ~ annehmen** *to give a conditional acceptance*
vorbehaltlos: *clean*
Vorbehaltspreis: *fall-back price; reserve price; upset price*
vorbeikommen: *call in*
Vorbestellungen: *dues*
vorbildlich: *model*
Vorderseite: *front*
Vordruck: *form*
Voreingenommenheit: *bias*
vorführen: *demonstrate*
Vorführer: *demonstrator*
Vorführmodell: *demonstration model*
Vorführung: *demonstration; presentation* **routinemäßige** *or* **stereotype ~** *canned presentation*
Vorhaben: *project*
Vorhand: *first option*
Vorhersage: *projection*
Vorlage: *presentation*
vorläufig: *provisional*
Vorrat: *stock; stockpile; store; supply* **einen ~ anlegen** *stock up*
Vorräte anlegen: *stockpile*
vorrätig: *in hand; in stock* **nicht ~** *out of stock*
Vorreiter: *pioneer*
vorsagen: *prompt*
Vorschau: *preview*
vorschießen: *to advance*
Vorschlag: *suggestion*
Vorschriften: *regulations*
vorschriftsmäßig: *in due form*
Vorschuß: *advance*
Vorsitzende(r): *leader*
Vorsitzender und Geschäftsführer: *chairman and managing director*
Vorspiegelung falscher Tatsachen: *false pretences; fraudulent misrepresentation*
Vorstand: *director*
Vorstandsgremium: *management committee*
vorstellen: *introduce*
Vorstellungsbild: *preparatory set*
Vorstellungsgespräch: *interview* **ein ~ führen** *to interview*
Vorsteuer: *input tax*
Vorteil: **absoluter ~** *absolute advantage*
vorübergehend: *transient* **nicht ~** *intransient*
Vorurteil: *bias*
Vorverkäufer: *advance man (US)*
vorverlegen: *advance*
Vorwahl: *area code*
Vorwärtsintegration: *forward integration*
vorzeitig: *early*
Vorzugsplatz: *preferred position; special position*

Ww

Waage: *scales*
waagerecht: *horizontal*
Wachstum: *growth*
Wachstumsbereich: *growth area*
Wachstumsbranche: *boom industry or growth industry*
Wachstumsindex: *growth index*
Wachstumsindustrie: *growth industry*
Wachstumsmarkt: **ein ~** *a growth market*
Wachstumsphase: *growth*
Wachstumsrate: *growth rate*
Waggon: *freight car (US); wagon or waggon* **frei ~** *free on rail*
Wagniskapital: *risk capital; venture capital*
Wahl: **zweite ~** *reject(s); second(s)*
Wahlhelfer: *canvasser*
wahllos: *at random*
Wahlwerbung: *canvassing*
Wahlwerbung betreiben: *to canvass*
Wahrnehmung: **selektive ~** *selective perception*
Wahrnehmungslandkarte: *perceptual map*
wahrscheinlich: *probable*
Wahrscheinlichkeit: *probability*
Wahrscheinlichkeitsauswahl: *probability sampling*
Währung: *currency* **frei konvertierbare ~** *convertible currency; free currency* **harte ~** *hard currency* **weiche ~** *soft currency*
Währungsausgleichsfonds: *Exchange Equalization Account (GB)*
Währungseinheit: *monetary standard; monetary unit*
Währungsfonds: **Internationaler ~** *the International Monetary Fund*
Währungsgarantie: *currency backing*
währungspolitisch: *monetary*
Währungssystem: **das internationale ~** *the international monetary system*
Wandel: *shift*
Wandergewerbe betreiben: *peddle*
Ware: *commodity; merchandise; product* **anonyme ~** *anonymous product* **verderbliche ~** *perishables*
Waren: *goods* **gesetzlich geschützte ~** *proprietary goods* **lose ~** *goods sold loose* **verzollte ~** *duty-paid goods*
Waren auf Lager: *stock in hand*

Warenaufzug: *freight elevator*
Warenausgangsbuch: *sales ledger*
Warenausgangsjournal: *sales book*
Warenauslage: alleinstehende ~ *island site or island display*
Warenbeschaffung: *purchasing*
Warenbestand: *stock; trading stock*
Warenbestände: *inventory*
Warenbestellung: *indent*
Warenbörse: *commodity market or commodity exchange*
Warencode: *stock code*
Wareneingangsbuch: *purchase book*
Warenhaus: *emporium; department store*
Warenkennzeichnung: *trade description*
Warenkennzeichnungsgesetz: *Trade Descriptions Act (GB)*
Warenkonzern: *giant retailer*
Warenlieferung: *delivery of goods*
Waren neu auszeichnen: *to re-sticker stock*
Warenpapier: *mercantile paper*
Warenposten: *job lot*
Warenprobe: *sample* **unverkäufliche** ~ *sample only - not for resale*
Warensendung: *consignment* **eine** ~ **annehmen** *to accept delivery of a shipment*
Warenständer: drehbarer ~ *spinner*
Warentermingeschäft: *commodity futures*
Warenterminhändler: *commodity trader*
Warentest: anonymer ~ *blind testing*
Waren übertragen: *to carry over stock*
Warenumsatzsteuer: *sales tax*
Waren unter Zollverschluß: *goods in bond*
Warenverkaufsbuch: *sales book*
Waren verpacken: *to package goods*
Warenverzeichnis: *stocklist*
Warenzeichen: *trademark or trade name*
Warenzustellung: *delivery of goods*
Warnhinweis: rechtsverbindlicher ~ *mandatory blurb*
Warnstreik: *token strike*
warten: *to service*
Wartung: *service*
Wartungs(hand)buch: *service handbook or service manual*
Wartungsvertrag: *service contract*
Wechsel: *agency bill; bill; bill of exchange* **akzeptierter** ~ *accepted bill* **einen** ~ **akzeptieren** *to accept a bill* **einen** ~ **diskontieren** *to discount a bill* **einen** ~ **einlösen** *to retire a bill* **einen** ~ **indossieren** *to endorse a bill* **einen** ~ **unterzeichnen** *to back a bill* **kurzfristige** ~ *short-dated bills* **langfristige** ~ *long-dated bills*
Wechselbürgschaft: eine ~ **leisten** *to guarantee a bill of exchange*
Wechsel diskontieren: *to discount bills of exchange*
Wechselforderungen: *bills receivable*
Wechselgarant: *backer of a bill*
Wechselgeld: *cash float*
Wechselkurs: *exchange rate or rate of exchange* **ungünstiger** ~ *unfavourable exchange rate*
wechseln: *exchange; switch*
Wechselprotest: *protest*
Wechselprotest einlegen: *to protest a bill*
wechselseitig: *reciprocal*
Wechselverbindlichkeiten: *bills payable*
Weg: *channel* **den** ~ **bahnen** *to pioneer*
Wegbereiter: *pioneer*
wegschnappen: *snap up*
Wegwerf-: *disposable*
Wegwerfpost: *junk mail*
Wehrmaterial: *military hardware*
Wein- und Spirituosenhandlung: *off licence*
weit: *extensive*
weiteres: bis auf ~ *until further notice; till countermanded (TC)*
Weiterverkauf: *resale*
weiterverkaufen: *resell*
weitverbreitet: *common*
Welthandel: *international trade*
Weltwährungsfonds: *The International Monetary Fund (IMF)*
weltweit: *worldwide*
Weltwirtschaftskrise: die ~ *the Great Depression; the Slump*
wenden: sich ~ **an** *approach*
wenig: zu ~ *short* **zu** ~ **berechnen** *undercharge* **zu** ~ **herausgeben** *short-change*
weniger werden: *decline*
Werbeabteilung: *design department; publicity department*
Werbeagentur: *advertising agency; publicity agency or publicity bureau; shop* **hauseigene** ~ *house agency* **künstlerische** ~ *creative shop*
Werbeaktion: *publicity campaign or advertising campaign*
Werbeanschlagfläche: *advertising hoarding*
Werbeaussage: *advertising message*
Werbebeilage: *insert in a magazine mailing or magazine insert; stuffer (US)*
Werbeblatt: *free paper or giveaway paper*
Werbebotschaft: *advertising message*
Werbebudget: *advertising appropriation or advertising budget*
Werbebudgetierung: finanzmittelbezogene ~ *affordable method*
Werbeetat: *account; advertising appropriation; advertising budget; promotional budget; publicity budget*
Werbefachmann: *adman (informal)*
Werbefläche: einzelne ~ *media option*
Werbegeschenk: *free gift; giveaway; premium offer*
Werbegrafik: *artwork*
Werbegrafiker: *commercial artist*
Werbegrundkonzept: *copy platform*
Werbehilfen: *sales aids*

Werbeinformationszeitschrift: **amerikanische** ~ *Standard Rate & Data Service (SRDS)*
Werbekampagne: *publicity campaign* or *advertising campaign* **explosionsartige** or **intensive** ~ *blitz*
Werbekanäle: *channels of influence*
Werbekontinuität: *continuity*
Werbekonzept: *copy platform*
Werbekosten: *publicity expenditure*
Werbeleiste: *channel strip*
Werbeleiter: *advertising manager; publicity manager*
Werbematerial: *publicity matter; sales literature*
Werbemedien: *advertising media*
Werbemelodie: *advertising jingle* or *publicity jingle*
Werbemittelkontakt: *exposure*
werben: *canvass; promote; publicize*
werben für: *endorse*
Werbepreis: *promotional price*
Werbeprobe: **unentgeltliche** ~ *"sample only - of no commercial value"*
Werbeprospekt: *publicity handout*
Werber: *advance man (US)*
Werberabatt: *promotional allowance*
Werberat: *Advertising Standards Authority (ASA)*
Werbesätze: **degressive** ~ *graded advertising rates*
Werbesendezeit: *advertising time; slot; TV spot*
Werbesendungplazierung: **feste** ~ *fixed break; fixed position; fixed spot*
Werbeslogan: **kurzer** ~ *shout*
Werbespot: *commercial* **einzelner** ~ *media option*
Werbespruch: *publicity slogan*
Werbetarif: *advertising rates*
Werbetextentwurf: *publicity copy*
Werbetexter: *copywriter*
Werbeträger: *advertising media; advertising medium; vehicle*
Werbeträgerforschung: *media research*
Werbeträger-Panelanalyse: *television consumer audit*
Werbetrick: *ploy*
Werbeversand: *mail-out* **selektiver** ~ *selective mailing*
Werbewesen: *advertising*
Werbewirkung: *message effect*
Werbezeit: *advertising time; air time*
Werbezettel: *broadside (US); flier; leave leaflet*
Werbung: *advertisement; advertising; commercial; publicity* **engagierte** ~ *advocacy advertising* **gemeinsame** ~ *co-operative advertising* **herabsetzende** ~ *disparaging copy; knocking copy* **informative** ~ *educational advertising* **kooperative** ~ *co-operative advertising* **landesweite** ~ *national advertising* **redaktionelle** ~ *editorial publicity* **reißerische** ~ *hype* **stoßweise** ~ *burst* **überregionale** ~ *national advertising* **übertriebene** ~ *hype* **unterschwellige** ~ *subliminal advertising* **vergütungsfähige** ~ *above-the-line advertising* **vergütungsunfähige** ~ *below-the-line advertising*
Werbung machen: *publicize*
Werbungsbranche: *advertising*
Werbungtreibender: *space buyer*
Werk: *works*
Werksspionage: *industrial espionage*
Werkstatt: *shop; workshop*
Werkszeitung: *house journal; house magazine*
Werktage: **drei** ~ *three clear days*
Wert: *value* **an** ~ **gewinnen** *gain* **angegebener** or **angemeldeter** ~ *declared value* **im** ~ **fallen** *to fall in value* **im** ~ **steigen** *to rise in value*
Wertpapier: **begebbares** or **übertragbares** ~ *negotiable instrument; negotiable paper*
Wertsteuer: *ad valorem duty*
wesentlich: *basic; essential; prime*
Wesentlichste: **das** ~ *bottom line*
Wettbewerb: *competition* **freier** ~ *free competition* **lauterer** ~ *fair trading* or *fair dealing* **monopolistischer** ~ *monopolistic competition* **mörderischer** ~ *cut-throat competition* **preisunabhängiger** ~ *non-price competition* **scharfer** ~ *keen competition* **unlauterer** ~ *unfair competition*
Wettbewerbsbeschränkung: *restraint of trade*
wettbewerbsfähig: *competitive*
Wettbewerbsfähigkeit: *competitiveness*
Wettbewerbsfreiheit: *free competition*
Wettbewerbsparität: *competitive parity*
Wettbewerbsvorteil: *competitive edge* or *competitive advantage*
Wichtigste: **das** ~ *bottom line*
wiederaufbereiten: *recycle*
Wiederauffinden von Information: *information retrieval*
Wiederausfuhr: *entrepot trade; re-export; re-exportation*
wiederausführen: *to re-export*
Wiederausfuhrhafen: *entrepot port*
Wiedereinfuhr: *reimport; reimportation*
wiedereinführen: *to reimport; to relaunch*
Wiedereinführung: *relaunch*
wiedererkennen: *recognize*
Wiedererkennungstest: *recognition test*
Wieder(holungs)kauf: *rebuy; repeat purchasing* **modifizierter** ~ *modified rebuy*
Wiederholungsrabatt: *no-change discount*
Wiederverkauf: *resale*
wiederverkaufen: *resell*
Wiederverkäufer: *distributor*
Wiederverkäufermarkt: *reseller market*
Wiederverkäuferrabatt: *trade discount; functional discount*
Wildanschlag: *fly-posting*
Wildkatzen: *wild cats*
willkürlich: *random*
Windschattenmarketing: *ambush marketing*
wirksam: *effective; effectual*

wirksam bleiben: *to remain in effect*
Wirksamkeit: *effectiveness*
wirksam werden: *operate*
Wirkung: *impact*
Wirtschaft: *economy* **staatlich gelenkte ~** *controlled economy*
wirtschaftlich: *commercial*
Wirtschaftlichkeit: *economy*
Wirtschaftsbüro: *trade bureau*
Wirtschaftsinstitut: *business college or business school*
Wirtschaftskorrespondent: *business correspondent; financial correspondent*
Wirtschaftskrise: *economic crisis*
Wirtschaftsplanung: *economic planning*
Wirtschaftspolitik: angebotsorientierte ~ *supply-side economics*
Wirtschaftsprüfer: *accountant* **amtlich zugelassener ~** *certified (public) accountant* **beeidigter ~** *chartered accountant*
Wirtschaftspublikation: *business publication*
Wirtschaftssanktionen: *economic sanctions*
Wirtschaftsspionage: *industrial espionage*
Wirtschaftsstagnation: *economic stagnation*
Wirtschaftssystem: kapitalistisches ~ *capitalist economy*
Wirtschaftsverband: *trade association*
Wirtschaftswachstum: *economic growth*
Wirtschaftswissenschaft: *economics; business science*
Wirtschaftswissenschaftler: *economist*
Wirtschaftszeitschriften: *business publications*
Wirtschaftszweig: *industry*
Wissenschaft: *science*
wissenschaftlich: *scientific*
Wochenzeitschrift: *weekly*
Wochenzeitung: *weekly*
Wohlstandsgesellschaft: *affluent society*
Wohltätigkeitsbasar: *jumble sale*
Wohltätigkeitsorganisation: *voluntary organization*
Wohnung: subventionierte ~ *subsidized accommodation*
Working Capital: *working capital*
Wucherer: *profiteer*
Wuchergeschäfte: *profiteering*
Wuchtplanung: *impact scheduling*
Wühlkorb or **Wühltisch:** *dump bin*
Wunsch: *desire* **auf ~ erhältlich** *optional*
Wurfsendung: *door drop*

Yy

Yard: *yard*
Yen: *yen*
Yuppies: *yuppies*

Zz

zahlbar: *payable*
Zahlen: gerade ~ *even numbers* **ungerade ~** *odd numbers*
zahlen: *pay*
zahlenmäßig: *numeric or numerical*
Zahler: *payer*
Zahlung: *payment* **aufgeschobene ~** *deferred payment* **eine ~ leisten** *to effect a payment* **in ~ geben** *trade in* **pünktliche ~** *prompt payment* **symbolische ~** *token payment*
Zahlungen: fällige ~ *payments which fall due*
Zahlungen einstellen: *to stop payments*
Zahlung gegen Dokumente: *cash against documents*
Zahlung gegen Nachnahme: *payment on delivery*
Zahlung nach Lieferung: *payment after delivery*
Zahlungsanweisung: *order*
Zahlungsbedingungen: *terms of payment or payment terms*
Zahlungsbilanz: *balance of payments*
Zahlungsbilanzdefizit: *balance of payments deficit or trade deficit*
Zahlungsempfänger: *payee*
Zahlungserleichterungen: *easy terms*
Zahlungsfrist: *days of grace*
Zahlungsgarant: institutioneller ~ *confirming house*
Zahlungsmittel: gesetzliches ~ *legal currency; legal tender*
Zahlungstermin: mittlerer ~ *average due date*
Zahlungsweise: *mode of payment*
Zauderer: *laggards*
Zehnertastatur: *numeric keypad*
Zeichen: *mark; token*
Zeichentrickfilm: *animation; cartoon*
Zeichnungsangebot: *offer for sale*
zeigen: *display; indicate*
Zeile: *line*
Zeilendrucker: *line printer*
Zeilenzahl: *lineage*
Zeilenzentimeter: *single column centimetre*
Zeit: *time* **in kurzer ~** *in the short term*
Zeitdauer einer Werbesendung: *timelength*
Zeit der Flaute: *slack season*
Zeitplan: *schedule*
Zeitreihenanalyse: *time series analysis*
Zeitschrift: *journal; magazine; periodical* **eine ~ abbestellen** *to cancel (a subscription to) a magazine* **eine ~ abonnieren** *to subscribe to a magazine; to take out a subscription to a magazine*
Zeitschriftenabonnement: ein ~ kündigen *to cancel a subscription to a magazine*
Zeitschriftenabonnent: *subscriber to a magazine or magazine subscriber*
Zeitschriftenausschnitt: *press cutting*

Zeitschriftenzustellung per Post: *magazine mailing*
Zeitsegment: *time segment*
Zeitspanne: *time*
Zeit- und Bewegungsstudie: *time and motion study*
Zeitung: *newspaper; paper* **überregionale ~** *national newspaper*
Zeitungsausschnitt: *press cutting*
Zeitungsbericht: *report in a newspaper or newspaper report*
Zeitungsblatt: großformatiges ~ *broadsheet* **kleinformatiges ~** *tabloid*
Zeitungsstand: *news stand*
Zentimeterpreis: *column-centimetre*
Zentralwert: *median*
zerbrechlich: *fragile*
zersplittern: *fragment*
Zersplitterung der Werbekampagne: *fragmentation*
Zeugnis: *testimonial*
Ziel: *aim; goal; objective; target* **ein ~ erreichen** *to meet a target*
Ziel-Aufgaben-Methode: *objective-and-task method*
Ziele: langfristige ~ *long-term objectives*
Ziele setzen: *to set targets*
Zielgruppe: *target audience*
Zielmarkt: *target market*
Zielpublikum: *target audience*
Zielsetzung: kurzfristige ~ *short-term objective* **langfristige ~** *long-term objective*
Zinsbelastung: *interest charges*
Zinsrückstand: *back interest*
Zinssatz: *interest rate or rate of interest*
Zinsschein: *interest coupon*
Zins und Zinseszins: *cumulative interest*
zitieren: *quote*
Zoll: *customs; customs duty or import duty* **den ~ passieren** *to go through customs*
Zollabfertigung: *customs clearance* **die ~ vornehmen** *to effect customs clearance*
Zollabfertigungsschein: *clearance certificate*
Zollabgabe: *customs duty*
Zollagent: *customs broker*
Zollager: *bonded warehouse*
zollamtlich abfertigen lassen: *to effect customs clearance*
Zollanmeldungsstelle: *customs entry point*
Zollbeamten: *customs officers or customs officials*
Zollbehörden: *customs*
Zolldeklaration or **Zoll(einfuhr)erklärung:** *bill of entry; customs declaration*
Zollfaktura: *customs invoice*
Zollformalitäten: *customs formalities*
zollfrei: *free of duty or duty-free*
Zollgebühren: *customs tariffs*
Zollniederlage: *customs warehouse*
zollpflichtig: *dutiable*
Zollrückvergütung: *drawback*
Zollschranken: *customs barriers or tariff barriers*
Zolltarife: *customs tariffs*
Zollunion: *customs union*
Zollverschluß: *customs seal*
Zone: *zone*
Zonen: in ~ aufteilen *to zone*
zufällig: *random*
Zufallsfehler: *random error; sampling error*
Zufallszahlentabelle: *table of random numbers*
Zufriedenheit: *satisfaction*
Zufriedenheit am Arbeitsplatz: *job satisfaction*
Zufriedenstellung: *satisfaction*
Zufriedenstellung des Kunden: *customer satisfaction*
zuführen: *feed*
Zugabeangebot: *premium offer*
Zugabeartikel zum Selbstkostenpreis: *self-liquidating offer*
Zugabenangebot: *premium offer*
Zugänglichkeit: *accessibility*
Zugeständnis: *concession*
zugreifen auf: *access*
Zugriffszeit: *access time*
Zuhauseverkauf: *in-home selling*
Zuhörerschaft: *audience*
zukleben: *seal*
Zukunft: *future*
zukünftig: *future*
Zukunftsforschung: *futurology*
Zulage: *bonus*
Zulassung: *recognition*
Zulassungsbescheinigung: *test certificate*
Zulassungspapiere: *registration*
Zulieferant or **Zulieferer:** *supplier*
zumachen: *close*
Zunahme: *gain; growth*
zurückerstattbar: *refundable*
Zurückführung in Privateigentum: *privatization*
zurückgeben: *return*
zurückgehen: *decline; drop; fall away; fall off; shrink*
zurückgreifen auf: *fall back on*
zurückkaufen: *buy back*
zurückschicken or **zurücksenden:** *return*
zurückstellen: *defer*
Zurückstellung: *deferment*
zurückzahlen: *refund*
Zusammenarbeit: *co-operation*
zusammenarbeiten: *co-operate*
Zusammenbau: *assembly*
zusammenfassen: *group together; integrate*
Zusammenfassung: *integration*
Zusammenhang: in ~ mit *in relation to*
zusammenlegen: *consolidate*
Zusammenlegung: *consolidation*
zusammenschließen: *integrate; merge*

Zusammenschluß: *integration*
Zusammenstellung: *assortment*
Zusammenstellung einer Bestellung: *order picking*
zusätzlich: *backup; extra*
Zuschauer: *viewer*
Zuschauerschaft: *audience*
Zuschlag: *surcharge*
zuschlagen: jdm etwas ~ *to knock something down to a bidder*
zuschneiden: *tailor*
zustellen: *deliver*
zustimmen: *agree*
zustimmend: *positive*
zuviel berechnen: *overcharge*
zuvorkommen: *pre-empt*
Zuwachs: *gain*
Zuweisung: *appropriation*
Zuwendung: *handout*
Zwangsverkauf: *forced sale*
Zweigstelle: *branch*
zweiseitig: *bilateral*
Zweiseitigkeit: *bilateralism*
zweistellig: *in double figures*
Zweitinserat: *readvertisement*
zweitklassig: *inferior*
zweitrangig: *secondary*
zwingen: *force*
Zwischenhändler: *middleman*
zyklisch: *cyclical*
Zyklus: *cycle*

Anhang

British Socio-Economic Groups

code	group	members
A	upper middle class	senior managers, administrators, senior civil servants, leading professional people (doctors, lawyers, architects, etc.)
B	middle class	middle managers & administrators, middle level civil servants & professional people
C1	lower middle class	junior managers & administrators, clerical staff
C2	skilled working class	workers with skills and qualifications
D	working class	unskilled workers, such as manual workers, in permanent jobs
E	lowest or subsistence level	pensioners, unemployed, casual manual workers

VALS Life style segmentation

group	*members*
Belongers	people living in a traditional way, who are happy to go on living as they have always lived
Achievers	successful people who have reached the top of their profession and are prosperous
Emulators	young people who want to become achievers
I-am-me	people who think of themselves as different from all others
Experiential	people who are attracted to others
Societally conscious	people who belong to groups, and who want to work with other groups
Survivors	old people. retired people, those who do not believe they have a future
Sustainers	people who live at subsistence level and are resentful of the fact that they cannot do better
Integrated	people who are satisfied with their way of living and have a strong inner life

Advertising Rates for a Periodical

RATE CARD

ADVERTISEMENT RATES: DISPLAY

Size	*Number of Insertions* 1	3	6
Black and White			
Full page	£1000	£950	£900
Half page	600	575	550
Third page	450	425	400
Quarter page	350	325	300
Four colour			
Full page	£1600	£1500	£1350
Half page	1100	1000	850
Two colour			
Full page	£1250	£1100	£1000
Half page	800	700	600
Inside covers full colour	£1900	£1500	£1250

Facing editorial: basic card rate plus 10%

Full page bleed: basic card rate plus 10%

Inserts

Preprinted inserts can be accepted folded

Rates:		
	one issue:	£1000
	three issues:	£2500
	six issues:	£4500

ADVERTISEMENT RATES: CLASSIFIED

Recruitment:	
Full page	£750
Half page	£400
Single column centimetre	£10.00
Double column centimetre	£19.00
Three column centimetre	£25.00

Classified under headings:

For Sale	Wanted	Property
Freelance offered	Technical Services	Marketing
Business Supplies	Personal	Educational

Single Column Centimetre	£9.00
Double Column Centimetre	£15.00

All advertisements must be pre-paid
Box numbers £5.00 per insertion
Copy required by 5p.m. four working days before publication

Technical Information for a Periodical

MECHANICAL DATA

Frequency:	Monthly
Publication day:	First Thursday in month
Printing process:	Offset litho
Binding:	Wire-stitched
Trim size:	285 x 210mm
Screen:	Black & White 120/48 line per cm Colour 150/60 lines per cm
Bleeds:	bleed trim on all trimmed edges is 3mm
Materials required:	
Colour:	screened positives, emulsion side down, right-reading, with progressives
Black & White:	screened positives, emulsion-side down, right-reading
Copy for setting:	double space typed

SWOT Analysis

Organization

Strengths

What are the services or products or skills which the organization is good at doing or making

Weaknesses

What are the things or products or skills which the organization can't do or doesn't do well

Market

Opportunities

Segments of the market which are attractive, and where changes in the market might work in favour of the organization

Threats

Segments of the market or changes taking place in the market which make it difficult for the organization to work there

Notizen

Notizen